The Defeat of
Barisan Nasional

The **ISEAS – Yusof Ishak Institute** (formerly Institute of Southeast Asian Studies) is an autonomous organization established in 1968. It is a regional centre dedicated to the study of socio-political, security, and economic trends and developments in Southeast Asia and its wider geostrategic and economic environment. The Institute's research programmes are grouped under Regional Economic Studies (RES), Regional Strategic and Political Studies (RSPS), and Regional Social and Cultural Studies (RSCS). The Institute is also home to the ASEAN Studies Centre (ASC), the Temasek History Research Centre (THRC) and the Singapore APEC Study Centre.

ISEAS Publishing, an established academic press, has issued more than 2,000 books and journals. It is the largest scholarly publisher of research about Southeast Asia from within the region. ISEAS Publishing works with many other academic and trade publishers and distributors to disseminate important research and analyses from and about Southeast Asia to the rest of the world.

The Defeat of Barisan Nasiona

Missed Signs or Late Surge?

EDITED BY

Francis E. Hutchinson
Lee Hwok Aun

CARTOGRAPHERS

Benjamin K.H. Hu
Pearlyn Y. Pang

 YUSOF ISHAK
INSTITUTE

First published in Singapore in 2019 by
ISEAS Publishing
30 Heng Mui Keng Terrace
Singapore 119614
E-mail: publish@iseas.edu.sg
Website: http://bookshop.iseas.edu.sg

ISEAS Library Cataloguing-in-Publication Data

Names: Hutchinson, Francis E., editor. | Lee, Hwok Aun, editor.
Title: The defeat of Barisan Nasional : missed signs or late surge? / editors, Francis E. Hutchinson and Lee Hwok Aun.
Description: Singapore : ISEAS – Yusof Ishak Institute, 2019. | Includes bibliographical references and index.
Identifiers: ISBN 9789814843898 (paperback) | ISBN 9789814843904 (PDF)
Subjects: LCSH: Malaysia. Parliament. Dewan Rakyat—Elections, 2018. | Elections—Malaysia. | Barisan Nasional (Organization). | Malaysia—Politics and government.
Classification: LCC JQ1062 A95D31

Photographs on the front and back covers reproduced with permission of *Malaysian Insight*.

Typeset by Superskill Graphics Pte Ltd

CONTENTS

LIST OF FIGURES

LIST OF TABLES

FOREWORD

For most Malaysian watchers, 9 May 2018 will go down as one of the most remarkable days in the country's history. For the first time ever, an opposition alliance succeeded in deposing the predominant Barisan Nasional (BN) coalition in a general election. The transition, characterized by a delayed swearing-in ceremony of the new prime minister, was peaceful if somewhat grudging. The losers were clearly shocked by their overwhelming defeat, but no less than the winners' surprise at their victory. After an initial spell of apprehension, a sense of buoyant optimism and idealism infected the mood of the country, though it would ultimately prove unsustainable after the real task of governing began.

The events of GE-14 are all the more remarkable because of how unlikely they seemed just a few years earlier. The opposition was in disarray after an earlier coalition fell apart when the Islamic Party broke off ties with another member party. Mahathir was still a highly distrusted figure by many key opposition stalwarts, not least because of what he had done to them in his previous stint as Prime Minister. Anwar Ibrahim, the most effective campaigner in the opposition, was in prison again and unable to run or campaign. Anwar and Mahathir were estranged, and the depth of disdain that they had for each other since the former's dismissal from the post of Deputy Prime Minister, his assault in custody and subsequent trial on questionable charges was seen as unbridgeable. Even the economy, while not performing at full potential, was still chugging along.

The only thing that the Pakatan Harapan had going for it was the simmering unhappiness over the 1MDB scandal. This undercurrent was strong enough to cause turbulence even within the dominant Malay party, UMNO, itself, and accounted for its incumbent Deputy President being dropped from his post and later stripped of his membership.

However, even with this, it took a combination of many factors for the upset of GE-14 to occur. It was aided by the ubiquity of social media that allowed the government-controlled media to be by-passed. There was also the political statesmanship displayed in the coming together of Mahathir, Anwar and Lim Kit Siang, among others, to form a political alliance. Also significant was Mahathir's effective campaigning and the strong symbolism of his return to active politics at the age of ninety-two against someone he had mentored in the past. These and many other factors, including several missteps by the ruling coalition, came together to deliver the result against all odds.

This book examines this remarkable historic event from the viewpoint of many researchers who have studied it as it was being played out and have spent many hours analysing the reasons that led to it. Readers may or may not agree with the conclusions drawn, but we hope that many will benefit from the numerous insights this collective work offers.

Choi Shing Kwok
Director, ISEAS – Yusof Ishak Institute
12 June 2019

ACKNOWLEDGEMENTS

This book is the result of a two-year collective journey. In early 2017, when the possibility—and to some extent, expectancy—of early elections permeated Malaysian political airspace, we started to plan a research programme and assemble a corps of contributors.

We thank the contributors from the ISEAS – Yusof Ishak Institute's Malaysia Studies Programme as well as our external researchers for their diligent research, thoughtful writing and constructive interactions that have resulted in this collection of original, engaging and insightful chapters.

We gratefully acknowledge funding from the Konrad Adenauer Stiftung (KAS), which enabled: the fieldwork that richly substantiates many of the chapters published here; the series of pre- and post-GE-14 conferences at the ISEAS – Yusof Ishak Institute, beginning in late 2017 and continuing through 2018; and the publication of this book. We thank Christian Echle and Frederick Kliem, in particular, for their personal support and intellectual investment in this project.

The maps within this book enhance our view of Malaysia's political panorama. We applaud the immense work of our cartographers, Benjamin Hu and Pearlyn Pang, in making such optically pleasing and informative maps. Data on election results and registered voters enabled us to numerically observe vote patterns and analyse relationships with electorate composition. We record our thanks to the NGO Tindak Malaysia, and Danesh Chacko specially, who generously shared their databases. Mohammad Syafiq Suhaini provided excellent translation work at short notice, for which we are very grateful. Ibrahim Suffian of the Merdeka Center has been an exceptional source of support and insight, sharing his in-depth knowledge of the country's continuously evolving context and making judicious recommendations. We thank Zaiem Irsyad for his help in interviewing Iskandar Abdul Samad and transcribing the text for Chapter 21.

The ISEAS Library, under Pitt Kuan Wah, have provided invaluable support, especially in curating materials and news updates relevant to our research. We are exceedingly thankful for ISEAS administration colleagues, especially Betty Tan, Karthi Nair, Chin Mui Lan, Kamala Ramachandran and Darron Hoon, providing logistics support that ensured our conferences ran seamlessly.

Our heartfelt thanks go to Ng Kok Kiong and Rahilah Yusuf of ISEAS Publishing who guided the manuscript preparation and stewarded the process through to this final product. For the iconic moments that grace the front cover, we note our appreciation to Jahabar Sadiq and Zainal Halim for availing photos from the *Malaysian Insight's* repository, as well as Su-Ann Oh for invaluable suggestions on the cover design.

This endeavour would also not be possible without the backing of the Senior Management of the ISEAS – Yusof Ishak Institute, particularly the Director, Mr Choi Shing Kwok, and Senior Advisor, Mr Tan Chin Tiong. We thank them for their fervent and steadfast support.

Francis E. Hutchinson
Lee Hwok Aun

CONTRIBUTORS

Adib Zalkapli is a Director at BowerGroupAsia Malaysia, where he advises multinational corporations on Malaysian political and government affairs. He previously worked as a Political Analyst at the British High Commission, Kuala Lumpur. Adib holds an MA in International Relations from the University of Nottingham Malaysia.

Tony Paridi Bagang has a Master's degree in Public Administration from Universiti Sains Malaysia and is currently attached to the Faculty of Administrative Science and Policy Studies, Universiti Teknologi MARA (UiTM) Sabah, Malaysia. He has contributed to a number of edited volumes including *Electoral Dynamics in Malaysia: Findings from the Grassroots* (2014) and *Constitutional Asymmetry in Multinational Federalism* (2019).

Danesh Prakash Chacko is the Mapping Advisor of Tindak Malaysia, an electoral reform group and member of the BERSIH Coalition. He trained as a spatial scientist at RMIT University (Australia). As a volunteer for Tindak, he has lent his expertise to the organization's Redelineation Project, launched Malaysia's Online Electoral Map Platform, and made presentations on redelineation and open electoral data in Australia, Singapore and Malaysia. He currently leads Tindak Malaysia's team of volunteers to contribute to the electoral reform process undertaken by the Election Commission of Malaysia.

James Chai is a columnist at *Malaysiakini*, *Sin Chew Daily* and *Oriental Daily*. He is an award-winning First-Class degree law student at Queen Mary University of London, and emerged top of his class at Oxford University. He is also the national best student of the Certificate of Legal Practice examination.

Fahmi Fadzil is a writer, performer, and Member of Parliament for Lembah Pantai. He is trained as a Chemical Engineer (Purdue University) and is an award-winning theatre practitioner. He is also the Communications Director for the People's Justice Party (PKR).

Anantha Raman Govindasamy is a Senior Lecturer in Politics at the Centre for the Promotion of Knowledge and Language Learning, Universiti Malaysia Sabah. His research area focuses on Malaysia and Southeast Asian politics. He has contributed to journals such as the *Australian Journal of International Affairs* and the *Asian Journal of Political Science*.

Francis E. Hutchinson is Senior Fellow and Coordinator of the Malaysia Studies Programme at the ISEAS – Yusof Ishak Institute, Singapore. He is the Managing Editor of the *Journal of Southeast Asian Economies*. Dr Hutchinson's research interests include: state-business relations, federalism, decentralization, elections, and industrialization in Southeast Asia. He has published on these topics in the *Journal of Contemporary Asia*, *Asian Journal of Political Science*, *Journal of the Royal Asiatic Society*, *Asian-Pacific Economic Literature*, *Bulletin of Indonesian Economic Studies*, *Journal of Southeast Asian Economies*, *Asian Affairs*, and *Southeast Asian Affairs*.

Iskandar Abdul Samad is the Treasurer of Parti Islam Se-Malaysia (PAS). He was its Vice-President from 2015 to 2019. He served the Selangor State Government in charge of housing for two terms (2008–18). He is a UK-trained architect and an alumni of The Malay College Kuala Kangsar.

Khaled Nordin was the 15th Menteri Besar of Johor (2013–18). Datuk Seri Khaled is a member of UMNO and current Vice-President of the party. He served as Member of Parliament for Johor Bahru (1990–2004) and Pasir Gudang (2004–18), as well as State Assembly person for Permas (2013–18). Datuk Seri Khaled also served as Minister of Entrepreneur and Cooperative Development (2004–08) and Minister of Higher Education (2008–13).

Jannie Lasimbang, a Kadazan from Penampang, is a first-term Kapayan elected representative and the Sabah Assistant Minister of Law and Native Affairs. She is also the DAP Sabah Women's Chief, DAP National Women Executive Committee and Central Executive Committee member. Before joining politics, Jannie was a member of the United Nations Expert Mechanism on the Rights of Indigenous Peoples, a Commissioner with the Malaysian Human Rights Commission, and the Secretary General of the Asia Indigenous Peoples Pact and the Indigenous Peoples Network of Malaysia. She is also an experienced grassroots trainer and organizer, having worked in this field for twenty years.

Cassey Lee is a Senior Fellow and Coordinator of the Regional Economic Studies Programme at the ISEAS – Yusof Ishak Institute, Singapore. Prior to joining ISEAS, Dr Lee held academic appointments at the University of Wollongong, Nottingham University Business School (Malaysia) and University of Malaya. Dr Lee received his PhD (Economics) from University of California, Irvine. Dr Lee specializes in industrial organization. His current research focuses on competition policy, regulatory reforms, institutional economics, algorithmic economics, and firm-level studies related to innovation, productivity and trade. He has published in peer-reviewed journals such as *Journal of Economic Dynamics and Control, Kyklos, Journal of Economic Surveys, Journal of Asian Economics,* and *Economic Modelling.*

Lee Hwok Aun is Senior Fellow and Co-coordinator of the Malaysia Studies Programme at ISEAS – Yusof Ishak Institute, Singapore. He holds a PhD in Economics from the University of Massachusetts, Amherst, and an MSc in Political Economy of Development from SOAS University of London. His main research interests are affirmative action, discrimination, inequality, labour and education. His recent articles have been published in *Journal of Contemporary Asia, Journal of Asian and African Studies, Journal of the Asia Pacific Economy, Journal of Southeast Asian Economies,* and in books published by ISEAS, Oxford University Press, Edward Elgar and Routledge.

Lee Poh Onn is Senior Fellow and member of the Malaysia Studies Programme at the ISEAS – Yusof Ishak Institute, Singapore. He works on economic development issues in East Malaysia and also on natural resource management and cooperation in Southeast Asia.

Ngu Ik Tien is Senior Lecturer in the Department of Chinese Studies at the University of Malaya. She obtained her PhD in Political Science from the Universiti Sains Malaysia. She has published in *Inter-Asia Cultural Studies, Asian Journal of Social Science, Universitas: Monthly Review of Philosophy and Culture* (Taiwan) and *Southeast Asian Affairs* (China). She has also contributed to a number of edited volumes including *Electoral Dynamics in Malaysia: Findings from The Grassroots* (2014) and *Electoral Dynamics in Sarawak: Contesting Developmentalism and Rights* (2017).

Norshahril Saat is Fellow and Co-ordinator of the Indonesia Studies Programme at the ISEAS – Yusof Ishak Institute, Singapore. In 2018, he published three books: *The State, Ulama, and Islam in Malaysia and Indonesia* (Amsterdam University Press); *Tradition and Islamic Learning: Singapore Students in the Al-Azhar University* (ISEAS Publishing); and edited *Islam in Southeast Asia: Negotiating Modernity* (ISEAS Publishing). Dr Norshahril's articles have been published in journals such as *Asian Journal of Social Science, Contemporary Islam: Dynamics of Muslim Life, Review of Indonesian and Malaysian Affairs,* and *Studia Islamika.*

Kai Ostwald is Assistant Professor at the University of British Columbia's School of Public Policy and Global Affairs and the Department of Political Science. He is also Director of UBC's Centre for Southeast Asia Research, Associate Editor of *Pacific Affairs,* and an Associate Fellow at the ISEAS – Yusof Ishak Institute, Singapore. He holds a PhD in political science from the University of California San Diego and an MA from the National University of Singapore. His research focuses primarily on elections, ethnic politics, and decentralization in Southeast Asia, and has been published in a range of political science and area studies journals.

Geoffrey K. Pakiam is Fellow at the ISEAS – Yusof Ishak Institute, Singapore. In April 2018, he received his PhD in History from SOAS University of London. His most recent publication was the Malaysia country overview chapter for the 2019 edition of *Southeast Asian Affairs*. His research draws on histories of commodities, migration, environment, food, farming, and health, with special attention to the Malay Peninsula. Amongst other things, he is currently working on his first monograph, a history of smallholder farming and environmental change in Johor, one of the world's leading agricultural frontiers since the nineteenth century.

Arnold Puyok is currently the Deputy Dean (Postgraduate and Research) and Senior Lecturer in Politics and Government Studies at the Faculty of Social Sciences and Humanities (FSSH), Universiti Malaysia Sarawak (UNIMAS). Dr Puyok's works on contemporary Malaysian politics especially Sabah and Sarawak have been published in *Asian Journal of Political Science, Journal of Contemporary Southeast Asia, Kajian Malaysia, Asian Politics and Policy*, and *Journal of Borneo-Kalimantan*. His research interests are the politics of federal-state relations, ethnic and regional politics, electoral competition, politics and society, and contemporary Southeast Asian politics. His first book is *Electoral Dynamics in Sarawak: Contesting Developmentalism and Rights* (2017), co-edited with Meredith L. Weiss.

Rafizi Ramli is the founder of INVOKE Malaysia, Vice-President of People's Justice Party (PKR), and the former Member of Parliament of Pandan. He graduated with a degree in Electrical and Electronics Engineering from Leeds University and qualified as a chartered accountant at Jeffreys Henry LLP in London. At twenty-five, he became the youngest manager appointed at PETRONAS and subsequently worked as a general manager at Pharmaniaga PLC, before joining the Economic Advisory Office for Selangor as Chief Executive Officer.

Serina Rahman studies rural and coastal community attitudes and behaviour with regards to politics, natural habitat use and urbanization. A Visiting Fellow at the ISEAS – Yusof Ishak Institute, her practice is in community empowerment for marine ecosystem preservation. She obtained her PhD in Science from Universiti Teknologi MARA, in collaboration with the Faculty of Education at Universiti Malaya. She has a Masters in Applied Linguistics from the University of Wales, Cardiff. Serina is Malaysia's Citizen Science Ambassador for Citizen Science Asia and an Iskandar Malaysia Social Hero Award Winner for Environmental Protection (2014).

Wan Saiful Wan Jan was Visiting Senior Fellow (2017–18) at the ISEAS – Yusof Ishak Institute, Singapore. Prior to that, he was Chief Executive Officer at the Institute for Democracy and Economic Affairs (IDEAS), Malaysia. He contested in Malaysia's 14th General Election for the parliamentary constituency of Pendang, Kedah, but did not win. Subsequently, he was appointed as Special Adviser to the Malaysian Minister of Education and Chairman of the National Higher Education Fund Corporation. He is also a member of Parti Pribumi Bersatu Malaysia's Supreme Council.

Meredith L. Weiss is Professor and Chair of Political Science at the Rockefeller College of Public Affairs and Policy at the University at Albany, SUNY. Her MA and PhD in Political Science are from Yale University. Dr Weiss has published widely on political mobilization and contention, the politics of identity and development, and elections in Southeast Asia. Her books include *Student Activism in Malaysia: Crucible, Mirror, Sideshow* (2011), *Protest and Possibilities: Civil Society and Coalitions for Political Change in Malaysia* (2006), a forthcoming book on the resilience of electoral-authoritarian praxis in Malaysia and Singapore, and a number of edited volumes. Her articles have appeared in *Asian Survey, Critical Asian Studies, Democratization, Journal of Contemporary Asia*, and other journals.

Yeah Kim Leng is Professor of Economics and Senior Fellow at Jeffrey Cheah Institute on Southeast Asia (JCI) and Jeffrey Sachs Center on Sustainable Development at Sunway University. He worked for over twenty years in the private sector, principally as chief economist at the country's leading domestic credit rating agency. Professor Yeah holds an MBA and a PhD in Agricultural and Resource Economics from the University of Hawai'i, both obtained as a degree participant at the East-West Center, Honolulu. He is currently a Deputy President of the Malaysian Economic Association, a trustee of the Malaysian Tax Research Foundation and one of the two external members appointed to the Monetary Policy Committee at Bank Negara Malaysia.

Young Syefura Othman is a first-term Democratic Action Party (DAP) state assemblywoman for Ketari, Pahang. She is also Assistant National Secretary for Wanita DAP and Pakatan Harapan (PH) Youth Chief for Pahang. The BERSIH movement spurred her to enter political activism in 2012 and subsequently to join public service, branching away from her training in nursing and health services. She served as councillor in the Kajang municipality before being fielded in the 2018 General Elections.

ABBREVIATIONS

AFC	Asian Financial Crisis
Alliance	precursor to Barisan Nasional, comprised of UMNO, MCA, and MIC
Amanah	Parti Amanah Negara (National Trust Party)
B40	Bottom Forty (low-income households)
BA	Barisan Alternatif (Alternative Coalition)
BARJASA	Barisan Rakyat Jati Sarawak (Sarawak Native People's Front)
BERJAYA	Parti Bersatu Jelata Sabah (United Sabah Folks' Party)
BERSIH	Coalition for Free and Fair Elections
BN	Barisan National (National Front)
BR1M	Bantuan Rakyat 1 Malaysia (1Malaysia People's Assistance)
bumiputra	term referring to Malays, indigenous people of Peninsular Malaysia and the natives of Sabah and Sarawak
ceramah	political rally
CPI	consumer price index
DAP	Democratic Action Party
Dong Jiao Zong	Malaysian Chinese Education Movement
DOS	Department of Statistics
EC	Election Commission, or SPR (Surahanjaya Pilihanraya)
ECRL	East Coast Rail Link
EIP	Electoral Integrity Project
FELDA	Federal Land Development Authority
FGD	Focus Group Discussions
FPTP	first-past-the-post electoral system
GBS	Gabungan Bersatu Sabah (United Sabah Coalition)
GDP	gross domestic product
Gerakan	Parti Gerakan Rakyat Malaysia (Malaysian People's Movement Party)
GLC	Government-linked corporation
GPS	Gabungan Parti Sarawak (Sarawak Parties' Coalition)

GS	Gabungan Sabah (Sabah Coalition)
GS	Gagasan Sejahtera (Alliance of Prosperity), the coalition comprised of PAS and several minor parties; contested in GE-14.
GST	goods and services tax
HINDRAF	Hindu Rights Action Force
huatuan	Malaysian Chinese associations
hudud	a set of punishments established under shariah law for offences such as theft, robbery, consumption of alcohol, apostasy and illicit sex
ICERD	International Convention on the Elimination of All Forms of Ethnic and Religious Discrimination
IDE	Institut Darul Ehsan
IPF	All Malaysia Indian Progressive Front
ISA	Internal Security Act, replaced by SOSMA in 2012
KDCA	Kadazandusun Cultural Association Sabah
KDM	Kadazan Dusun Murut
KLCI	Kuala Lumpur Composite Index
LDP	Liberal Democratic Party
LTTE	Liberation Tigers of Tamil Eelam
M40	Middle Forty (middle-income households)
MACC	Malaysian Anti-Corruption Commission
MARA	Majlis Amanah Rakyat (People's Trust Council)
MA 63	Malaysia Agreement 1963
MCA	Malaysian Chinese Association
MIB	Malaysian Indian Economic Blueprint
MIC	Malaysian Indian Congress
Menteri Besar	Chief Minister of a state government
MP	Member of Parliament
NCR	Native Customary Rights
NDP	National Development Policy
NEP	New Economic Policy
NGO	non-governmental organization
NVP	National Vision Policy
1MDB	1 Malaysia Development Berhad
OPOVOV	One Person One Vote One Value
OSA	Official Secrets Act
PAADIAN	Persatuan Kadayan Sabah (Sabah Kadayan Association)
PANAS	Parti Negara Sarawak (Sarawak National Party)
PAP	People's Action Party (Singapore)
PAS	Parti Islam Se-Malaysia (Islamic Party of Malaysia)
PBB	Parti Pesaka Bumiputera Bersatu (United Bumiputera Heritage Party)
PBDS	Parti Bansa Dayak Sarawak (Sarawak Dayak People's Party)

PBRS	Parti Bersatu Rakyat Sabah (United Sabah People's Party)
PBS	Parti Bersatu Sabah (United Sabah Party)
PCS	Parti Cinta Sabah (Love Sabah Party)
PDP	Progressive Democratic Party
PESAKA	Parti Pesaka Anak Sarawak (Sarawak Native's Heritage Party)
Perkasa	Pertubuhan Pribumi Perkasa Malaysia (Malaysian Indigenous Empowerment Organization)
PH	Pakatan Harapan (Alliance of Hope), the coalition comprised of PKR, DAP, Amanah and PPBM; founded in 2015
PHRS	Parti Harapan Rakyat Sabah (Sabah People's Hope Party)
PKR	Parti Keadilan Rakyat (People's Justice Party)
PKS	Parti Kebangsaan Sabah (Sabah National Party)
PMIP	Pan-Malaysian Islamic Party; the precursor to PAS
PNB	Permodalan Nasional Berhad (National Equity Limited)
PPBM	Parti Pribumi Bersatu Malaysia (Malaysian United Indigenous Party)
PPP	Parti Progresif Penduduk Malaysia (Malaysian People's Progressive Party)
PPPA	Printing Presses and Publications Act
PPRS	Parti Perpaduan Rakyat Sabah (Sabah People's Unity Party)
PR	Pakatan Rakyat (People's Alliance); the coalition comprised of PKR, DAP and PAS; in operation from 2008 to 2015.
PRS	Parti Rakyat Sarawak (Sarawak People's Party)
PSRM	Parti Socialis Rakyat Malaysia (Malaysian People's Socialist Party)
PTPTN	Perbadanan Tabung Pendidikan Tinggi Nasional (National Higher Education Fund Corporation)
RM	ringgit Malaysia
ROS	Registrar of Societies
SAPP	Sabah Progressive Party
Sarawak BN	Sarawak Barisan Nasional
SCA	Sabah Chinese Association
SCA	Sarawak Chinese Association
SIC	Sabah Indian Congress
SLA	State Legislative Assembly
SNAP	Sarawak National Action Party
SOSMA	Security Offences (Special Measures) Act
SPDP	Sarawak Progressive Democratic Party
SPR	Surahanjaya Pilihanraya, or EC (Election Commission)
STAR	State Reform Party
STAR	Parti Solidariti Tanahair Ku (Sabah Homeland Solidarity Party)
SUF	Sarawak United Front
SUPP	Sarawak United People's Party
TERAS	Parti Tenaga Rakyat Sarawak (Sarawak People's Energy Party)

Ubah	Change (campaign slogan)
UEC	United Examination Certificate
UMNO	United Malays National Organization
UPKO	United Pasokmomogun Kadazandusun Organization
UPP	United People's Party
USA	United Sabah Alliance
USNO	United Sabah National Organization
VP	Vote Popularity
Warisan	Parti Warisan Sabah (Sabah Heritage Party)

Introduction

1

9 MAY 2018
The Unexpected

Francis E. Hutchinson and Lee Hwok Aun

INTRODUCTION

The results of Malaysia's 14th General Elections (GE-14) held in May 2018 were unexpected and transformative. Against conventional wisdom, the newly reconfigured opposition grouping Pakatan Harapan (PH) decisively defeated the incumbent Barisan Nasional (BN), ending six decades of uninterrupted dominant one-party rule.

Despite a long-running financial scandal dogging the ruling coalition, an opposition victory had been all but discarded due to: the advantages of incumbency; fissures amongst opposition ranks well into 2018; and a favourable economic outlook. Indeed, prominent pollsters and commentators predicted a solid BN victory or, at least, a narrow parliamentary majority.

Yet, on the day, deeply rooted political dynamics and influential actors came together, sweeping aside many prevailing assumptions and reconfiguring the country's political reality in the process. Voter turnout was significant, economic handouts were disregarded, and the effects of the redelineation of parliamentary and state constituencies were limited.

Beyond consolidating their support in ethnically mixed, urban areas, PH took most semi-urban areas and made important incursions into rural constituencies in the Peninsula's south and west. In addition to losing their parliamentary majority, BN's seemingly impregnable hold on many state governments was breached, and its East Malaysian fortresses capitulated. In addition, against all predictions, Parti Islam se Malaysia (PAS) thrived, retaining Kelantan, toppling Terengganu and making important inroads in Pahang and Kedah.

Due to its long tenure in power, up until 2018, BN was the only government most Malaysians have ever known. It is formally a parliamentary democracy, but has been variously labelled a semi-democracy (Case 2002), pseudo-democracy (Case 2004) or an electoral authoritarian regime (Ufen 2009). Mostly recently, Lopez and Welsh (2018) labelled it a "resilient regime", implying one that is strong—though not invincible.

The Alliance-BN's hold on power for more than six decades was aided by massive structural advantages, including deployment of public resources for partisan campaigning, control over mainstream media, and a compliant electoral commission able and willing to tilt the playing field in their favour (Weiss 2014; Ostwald 2017).

These incumbent advantages were demonstrated in the 2013 elections, when expectations of change were dashed and BN held on—despite winning fewer votes than the opposition. These systemic factors, and perhaps recent electoral history, led many commentators to be overly conservative in their analyses of Malaysia's 14th general election (GE-14).

Malaysia is a complex country, with important urban and rural realities, and different communities spread across its vast territory. New developments in society and technology have been underway. While BN exerted strong control over traditional media, new media is reconfiguring the country in distinct and unexpected ways. Traditional voter blocs are becoming more heterogeneous in outlook and voting patterns. Diverse geographical patterns of political expression, as well as localized history, refract national issues differentially. Social media posting, and the growing industries of public opinion polling and big data analysis, constitute new arenas for gauging electoral sentiment and influencing public opinion.

Through these means, as well as anecdotal observations in the run-up to GE-14, many discerned a tide of public discontent regarding: the cost of living and economic hardships; perceived corruption of the regime; and a self-serving ruling elite. Some parties were certain that sentiments had reached a decisive point, yet it was widely held that BN's cohesion and economic management, coupled with Pakatan's uncertainty and inexperience, had curtailed the latter's momentum. Public polls reflected a BN buffer—but also large proportions of undecided voters. In combination, the above presaged the sense of shock and disbelief that greeted the results of 9 May.

This book *The Defeat of Barisan Nasional: Missed Signs or Late Surge?* seeks to establish the underlying drivers for change in this election and so contribute to the literature on Malaysia's political context as well as wider debates on transitions from compromised democracies. An important subsidiary enterprise is to investigate the reasons behind the misplaced expectations regarding GE-14's results and the untrammelled surprise generated by its denouement.

By way of introduction, this chapter sets out the various themes and sub-themes guiding this book. To this end, the next section will briefly review Malaysia's electoral history up until the 2013 general election. The subsequent part will set out the salient issues and drivers in the run-up to the May 2018 general election. The following section will then briefly review the results of that year's election at the national and state levels. The final section will lay out the aims and research design of the GE-14 project before relating it to the structure of the book.

TILTING THE PLAYING FIELD: ELECTIONS IN MALAYSIA

Up until 2018, the ruling regime's longevity—including the Alliance era of 1957–69 as well as BN's post-1974 continuous reign—and ability to eke out victories in the face of formidable challenges were underpinned by several elements. These included the coalition's track record in maintaining social cohesion, stewarding economic growth and overseeing a generous redistribution system. However, its political dominance had deeper roots.

One key element of the Alliance-BN's electoral success was its consociational nature. According to Lijphart (1977), this framework can be used to govern plural societies, namely those characterized by cleavages due to language, religion or ethnicity. Under this arrangement, the representation of the main interest groups in government, as well as effective negotiation between the leaders of these groupings allows stability to be preserved and conflict to be avoided.[1]

Consequently, the Alliance-BN coalition brought together the representatives of the country's primary ethnic groups into one grouping, namely: the United Malays National Organization (UMNO), the Malaysian Chinese Association (MCA), and the Malaysian Indian Congress (MIC).[2] In electoral terms, this arrangement entailed several advantages. First, it allowed the coalition to pool candidates and deploy them strategically, usually matching them with the predominant ethnic community in each constituency. Second, even where individual candidates did not match the largest ethnicity of a given seat, many voters could still be persuaded to vote across ethnic lines for BN. This was due to the belief that the coalition's multiethnic leadership meant that their interests were still represented within the grouping and the country at large. Despite their nominal equality, UMNO was the *primus inter pares* of the coalition, as it represented the largest and most politically active demographic at independence. Its power relative to the other coalition members has increased over time, particularly after the civil unrest of 1969 (Mauzy 1993).

Nonetheless, the electoral system furnished various advantages to the incumbent, which BN consistently and effectively utilized. While Malaysia has held regular elections since independence and the BN has secured "performance legitimacy" through competing and winning them, the electoral contests have taken place on a tilted "playing field". The country's first past the post (FPTP) system disproportionately rewards winners by awarding an entire parliamentary seat to the winner—regardless of how narrow the victory. This system helped BN maintain a two-thirds majority in parliament up until 2008. This majority, in turn, allowed the coalition to table frequent amendments to the Constitution, including through interventions that undermined the Election Commission's (EC) authority and independence (Saravanamuttu 2016; Chacko, this volume).

A compliant EC oversaw continuous malapportionment, resulting in the persistence of oversized urban constituencies and undersized rural constituencies, and a ratio of rural to urban legislative seats not aligned to Malaysia's urbanizing demographics. Malapportionment has especially benefited UMNO in the rural Malay heartland, as well as indigenous-based parties in Sarawak and Sabah. Gerrymandering, by redrawing boundaries to "pack" districts with concentrations of supporters and "crack" opposition-leaning areas, has further biased the terms of engagement, as part of redelineation exercises conducted about once every decade. Voter irregularities have also marred BN wins in some elections (Ostwald 2017).

In power, BN also possessed various coercive instruments at its disposal. This included control over traditional media: directly via ownership of news outlets by BN member parties; or indirectly through licensing via the Printing Presses and Publications Act controlled by the Ministry of Home Affairs (Tapsell 2013). The government has detained persons without trial and prosecuted dissidents under national security pretexts but clearly with political motivation, most aggressively under the Internal Security Act (subsequently the Security Offences (Special Measures) Act (SOSMA)), and the Sedition Act. The power to take disciplinary action against dissenting university students, enabled by the University and University Colleges Act, contained student activism. The Registrar of Societies (ROS) has also occasionally harassed opposition parties (International Crisis Group 2012).

Barisan Nasional's consociational mode of campaigning worked especially well in Peninsular Malaysia, but began to lose effectiveness from the late 1990s when its popularity in urban, multiethnic areas began to wane, prompting a search for alternative methods of appealing to voters. Thus, BN increasingly depended on East Malaysian coalition partners as well as "developmentalism" (Loh 2002) to appeal to the country's expanded middle class, while continually dispensing patronage to secure party factions and enhance electoral popularity (Gomez and Jomo 1997).

This process was hastened by the developments of 1997. Prime Minister Mahathir's sacking of his deputy, Anwar Ibrahim, in the aftermath of the Asian Financial Crisis, triggered a political crisis as well as the genesis of the *Reformasi* social movement (Pepinsky 2009). A more permanent result from this period of turbulence was the establishment of the Keadilan party—later renamed Parti Keadilan Rakyat (PKR)—by disgruntled elements of UMNO, led by Anwar Ibrahim. UMNO's past schisms had been short-lived, but new opposition forces were sustained post-1998—albeit with shifts over time.

The *Reformasi* movement along with the mistreatment of Anwar Ibrahim and formation of the Barisan Alternatif, galvanized a protest wave against UMNO—which did poorly in the 1999 general elections. However, while Keadilan and PAS increased their electoral foothold, the Democratic Action Party (DAP) received a rebuke from non-Malay, especially Chinese, voters apprehensive over the cobbled opposition coalition (Felker 2000). Nonetheless, the opposition coalition did well enough to threaten BN's permanence in power, prompting Mahathir's decision to retire in 2003 and hand over to Abdullah Badawi (Wain 2009).

The handover to Abdullah Badawi was warmly received, and rapturously reflected in the 2004 election results which gave BN its best ever showing. That swing, however, was more issue- than loyalty-driven. This factor, as well as the shortfalls in Abdullah's administration, coupled with increased cohesion in the DAP-PKR alliance, delivered the 2008 shock. That year, BN lost its customary two-thirds majority and relinquished five state governments. Subsequently, the opposition banded together in the PKR-DAP-PAS Pakatan Rakyat coalition (Weiss 2013).

In 2009, Abdullah Badawi, in turn, passed stewardship of UMNO and BN to Najib Razak, a political blue-blood and son of Malaysia's second Prime Minister Tun Abdul Razak. Najib vigorously moved to define his administration, courting international opinion, pronouncing a reformist New Economic Model, and rolling out cash handouts to poor families (BR1M) as well as setting up subsidized shops and more health clinics (Nelson 2012; Brown 2013).

The most captivating of reforms concerned a nebulous shift from "race-based" affirmative action to "need-based" affirmative action, including a roll-back of ethnic equity requirements in various services sectors. However, the lack of coherence, clarity and foresight provoked Malay nationalist backlash at perceived loss of privilege, to which Najib responded by introducing new pro-bumiputra programmes. Simultaneously, the failure to truly replace pro-bumiputra race-based preferences deepened disaffection among non-bumiputras (Nelson 2012; Abdillah 2014).

In the 2013 election, Najib's first, BN secured only 47 per cent of the popular vote—less than Pakatan Rakyat—and lost more parliamentary seats. However, the coalition retained power due to the FPTP system and the over-representation of rural Malay-majority seats. Due to this latter factor, UMNO paradoxically obtained a higher number of parliamentary seats than it did in 2008, and also managed to recapture the Kedah and Terengganu state governments (Ostwald 2013). That said, many of UMNO's victories were slim.

With non-Malay support crumbling and BN's Peninsular-based non-Malay parties decimated, the coalition became unprecedentedly UMNO-dominant and more dependent on its Sarawak and Sabah parties in order to secure a parliamentary majority (Chin 2014). Najib's 2013–18 term retained a raft of social assistance programmes targeted at the bottom 40 per cent (B40), especially the BR1M cash transfers, but politically leaned increasingly towards the Malay base (Abdillah 2014).

Barisan Nasional was initially helped by turmoil in Pakatan Rakyat, as PAS left and then, in turn, split into two, with the more progressive faction Parti Amanah Negara (Amanah) joining PKR and the DAP to form Pakatan Harapan. Yet, Amanah's genesis as a splinter party from PAS was fraught with uncertainty, given the fierce loyalties towards its parent party and uncertainty on how to split resources and assets (Wan Saiful 2017).

The Najib administration also became embroiled in a series of scandals, most prominently revolving around the strategic wealth fund, 1MDB. The fund was established in 2009 and directly supervised by the Ministry of Finance—a portfolio held by Najib Razak himself. By June 2014, the organization had liabilities in excess of US$10 billion linked to real estate speculation, acquisition of power plants, and debt-funded growth. US$4.5 billion was allegedly misappropriated by 1MDB's senior management and associates, and US$700 million was found in Najib Razak's personal bank accounts (*Sunday Times*, 3 June 2018).

The 1MDB scandal acquired an international dimension when the US Department of Justice launched an investigation in 2015. This led to further probes of 1MDB and affiliated companies being launched in six countries. Domestically, additional allegations of mismanagement were made of apex government bodies such as Majlis Amanah Rakyat (MARA), Federal Land Development Authority (FELDA), and Tabung Haji—institutions of deep significance to the Malay community (*Sunday Times*, 3 June 2018; *The Edge Malaysia Weekly*, 24 October 2017).

An elite schism took place within UMNO as a result of this. Senior party figures such as Mahathir Mohamad, Muhyiddin Yassin, and Shafie Apdal openly criticized Najib Razak's handling of the 1MDB issue. In mid-2015, Muhyiddin and Shafie lost their Cabinet positions and were expelled or suspended from UMNO the subsequent year. For his part, Mahathir left the party in early 2016 (Hutchinson 2018).

Mahathir and Muhyiddin, along with a number of other ex-UMNO leaders, formed Parti Pribumi Bersatu Malaysia (PPBM) in September 2016. Through focusing on language, religion, and affirmative action, the new party sought to compete directly with UMNO for Malay votes (Wan Saiful 2018). In March 2017, the party joined PKR, DAP and Amanah in the newly reconfigured alliance Pakatan Harapan.

THE RUN-UP TO GE-14

In early 2018, BN's electoral prospects were looking favourable. The benefits of incumbency were thought to carry the day and there was relatively little that hinted at the prospect of regime change.

The economy was doing well, with predictions from the Central Bank that the economy was on course to grow 5.5–6 per cent in 2018. Inflation was a moderate 2–3 per cent, and unemployment a commendable 3.4 per cent (*The Edge Financial Daily*, 29 March 2018). An election budget released in October 2017 increased subsidies and social assistance for the B40, and was accompanied by tax reductions and cash transfers to influential interest groups such as farmers, civil servants, and retirees (Yeah 2017).

From BN's perspective, the 1MDB issue seemed to have been brought under control. Difficulties in communicating the arcane intricacies of kleptocratic dealings in a simple fashion and in categorically incriminating Najib Razak, made the electoral impact of these allegations unclear. Moreover, leaders from key supervisory organizations such as the Central Bank and Attorney-General's office had been replaced. An internal probe carried out by the new Attorney-General absolved Najib Razak of any responsibility in 1MDB's financial irregularities, and that investigation along with a subsequent report drafted by Parliament's Public Accounts Committee were kept under wraps by the Official Secrets Act (*Sunday Times*, 3 June 2018).

In electoral terms, BN held wide swathes of rural territory, particularly along the eastern flank of the Peninsula in Johor and Pahang, and in the northwest in Kedah and Perlis. Sabah and Sarawak constituted other redoubts of consequence. Furthermore, the incumbent coalition held no less than ten out of thirteen state governments.

In March 2018, the ruling coalition pushed through a parliamentary redelineation exercise. In the past, such exercises corresponded with a bump in BN's electoral performance, but this time the coalition lacked the two-thirds majority necessary to increase the total number of parliamentary seats. Nonetheless, the redelineation amended boundaries in ninety-eight seats in West Malaysia, yet it did not address structural issues such as malapportionment or gerrymandering. Instead, it increased the ethnic concentration of a number of key seats, particularly in Selangor (Ooi 2018). The effect of these changes was taken to increase the vulnerability of key PH-held seats or shore up support in marginal BN-held seats.

The following month, the BN majority in parliament approved the Anti-Fake News Bill. Overlooking concerns raised by the Malaysian Bar Council and civil society organizations about freedom of expression, the Bill provided for up to six years' jail and hefty fines for news deemed to be fake. The Anti-Fake News Bill applied to traditional, online, and social media, as well as news regarding Malaysia published locally or overseas. The Bill covered those generating news as well as third parties who hosted information that was classified as fake (*Straits Times*, 2 April 2018).

Poll watchers also pointed to the potential boost to BN's electoral chances accruing from three-way contests, which were anticipated to favour the incumbents by splitting the protest vote. Barisan Nasional tacitly encouraged PAS to run as a third electoral force, and held out the promise of a pact between the two in the aftermath of the election (*Asia Sentinel*, 9 February 2018).

With these factors as a backdrop, conventional wisdom held that BN would retain a parliamentary majority even if it lost the popular vote—much as it had in 2013. Other more optimistic projections held that the incumbents would retain their grip over their "fixed deposits" and rural strongholds, and perhaps even claw back some seats from PH or PAS (*The Sun Daily*, 7 May 2018).

Nonetheless, Pakatan Harapan was not without its electoral assets. Since its inception in 2008, PH's precursor, Pakatan Rakyat, had gained experience in managing coalitional relations, forging common platforms, cultivating ties with activist groups, and sustaining dissent (Khoo 2018). The grouping was also able to refer its credible achievements in Selangor and Penang (Yeoh 2012).

Pakatan Harapan built on these assets in important ways, mostly notably by hammering out an apex organizational structure for the fledgling coalition. In July 2017, the grouping appointed Mahathir as chairman and Wan Azizah, Anwar Ibrahim's wife and PKR Head, as president. The other party leaders were made deputy presidents. In January 2018, PH nominated Mahathir Mohamad as its prime ministerial candidate—marking a first for Pakatan Rakyat and Pakatan Harapan members, who previously could not reach consensus, and this time were saddled with a dilemma due to Anwar Ibrahim's incarceration and hence ineligibility for the position. In the early part of 2018, the PH campaign also grew more disciplined and its messages clearer and simpler. This was aided by agreements within the coalition on a common logo and campaign platform.

In East Malaysia, the dynamics worked somewhat differently. The 2016 state elections in Sarawak bolstered BN's hopes of a repeat performance in 2018—albeit without the popular Adenan Satem at its head, as the late Chief Minister had been widely credited with that year's stellar results. However, less compelling leadership in subsequent years raised questions as to the solidity of BN's hold on the state. The increasingly strident calls for state autonomy and respect for indigenous land and local issues also suggested that election contenders' chances would be influenced by their credibility on these specific issues (Lee Poh Onn, this volume).

Sabah, for its part, looked decidedly less sure. Shafie Apdal sought to make inroads in his native state by founding Parti Warisan Sabah (Warisan), which sought to cater to both Muslim and non-Muslim bumiputras. In a further twist, Warisan allied with PH, enabling it to pool resources and field candidates in all of the state's constituencies (Bagang and Puyok, this volume).

The prevalence of UMNO rural strongholds, as well as PH's consolidated presence in urban constituencies, set up semi-urban/semi-rural constituencies as key battlegrounds. Indeed, fifty-four seats were identified as marginal UMNO-held constituencies, which were won by narrow majorities in 2013. In addition, we should note that, while rural constituencies disproportionately outnumber urban ones, 70 per cent of Malaysia's population is classified as urban. Consequently, a significant proportion of rural voters are actually urban residents who return to their towns and villages to vote. Hence, a broader range of electoral issues more commonly associated with the urban electorate concerning governance, corruption, and the like can also gain traction among a significant share of voters registered in rural areas. Thus, relative to past elections, patronage-oriented campaigns frontloaded with giveaways and development promises, might be less effective in rural areas than they used to be.

In addition, despite the positive aggregate economic data, surveys consistently reflected the primacy of cost of living issues for voters. This was due to, among other things, the depreciating ringgit, which made imported items more expensive, and the federal government's phasing out of subsidies on oil, sugar, gas, flour, and other staples. The imposition of goods and services tax (GST) from April 2015 further compounded frustrations, as it visibly increased costs for a wide range of items, including basic necessities that contained some form of value-added processing (Hutchinson 2018).

The electoral gains offered by cost of living issues and GST were also ably perceived by PAS, the third competitor in the elections. Consequently, the party sought to increase its hold over Kelantan and expand its reach into new territory. As for Kelantan, the state had been continuously ruled by the Islamic party since 1990. While it was among Malaysia's poorest states, PAS could point to popular local legislation and make credible claims that the state had been deprived of its fair share of royalties from petroleum (Norshahril, this volume; Hutchinson 2014). For audiences in other parts of the Peninsula, the party made much mileage out of rising prices, wage levels, and GST.[3]

While BN looked to be competing from a position of strength, some unique developments in the campaign's final days resulted in greater uncertainty and flux than anticipated.

In a first for the country, polling day was declared on a Wednesday, ostensibly to lower voter turnout, which was deemed to benefit BN (*Today*, 13 April 2018). This generated a public outcry from diverse segments of society, including the civil servants' union, CUEPACS, as well as a petition to the King signed by more than 100,000 people (*Straits Times*, 11 April 2018). Those particularly inconvenienced included voters from Sabah and Sarawak working on the Peninsula, as well as Malaysians working in Singapore, who would have to travel home to vote (*Malay Mail*, 10 April 2018; *Today*, 13 April 2018).

This was partially addressed by the Najib administration's decision to make the day a public holiday. However, the date still had an impact on outstation voters, particularly those living overseas. Unlike in recent elections, when foreign missions processed the ballots of overseas Malaysians, this provision was denied in 2018; in many countries, voters were responsible for delivering their ballot sheets to their district. However, the sheets were only available after nomination day on 29 April—making postage or even express courier services unfeasible. This generated widespread resentment, spurring Malaysians overseas to organize collectively to deliver their ballots, or car-pool to travel back to vote (*The Star*, 7 May 2018; *Channel NewsAsia*, 10 April 2018).

Decisions taken by state organs also compounded feelings of frustration. During the campaign, the Registrar of Societies (ROS) refused to register PH as a coalition and also provisionally deregistered Bersatu as a political party (*Straits Times*, 6 April 2018; *New Straits Times*, 15 May 2018). While this temporarily wrong-footed PH, it forced the component parties to negotiate and ultimately accept to collectively contest using PKR's logo (*The Star*, 27 April 2018). This was complemented by the EC's egregious ruling that only the official president of the contesting party and local candidates could appear on campaign posters (*The Star*, 1 May 2018). This was clearly a tactic to prevent the propagation of Mahathir's image as the de facto leader of non-registered Pakatan Harapan. These moves themselves became election storylines, and may have even backfired on BN, which came across as petty and mean-spirited.

Despite these pivotal developments, there was still a generalized feeling that PH did not inspire overwhelming confidence. Polling firms such as Merdeka Center, Ilham Centre, and Kajidata Research consistently reported low levels of confidence in the new coalition (*Free Malaysia Today*, 27 March 2018; *Malay Mail Online*, 14 February 2018), as did more targeted surveys in key battlegrounds such as Johor (Chong et al. 2017). Indeed, in a press release on 8 May, the eve of the election, the Merdeka Center predicted a narrow win for the incumbents (Merdeka Center 2018). The only exception to this trend was INVOKE, who forecasted a PH victory (Rafizi and Chai, this volume). However, given that organization's affiliation with PKR, its findings were seen as partisan—limiting its diffusion and impact.

The state of affairs on 6 April 2018, the eve of the dissolution of parliament, is illustrated in the front and back endpapers of this book. The maps depict the seats held by BN, PH, PAS, and Parti Warisan Sabah, as well as five constituencies whose MPs switched their party affiliation to independent status. This includes: Cameron Highlands, Kota Melaka, and Bandar Tun Razak on the Peninsula; as well as Lubok Antu and Selangau in Sarawak.

THE RESULTS: DECISION AND DIVISION

Against expectations of a lower turnout rate, polling on 9 May proceeded with a relatively high turnout of 82 per cent and without significant anomalies. Beyond the thousands of volunteers who manned the polling stations and monitored proceedings, there were also international observers from nine countries (*Malay Mail*, 7 May 2018; *The Star*, 11 May 2018). There were, however, isolated cases of irregularities, notably the refusal of some EC officials to countersign and officially endorse the vote counts of ballot boxes (*Malaysiakini*, 10 May 2018).

While the voting process proceeded without significant incident, the release of official results descended into some chaos with the EC straggling to pronounce winners in a timely manner. Early waves of results, swiftly disseminated through the online and social media and eventually declared by the EC, indicated a massive collapse of confidence in UMNO and BN. However, a period of limbo ensued in the wee hours of the morning of 10 May, during which unofficial results based on the tallying by PH campaigns and reporting of district counting centres clearly showed PH winning—but the EC central command stalled confirmation.

In the end, GE-14's verdict could be delayed but not denied. Malaysia and Malaysians were numb, as they took in the new political order and resulting electoral lay of the land. The popular votes were cast: 48.3 per cent for PH (with Warisan); 33.8 per cent for BN; and 17.0 per cent for PAS. Relative to GE-13, BN's vote share fell the most, from 47.4 per cent in GE-13. The three-way contest also affected the other two parties, as Pakatan Rakyat, which included PAS in 2013, also garnered less than the 50.9 per cent it did in GE-13.

Malaysia's political reconfiguration is spatially staggering. The incumbents and GE-14 winners are illustrated, respectively, on this book's front and back endpapers, with additional permutations in Figures 1.1 and 1.2. On the Peninsula, PH carried urban areas and the west coast, BN held on to vast rural swathes notably in eastern Pahang and Johor, and much of Perak, while PAS became more concentrated in portions of Kedah and coastal Kelantan and Terengganu.

The realignment was driven by decisive, overwhelming support of some groups, notably Chinese and Indian voters, and stark divisions in others, especially in the Malay and indigenous electorate (Figure 1.1). Expectations that multicornered fights would split the opposition vote and play into BN's hands were thoroughly

FIGURE 1.1
Parliamentary Seats in Peninsular Malaysia by Ethnicity and Winning Party (GE-14)

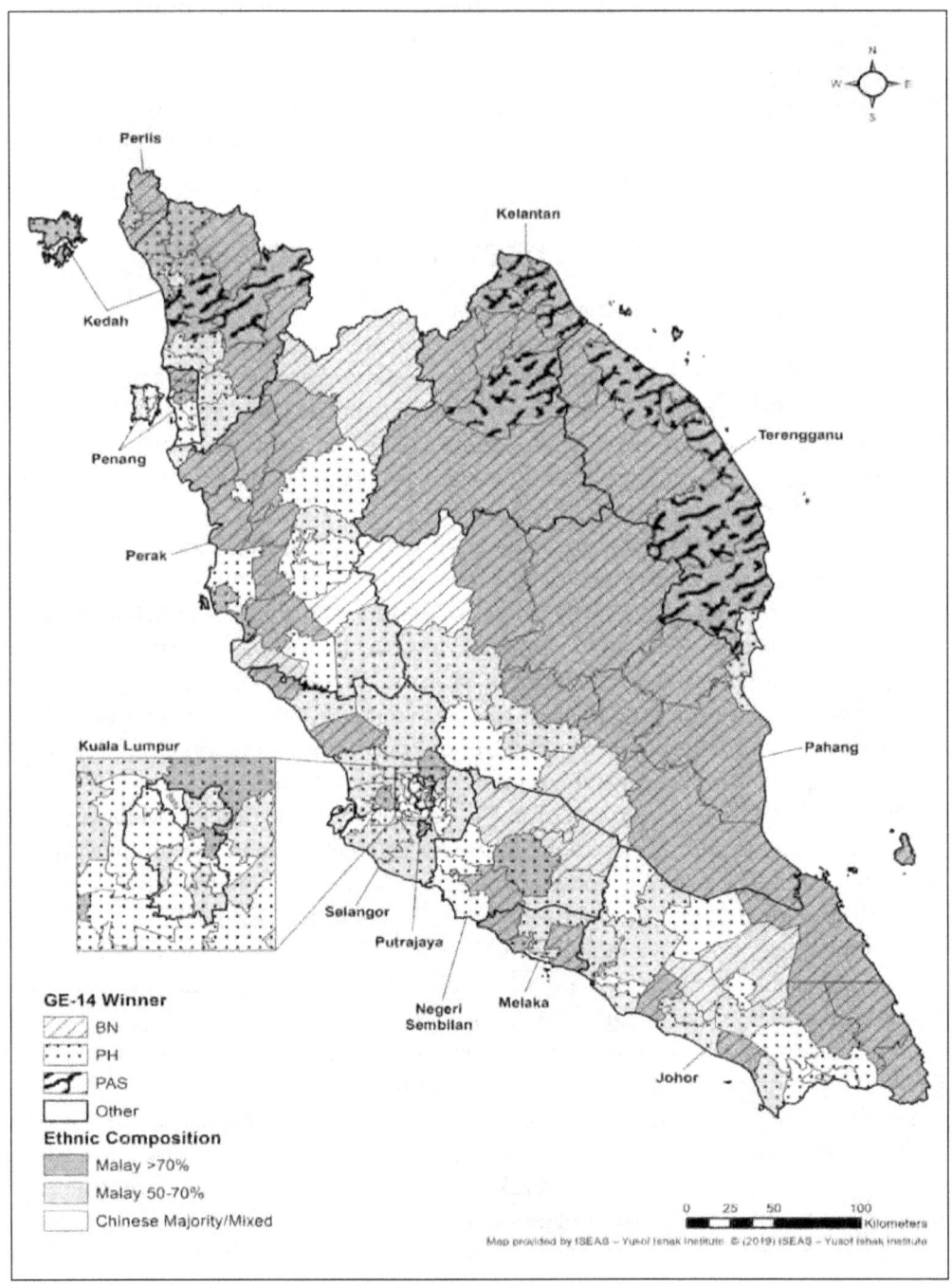

FIGURE 1.2
Parliamentary Seats in Sabah and Sarawak by Ethnicity and Winning Party (GE-14)

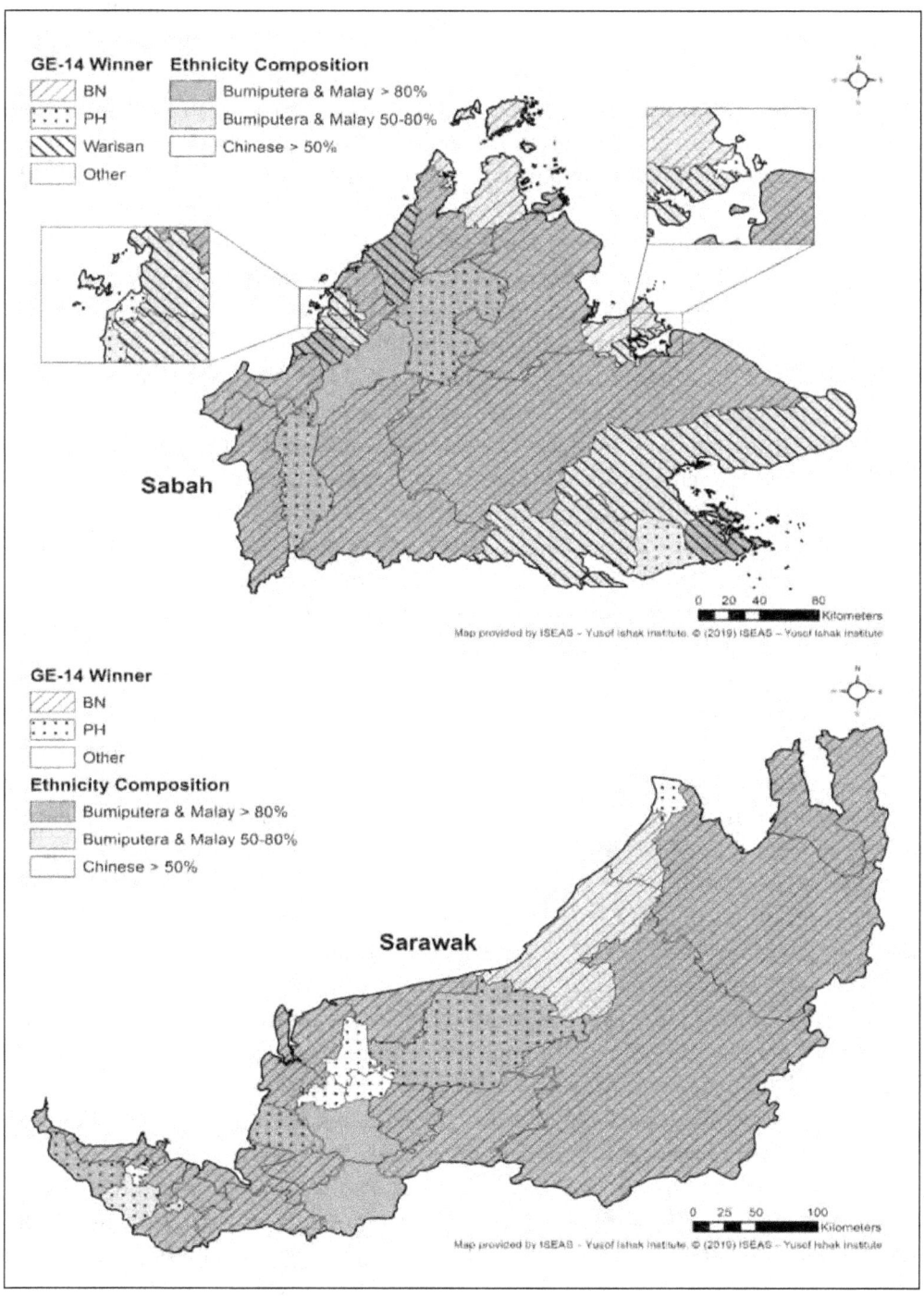

confounded; PH generally won by wide margins. On the Peninsula, UMNO sustained its loyal following in the rural Malay heartland, but PAS also held its ground, and both PAS and PH made some inroads. PH was competitive in constituencies with 50–70 per cent Malay voters, in which UMNO and PH did evenly well. UMNO's popularity held in constituencies where Malays constituted 70 per cent or more, with PAS also securing wins in this demographic. However, in Kedah as well as a small number of seats in other states, PH made some inroads in these seats. PH won all but two Chinese-majority or mixed constituencies without a majority group.

In Sabah and Sarawak, mixed and Chinese-majority seats were also carried by PH or Warisan, without clear patterns based on the indigenous share of the electorate (Figure 1.2). This generalized portrayal of course overlooks the highly heterogeneous composition of East Malaysia's indigenous peoples.

Tables 1.1 and 1.2 shed further light on the GE-14 results. Table 1.1 sets out the change in parliamentary seats between 6 April and 9 May 2018. BN recorded a total loss of fifty seats with a particularly large number of seats, thirty-five, concentrated on the Peninsula—leaving the coalition with a mere seventy-nine seats. Pakatan Harapan gained in similar measure, netting forty additional seats, with most of these also on the Peninsula. By itself, the coalition had enough seats to secure a narrow majority in parliament. However, its majority was complemented by Warisan's seats, which had also increased from two to eight. For its part, PAS built upon its base of thirteen seats with the acquisition of another five—all on the Peninsula.

The win rates for BN shrank from 60.2 per cent in GE-13 to 35.6 per cent in GE-14, while those of PKR and DAP burgeoned from 30.3 per cent to 67.6 per cent, and from 74.5 per cent to 89.4 per cent, respectively. In contrast, PAS fared much worse outside of Pakatan Rakyat, with its win rates plummeting from 28.8 per cent to 11.5 per cent. In terms of the new entrants, Warisan did the best, winning almost half of its contests, while PPBM and Amanah won only a quarter and a third of their respective contests.

At the state level, the change is even more striking. From its initial holdings of ten state governments, BN was eventually only left with two, Pahang and Perlis. PH retained Selangor and Penang and, with its new holdings, secured a continuous line of control along the west coast from Johor in the south to Kedah in the north. PAS kept Kelantan and secured Terengganu (Figure 1.3). In East Malaysia, Warisan and PH allies mustered a majority in the Sabah state assembly, and in terms of the balance of Sarawak parliament seats, BN affiliates left the coalition to form an independent state-based coalition, Gabungan Parti Sarawak (GPS).

GE-14 has thus vastly reconfigured Malaysia's political panorama and on a scale far beyond anything most imaged. There are many moving parts to this phenomenon, with certain elements channelling the desire for change and others generating a movement away from the incumbents. The next section will lay out how this book seeks to approach the elections.

TABLE 1.1
Parliament of Malaysia: GE-14 Change in Seats

6 April (Incumbents)					
	BN	*PH*	*PAS*	*Warisan*	*Other*
Peninsula	84	65	13		3
Sabah	22	2		2	
Sarawak	23	6			2
Total	*129*	*73*	*13*	*2*	*5*
9 May (GE-14 Winners)					
	BN	*PH*	*PAS*	*Warisan*	*Other*
Peninsula	49	97	18		1
Sabah	11	6		8	1
Sarawak	19	10			2
Total	*79*	*113*	*18*	*8*	*4*
Change (Gain/Loss)					
	BN	*PH*	*PAS*	*Warisan*	*Other*
Peninsula	−35	+32	+5		−2
Sabah	−11	+4		+6	+1
Sarawak	−4	+4			
Total	*−50*	*+40*	*+5*	*+6*	*−1*

TABLE 1.2
Parliament of Malaysia: Wins and Win Rates, by Party

GE-13			
	Won	*Contested*	*Win Rate*
BN	133	221	60.2%
PKR (PR)	30	99	30.3%
DAP (PR)	38	51	74.5%
PAS (PR)	21	73	28.8%
GE-14			
	Won	*Contested*	*Win Rate*
BN	79	222	35.6%
PKR (PH)	48	71	67.6%
DAP (PH)	42	47	89.4%
PAS	18	157	11.5%
PPBM (PH)	12	52	23.1%
Amanah (PH)	11	34	32.4%
Warisan	8	17	47.1%

FIGURE 1.3
Peninsular Malaysia: State Governments in GE-13 and GE-14

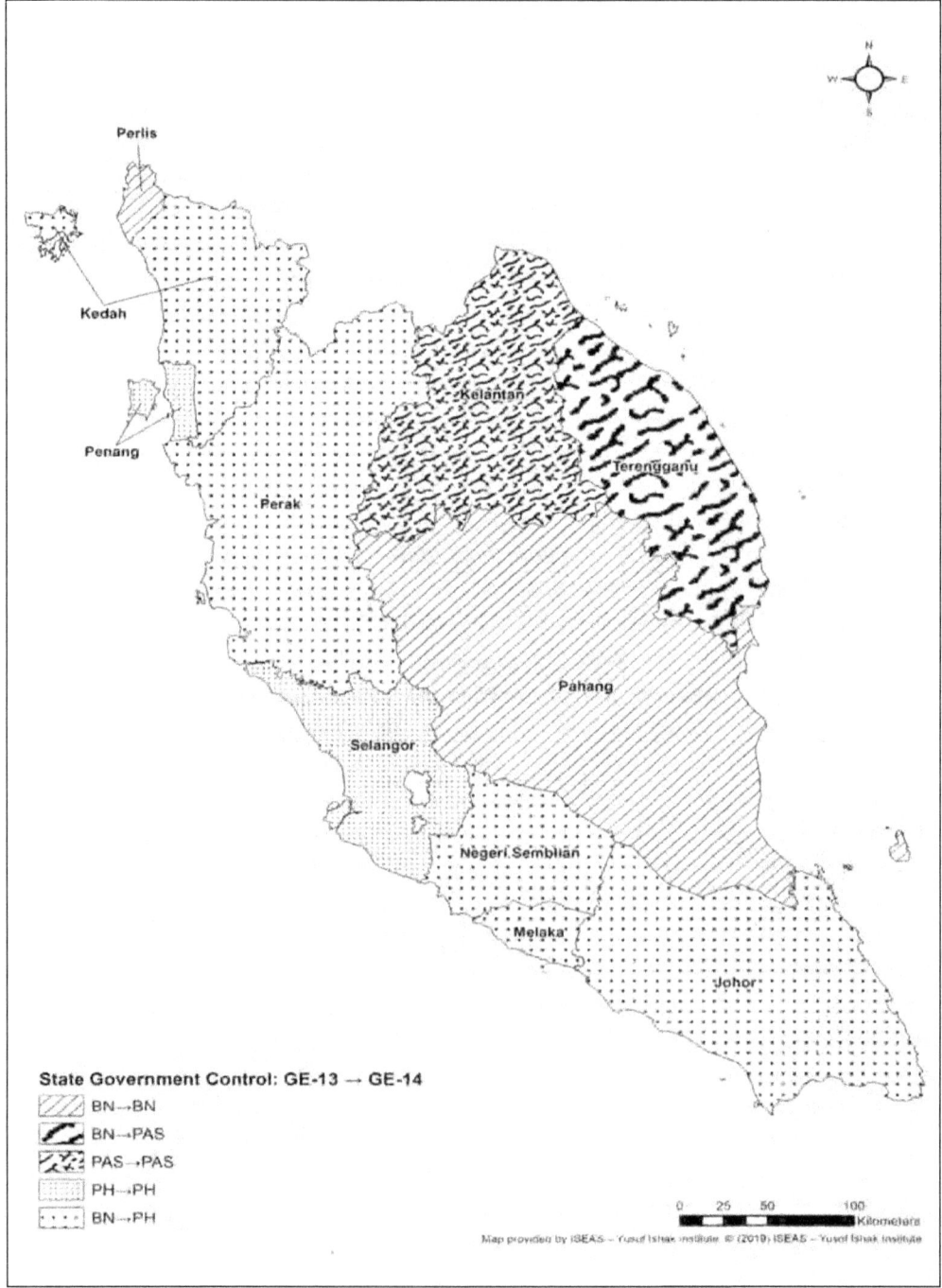

THE STRUCTURE OF THIS BOOK

The ISEAS – Yusof Ishak Institute has a well-established Malaysia Studies Programme, which seeks to provide informed analysis on key economic, social, and political issues facing the country.

Researchers based at the Institute have followed and carried out research on the conduct of elections in Malaysia over the past decades. The fruits of this work have been shared through monographs published by the Institute as well as, more recently, research products such as *ISEAS Perspectives* and the *Trends in Southeast Asia* series. Over the last ten years, the Malaysia Studies Programme has produced books on the 2008 and 2013 general elections, as well as the conduct of elections more generally.

In *March 8: Eclipsing May 13* (2008), Ooi, Saravanamuttu, and Lee provided a grounded perspective on the 2008 parliamentary elections in the country, discussing the key issues in the campaign on one hand, and providing observations on key contests in Selangor, Putrajaya, Kuala Lumpur, Penang, and Kelantan on the other.

Saravanamuttu, Lee, and Mohamed Nawab's *Coalitions in Collision: Malaysia's 13th General Elections* (2015) looks at the 2013 general election from a variety of perspectives, including: systemic issues such as electoral malapportionment, the role of FELDA in key parliamentary seats, and the role of the media; as well as specific electoral battles in states such as Sabah, Sarawak, and others in Peninsular Malaysia.

Saravanamuttu's 2016 work *Power Sharing in a Divided Nation: Mediated Communalism and New Politics in Six Decades of Malaysia's Elections* (2016), provides a longer-term perspective on the conduct of elections in the country, looking at the initial design of the electoral system, its subsequent development, as well as the issues and performance of the various parties and coalitions in each electoral contest up to and including the 2013 general election.

Consequently, *The Defeat of Barisan Nasional: Missed Signs or Late Surge?* seeks to continue this tradition of collectively analysing the elections. Seven researchers based at the ISEAS – Yusof Ishak Institute participated in the GE-14 project, from design to completion. This core was complemented by a group of selected researchers, largely, but not exclusively, based in Malaysia.

The GE-14 project drew on the past approaches adopted to study the elections, but complemented them with additional lines of enquiry. This collective research design was developed in late 2017, as the momentum for the elections began to gather. The framework entailed studying the conduct of the elections and analysing their results from three angles.

The first angle was a systemic one, seeking to examine the broad context within which the elections were being carried out. This included the electoral process per se, specifically the "rules of the game" and the resulting advantages or disadvantages for the parties contesting, as well as more granular aspects such as how the 2016–18 parliamentary redelineation exercise was carried out and what its implications were. This was complemented by specific explorations of the country's economic context, and more direct analyses of the linkage between economic benefits and voter preferences as well as the implications of money politics in shaping voter behaviour.

The second angle consisted of analysing key trends among major interest groups. This category was defined broadly in ethnic trends, but in certain cases disaggregated further by geographic variables or institutional affiliation. Consequently, members of the team looked at electoral trends and political dynamics among rural Malays, urban Malays, FELDA settlers, in addition to Chinese and Indian voters, respectively.

The third angle consisted of studying the confluence of national and local-level issues, trends, and political dynamics in key states across the country. Consequently, on the Peninsula, researchers focused on the larger and more politically salient states of Selangor, Johor and Kelantan, as well as Sabah and Sarawak in East Malaysia.

This overarching structure enabled the research team to have a shared understanding for approaching the elections and locating their specific inquiry within it. It also allowed for comparison within each axis of enquiry, and lent itself for generating a larger, macro picture across the three aspects.

These findings were shared in a series of four public conferences held at the ISEAS – Yusof Ishak Institute. These events, with the first held on 13 December 2017 and the subsequent three on 16 March, 2 May, and 27–28 September 2018, were timed to coincide with key junctures in the electoral process. In addition, they served to coordinate the method and substance of differently authored chapters.

In addition to the research team itself, the GE-14 project included two in-house geographic information system (GIS) specialists who worked to develop more than thirty bespoke maps found through this book. Beyond portraying specific results, the maps were invaluable in helping researchers tease out patterns and relations as well as explore specific regional dynamics.

Consequently, the first three sections of the book—Campaign Dynamics, Interest Groups, and States—mirror the framework set out above. This book also has a fourth section entitled "Personal Perspectives", comprising a selection of essays solicited by the GE-14 team following the 2018 election. While not comprehensive, the section seeks to capture the voices of a range of "players" from different backgrounds and political affiliations, and thus complement the structural analyses in the first three sections with a ground-level perspective.

In the conclusion, this book brings together the themes raised by the various chapters. In addition, it seeks to deal with the central question of whether the unexpected denouement of GE-14 was the result of well-established and misread signs of discontent among Malaysia's voters or a last-minute movement away from BN towards PH and PAS.

Notes

1. This arrangement can work if three additional requirements are met. First, there is a mutual veto in decision-making, preventing the majority from imposing its will unilaterally on all groups. Second, important positions including public office and the civil service are allocated proportionally. Third, the various groups possess a significant degree of autonomy to manage their own affairs (Lijphart 1977, p. 25). For literature on how this applies to Malaysia, consult Milne and Mauzy (1999) and Crouch (1996).

2. The United Malays National Organization (UMNO) and the Malayan Chinese Association
    (MCA) formed an electoral alliance in 1952, and the Malayan Indian Congress then
    joined in 1954. This coalition was named the Alliance until 1971, when the formation
    was renamed Barisan Nasional and expanded to include more political parties.
3. PAS Johor Manifesto, https://www.facebook.com/paskawbakri/videos/
    1616693205113262/?epa=SEARCH_BOX (accessed 26 December 2018).

References

Abdillah Noh. 2014. "Malaysia's Dilemma: Economic Reforms but Politics Stay the Same".
    In *Southeast Asian Affairs 2014*, edited by Daljit Singh. Singapore: Institute of Southeast
    Asian Studies.
Bagang, Tony P., and Arnold Puyok. 2019. "Sabah: The End of BN and a New Order?". In *The
    Defeat of Barisan Nasional: Missed Signs or Late Surge?*, edited by Francis E. Hutchinson
    and Lee Hwok Aun, pp. 402–22. Singapore: ISEAS – Yusof Ishak Institute.
Brown, Graham K. 2013. "Malaysia in 2012: Promises of Reform; Promises Met?". In *Southeast
    Asian Affairs 2013*, edited by Daljit Singh. Singapore: Institute of Southeast Asian Studies.
Case, William. 2002. *Politics in Southeast Asia: Democracy or Less*. London: Curzon Press.
———. 2004. "New Uncertainties for an Old Pseudo-Democracy: The Case of Malaysia".
    Comparative Politics 37, no. 1: 83–104.
———. 2007. "Semi-Democracy and Minimalist Federalism in Malaysia". In *Federalism in Asia*,
    edited by Baogang He, Brian Galligan, and Takashi Inoguchi. London: Edward Elgar.
Chacko, Danesh Prakash. 2019. "Defeating the Rigged Borders: Redelineation meets its
    Match". In *The Defeat of Barisan Nasional: Missed Signs or Late Surge?*, edited by Francis
    E. Hutchinson and Lee Hwok Aun, pp. 49–84. Singapore: ISEAS – Yusof Ishak Institute.
Chin, James. 2014. "Malaysia in 2013: Najib's Pyrrhic Victory and the Demise of 1Malaysia".
    In *Southeast Asian Affairs 2014*, edited by Daljit Singh. Singapore: Institute of Southeast
    Asian Studies.
Chong, Terence, Lee Hock Guan, Norshahril Saat, and Serina Rahman. 2017. *The 2017 Johor
    Survey: Selected Findings*. Trends in Southeast Asia, no. 20/2017. Singapore: ISEAS – Yusof
    Ishak Institute.
Crouch, Harold. 1996. *Government and Society in Malaysia*. Ithaca and London: Cornell University.
Felker, Greg. 2000. "Malaysia in 1999: Mahathir's Pyrrhic Deliverance". *Asian Survey* 40,
    no. 1: 49–60.
Gomez, Edmund Terence, and K.S. Jomo. 1997. *Malaysia's Political Economy: Politics, Patronage
    and Profits*. Cambridge: Cambridge University Press.
Hutchinson, Francis E. 2014. "Malaysia's Federal System: Overt and Covert Centralisation".
    Journal of Contemporary Asia 44, no. 3: 422–42.
———. 2018. "Malaysia's 14th General Elections: Drivers and Agents of Change". *Asian Affairs*
    49, no. 4: 582–605.
International Crisis Group. 2012. "Malaysia's Coming Election: Beyond Communalism?".
    Asia Report No. 235. Brussels: ICG.
Khoo, Boo Teik. 2018. "Borne by Dissent, Tormented by Divides: The Opposition 60 Years
    after Merdeka". *Southeast Asian Studies* 7, no. 3: 471–91.
Lee, Poh Onn. 2019. "Sarawak: An Electoral Tremor with Far-Reaching Consequences". In
    The Defeat of Barisan Nasional: Missed Signs or Late Surge?, edited by Francis E. Hutchinson
    and Lee Hwok Aun, pp. 364–401. Singapore: ISEAS – Yusof Ishak Institute.

Lijphart, Arend. 1977. *Democracy in Plural Societies: A Comparative Exploration*. New Haven: Yale University Press.

Loh, Francis. 2002. "Developmentalism and the Limits of Democratic Discourse". In *Democracy in Malaysia: Discourses and Practices*, edited by Francis Loh and Khoo Boo Teik. Richmond: Curzon Press.

Lopez, Greg, and Bridget Welsh. 2018. *Regime Resilience in Malaysia and Singapore*. Kuala Lumpur: Strategic Information and Research Development Centre.

Malaysiakini. 2018. "GE14 Live Reporting by Malaysiakini". 10 May 2018. https://live.malaysiakini.com/ge14/en/ (accessed 29 May 2019).

Mauzy, Diane K. 1993. "Malaysia: Malay Political Hegemony and 'Coercive Consciationalism'". In *The Politics of Ethnic Conflict Regulation*, edited by J. McGarry and B. O'Leary. London: Routledge.

Merdeka Center. 2018. *Malaysia General Elections XIV Outlook. Prospects and Outcome III*. 8 May 2018. Kuala Lumpur: Merdeka Center.

Milne, R.S., and Diane K. Mauzy. 1999. *Malaysian Politics under Mahathir*. London: Routledge.

Nelson, Joan M. 2012. "Political Challenges in Economic Upgrading: Malaysia Compared with Korea and Taiwan". In *Malaysia's Development Challenges: Graduating from the Middle*, edited by Hal Hill, Tham Siew Yean, and Ragayah Haji Mat Zin. London and New York: Routledge.

Norshahril Saat. 2019. "Kelantan: PAS Settles in on the Balcony of Mecca". In *The Defeat of Barisan Nasional: Missed Signs or Late Surge?*, edited by Francis E. Hutchinson and Lee Hwok Aun, pp. 342–63. Singapore: ISEAS – Yusof Ishak Institute.

Ooi, Kee Beng, Johan Saravanamuttu, and Lee Hock Guan. 2008. *March 8: Eclipsing May 13*. Singapore: Institute of Southeast Asian Studies.

Ooi, Kok Hin. 2018. "How Malaysia's Election is being Rigged". *New Naratif*. 19 March 2018. https://newnaratif.com/research/malaysias-election-rigged/ (accessed 5 July 2018).

Ostwald, Kai. 2013. "How to Win a Lost Election: Malapportionment and Malaysia's 2013 General Election". *The Round Table* 102, no. 6: 521–32.

———. 2017. *Malaysia's Electoral Process: The Methods and Costs of Perpetuating UMNO Rule*. Trends in Southeast Asia, no. 19/2017. Singapore: ISEAS – Yusof Ishak Institute.

Pepinsky, Thomas B. 2009. *Economic Crises and the Breakdown of Authoritarian Regimes: Indonesia and Malaysia in Comparative Perspective*. New York: Cambridge University Press.

Rafizi Ramli, and James Chai. 2019. "Big Data and Bold Calls: How INVOKE Saw What Everyone Missed". In *The Defeat of Barisan Nasional: Missed Signs or Late Surge?*, edited by Francis E. Hutchinson and Lee Hwok Aun, pp. 458–76. Singapore: ISEAS – Yusof Ishak Institute.

Saravanamuttu, Johan. 2016. *Power Sharing in a Divided Nation: Mediated Communalism and New Politics in Six Decades of Malaysia's Elections*. Singapore: ISEAS – Yusof Ishak Institute.

———, Lee Hock Guan, and Mohamed Nawab Mohamed Osman. 2015. *Coalitions in Collision: Malaysia's 13th General Elections*. Singapore: Institute of Southeast Asian Studies.

Tapsell, Ross. 2013. "The Media Freedom Movement in Malaysia and the Electoral Authoritarian Regime". *Journal of Contemporary Asia* 43, no. 4: 613–35.

Ufen, Andreas. 2009. "The Transformation of Political Party Opposition in Malaysia and its Implications for the Electoral Authoritarian Regime". *Democratization* 16, no. 3: 327–50.

Wain, Barry. 2009. *Malaysian Maverick: Mahathir Mohamad in Turbulent Times*. London: Palgrave Macmillan.

Wan Saiful Wan Jan. 2017. *Parti Amanah Negara in Johor: Birth, Challenges, and Prospect*. Trends in Southeast Asia, no. 9/2017. Singapore: ISEAS – Yusof Ishak Institute.

———. 2018. *Parti Pribumi Bersatu Malaysia in Johor: New Party, Big Responsibility*. Trends in Southeast Asia, no. 2/2018. Singapore: ISEAS – Yusof Ishak Institute.

Weiss, Meredith. 2013. "Coalitions and Competition in Malaysia – Incremental Transformation of a Strong-Party System". *Journal of Current Southeast Asian Affairs* 23, Issue 2.

———. 2014. *Electoral Dynamics in Malaysia: Findings from the Grassroots*. Singapore: Institute of Southeast Asian Studies.

Yeah Kim Leng. 2017. "Malaysia's 2018 Budget: Balancing Short Term Needs and Long Term Imperatives". *ISEAS Perspective*, no. 2017/88, 24 November 2017.

Yeoh, Tricia. 2012. *States of Reform: Governing Selangor and Penang*. Kuala Lumpur: Genta Media.

Periodicals
Asia Sentinel
Channel NewsAsia
Free Malaysia Today
Malay Mail
New Straits Times
The Edge Financial Daily
The Edge Malaysia Weekly
The Star
The Straits Times
The Sun Daily
The Sunday Times
Today

I

Campaign Dynamics

2

AGAINST THE ODDS
Malaysia's Electoral Process and Pakatan Harapan's Unlikely Victory[1]

Kai Ostwald

INTRODUCTION

The outcome of Malaysia's 14th General Elections (GE-14) in May 2018 was an almost universal surprise, not least to its two main protagonists, incumbent Prime Minister Najib Razak and challenger Mahathir Mohamad.[2] The source of Najib's confidence is clear: he inherited a vast political machine that consistently delivered electoral victories to the United Malays National Organization (UMNO) and its coalition partners over Malaysia's six-decade-long independent history. Mahathir's doubts were likewise well founded: as one of the primary architects of that political machine during his two decades as UMNO president and prime minster, he understood well how grossly the odds were stacked against the party's challengers.

In its six decades at the helm of Malaysia's high-capacity state, UMNO strategically reshaped the electoral process in ways that reinforced its dominance of Malaysian politics. In doing so, it created a quintessential single-party dominant regime (Case 1996) in which elections were held regularly and contested by opposition parties, but were also biased to a degree that effectively prevented the transition of power.[3] The electoral process, in short, was designed to prevent an outcome like Pakatan Harapan's (PH) unlikely victory in GE-14.

How the Mahathir-led PH coalition achieved this victory against seemingly impossible odds has already drawn significant scholarly attention.[4] This chapter acts as a backdrop for those explanations by systematically examining the partisan bias in Malaysia's electoral process, including in the run-up to GE-14. In doing so, it provides comprehensive context for making sense of both UMNO's defeat and the myriad reform challenges facing the new government.

The first section of the chapter reviews Malaysia's institutional structure and electoral history. The second section brings Malaysia's electoral process into comparative perspective using recent data from the Electoral Integrity Project (Norris and Grömping 2017a). By these and other measures, Malaysia's electoral process was significantly more biased than other countries with comparable levels of development and institutionalization. The third section uses a theoretical framework from Birch (2011) to provide a structured overview of manipulations in each phase of Malaysia's electoral process. The final section briefly discusses the ongoing costs entailed by the electoral manipulations, including significantly impeding the reform process.

One important clarification is necessary. The transition to PH was not only unlikely, but also unprecedented—Malaysian politics may not return to a steady state for a considerable time, producing significant ambiguity around the transition. In that ambiguity, it is also uncertain how many of PH's reform aspirations will be realized. Since this chapter focuses on describing the electoral manipulations facing PH in GE-14, they are described in the past tense. This should not be read as an assertion that GE-14 represents a clean break in Malaysian politics. Rather, it is a conservative approach that reflects the uncertainty of Malaysian politics in the immediate post-transition period. Only in the years to come will it be clear whether the electoral manipulations described below are relics of the UMNO era, or enduring features of Malaysian politics.

MALAYSIA'S POLITICAL INSTITUTIONS AND ELECTORAL HISTORY

Malaysia is a constitutional monarchy that uses a Westminster-style parliamentary system inherited from the British. It has a federal structure with power nominally divided between federal and state levels, though in practice it is highly centralized (Hutchinson 2014; Ostwald 2017b). The King (Yang di-Pertuan Agong) acts as the largely ceremonial head of state and is elected for a five-year term by and from among the country's nine hereditary sultans. The federal parliament is bicameral, comprised of an appointed senate (Dewan Negara) with limited powers and an elected lower house (Dewan Rakyat). The Dewan Rakyat currently has 222 seats, a substantial increase from the 98 at the time of the first general election. The prime minister is the chief executive and head of government. Elections follow first-past-the-post (FPTP) rules in single-member districts, and must be held at least once every five years.[5] The Yang di-Pertuan Agong can dissolve parliament upon the request of the prime minister, triggering new elections. The minimum campaign period is currently a short eleven days, which provides a significant incumbent advantage (Lim and Ong 2006).

Malaysia's population is highly diverse, being comprised of ethnic Malays (55 per cent), Chinese (23 per cent), Indians (7 per cent), and others (15 per cent). Malays and other indigenous groups are categorized as bumiputra (sons of the soil) and receive significant privileges and special rights. The monarchy is comprised exclusively of Malays. It is widely conceded that the head of government is also reserved for Malays.

From the run-up to independence through 2018, Malaysia's politics were thoroughly dominated by UMNO, which was founded in 1946 to represent the interests of ethnic Malays. While UMNO always governed as part of a coalition, it was the clear hegemonic partner and largely dictated the terms of power sharing. Its coalition partners—the Malaysian Chinese Association (MCA), the Malaysian Indian Congress (MIC), and numerous smaller parties from East Malaysia—are also predominantly structured along ethnic lines. Table 2.1 shows the percentage of popular vote and parliamentary seats captured by UMNO's coalition in each of Malaysia's fourteen general elections. It is noteworthy that aside from the three most recent elections and the contentious 1969 election, UMNO's coalition always secured a two-thirds parliamentary supermajority, allowing it to easily amend the Constitution.

Malaysia's electoral institutions and procedures have been subject to continuous partisan pressure from the moment of their creation. Several critical junctures, however, are noteworthy. Ethnic riots in 1969 catalysed far-reaching restrictions on campaigning and media independence that were used to impede opposition activity. Mahathir's first tenure as prime minister from 1981 to 2003 also significantly affected Malaysia's political landscape, in particular by undermining the independence of key institutions and personalizing power in the prime minister (Slater 2003). Moreover,

TABLE 2.1
General Elections in Malaysia: Dominance of UMNO-led Coalitions

Year	Percent of Votes	Percent of Seats	Total Number of Seats
1959	63.7	73.5	98
1964	58.2	84.6	104
1969	45.3	52.1	142
1974	60.8	87.7	154
1978	57.3	85.3	163
1982	60.5	85.1	148
1986	57.3	83.6	177
1990	53.1	70.6	180
1995	63.2	84.4	192
1999	56.8	76.7	193
2004	63.8	90.4	219
2008	51.4	63.1	222
2013	47.4	60.0	222
2018	33.8	35.6	222

extensive economic restructuring created a tight nexus between the state and private sector that substantially increased the role of money in politics, favouring the resource-rich incumbent coalition (Gomez 1996, 2012). More broadly, a series of constitutional amendments altered the basic parameters governing Malaysia's elections, each time granting the government greater leeway in shaping the process in its favour.

ELECTORAL MANIPULATIONS IN COMPARATIVE PERSPECTIVE

International comparisons can provide useful perspective. Of the available datasets that address elections, the Electoral Integrity Project's "Global Perceptions of Electoral Integrity (PEI)" focuses most explicitly on partisan electoral manipulations (Norris and Grömping 2017a).[6] Its main PEI score reflects the overall partisan bias of an electoral system by aggregating measures of bias in electoral laws, electoral procedures, district boundaries, voter registration, party registration, media coverage, campaign finance, the voting process, and the vote count. Based on the PEI score, countries are grouped into "Very High", "High", "Moderate", "Low/Flawed", "Very Low/Failed" categories of electoral integrity.

Table 2.2 shows a selection of countries ranked according to PEI score. In 2017, Malaysia fell in the "Very Low/Failed" category, ranking 142nd out of the 158 assessed countries. Nearly all other countries in this category have experienced deep social and political instability (like Afghanistan and Zimbabwe) or have single-party systems (like Vietnam) that preclude meaningful electoral competition. Neither of these are true for Malaysia, making it a clear outlier in the category. To the contrary, the country has a strong and well-institutionalized state that has provided relative social stability, a high level of human development, and robust economic development. This developmental success brings Malaysia's poor electoral

TABLE 2.2
Electoral Integrity PEI scores

Country	Global Rank	PEI score	Category
Denmark	1	86	Very high
Canada	17	75	Very high
Japan	32	68	High
India	62	59	Moderate
Indonesia	68	57	Moderate
Myanmar	83	54	Moderate
Singapore	94	53	Moderate
The Philippines	101	52	Moderate
Pakistan	106	49	Low/Flawed
Malaysia	*142*	*35*	*Very Low/Failed*
Zimbabwe	143	35	Very Low/Failed
Vietnam	147	34	Very Low/Failed
Afghanistan	150	31	Very Low/Failed

integrity into stark contrast and suggests that its deviations from recognized norms are the result of deliberate partisan manipulations, rather than a by-product of developmental strife.

Figure 2.1 disaggregates the electoral process into the key components and compares Malaysia against its Southeast and East Asian neighbours. It clearly illustrates the breadth of electoral manipulations in Malaysia, as only Party Registration and the Vote Process on polling day reach regional standards. When the less developed countries of Cambodia, Laos, Myanmar and Vietnam are excluded, however, the gap reappears even in these areas. In other areas like Electoral Laws and Electoral Boundaries, Malaysia's score is among the lowest in the world.

ELECTORAL MANIPULATIONS

Both academics and the general public focus much of their attention on brazen polling day malpractices like ballot rigging, alteration of vote counts, or violence at the polls. Despite the intense reactions these malpractices elicit, the more banal pre-election manipulations often have a greater impact on election outcomes, as they fundamentally tilt the playing field in favour of the incumbent. This was certainly true for Malaysia under UMNO rule, as nearly every aspect of electoral competition

FIGURE 2.1
Perceptions of Electoral Integrity: East Asia, Southeast Asia and Malaysia Compared[a]

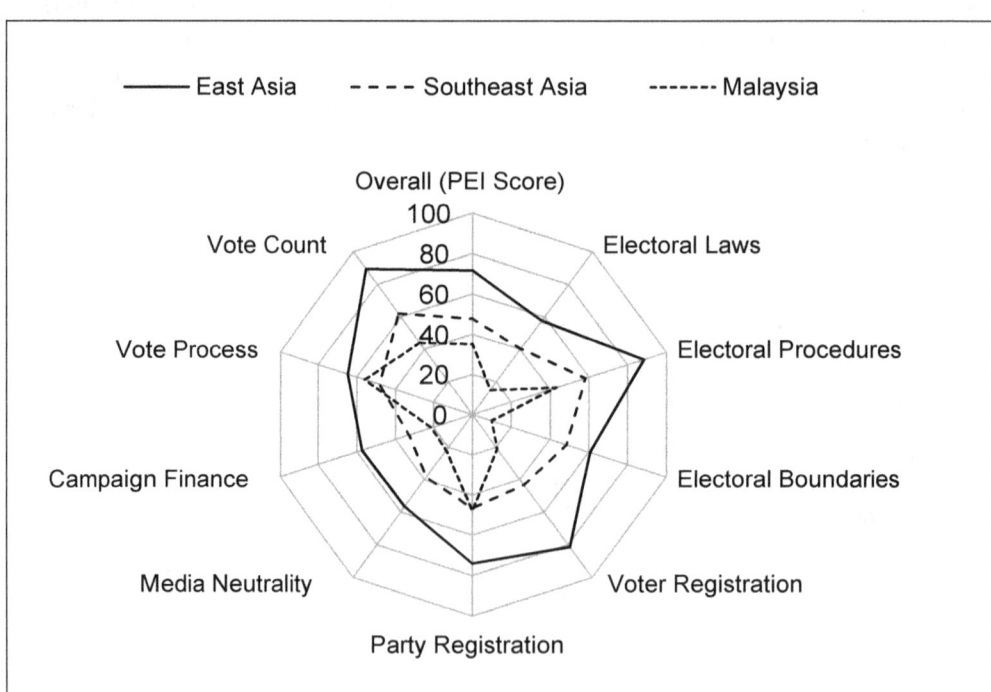

Note: a. In Southeast Asia, Brunei and East Timor are excluded. In East Asia, China is excluded.

was biased in favour of the BN through institutions and procedures that fell far short of neutral.

This chapter is loosely structured around the electoral malpractice framework proposed by Birch (2011). As such, the next section focuses on bias in the *institutional and legal framework*, while the subsequent section addresses systematic manipulations of *voter preferences*. Both of these are most pronounced in the pre-election phase. The following section focuses on polling day malpractices, and the final part addresses the post-election phase.

The Institutional and Legal Framework of Elections

Slater and Fenner (2011, p. 16) argue that *"state power* is the strongest institutional foundation for authoritarian regimes' *staying power"*, meaning control of a high-capacity state can be leveraged towards entrenching a party and staving off political challenges. In short, dominance begets dominance (Pempel 1990). In the greater than half century during which UMNO helmed the Malaysian state, it penetrated nearly all of the state's appendages, rendering the line between UMNO and the state essentially indistinguishable in many areas. The result of this state capture was a fundamental bias towards UMNO and the BN in many institutions central to the electoral process.

The Election Commission (EC), which is tasked with maintaining electoral rolls, establishing electoral boundaries, and administering the elections themselves, is among the most important of these (Lim 2002). The Constitution stipulates that the EC is to be a neutral body that maintains the public's confidence. As such, it is nominally independent and non-partisan. Lim (2002, p. 113) notes, however, that from the early 1960s onwards the EC was under constant pressure "to consult the government while carrying out its functions", thereby undermining its neutrality in practice. Furthermore, the EC is constituted by the prime minister and was comprised largely of retired civil servants with UMNO connections. Hence it is little surprise that "former and current commissioners [of the EC] have publicly claimed loyalty to UMNO" (Welsh 2014, p. 17) and have, upon retirement, been forthright about their attempts to influence electoral outcomes.

The partisan leanings of the EC were evident in several areas. A clear example is in the delineation of electoral boundaries, which occurs at regular intervals of not less than eight years. That involves the EC submitting a proposal for new district boundaries to the prime minister for amendment, before the proposal is approved through a simple majority parliamentary vote.[7]

Partisan manipulation of district boundaries, particularly in single-member FPTP systems like Malaysia's, can impact electoral outcomes through both malapportionment and gerrymandering. Malapportionment is the creation of electoral districts with dissimilar ratios of voters to representatives. In practice, it amplifies the influence of voters in districts with fewer voters and dilutes the influence of voters in districts with more voters. While some degree of overrepresentation in rural areas is a common feature of electoral systems, high levels of malapportionment can significantly distort the translation of votes into parliamentary seats.

Constitutional limits on malapportionment in Malaysia were relaxed in 1962 and removed entirely in 1973 (Lim 2002). Levels of malapportionment are now among the highest in the world; in fact, the EIP ranks Malaysia's electoral boundaries as the most biased of the 155 countries assessed (Norris and Grömping 2017a). The boundaries used to contest GE-13 substantially diluted the influence of voters in opposition-leaning areas and biased outcomes in favour of the BN (Ostwald 2013; Lee 2015; Ong, Kasuya, and Mori 2017). Remarkably, the BN won eighty-three of the eighty-six smallest districts (where the impact of a vote is magnified), while the opposition Pakatan Rakyat (PR) secured a substantial majority of the largest one-third of districts (where it is diluted). As a result, the median number of voters in BN-held districts was 43,876, relative to 78,148 for PR. There is compelling evidence that this distribution of seats reflects intentional partisan bias in the drawing of boundaries, rather than differences in party appeal based on the structural characteristics of districts: even when controlling for voter density (rural bias) and percentage of bumiputra voters, BN-held districts still had on average over 20,000 fewer voters than their opposition-held counterparts (Ostwald 2013).

The EC concluded a redelineation exercise shortly before parliament was dissolved to trigger GE-14. It was widely seen as maintaining—and in some cases even exacerbating—the already grossly partisan boundaries (Wong 2018). Two differences between GE-13 and GE-14 had the potential to shake the BN's stranglehold on smaller districts. First, the Mahathir-headed UMNO-clone Parti Pribumi Bersatu Malaysia (PPBM) was to make PH competitive in overweighted Peninsular districts, while Warisan was to do the same in Sabah. Second, PAS' decision to contest the election as a third-party was seen as an attempt to split the Malay anti-incumbent vote (Ostwald, Schuler, and Chong 2018).

Despite these changes and the BN's dramatic decline in popular vote share, the BN continued to be overrepresented in the smallest one-third of districts, while PH and PAS were overrepresented in the largest one-third of districts. Figure 2.2 illustrates that distribution by dividing the 222 parliamentary districts into sextiles of 37 districts each and arranging them from smallest to largest in terms of number of voters. In other words, the first sextile contains the smallest 37 districts, while the last contains the largest 37 districts. The bars indicate the number of seats won by the BN, PH and PAS.

While the BN was forced to concede GE-14, the continuation of this pattern meant that they captured a larger number of seats than would be expected given their vote share. FPTP systems like Malaysia typically provide a mechanical seat bonus to the most successful party or coalition, which grants them a seat share above their vote share. By contrast, losing parties/coalitions receive a penalty that results in a smaller seat share than vote share. Remarkably, the extensive malapportionment in Malaysia led to the BN receiving a seat bonus above its vote share *despite losing the popular vote to PH by 15 per cent*. The simple conclusion is that—despite losing—biased electoral boundaries in GE-14 continued to help the

FIGURE 2.2
Malapportionment of Districts in the 2018 General Election

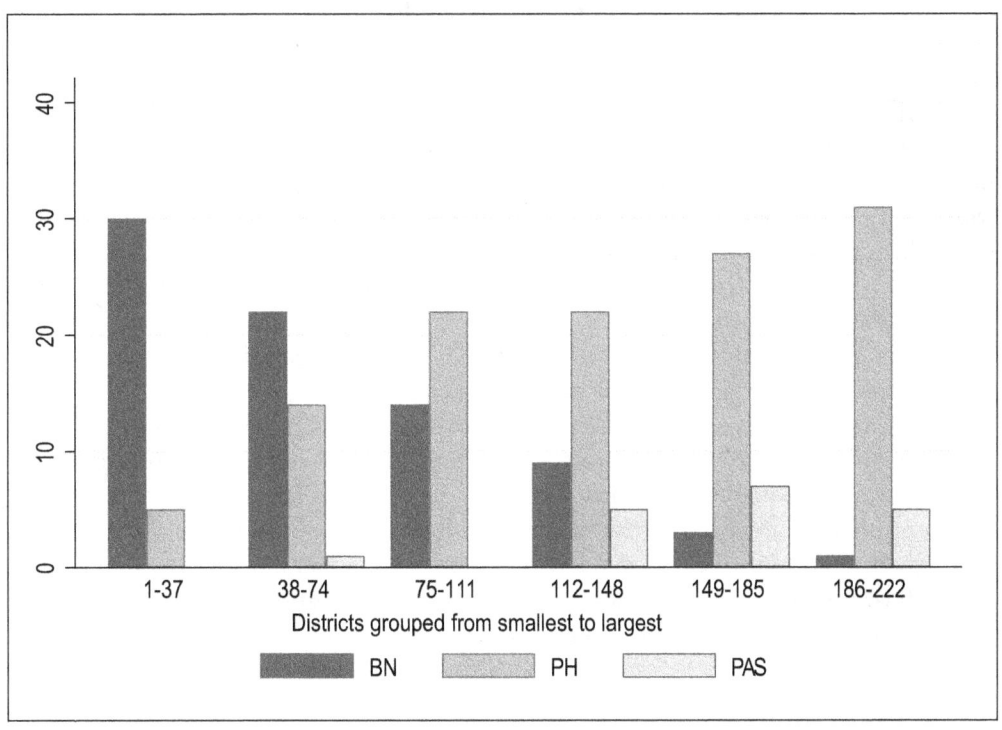

BN, which would have had significantly fewer seats if electoral boundaries were unbiased.

Independent of electorate size, electoral boundaries can also be manipulated through gerrymandering to advantage the incumbent by strategically dividing (cracking) or concentrating (packing) opposition supporters. Both forms are prevalent in Malaysia, where electoral boundaries frequently deviate from municipal boundaries or natural community clusters (Wong 2018). An additional objective of these interventions is to shape the demographics of districts in ways that advantage the incumbent. The redelineation exercise concluded just prior to GE-14, for example, reduced the average ethnic diversity of districts, thereby increasing the number of Malay-majority districts in which the BN's bumiputra-centric agenda would presumably resonate most strongly.

The EC is also tasked with preparing and maintaining Malaysia's electoral rolls. These were subject to extensive criticism, with allegations that they contained widespread inaccuracies and reflected partisan bias (Lim 2002; Wong, Chin, and Othman 2010; MERAP 2013; Bersih 2014). Involuntary voter deregistrations, specifically eligible voters missing from the electoral roll, were prevalent. Lim (2002, p. 116), for example, writes that "more than 300,000 persons were removed as electors ..." just prior to the 1974 election. Since most of those removed were non-Malays, the "proportion of Malay electors increased from 55.7 to 57.9 per cent". As Malay voters were disproportionately likely to support UMNO, this provided an important advantage to the BN (Crouch 1996). Unwarranted removal of voters, including without the required public notification, was widely noted in GE-13 (MERAP 2013).

Presumably inaccurate entries on the electoral rolls were also a concern, as they potentially enabled "phantom voters" or multiple voting. Close analysis of the rolls used for the 2013 general election, for example, found numerous instances of multiple entries with the same name and either the same or very similar birth dates (Ong 2012). Other entries had incomplete or missing addresses, or were otherwise questionable: 324 addresses, for example, had more than 100 voters registered to them. Also noted were the large number of older voters, including more than 1,000 above 100 years old and one with an 1890-birth year.

It is difficult to assess the extent to which those inaccuracies reflect clerical errors, or explicit attempts to alter the electorate. The history of strategic manipulation of electoral rolls in Malaysia justifies concerns of the latter. There is strong evidence, for example, that several hundred thousand illegal immigrants to the state of Sabah were given the identity cards needed to secure voting rights, despite many native (and non-Muslim) Sabahans lacking the required documentation to vote (Sadiq 2005). This "importation" of Muslim voters from Indonesia and the Southern Philippines—sometimes referred to as "Project IC"—significantly increased the size of Sabah's Muslim electorate, which votes disproportionately for the BN (Chin 2012; Welsh 2013).

MERAP (2013) also documented a large number of voters whose assigned constituency changed in ways that appeared to benefit the BN. In numerous instances, the constituencies of the BN's key leaders gained additional and presumably safe voters to decrease the probability of their defeat. In other instances, districts that were decided by a slim margin in the previous election received new voters from safe districts. These tactics were clearly employed prior to GE-14 as well. A large number of military personnel, for example, were reassigned to vote in competitive districts—at least two of which belonged to BN ministers—where new army camps were being constructed, despite the targeted completion dates for those camps—and actual residence in the camps—coming long after the election. In aggregate, the biased electoral boundaries and documented issues with the electoral rolls clearly advantaged the BN and undermined the nominal neutrality of the EC.

The Registrar of Societies (ROS), which falls under the Ministry of Home Affairs, likewise showed consistent pro-BN institutional bias. The ROS is responsible for overseeing the registration and operation of societies, including political parties. It has the power to block the formation of new parties or deregister parties that do not follow its dictates, which cover a wide range of areas from the internal governance of parties to their names and symbols. The ROS' decisions frequently appeared partisan and politically tainted (Welsh 2014; Gomez 2012). Several recent examples are illustrative. The PH constituent Democratic Action Party (DAP) held internal elections for its central executive committee in late 2013. In mid-2017, as tensions between UMNO and the DAP grew with GE-14 on the horizon, the ROS revisited those elections and declared them illegal. This required the DAP to divert focus and resources from election preparations to the legal dispute. Almost concurrently, the ROS declared the logo of the newly formed opposition coalition Pakatan Harapan (PH) invalid on technical grounds. While the fix was relatively simple, it likewise required the remaking of campaign materials, the original versions of which had just been revealed. More dramatically, the ROS provisionally dissolved Bersatu—the party of prime minister designate Mahathir—less than a month before the start of campaigning based on a minor technicality, causing a rethink of campaign strategies. Interestingly, UMNO's breach of its own internal constitution likewise came to light at the eleventh hour, but in stark contrast the ROS seamlessly approved its request for an additional extension of internal elections, thereby minimizing the impact. The same asymmetric scrutiny appeared at the candidate level, where several PH candidates were disqualified from the election on technicalities while the BN faced few comparable challenges.

The judiciary's independence and partiality were also widely questioned. Its partisan leanings were evident in the selective usage of powerful coercive mechanisms (Means 1996). The Sedition Act—originally intended to curb opposition to colonial rule—prohibits speech or action with "seditious tendencies", which are vaguely defined as "any act" that "excite[s] disaffection against any Ruler or … any government"; that "raise[s] discontent amongst subjects"; "promote[s] ill-will and hostility … between races or classes of the population"; or "question[s] sensitive matters", including "any provisions dealing with the right, status, position, [or] privilege … in relation to citizenship, language, the special position of the Malays … [and] the Malay Rulers." Moreover, "the intention of the person charged at the time he did or attempted [a seditious act] … shall be deemed to be irrelevant if in fact the act had, or would, if done, have had … a seditious tendency." The strikingly broad nature of the law, together with the low bar for guilt, facilitated its usage against political opponents. It was regularly applied towards this end, including on senior opposition figures, with those found guilty sentenced up to 3 years in jail or at least tied up in consuming legal processes. In 2015 alone, for example, over ninety individuals were arrested, charged, or investigated for sedition, with nearly all having ties to the opposition. While the law was amended in 2015, it continued to constrain the operating space for opposition figures. A controversial and powerful anti-fake news bill, which was widely seen as an additional measure to curb commentary critical of the government, was hastily implemented in the month prior to GE-14. Just days before the election, police announced that Mahathir himself was under investigation for violating the act.

The more draconian Internal Security Act (ISA) of 1960 allowed preventive detention without trial under specified circumstances. Though it was initially intended to counter communist activities in the wake of the Malayan Emergency of 1948 to 1960, it was regularly directed against opposition and civil society leaders in subsequent decades. The ISA was replaced by the Security Offences (Special

Measures) Act (SOSMA) in 2012, though many of its core features were retained. While SOSMA did not directly factor into GE-14, it and other coercive mechanisms continued to have chilling effect across all levels of opposition politics.

A host of additional legal measures are relevant to the electoral process. The 13 May 1969 riots, for example, prompted a ban on political marches. As a result, political rallies have been tightly controlled and limited to *ceramahs* held in enclosed spaces. While these constraints ostensibly applied to all political parties, in practice the partiality of adjudicating institutions often placed far greater burdens on the opposition than on their BN counterparts. Other legal measures address the candidate level. All candidates, for example, are required to pay an election deposit in order to appear on the ballot. The deposit, which was among the highest in the world in recent elections, was forfeited if the candidate did not secure one-eighth of votes cast in the constituency. In addition, candidates were given only one hour to complete nomination forms on nomination day. That tight window regularly led to the disqualification of opposition candidates (Brown 2008). In aggregate, the pro-BN bias present in many of Malaysia's institutions hampered the ability of the opposition to challenge elections on a level playing field.

Manipulation of Voters

Aside from biasing the playing field for political parties and their candidates, institutional bias also directly affected voter preferences. Three channels stand out in UMNO-era Malaysia. The first is the traditional mass media, which showed pervasive pro-BN bias. Second is the monetization of politics, which advantaged the BN due to its far greater access to resources. Third is the pervasive narrative, often enforced by state appendages, the media, and UMNO-aligned activist groups, that everything from continuation of bumiputra privileges to Malaysia's ongoing development and stability were conditional on the BN maintaining power. I address each of these channels in turn.

Media bias was consistently identified as an important factor in the BN's electoral resilience, as the print media—long the major source of information for Malaysia's voters—generally provided positive coverage of the BN while undermining the opposition's attempts to build credibility through negative coverage (Abbott and Wagner Givens 2015; Brown 2005). The legal framework overseeing the mass media was the first major source of bias. The Official Secrets Act (OSA) of 1972, for example, prohibits the publication of any information that the government deems confidential or sensitive, unless explicitly authorized. Given that discretion to determine what constitutes confidential and sensitive remains with the government, the OSA effectively grants the state broad powers to criminalize non-approved dissemination of information on its own activities. These powers were frequently directed at journalists, effectively preventing the development of domestic investigative journalism. The OSA was also used to target opposition politicians: prior to the transition, for example, the only major domestic prosecution in Malaysia's notorious 1MDB financial scandal was of opposition lawmaker Rafizi Ramli, who was handed an 18-month prison sentence for revealing passages of the Auditor General's findings. The OSA's effect, in short, was to muzzle information critical of the government.

The Printing Presses and Publications Act (PPPA) of 1984 further selectively constrains media activity. This requires all printing presses to renew licences on a yearly basis through the Ministry of Home Affairs, which was under UMNO control and closely followed the prime minister's directives. The PPPA gave the Minister of Home Affairs the "absolute discretion" to grant and revoke printing licences. Furthermore, it punishes with a prison sentence any attempt to print, import, or distribute a newspaper in the absence of an appropriate licence, as well as imposes a fine on anyone found in possession of such a newspaper. Amendment 13A prevents court challenges against the minister's decisions. The Act was regularly invoked against newspapers and journalists that were deemed critical of the government. The risk of prosecution induced substantial self-censorship on matters that could be construed as sensitive.

The ownership structure of Malaysia's traditional mass media contributed to bias as well. As has been widely noted, most of the country's major newspapers were either directly owned by the BN or closely linked to key BN figures, placing them effectively under the BN's control. UMNO, for example, is the majority owner of the company that publishes dominant Malay-language papers like *Utusan Melayu* and *Kosmo*. Other major papers like the *New Straits Times* and *Berita Harian* are tied to UMNO through government holdings and personal connections. The BN-constituent party Malaysian Chinese Association (MCA) directly controls *The Star*, an English daily. The Malaysian Indian Congress (MIC) is closely associated with the country's Tamil newspapers. Several television and radio stations are likewise tied to the BN.

As a consequence of the legal environment and ownership structure, Malaysia's print press frequently biased reporting in favour of the BN and often assumed the role of the government's mouthpiece. Several studies have empirically examined the extent of that bias. *Watching the Watchdog*, for example, assessed news coverage of the 2013 general election across major outlets (Houghton 2013). For every one "positive" mention of the BN in the Peninsular English-language print media, there were only 0.026 "positive" mentions of the opposition—i.e., nearly forty times fewer. By contrast, for every one "negative" mention of the BN, there were over fourteen of the opposition. The numbers were similar in Malay-language print and only slightly less biased in television coverage. Among the traditional media, only the Chinese-language press showed a semblance of balance. Other studies reach similar conclusions in their analysis of major newspapers (Abbott and Wagner Givens 2015; Abbott 2011). While privately owned media has some degree of partisan bias in most countries, its magnitude in Malaysia was unusually high. In addition, publicly funded media like Radio Televisyen Malaysia (RTM)—which are non-partisan in mature democracies—displayed the same pro-BN bias in Malaysia. In a context where the traditional mass media was long the dominant source of information, the impact of this bias on public opinion formation and party attachment should not be underestimated. The transition appears to have altered coverage in some

BN-aligned outlets, but others like *Utusan Melayu* have largely maintained their previous orientation.

The growth of online media increased access to alternative sources of information and opened a space for the vibrant exchange of political views (Tapsell 2013). While online media was embraced by many Malaysians, it provided only a partial counterbalance to the bias introduced through the traditional mass media (Weiss 2013; Pepinsky 2013). Its potential was limited by several factors. Internet penetration and media consumption patterns favoured the BN, since the electorally crucial Malay heartland continued to rely on the mainstream media at disproportionally greater rates than opposition-leaning areas. New media was also subject to some of the same restrictions as the print media. The case of the *Malaysian Insider*, previously one of Malaysia's primary online news sources, is illustrative: following reporting on the 1MDB scandal in early 2016, its website was blocked (in Malaysia) by the Malaysian Communications and Multimedia Commission (MCMC), eventually prompting a decision to close the organization. Furthermore, the rise of pro-BN "cybertroopers" also injected the government's messaging into the online space (Hopkins 2014).

Money politics also biased the preferences of Malaysia's voters. This channel grew dramatically in scope and importance following the emergence of a tight state-business nexus in the late 1980s, in which the state, BN-connected business elites, and BN-constituent parties became central players in the economy (Gomez and Jomo 1999; Gomez 2012). Through this, the BN gained access to far greater financial resources than were available to opposition parties.[8]

The BN's plethora of resources brought all manner of day-to-day advantages over its challengers. This included the ability to maintain more extensive permanent staff and offices, to conduct ongoing research on the political climate, and to lead political education between campaign periods. The advantages were pronounced during the election period as well. While there are legally defined limits on campaign spending at the candidate level, the limits do not apply to general party spending, allowing the BN to vastly outspend its challengers during the election run-up. This took many forms. In the absence of large public rallies, door-to-door canvassing is the dominant method of campaigning in Malaysia. The BN had resources to pay a substantial number of these canvassers, while the opposition was forced to depend largely on volunteers (Gomez 2012). The BN was also able to flood various media channels with its messaging, as well as to completely overwhelm even opposition strongholds with BN banners, flags, and posters during the campaign period.

Campaign goodies were likewise ubiquitous. Watchdog groups like PEMANTAU (2018) compiled an extensive list of election offences in the run-up to GE-14, including giveaways of low-cost items like cooking oil, rice, petrol and groceries, as well as big ticket items like washing machines, bicycles, televisions and computers. While all sides engaged in such practices, the scope and scale of the BN's handouts reflected its much greater resources.

Other expenditures were more systemic in nature. Just prior to GE-14, for example, the BN Health Minister announced incentives of RM4,000 for selected FELDA settlers, who constituted an important voting bloc for the BN.[9] Likewise right before GE-14, Najib announced that Malaysia's 1.6 million strong civil service—another key BN voting bloc—would receive a bonus salary increment equivalent to one annual raise, as well as a one-time pension increase, additional religious leave, new medical coverage and other benefits. Cash payments to low-income households through the BR1M programme were implemented just prior to GE-13; the BN's GE-14 election manifesto called for them to be doubled. Lim and Ong (2005, p. 63) describe more localized but similarly strategic expenditures like "[t]he sudden widening and tarring of dilapidated roads, the provision on new facilities at the local park, the clearing of drains and rubbish dumps, the sudden allocation of grants to an area …" in competitive areas. In aggregate, these leave tell-tale signs of electoral cycle spending (Pepinsky 2007).

The New Economic Policy (NEP) and its successor programmes—which provide economic and social advantages to the bumiputra—often blurred the line between UMNO and the state for voters, thereby fostering party loyalty among a significant portion of Malays (Gomez and Saravanamuttu 2013). Those programmes remain popular with many bumiputra voters, who are consequently responsive to the UMNO-led narrative that an opposition government—especially one that contains "progressive" parties like the DAP and PKR—would bring about the end of their economic and social privileges. That narrative, in short, was a clear attempt to position UMNO as the patron and protector of the Malays. As stated dramatically by Najib himself prior to GE-14, if UMNO is voted out, "Malays will no longer have anywhere to hang their hopes, they will fall and lie prone, and will be considered lowly and be vagabonds, beggars and destitutes in their own land", as "the rights and privileges advocated and defended by UMNO over the years … will become extinct and disappear" (Bloomberg 2016). Against that backdrop, it is noteworthy that only an estimated 25 to 30 per cent of Malay voters supported PH in GE-14 (Hutchinson 2018).

As UMNO increasingly sought to portray itself as the true defender of Islam in Malaysia over the last decades (Liow 2004; Ahmad Fauzi 2013), it voiced similar warnings about the religion's potential demise in the wake of a political transition. In addition to bolstering support among its base, the Islamic appeals also reduced the space for religious pluralism in the public sphere (Barr and Govindasamy 2010), particularly following the conservative turn in Malaysia's Islamic discourse (Nawab 2017). This left the more vocally multiracial and multireligious opposition coalition vulnerable to criticism from religious conservatives, and eventually precipitated PAS' departure.

Accompanying the religious rhetoric were regular references—sometimes veiled, sometimes explicit—to Malaysia's past ethnic violence, typically followed by the assertion that only UMNO could maintain the peace between the country's ethnic groups. With GE-14 on the horizon, for example, Najib reminded a large audience that the Chinese community would be targeted first if Malaysia descended into chaos, after which he offered assurances that his was a moderate government committed to maintaining stability.[10] Other statements by UMNO and UMNO-linked figures were intended to demobilizing ethnic minorities by suggesting the potential for unrest if too many concessions were demanded from the Malays. At UMNO's 2005 annual general meeting, for example, then UMNO Youth leader Hishammuddin Hussein brandished a *keris* (traditional Malay dagger) while reminding Malaysia's minority groups of the rightful dominance and limited patience of the Malay community. Najib allegedly made similar statements at a 1987 UMNO rally, vowing to soak the *keris* in Chinese blood.[11]

Some media outlets adopted similar narratives. The UMNO-owned *Utusan Malaysia* newspaper regularly referenced the potential for interethnic conflict through a pro-UMNO lens, as well as resorted to dehumanizing language, especially vis-à-vis ethnic minorities (Fong and Ishak 2014; Christie and Noor 2017). A notorious headline following GE-13, for example, bluntly asked "*Apa Lagi Cina Mahu?*" (What More Do the Chinese Want?). A subsequent story called on the Chinese to "Wake Up", suggesting that a majority in the community were racist, greedy, and unable to recognize how much the government had done for them.[12] Other work has noted the growing "politics of offence and outrage" in which relatively minor transgressions by ethnic minorities are cause for substantial unrest among the Malay population (J. Lee 2018).

The rise of Malay rights NGOs like Pertubuhan Pribumi Perkasa (Perkasa) or the so-called Red Shirts, who style themselves as defenders of Islam and the Malays, added to the volatile mix through occasionally violent rhetoric and confrontational postures. Perkasa president Ibrahim Ali pronounced in 2011, for example, that his group was prepared to wage a "crusade" against the country's Christians, in which Perkasa's "leaders will … lay down their lives and die sprawling in blood".[13] The linkages to UMNO were clear with both groups, making them, in effect, a radical, grassroots activist arm of UMNO. Perhaps because of this, their aggressive and inflammatory actions were rarely prosecuted, even during periods when the Sedition Act was regularly applied to opposition-linked figures.

Despite the recurrent threats of unrest or loss of privilege, many voters cast ballots against UMNO, especially in urban areas and among ethnic minority communities. This does not mean that the strategy had no effect. To the contrary, fear of losing status and privilege is a likely factor in Malay reluctance to support coalitions that have an assertive non-Muslim component, including PH in GE-14. Moreover, the backdrop of threats created widespread unease that "normal" politics could provoke a destabilizing backlash. Following the DAP's 2008 state-level victory in Penang, for example, the streets of otherwise lively George Town were deserted for fear of an angry reaction by BN supporters. The general trepidation, at least among non-Muslims, to directly confront UMNO also helps explain why PH contested GE-14 with Mahathir as prime minister designate and an UMNO-clone party at its centre. That decision likely allowed for a smooth transition, but it also ensures at least a partial continuation of UMNO's interests, with clear implications for reform efforts.

Polling Day Manipulations

The range of pre-election manipulations ensured that electoral competition, including in GE-14, does not occur on a level playing field. As the ultimate outcome in many of Malaysia's past elections was all but guaranteed, there were few incentives to extensively manipulate the elections themselves. In that sense, GE-12 and GE-13 were unusual for their more competitive nature and smaller margins of victory. In GE-13, eight seats were decided by a margin of less than 1 per cent of votes and twenty seats by a margin of 2 per cent or less. While the BN had a relatively safe winning margin of forty-four seats, growing political pressure during and after the election increased the incentives to ensure that close contests went in its favour.[14]

Anecdotal evidence from several monitoring initiatives suggests that polling day manipulations were common in GE-13 and GE-14 (see, for example, Bersih 2014; IDEAS and CPPS 2013; PEMANTAU 2013 and 2018). Many of those manipulations stem directly from the aforementioned institutional biases. They were particularly pronounced in regards to the electoral rolls: PEMANTAU (2013) notes that in GE-13, 8 per cent of observed constituencies had instances of voters being reassigned to a different constituency for unexplained reasons, while 14 per cent of observed constituencies had instances of eligible voters not appearing in the rolls. Dubious voters whose identity observers distrusted were reported in over a quarter of observed constituencies. These raised fears of multiple voting or voting in place of rightful voters. Suspicions were exacerbated by widespread irregularities with indelible ink: instances of it easily washing off, in some cases with water alone just outside the polling station, were reported in 24 per cent of observed constituencies. A subsequent discussion in parliament revealed that the ink contained only 1 per cent silver nitrate, far less than the 10 per cent to 18 per cent needed to make the ink indelible for the intended three to five days (Bersih 2014). While the ink functioned more effectively in GE-14, roll-related issues remained widespread. Prohibitively long queues at polling stations, especially in opposition-leaning areas, were noted. In several instances, voters were prohibited from casting a ballot upon close of the polls, even when legally entitled to do so. More egregiously, the EC's voting procedures effectively prohibited a large number of overseas voters—who tend to oppose the BN—from casting a ballot.

Concerns of malpractice were also raised around the vote-counting process (Bersih 2014). Those stem in part from the observed failure to ensure the safe custody of electoral materials: credible reports indicate, for example, that some ballot boxes from advanced voting in GE-13 were kept unsecured, potentially compromising their integrity prior to the tallying process. The poor training of election officers and suspicions around their impartiality compounded the concerns. Discrepancies in the actual tallying process, for example the number of recorded votes not matching the number of ballots distributed, were likewise reported (Bersih 2014). PH's success in training several thousand volunteer polling and counting agents (PACAs) to monitor polling day procedures—especially in marginal seats—is thought to have reduced opportunities for such malpractices in GE-14 (T.W. Lee 2018).

Attempts to influence voter preferences continued on polling day in both elections. In GE-13, PEMANTAU (2013) observers reported continued campaigning—which is expressly forbidden on polling day—in 44 per cent of observed constituencies; in roughly a quarter, this occurred within the 50-metre perimeter that is legally off limits for non-authorized individuals. Various forms of vote buying were witnessed: instances of cash, cash vouchers, travel allowances or travel reimbursements being illegally distributed were reported in 18 per cent of observed constituencies. This rose to 24 per cent for prohibited distribution of food and drinks. In GE-14, government machinery was extensively used to sway voters towards the BN, as well as to turn out the vote in BN strongholds.

It is unclear to what extent these polling day malpractices result from inadequate training of election officers, or are deliberate manipulations intended to skew the outcome of the election. In either case, their visibility undermined confidence in the electoral process for many voters, even if their immediate effect on election outcomes was likely modest relative to the more systematic pre-election manipulations.

Post-election Manipulations

Prior to GE-14, there were serious concerns that even an opposition victory—in the sense of securing a majority of parliamentary seats—would not result in a clean turnover of power. Previous state-level interventions provided a template for interference. In Perak's 2008 election, the opposition Pakatan Rakyat secured 52.5 per cent of the popular vote and a narrow seat margin of thirty-one to twenty-eight seats against the incumbent BN. Not long after the formation of the new government, three PR legislators were persuaded to defect and support the BN in votes of confidence. A request by the Speaker to dissolve the legislature and hold fresh elections was denied by the Sultan, who instead supported the formation of a new BN state government (Chin and Wong 2009). Legal challenges eventually favoured the BN, effectively overturning the results of the election and granting the BN full control of the state. A similar scenario played out in Sabah in 1994, where the BN likewise assumed control of the government after securing defections (Chin 1994).

While PH's assumption of power post-GE-14 appeared relatively seamless, numerous rumours hint at extensive manoeuvring behind the scenes. First, it appears that Najib sought to bring over defectors during the night of 9 May. PH took measures to forestall this, including a lock-in of its candidates at a Klang Valley hotel and explicit instructions on communication. Ultimately, the seat gap was sufficiently large to make forming a parliamentary majority through individual defections unrealistic for Najib. While rumours also suggest pre-election discussions between Najib and key PH members to arrange alternative governing structures, events unfolded too rapidly post-election for them to gain serious traction. Second, the Agong appeared reluctant to appoint Mahathir as prime minister. Rumours suggest that alternative arrangements were floated in the uncertain post-election hours, including different candidates for prime minister and a joint transitional government. Mahathir's decision to give a public ultimatum on the morning of 10 May—which warned of instability and lawlessness if he was prevented from forming a government as per the Constitution—appears to have taken those alternatives out of play. Third, rumours suggest extensive communication between the prime minister's office and key state institutions in the immediate aftermath of the election, many in an attempt to buy time for the BN. Mahathir's larger-than-life stature in the state appears to have prevented outright interference, though numerous accounts suggest that areas of the state remained unresponsive to political instruction even months after the election. If these rumours are accurate, they lend credibility to the notion that a smooth transition would have been unlikely without the presence of an UMNO-splinter party to assume the reins and offer assurances of continuity to a deeply UMNO-dependent state.

DISCUSSION

UMNO faced an increasingly challenging political landscape in the last two decades of its rule. The vast developmental strides that gave it strong performance legitimacy from independence through the late 1980s slowed as Malaysia attained middle-income status. Simultaneously, the previously fragmented opposition coalesced and gained in credibility, having demonstrated its abilities at the state-level. Against this evolving backdrop, UMNO struggled with factionalism and recurring scandals. To ensure its grip on power against the mounting challenge, UMNO leveraged control of Malaysia's high-capacity state to bias nearly every aspect of the electoral process in its favour.

Those measures created what had the appearance of an impenetrable political fortress that could withstand any electoral challenge. GE-13 illustrated that well. The conditions seemed ideal for achieving a transition: the opposition coalition coordinated its efforts more effectively than ever before, had access to new resources that narrowed the gap with the BN, and benefited from what looked like ideal timing. The sense of a perfect storm brewing against the BN reinvigorated interest in opposition politics and mobilized a broad base of dissatisfied citizens. The result—a victory margin of 4 per cent in the popular vote for PR—was a remarkable feat given the BN's countless advantages. Yet such was the extent of pro-BN bias in the translation of votes into seats that even that outcome was insufficient to topple the government.

For many opposition supporters, Pakatan Rakyat's defeat reinforced the notion that change through the ballot box was impossible.[15] The sense of resignation was compounded by the government's increasingly narrow agenda, in which Islam grew in prominence while the MCA and MIC dwindled into insignificance, leaving few signs of broad-based representation. Many Malaysians, especially among ethnic minorities, expressed a strong desire to leave a country they struggled to see a future in (Al-Ramiah, Hewstone, and Wölfer 2017).

As Birch (2011) argues, a biased electoral process enables corruption and potentially imposes other indirect costs. Ample examples can be found in Malaysia. UMNO's attempts to buy votes through local party machinery deepened illicit forms of clientelism, hastening the party's internal decay. The increasing number of populist initiatives, including the BR1M programme and the civil service's regular salary increases, placed substantial financial strains on the state (Gomez 2016), prompting risky financial initiatives and requiring a helping hand from foreign partners, including China. Hindsight, in fact, may reveal a rather direct connection between the pervasive electoral manipulations and the BN's ultimate downfall.

The effects of Malaysia's biased electoral process do not end with GE-14. To the contrary, they have already shaped the composition of the new government and its agenda. Extreme malapportionment substantially amplifies the importance of voters in traditionally BN-leaning peninsular rural Malay districts and East Malaysian districts, making electoral success conditional on winning support from that electorate. Despite its many breakthroughs, PH largely failed on that front. Mahathir, with his fellow UMNO defectors and UMNO-clone PPBM party, was more effective, especially with the partnership of BN-defectors Warisan in Sabah. Making Mahathir and his fellow establishment Malay elite the public face of PH also effectively undermined UMNO's alarmist rhetoric around race and religion, allowing focus to shift towards their governance blunders. Furthermore, it offered a semblance of continuity to anxious state institutions that may otherwise have blocked a transition.

In essence, Malaysia's electoral process was designed to produce victories for UMNO and its coalition partners. Defeating the BN through that process required a coalition that cloned many of its key attributes, including the bumiputra-centric orientation. That importance is reflected not only in Mahathir's premiership, but also the initial Cabinet composition of the new government. Bersatu, Amanah, and Warisan—who can attract the disproportionately valuable rural Malay and East Malaysian vote—received over half of the Cabinet positions (14 of 27) despite securing only about a one-quarter (32 of 121) of PH's total seats. In other words, the (at least nominally) multiracial PKR and DAP received approximately one Cabinet position for every seven of their parliamentary seats, relative to a ratio of just over 1:2 for Bersatu, Amanah, and Warisan. Given that relative distribution of power, reform aspirations that do not align with the latter's interests are unlikely to proceed. That includes a fundamental reform of the electoral system itself, as a more equitable distribution of voters across districts would shift power to PKR and the DAP within PH. Reducing malapportionment would also alter the balance point of Malaysian politics by increasing the electoral influence of ethnically diverse urban areas at the expense of currently overrepresented bumiputra-majority areas. Such a move carries substantial political risks, since it can easily be depicted as a betrayal of PH's implicit commitment to maintain aspects of Malay and Islamic primacy.

It is important to keep the larger picture in mind. The post-GE-14 transition opens up new political space in Malaysia and has already produced meaningful reforms. But as it was enabled by moulding a political challenge into the form required by the deeply biased electoral process, it cannot avoid reflecting elements of that process. Ultimately, while Malaysia's electoral system could not save UMNO, it did ensure that the core of UMNO's agenda survived into the next chapter of Malaysia's political history.

Notes

1. This chapter is based Ostwald (2017a), also published by ISEAS – Yusof Ishak Institute.
2. Najib noted in a Reuters (2018) interview: "I didn't expect it to be this catastrophic. I thought we could possibly lose some seats, but I didn't expect this sort of dramatic result, this calamitous result." Mahathir admitted on numerous occasions being "very surprised" by his coalition's victory, including in an interview with Thai broadcaster ThaiPBS (2018).
3. Malaysia had alternatively been categorized a one-party state (Wong, Chin, and Othman 2019), electoral authoritarian (Ufen 2009), and competitive authoritarian (Levitsky and Way 2010).
4. Aside from chapters in this volume, see Chin (2018), Hutchinson (2018), and Lemière (2018), for early accounts.
5. See Lim (2002) and Welsh (2014) for comprehensive discussions of Malaysia's electoral system.
6. The "Varieties of Democracy" (www.v-dem.net) dataset considers fewer dimensions of electoral manipulations, but has greater temporal coverage.
7. A two-thirds majority is required to approve an increase in the number of seats.
8. The was more successful in securing support from the private sector following the watershed 2008 election.
9. FELDA is the Federal Land Development Authority, which resettled more than 100,000 landless Malay families beginning in the 1950s. FELDA settlers constitute nearly 1.2 million voters distributed across 54 of Malaysia's 222 districts. Prior to GE-14, these voters were a virtual "fixed-deposit" for the BN (Maznah 2015).
10. See *Malaysiakini*, "Chinese the First to Be Targeted if There Is No Peace, PM Fears", 16 September 2017.
11. See *Malaysian Insider*, "Dr M Chided Najib for Stoking Racial Tensions", 17 April 2012.
12. See *Utusan Malaysia*, "Apa Lagi Cina Mahu", 6 May 2013 and "Sedarlah Cina", 9 June 2013, respectively.
13. See Aidila Razak, "Perkasa Ready to Crusade against Ungrateful Christians", *Malaysiakini*, 15 May 2011.
14. The BN won thirteen of the twenty seats decided by a margin of 2 per cent or less, and eighteen of the thirty-one decided by a margin of 3 per cent or less.
15. A Merdeka Center (2017) poll found that over 70 per cent of respondents in the 21–30 year old age bracket felt they had no influence over government policy-making. Less than one-third indicated an interest in politics, with a staggering 40 per cent of eligible voters choosing not to register to vote.

References

Abbott, Jason. 2011. "Electoral Authoritarianism and the Print Media in Malaysia: Measuring Political Bias". *Asian Affairs: An American Review* 38, no. 1: 1–38.

———, and John Wagner Givens. 2015. "Strategic Censorship in a Hybrid Authoritarian

Regime? Differential Bias in Malaysia's Online and Print Media". *Journal of East Asian Studies* 15, no. 3: 455–78.

Ahmad Fauzi Abdul Hamid. 2013. *Political Islam and Islamist Politics in Malaysia*. Trends in Southeast Asia, no. 2/2013. Singapore: Institute of Southeast Asian Studies.

Al-Ramiah, Ananthi, Miles Hewstone, and Ralf Wölfer. 2017. "Attitudes and Ethnoreligious Integration: Meeting the Challenge and Maximizing the Promise of Multicultural Malaysia". Report to the Board of Trustees, CIMB Foundation, Kuala Lumpur.

Barr, Michael, and Anantha Raman Govindasamy. 2010. "The Islamisation of Malaysia: Religious Nationalism in the Service of Ethnonationalism". *Australian Journal of International Affairs* 64, no. 3: 293–311.

Bersih. 2014. "Findings of the People's Tribunal on Malaysia's 13th General Elections". http://www.bersih.org/wp-content/uploads/2014/03/Peoples-Tribunal-on-GE-13-Findings-Report.pdf (accessed 8 February 2019).

Birch, Sarah. 2011. *Electoral Malpractice*. Oxford: Oxford University Press.

Bloomberg. 2016. "Najib Warns Malay Base of Threat to Islam if Opponents Win Power". 30 November 2016.

Brown, Graham. 2005. "The Rough and Rosy Road: Sites of Contestation in Malaysia's Shackled Media Industry". *Pacific Affairs* 78, no. 1: 39–56.

———. 2008. "Federal and State Elections in Malaysia, March 2008". *Electoral Studies* 27, no. 4: 740–73.

Case, William. 1996. "UMNO Paramountcy: A Report on Single-Party Dominance in Malaysia". *Party Politics* 2, no. 1: 115–27.

———. 2017. "Stress Testing Leadership in Malaysia: The 1MDB Scandal and Najib Tun Razak". *Pacific Review* 30, no. 5: 633–54.

Chin, James. 1994. "Sabah State Election of 1994: End of Kadazan Unity". *Asian Survey* 34, no. 10: 904–15.

———. 2012. "Forced to the Periphery: Recent Chinese Politics in East Malaysia". In *Malaysian Chinese: Recent Developments and Prospects*, edited be Lee Hock Guan and Leo Suryadinata. Singapore: Institute of Southeast Asian Studies.

———. 2018. "The Comeback Kid: Mahathir and the 2018 General Elections". *The Round Table* 107, no. 4: 535–37.

———, and Wong Chin Huat. 2009. "Malaysia's Electoral Upheaval". *Journal of Democracy* 20, no. 3: 71–85.

Christie, Daniel, and Noraini Noor. 2017. "Humanising and Dehumanising the Other: Ethnic Conflict in Malaysia". In *Enlarging the Scope of Peace Psychology*, edited by Mohamed Seedat, Shahnaaz Suffla, and Daniel Christie. Springer International Publishing.

Crouch, Harold. 1996. *Government and Society in Malaysia*. St. Leonards: Allen and Unwin.

Diamond, Larry. 1996. "Thinking About Hybrid Regimes". *Journal of Democracy* 13, no. 2: 21–35.

Fong, Yang, and Md Sidin Ahmad Ishak. 2014. "Framing Interethnic Conflict in Malaysia: A Comparative Analysis of Newspaper Coverage on the *Keris* Polemics". *Ethnicities* 14, no. 2: 252–78.

Gomez, Edmund Terence. 1996. "Electoral Funding of General, State and Party Elections in Malaysia". *Journal of Contemporary Asia*, no. 1: 81–99.

———. 2012. "Monetizing Politics: Financing Parties and Elections in Malaysia". *Modern Asian Studies* 46, no. 5: 1370–97.

———. 2016. "Resisting the Fall: The Single Dominant Party, Policies and Elections in Malaysia". *Journal of Contemporary Asia* 46, no. 4: 570–90.

———, and Jomo K.S. 1999. *Malaysia's Political Economy: Politics, Patronage and Profits*. Cambridge: Cambridge University Press,

———, and Johan Saravanamuttu, eds. 2013. *The New Economic Policy in Malaysia: Affirmative Action, Ethnic Inequalities and Social Justice*. Singapore: NUS Press and Institute of Southeast Asian Studies.

Hopkins, Julian. 2014. "Cybertroopers and Tea Parties: Government Use of the Internet in Malaysia". *Asian Journal of Communication* 24, no. 1: 5–24.

Houghton, Tessa. 2013. "Malaysian Media—Watchdog or Running Dog?". *New Mandala*, 17 November 2013. http://www.newmandala.org/malaysian-media-watchdog-or-running-dog/ (accessed 8 February 2019).

Hutchinson, Francis E. 2014 "Malaysia's Federal System: Overt and Covert Centralisation". *Journal of Contemporary Asia* 44, no. 3: 422–42.

———. 2018. "Malaysia's 14th General Elections: Drivers and Agents of Change". *Asian Affairs* 49, no. 4: 582–605.

IDEAS and CPPS. 2013. "Was GE-13 Free and Fair? An Interim Observation Report on Malaysia's 13th General Election". Jointly prepared by Institute of Democracy and Economic Affairs (IDEAS) and the Centre for Public Policy Studies (CPPS).

Lee Hock Guan. 2015. "Malapportionment and the Electoral Authoritarian Regime in Malaysia". In *Coalitions in Collision: Malaysia's 13th General Elections*, edited by Johan Saravanamuttu, Lee Hock Guan, and Mohamed Nawab Mohamed Osman. Singapore: Institute of Southeast Asian Studies.

Lee Hwok Aun. 2017. "Fault Lines—and Common Ground—in Malaysia's Ethnic Relations and Policies". *ISEAS Perspective*, no. 63/2017, 15 August 2017.

Lee, Julian C.H. 2018. "Outrage in Malaysia: The Politics of Taking Offence". *East Asia* 35, no. 3: 249–65.

Lee Tak Wee. 2018. "Making Sure Votes Count: Polling and Counting Agents in Malaysia". *The Round Table* 107, no. 6: 803–4.

Lemière, Sophie. 2018. "The Downfall of Malaysia's Ruling Party". *Journal of Democracy* 29, no. 4: 114–28.

Levitsky, Steven, and Lucan Way. 2010. *Competitive Authoritarianism: Hybrid Regimes after the Cold War*. New York: Cambridge University Press.

Lim Hong Hai. 2002. "Electoral Politics in Malaysia: 'Managing' Elections in a Plural Society". In *Electoral Politics in Southeast and East Asia*, edited by Auriel Croissant, Gabriele Bruns and Marie John. Singapore: Friedrich Ebert Stiftung.

——— and Ong Kian Ming. 2006. "Electoral Campaigning in Malaysia". In *Electoral Campaigning in East and Southeast Asia*, edited by Christian Schafferer. Aldershot: Ashgate.

Liow, Joseph Chinyong. 2004. "Political Islam in Malaysia: Problematising Discourse and Practice in UMNO-PAS 'Islamisation Race'." *Commonwealth & Comparative Politics* 42, no. 2: 184–205.

Maznah Mohamad. 2015. "Fragmented but Captured: Malay Voters and the Felda Factor in GE-13". In *Coalitions in Collision: Malaysia's 13th General Elections*, edited by Johan Saravanamuttu, Lee Hock Guan, and Mohamed Nawab Mohamed Osman. Singapore: Institute of Southeast Asian Studies.

Means, Gordon. 1996. "Soft Authoritarianism in Malaysia and Singapore". *Journal of Democracy* 7, no. 4: 103–17.

MERAP. 2013. "Malaysian Electoral Roll Analysis Project, 2013". http://malaysianelectoral rollproject.blogspot.ca (accessed 8 February 2019).

Merdeka Center. 2017. "Youth Perception of Economy, Leadership and Current Issues", 20 September 2017.

Mohamed Nawab Mohamed Osman. 2017. "The Islamic Conservative Turn in Malaysia: Impact and Future Trajectories". *Contemporary Islam* 11, no. 1: 1–20.

Norris, Pippa, and Max Grömping. 2017a. "The Expert Survey of Perceptions of Electoral Integrity". Release 5.0, (PEI_5.0), www.electoralintegrityproject.com (accessed 8 February 2019).

———, and Max Grömping. 2017b. "Populist Threats to Electoral Integrity: The Year in Elections 2016–2017". In "The Expert Survey of Perceptions of Electoral Integrity". Release 5.0, (PEI_5.0).

Ong Kian Ming. 2012. "10 Major Problems in EC's Electoral Roll". *Malaysiakini*, 7 April 2012. https://www.malaysiakini.com/news/194373 (accessed 9 February 2019).

———, Yuko Kasuya, and Kota Mori. 2017. "Malapportionment and Democracy: A Curvilinear Relationship". *Electoral Studies* 49: 118–27.

Ostwald, Kai. 2013. "How to Win a Lost Election: Malapportionment and Malaysia's 2013 General Election". *The Round Table* 102, no. 6: 521–32.

———. 2017a. *Malaysia's Electoral Process: The Methods and Costs of Perpetuating UMNO Rule*. Trends in Southeast Asia, no. 19/2017. Singapore: ISEAS – Yusof Ishak Institute.

———. 2017b. "Federalism without Decentralization: Power Consolidation in Malaysia". *Journal of Southeast Asian Economies* 34, no. 3: 488–506.

———, Paul Schuler, and Jie Ming Chong. 2018. "Triple Duel: The Impact of Coalition Fragmentation and Three-Corner Fights on the 2018 Malaysian Election". *Journal of Current Southeast Asian Affairs* 37, no. 3: 31–55.

PEMANTAU. 2013. "An Election Observation Report for GE-13: Clean and Fair?". Petaling Jaya: Persatuan Kesedaran Komuniti Selangor (EMPOWER).

———. 2018. "Election Offenses Listing 3". https://pemantau.org/wp-content/uploads/Election-Offences-GE-14_25042018-edited.pdf (accessed 8 February 2019).

Pempel, John. 1990. *Uncommon Democracies: The One-Party Dominant Regimes*. Ithaca, NY: Cornell University Press.

Pepinsky, Thomas. 2007. "Autocracy, Elections, and Fiscal Policy: Evidence from Malaysia". *Studies in Comparative International Development* 42, nos. 1-2: 136–63.

———. 2013. "The New Media and Malaysian Politics in Historical Perspective". *Contemporary Southeast Asia: A Journal of International and Strategic Affairs* 35, no. 1: 83–103.

Reuters. 2018. "Former Malaysian Premier Najib Talks about 1MDB Scandal, Seized Assets". 20 June 2018.

Sadiq, Kamal. 2005. "When States Prefer Non-Citizens Over Citizens: Conflict Over Illegal Immigration into Malaysia". *International Studies Quarterly* 49, no. 1: 101–22.

Slater, Dan. 2003. "Iron Cage in an Iron Fist: Authoritarian Institutions and the Personalization of Power in Malaysia". *Comparative Politics* 36, no. 1: 81–101.

———, and Sofia Fenner. 2011. "State Power and Staying Power: Infrastructural Mechanisms and Authoritarian Durability". *Journal of International Affairs* 65, no. 1: 15–29.

Tapsell, Ross. 2013. "The Media Freedom Movement in Malaysia and the Electoral Authoritarian Regime". *Journal of Contemporary Asia* 43, no. 4: 613–35.

ThaiPBS. 2018. "Dr Mahathir: We Were Very Surprised We Won". 23 August 2018. https://www.kinitv.com/video/6493908 (accessed 8 February 2019).

Ufen, Andreas. 2009. "The Transformation of Political Party Opposition in Malaysia and

Its Implications for the Electoral Authoritarian Regime". *Democratization* 16, no. 3: 604–27.

Weiss, Meredith. 2013. "Parsing the Power of 'New Media' in Malaysia". *Journal of Contemporary Asia* 23, no. 4: 591–612.

Welsh, Bridget. 2013. "Malaysian Elections 2013: A Step Backward". *Journal of Democracy* 23, no. 4: 136–50.

———. 2014. "Elections in Malaysia: Voting Behaviour and Electoral Integrity". In *Routledge Handbook of Contemporary Malaysia*, edited by Meredith Weiss. London: Routledge.

Wong Chin Huat. 2018. "Constituency Delimitation and Electoral Authoritarianism in Malaysia". *The Round Table* 107, no. 1: 67–80.

———, James Chin, and Norani Othman. 2010. "Malaysia: Towards a Topology of an Electoral One-Party State". *Democratization* 17, no. 5: 920–49.

3

WINNING ELECTIONS BY RIGGING BORDERS?
Barisan Nasional's Brazen, and Failed, Attempt

Danesh Prakash Chacko

INTRODUCTION

Redelineation has often been used as a tool by the former ruling coalition, Barisan Nasional (BN), to hold on to power. Past analyses observed that, by increasing the number of constituencies and redrawing their borders, redelineation exercises have boosted the former ruling coalition's electoral performance, most notably in the general elections of 1974, 1986, 1995 and 2004.

During Malaysia's 2016–18 redelineation exercise, the Election Commission (EC)—the organization tasked with carrying out this exercise—provided many illustrations of unfair practice and violation of constitutional norms, clearly with a view to provide electoral advantage to BN.

Unlike its antecedents, the 2016–18 redelineation exercise did not involve increasing the number of parliamentary or state seats. However, the review had long-reaching implications. First, it left malapportionment, which disproportionately favours small, rural, and Malay-majority constituencies, unaddressed. Second, the exercise extensively gerrymandered parliamentary and state constituencies with the aim of increasing the share of registered Malay voters in select seats, as well as concentrating non-Malay voters in a number of oversized constituencies.

While these changes further tipped the "playing field" towards BN and were expected to increase the incumbent's share of parliamentary seats, their intended effect in the 2018 general election was underwhelming. The redrawn borders delivered just one additional seat to BN and could not stop Pakatan Harapan (PH) from forming a supermajority in the Legislative Assembly of Selangor—the most aggressively gerrymandered state. However, while the 2016–18 redelineation exercise did not alter the outcome of the 14th General Elections (GE-14), the misdeeds of the EC and BN members of parliament must not be overlooked.

The chapter seeks to identify what electoral violations were committed and analyse why these did not have the expected outcome. The chapter comprises five sections. Following this introduction, the second section will examine the principles of redelineation according to the Malaysian Constitution. The subsequent section will review the history and implementation of redelineation exercises in Malaysia in order to see what advantages the exercises have provided to BN at the parliamentary and state levels. The fourth section will assess changes introduced since GE-13 and in the run-up to GE-14, seeking to understand why this round of border-rigging did not deliver as before. The final section will conclude.

REDELINEATION IN MALAYSIA: PRINCIPLES

Although the Constitution does not stipulate a particular electoral system, Malaysia has adopted the first-past-the-post (FPTP) system to elect individual representatives for each parliamentary and state constituency. Since this is a winner-takes-all system, the outcome of election results can be heavily influenced by the alteration of electoral boundaries.

The delineation process usually involves two determinations, namely: the number of electoral constituencies; and the shape of their borders (Wong 2014). With regard to the number of electoral constituencies, Article 46 of the Constitution stipulates the total number of representatives in the Parliament as well as for each state in Malaysia (Federal Constitution 2010). Changing the number of members of parliament (MPs) requires a constitutional amendment passed by a two-thirds majority vote in the federal parliament. The same principle applies at the state level, where two-thirds of the elected representatives must approve an amendment to the respective state constitution to increase the number of seats in the State Legislative Assembly.

With regard to the drawing of electoral boundaries and redistricting seats, according to the 13th Schedule of the Constitution, the EC is the responsible party. The Constitution initially implied the principle of voter equality by: ensuring each state's share of parliamentary seats was proportionate to its population; and limiting disparities between the number of voters in rural and urban seats. However, such safeguards have been weakened over time. Nonetheless, the process can and should uphold democratic principles of "One Person, One Vote, One Value" (OPOVOV) (Tindak Malaysia 2014).

In Malaysia, there are three units of review when conducting a redelineation exercise: Peninsular Malaysia (including the Federal Territory of Labuan); Sabah;

and Sarawak. The redelineation exercises for Peninsular Malaysia and Sabah, by precedent and continuing practice, happen concurrently. Sarawak follows its own schedule, as its state government elections do not coincide with the rest.

The Constitution provides two grounds for performing redelineation: to ensure constituencies adhere to the principles of the 13th Schedule; and to comply with changes in the total number of constituencies as approved by the national parliament and respective state assemblies. According to the Constitution, redelineation is to be done no less than eight years from the previously gazetted exercise and completed within two years from the date of its commencement (Suruhanjaya Pilihan Raya 2018a).

Since 1962, the principles of redelineation have been set out in section 2 of the 13th Schedule, which are worth reproducing here (italics added):

(a) while having regard to the desirability of giving all electors reasonably convenient opportunities of going to the polls, constituencies ought to be delimited so that *they do not cross state boundaries* and regard ought to be had to the inconveniences of state constituencies crossing the boundaries of federal constituencies;

(b) regard ought to be had to the *administrative facilities available within the constituencies* for the establishment of the necessary registration and polling machines;

(c) the number of electors within each constituency in a state *ought to be approximately equal* except that, having regard to the greater difficulty of reaching electors in the country districts and the other disadvantages facing rural constituencies, a measure of weightage for area ought to be given to such constituencies;

(d) regard ought to be had to the inconveniences attendant on alterations of constituencies, and to the *maintenance of local ties* (Federal Constitution 2010).

The Constitution stipulates that the redelineation exercise is to be conducted if there are non-compliances with the principles of the 13th Schedule, for example due to large movements of people between parliamentary constituencies (Suruhanjaya Pilihan Raya 2018). These principles give broad latitude to the authorities' discretion. Given these conditions, it is imperative that the Election Commission is vested with independence and integrity, and that it executes its mandate in a free and fair manner (Malaysian Bar Council 2016).

In practice, of the four fundamental principles above, only section 2(a) which stipulates that parliamentary constituencies must not straddle different states and state seats must not cross parliamentary constituency lines has been systematically observed by the EC. Compliance with section 2(b), which requires constituencies to have facilities such as post offices and EC offices to register voters as well as schools and halls to conduct the polling, is difficult to assess. Elections have generally proceeded without delays or bottlenecks due to the adequate provision and management of polling centres, but accessibility for remotely located voters and reliability of the postal balloting process have been questioned. The sizeable number of unregistered voters (3.6 million as of 2017 (Bernama 2018)) also raises questions over the adequacy of the EC's efforts to register voters.

The EC has clearly and consistently violated section 2(c), which upholds voter equality across electoral districts. Malapportionment, or inequalities of voter populations between constituencies which have the same number of representatives, is the first fundamental problem of Malaysia's electoral system (Tindak Malaysia 2014). To illustrate, if Constituency A has 10,000 voters and Constituency B has 50,000 voters but each elect one representative, then the value of Constituency A votes outweighs that of Constituency B. This is the most common form of malapportionment, and it is an issue that needs to be addressed in an *intra*state context, specifically between rural and urban constituencies *within* states.[1]

In any democracy with uneven population distribution and varying densities, it is virtually impossible to redistrict every constituency to have equal numbers of voters. The Venice Commission of 2002, which formulated the code of good electoral practices in Europe, prescribed that the permissible departure for constituencies from the average in order to protect minorities and foster fair representation of rural areas should ideally be not be more than 10 per cent and should not exceed 15 per cent (Tindak Malaysia 2014).

In Malaysia, the empowerment of Parliament rather than the EC to determine the number of constituencies and the unspecific wording of section 2(c)'s stipulation that constituencies be "approximately equal", have unduly politicized what should be a technical procedure and have also permitted inordinate flexibility in interpreting these terms. Since the 1970s, interstate and intrastate malapportionment have become entrenched (including the reduction in the proportion of East Malaysian seats in Parliament) resulting in BN holding many smaller, rural constituencies. The Electoral Integrity Project (EIP), an independent academic project between Harvard University and University of Sydney, concluded that Malaysia ranks at the bottom when it comes to disparities in the size of electoral constituencies (Lyn 2014).

Malapportionment, together with gerrymandering, also contributed to the ability of BN to effectively form government with a miniscule share of the popular vote. Specifically, the number of votes for BN in the smallest 112 constituencies (necessary to secure a majority) that it won in the 2008 and 2013 general elections amounted to 15.4 per cent and 16.5 per cent of total votes, respectively (Tindak Malaysia 2014).

The second fundamental problem of redelineation concerns gerrymandering, or the drawing of boundaries for electoral advantage. Gerrymandering specifically operates in two ways to enhance one party's chances: "cracking" the opponent's support base and dispersing its downsized blocks across two or more constituencies; and "packing" one's support base into targeted constituencies to augment the expected vote share. Constitutionally, constituencies ought to be drawn such that the process preserves "local ties" (section 2(d)). This provision is interpreted as referring to borders that recognize existing communities, interconnected residential areas, and administrative jurisdictions (Suruhanjaya Pilihan Raya 2018a). When a constituency spans two or more local authority areas, it creates greater inconveniences for elected representatives to liaise with the local authorities.

REDELINEATION IN MALAYSIA: HISTORY

The history of electoral redelineation in Malaysia has been marked by: tensions between the EC and the federal executive; steady erosion of the EC's independence; and expansion of the EC's discretionary powers alongside removal of constitutional safeguards for voter equality. The following paragraphs will trace the evolution of these tensions over time and punctuated by major milestones.

The Early Days

After convincingly winning local council elections in the early 1950s in Malaya, United Malays National Organization (UMNO) and Malaysian Chinese Association (MCA) pressed the British to convene federal elections (Lim 2002). A committee, commissioned to draw up an electoral system for Malaya, recommended FPTP for determining the winner in each seat. In terms of redelineation, constituencies ought to be drawn with approximately equal sizes of voter population with some weightage for rural seats (Lim 2002). The acceptable deviation from the norm for constituencies was set at 33 per cent. Fifty-two seats were apportioned and redistricted for the 1955 Federal Legislative Council, which was held under the auspices of the British in the run-up to independence.

After the Alliance—comprising UMNO, MCA, and Malaysian Indian Congress (MIC)—swept fifty-one out fifty-two seats of the Federal Legislative Councils in 1955, the process of drafting the Constitution for self-governing Malaya commenced. The Reid Commission laid out key principles for the redelineation exercise, which were incorporated into the 1957 Malayan Constitution:

1. Article 116(3): The number of constituencies allocated to each state should correspond with its population size;
2. Article 116(4): To curb within-state malapportionment, the size of constituencies should not exceed or fall short of a baseline by more than 15 per cent. This baseline is derived from the statewide average constituency size;[2]
3. A new redelineation exercise was to be initiated 8–10 years after the preceding exercise.

The above principles were adopted in the 1957 Malayan Constitution. Then, Article 46(1) stipulated that the lower house would consist of 100 elected members—with the exception that the first lower house would have 104 elected members. To simplify the transition from the pre-independence Federal Legislative Council to the post-independence Parliament, the EC divided the Council's 52 seats into two, forming 104 constituencies in 1958. At this point of time, the process of allocating the number of seats and drawing borders was completely in the hands of the EC (Federal Constitution 2010).

For the 1958 redelineation, the following principles were adopted (Election Commission 1958):

1. Constituencies ought to be drawn such that the constituency hosts sufficient facilities to conduct voter registration and polling machinery;
2. Constituencies ought to be drawn where all seats have approximately equal numbers of inhabitants, with some weightage to rural areas;
3. The EC was not bounded by strict principles on redistricting as stipulated in Article 116(4); however, it took population density, community types and existing communication methods into consideration for this exercise.

Figures 3.1 and 3.2 demonstrate the EC's efforts to adhere to these guidelines particularly regarding the size of constituencies in predominantly rural Kelantan and the more urbanized state of Selangor. The population comparisons in both states demonstrate substantial variation but—with the exception of two large constituencies in Selangor—remain within the broad contours of 33 per cent above and below the average constituency size in each state (Election Commission 1960).

The first post-independence election of Malaya in 1959, based on the 1958 redelineation exercise, witnessed the ruling Alliance winning most states. Despite this, the coalition lost ground to Pan-Malaysian Islamic Party (PMIP; the precursor to PAS) in Kelantan and Terengganu, as well as other opposition forces in urban areas. The loss of non-Malay support in the 1959 elections may have created anxieties in the ruling Alliance coalition and provided the impetus for undermining the EC's independence.

In 1960, the EC proceeded with another redelineation exercise, triggered by the reduction in the number of legislative seats from 104 to 100. The new exercise strictly followed the principles laid out in the 1957 Constitution, in that constituencies within a state could not deviate 15 per cent from the baseline (Election Commission 1960).[3] The 1960 exercise also set out demographic guidelines, seeking to redraw boundaries such that constituencies would be racially mixed and reflective of the Federation's ethnic composition (Election Commission 1960) (see Table 3.1).

Alarmed by the prospects of greater electoral empowerment of non-Malays based on the EC's 1960 proposal, UMNO—the main component party in Alliance— looked for ways to curb the Commission's independence. In 1962, key constitutional amendments with regard to redelineation were implemented, which worsened malapportionment and expanded executive control over the EC. First, the number of elected members in the lower house was maintained at 104, thus nullifying the grounds for the 1960 redelineation proposal. Second, sections 3, 4 and 5 of Article 116 of the Constitution were repealed, and the 13th Schedule was added as a new set of redelineation principles. These changes eliminated the requirement that states' seat allocations should correspond with population size, and reduced constraints against malapportionment among constituencies within states. In addition, Parliament— rather than the EC—would determine any change in the number of seats, provided the proposal secured a two-thirds majority. Third, rural constituencies were permitted to have populations as little as half that of urban seats.[4]

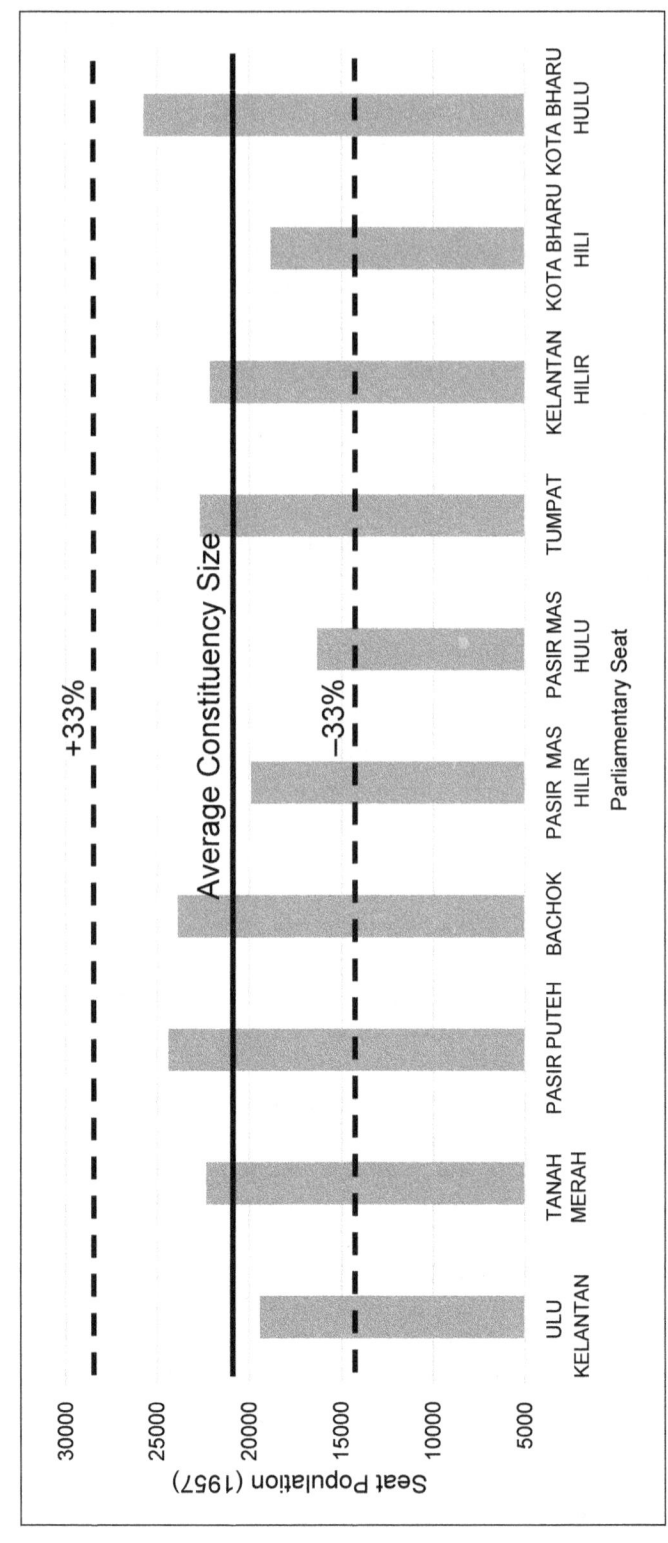

FIGURE 3.1
Variation of Voter Population in Redistricted Parliamentary Seats in Kelantan, 1958

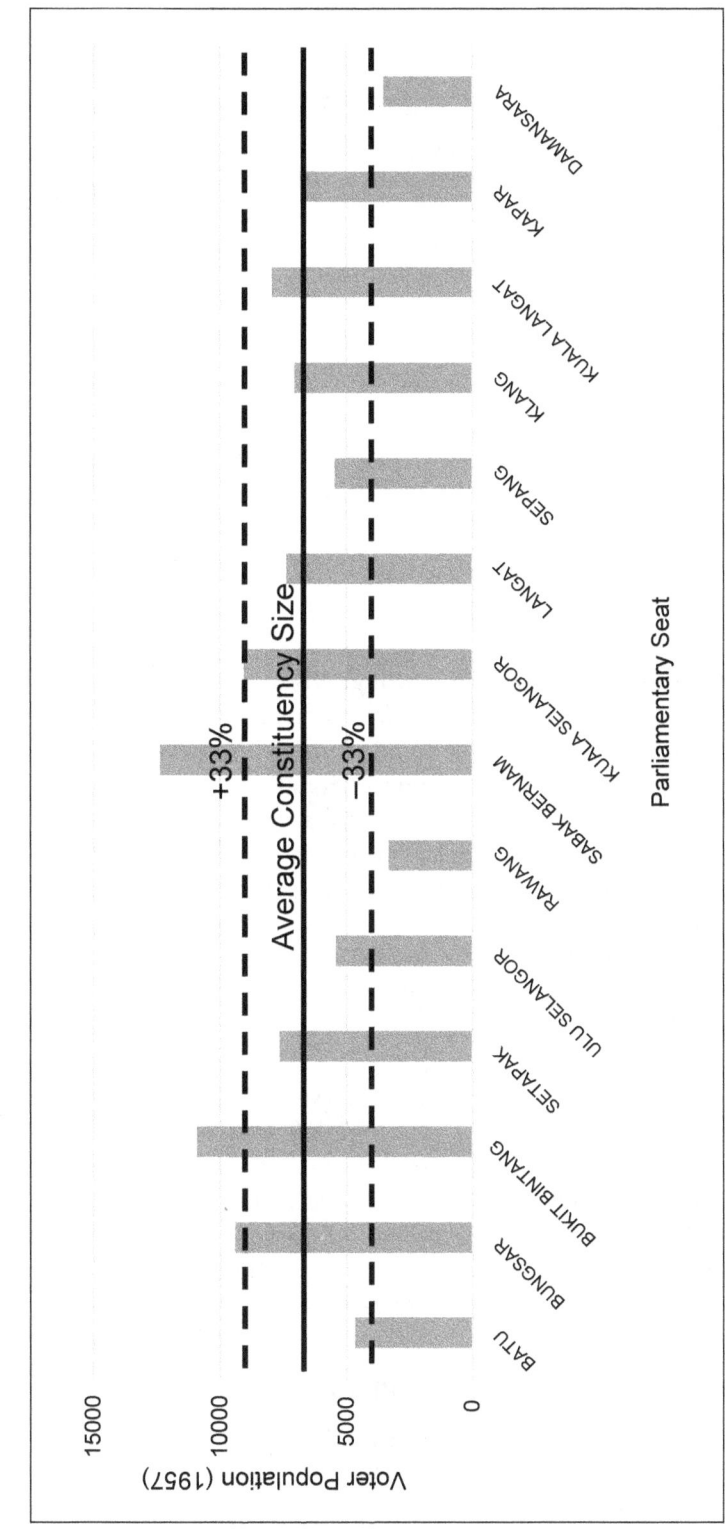

FIGURE 3.2
Variation of Voter Population in Redistricted Parliamentary Seats in Selangor, 1958

TABLE 3.1
Proposed Change in Representations for States of Malaya in 1960

State	1958 Number of Federal Seats	1960 Number of Federal Seats	1958 Number of State Seats	1960 Number of State Seats
Perlis	2	2	12	12
Kedah	12	12	24	24
Penang	8	9	24	27
Perak	20	19	40	38
Selangor	14	14	28	28
Negri Sembilan	6	5	24	25
Malacca	4	5	20	20
Johor	16	14	32	28
Pahang	6	5	24	25
Terengganu	6	5	24	25
Kelantan	10	10	30	30

Source: Election Commission (1960).

In 1963, Malaysia was created through the merger of Peninsular Malaysia, Sabah, Sarawak and Singapore. Political calculations motivated the allocation of seats to states. To contain the influence of Singapore, the city was assigned disproportionately lower representation relative to its population (fifteen seats). To safeguard the political weight of the East Malaysian regions, and in accordance with the Malaysia Agreement 1963, Sabah and Sarawak were accorded disproportionately higher representation and assigned sixteen and twenty-four seats, respectively. When Singapore left in 1965, Singapore's fifteen seats were all transferred to Peninsular Malaysia. Sabah (1966) and Sarawak's (1968) subsequent redelineation exercises adopted the prevailing guidelines. Most constituencies lay within 33 per cent of the average, but clearly had departed from the 15 per cent margin that operated from 1957 to 1962 (Figure 3.3).

The EC commenced a redelineation exercise for Peninsular Malaysia in 1967. The redelineation exercise was not completed before the 1969 elections and was delayed due to the political unrest and ensuing declaration of emergency. The EC resumed the redelineation study in 1971 and just as it tabled its report in Parliament on 13 June 1973, Parliament increased representation for Peninsular Malaysia from 104 to 114 (Suruhanjaya Pilihan Raya 1974). The report, which was based on the previous total number of MPs, was discarded.

Institutionalizing Malapportionment

On 23 August 1973, the Constitutional (Amendment) (No. 2) Act (A206) was enforced, thereby institutionalizing interstate and intrastate malapportionment. First, the discretionary power to determine the number of parliamentary

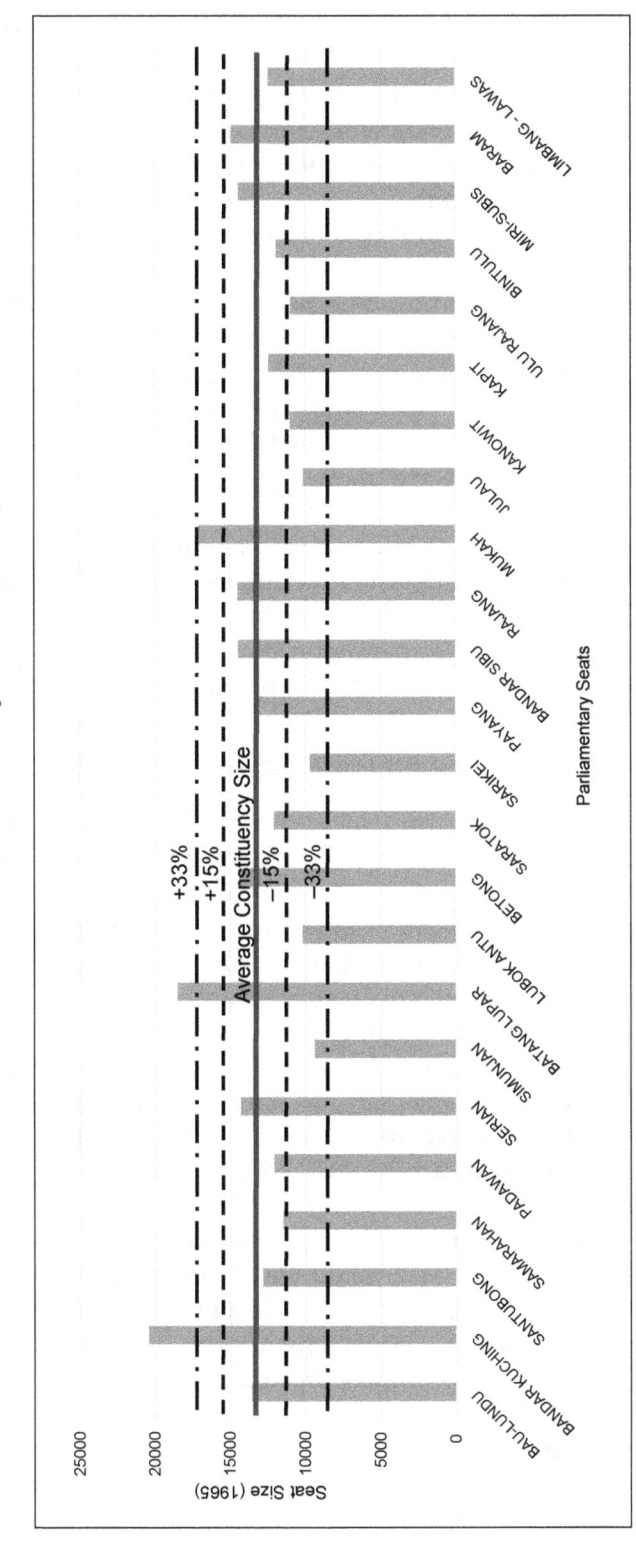

FIGURE 3.3
Variation of Redistricted Parliamentary Seats in Sarawak, 1968

constituencies across the country, and the number within each state, was taken away from the EC and transferred to national and state legislatures (Lim 2002). Henceforth, Article 46 stipulated the number of constituencies for each state through parliamentary amendments, without the EC providing any advice or recommendation. This led to unevenness of voter values across different states (interstate malapportionment).

Second, the remaining constitutional limits on equal electorate sizes (as per the 1962 amendments) within a state were removed. The general principle that constituencies should be "approximately equal" remained, but whereas the previous 1962 regulations stipulated that urban seats could not be more than double the size of rural seats, the 1973 amendment merely stipulated that some weightage should be given to rural constituencies—with no specified amounts or limits. Larger disparities ensued. For example, the 1977 Sarawak redelineation exercise resulted in the urban Bandar Kuching seat being three times bigger than rural Julau.

Third, the amendment laid the grounds for the electoral excision of Kuala Lumpur from Selangor. Kuala Lumpur was a hotbed of opposition Chinese voters who contributed to the near-defeat of the Alliance in the Selangor state elections in 1969 (Lim 2002). Combined with rural weightage and the excision of Kuala Lumpur, as well as the absorption of former opposition party Gerakan into the Alliance[5] in 1972, Selangor remained in the hands of BN until 2008 (Lim 2002).

Redelineation during Mahathir's First Tenure (1981–2003)

The Constitution (Amendment) (No. 2) Act of 1984 conferred more discretionary power to the ruling government on redelineation matters. First, Labuan was excised from Sabah and converted into a Federal Territory (Lim 2002). Second, the ten-year upper limit for redelineation to be conducted was removed, but the lower limit retained. The elimination of the upper limit meant that boundaries could be retained for a longer time, with no governmental obligation to align constituencies with population growth and demographic change. Third, clause 3A was added to the 13th Schedule, stipulating that redelineation can be carried out at any time when the number of parliamentary or state representations is amended. More consequentially, clause 3A exempted the EC from strictly following the principles of the 13th Schedule when carrying out redelineation for change in the number of seats (Lim 2002).

The 1984 redelineation resulted in further ethnically based gerrymandering of constituencies, in Peninsular Malaysia as well as Sabah. A 1986 study by the National Union of Journalists concluded that fifteen out of nineteen new parliamentary seats in Peninsular Malaysia were Malay-majority in composition, although much population growth was taking place in urban, ethnically mixed areas (National Union of Journalists 1986). Ten of those fifteen seats were won by UMNO in the 1986 elections. In Sabah, to curb the influence of the then opposition Parti Bersatu Sabah (PBS), the 1994 redelineation exercise reduced the number of non-Muslim bumiputra and Chinese-majority seats—vote bases for PBS—at the parliamentary and state level (Lai 2002). The moves clearly paid off in the 1995 elections, when BN wrested two parliament seats from PBS, which lost further ground at the state level in 1999 (Lai 2002).

The sacking of Anwar Ibrahim in September 1998 and consolidation of PAS as the biggest opposition force in the 1999 elections signalled that the Malay vote shifted from UMNO to the Islamic party. The 2003 redelineation exercise witnessed zero growth in parliamentary seats in PAS-dominated areas of Kedah, Kelantan and Terengganu, while the government added six new seats in UMNO-dominated Johor (Suruhanjaya Pilihan Raya 2018a). Notably, the 2003 redelineation exercise was characterized by increases in mixed seats, both in new and existing seats, to dilute PAS' potential Malay voter base. In addition, rural seats which supported UMNO were manipulated, with the result that rural seats held by UMNO have a smaller population than those counterparts held by PAS (Lim 2003).

In the 2003 redelineation exercise, the gerrymandering of key parliamentary seats in Kedah resulted in more ethnically mixed seats. Given that non-Malays overwhelmingly refused to vote for PAS, this benefited BN and affected the support levels of key PAS leaders. Thus, leaders of the Islamic party such as Mahfuz Omar and Mat Sabu were defeated in the 2004 general elections.

Table 3.2 summarizes the implications of malapportionment and gerrymandering of each redelineation exercise. Not all exercises follow the same logic. For example,

TABLE 3.2
Malapportionment and Gerrymandering in Malaysia's Redelineation Exercises, 1958–2018: Constitutional Amendments and Electoral Implications

Redelineation Exercise	Constitutional Amendments Affecting Malapportionment	Electoral Implications of Gerrymandering
1958	Exempted from 15 per cent deviation from state baseline	
1960 (Aborted)	15 per cent deviation from state baseline	
1962	33 per cent deviation from state baseline	
1973	Removal of apportionment margins	
1984	10-year maximum limit on initiation of redelineation removed; more than 10 years can lapse between exercises	Concentration of majority/ supermajority ethnic group
1994		Concentration of majority/ supermajority ethnic group
2003		Increase of ethnically mixed seats
2016–18		Concentration of majority/ supermajority ethnic group

the 2003 redelineation exercise increased the number of ethnically mixed seats on the Peninsula to capitalize on BN's strategy of that time. However, the equation was reversed from 2008. This is because mixed seats then became BN's Achilles heel and Malay-majority seats its continual bastion, even more so in 2013 when UMNO rebounded.

Figure 3.4 establishes the relationship between redelineation exercises and subsequent electoral performance, showing that each redrawing of electoral boundaries—barring the last—was followed by an increase in BN-held seats.

In all redelineation exercises until recent years, the BN government was able to bulldoze constitutional amendments and redelineated boundaries through Parliament with haste, facing limited resistance from the opposition or civil society. With the rise of the electoral reform movement Bersih in 2007, the public became more aware about the implications of redelineation. BN's loss of its two-thirds majority in the 2008 general elections, and the formation of Pakatan Rakyat (PR) as a cohesive opposition, also meant that the incumbent coalition could no longer redelineate at will. According to the precedent of previous decades, a new exercise was due around 2013 but it did not proceed.

In GE-13, the issue of malapportionment became more apparent than ever. For the first time in Malaysian history, BN was able to form the government although it failed to garner the popular vote. Figure 3.5, showing parliamentary seats arranged from smallest to biggest, demonstrates the wide gaps in size and the scope for taking power by carrying small constituencies. Indeed, a winning coalition can conceivably form government with a mere one-third of the overall popular vote. In GE-13, BN managed to win 99 of the 112 smallest seats in the country and PR—the predecessor to Pakatan Harapan—only managed to get 13 of the 112 smallest seats (Ostwald 2013). PR garnered the popular vote largely due to its ability to win large urban constituencies in West Malaysia. However, malapportionment, which favoured smaller rural seats, ultimately delivered another victory for BN.

The 2015 Sarawak Redelineation: The First Glimmer of Resistance

Barisan Nasional held a two-thirds majority in the state assembly of Sarawak and embarked on a redelineation exercise in 2015, ten years after the previous such episode. The exercise sought to redistrict state constituencies and create eleven new state seats. As soon as the notice of the recommendation was issued to the public, civil society and opposition politicians condemned the process on the following grounds (Aliran 2015a and b):

1. Failure to use the latest electoral roll for the redelineation exercise (violation of the Constitution).
2. Lack of detailed maps to inform the public about the relocation of voting districts.
3. Failure to address rampant malapportionment. Most of the new and existing seats are undersized in nature. To illustrate, it was possible that only one-

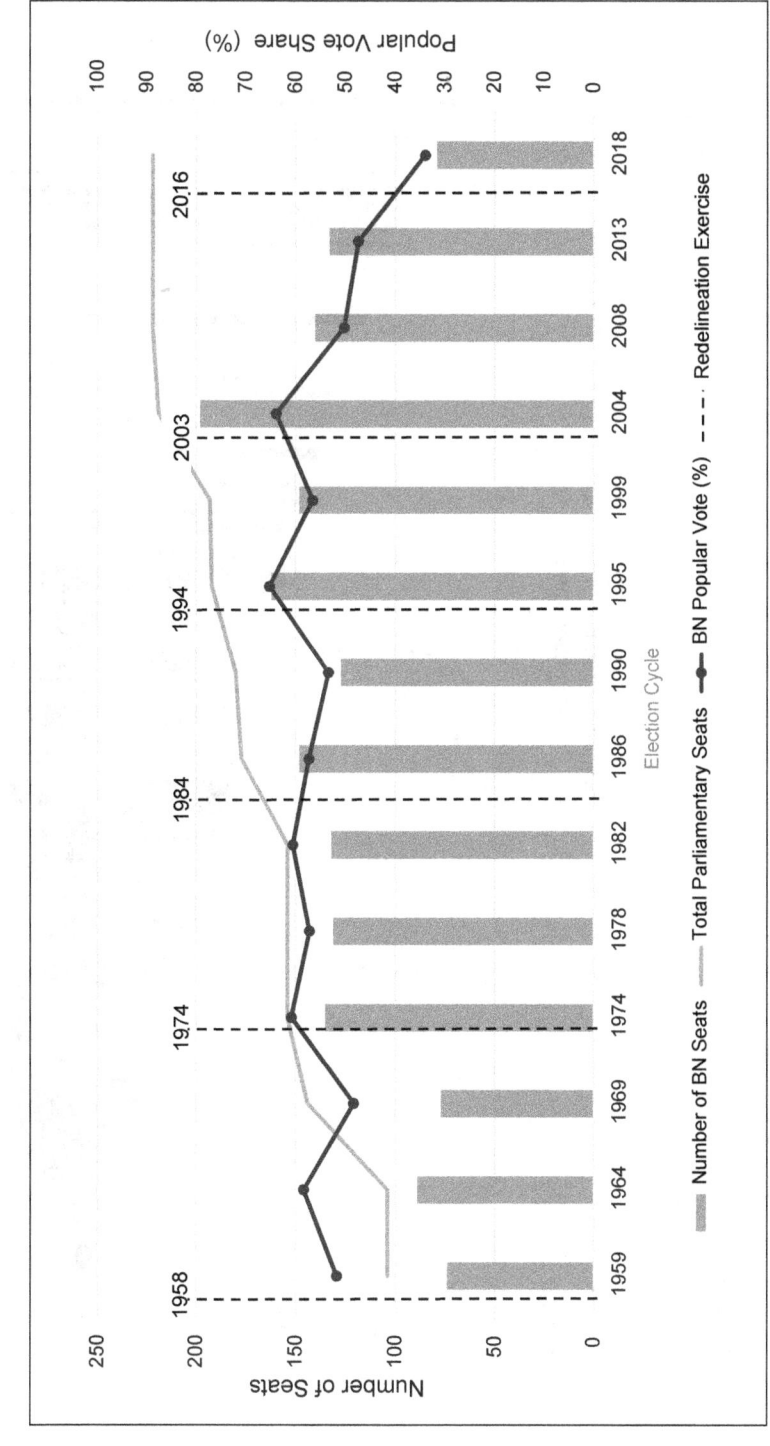

FIGURE 3.4
Redelineation Exercises, Seat Creation and BN's Electoral Performance, 1964–2018

Source: Tindak Malaysia (2014); Wikipedia (2019).

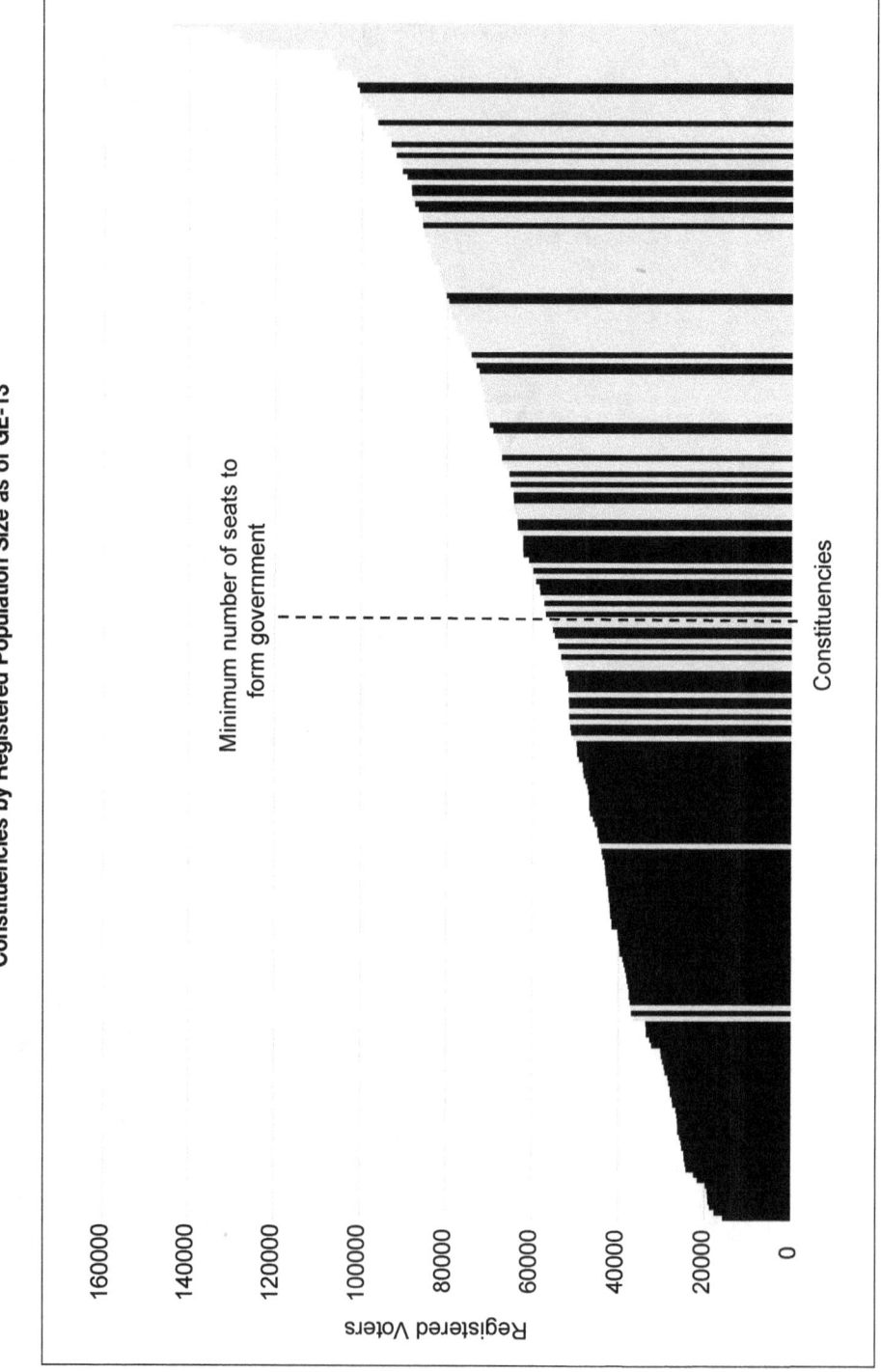

FIGURE 3.5
Constituencies by Registered Population Size as of GE-13

Minimum number of seats to form government

Registered Voters

Constituencies

160000
140000
120000
100000
80000
60000
40000
20000
0

Note: Black indicates BN won the seat while grey indicates PR won the seat

third of Sarawakian voters would be needed to win the smallest forty-two out of total eighty-two constituencies and form government.

4. Pattern of bias: based on past election results, nine out of eleven new seats could be won by BN in the subsequent state elections (Steering Committee of Bersih 2.0 and the Malaysian Electoral Roll Analysis Project 2016).

On 29 January 2015, See Chee How (State Legislative Assembly (SLA) member for Batu Lintang) and a voter filed a court case against the EC on the grounds of non-compliance with the 13th Schedule, and that the Commission did not have the power to alter parliamentary boundaries (Tawie 2015).

Despite the judicial review, the EC proceeded with two rounds of community consultations. In May 2015, the Kuching High Court declared the EC's proposals were null and void (Nazlina 2015). However, the Court of Appeal overturned the High Court's verdict in August 2015 and the Federal Court upheld the Court of Appeal's ruling in October 2015—rendering the EC's proposals as constitutional (Bernama 2015). The ruling declared the redelineation matter academic, as the EC's report was tabled at the hands of the prime minister. Redelineation was gazetted on 19 December 2015, just in time for the 2016 Sarawak State Elections. Despite the violation of democratic principles and setback to the electoral reform movement, the episode signalled to the EC and the BN government that redelineation exercises could no longer be bulldozed with haste.

CRITICAL REVIEW OF THE REDELINEATION EXERCISE OF 2016–18

After a thirteen-year interval following the previous 2003 redelineation exercise— the second longest interval in Malaysian history after the interim between the 1958 and 1974 exercises—the Election Commission issued the redelineation notice for Peninsular Malaysia (and all Federal Territories) and Sabah on 15 September 2016. It was tasked with completing the exercise within two years.

While redelineation in Peninsular Malaysia has proceeded in tandem with the creation of new seats since the 1960s, this exercise focused only on the redistricting aspect. This is because BN no longer had a two-thirds majority in Parliament to approve an increase in the number of constituencies. For Sabah, the state legislature— where BN commanded a two-thirds majority—amended the Constitution on 9 August 2016 to increase the number of state seats from sixty to seventy-three (Unnip Abdullah 2018). Hence, the Sabah redelineation notice included both redistricting existing boundaries and apportioning thirteen new state seats.

The redelineation notice for Peninsular Malaysia and Sabah came on the backdrop of impending general elections and heightened electoral awareness. The EC notices stated that the redelineation would adhere to constitutional principles (Suruhanjaya Pilihan Raya 2018a), but upon critical examination, we find numerous and serious acts that amount to non-compliance.

Uneven Redelineation: Targeted and Omitted States

The EC's 2016–18 redelineation of Peninsular Malaysia was limited to redistricting, which entailed some movement of voters across constituencies. Overall, around 5 per cent of the voter population were moved from one parliamentary seat to another, while around 6 to 7 per cent of the voter population were moved from one state seat to another (Suruhanjaya Pilihan Raya 2018a).

Moreover, when we observe these movements state by state, it becomes clear that some states were targeted. Figures 3.6 and 3.7 show the proportion of voters shifted at the parliamentary and state assembly levels.

Around 52 out of 165 parliamentary constituencies in Peninsular Malaysia were excluded from any form of boundary alterations (Wong, Yeong, and Ooi 2016). Thus, no parliamentary boundary changes were made in Pahang, and Penang and Perlis had no redelineation of either parliamentary or state seats.

Persistent Malapportionment and Its Detriments

Like its predecessors, Malaysia's redelineation exercise of 2016–18 refused to address the inequality of population size between constituencies—violating the constitutional directive for approximately equal constituencies with allowance for some urban-rural disparity. Hence, the process not only failed to rectify malapportionment, it aggravated the problem.

While section 2(c) of the 13th Schedule does not quantify the acceptable range of disparity, we can measure the gravity of malapportionment using historically stipulated deviations from average constituency size, officially termed the Electoral Quota (EQ). We adopt the previously stipulated EQs in the Constitution of 15 per cent (1957–62) and 33 per cent (1962–73). These are reasonable baselines for determining moderate and high malapportionment, which applies to both undersized and oversized constituencies. Thus, the ratio of voters in oversized constituencies can be computed as a percentage of the average, from highly undersized (<67 per cent), to moderately undersized (67–85 per cent), and approximately equal (85–100 per cent or 100–115 per cent). Likewise, we establish the parameters for moderately oversized (115–133 per cent) and highly oversized (>133 per cent).

Table 3.3 compares the deviations from the EQ of GE-13 (pre-redelineation) and GE-14 (post-redelineation). Clearly, the redelineation did not rectify many seats in Peninsular Malaysia that are oversized or undersized (those in the category of having 33 per cent more or 33 per cent less than the average). The only state with minimal malapportionment is Perlis, while Johor, Selangor and Negeri Sembilan witnessed increases in voter inequality.

If the aim of the redelineation is to rectify voter inequality, boundaries should have been altered in order to rebalance populations in the various constituencies. Notably, the borders of many undersized rural constituencies were not touched. This is warranted to some extent, in view of the land area that representatives will need to cover. However, the 2016–18 exercise exhibited a stark pattern of minimal, or zero, redelineation in BN bastions.

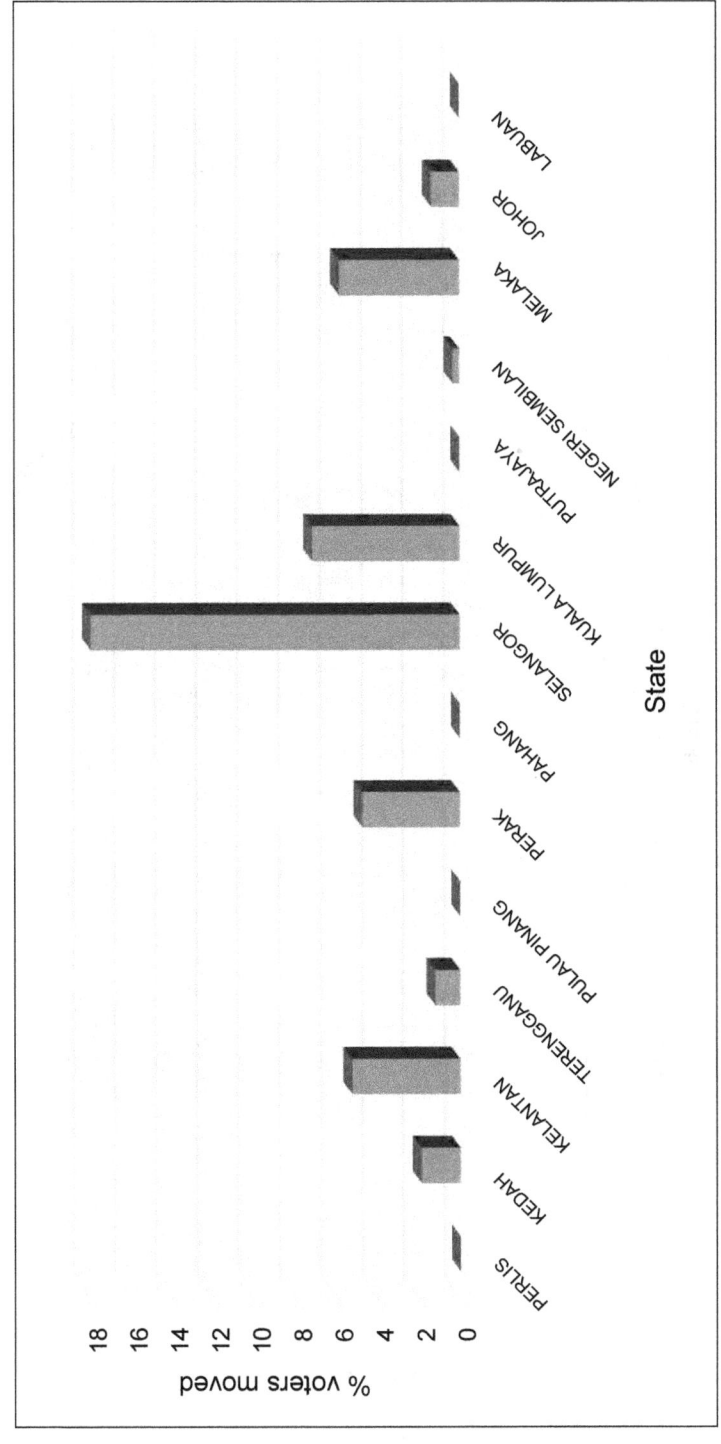

FIGURE 3.6
Parliamentary Seats in Peninsular Malaysia and the 2018 Redelineation:
Percentage of Voters Moved from One Seat to Another

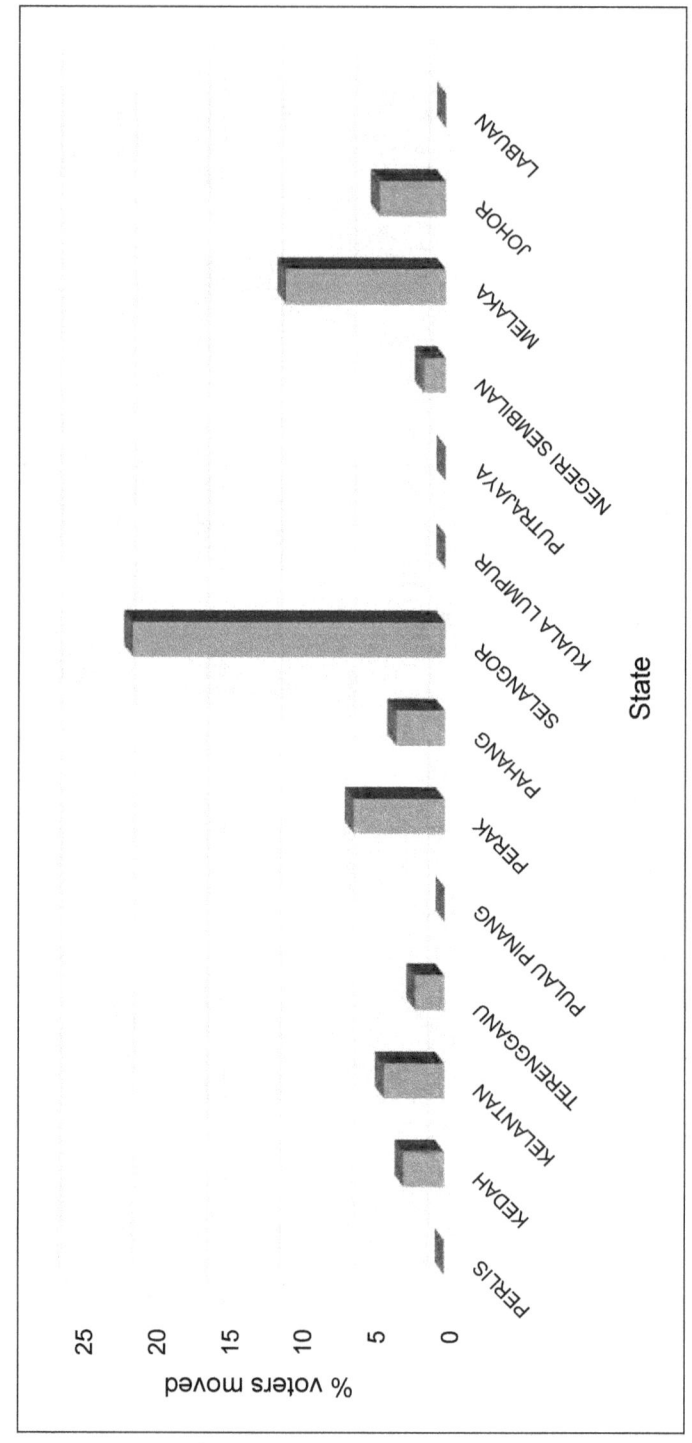

FIGURE 3.7
State Legislative Assembly Seats in Peninsular Malaysia and the 2018 Redelineation: Percentage of Voters Moved from One Seat to Another

TABLE 3.3
Malapportionment of Parliamentary Seats in Peninsular Malaysia, GE-13 and GE-14

State	GE-13			GE-14		
		Degree of Malapportionment			Degree of Malapportionment	
	Approx. Equal[a]	Moderate[b]	High[c]	Approx. Equal[a]	Moderate[b]	High[c]
Perlis	3	0	0	3	0	0
Kedah	6	4	5	8	2	5
Kelantan	7	4	3	9	3	2
Terengganu	4	2	0	6	2	0
Penang	6	7	0	6	7	0
Perak	7	6	11	8	6	10
Pahang	6	5	3	9	2	3
Selangor	13	1	8	11	2	9
Kuala Lumpur	6	5	0	8	3	0
Negeri Sembilan	3	3	2	3	2	3
Melaka	3	1	2	4	0	2
Johor	2	11	12	3	7	16
Total	66	49	46	78	36	50

Note: Relative to average size of constituencies within each state: a. 85–115 per cent; b. 67–85 per cent or 115–133 per cent; c. <67 per cent or >133 per cent.

The implications are peculiar to each state, even those that on face value appear unchanged. Penang and Perlis were not redelineated, but experience ongoing or foreseeable malapportionment. For Perlis, all the three federal seats have voter populations between 85 per cent and 115 per cent of the average (hence, approximately equal). At the state level, all seats are within the 67–133 per cent range, but the EC did not take into account growth projections and urbanization trends. Two state seats within the federal parliament seat of Kangar, Perlis's capital, are very close to the 33 per cent threshold and may soon be oversized. Redelineation should have been done on these seats to moderate the mild malapportionment gap in Perlis.

Penang exemplifies the case of the EC tolerating non-compliance of the Constitution's mandate to mitigate malapportionment, as there was virtually no redelineation in the state. As a result, at least seven states seats out of forty in Penang are on a path to becoming highly undersized or oversized. Seats in the city centres of George Town, Perai and Bukit Mertajam will only become more oversized in the years to come, as they have high voter growth rates (Wong et al. 2016). The biggest state seat in Penang (Paya Terubong) is nearly three times bigger than the second smallest seat (Air Putih)—and they are neighbours to each other. Table 3.4 shows the malapportionment ranges in Penang. Strikingly, the number of highly undersized seats doubled. In short, the EC failed to comply with section 2(c) for the state of Penang.

TABLE 3.4
Penang State Assembly: Degree of Malapportionment, 2013 and 2018

Degree of Malapportionment (Number of Voters per Average)	Seats Affected (2013)	Seats Affected (2018)	Average Voter Population Growth (2013–18)
Highly undersized (<67%)	2	4	–0.20%
Moderately undersized (67–85%)	10	10	1.93%
Approximately equal, below average (85–100%)	10	8	2.68%
Approximately equal, above average (100–115%)	8	10	2.74%
Moderately oversized (115–133%)	5	3	1.59%
Highly oversized (>133%)	5	5	3.63%

Unlike Penang, Melaka was redelineated, notably resulting in an increase in the number of moderately malapportioned seats in its state assembly (Table 3.5). However, the redelineated boundaries hardly addressed the highly undersized seats in the Masjid Tanah area and highly oversized seats in the greater Kota Melaka area, which further absorbed voters from neighbouring Hang Tuah Jaya (formerly Bukit Katil) constituency. The exercise slightly reduced the number of "approximately equal" seats in the range of 85 per cent to 115 per cent relative to the average. However, on the whole, the EC failed to redress malapportionment in Melaka.

Selangor was subjected to the most blatant disregard for the constitutional principles concerning malapportionment. In 2013, then EC chairman Tan Sri Abdul Aziz Mohd Yusof stated that constituencies exceeding over 100,000 voters would be split. Selangor is home to nine such constituencies, including Kapar, the largest seat in 2013 (*Malay Mail*, 26 December 2013). However, the 2016–18 redelineation exercise did not focus on these oversized seats. And, although they were undersized, parliamentary seats in northern and rural Selangor held by BN were largely untouched. Conversely, a number of larger seats, held by PH, were made to absorb even more voters. Currently, Bangi is the largest parliamentary seat in the country with a whopping 178,000 voters. And, although larger seats such as Kapar and Puchong had their voter population reduced, their redelineation involved the relocation of various state assembly seats and districts that disrupted administrative functionality or community cohesion. The EC did not provide sufficient explanation why some grossly oversized seats grew further or some shrank, and why state assembly seats and districts were moved around.

TABLE 3.5
Melaka State Assembly: Degree of Malapportionment, 2013 and 2018

Degree of Malapportionment (Number of Voters per Average)	Seats Affected (2013)	Seats Affected (2018)
Highly undersized (<67%)	7	3
Moderately undersized (67–85%)	5	6
Approximately equal, below average (85–100%)	4	4
Approximately equal, above average (100–115%)	4	3
Moderately oversized (115–133%)	4	4
Highly oversized (>133%)	4	8

Gerrymandering: Disruption of Local Ties and Ethnicized Constituencies

The intensity of gerrymandering varied from state to state in the 2016–18 redelineation exercise. In Selangor, multiple state constituencies were shifted from one parliamentary seat to another while breaking rules on voter inequality. In other states like Kedah, safe PH seats were made to absorb adjoining polling districts while making other seats more vulnerable to the effect of three-cornered fights.[6] Shifts were done either on past political preferences, ethnic tendencies and presence of early and postal voters. For states that experienced minimal or no redelineation like Penang and Pahang, past gerrymandered boundaries were retained.

Arbitrary Redistricting of Constituencies Disrupting Administration and Cohesion

In Selangor, some of the constituencies redrawn in 2003 in violation of the local ties condition were made even more irregular in shape. For example, seats such as Seri Serdang and Sungai Kandis (formerly Seri Andalas) continually straddle municipal boundaries and hence unduly inconvenience the relationships between elected representatives and constituents, who have to deal with two local governments.

It is instructive to look at the specific example of Sungai Kandis. Figure 3.8 shows the boundaries (in black dashed lines) that applied until the 2016–18 redelineation exercise. The constituency was split in the middle, with the eastern half falling under the Shah Alam City Council and the western half under the Klang equivalent. Post-redelineation, this division not only persists, but further complicates effective and cohesive representation (Figure 3.9).

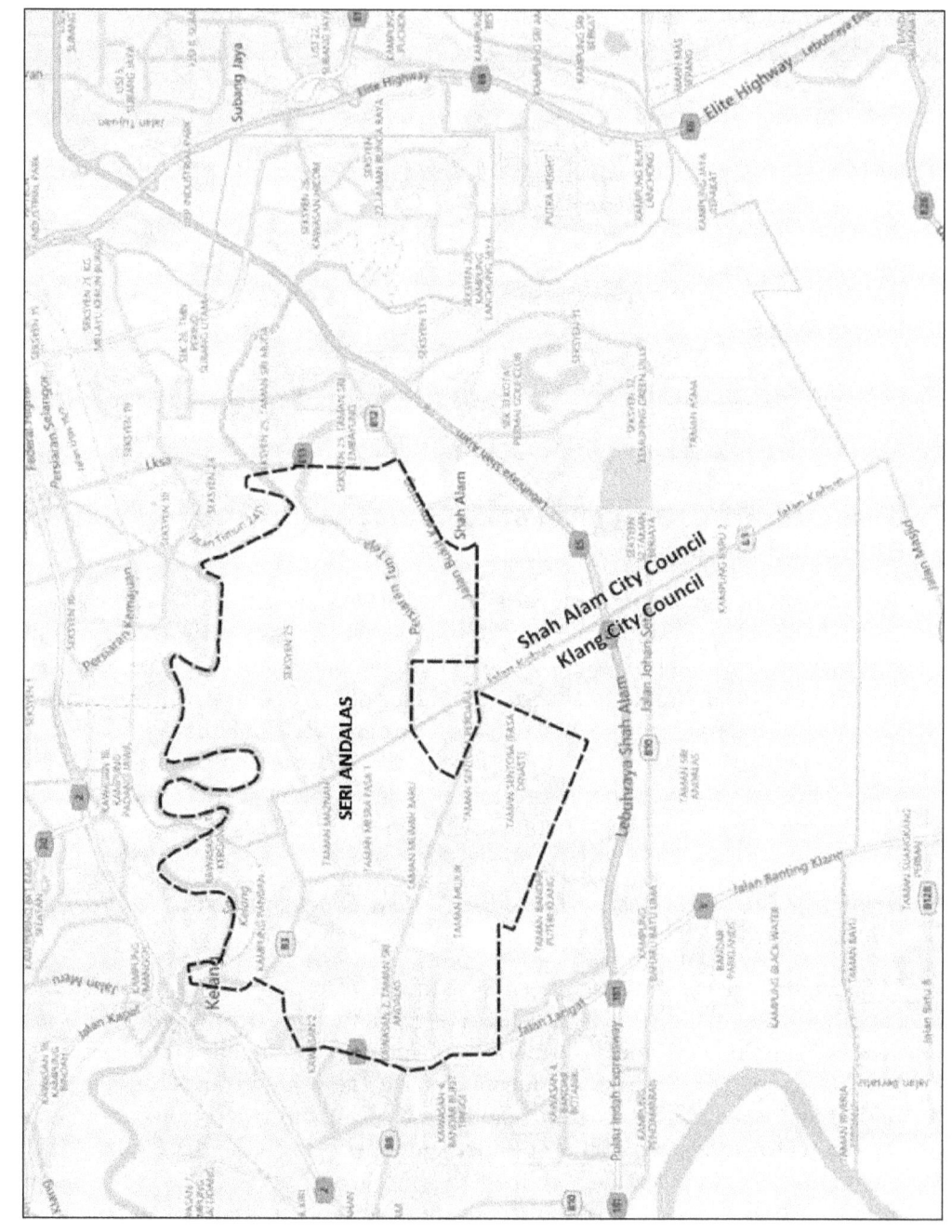

FIGURE 3.8

Seri Andalas (Now Sungai Kandis) State Assembly Seat (Selangor), Prior to 2018 Redelineation

FIGURE 3.9

Sungai Kandis (previously, Seri Andalas) State Assembly Seat (Selangor), After 2018 Redelineation

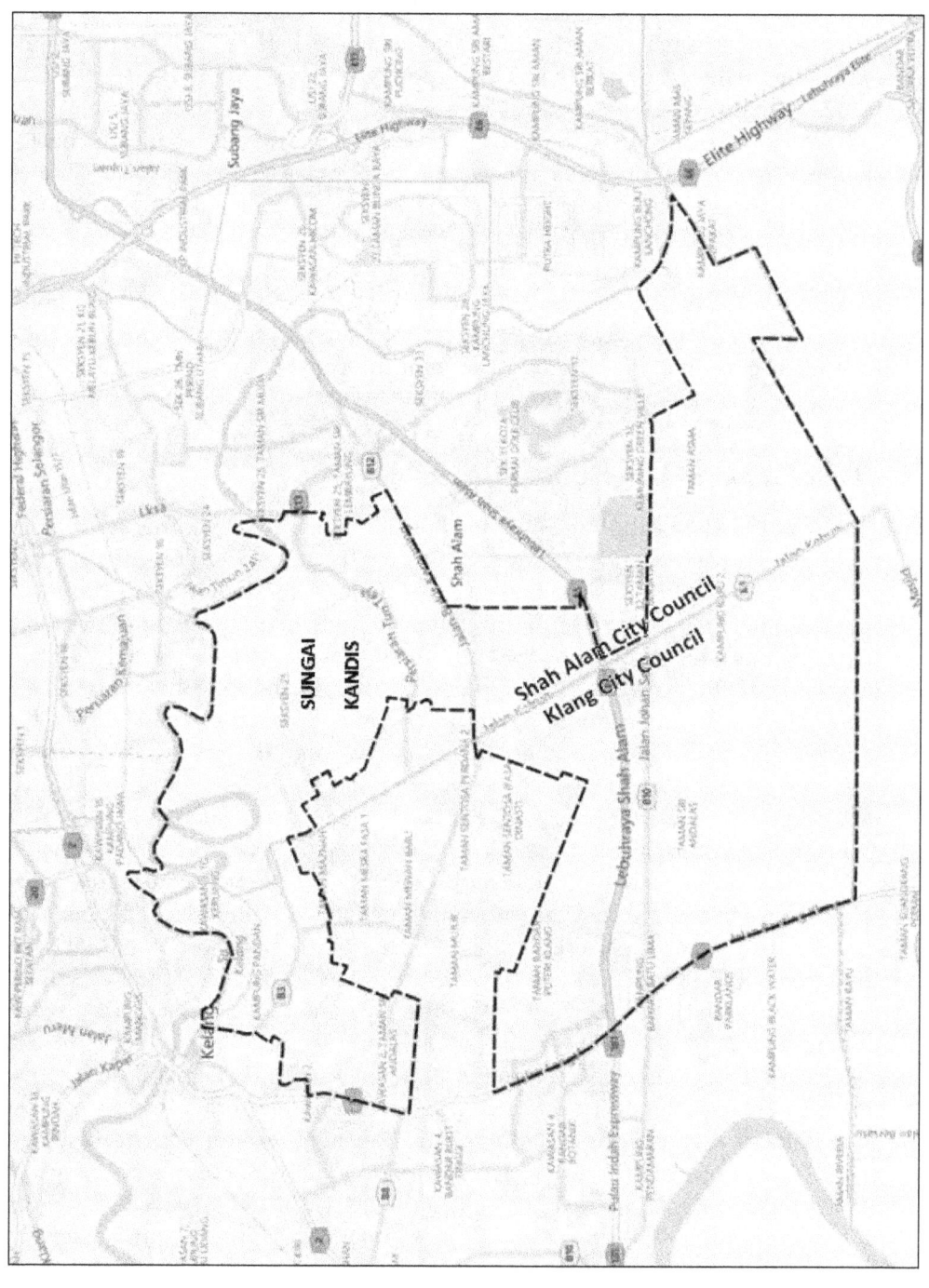

In practice, the redelineation of Sungai Kandis arbitrarily lumped together constituents from southern Kota Raja, the parliament constituency in which Sungai Kandis is located. The state constituency doubled in its east-west span and grew 1.5 times along its north-south axis. The oddity of the shape could be explained by: past voting patterns of newly absorbed polling districts where BN won a majority in GE-13; and the change in ethnic composition.

Among constituencies that saw increases in the Malay share of voters—the sharpest trend of the redelineation exercise—Sungai Kandis recorded one of the biggest changes. Institut Darul Ehsan (IDE), the Selangor government think-tank, concluded in January 2018, that redelineated Sungai Kandis would reduce support for Parti Keadilan Rakyat (PKR) in the seat by a factor of eight (IDE 2018a) and make the seat vulnerable to a three-cornered fight. Despite this, PKR's hold was maintained reasonably well in GE-14 and consolidated further in a by-election not long after. However, the irregular shape of the constituency probably contributed to low voter turnout (IDE 2018b).

Ethnicization of Voter Composition

The 2016–18 redelineation resulted in considerable shifts in the ethnic composition of a number of state and parliamentary constituencies. The EC Chief responsible for the 2016–18 redelineation exercise, Tan Sri Mohd Hashim, admitted that redelineation took geographical and ethnic aspects into consideration and argued that constituencies should not split up ethnic groups (*Malay Mail*, 29 March 2018). However, the final proposed boundaries continued the long-established trend of ethnically based redelineation. It is important to note that the expansion of Chinese-majority and mixed urban constituencies has favoured the PH component member, the Democratic Action Party (DAP), making it harder for Gerakan and MCA to win new seats. This has prompted even BN component parties such as MIC, MCA, and Gerakan to echo PH's objections.

Digging deeper into each state and observing at a greater detail shows growing ethnic concentration at the state assembly level. Out of thirteen redelineated state seats in Kedah, nine experienced a slight increase in the proportion of Malay voters. In Perak, out of thirty-five state seats, fifteen witnessed a rise of Malay voters and twenty witnessed a rise of Chinese voters. In some instances, significant shifts of polling districts caused the overall ethnic composition of mixed seats to change: the Tebing Tinggi state seat became Malay-majority and Astaka became Chinese-majority. These patterns closely correspond with past electoral preferences. Districts with Chinese voter majorities and opposition-leaning records were packed together, while Malay populated districts were moved to inflate the group's majority in some state seats in order to boost BN's, and particularly UMNO's, prospects. However, due to evolving political preferences since late 2016 until GE-14 among all groups, but most momentously among ethnic Malays and Indians, the effect of ethnic-based redelineation was neutralized.

Shifting of Polling Districts Along Partisan and Ethnic Lines: The Case of Kedah

The movement of polling districts between the parliamentary seats of Kuala Kedah, Alor Setar (previously Alor Star) and Pokok Sena is a classic case of political gerrymandering to curb the ability of major contenders to effectively challenge BN. In 1999, in the wake of Anwar Ibrahim's ouster and the rise of *Reformasi*, PAS (then under Barisan Alternatif) captured the Malay-majority areas of Kuala Kedah and Pokok Sena for the first time. BN held on to Alor Star with a reduced majority. The 2003 redelineation exercise resulted in Kuala Kedah and Pokok Sena losing polling districts and even one state seat to Alor Star, thus reducing opposition-inclined Malay voters. In 2004, BN wrested back Kuala Kedah and Pokok Sena from PAS. The 2008 and 2013 "political tsunamis" indicated a shift among non-Malay voters favouring the opposition and resulted in PAS capturing Kuala Kedah, Alor Star and Pokok Sena in those election cycles.

The 2016–18 redelineation exercise initiated the absorption of urbanized opposition polling districts into Alor Setar from Kuala Kedah and Pokok Sena. This time, non-Malay voter presence was reduced in the latter two seats. In the event of a three-cornered fight in the predominantly Malay Kuala Kedah and Pokok Sena seats, BN could have won. However, due to shifting political preferences, PH retained Alor Setar, Kuala Kedah and Pokok Sena.

Relocation of Early Voters: Lembah Pantai, Kuala Lumpur

Lembah Pantai experienced a recurrent gerrymandering tactic: relocating early and postal voters to expand BN's vote base. Historically, the police and military personnel—who constitute the bulk of early and postal votes—were considered as solid vote banks for BN. In 2008, Nurul Izzah Anwar trounced prominent BN MP Shahrizat Abdul Jalil. In 2013, Nurul Izzah retained the seat with a slightly lower margin, carried by strong support in the Bangsar area and Kampong Bahagia and Kampung Bohol on the southern tip of the constituency. The 2016–18 redelineation carved out some strong PH areas from Lembah Pantai, but included the Bukit Aman police headquarters, consisting of 6,598 voters in a constituency of 72,450 voters (Figure 3.10).

The influx of presumably pro-BN early votes was engineered to help BN to wrest back Lembah Pantai. However, in GE-14, there was a 9 per cent shift of police voters from BN to PH and PAS, and their voter turnout declined by 6 per cent. Meanwhile, low-income housing areas (PPR, Program Perumahan Rakyat) which used to be another vote bank for BN witnessed a 14 per cent decline in BN vote share, due to a heavy shift towards PAS. This resulted in PKR winning the seat for the third consecutive time—and BN further losing its vote share.

Similar political shifts among police and military voters were seen in Setiawangsa in Kuala Lumpur where votes largely gravitated from BN to PAS. The redelineation based on political preferences of police and military markedly failed.

FIGURE 3.10
Lembah Pantai: Gerrymandering and Evolving Voter Preferences

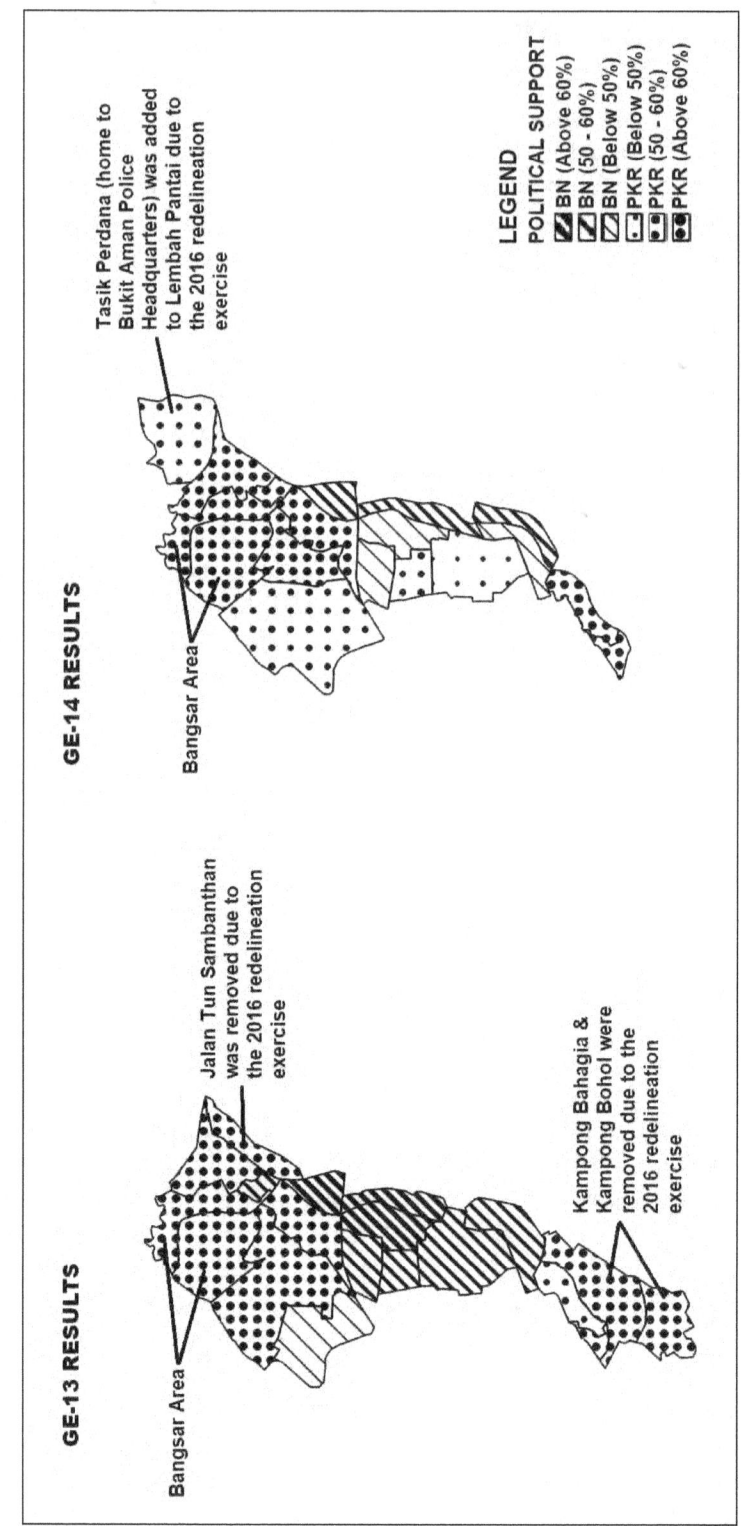

General Shifts in Voter Preference

As noted earlier, prior to GE-14, history strongly suggested that malapportionment and gerrymandering would boost the electoral prospects of the BN coalition. The long-ruling coalition prevailed in every election that followed a redelineation exercise, significantly on the back of increased number of seats and redrawn borders. We now zoom out, to consider broader trends in voter preference, and in doing so we observe how the rigging of boundaries finally met its match.

GE-14 may be termed a "Malaysian tsunami' where voter preference in all ethnic groups shifted away from BN to PH and PAS in Peninsular Malaysia. In GE-13, BN and PAS-Pakatan Rakyat dominated in constituencies with more than 60 per cent Malay voters, with PKR-Pakatan Rakyat making a few inroads. Where Malays constituted more than 80 per cent of voters, only PAS could contend against UMNO (Figure 3.11). In GE-14, PAS captured new territories from previously BN-held seats with more than 80 per cent Malay voters, and PH made breakthroughs in numerous Malay-majority seats (Figure 3.12). PH's wins were mainly on the west coast.

For non-Malay voters, PH consolidated its position by capturing additional mixed seats, as shown in scatterplots and fitted lines of Chinese and Indian shares of voters and support for Pakatan in GE-13 and GE-14 (Figures 3.13 and 3.14). The lines suggest that the higher presence of Chinese and Indian voters corresponded with a higher share of votes for PH in both elections—but the relationship was steeper in GE-14. Non-Malay voters became more inclined to vote for PH.

Due to the shifting of political preferences across the board, among the seats redelineated to increase Malay voter presence and thereby confer advantage on BN, redelineation was only able to deliver one seat to BN's hands (Bukit Gantang) while not altering the status quo for other redelineated seats. The impact of this variant of redelineation was limited to reducing winning majorities for PH and PAS. Redelineation that created oversized urban constituencies, mostly mixed or Chinese-majority, yielded supermajorities in safe DAP and PKR seats.

CONCLUDING REMARKS

The 2016–18 redelineation exercise of Peninsular Malaysia and Sabah violated the key constitutional principles of the 13th Schedule of the Constitution, especially the preservation of equality of voters and of local ties. The general aim of redelineating borders should be to uphold One Person, One Vote, One Value (OPOVOV) for all Malaysians, but this recent exercise further undermined this principle.

The exceedingly large number of undersized constituencies can enable a government in Malaysia to be elected with a mere 16.5 per cent of the popular vote—severely diluting the effect of votes cast in oversized constituencies. This latest redelineation exercise continued the long-established trend of reinforcing ethnicity-based politics—assuming that historical political preferences would keep the incumbents in power. However, unlike the 2015 Sarawak redelineation, the national 2016–18 exercise could not increase the total number of parliamentary

FIGURE 3.11
Parliamentary Seats in Peninsular Malaysia (GE-13): Malay Voter Presence and Winning Coalition

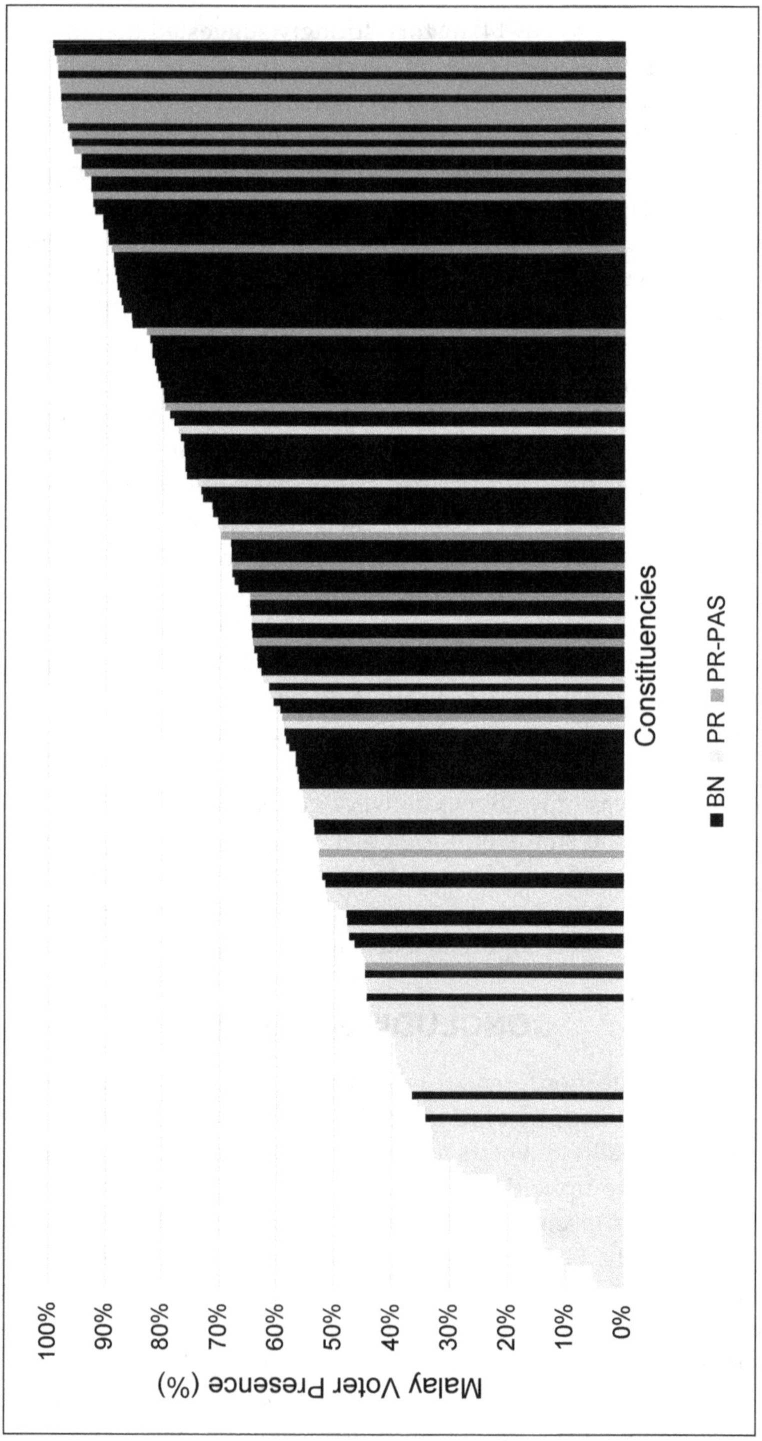

Malay Voter Presence (%)

Constituencies

■ BN   PR   ■ PR-PAS

Source: Rui Yang Fann, Tindak Malaysia.

FIGURE 3.12

Parliamentary Seats in Peninsular Malaysia (GE-14): Malay Voter Presence and Winning Coalition

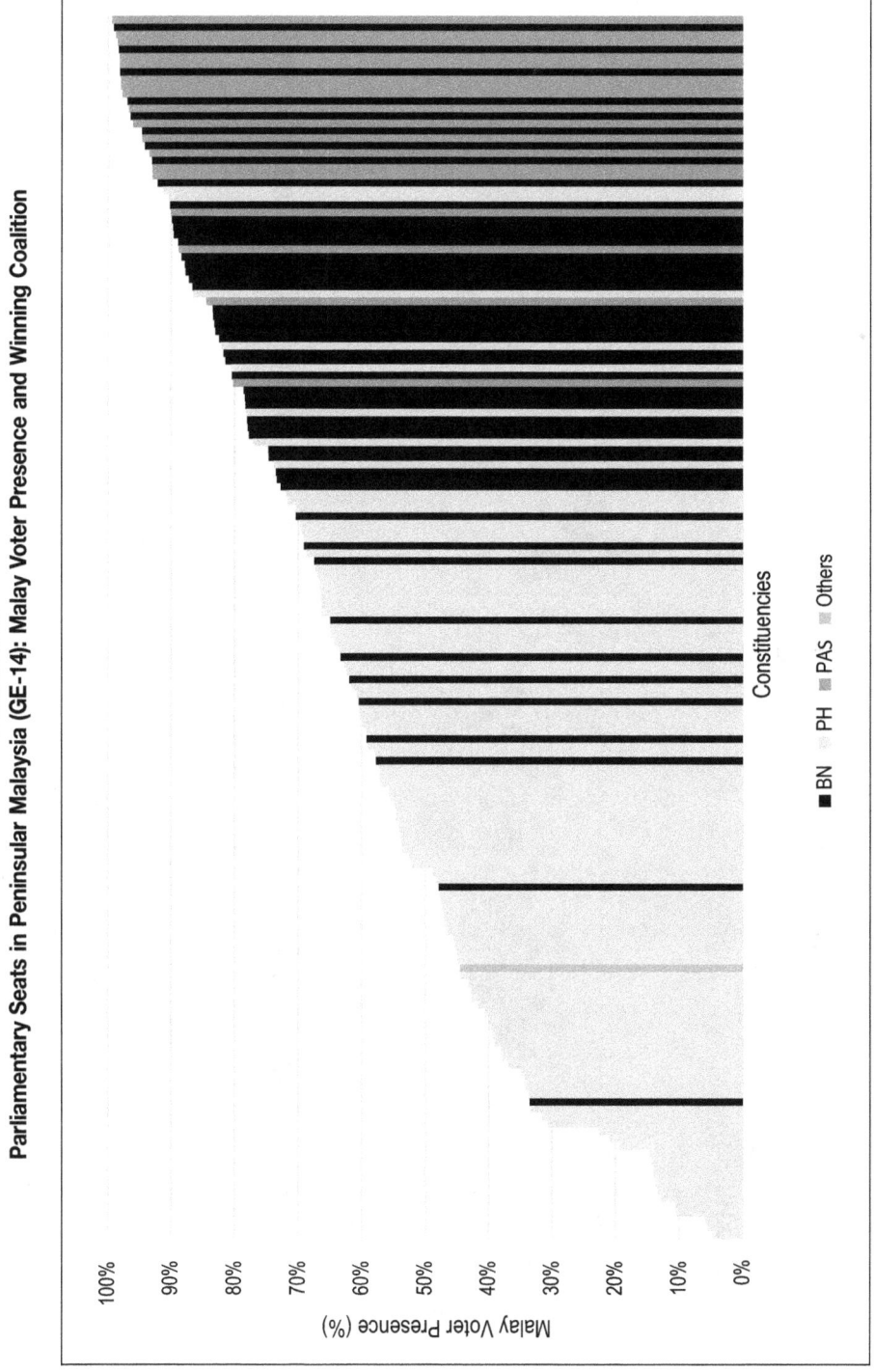

Source: Rui Yang Fann, Tindak Malaysia.

FIGURE 3.13
Level of Support for PR/PH among Chinese Voters (Peninsular Malaysia)

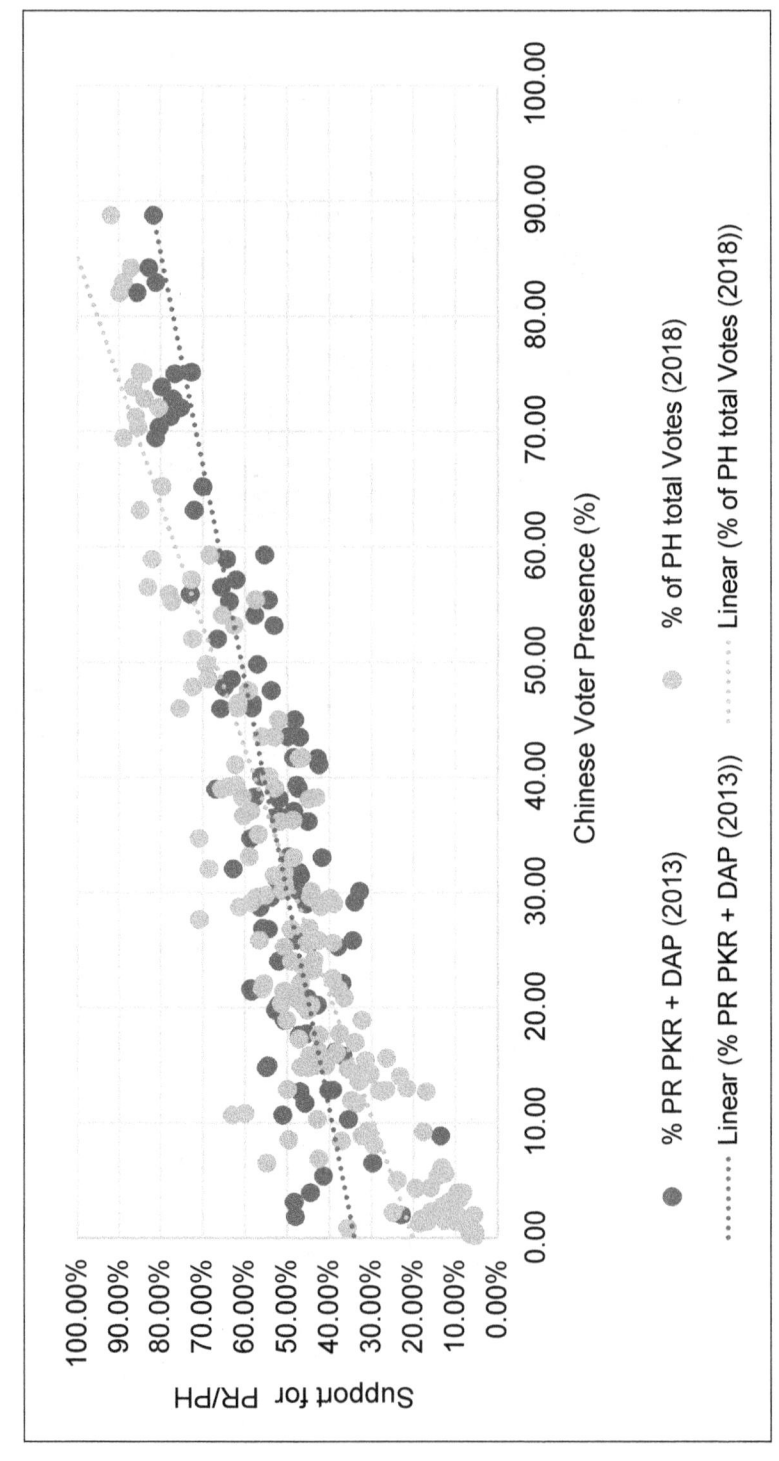

FIGURE 3.14
Level of Support for PR/PH among Indian Voters (Peninsular Malaysia)

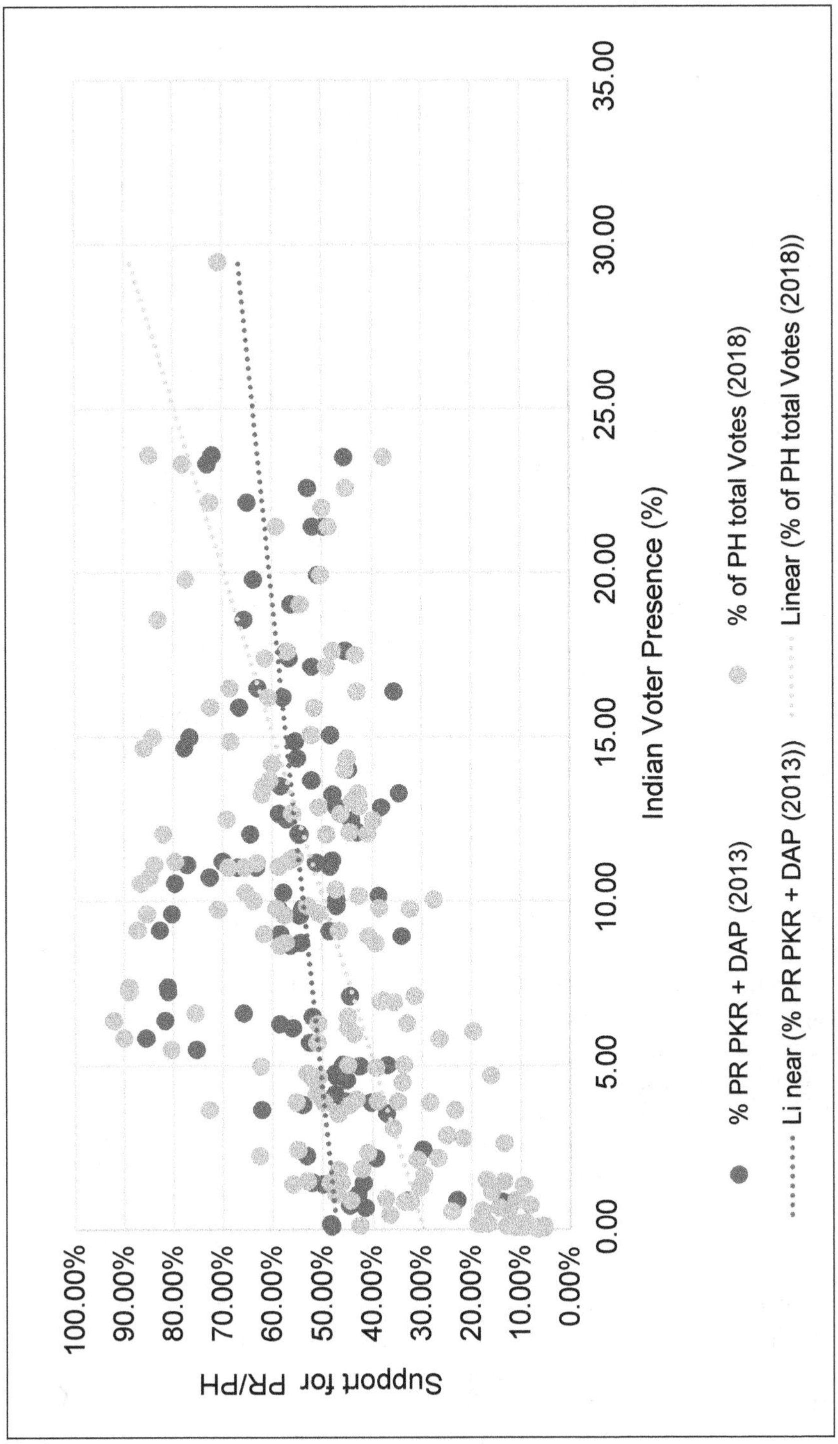

seats, instead relying on gerrymandering to further tilt the "playing field" to BN's advantage.

Despite the expected advantages of the redrawn boundaries, GE-14 was shaped by the themes felt by voters and contested in the election. The introduction of GST, the increased cost of living, and broad discontent with economic conditions under BN's watch were key campaign themes. In addition, elite fractures within UMNO and the creation of Parti Pribumi Bersatu Malaysia (PPBM) on the Peninsula and Warisan in Sabah reshaped traditional voter calculations. Pakatan Harapan benefited from a further gravitation away from BN in urban areas, and PAS enjoyed the benefit of the protest vote in Malaysia's north. These dynamics, among others, neutralized the impact of redelineation.

Thus, multicornered fights and shifting political preferences—rather than redrawn borders and altered ethnic composition—ultimately decided the outcome of GE-14. The 2016–18 exercise may not have had pivotal impact on the election, and indeed its intended effects were negated, but various consequences linger. Malapportionment which disproportionately favours rural areas and small constituencies in predominantly Malay areas, and gerrymandering which accentuates ethnic majorities, stand to perpetuate ethnic politics.

The EC's absolute co-optation by the former BN regime, underscore the need for clarity, autonomy and integrity in the institutions administering elections and in voting outcomes. For now, Malaysians have to exercise their democratic voice within the new redelineated borders, but the public can take comfort that heightened electoral awareness is one of the catalysts for negating the effects of the electoral system's rigged boundaries.

Notes

1. In Malaysia, malapportionment can also be seen at the *inter*state level, in terms of the disproportionality between the share of a state's share of parliament seats and its share of the overall population. In view of its predominance, this chapter will focus on *intra*state malapportionment, and when used, the term malapportionment will refer to this *intra*state context, unless specified otherwise.

2. This is an Electoral Quota (EQ), which is the total population divided by the number of seats. In a state averaging 10,000 voters per constituency, constituencies should not have fewer than 8,500 voters or greater than 11,500 voters.

3. This was stipulated in Article 116 of the Constitution, which was subsequently repealed in 1962.

4. This corresponded with the 33 per cent limit of deviation from the average constituency size, as applied in the 1955 elections.

5. The Alliance coalition was renamed Barisan Nasional in 1974.

6. While the public is largely aware on manipulations during the redelineation, few are cognizant of periodic "silent" redelineation that pose inconveniences on polling day. Even though some constituencies were not touched by the 2016 redelineation (e.g., Hulu Selangor), they experienced a stealthy form of redelineation in early 2016. The EC can reassign voters to different polling districts, for the purpose of easing their accessibility

to polling centres. However, the recent exercise resulted in the relocation of up to 118,774 voters to a polling centre in another constituency (BERSIH 2.0 2016). Instead of moving the borders, the process moved voters, exploiting a loophole that allows such measures to be taken without even informing Parliament.

References

Aliran. 2015a. "Sarawak Constituency Boundary Review Proposals Deeply Flawed, Violate International Conventions". 5 February 2015. https://aliran.com/civil-society-voices/2015-civil-society-voices/sarawak-constituency-boundary-review-proposals-deeply-flawed-violate-international-conventions/ (accessed 12 September 2018).

———. 2015b. "Sarawak Redelineation Exercise Seriously Stymied". 25 February 2015. https://aliran.com/coalitions/clean-and-fair-elections/sarawak-redelineation-exercise-seriously-stymied/ (accessed 12 September 2018).

Attorney General's Chambers. 2016. "Act 19 Election Act 1958". The Commissioner of Law Revision, Malaysia, 1 December 2016. http://www.agc.gov.my/agcportal/uploads/files/Publications/LOM/EN/Act%2019%20-%20Reprint%202016.pdf.

Bernama. 2015. "Apex Court upholds Courts of Appeals' verdict on EC's Sarawak redelineation exercise". *The Sun Daily*, 15 October 2015. http://www.thesundaily.my/news/1582767 (accessed 12 September 2018).

———. 2018. "EC: 3.6 Million yet to Register as Voters". *Free Malaysia Today News*, 17 January 2018. https://www.freemalaysiatoday.com/category/nation/2018/01/17/ec-3-6-million-yet-to-register-as-voters/ (accessed 11 April 2019).

BERSIH 2.0. 2016. "Media Statement: Moving of Voters Across DUN and Parliament Constituencies Is Against the Federal Constitution". 1 July 2016. http://www.bersih.org/media-statement-moving-of-voters-across-dun-and-parliament-is-against-the-federal-constitution/ (accessed 5 March 2019).

Bhattacharjee, Rash Behari. 2018. "Remaking Malaysia: Flaws That Need Fixing in First Past the Post Polls". *The Edge Markets*, 7 September 2018. http://www.theedgemarkets.com/article/remaking-malaysia-flaws-need-fixing-firstpastthepost-polls (accessed 12 September 2018).

Chacko, Danesh Prakash. 2018. "Mapping out elections for victory". *New Mandala*, 26 April 2018. http://www.newmandala.org/mapping-elections-victory/ (accessed 10 September 2018).

Election Commission. 1958. *Report of the Election Commission on the Delimitation of Constituencies for the First Elections to the House of Representatives and That State Legislative Assemblies*. Kuala Lumpur: Government Press.

———. 1960. *Report of the Election Commission on the Delimitation of Parliamentary and State Constituencies Under the Provisions of the Constitution of Persekutuan Tanah Melayu*. Kuala Lumpur: Government Press.

Institut Darul Ehsan (IDE). 2018a. "Sidang Media: Proses Persempadanan & Pilihan Raya Ke-14". 2 January 2018. https://www.ideselangor.org/index.php/berita-footer/item/384-proses-persempadanan-pilihan-raya-ke-14 (accessed 11 September 2018).

———. 2018b. "Peratusan Turun Mengundi: Pengalaman Sungai Kandis, Pengajaran Buat Seri Setia". 6 September 2018. https://www.ideselangor.org/index.php/penyelidikan-footer/item/423-prk-serisetia-faktor-persempadanan (accessed 11 September 2018).

———. 2018c. "PRU 14: Pakatan Harapan Dijangka Menang Besar di Selangor". 8 May 2018. https://www.ideselangor.com/index.php/penyelidikan-footer/item/414-pru-14-ph-menang-besar-selangor (accessed 31 January 2019).

Lim, Hong Hai. 2002. "Electoral Politics in Malaysia: 'Managing' Elections in a Plural Society". *Ace Project*. January 2002. http://aceproject.org/ero-en/regions/asia/MY/01361005.pdf (accessed 12 September 2018).

——. 2003. "New Rules and Constituencies for new Challenges". *ALiran*, pp. 7–9.

Lai, Yew Meng. 2002. *The 1999 Sabah State Elections: A Vote for Continuity, Chage and Development*. Kota Kinabalu: Universiti Malaysia Sabah.

Loh, Andrew Zhu An. 2018. "Malapportionment in GE-14". 31 May 2018. https://datatarik. com/home/2018/5/31/malapportionment-in-GE-14 (accessed 13 September 2018).

Lyn, Boo Su. 2014. "Malaysia Bottom of the Pile in Global Study on Electoral Boundaries". *Malay Mail*, 3 March 2014. https://www.malaymail.com/s/628183/malaysia-bottom-of-the-pile-in-global-study-on-electoral-boundaries (accessed 10 September 2018).

Malay Mail. 2013. "In upcoming redelineation, EC seeks to balance unequal-sized election seats". 26 December 2013. https://www.malaymail.com/s/587901/in-upcoming-redelineation-ec-seeks-to-balance-unequal-sized-election-seats (accessed 11 September 2018).

——. 2018. "EC Chief Admits Racial Redelineation, Says Ethnic Groups Can't Be Split". 29 March 2018. https://www.malaymail.com/s/1610117/ec-chief-admits-racial-redelineation-says-ethnic-groups-cant-be-split (accessed 11 September 2018).

Malaysian Bar Council, Constitutional Law Committee 2016/17. 2016. "Guide on Redelineation of Electoral Boundaries 2016". *Malaysian Bar*, 13 October 2016. http://www.malaysianbar. org.my/constitutional_law_committee/guidelines_on_redelineation_of_electoral_ boundaries_.html (accessed 10 September 2018).

National Union of Journalists. 1986. "1986 Malaysian Parliamentary & State Elections Held on August 2nd & 3rd 1986 Including Analysis of 1984 Electoral Delineation Exercise". Office Automation Sdn Bhd.

Nazlina, Maizatul. 2015. "Appeals Court rules Sarawak's re-delineation exercise valid". *The Star*, 7 August 2015. https://www.thestar.com.my/news/nation/2015/08/07/court-of-appeal-ec-recommendations/.

Ong, Kian Ming. 2018. "EC Redelineation: Unfair, Unprecedented, and Dangerous". *Malaysiakini*, 28 March 2018. https://www.malaysiakini.com/news/417496 (accessed 18 September 2018).

Ooi, Kok Hin. 2018. "How Malaysia's Election Is Being Rigged". *New Naratif*. 19 March 2018. https://newnaratif.com/research/malaysias-election-rigged/ (accessed 11 September 2018).

Ostwald, Kai. 2013. "How to Win a Lost Election: Malapportionment and Malaysia's 2013 General Election". *The Round Table: The Commonwealth Journal of International Affairs* 102, no. 6: 521–32. https://doi.org/10.1080/00358533.2013.857146.

Steering Committee of Bersih 2.0 and the Malaysian Electoral Roll Analysis Project. 2016. "MERAP Analysis Reveals Shcoking Results on Sarawak Delineation". 21 January 2016. https://www.bersih.org/merap-analysis-reveals-shocking-results-on-sarawak-delineation/ (accessed 12 September 2018).

Suruhanjaya Pilihan Raya. 1969. *Report of the Election Commission on the Delimitation of Parliamentary and State Constituencies in the State of Sarawak*. Kuala Lumpur: Suruhanjaya Pilihan Raya.

——. 1974. *Lapuran Suruhanjaya Pilihanraya Malaysia atas pensempadanan Bahagian-bahagian pilihanraya Persekutuann dan negeri bagi negeri-negeri Tanah Melayu (Semenanjung Malaysia)*. Suruhanjaya Pilihan Raya.

——. 2018a. *Laporan Kajian Semula Pensempadanan Mengenai Syor Syor yang Dicadangkan bagi*

Bahagian-Bahagian Pilihan Raya dan Negeri di Dalam Negeri-Negeri Tanah Melayu Kali Keenam Tahun 2018 Jilid 1. Vol. 1. Kuala Lumpur: Suruhanjaya Pilihan Raya Malaysia.

———. 2018b. "Kajian Semula Pensempadanan". 11 April 2018. http://www.spr.gov.my/ms/pilihan-raya/kajian-semula-persempadanan (accessed 12 September 2018).

———. n.d. "Keputusan Pilihan Raya Umum Parlimen/Dewan Undangan Negeri". http://semak.spr.gov.my/spr/laporan/5_KedudukanAkhir.php (accessed 13 September 2018).

Tawie, Joseph. 2015. "Sarawak PKR Files Review Bid to Stop Redelineation". *Malaysiakini*, 28 January 2015. http://www.malaysiakini.com/news/287622 (accessed 12 September 2018).

Tindak Malaysia. 2014. "Towards a Fairer Electoral System: Feb 2014 Forum". 15 February. http://www.tindakmalaysia.org/persempadanan/towards-a-fairer-electoral-system-feb-2014-forum (accessed 10 September 2018).

Unnip Abdullah, Mohd Izham. 2018. "DUN Sabah Lulus Tambahan 13 kerusi DUN". *Berita Harian*, 9 August 2018. https://www.bharian.com.my/node/181421 (accessed 11 September 2018).

Utusan Malaysia. 2018. "Keputusan PRU14". http://www.utusan.com.my/berita/politik/pilihan-raya/pilihan-raya-umum-ke-14/keputusan (accessed 13 September 2018).

Wikipedia. 2019. "Elections in Malaysia". https://en.wikipedia.org/wiki/Elections_in_Malaysia (accessed 11 April 2019).

Wong, Chin Huat. 2014. "Uncommon Sense with Wong Chin Huat: Constituency Redelineation and Citizen Vigilance". *The Nut Graph*, 7 January 2014. http://www.thenutgraph.com/uncommon-sense-with-wong-chin-huat-constituency-redelineation-and-citizen-vigilance/ (accessed 10 September 2018).

———, Pey Jung Yeong, and Ooi Kok Hin. 2016. "Malapportionment of Constituencies: Analysis of the 2016 Redelineation Proposal (First Display) for Peninsular and Sabah and 2015 Redelineation Exercise for Sarawak". *Penang Institute*, 14 October 2016. https://penanginstitute.org/wp-content/uploads/jml/files/malapportionment/Malapportionment-Report-2.0-20161022.pdf (accessed 12 September 2018).

———, Pey Jung Yeong, Nidhal Mujahid, and Ooi Kok Hin. 2016. "The Effects of the 2016 Delimitation Exercise". *Penang Institute*, 13 October 2016. https://penanginstitute.org/wp-content/uploads/jml/files/malapportionment/Penang-Report_20161013_Final.pdf (accessed 11 September 2018).

4

ECONOMIC DYNAMICS AND THE GE-14 SURPRISE
Statistics, Realities, Sentiments[1]

Yeah Kim Leng

INTRODUCTION

Despite solid macroeconomic data, power of incumbency and unlimited political funding, the coalition party that had ruled Malaysia for over six decades and was widely expected to win the 14th General Elections (GE-14), lost to a newly constituted opposition coalition led by a ninety-three-year-old former prime minister of the country. Various social, economic, political and psychological dynamics have been advanced to explain the surprise victory. A primary factor is the influence of the state of the economy and how voters perceive their economic well-being is being taken care of by the ruling government.

Public opinion polls had consistently identified economic issues, specifically the rising cost of living, as a key voting factor. However, positive macroeconomic conditions prevailed at the time of the election. The surprise election outcome seems at odds with what we would expect of economic voting—whereby voters reward the incumbents for bringing economic prosperity. The influence of economics on election outcomes in democratic countries has been found to be pervasive across countries and over different time periods although the relative importance of the economic variables such as income growth, inflation and unemployment may vary depending on the country's prevailing socio-economic conditions.

Were voters in Malaysia less concerned about how the economy performed? Could it be that the economic indicators such as national income, inflation and unemployment did not reflect on-the-ground realities? In other words, the country's positive overall economic indicators masked the variation in performance across industries, income groups and rural-urban divide. Or, could it be that economic issues are much more complex in relation to election outcomes?

This chapter will discuss these three themes to better understand the influence of the economy on voting behaviour, particularly the extent to which economic factors could have provided early indicators on vote swings that resulted in the unexpected change in government. Given the strength of the overall economy prevailing at the time when the ruling government called the election, a primary focus of the analysis is the extent to which unevenness in growth, income inequality and distributional issues have contributed to the divergence between the economic indicators and voters' economic realities and discontent.

The weak statistical relationship between economic performance and voting outcomes is contrary to pre-election poll results that consistently showed the high importance voters placed on economic issues and well-being. The lack of statistical evidence at the national level can be attributed to the small sample size as well as the presence of outliers that include the 2018 election outcome.

In examining the extent to which national economic aggregates mask the distribution effects, the analysis suggests that economic discontentment as revealed by opinion surveys could be attributed to uneven growth and disparities in wage growth, employment and other economic issues such as unaffordable housing and cost of living. The complexities of economic dynamics and how the economic issues could have been viewed with different lenses among heterogeneous voter groups as well as being exploited by the incumbent and opposition parties to advance their respective agenda through various media and political campaigns.

These complexities and dynamics of economic issues and realities have contributed to the surprise election result. With the peaceful change in government signalling democratic coming of age, the relationship between the management of the economy and election outcome will continually evolve and mature.

THE INFLUENCE OF ECONOMIC FACTORS ON VOTER BEHAVIOUR

The influence of economic factors on voter behaviour has been extensively studied since the seminal work by Downs (1957) who applied the rational choice theory to voting in democratic elections. Economic voting, as the research paradigm is called, also draws its theoretical underpinnings from the responsibility hypothesis in political science theory of democracy which contends that voters hold the government accountable for the country's economic performance.

According to the rational choice theory, voters adopt a cost-benefit approach and utility maximization framework in voting for candidates and parties akin to making market choices. Its integration with the logic of responsibility theory that presupposes voters have the freedom to act rationally has provided the initial theoretical foundation to explain how economic conditions and performance influence voter behaviour. Subsequent extensions and modifications, addressing criticisms of the rational choice theory and incorporating individual decision-making under uncertainties, have strengthened the economic voting theory and spawned a vast empirical literature that has now spread to developing countries where democracy traditions and practice are more limited.

Extensive empirical studies on the influence of the economy on election outcomes show robust evidence of economic voting in democratic countries particularly in the developed world. Aptly summed by a leading researcher in the field, "Good times keep parties in office, bad times cast them out", it highlights the considerable emphasis voters place on economic issues. As to whether voters consider economic issues based on past performance of the incumbent government ("retrospective economic voting") or future economic policies and outlook ("prospective economic voting"), the main finding is that the difference is small.[2] However, voters in developing countries tend to be prospective (forward-looking) and sociotropic (nationally oriented) rather than retrospective and pocketbook types with varying degree of country differences.[3]

Single and cross-country studies, employing the econometric-based vote-popularity (VP) functions, assert that voters have a short time horizon ("myopic"), economic changes account for a third of the change in vote, and national ("sociotropic") economic voting is stronger than personal ("egotropic" or pocketbook) economic voting although there are country exceptions.

The VP functions are however found to be unstable in cross-country studies as well as in a country over time, suggesting a more complex interaction between economic variables and the other institutional and political factors that shape voter behaviour.[4]

Other country-specific variations in economic voting behaviour are found in Latin American studies showing voters have a longer time horizon in that they punish both current and past incumbents. Voters' priorities also shifted from inflation crisis during the 1980s and 1990s to growth issues in the 2000–10 period. The institutional context also plays a role in that support for the president was lower during bad economic times under a divided government. Another study revealed variation across different groups. The elderly are the least likely to vote based on economics, women are more likely to decide based on their opinion of the incumbent; while the poor voters care about unemployment rate and the rich are more concerned about inflation.[5]

In single and cross-countries studies in Africa and Asia, the importance of economic factors and sociotropic and prospective voting behaviour were established. The studies also found country-specific differences. In South Korea, for instance, voters were influenced by economic factors only after the 1997–98 Asian Financial Crisis especially in the 2007 election.[6]

The consistent pattern of economic voting revealed in the country studies suggests that Malaysian voters would likely exhibit similar tendencies. To examine this, the issues that voters are most concerned about based on pre-election polling are analysed. To answer the first question posed earlier as to whether economic issues have become less important in the 2018 election, we will examine the changes in emphasis placed by voters on the various election issues.

Voters' concerns over the economy may not have a strong relationship with election outcomes particularly if the different groups such as the low- and middle-income groups, categorized as B40 and M40 households in the Malaysian socio-economic landscape, are affected differently. Consequently, the second question pertaining to the strength of the relationship between national economic indicators and election outcomes could be influenced by varying economic performance and outcome across regions, industries or income groups. To this end, the national statistics will be further disaggregated to determine if the differences are large enough to mask the evidence of economic voting at the national level as well as to cause the seismic shift in voting behaviour in the 2018 election.

The third question about the complexity of economic issues is examined from the angle of the varied responses of voters to local and national-level issues and the extent to which their concerns are predominantly short term or long term, including the likelihood that such concerns could switch over time and under different economic conditions. Such complexities would not be adequately captured by economic indicators, thereby clouding the relationship between economic factors and voting decisions.

MALAYSIA'S ECONOMIC PERFORMANCE AND ELECTION OUTCOMES

Following a soft patch in 2016 whereby real GDP growth slowed to 4.5 per cent, the Malaysian economy rebounded in 2017 to register a growth of 5.9 per cent on the back of an export surge and synchronized global growth. Most economic indicators point to a continuing growth momentum and a generally positive economic environment under which the country's 14th general election was held on 9 May 2018 and one which was strongly in favour of the incumbent coalition party that had ruled the country since its independence in 1957.

As shown in Table 4.1, most of the indicators in the run-up to the general election pointed to a favourable economic environment for the ruling coalition. Given the favourable economic environment, the incumbent party would have an edge over the opposition as predicted by the economic voting theory which contends that voters are inclined to favour the political party that can better fulfil their economic needs. The relationship is tested using correlation analysis and regression techniques, bearing in mind that the small number of observations will render the results less reliable.

The statistical results are presented in the Appendix. As illustrated in Figure 4.1, the relationship with election outcome in terms of the percentage seats and votes obtained by the incumbent party is relatively weak for all the common economic indicators. It is noted that the three-year average real GDP growth and three-year average per capita income growth have a stronger positive relationship with election outcome compared to the one-year variable. It suggests that sustained GDP growth performance is more important in influencing voters than shorter term performance.

TABLE 4.1
Malaysia's Macroeconomic Setting in the Run-up to GE-14 on 9 May 2018

	Macroeconomic Indicators					Weighted Average Bank Lending Rate (%)
	World GDP Growth (%)	Malaysia's GDP Growth (%)	Per capita Income Growth (%)	Inflation (CPI %)	Unemploy- ment Rate (%)	
2016	3.2	4.5	2.6	2.1	3.4	5.31
2017	3.7	5.9	4.6	3.7	3.4	5.21
2018 (end April)	–	–	–		3.3	5.39
2018 (forecast)	3.9	5.0	4.2	2.2	3.3	–

Note: * Quarter 1.
Source: Department of Statistics Malaysia, Bank Negara Malaysia's Monthly Statistical Bulletin; forecasts from IMF and domestic official and market sources.

Excluding the elections whereby there were shocks to the economy (oil shock in 1974, recession in 1986 and 1999), the positive relationship between economic growth and votes or seats won by the incumbent party improved substantially.

In the case of inflation as measured by the Consumer Price Index (CPI), the relationship was positive with election outcome, contradicting the expectation that a rise in inflation would lead to a poorer performance by the incumbent party. Excluding the outliers, the relationship remains positive, indicating that inflation as measured by the official CPI is correlated with election outcome in a perverse way. Likewise, given that food is a major component in accounting for the rising cost of living, the food CPI also showed weak and positive relationship with election outcome.

Unemployment shows a similarly weak relationship with election outcome in terms of percentage of seats won and an even weaker relationship with the percentage of votes obtained. Contrary to expectations, employment growth is negatively correlated for the one- and two-year variables, again reiterating the weak relationship between the national economic variables and election outcome.

As illustrated in Figure 4.1, the 2018 election surprise further skewed the relationship between the various macroeconomic indicators and election outcomes, standing out as an outlier as displayed in all the charts. Overall, bearing in mind the small sample size, the results point to the weak correlation between the key economic indicators and election outcome.

This finding is consistent with the regression estimated results shown in Table 4A.2 in the Appendix where the individual economic indicators and their various combinations are found to lack the ability to explain the election results. Including a dummy to take into account the outliers (1974, 1986, 1999 and 2018), the regression fit improved but again there is low confidence in the results. The poor regression model results are not surprising given the small sample size (maximum 13). None of the national economic variables—GDP growth, per capital income growth, inflation and unemployment, which are the common variables employed in

FIGURE 4.1
**Scatter Plot of Macroeconomic Variables That Votes and Seats Obtained by
the Incumbent Party Which Lost the Election**

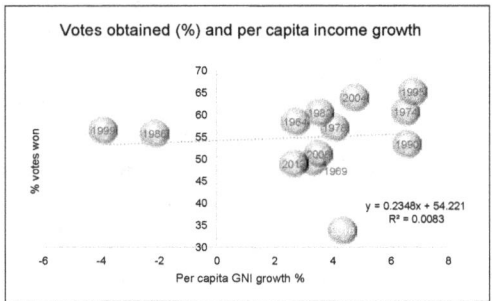

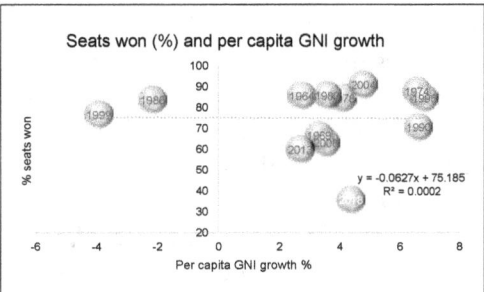

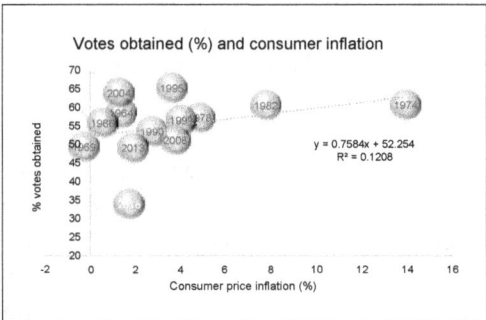

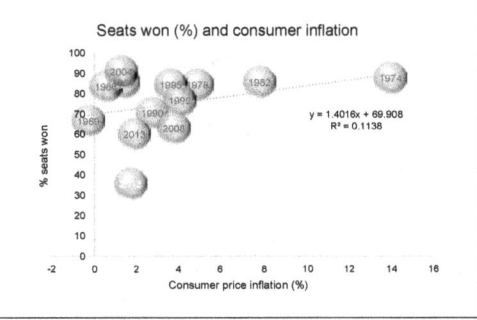

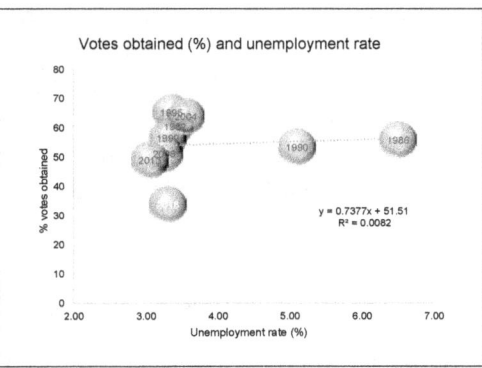

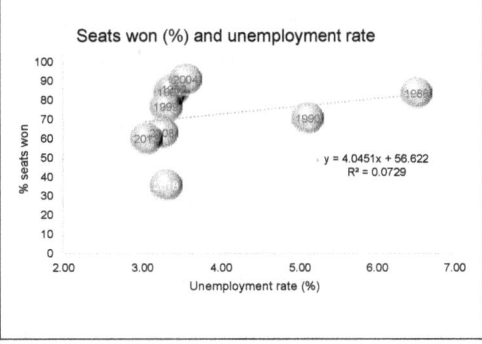

single and cross-country studies on economic voting—were found to be statistically significant in single and multiple variable regression models to explain the election outcomes using either seats won or votes obtained as the dependent variable.

Given the limitations imposed by small sample size and the poor fit of the models, the statistical evidence to reject the hypothesis that there is no relationship between voting outcome and the macroeconomic variables is not also conclusive.[7] In the following sections, we explore various plausible explanations for weak relationship between national aggregate performance and electoral outcomes.

ECONOMIC DYNAMICS AND THE ELECTION PARADOX

The absence of a correspondence between national economic performance and election outcome as predicted by economic voting theory suggests several avenues for further investigation, of which three lines of inquiry are pursued. The first line of inquiry examines the hypothesis that voters could be less concerned about economic issues as other issues could have become "national" and turned pocketbook or egotropic voters into sociotropic voters. These issues include financial scandals (e.g., 1MDB, FELDA) and social issues such as religion, ethnic relations, among others, that had dominated political campaigns of the multitude of ethnic and religious-based parties. To determine if economic matters have taken a backseat in voters' decision-making, the pre-election opinion poll reports are used to examine the issues that were most important to voters.

The second line of inquiry is to examine the extent to which the aggregate economic measures may not be reflective of on-the-ground realities. A disaggregated analysis will be conducted to examine the dispersion or unevenness of growth, inflation and unemployment.

The third line of inquiry, discussed in the next section, is that economic issues are much more complex than could be correlated with election outcomes since there are different dimensions in which the economic issues could be perceived by different voting groups depending on their economic status, needs and aspirations.

Further compounding the heterogeneity of voter groups is ethnicity, rural/urban divide and gerrymandering in the redelineation exercise of constituencies just before the election. The varying perceptions and realities invariably lead to unpredictable changes in voting patterns of the different voter groups such as between rural and urban voters and between those in different socio-economic strata. The issues are also shaped by the different narratives and media strategies mounted by the ruling party and the opposition to the extent of eroding party identification, ideologies and ethnicity as key determinants of the election outcome.

Election Issues and the Importance of Economic Matters to Voters

In polls carried out periodically by the Merdeka Center for Opinion Research, economic concerns topped the issues list for the 2018 election as well as in previous elections. As compiled in Table 4.2, economic concerns were found to be the top issue in all four pre-election polls between 2004 and 2019. The other major issues cited were crime and public safety, political instability/problems, social problems, quality of national leadership and corruption/abuse of power. The relative importance of these issues fluctuate over the different elections. It is noted that voters' concerns over the economy increased in the 2018 election (43 per cent) compared to the previous elections in 2004 (18 per cent) and in 2013 (25 per cent).

The relatively high percentage of 43 per cent of respondents citing economic concerns in 2018 was only topped by the 50 per cent polled in the 2008 election year just when the adverse impact of the global financial crisis on the economy was

TABLE 4.2
Issues Identified in Pre-Election Opinion Polls

Key Issues	2004	2008	2013	2018
Economic concerns	18%	50%	25%	43%
Crime and public safety	15%	4%	7%	—
Political instability/problems	14%	21%	9%	4%
Social problems	9%	11%	7%	—
Quality of national leadership	8%	1%	—	8%
Corruption, abuse of power, etc.	4%	3%	6%	21%
Traffic accidents	7%	—	—	—
Education	5%	—	4%	—
Election	5%	—	—	—
Racial inequality	—	3%	—	3%
Ethnic relations	—	2%	—	—
Lack of national unity	—	1%	—	—
Lack of education opportunities for own race	—	1%	—	—
Development & public infrastructure	—	—	2%	1%
Religion issues/Implementation of *hudud* law	—	—	2%	2%
Housing	—	—	—	5%
Preservation of Malay rights/Fair treatment	—	—	—	8%

Source: Merdeka Center for Opinion Research.

beginning to be felt. While the incumbent government lost its two-thirds majority in the 2008 election for the first time since the 1969 election, the high concerns about the economy as expressed in the opinion poll could be a dominating factor contributing to the erosion of support. The poll results also suggest that the public perception was prospective, being concerned about the growing economic uncertainties at the early stage of the global financial crisis in 2007–09, rather than retrospective as the economy was doing well in the run-up to the election in March 2008. The economy grew by 5.6 per cent in 2006 and improved to 6.3 per cent in 2007 before easing to 4.8 per cent in 2008 and contracting by 2.5 per cent in 2009 due to the global financial crisis.

On the contrary, GDP growth in 2017 surged to 5.9 per cent from 4.2 per cent in 2016 and the growth momentum going into the May 2018 election was reasonably strong as suggested by various leading indicators and private sector forecasts. The high concerns related to economic issues expressed in the poll despite the positive state of the economy in early 2018 point to a divergence between the macro indicators and the actual economic conditions being felt at the micro level involving individuals, households, businesses and industries.

Besides a near doubling of respondents (43 per cent) in the 2018 poll being concerned about the economy compared to the previous election in 2013 (25 per cent), another key result stood out. Compared to only 6 per cent of the respondents who listed corruption and abuse of power as issue in the 2013 election, 21 per cent identified it as an issue in 2018, elevating it to be the second most important issue in the 2018 election compared to its seventh placing in the previous poll in 2013. Two other new issues not cited in the 2013 poll were found in the 2018 poll: preservation of Malay rights/fair treatment for all (8 per cent) and housing (5 per cent). Housing emerged as an election issue following the property market boom between 2012 and 2015 that led to affordability becoming an issue and elicited a policy response from the government which embarked on a national affordable housing drive. Despite launching a special body called PR1MA Corporation to build affordable homes for middle-income households with monthly income of between RM2,500 and RM15,000 in various urban areas in 2012, the issue persisted through the 2018 election and this could have added to the growing discontentment among low- and middle-income groups on the state of the economy.

A more telling public sentiment against the incumbent government was regarding the direction of the economy. Except for the income group below RM2,000 a month, respondents from the higher income groups perceived the economy to be going in the wrong direction, with a whopping 72 per cent among those with a monthly income of RM7,000 and above expressing the same view compared with 55 per cent and 56 per cent for the other two middle-income groups (Figure 4.2). A majority of private sector respondents (56 per cent) and business owners and self-employed (55 per cent) expressed the sentiment that the economy is heading in the wrong direction. By contrast, employees of the government and government-related companies not surprisingly believed the economy is headed in the right direction.

The poll results unambiguously highlighted economic issues as the main concern for the public, a finding that is consistent for polls in all the previous elections. It corroborates the important link from perception of the economy to voter intention. However, whether voter intention translates into votes cast is also shaped by institutional and political factors, including the media and campaign strategy mounted by the incumbent party and opposition parties.

Uneven Growth and Distributional Effects

To answer the second question, the disaggregated performance is examined with the focus on the extent to which unevenness in growth, income distribution, inflation, wage and employment could have contributed to the divergence between the macroeconomic indicators and realities faced by the public leading to the rejection of the incumbents at the poll.

Variation in Growth Performance among Industries

Disaggregated data for eighteen broad sectors of the economy show that growth is more pervasive in the year preceding the 2018 election compared to the previous election in 2013. However, growth performance at the more disaggregated industry level has been uneven. Dissecting the output performance of the 105 industries, it is seen that besides lower overall average growth in 2016, their performance in 2017 was more variable, and growth was less pervasive (as indicated by the higher

FIGURE 4.2
Opinion Poll on the Direction of the Economy in the 2018 Election

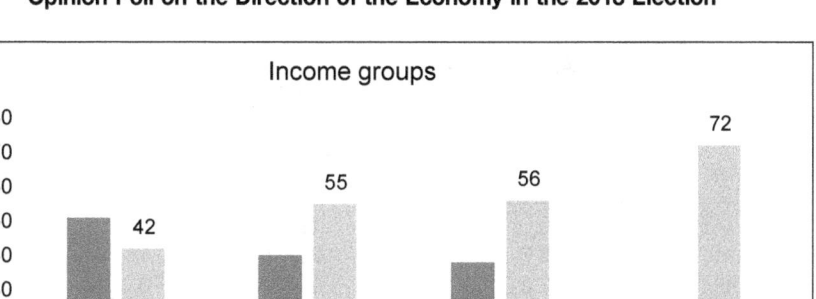

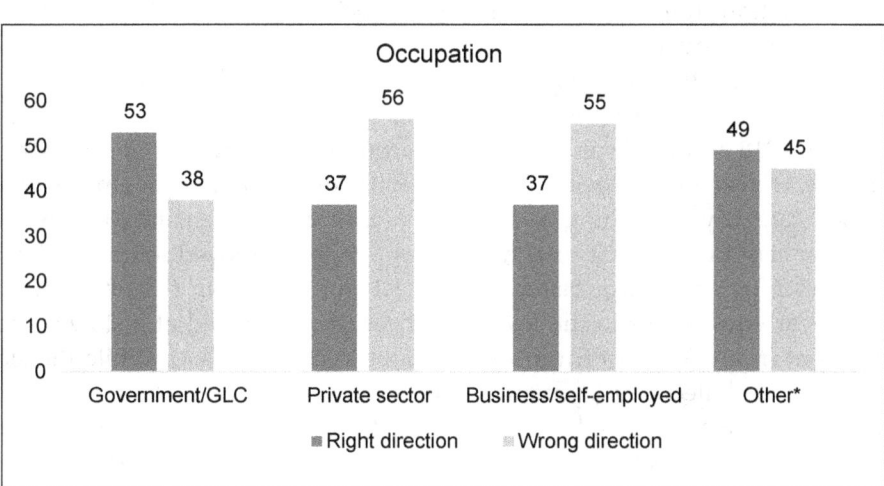

Source: Merdeka Center for Opinion Research.

coefficient of variation of 201.0 per cent in 2017 compared to 190.2 per cent in 2016 and the lower diffusion index which indicates that fewer industries are expanding) (see Table 4.3). Despite the improving overall performance of the economy and higher pervasiveness of growth at the sectoral level, increased unevenness in growth could have contributed to divergence between the GDP growth numbers and actual growth experienced by the various industries.

Variation in Employment, Wage Growth and Income Distribution

The country's total employment increased by 1.0 per cent in 2017 compared to a 0.2 per cent decline in the previous year, bringing the total number employed to

TABLE 4.3
Dispersion in Monthly Output Performance of 105 Manufacturing Industries

	Average Annual Growth (%)	Average Standard Deviation	Average Coefficient of Variation (%)	Average Minimum Monthly Growth (%)	Average Maximum Monthly Growth (%)	Diffusion Index
2016	6.0	11.1	190.2	−24.8	53.8	79.3
2017	5.7	10.9	201.0	−20.1	74.1	78.1
2018 (Jan–Apr)	7.0	12.3	184.0	−25.9	53.2	73.3

Source: Computed using industrial production data published by the Department of Statistics Malaysia.

8.48 million. The positive employment growth trend is accompanied by an increase in labour force participation rate from 67.7 per cent in 2016 to 68.1 per cent in 2017 with a further rise to 68.2 per cent as at end April 2018. Compared to 2016 which saw consolidation in a number of industries such as the oil and gas, airline and banking, labour market conditions were improving in 2017 and the positive trend continued through the election in May 2018. Likewise, the unemployment rate remained unchanged at 3.4 per cent in 2016 and 2017 but improved to 3.3 per cent in February 2018 and this was maintained through the election held on 9 May.

There was also an improvement in the skills composition with employment in the skilled category expanding at a higher rate of 2.3 per cent in 2017 compared with 1.3 per cent in 2016. The total number of people employed in the semi-skilled category also increased at a faster pace of 1.1 per cent from 0.3 per cent in the previous year while those in the low-skilled category declined at a slower pace of −1.2 per cent from −5.0 per cent in the previous year (Table 4.4). While the slower increase in low-skilled employment is a positive sign of a shift to a higher wage economy, which would have been favourable to the incumbent government in its ability to create better paying jobs, the preponderance of semi-skilled employment which accounts for 62.1 per cent of the total employment suggests a vulnerability especially when viewed in tandem with the rising cost of living.

Although the yearly increase in national mean monthly wage (nominal) shows a rising trend from 4.6 per cent in 2015 to 6.8 per cent in 2016 and 8.4 per cent in 2017, the disaggregated sectoral and industry data reveal significant variation across and within sectors. The variability in wages is evidenced by the wide range (minimum of RM1,754 and maximum of RM5,709 for mean monthly wages) across sectors. Further disaggregated analysis of the wage trends in the two largest sectors of the economy, manufacturing and services, show diverging trends. For manufacturing, the increase in average nominal wage per employee exceeded the CPI inflation rate but that for services slipped below inflation, indicating that employees in the services sector experienced negative real wage growth in the three years preceding the general election. Given the larger number of employees in the services amounting to 3.94 million in 2017 compared to 1.06 million in manufacturing, the lower wage

TABLE 4.4
Labour Market Conditions

	Total Employed ('000) Share of Total/Sub-total (%)		
	2015	2016	2017
All sectors ('000)	8,412	8,393	8,481
All sectors (%)	100.0	100.0	100.0
Skilled	23.6	23.9	24.2
Semi-skilled	61.8	62.1	62.1
Low-skilled	14.7	14.0	13.6
1. Agriculture	5.7	5.6	5.7
Skilled	5.8	6.9	6.6
Semi-skilled	85.7	85.4	85.9
Low-skilled	8.5	7.7	7.5
2. Mining & quarrying	1.0	1.0	1.0
Skilled	29.4	29.8	30.0
Semi-skilled	57.4	57.7	57.6
Low-skilled	13.2	12.6	12.4
3. Manufacturing	26.3	26.2	26.2
Skilled	18.2	18.5	18.9
Semi-skilled	74.0	74.0	73.8
Low-skilled	7.8	7.5	7.3
4. Construction	15.5	15.7	15.6
Skilled	11.0	11.7	11.8
Semi-skilled	84.9	84.2	84.3
Low-skilled	4.1	4.1	3.9
5. Services	51.5	51.5	51.4
Skilled	32.0	32.2	32.6
Semi-skilled	46.0	46.8	46.8
Low-skilled	22.1	21.0	20.6

Source: Department of Statistics Malaysia.

level and small wage increase in the services sector would be a major contributing factor to the disconnect between the relatively good national economic performance and a large segment of the population facing low salary levels and smaller wage increases (Table 4.5).

Average wage increase per employee for those in the lower categories were generally smaller than those in the higher wage categories in both the manufacturing and services sector (Figure 4.3). Since the wage statistics were compiled at the industry level, the stronger wage increases for those in the higher wage ranges also indicate that industries that pay higher wages were also able to give larger wage increases. It is noted that the growth in average wage per employee by industry as derived is biased downwards especially for industries that expand by increasing the number of lower skilled and therefore lower wage workers which has the effect of lowering the industry average wage per employee.

TABLE 4.5
Divergence in Monthly Wage per Employee and Wage Increases in the Manufacturing and Services Sectors

	Average Monthly Wage (RM)				Average Salary Increase (%)			
	2015	2016	2017	2018*	2015	2016	2017	2018*
Manufacturing sector (105 industries)								
Minimum (RM)	1,312	1,400	1,263	1,541	−41.0	−25.0	−30.0	−26.4
Maximum (RM)	14,823	18,925	20,916	24,192	58.0	61.0	94.0	123.6
Average (RM)	3,158	3,416	3,723	4,021	5.8	6.8	10.0	10.4
Standard deviation	1,957	2,447	2,761	3,106	15.5	16.0	16.9	17.9
Coefficient of variation (%)	62.0	71.6	74.2	77.2	267.2	235.3	169.0	172.1
Services sector (30 subsectors)								
Minimum (RM)	250	254	258	261	−2.2	−1.9	−1.9	−2.0
Maximum (RM)	5,502	5,399	5,572	5,412	8.5	8.2	7.3	5.6
Average (RM)	2,300	2,339	2,398	2,430	3.4	1.8	2.3	1.2
Standard deviation	1,026	1,025	1,071	1,071	2.7	2.1	1.8	1.8
Coefficient of variation (%)	44.6	43.8	44.7	44.1	78.3	112.6	77.6	144.8

Note: * Jan–April for manufacturing and first two quarters of 2018 for services.

The highly skewed wage distribution both in terms of level and increment suggests that a large segment of the working population are low wage employees. They would find the economic situation challenging when faced with the rising cost of living. This segment of voters would likely express bread-and-butter or pocketbook issues as a key concern despite the healthy performance of the economy from a national perspective. It also affirms the strong manifestation of economic concerns in the pre-election polls.

Cost of Living and GST

The abolition of the goods and services tax (GST) was a central campaign issue adopted by the PH coalition to galvanize voters' concerns on the rising cost of living. Implemented in April 2015, the consumption tax has a broader coverage of goods and services tax, amounting to 60 per cent of the consumer price index (CPI) basket compared to the old sales and services tax (SST) which is likely to be slightly above the 38 per cent cited by the government for the new SST as more items are exempted by the new government.

The one-off rise in consumer inflation seen in other countries that had implemented the consumption tax system is not evident in Malaysia. Its overall CPI remained stable at 2.1 per cent in 2015 as well as in 2016 largely due to falling oil prices which resulted in a fall in transport cost (−4.5 per cent in 2015 and −4.6 per cent in 2016) (Table 4.6). The reversal in oil price from US$46 a barrel in 2016 to US$57 a barrel[8] in 2017 led to a 13.2 per cent rise in transport cost in the CPI basket and an above trend, one-off 3.7 per cent rise in CPI in 2017. In the months preceding the May

FIGURE 4.3
Distribution of Mean Monthly Wages and Wage Increases in
Manufacturing and Service Industries in 2017

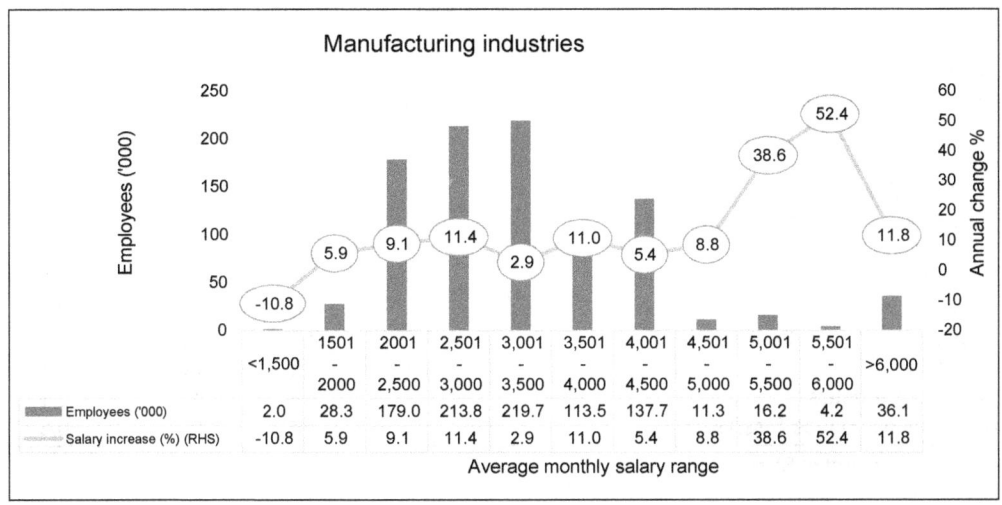

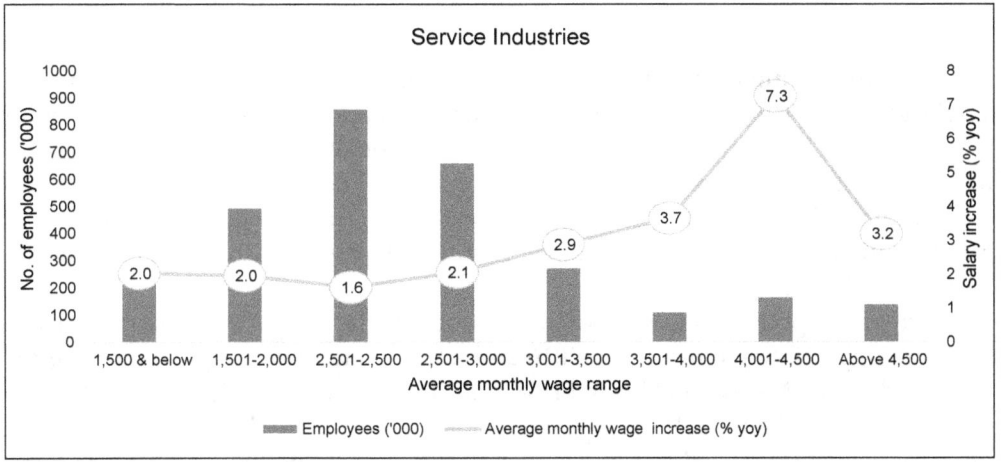

Source: Computed from Department of Statistics Malaysia's Monthly Manufacturing Survey and Services Survey.

election in 2018, inflation was on a downtrend, easing to 1.7 per cent. Despite the benign inflation environment as indicated by the official CPI measure, the rising cost of living was a core campaign issue that resonated well with the general public. Besides the low wage level and smaller wage increases for low-wage employees as discussed in the preceding sections, there are obviously other dynamics at work.

Despite being a leading election campaign issue, there is a dearth of studies on the rising cost of living and how divergent it is from consumer price inflation as measured by the official CPI for the different income groups. An instructive study by the central bank revealed that about 27 per cent of the households in Kuala

TABLE 4.6
CPI Inflation Trends Prior to GE-14 (% change year-on-year)

Items	2015	2016	2017	2018 (Jan–Apr)
All groups	2.1	2.1	3.7	1.7
Food & non-alcoholic beverages	3.6	3.7	3.9	3.0
Alcoholic beverages & tobacco	13.5	17.2	0.2	0.2
Clothing & footwear	0.5	–0.4	–0.4	–0.6
Housing utilities	2.4	2.4	2.2	2.0
Furnishings & household equipment	2.7	2.4	2.2	2.1
Health	4.4	2.7	2.6	2.1
Transport	–4.5	–4.6	13.2	1.0
Communication	2.0	–1.6	–0.3	–0.6
Recreation services & culture	1.7	2.5	1.9	0.5
Education	2.4	2.2	1.6	1.1
Restaurant & hotels	4.2	2.8	2.5	2.1
Miscellaneous goods & services	4.2	2.9	1.2	0.5

Source: Department of Statistics Malaysia.

Lumpur are earning below the living wage estimated at RM2,700 per month for a single adult, RM4,500 for a couple without children and RM6,500 for a couple with two children. This suggests that a sizeable proportion of households are vulnerable to rising cost of living pressures despite the low CPI inflation averaging 2.4 per cent annually between 2013 and 2016. Nonetheless, the 3.7 per cent rise in CPI inflation in 2017 could have raised the living cost pressures in the run-up to the 2018 general election.

Further compounding the cost of living issues are the escalating house prices since 2011 and depreciating currency in 2016 and 2017. Average house price increases as measured by the Malaysian House Price Index exceeded income growth in all years except for 2014 (Figure 4.4). As a result, housing affordability based on the house price-to-income ratio has remained above 4 times, exceeding the widely considered affordable threshold of 3 times.

The voters' concern over the rising house prices was reflected in the public opinion poll, being ranked fourth among the top election issues in 2018 (see Figure 4.2). It was either absent or lowly ranked in previous election polls.

Household Indebtedness

Another economic reality confronting households despite the positive macroeconomic environment was high household indebtedness. Total household debt-to-GDP ratio rose from 60.4 per cent in 2008 to 86.2 per cent in 2013. It peaked at 89.1 per cent in 2015 before easing to 84.3 per cent in 2017 (Bank Negara Malaysia 2018). An analysis of the issue by staff of the central bank's Financial Surveillance Department shows

FIGURE 4.4
House Price and Household Income Trends

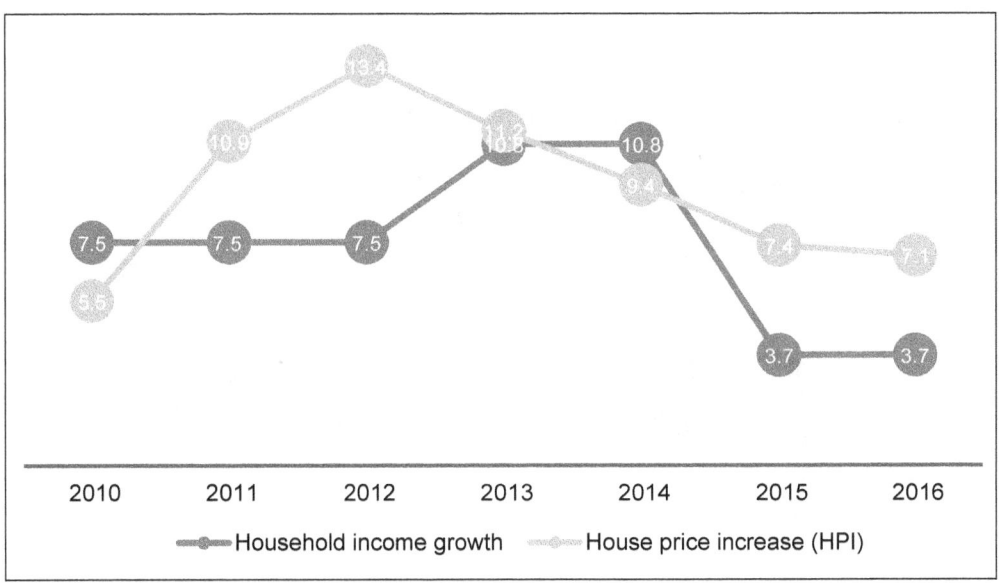

Source: National Property Information Centre (NAPIC) and Department of Statistics Malaysia.

that the bulk of households' borrowings were for purchases of residential properties, motor vehicles and personal financing. For middle- and high-income groups, residential property purchases comprised more than half of the debt. Low-income households are also highly exposed to personal financing and vehicle loans (28 per cent). The same study also revealed that there were 554,000 borrowers or 6.5 per cent of the total with negative financial margin whereby the individual's monthly disposable income and liquid financial assets, after deducting debt repayments and expenditure on basic necessities, is negative (Figure 4.5).

Unevenness in growth across sectors and industries, relatively low wage levels and small salary increase in a sizeable proportion of the workforce engaged in the services sector, and rising cost of living that was further exacerbated by property price escalation and currency depreciation appear to fit the puzzle that despite strong economic performance denoted by macroeconomic indicators, a sizeable segment of the society had not benefitted from the growth spillovers.

From an economic perspective, the discontentment at the lower segment of the income spectrum (pocketbook or retrospective economic voters) combined with those in the middle-and high-income segments who believe that the economy is heading in the wrong direction (prospective economic voters) created a potent or "tsunami" force that changed the government that had ruled the country since its independence.

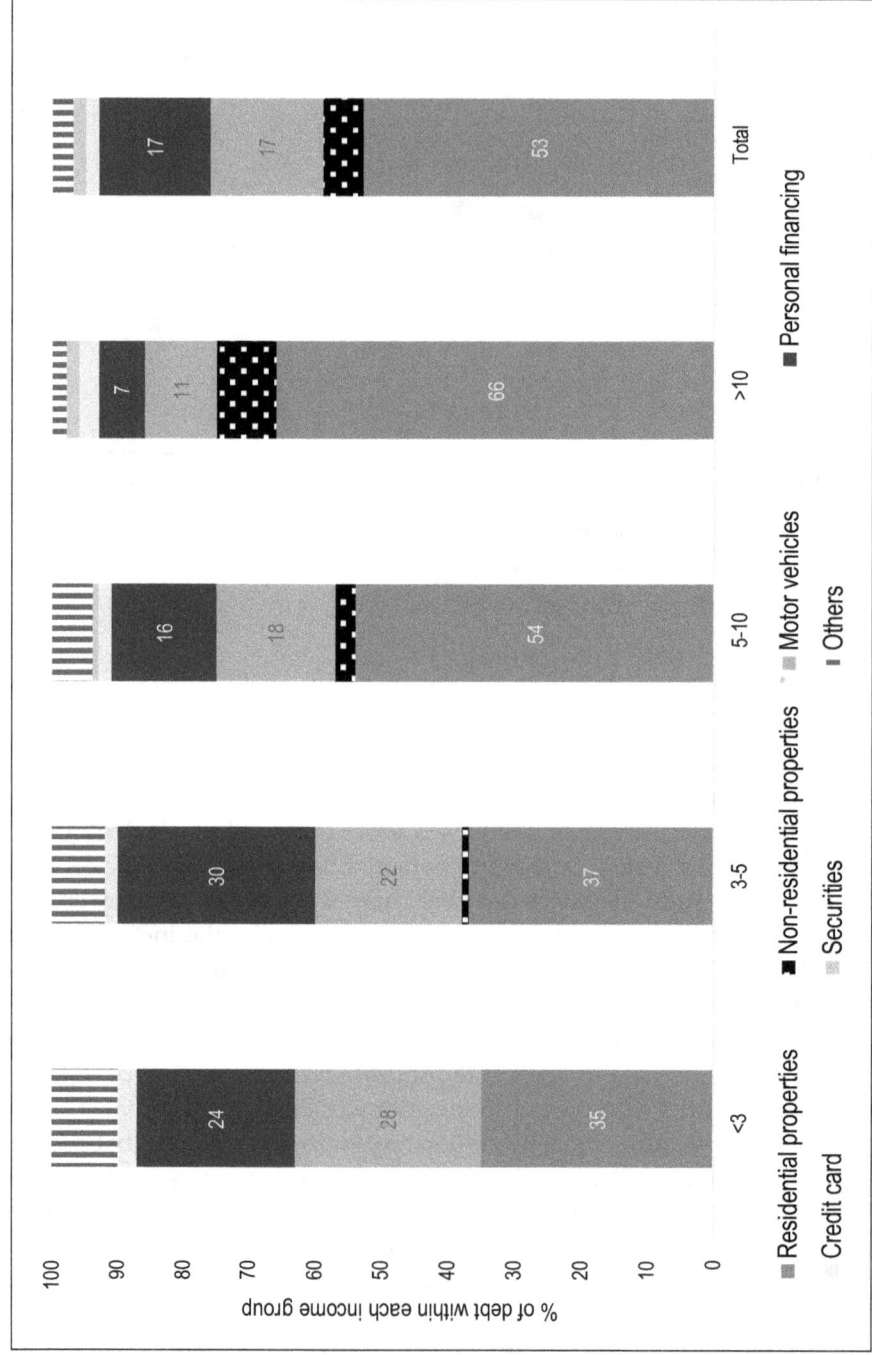

FIGURE 4.5
Type of Household Debt by Income Group (RM thousands per month)

Source: Siti Hanifah, Lim and Muizz (2018).

COMPLEXITY OF ECONOMIC ISSUES AND
THEIR INFLUENCE ON VOTER GROUPS

Aggregated economic variables such as income, wages, employment and prices do not reveal the variation and patterns at lower or disaggregated levels of analysis. The unequal, varying or distributional effects give rise to the different economic realities faced by various voter groups. Their economic priorities and concerns are also being shaped by the policies and strategies employed by the ruling government and alternatives offered by the opposition.

The complexity of economic issues arises from three dimensions, namely, time period (short, medium and long term), trade-offs (short-term "pain" versus long-term "gain", local or regional versus national) and opportunity costs ("funding public transportation rather than fuel subsidies", "cheaper to build now than later when prices are higher"). Importantly, the understanding of complex economic issues and their relative importance in shaping voting decisions are dependent on the voters' socio-economic background and educational level.

The ability of the political parties to identify the "hot button" issues and the effectiveness of their campaign in addressing the various concerns that vary across voter groups is one of the keys to electoral success. It is posited that arising from the complexity of economic issues, the type and relative importance of "hot button" issues vary across voter groups according to the different dimensions of the economic issues. Voters are presumed to take into consideration how the party they vote in can best address the spectrum of economic issues that affect them in various dimensions depending on their level of understanding and concerns which range from immediate and local bread-and-butter issues to the long term, national-level country direction and economic security concerns.

A characterization of the complexity of economic issues confronting the nation and how they shape the ruling government's response and campaign strategies in terms of being an advantage (tailwind), disadvantage (headwind) or two-way (crosswind) whereby the net balance of contrasting effects could tilt to the incumbent or opposition, is summarized in Table 4.7 and the issues' nexus are discussed in the following sections.

Economic Growth, Direction and Economic Security Nexus

The country's economic performance in 2016 and 2017 was healthy and the prevailing outlook for 2018 was positive in the run-up to the May 2018 election. The economic stability and commendable performance, which was highlighted by the International Monetary Fund as among the top percentile in per capita income growth among upper middle-income countries, has enabled the incumbent government to tout its track record in the management of the economy. While the short-term growth performance and prospects was a tailwind to the incumbent's media and political campaign, there were a number of longer term issues that surfaced to the fore as reflected in the angst of poll respondents on the direction of the economy.

TABLE 4.7
Complexity of Economic Issues and How They Contributed to the Change in Government

Pre-GE Conditions	Expected Effects on Incumbent/Ruling Government		
	Tailwind (+)	Headwind (–)	Crosswind (?)
Economic growth and direction: Sustained GDP growth of 5.5–6.0%, slightly weaker than 2017's 5.9%	• Economic stability • Buoyant business sentiments	• Wide income gap between rural-urban, regional and intra-ethnic groups • Improving but not optimistic consumer sentiments • Increasing number of lagging industries • Negative public view on large scale investments from China and large infrastructure projects awarded to Chinese firms based on negotiated contracts	• Avoidance of long-term middle income trap versus the short-term "pain" of hard structural reforms • Costs versus benefits of mega infrastructure projects
Employment and wages: Decline in unemployment rate to 3.3% while wage growth remains firm at 5–7%	• Full employment • Improving wages • Less intense industry consolidation	• Depressed wage levels • Prevalence of low skills, low wage labour • Weak services wage growth • High graduate unemployment • High reliance on unskilled foreign labour	• Creation of skilled jobs versus displacement by disruptive technologies and foreign competition

continued on next page

TABLE 4.7 – cont'd

Pre-GE Conditions	Expected Effects on Incumbent/Ruling Government		
	Tailwind (+)	Headwind (–)	Crosswind (?)
CPI and cost of living: Decline in headline inflation to 2–2.5% while core inflation remains stable at 2%.	• Lower cost of living • Reduced production cost pressures	• Stronger impact of energy and food inflation on low-income voters • Higher cost of living among urban voters • Unaffordable housing	• Positive wealth effects of rising asset and commodity prices versus negative impact on cost of living
Financial and credit conditions: Stable financial environment, ample liquidity and improving bank lending; stronger ringgit amid marginally higher interest rate	• Domestic financial stability that shielded the real sector from global financial market volatility • Low and stable interest rate environment following the 25 basis points hike in the Overnight Policy Rate in January 2018	• Slower credit growth with first-time house owners facing difficulties in obtaining bank loans • Credit rationing to SMEs and low income households	• Access to global capital and other positive effects of foreign capital inflows versus increased financial market volatility through contagion and exposure to capital flow reversals
Government spending: Fiscal deficit target of 2.8% on target with debt level kept at below 55% of GDP	• Increased people-friendly spending, including income transfers to boost "feel good" factor • Fiscal discipline reflected in limiting deficit and debt levels	• Spending inefficiencies and leakages • Continuing opposition to GST over slower refunds • Increased revenue risk as tax buoyancy declines • Rising contingent liabilities • High NFPEs debt level raises government's future contingent liabilities	• Preserving fiscal space (reduce spending) versus vulnerability to growth slowdown if public spending is curtailed

These headwinds to the incumbent party's political campaign include the development gap between the Bornean states and West Malaysia, rural and urban constituencies, middle-income trap risk, increasing number of lagging industries and negative public sentiments on the large scale infrastructure projects awarded on the basis of direct negotiation especially to the Chinese firms. Growing concerns over the future direction of the economy would have been triggered by a combination of these factors and developments. The opposition party offered a simple alternative policy in its manifesto, which is to review all mega projects that had been awarded by the ruling government. The significance of corruption as an issue to voters is supported by the spike in the percentage of respondents citing it in Merdeka Center polls from 6 per cent in the 2013 election to 21 per cent in the 2018 election.

Employment, Wages, Inflation and Cost of Living Nexus

The disaggregated analyses of growth, employment, wages and salary increases, inflation and cost of living in the preceding section reveal a wide dispersion across sectors and industries that lend credence to the observation that the national-level economic performance is not reflective of the economic situation faced by a majority of the population. A national public opinion poll on economic hardships revealed that nearly two-thirds of the respondents felt stressed about the future while 40 per cent experienced delays or were unable to settle utility bills (Merdeka Center 2017). It is not surprising therefore that there was widespread economic discontentment to the extent the abolition of the GST system, despite being supported by economists and professionals as well as being acknowledged subsequently by the winning opposition party as being more broad-based and efficient, was employed effectively by the latter in political campaigns to swing the votes.

Nonetheless, besides being blamed for the rising cost of living, there were a number of factors that had led to the unpopularity of the GST. The slow refund and cascading effects of GST affecting all stages of the supply chain as well as its regressive impact on small and medium-size enterprises were among the factors contributing to its opposition by the business sector.

Government Spending, Financial and Credit Conditions Nexus

Inefficient and wasteful government spending, income transfer payments (cash handouts) to low-income households and difficult access to bank credit faced by first time home buyers were some of the issues that are multidimensional as they have unequal effects on different stakeholders. The broadening of cash handouts by the previous government, while aimed at reducing the cost of living burden faced by low income households, led to concerns over subsidy dependency on the one hand, and wasteful, untargeted and inefficient spending on the other. Not surprisingly therefore, those in the low-income groups who think the economy is heading in the right direction exceeded those who hold the contrary view. By contrast, those in the higher income groups who believed the economy is heading in the wrong direction far exceeded those who do not think so. For the middle-income groups who are not eligible under the direct income transfer programme (BR1M), but continued to be burdened by income and consumption taxes, a majority hold the view that the economy is heading in the wrong direction, a perception fuelled by the corruption, cronyism and race-based policies. These national-level issues are related more to governance and policy and would have dominated the material economic conditions and rendered recent economic performance less pertinent in their voting decisions.

CONCLUSIONS

This chapter's narrowly constructed analyses point to a number of "hidden" economic signs of a surprise election outcome. The signs include the wide dispersion in growth performance when analysed at the industry level. There was wide disparity in wage levels and salary increases between the services and manufacturing sectors and sizeable interindustry differences within each sector. Being lower in the services sector, the low wage and salary increases affected a wider segment of the population given that services employment accounted for slightly over 4 million employees compared to over a million for manufacturing.

Despite cash handouts for the low-income group, there remained a sizeable number of pocketbook voters who were economically discontented due to depressed wages and rising cost of living especially in urban constituencies. The middle- and high-income voters, in exhibiting prospective economic voting behaviour, were predominantly of the view that the country was heading in the wrong direction under the incumbent government. The alignment of the economic voting behaviour across all income groups in punishing the incumbent government could have set the stage for a surprise change in government despite the solid macroeconomic fundamentals.

By themselves, these economic signals would not be able to fully account for the total surprise without considering the institutional and political winds of change. Other institutional, political and personality factors have added to the change momentum. These included pervasive corruption afflicting the ruling government, the emergence of a viable opposition coalition party (Pakatan Harapan) and trust in a former leader, all of which could be better analysed through the lenses of political science and human psychology.

Going forward, the relationship between the state of the economy, economic management and election outcomes in Malaysia will likely evolve and mature further, given the country's breakthrough to become a higher functioning democracy. Future research on the influence of the economy on voter behaviour will have to be micro-level to take into consideration the strong divergence between national economic performance and on-the-ground realities. Another important consideration in future studies is the heterogeneity of the voter base particularly ethnicity and regionalism along with commonly studied income and demographic (age and gender) dimensions. These dimensions will have to be overlaid with institutional and political factors such as party identification and coalition politics.

APPENDIX
Statistical Analysis

Correlation Analysis

The correlation coefficient measures the strength of the linear relationship between two variables whereby –1 denotes perfect negative correlation, +1 perfect positive correlation and 0 no correlation. In the analysis below, the correlation coefficient of election outcome based on either percentage seats won or votes and each selected economic indicator is computed in three different ways. The first correlation relates the election result to the economic indicator for the previous year based on the finding that voters tend to be myopic (Lewis-Beck and Paldam 2000). The second correlation covers a two-year period where the average of the indicator for the prior year and the election year based on the actual out-turn for past elections and official or market forecasts for the 2018 election is used. The third correlation extends to two years before the election year on the assumption that retrospective voters are shaped by longer term performance that is reflective of the underlying trend. The same set of correlations is computed for the series that exclude the outlier years, namely, 1974, 1986, 1999 and 2018 where the economy was hit by shocks that resulted in a pronounced slowdown or recession. The two sets of results are displayed in Table 4A.1.

TABLE 4A.1
Correlation Coefficient between Macroeconomic Variables and Election Outcomes

Full sample

Variable	Sample Size	Economic Indicator for Year Prior to GE		Average Economic Indicator for Election Year and Previous Year		Average Economic Indicator for Election Year and Previous 2 Years	
		% Seats Won	% Votes Obtained	% Seats Won	% Votes Obtained	% Seats Won	% Votes Obtained
Real GDP growth	13	0.00	0.06	0.09	0.18	0.25	0.33
Per capita income growth	13	-0.02	0.04	-0.01	0.09	0.10	0.21
CPI inflation	13	0.28	0.28	0.34	0.35	0.26	0.28
Food CPI inflation	11	0.24	0.26	0.39	0.34	0.37	0.32
Unemployment	8	0.29	0.14	0.27	0.09	0.22	0.08
Employment growth	8	-0.09	-0.05	-0.22	-0.18	0.05	0.15

Excluding outliers (1974, 1986, 1999, 2018)

Variable	Sample Size	Economic Indicator for Year Prior to GE		Average Economic Indicator for Election Year and Previous Year		Average Economic Indicator for Election Year and Previous 2 Years	
		% Seats Won	% Votes Obtained	% Seats Won	% Votes Obtained	% Seats Won	% Votes Obtained
Real GDP growth	9	-0.17	-0.05	0.26	0.41	0.34	0.44
Per capita income growth	9	0.26	0.37	0.26	0.47	0.27	0.46
CPI inflation	9	0.45	0.42	0.30	0.33	0.18	0.23
Food CPI inflation	7	0.28	0.23	0.14	0.10	-0.07	-0.09
Unemployment	4	0.10	0.00	0.01	-0.08	-0.03	-0.09
Employment growth	4	-0.31	-0.51	-0.55	-0.64	-0.50	-0.51

Source: Author's computations.

Regression Analysis

The ordinary least squares (OLS) regression and the more sophisticated autoregressive distributed lag (ARDL) technique that is suitable for small sample size and non-stationary variables are used to examine the statistical relationship between the economic variables (GDP, GNI per capita, CPI, unemployment, and employment growth) and the election outcome as measured by the percentage of seats or votes won (dependent variables) by the ruling coalition party. All the dependent and explanatory variables are found to be non-stationary and they are either integrated of the order 1 or 2, i.e., I(1) or I(2) variables. OLS regression tests will be spurious in the presence of non-stationarity. The ARDL regression is valid for non-stationary variables provided the variables that are either I(0) or I(1) but not I(2). For I(2) variables, the difference of the variable (transformed into I(1) variable) is used in the ARDL estimation to ensure the diagnostic tests are valid. A dummy is created for the outlier years (1974, 1986, 1999 and 2018) to determine if the shocks are significant statistically in explaining the election outcome. The selected results are summarized in Table 4A.2.

TABLE 4A.2
Regression Results of Economic Voting Models

Dependent Variable: Seats won

Method:	ARDL	ARDL	ARDL	OLS
Number of models evaluated:	4	8	4	1
Selected Model:	ARDL(1, 0, 1)	ARDL (1,1,0,1)	ARDL (1,0,1)	
Included observations:	12	12	10	13
Seats (–1)	–0.584	–0.792	–0.533	
	(p=0.0768)	(p=0.073)	(p=0.221)	
Real GDP growth	0.879	–0.685	0.725	1.688
	(p=0.624)	(p=0.814)	(p=0.721)	(p=0.432)
CPI inflation	1.683	1.910		1.120
	(p=0.344)	(p=0.464)		(p=0.570)
CPI inflation (–1)	2.154			
	(p=0.183)			
Food CPI			0.027	
			(p=0.992)	
Food CPI (–1)			1.729	
			(p=0.255)	
Dummy		3.117		
		(p=0.795)		
Dummy (–1)		21.177		
		(p=0.167)		
Constant	–24.379	–31.744	–19.080	–17.501
	(p=0.084)	(p=0.180)	(p=0.314)	(p=0.194)
Observations	12	13	10	13
R-squared	0.563	0.643	0.403	(p=0.154)
F-statistic	2.257	1.502	0.844	0.912
Prob (F-statistic)	(p=0.164)	(p=0.336)	(p=0.553)	(p=0.433)
Breusch-Godfrey Serial				
Correlation LM Test:	0.781	0.029	12.833	2.430
	(p=0.507)	(p=0.972)	(p=0.034)	(p=0.150)
F-Bounds Test	9.322	6.035	5.015	na
Critical value at 1%	5.000	4.660	5.000	na

Note: na: not applicable; p-value in parentheses.

Notes

1. The author wishes to thank Francis E. Hutchinson and Lee Hwok Aun for helping to shape the ideas and content of this chapter. All remaining errors are the writer's responsibility.
2. See Lewis-Becker and Stegmaier (2000) and Lewis-Becker and Paldam (2000) for an exposition of the economic voting research paradigm.
3. For example, Venezuelan voters who exhibited pocketbook economic voting became sociotropic in character in the post-election period. In Mexico, voters were found to be policy-oriented rather than incumbency-oriented (Brophy-Baermann 1994) and those who received remittance income from abroad were less likely to engage in economic voting, being less affected by the domestic economic conditions according to Germano (2013).
4. As reported by Duch and Stevenson (2006). However, Lewis-Becker and Paldam (2000) opined that much of the instability in VP functions can be attributed to measurement or specification errors.
5. See studies by Benton (2015), Singer (2013) and Johnson and Schwindt-Bayer (2009).
6. Bratton (2010); Hsieh, Lacy, and Niou (1998); Choi (2010); Lee (2011); Lee, Yong, and Glasure (2012).
7. For some diagnostics in the Autoregressive Distributed Lag (ARDL) model, a minimum of twenty observations is needed for the results to be reliable. The poor model fit is reflected in the low F-statistic which is not significant at the 10 per cent level.
8. Weighted average as reported in the central bank's Monthly Statistical Bulletin.

References

Bank Negara Malaysia. 2018. *Financial Stability and Payment Systems Report 2017*. Kuala Lumpur: Bank Negara Malaysia.

Benton, Allyson Lucinda. 2005. "Dissatisfied Democrats or Retrospective Voters? Economic Hardship, Political Institutions and Voting Behaviour in Latin America". *Comparative Political Studies* 38, no. 4: 417–42.

Bratton, Michael, Ravi Bhavnani, and Tse-Hsin. 2012. "Voting Intentions in Africa: Ethnic, Economic or Partisan". *Commonwealth and Comparative Politics* 50, no. 1: 27–52.

Brophy-Baermann, Michelle. 1994. "Economics and Elections: The Mexican Case". *Social Science Quarterly* 75, no. 1: 125–35.

Choi, Eunjung. 2010. "Economic Voting in Taiwan: The Significance of Education and Lifetime Economic Experience". *Asian Survey* 50, no. 5: 990–1010.

Downs, Anthony. 1957. *An Economic Theory of Democracy*. New York: Harper and Row.

Department of Statistics Malaysia. 2018. *Salaries and Wages Report 2017*. Kuala Lumpur: Department of Statistics, Malaysia.

Duch, Raymond, and Randy Stevenson. 2006. "Assessing the Magnitude of the Economic Vote over Time and Across Nations". *Electoral Studies* 25, no. 3: 528–47.

Germano, Roy. 2013. "Migrants' Remittances and Economic Voting in the Mexican Countryside". *Electoral Behavior* 32, no. 4: 875–85.

Hsieh, John Fuh-Sheng, Dean Lacy, and Emerson Niou. 1998. "Retrospective and Prospective Voting in a One-Party Dominant Democracy: Taiwan's 1996 Presidential Election". *Public Choice* 97, no. 3: 383–99.

Johnson, Gregg, and Leslie Schwindt-Bayer. 2009. "Economic Accountability in Central America". *Journal of Politics in Latin America* 1, no. 3: 33–56.

Lee, Sophie Jiseon. 2011. "Economic Voting and Regionalism in South Korea: A Statistical Analysis of the 2007 Presidential Elections". PhD dissertation, Department of Political Science, Duke University.

Lee, Aie-Rie, and Yong U. Glasure. 2012. "Economic Voting in South Korea: Pocketbook or Sociotropic". *Japanese Journal of Political Science* 13, no. 3: 337–53.

Lewis-Beck, Michael S., and Richard Nadeau. 2011. "Economic Voting Theory: Testing New Dimensions". *Electoral Studies* 30: 288–94.

———, and Martin Paldam. 2000. "Economic Voting: An Introduction". *Electoral Studies* 19: 113–21.

———, and Mary Stegmaier. 2000. "Economic Determinants of Electoral Outcomes". *Annual Review of Political Science* 3: 183–219.

Merdeka Center. "National Public Opinion Survey on Economic Hardship Indicators", Survey Period, 4–14 November 2017. http://merdeka.org/v4/index.php/downloads/category/2-researches?download=181:nov-2017-economic-hardship-indicators (accessed 20 September 2018).

Nannestad, Peter, and Martin Paldam. 1994. "The VP-Function: A Survey of the Literature on Vote and Popularity Functions after 25 Years". *Public Choice* (Springer) 79, no. 3–4: 213–45.

Ministry of Finance Malaysia. 2018. Media Release, 19 July 2018. http://www.treasury.gov.my/index.php/en/gallery-activities/press-release/item/4092-media-release-gst-is-a-cradle-to-grave-tax-that-covers-60-of-the-cpi-basket-of-goods-and-services-compared-to-sst-that-is-taxable-on-only-38-of-the-cpi-basket-of-goods.html (accessed 20 September 2018).

Oganesyan, Rafael. 2014. "Economic Voting in the Developing World". University of Nevada, Las Vegas, UNLV Theses, Dissertations, Professional Papers, and Capstones 2201.

Posner, Daniel, and David Simon. 2002. "Economic Conditions and Incumbent Support in Africa's New Democracies: Evidence from Zambia". *Comparative Political Studies* 35, no. 3: 313–36.

Siti Hanifah Borhan Nordin, Lim S.L., and M.K. Muizz Abd Aziz. 2018. "Indebted to Debt: An Assessment of Debt Levels and Financial Buffers of Households". Financial Surveillance Department, Bank Negara Malaysia.

Singer, Matthew M. 2013. "Economic Voting in an Era of Non-Crisis: The Changing Electoral Agenda in Latin America 1982–2010". *Comparative Politics* 45, no. 2: 169–85.

———, and Francois Gelineau. 2010. "Heterogeneous Economic Voting: Evidence from Latin America 1995–2005". Paper prepared for the Latin American World Association for Public Opinion Research.

Weyland, Kurt. 2003. "Economic Voting Reconsidered: Crisis and Charisma in the Election of Hugo Chavez". *Comparative Political Studies* 47, no. 7: 822–48.

Youde, Jeremy. 2005. "Economics and Government Popularity in Ghana". *Electoral Studies* 24, no. 1: 1–16.

5

ECONOMIC VOTING AND THE END OF DOMINANT PARTY RULE IN MALAYSIA

Cassey Lee[1]

INTRODUCTION

The 14th General Elections (GE-14) in May 2018 witnessed the defeat of Malaysia's ruling political coalition Barisan Nasional (BN) by Pakatan Harapan (PH). Of the 222 parliamentary seats contested, the PH coalition secured 113 seats (52 per cent) compared to BN's 79 seats (36 per cent). BN's defeat was unexpected with most political pundits predicting the continuation of its rule, albeit with a slimmer majority.[2] The BN coalition had governed Malaysia continuously since the country's first general election in 1955 and its independence in 1957. Thus, the election marked the end of one of the longest periods of continuous rule in modern times.[3]

This leads to the question of what accounts for the defeat of BN in GE-14. In other words, what are the factors that can explain the outcome of the election? Did economic factors such as economic growth and inflation play a role in GE-14? Was the change in political regime brought about by the re-entry and active campaigning of the country's former Prime Minister Mahathir Mohamad? Did the party splits in Malay-based parties such as Parti Islam Se-Malaysia (PAS) and the United Malays National Organization (UMNO) contribute to PH's victory in GE-14? Was there a decline in the support of the bumiputra community for UMNO which contributed to BN's defeat?

The aim of this essay is to empirically examine economic and non-economic factors that determined the outcomes of the 2018 election. GE-14 was different from previous elections in Malaysia in that it involved regime transition, namely, the end of dominant party rule. As such, although the economic voting model is used to investigate the determinants of electoral outcomes in Malaysia, attention is also paid to factors identified in the empirical literature on the end of dominant party rule.

The outline of the rest of this chapter is as follows. The next section frames the research problem by reviewing the literature on economic voting as well as the end of dominant party rule. This is followed by qualitative discussions on the economic conditions and political changes leading up to GE-14 in Malaysia. An econometric analysis of the determinants of electoral outcomes is carried out in the subsequent section. The final section concludes.

FRAMING THE RESEARCH PROBLEM: ECONOMIC VOTING, DEMOCRATIZATION AND THE END OF DOMINANT PARTY RULE

Changes in political regimes are complex and driven by a multitude of factors. Therefore, it is useful to draw from different bodies of research related to political regime change or transitions. There are three strands of literature from political science that might be relevant: economic voting; regime change and inequality; and the end of dominant party rule. Each is briefly reviewed to draw relevant insights.

Economic factors have long been considered to be important determinants of electoral outcomes. The economic voter hypothesis (or economic voting model) can be stated as follows: "The citizen votes for the government if the economy is doing all right; otherwise, the vote is against" (Lewis-Beck and Stegmaier 2000, p. 183). This hypothesis has been tested within the empirical literature using two different approaches. In the first approach, the outcome or dependent variable is measured in terms of popularity such as job approval rating. In the second approach, the actual vote count in the form of vote/seat share is used as a measure of electoral outcome. The overall findings from the empirical literature support the hypothesis. In other words, economic conditions matter in elections. Economic variables that matter in elections include economic growth, the rate of inflation, and unemployment (Lewis-Beck and Stegmaier 2000 and Fair 1996). Higher economic growth, lower inflation and lower unemployment are positively associated with political support for the incumbent party in elections.

Unlike economic voting models, the explanations or theories of change in political regimes are more varied and complex. One important strand of literature focuses on regime change, more specifically democratization and the role of social conflict. The role of economic inequality plays a central role in the work on regime change and distributive conflicts. Boix (2003), for example, argued that greater inequality can lead to an increase in demands for redistribution of economic resources. The elite is likely to resist such redistribution resulting in a more authoritarian government and a decline in democratization. Acemoglu and Robinson (2006) also focus on distributive conflicts but make a distinction between *de facto* and *de jure* political power. They argue that the masses have the ability to mobilize and challenge the elite. The elite, on the other hand, can promise to make concessions to the masses but ultimately such promises are not credible. Thus, democratization is more likely if inequality is at moderate levels. Ansell and Samuels (2010) argue that median voters are poor and politically inert. More importantly, the rising elite fear expropriation by the incumbent governing elite and therefore the former group demands political power to prevent this from happening. Thus, democratization is more likely to emerge when the new elite owns an increasingly larger share of national income. For Haggard and Kaufman (2012), even though distributive conflict is an important source of regime change, democratic transitions can only occur when masses overcome barriers to collective action. Otherwise, regime change will only involve narrow intra-elite conflicts. Furthermore, collective action in terms of the mobilization of masses is facilitated in industrialized and urbanized setting.

The BN coalition that ruled Malaysia prior to its electoral defeat in May 2018 was clearly a dominant party. It had longevity in power (sixty-one years), was associated with the nation's independence, dominated the political scene and was unassailable to opposition parties.[4]

How has the end of dominant party rule been theorized and empirically researched? Greene (2007, 2010) argues that dominant parties lose power when their ability to politicize public resources decline. This can take place through privatization measures, which results in a decline in tax revenues. For Magaloni (2006), hegemonic party autocracies can be quite resilient to economic recessions. However, voter dissatisfaction can lead to elite/party splinters that challenge the governing regime. One such potential source or factor is economic deterioration. Voters and some members of the elite will defect when they believe economic deterioration to be systemic. The role of economic performance is also featured in the work of Reuter and Gandhi (2010) who argue that poor economic performance can lead to defection of party elites and mobilization of support to challenge the incumbent/dominant party.

To summarize, general economic conditions such as economic growth, inflation and unemployment do seem to matter in elections. The role of inequality is slightly more ambiguous and is tied to the presence of social conflict and mobilization. The impact of economic factors on elections may be due to structural changes, e.g., privatization. Economic performance may also affect elections through intra-elite defections and competition.

ECONOMIC CONDITIONS AND POLITICAL CHANGES LEADING UP TO GE-14

Economic Conditions

In 2018, BN's share of seats in the parliamentary elections dropped sharply to 35.6 per cent from 59.9 per cent in GE-13 (Figure 5.1). This sharp deterioration in the electoral performance of BN took place amidst relatively robust economic growth.

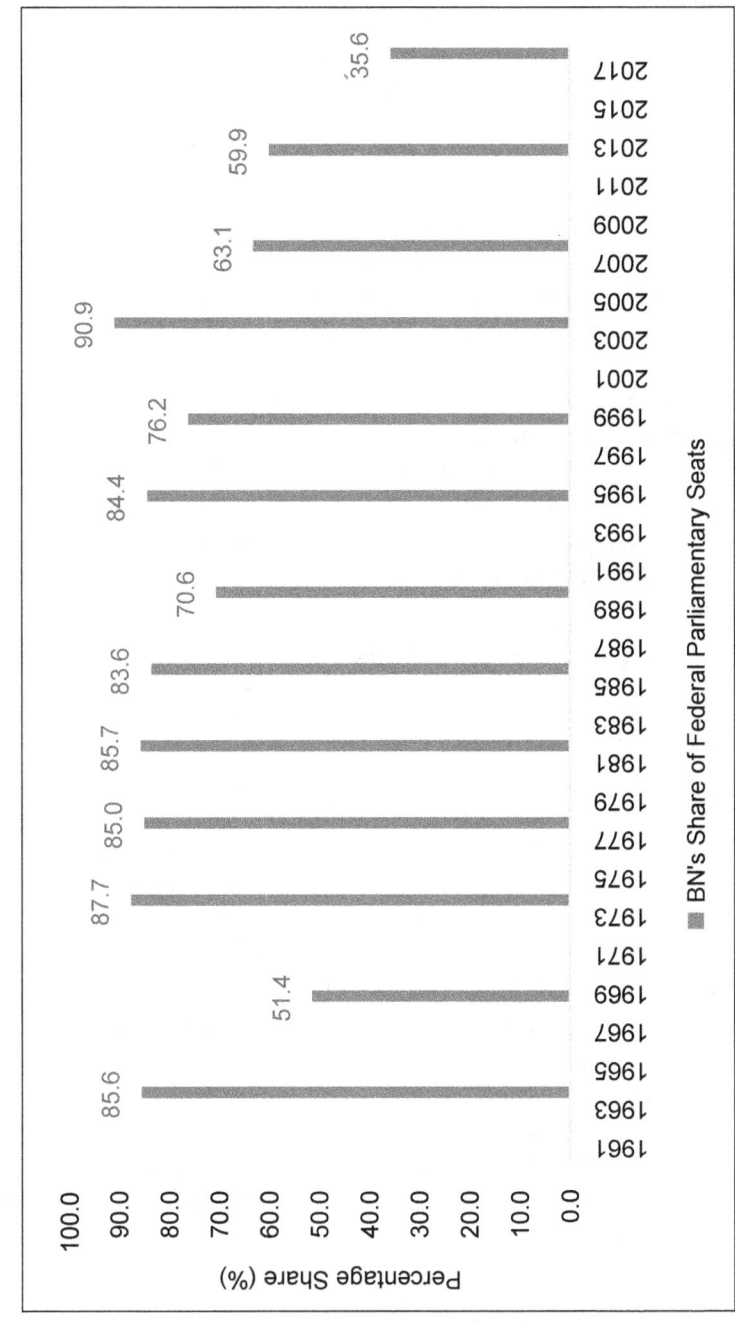

FIGURE 5.1
BN's Performance in General Elections, 1964–2018

In the four quarters prior to the election in May 2018, the quarterly growth rate for the country's national income (GDP) exceeded 5 per cent (Figure 5.2).

The rising cost of living was another issue highlighted during GE-14. This was linked to the implementation of the goods and services tax (GST) which took effect on 1 April 2015, some three years before the elections. Inflation did spike for nine months after the implementation of the GST but its effect is likely to have subsided thereafter (Figure 5.3). There was, however, a sharp increase in the inflation rate from the third quarter of 2016 to the first quarter of 2017. This rise in inflation coincided and is likely to have been caused by the ringgit depreciation (Figure 5.4). The rate of inflation declined thereafter for nine months but remained above 3.5 per cent until GE-14. Price increases are often irreversible, resulting in ratchet effects that might affect cost of living. Another indicator, the unemployment rate increased from 2.7 per cent in the third quarter of 2014 to 3.5 per cent in third quarter of 2016 (Figure 5.5). It remained at around 3.3 per cent until the first quarter of 2018. In comparing with historical data since 2009, the unemployment rate was relatively high in 2018.

To sum up, even though economic growth was relatively robust in the months prior to GE-14, both the inflation rate and unemployment rate do suggest a deterioration in economic conditions. The former, however, is likely to have been caused by a deterioration in the exchange rate rather than the imposition of GST. These economic factors could have adversely affected BN's performance in GE-14.

Politicization of Public Resources

One of the factors identified in the end of dominant party rule is the deterioration in a party's ability to politicize the use of public resources (Greene 2006, 2010). Has there been a decline in BN's ability to politicize public resources? The share of government expenditure as percentage of national income (GDP) has declined from a peak of 43 per cent in 1981 (when Mahathir first came to power) to 26 per cent in 2012 and 19 per cent in 2017 (Figure 5.6). This has been accompanied by a decline in government revenues. These trends suggest that the ruling coalition's access and ability to politicize public economic resources has declined in recent years. As a result, the BN-led government was likely to have resorted to alternative sources of funds that are off-budget including the 1 Malaysia Development Berhad (1MDB) investment fund. Media investigations indicate that funds originating from 1MDB were used by BN in the 13th General Elections (GE-13).[5] From the perspective of dominant party rule, 1MDB investments in the energy sector generated minimal spillover to the masses (voters). It also led to the creation of systemic economic problems in the form of high debt levels. These issues and allegations of corruption are likely to have reduced support for BN in GE-14.

Elite Defections and Voter Mobilization

Elite defections and voter mobilization are key factors in the literature on the end of single-party dominance. It is plausible to argue that these factors are relevant

FIGURE 5.2
Nominal GDP Growth, 2016–18

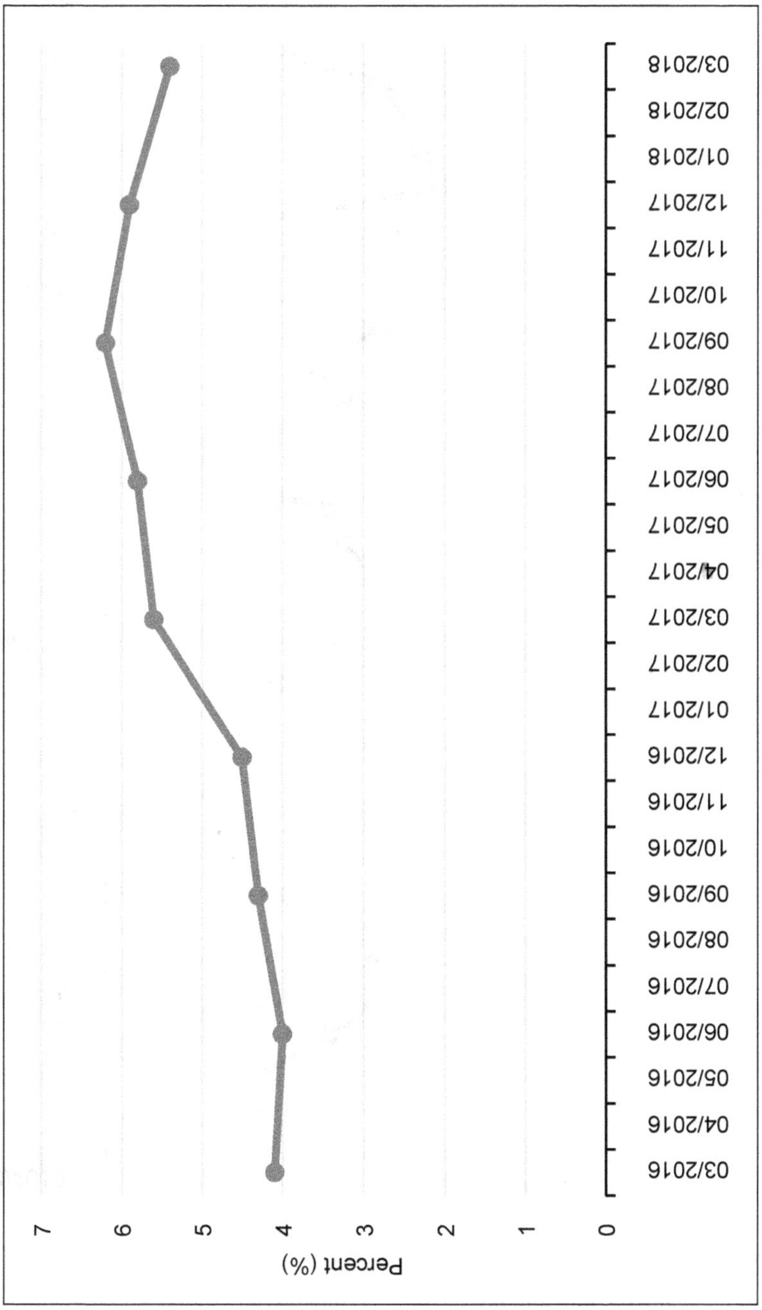

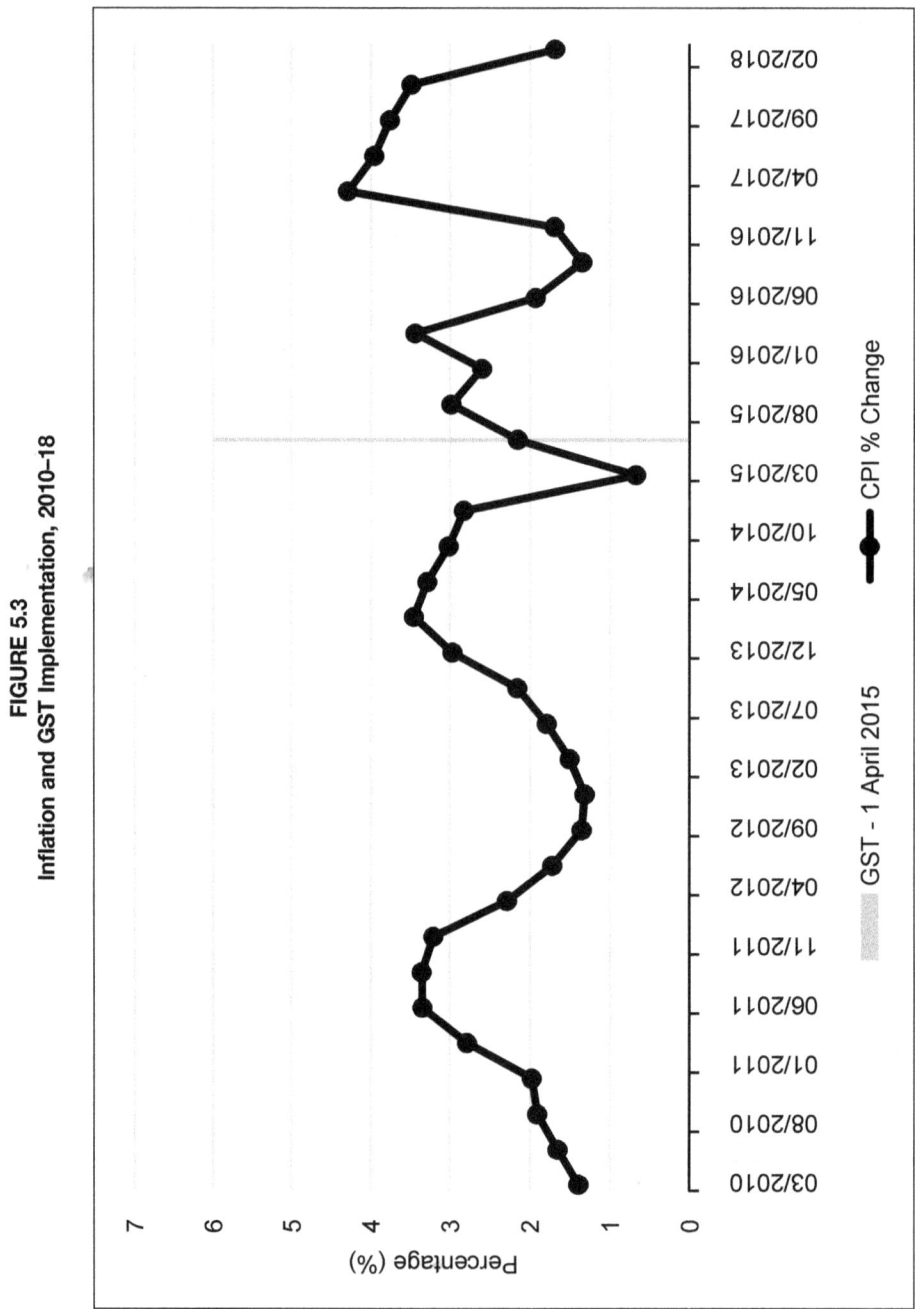

FIGURE 5.3
Inflation and GST Implementation, 2010–18

FIGURE 5.4
Inflation and Exchange Rate, 2010–18

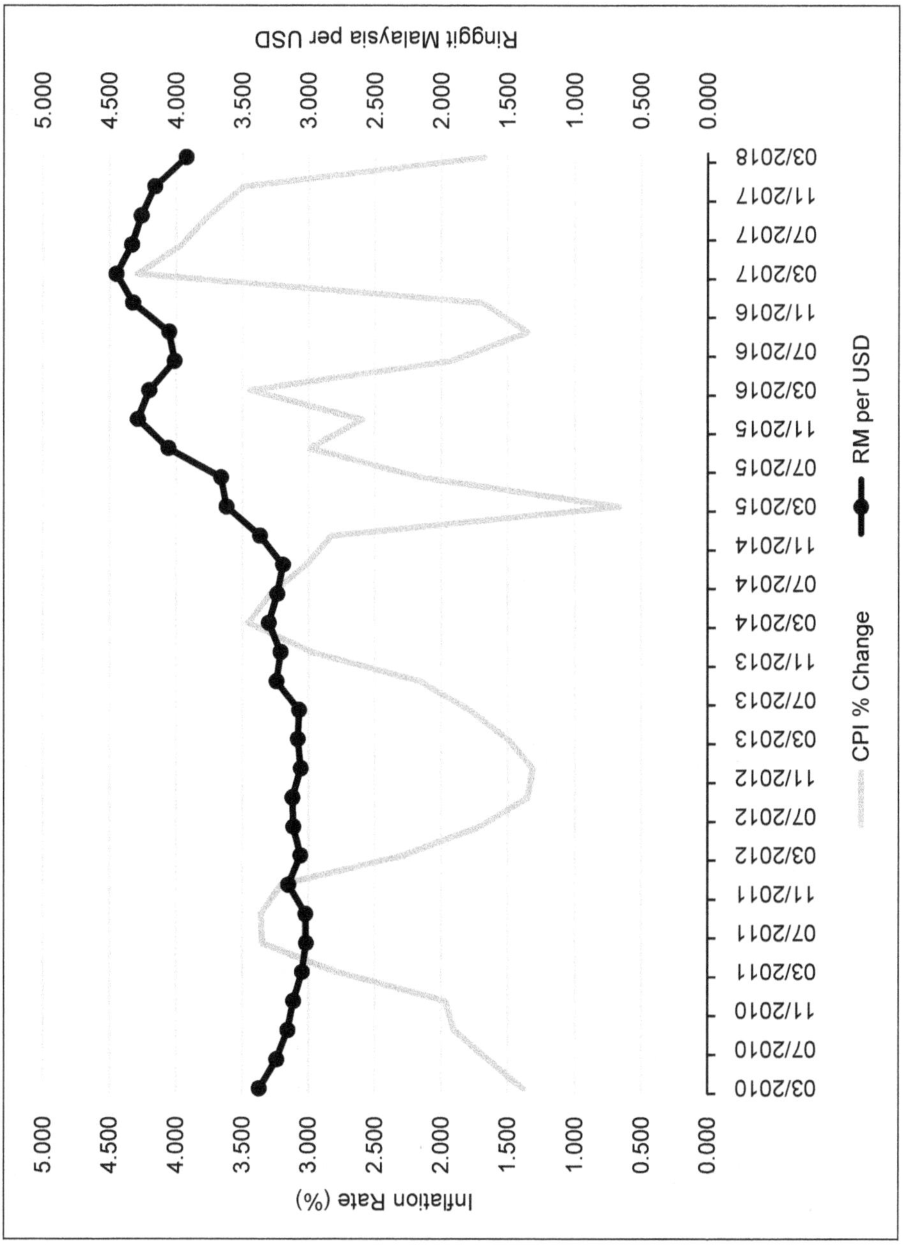

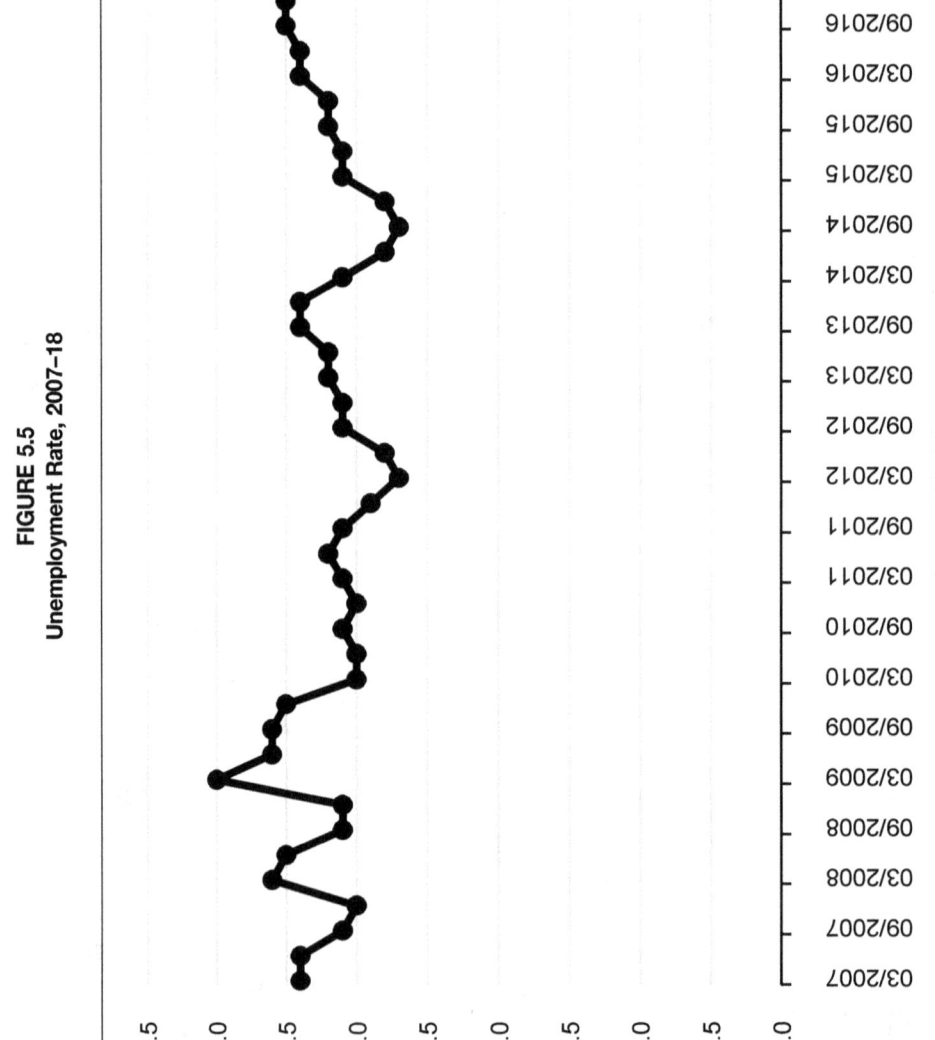

FIGURE 5.5
Unemployment Rate, 2007–18

FIGURE 5.6
Government Expenditure and Revenue, 1970–2016

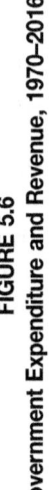

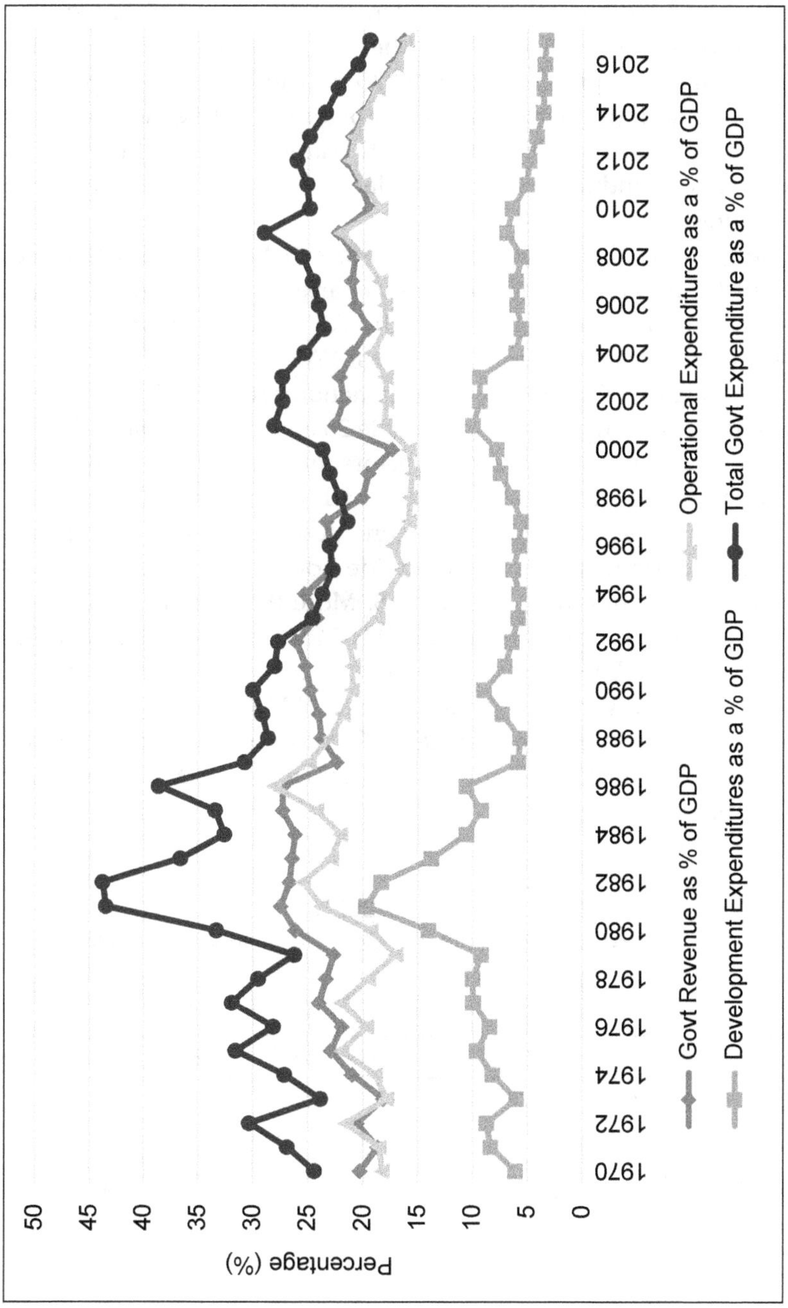

in the case of GE-14 (Figure 5.7). A key member of the PH coalition is the Parti Pribumi Bersatu Malaysia (PPBM) which was formed on 8 September 2016. It was primarily formed from elite and splinter members from UMNO. The party was led by Mahathir Mohamad, former president of UMNO and Malaysia's longest-serving prime minister from 1981 to 2003. Other key leaders of PPBM include Muhyiddin Yassin (former vice-president of UMNO and former deputy prime minister) and Mukhriz Mahathir (former Menteri Besar of the state of Kedah). Another party formed by an elite splinter from UMNO is Parti Warisan Sabah which was established on 17 October 2016 and led by Shafie Apdal, a former vice-president of UMNO and a former minister.[6]

Elite splinters also affected the opposition. After PAS became more conservative in the 1980s, moderate party leaders departed to form the Parti Amanah Rakyat (Amanah) on 16 September 2015. With PAS no longer part of the PH coalition in GE-14, Amanah leaders contested against PAS politicians in GE-14.

Examining the distribution of parliamentary seats in GE-14, the defector parties' share of PH seats amounted to a sizeable 25.6 per cent (Table 5.1). The BN coalition lost some nineteen seats to party defectors (or 14.3 per cent of BN's seats in GE-13).

In terms of voter mobilization, Mahathir Mohamad visited and campaigned in at least thirty-six parliamentary constituencies in the four months leading to GE-14. This culminated in a nationwide address by Mahathir on Facebook live on the eve of election day, 8 May 2018. More than 3.3 million people viewed the event on Facebook. Aside from Mahathir Mohamad and Muhyiddin Yassin, other elite former members of UMNO were actively involved in mobilizing voters (especially Malay voters) to vote against UMNO and BN during the campaign period of the elections. These included Rafidah Aziz (former Wanita UMNO chief and former minister) and Daim Zainuddin (former UMNO treasurer and former finance minister).

TABLE 5.1
Parliamentary Seats Won by Parties in GE-13 and GE-14

Seats Won in GE-14

		BN	PKR	DAP	PAS	PPBM	Amanah	Warisan	Other
Seats Won in GE-13	BN	78	21	4	5	12	3	7	3
	PKR	0	27	0	0	0	1	1	1
	DAP	0	0	38	0	0	0	0	0
	PAS	1	0	0	13	0	7	0	0
	PPBM	0	0	0	0	0	0	0	0
	Amanah	0	0	0	0	0	0	0	0
	Warisan	0	0	0	0	0	0	0	0
	Other	0	0	0	0	0	0	0	0

FIGURE 5.7
Elite Defections and Electoral Outcomes

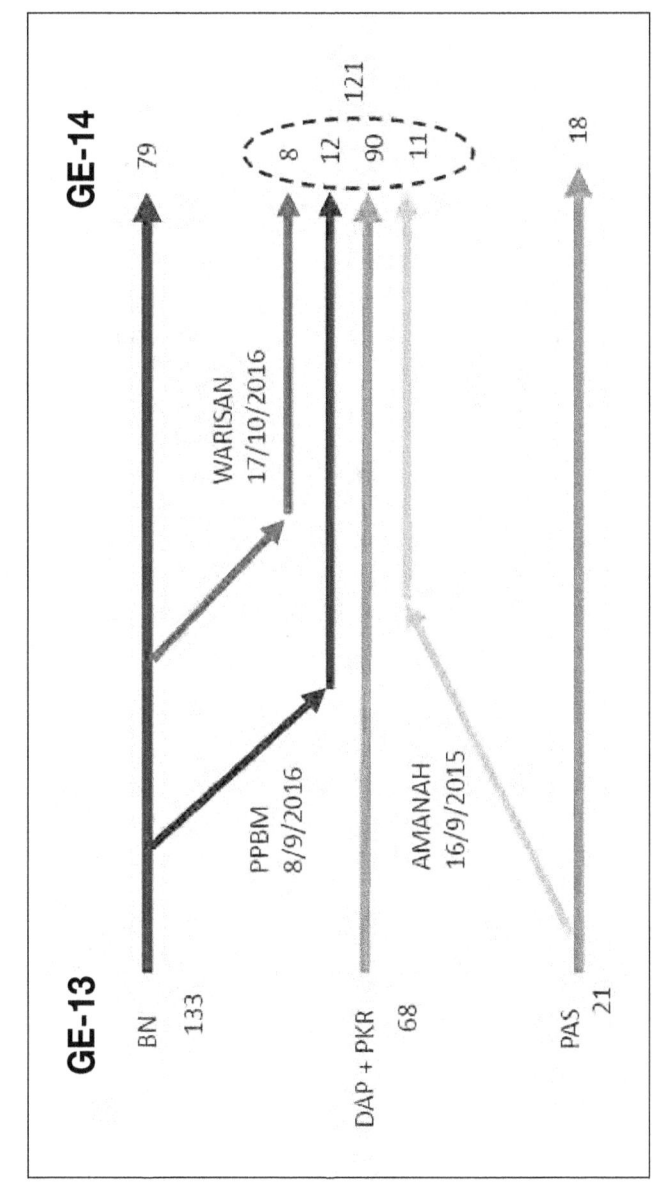

ECONOMETRIC ANALYSIS OF ECONOMIC VOTING MODEL

An econometric estimation of a voting equation can be used to quantitatively untangle the multitude of factors determining electoral outcomes. The selection of variables is drawn from the literature employing economic voting models.

The incumbent coalition BN's share of votes in a parliamentary constituency i located in state j and year t can be modelled as follows:

$$V_{it} = \alpha_1 + \alpha_2 GDP_{j,t-1} + \alpha_3 INF_{j,t-1} + \alpha_4 UNEMP_{j,t-1} + \alpha_5 GINI_{j,t-1} + \alpha_6 BUMI_{it} +$$
$$\alpha_7 EAST_{jt} + \alpha_8 VTURN_{it} + \alpha_9 INCUMBIND_{it} + \alpha_{10} INCUMBPTY_{it} +$$
$$\alpha_{11} DENSITY_{it} + \alpha_{12} MAHA_{it} + \varepsilon_{it}$$

where GDP is the growth rate of Real GDP per capita (lagged by one year, state), INF the inflation rate (lagged by one year, state), UNEMP the unemployment (lagged by one year, state), GINI the Gini coefficient (lagged by one year, constituency), BUMI the share of bumiputra voters (constituency), EAST a dummy variable for East Malaysia (Sabah and Sarawak), VTURN voter turnout, INCUMBIND individual incumbency, INCUMBPTY party incumbency, DENSITY population density, and MAHA a dummy variable representing Mahathir's visit to a constituency during the election campaign.

The above equation is estimated using the ordinary least squares method and data from two elections, namely GE-13 in 2013 and GE-14 in 2018.[7] There are 222 parliamentary constituencies in both elections. The results are summarized in Table 5.2. The economic data are based on state-level statistics from the Department of Statistics. Constituency-level data such as Gini coefficient, share of bumiputra population and population density are also sourced from the Department of Statistics. The constituency-level data are obtained by matching district with parliamentary constituency. Election results such as BN's voter share, voter turnout and incumbency are sourced from the Elections Commission. The variable for Mahathir's visits to parliamentary constituencies is constructed based on Facebook postings featuring campaign posters for these visits.

Overall, the model has a fairly good explanatory power. The estimation using the pooled data from GE-13 and GE-14 can explain close to 73 per cent of the outcome of the elections.[8] Comparing the estimations for GE-13 and GE-14, the results for economic voting are very different. Economic growth is positively correlated to the vote share of UMNO in GE-13 but the sign is reversed in GE-14. Inflation is statistically significant in the pooled data but insignificant in the both elections separately. Higher unemployment is negatively correlated with BN's vote share in GE-14 but is statistically insignificant in GE-13. Higher inequality, as measured by the Gini coefficient, is negatively correlated with BN's vote share in both GE-13 and GE-14.

For non-economic variables, ethnic voting is important in both elections as higher share of bumiputra voters is associated with higher BN's vote share. However, the smaller size of the coefficient in GE-14 compared to GE-13 suggests that bumiputra

TABLE 5.2
Determinants of BN's Vote Share in GE-13 and GE-14

	GE-13 & GE-14	GE-13	GE-14	GE-14 + MAHA	GE-14 + MAHA + PM
VARIABLES	BN Vote Share	BN Vote Share	BN Vote Share	BN Vote Share	BN Vote Share
GDP(–1)	0.0277	0.178***	–0.168**	–0.172**	0.117*
	(0.0233)	(0.0296)	(0.0672)	(0.0679)	(0.0701)
INF(–1)	–0.403***	0.0422	–0.266	–0.264	0.393*
	(0.0316)	(0.0715)	(0.213)	(0.214)	(0.205)
UNEMP(–1)	–0.187***	0.00773	–0.164**	–0.168**	0.0510
	(0.0357)	(0.0252)	(0.0650)	(0.0656)	(0.0667)
GINI	–0.370***	–0.373***	–0.425**	–0.430**	–0.563***
	(0.119)	(0.0908)	(0.178)	(0.179)	(0.181)
BUMI	0.181***	0.400***	0.128***	0.129***	0.399***
	(0.0185)	(0.0177)	(0.0246)	(0.0248)	(0.0384)
EAST	0.197***	0.436***	0.226***	0.225***	
	(0.0477)	(0.0745)	(0.0694)	(0.0695)	
VTURN	–1.585***	–0.674**	–1.198***	–1.197***	–2.296***
	(0.279)	(0.277)	(0.416)	(0.417)	(0.580)
INCUMBIND BN	0.0367	0.0385*	–0.0270	–0.0268	–0.0153
	(0.0375)	(0.0230)	(0.0681)	(0.0682)	(0.0765)
INCUMBPTY BN	0.166***	0.0902***	0.261***	0.258***	0.190**
	(0.0401)	(0.0265)	(0.0697)	(0.0701)	(0.0768)
INCUMBIND Non-BN	–0.0768**	0.0344	–0.191***	–0.189***	–0.120**
	(0.0351)	(0.0279)	(0.0490)	(0.0493)	(0.0466)
INCUMBPTY Non-BN	–0.198***	–0.144***	–0.205***	–0.207***	–0.155***
	(0.0362)	(0.0295)	(0.0501)	(0.0506)	(0.0478)
DENSITY	–4.14e-05***	–8.28e-06	–4.64e-05***	–4.59e-05***	–2.49e-05**
	(7.30e-06)	(5.55e-06)	(1.17e-05)	(1.18e-05)	(1.08e-05)
MAHA				–0.0200	–0.0248
				(0.0480)	(0.0411)
Constant	2.821***	1.427***	3.156***	3.160***	0.123
	(0.187)	(0.160)	(0.486)	(0.487)	(0.573)
Observations	410	189	221	221	165
R-squared	0.732	0.899	0.737	0.737	0.802

Notes: PM – Peninsular Malaysia; Standard errors in parentheses; *** $p < 0.01$, ** $p < 0.05$, * $p < 0.1$.

support for BN has declined. The state of Sabah and Sarawak were long considered to be BN's "safe deposits" for their track record of supporting BN in previous successions. This variable is statistically significant though the sizes of the coefficients suggest a decline in the support for BN in GE-14 compared to GE-13. The voting day for the GE-14 was set on a Wednesday (originally a working day) to dampen the negative effect of high voter turnout on support for BN. The sign and size of the coefficient for voter turnout variable does indicate that the strengthening of the negative correlation between voter turnout and support for BN in GE-14. Incumbency—both at the individual and party level—remained important in both GE-13 and GE-14 except for individual incumbency for BN politicians. Finally, a dummy variable was created to capture the effects of Mahathir's campaigning in GE-14. This variable is not statistically significant in the full sample.

A key feature of GE-14 was the prevalence of three-cornered fights for parliamentary seats involving BN, PH and PAS. About 71 per cent of the seats contested in GE-14 involved three-cornered fights. In the GE-13, most of the seats were contested by parties from the two coalitions, namely, BN and Pakatan Rakyat (PR was a precursor to PH). The Islamic party PAS was then part of the PR coalition. Due to the demographics of the parliamentary constituencies, specific component parties of PR are likely to have strategically chosen to compete with BN and PAS in GE-14. For example, the Democratic Action Party (DAP) and Parti Keadilan Rakyat (PKR) might be chosen to contest against BN and PAS in urban constituencies. For rural Malay constituencies, PPBM and Amanah are more likely to be effective competitor against UMNO and PAS. It is thus useful to re-examine the determinants of voter support for BN for each of these specific contestations. There are four possible configurations, namely:

- BN vs. PKR vs. PAS
- BN vs. DAP vs. PAS
- BN vs. PPBM vs. PAS
- BN vs. Amanah vs. PAS

What matters when different set of parties compete against each other? The estimates for the four types of three-cornered fights are summarized in Table 5.3. The economic variables were not statistically significant. In terms of incumbency effects, BN's party incumbency has the greatest positive effect when competing with PAS. PKR's incumbency is significant when competing with BN and PAS. PKR did not lose any seat it won in GE-13 to BN or PAS in GE-14. Mahathir's campaign visits only had a negative effect on BN when PKR was competing with BN and PAS. However, when Amanah was competing with BN and PAS, Mahathir's visit may have had a negative effect on voter support for Amanah. This could be explained by the lack of Mahathir's popularity amongst voters in PAS stronghold in Terengganu and Kelantan.[9] Finally, voter support for BN was not affected by any factors when DAP is a competitor. In GE-14, DAP did not lose any of the seats it won in GE-13.

Elite defection was a key feature of political change leading to GE-14. This issue is re-examined by analysing the election data on BN seats won by politicians from the two political parties associated with defectors from UMNO, namely PPBM. A Probit version of the economic model is estimated and the results are summarized in Table 5.4. The dependent variable is a binary variable with a numerical value of one for a BN win and zero otherwise. For seats where BN competed with PPBM, the probability of BN winning is negatively correlated with the mobilization of vote by elite defectors (the Mahathir variable). This clearly indicated that Mahathir played an important role in political contestations involving BN and BN defectors.

TABLE 5.3
Determinants of BN's Vote Share in Three-Cornered Fights in GE-14

VARIABLES	BN-PKR-PAS BN Vote Share	BN-DAP-PAS BN Vote Share	BN-PPBM-PAS BN Vote Share	BN-AMANAH-PAS BN Vote Share
GDP(–1)	–0.149	–0.331	0.131	–0.452
	(0.150)	(0.953)	(0.108)	(0.281)
INF(–1)	–0.506	–0.277	0.0998	0.214
	(0.530)	(1.715)	(0.332)	(0.614)
UNEMP(–1)	–0.111	0.191	0.0945	0.0684
	(0.134)	(0.950)	(0.107)	(0.261)
GINI	–0.630	–0.460	–0.314	–0.610
	(0.433)	(1.046)	(0.245)	(0.805)
BUMI	0.140	0.559	–0.0129	0.301
	(0.146)	(0.540)	(0.193)	(0.361)
EAST	0.194			0.484*
	(0.169)			(0.268)
VTURN	–0.163	–2.399	0.143	–0.181
	(1.526)	(4.728)	(1.010)	(1.269)
INCUMBIND BN	–0.0104	0.151	0.0284	0.0383
	(0.193)	(0.338)	(0.0922)	(0.233)
INCUMBPTY BN	0.241		0.197*	0.220
	(0.193)		(0.104)	(0.146)
INCUMBIND Non-BN	–0.0553	–0.0945	–0.0113	0.00153
	(0.0949)	(0.214)	(0.170)	(0.0977)
INCUMBPTY Non-BN	–0.264***	–0.213	0.0884	–0.111
	(0.0892)	(0.258)	(0.116)	(0.191)
DENSITY	2.14e-05	–6.24e-05	–4.30e-06	–0.000125*
	(2.19e-05)	(8.71e-05)	(2.25e-05)	(6.95e-05)
MAHATHIR	–0.147*	–0.155	–0.0167	0.307*
	(0.0849)	(0.314)	(0.0684)	(0.162)
Constant	3.302*	1.169	2.947*	1.857
	(1.638)	(4.143)	(1.466)	(2.511)
Observations	51	19	49	31
R-squared	0.692	0.804	0.479	0.815

Notes: Standard errors in parentheses. *** $p < 0.01$, ** $p < 0.05$, * $p < 0.1$.

CONCLUSIONS

The 14th General Elections in Malaysia was a watershed event. The election witnessed the defeat of the BN coalition which had ruled the country since its independence in 1957. A number of factors are likely to have driven the outcomes in the GE-14. Overall, the robust economic growth was not a positive factor in voter support for BN in the election. Unemployment and inequality (measured by Gini coefficient) are likely to have negative effects on voter support for BN. Contrary to the findings of media reports and surveys, inflation was not a significant determinant. It is possible that official CPI did not capture cost of living issues adequately.

TABLE 5.4
Probit Estimates of BN Win in GE-14

VARIABLES	BN-PKR-PAS Prob(BN Win)	BN-PPBM-PAS Prob(BN Win)
GDP(–1)	–1.453	–0.935
	(1.776)	(1.141)
INF(–1)	–10.80*	–2.756
	(6.147)	(3.098)
UNEMP(–1)	–5.720*	–1.566
	(3.232)	(1.162)
GINI	10.63	–4.544*
	(7.310)	(2.604)
BUMI	1.872	0.731
	(1.462)	(1.785)
VTURN	1.135	–6.880
	(11.24)	(8.497)
DENSITY	–0.00981	–0.000818
	(0.00610)	(0.000768)
MAHA	+	–1.820***
		(0.699)
Constant	27.43	–1.739
	(19.61)	(13.69)
Observations	40	49

Notes: + Omitted due to failure to predict; Standard errors in parentheses; *** $p < 0.01$, ** $p < 0.05$, * $p < 0.1$

In terms of non-economic factors, there was also a decline in voter support for BN in the bumiputra community and in East Malaysia. Another key feature of GE-14 was the defections amongst the political elite from UMNO leading up to the election. The formation and participation of former UMNO members in PPBM and Warisan helped strengthened the opposition coalition. There is quantitative evidence that Mahathir's political campaigning prior to GE-14 mobilized and consolidated voter support for PH.

Notes

1. The author thanks Francis Hutchinson, Lee Hwok Aun, Norshahril Saat and Pritish Bhattacharya for their comments and suggestions. The usual caveat applies.
2. "GE-14 Results: How It Went So Wrong for Pundits", *Malay Mail*, 29 June 2018.
3. BN effectively ruled Malaysia for sixty-for years from 1955 to 2018. In comparison, the Indian National Congress ruled India for thirty-two years (1946–77), the Liberal Democratic Party in Japan for thirty-nine years (1952–90), the Institutional Revolutionary Party in Mexico for seventy-one years (1929–2000) and the Kuomintang party in Taiwan for fifty-three years (1948–2000).
4. See De Jager and Du Toit (2013) for definitions of dominant party systems.
5. "WSJ: Najib Used 1MDB's funds for GE-13", *Malaysiakini*, 19 June 2015.

6. PPBM also drew some of its members, especially relatively junior leaders, from non-UMNO party members such as Maszlee Malik, Syed Saddiq Syed Abdul Rahman and Wan Saiful Wan Jan.
7. The OLS approach was used rather than panel estimation as this study is interested to compare the determinants of GE-13 and GE-14.
8. Alternative specifications were also experimented using interactive variables for BUMI and VTURN, and INCUMBIND and INCUMBPTY. The inclusion of these variables did not alter the results.
9. The author thanks Norshahril Saat for useful insights on this.

References

Acemoglu, Daron, and James A. Robinson. 2006. *Economic Origins of Dictatorship and Democracy.* Cambridge MA: MIT Press.

Ansell, Ben, and David Samuels. 2010. "Inequality and Democractization". *Comparative Political Studies* 43, no. 12: 1543–64.

Boix, Carles. 2003. *Democracy and Redistribution.* New York: Cambridge University Press.

De Jager, Nicola, and Pierre Du Toit, eds. 2013. *Friend or Foe? Dominant Party Systems in Southern Africa.* South Africa: UCT Press.

Fair, Ray. 1996. "Econometrics and Presidential Elections". *Journal of Economic Perspectives* 10, no. 3: 89–102.

Greene, Kenneth F. 2007. *Why Dominant Parties Lose: Mexico's Democratization in Comparative Perspective.* New York: Cambridge University Press.

———. 2010. "The Political Economy of Authoritarian Single-Party Dominance". *Comparative Political Studies* 43, no. 7: 807–34.

Haggard, Stephan, and Robert R. Kaufman. 2012. "Inequality and Regime Change". *American Political Science Review* 106, no. 3: 495–516.

Lewis-Beck, Michael S., and Mary Stegmaier. 2000. "Economic Determinants of Electoral Outcomes". *Annual Review of Political Science* 2: 183–219.

Magaloni, Beatriz. 2006. *Voting for Autocracy: Hegemonic Party Survival and Its Demise in Mexico.* New York: Cambridge University Press.

Reuter, Ora John, and Jennifer Gandhi. 2010. "Economic Performance and Elite Defection from Hegemonic Parties". *British Journal of Political Science* 41: 83–110.

6

MONEY, MALFEASANCE, AND A MALAYSIAN ELECTION

Meredith L. Weiss[1]

INTRODUCTION

Voting based on personal economic progress or standing is common anywhere. However, the considerations that enter into such calculations vary, complicating assessment. In Malaysia, complex phenomena glossed as "money politics" are especially germane to the extent and nature of "economic voting": the links between business and political parties, the partisan use of "slush funds" from oil and other resource wealth, and the preponderance of patronage appeals in elections.

However, their electoral implications are obdurately opaque, especially at the hazy intersection of illicit and beneficent behaviour. That murkiness makes it difficult to predict, too, how the recent change of government will affect patterns of money politics, though some predictions are plausible. On the most obvious level, up until now, we have been able to track the proximity of elections through increasingly bloated government budgets full of enticements for key constituencies. This has taken the form of public resources' being used to make the incumbent Barisan Nasional (BN, or National Front) popular and beloved, but in a manner that is sufficiently public and wealth-sharing to be legal and basically acceptable.

There is no reason to expect the new Pakatan Harapan (PH) government to shirk such politically useful budgeting—and its state-level budgets have followed similar templates. However, some of the more problematic dimensions of money politics are likely to diminish, now that the BN lacks access to resources and PH so significantly differentiates itself in terms of being "clean" and accountable. In other words, given similarities in welfare programmes and commitment to racially defined preferential policies, the question in 2018 was less of who had better policies than who could be trusted, given concerns with financial probity and seemingly out-of-touch ruling-party elites.

But troubling dimensions of money politics, developed over decades of BN governance, have broad reach. They extend not only to the confluence of massive corruption scandals such as that revolving around the 1Malaysia Development Berhad (1MDB) sovereign wealth fund, but also to the ways in which government programmes are turned to partisan advantage, as (or appearing to be) conditional patronage. Indeed, the explanation used to justify the transfer of large payments to former Prime Minister Najib Razak's accounts in connection with the 1MDB scandal is that those funds were for elections. (We lack reliable data on how much credence voters gave to Najib's claim that these funds were for the common good rather than for his personal benefit, particularly before media-sensationalized post-election revelations of the precise extent of Najib and wife Rosmah Mansor's wealth accumulation.) Not only, then, were members of the prime minister's party and coalition complicit as the recipients of campaign resources, but the public itself could see a benefit, through campaign-period spending and promises.

But do these pay-outs, whether in the course of the campaign or, for instance, through cash transfer schemes such as Bantuan Rakyat 1Malaysia (BR1M, or 1Malaysia People's Aid), matter? Beyond the relative pull of material lures, if the public purse loses more overall through mismanagement and graft, or if the flows are in both directions, given new taxes, does ire at those losses outweigh gratitude for handouts? (The goods and services tax (GST) BN introduced in 2015 turned a previously mostly exempt mass of voters into taxpayers.)

And at what point does clear malfeasance—in this case, increasingly undeniable evidence of Najib's corruption and the plausible framing of 1MDB as straight-out theft—independently counter positive economic effects? This chapter probes these issues through the lens of the 14th General Elections (GE-14), drawing primarily on survey data, media accounts, interviews, and secondary literature. The twin goals are to determine how much of an electoral issue either 1MDB or BR1M payments (and related scandals or distributions) are among the Malaysian public and to assess the reasons for those relative emphases. Is corruption accepted, for instance, if some of its proceeds are parcelled out among voters? Will voters forgive the slow seepage of a new tax in light of stepped-up, lump-sum cash transfers or patronage rewards? And inasmuch as concern with corruption affects voting patterns, is it the party or an individual who gets tarred? Can we see a distinction between the effects for voting behaviour between long-term, iterated clientelism versus one-off payments?

Malaysia's GE-14 campaign saw the usual barrage of inducements to vote along economic lines. Both coalitions' manifestos offered measures to address rising costs of living, both offered infrastructure development and targeted welfare policies, both sweetened the deal with on-the-spot grants, and both had been cultivating support long-term through various forms of grassroots, individualized support. And yet material considerations—as opposed to culturally pitched identity-based claims, religious promises, or other bases for voting—took on especial salience this time, making GE-14 an ideal opportunity to test the extent and character of "economic voting" in Malaysia, which may not look quite like its counterparts elsewhere. To explore these issues, we begin by examining what "economic voting" entails generally, the better to situate the patterns we find in Malaysia. The chapter then turns to the nature of promises made and policies pursued, and the electoral impact of these patterns for both the BN and PH. Three perspectives offer insight into these dimensions: the relative balance of macroeconomic or programmatic versus particularistic promises; the influence of retail-level vote-buying and similar campaign-period gifts, as well as post-polls scrambling to pay off potential party-jumpers; and the framing of corruption as an economic rather than a moral or governance issue.

ECONOMIC VOTING DEFINED

The concept of economic voting is neither new nor country-specific, though the literature first really took root in the United States in the 1970s (e.g., Tufte 1978; Monroe 1979). The basic premise is that voters prioritize economic progress above all, and particularly their *own* prosperity rather than the country's as a whole. They reward incumbents under whose governance they have done well—the classic question in US surveys is whether the respondent's economic position is better or worse than it was X years ago—and punish those during whose tenure their position has declined. Of course, even where economic voting is prevalent, not all citizens will vote accordingly; many rank other priorities higher. In practice, however still salient, economic voting is inconsistent, given the weight of other considerations.

There is no reason to assume that Malaysians are fundamentally different from voters elsewhere in their propensity for economic voting. Indeed, surveys consistently show economic concerns to be far and away the issues Malaysians deem most important in elections; these concerns almost always rank first among a clear majority of Malaysians.[2] It is hardly surprising, then, that parties perennially court votes by counting on an economic logic. Just as economic voting yields a push/pull logic elsewhere, in which politicians do what they can to step up short-term prosperity with elections looming, we might expect the same for Malaysia. Yet analysts have given relatively little concerted attention to economic voting per se.[3]

Parties' efforts are both retrospective, calling attention to their infrastructural and other achievements thus far, and prospective, promising goodies to be had if they win. The BN had a challenging economic case to make among voters in 2018. Introduction of a 6 per cent GST since the last election,[4] plus removal of fuel subsidies and rising costs for higher education (in a polity with a preponderance of comparatively young voters), housing, road tolls, and other daily expenses had meant most Malaysians were now paying into the system *and* receiving reduced benefits from it.

Prior to that point, the income of only one in eleven working adults was taxed (Narayanan 2014, p. 1). That the GST might carry political costs hence could not have been a surprise. Promise of a GST, for instance, after previous false starts, was the leading issue in Australia's 1998 election and arguably not just cost the Liberal Party votes, but also may have shunted defectors to the far-right One Nation Party (McAllister and Bean 2000, pp. 377–91, 395–96; Lau, Tam, and Heng-Contaxis 2013, p. 19).

However popular among tax experts and useful economically, such taxes may carry regressive effects, especially if not accompanied by targeted exemptions and strengthened social safety nets; may have contractionary effects if inflation kicks in (estimated as likely if the GST rate reached 7 per cent in Malaysia); and change requirements for business reporting. The Malaysian government first mooted the GST in 1989 to reduce deficits swollen by government spending, stabilize the oil and gas–dependent budget (alongside fuel subsidy cuts), and broaden the limited tax base. However, for both political and implementation-readiness reasons, the government delayed its initial roll-out, planned for 2007. The proposal then appeared in the BN's 2014 federal budget—safely beyond the 2013 general election. The plan initially was for a 4 per cent tax rate, to be implemented within two years.[5] Even at 6 per cent by 2018, Malaysia's GST remained the lowest in the region, and far lower than rates in Europe (Lau, Tam, and Heng-Contaxis 2013, pp. 2–6, 9, 13–14, 18, 21–22; Narayanan 2014).

Meanwhile, the benefits of perceived pro-business policies and "trickle-down economics"—the notion that fiscal policies to favour the wealthy ultimately benefit the poor when businesses increase jobs, wages, and other contributions—were unconvincing. Survey data as of late 2017 suggested a pervasive sense of economic hardship and precarity, notwithstanding macroeconomic growth. Despite a slight improvement since the start of the year, as 2017 neared its end, almost two-thirds still said they felt stressed thinking about the future, 40 per cent had experienced difficulty in paying their bills, and 29 per cent lacked at least RM500 in emergency savings.[6]

Overall, a daunting share of Malaysians indicated in surveys in the run-up to GE-14 that they felt the economy was moving in the "wrong direction": less than one month out, 47 per cent characterized economic concerns as their top such item; only 10 per cent deemed the economy, at least in terms of macroeconomic conditions, to be heading in the right direction. Those displeased with the state of the economy cited the high cost of living above all, followed by overall unfavourable economic conditions, notwithstanding generally positive national indicators.[7] Asked at the time to identify the two issues most important to them, a majority across all ethnic categories except Chinese (but still 49 per cent even among them) said inflation; next across racial categories was either job opportunities or corruption, then housing.[8]

Parsing these data differently as the campaign began, the Merdeka Center for Opinion Research found the same top three most important issues (economic concerns, corruption, housing) nationally and in each state they surveyed.[9] Particularly since evidence from elsewhere suggests citizens may demand greater accountability when government revenues come heavily from taxes rather than non-tax sources (e.g.,

Prichard 2009), the fact of the new GST may have increased voters' expectations, compared with past years. And indeed, rising public debt as well as financial irregularities and extravagance lent analysts and the public little confidence that the BN government would spend revenues prudently (Narayanan 2014, p. 11).

Yet, diagnoses of solutions to economic decline are tempered in Malaysia by communal politics, such that after decades of BN policies that specifically favour bumiputra (Malay and other indigenous) voters, it was not clear whether economic dissatisfaction would spur voting for change or for the status quo. Merdeka Center surveys for 2017 found that a plurality of over one-third of ethnic Malays prioritize Malay rights, versus only 13.1 per cent who prioritize economic performance (generating economic growth and development, creating jobs, and raising incomes). But the factor with the highest value in that "Malay rights" cluster (after the front-runner of maintaining Malay control of politics and government) is helping Malays compete effectively in the economic arena.[10] In other words, concern over Malay rights is inseparable from issues of economic anxiety, given the structure of the Malaysian economy. Currently, though, we lack detailed information on how Malays, other bumiputra (who likewise benefit from preferential policies), and others in Malaysia parse these perspectives. In the future, more targeted surveys, with greater attention to question-phrasing and response-coding, as well as electoral exit polls, may help us to disaggregate motivations for voting behaviour with a level of confidence not currently possible.

Responses from non-Malay respondents, too, revealed at least limited ethnic patterns in specific economic preferences. As of 2017, 23.1 per cent of ethnic Chinese Malaysian voters emphasized economic performance, a significantly larger share than among Malays, with the largest concern being creating jobs and boosting incomes. However, they ranked a cluster of issues comprising governance and service delivery even higher (39.9 per cent).[11] The pattern among Indian voters was comparable: 25.1 per cent prioritized economic performance and 41.5 per cent, governance and service delivery.[12] By February 2018, with elections approaching, those percentages had hardly changed, although Indian voters' concern for governance and service delivery had declined after new BN measures to address Indian socioeconomic concerns.[13] In short, for all three communities, despite the usual reading of economics as paramount, disentangling perspectives differently reveals that a cluster of governance and service delivery issues outranks the economic performance cluster. Moreover, for Malays, a Malay rights cluster dominates, but those indicators include ones specific to economic well-being.[14]

Interestingly, while the main thrust of PH's economic promises—the "populist" measures that have given observers pause[15]—seem tailored towards the lower end of the economic spectrum, Merdeka Center's final survey during the GE-14 campaign found dramatically higher dissatisfaction with the "direction of the country" as income increased. A majority (51 per cent) of only the poorest of voters deemed the country to be going in the right direction, possibly indicating support for welfare policies (appreciated even if inadequate), and household economics (inflation, jobs, income, and so forth) remained by far the leading single most important issue overall.[16]

This priority was nearly stable across age categories, but was significantly higher among Malays than Chinese (with Indians in between) and highest of all among women (50 per cent, versus 37 per cent for men).[17] That difference suggests a rationale behind PH's campaign efforts to emphasize rising costs of living among women and proposals such as pensions for housewives, and to break down the costs of corruption in terms of personal financial burdens (e.g., the GST) for Malay crowds, to encourage economic angst to turn them away from the BN. If that messaging was indeed the strategy, it seems to have worked; the share of Malay voters prioritizing economic improvement increased after nomination day, though less substantially than "having a clean government" decreased and "having credible leadership"—presumably a veiled indicator for the "Mahathir factor"—soared. (That defending the position of Malays and Islam likewise declined surely reflects the fact of there being at least one self-defined bumiputra-communal party in each coalition.[18])

It seems clear that we can conclude that there was at least some extent of economic voting in Malaysia in GE-14. But given mixed priorities and signals, to determine how that pattern plays out requires deeper exploration.

PROGRAMMES OR PARTICULARISM?

The two coalitions' published platforms are similar enough in their welfare plans and related provisions that it would be difficult for the average voter to say with certainty which would benefit her more (see Table 6.1). That similarity no doubt helps to account for the extent to which probity, rather than policies per se, mattered to voters' decisions, beyond simple ire over BN (or Najib's) predation. Both coalitions could count on both retrospective and prospective voting—with the caveat that voters might find clear assessments of progress to date challenging.

The BN's manifesto, launched just over a month before polling day, promised benefits for all manner of constituents. Included among its pledges were creation of 3 million new jobs; sustained infrastructure and social assistance spending; and benefits for women, youths, specific states, and groups such as bumiputra Federal Land Development Authority (FELDA) settlers. Introducing the manifesto, Najib also announced increased and more widely distributed BR1M payments for 2018.[19] The BR1M component was especially noteworthy, not just for its transparent expense, but as a concrete manifestation of the extent to which the BN turned state spending to partisan advantage.

BR1M, an unconditional cash transfer scheme launched in 2012, anchored a set of ideological and instrumental "1Malaysia" programmes,[20] promoting a sort of nation-building through shared economic mission or progress. A headline-grabbing 2017 study found the "1Malaysia" label, or simply the notion of being "Malaysian", promoted an inclusive nationalist vision only among non-Malays; among Malays, it tended instead to reinforce in-group ethnic identity (Al Ramiah, Hewstone, Wölfer 2017, p. 60). Regardless, the share of households or individuals receiving even just BR1M subsidies has expanded yearly; benefit levels also increased regularly until 2017. By now, most Malaysians have received BR1M payments at least once, with at least some benefits (especially for education) reaching even those in the wealthiest decile. Successive studies suggest most voters saw the BN government as sincere in

TABLE 6.1
Partial Comparison of Barisan Nasional and Pakatan Harapan Manifestos

	Barisan Nasional	Pakatan Harapan
New jobs	3 million (1.3 million via development of the Malaysian Vision Valley, plus reduced reliance on foreign labour); graduate apprenticeship programme and training schemes to increase employability; GLC funds for 10,000 social entrepreneurship jobs	1 million (through reduction from 6 million to 4 million foreign workers); retraining for unemployed; 1 million jobs with minimum RM2,500 per month salary
Minimum wage	RM1,500 per month within 5 years	RM1,500 per month within 5 years, then reviewed every 2 years; government to pay 50 per cent of increase
Housing	Special bank for loans for housing priced below RM300,000; tax incentives to encourage rent-to-own schemes; public housing assistance for poor or disabled renters; ending bumiputra discounts for property valued above RM1 million; low-cost housing for retired public servants (including 10,000 units for police); 10,000 affordable housing units for armed forces and 45,000 units military family housing; housing maintenance and revival of abandoned/failed projects	1 million affordable houses within 2 years; expanded rent-to-own scheme; incentives to develop affordable housing; take over low-cost housing maintenance
Internet and media	Reduce broadband costs by 50 per cent and double speed	Improve broadband speed/ access and cut cost by half; free broadcasts of major sports leagues (including English Premier League)
Social welfare	Make BR1M conditional on behaviour (e.g., skills training, children's immunization); extended insurance coverage, healthcare benefits, and cost-of-living allowance for GLC/GLIC employees earning below RM2,500 per month; electricity subsidies for over 1 million consumers	Social-security programme for poor; maintain BR1M (distributed through non-partisan agencies); RM4 billion over 10 years for Indian community's socioeconomic development; RM150 per month for seniors
Women	Easier access to loans; tax incentives when return to job market; flexible hours and accommodations for child/ family care	Housewives' pension: RM50 per month government contribution + 2 per cent of husbands' Employee Provident Fund payments; 90 days' maternity leave and subsidized/coordinated childcare services; microcredit for female entrepreneurs

continued on next page

TABLE 6.1 — *cont'd*

	Barisan Nasional	*Pakatan Harapan*
Students and education	RM1,500 for children of BR1M recipients who enrol in higher education; RM12 million rural education programme (benefitting 615,000); RM1,000 matching grant for education savings scheme; student discount cards for education, government services, and supplies; funds to upgrade religious schools	Free public education from pre-school to tertiary levels; RM300 per year per student for non-national schools (e.g., religious, "national-type" Chinese, Tamil, private); deferred student loan payments for graduates earning less than RM4,000 per month; incentives to employers to repay student loans
Healthcare	Doubling tax exemption for parents' medical expenses to RM10,000	RM500 per year for primary care in private clinics for low-income families
Taxes	Revise individual and corporate taxes for competitiveness; tax exemptions for rental income; tax incentives to employ people with disabilities	Eliminate GST; raise floor for 26 per cent tax rate from income exceeding RM250,000 to RM400,000; tax deductions for seniors who return to work
Veterans	1,800 housing units for veterans; home-repair assistance for 1,800 veterans; microfinance scheme for veteran entrepreneurs; RM600/year for veterans over 60 without pensions or BR1M	RM2,000 per year to non-pensionable veterans; government contribution to Armed Forces Fund Board increased; RM500 million for veterans' entrepreneurship fund
Public transportation	Public-transport pass for RM50–150 per month for students, working youths, seniors, disabled; improved train-tracks and buses; over RM2 billion to upgrade/build airports; Kuala Lumpur–Singapore high-speed rail and East Coast Rail Line; expansion of Klang Valley LRT/MRT	10,000 more public buses; initiate high-speed rail development; monthly RM100 transport pass in cities
Private transportation	Subsidies for rural youths applying for motorcycle licences	Lower excise taxes for imported cars; eliminate highway tolls; targeted petrol subsidies; cancel motor vehicle licence renewal fees; urban bicycle routes
Small businesses	Support for Chinese entrepreneurs, food trucks, small and medium enterprises	Microcredit and other schemes for Indian small traders
Agriculture	Price supports, cost reductions, and subsidies for smallholders, farmers, and fishermen; building/upgrading plantation, paddy-area, and FELDA roads; upgrading rural drainage, sewerage, and irrigation; RM250 million to install/maintain rural streetlights	Grants, subsidies, and improved prices for farmers; limits on rice imports

FELDA	RM5,000 to each settler; replanting grant up to RM7,500 per hectare; write off settlers' debt from purchase of FGV shares; RM300 million fund to write off other extraordinary debts	Improved administration; subsistence allowance of up to RM2,000 per month during replanting; faster payment for produce; expedited settlement (and 50 per cent disposal) of existing debts; scholarship/training schemes
East Malaysia	RM2 billion for telecommunications; RM2.3 billion for electrification; upgrading 12,500 km rural roads; equalization of prices nationwide; build RM4.3 billion Trans-Sabah Gas Pipeline	Increase petroleum royalty to 20 per cent; infrastructure development, including Pan-Borneo Highway; Borneoization of public sector; improvements to education, healthcare, employment; protection of customary land
Arts	RM3 million every 5 years for Art Practitioners Welfare Fund; RM1,000 per year tax incentive for contributing to arts development; RM5 million for heritage bodies; RM10 million for cultural groups and creative industries	To be developed via youth empowerment
Youth	RM3 million for parenting workshops	RM500 marriage incentive for first marriage (under age 35); RM1 billion per year annually for young entrepreneurs

Source: Barisan Nasional (2018); Pakatan Harapan (2018).

addressing their well-being, supported distribution of subsidies (particularly BR1M, among federal welfare programmes), and found the approach at least reasonably effective.[21] Nevertheless, given the GST and rising costs of living, the programme seems to have made little impact in reducing inequality, even if overall progressive (Gil Sander 2014, pp. 74–75, 84–85).

Less than six months before announcing its campaign manifesto, in late October 2017, the BN government had released its federal "election budget", likewise chock-full of goodies. The budget, which Najib introduced in Parliament as "happy news that will put a smile on everyone's faces", decreased taxes and increased social assistance, taking advantage of economic growth to fund a spending increase of 7.5 per cent over 2017 levels.[22] Included were benefits and bonuses for 1.6 million civil servants; profit-sharing and other benefits for employees of government-linked corporations (GLCs); better childcare facilities, maternity leave, and other provisions to support women; reduced income tax rates for 2.3 million middle-income taxpayers; increased allowances for groups such as FELDA settlers, senior citizens, the disabled, and caretakers; billions of ringgit in subsidies and other aid for farmers, fishers, rubber-tappers, and oil-palm workers; additional spending on, for instance, healthcare, housing, Orang Asli villages, small and medium enterprises, scholarships and student loans, and hospitals; and construction of a range of new airports, special economic zones, roads, sports complexes, schools, and other infrastructure.

Earlier in the year, Najib had announced additional benefits, from cash incentives for FELDA families to free television decoders for BR1M recipients.[23] The BN proffered further promises still during the campaign, including Najib's election eve proclamation of a tax holiday for anyone aged twenty-six and under and of plans to allow affordable housing residents to purchase their flats.[24] Subnational manifestos added yet more perks—for instance, removal of tolls for motorcycles on the Penang Bridge for that state,[25] sponsored mass weddings, free commuter buses, and housing-related measures for the Federal Territories.[26] The budget, too, left ample openings for projects to be announced just in time for the campaign. Shortly before the campaign kicked off, caretaker Transport Minister Liow Tiong Lai, for example, promised his constituency a service-providing, job-generating Urban Transformation Centre if the BN won.[27]

Pakatan Harapan offered many of the same sorts of benefits. Like the BN, PH pledged to increase the availability and quality of affordable housing; to expand access to funding for students, entrepreneurs and small businesses; to improve public transportation and healthcare access; to increase the minimum wage; and to introduce a range of agricultural supports. Yet it also promised a fairer taxation system; taking on monopolies (for instance, for rice and satellite television); a pension scheme for housewives; and, especially, a concerted focus on eradicating corruption and investigating past scandals, including in 1MDB, FELDA, the Tabung Haji pilgrimage fund, and bumiputra support agency Majlis Amanah Rakyat (MARA, or Council for the People's Trust). PH promised to rectify those and other government agencies' and GLCs' management, and to improve transparency and governance. It set an ambitious (and ultimately, unsurprisingly, unworkable) agenda of ten promises for its first hundred days in office, prioritizing key economic and other goals, such as eliminating the GST, introducing petrol and healthcare subsidies, and forgiving or deferring FELDA settlers' and low-income students' loans.[28] Both the Democratic Action Party (DAP) and Parti Keadilan Rakyat (PKR), too, had been pursuing small-scale infrastructure initiatives such as micro-hydro and micro-solar projects in East Malaysia, plus promoted new projects in the states they controlled closer to campaign time. However, they had far less capacity to offer projects than did the BN.

Not to be outdone, the Gagasan Sejahtera (literally, Idea of Prosperity) coalition—dominated by Parti Islam seMalaysia (PAS, or Pan-Malaysian Islamic Party)—echoed these themes and proposals. Their manifesto, too, offered such pledges as replacing the GST with corporate and capital gains taxes, eliminating student loans, subsidizing first-time car purchases, and restructuring road tolls. Like PH, Gagasan also stressed themes of anti-corruption and public trust, but with a strong emphasis on redressing inequality and increased costs of living.[29]

But the chief contest at the federal level remained between the BN and PH. Both coalitions promised to promote bumiputra specifically in economic policy, although within PH, only Mahathir's Parti Pribumi Bersatu Malaysia (PPBM, or Malaysian United Indigenous Party) has a communal basis. Yet needing votes from across communities, both sides also emphasized the benefits they offered non-Malay, non-Muslim communities. Women represented another specific target. Not only did PH offer social welfare policies and launched a *"Bangkit dan Ubah"* (Arise and Change) campaign to mobilize female voters, but in his final-night rally address, broadcast nationally from Langkawi, Mahathir emphasized equalizing pay and opportunities for women. Meanwhile, the BN peppered the highways with billboards stressing its respect for and programmes targeting women. All told, a female voter might have been hard-pressed to conclude which coalition would give greater attention to improving her lot. Both coalitions, too, proffered more goodies for post-election delivery, to woo specific local communities.

However, each coalition took on more defining than usual key aspects of macroeconomic policy. PH, for instance, stressed aggressively its plan to repeal the GST (more likely to matter across the board than income taxes that only some pay) and to restore the less widely applicable sales and services tax; closer scrutiny of the large-scale foreign investment essential to capital-intensive growth and the megaprojects that punctuate the Malaysian landscape; and the downward pressure on wages, plus competition for jobs, from excessive importation of foreign workers. PH also went further than the BN in promising enhanced income-sharing with states, particularly Sabah and Sarawak—although the BN doubled down with assurances of massive investment in electrification, telecommunications, water supply, and other infrastructure there.

The question remained whether PH's promises, being less par-for-the-course on their part (and including provisions inimical to generating government revenue) were feasible,[30] as well as of whether key groups, particularly bumiputra, stood to gain or lose from a change of government. Here the inclusion of Mahathir Mohamad as opposition standard-bearer lent PH credibility: the developmentalist visionary of the 1980s–90s, as well as the author of the 1970 book, *The Malay Dilemma*, that most clearly inspired the New Economic Policy's affirmative-action strategy launched that same year, Mahathir validated PH's plans, reinforced messages of BN corrupt economic mismanagement, and reassured beneficiaries of preferential policies that they would not lose out by rejecting the BN. Furthermore, Mahathir's own record of megaprojects in decades past surely undercut what political capital Najib and the BN could derive from their more recent glamour projects, such as Kuala Lumpur's swank new MRT line or towering, incomplete Tun Razak Exchange. In short, then, while both the BN and PH banked on economic voting, they did so in strikingly similar ways, likely limiting the clarity with which household economics and personal financial prospects could actually influence votes. In the process, they left open the chance for governance and corruption, as higher order economic concerns, to matter.

BUYING AND SELLING VOTES AND SEATS

Compared with neighbouring Indonesia or the Philippines (Aspinall and Sukmajati 2016; Hicken, Aspinall, and Weiss forthcoming), individual-level (also termed "retail") vote-buying is relatively rare in Malaysia and far less dominant a strategy than elsewhere. Rather, what critics lambaste as vote-buying in Malaysia tends to be the sorts of politically pitched government programmes described above. For instance, Najib defended his February 2018 announcement of over RM6 billion in aforementioned extra BR1M payments, reaching 7 million voters, as an aid scheme proposed by Bank Negara (Malaysia's central bank), intended to regularize welfare assistance and curb the slippage and regressive aspects that come with subsidizing goods. The timing of the payments—in three tranches, before and after the deadline for calling elections—drew derisive dismissals as *dedak* (chicken feed).[31] By that point, the BN had already distributed over RM2.5 billion in payments since July 2017, to millions of recipients, including the poor, rural workers, civil servants, religious teachers, and village heads. The BN's strategy mimicked its playbook in the year leading up to the 2013 election: its incentives then totalled an estimated nearly RM2,000 per person, with additional bonuses paid after the polls.[32] In late February 2018, BERSIH activist Ambiga Sreenivasan complained, "money is being promised all over".[33] Lax campaign finance laws, together with availability of funds from GLCs and other state-linked enterprises, party-specific assets, usually untallied donations from businesses and supporters, and increased oil, natural gas, and palm oil earnings meant the BN would have plenty to spend—and PH was also in a better financial position this time than previously, given its state-level authority and increasingly open backers.

Yet these welfare strategies blur the line between patronage and programmatic policies—and as with the coalitions' manifestos, that both coalitions offer cognate schemes makes the pull of either less certain. PH's state-level governments offered their own BR1M-like programmes (for instance, Selangor's Merakyatkan Ekonomi Selangor, rebranded in 2017 as Initiatif Peduli Rakyat). Supplementing these programmes were additional payments, such as to households affected by devastating floods in Penang in 2017. What is key may be the mode of delivery, as with a social media firestorm in response to photos of a BN Cabinet minister distributing cash at parent–teacher association meetings. These federal schooling assistance funds were intended to be channelled to schools to distribute to parents; that a politician handed them out directly made the payments "akin to bribes" rather than legitimate welfare.[34] A 2014 study suggests state government programmes to have been slightly better received than the federal BR1M initiative in Selangor, though respondents looked favourably on both (Muhammad Shamshinor et al. 2014).

Regardless, more traditional vote-buying does also happen. Corruption-watchdog C4 noted in mid-April "numerous reports on vote buying by both sides of the political divide"; they included in that category the increased BR1M payments, but also more dubious "discounted groceries, promises of free gym membership, free tablets, bonuses and other goodies".[35] The risk consulting firm Kroll predicted that Malaysia could expect "significant 'vote-buying' exercises where exposed companies may be instructed to donate to UMNO-related causes".[36]

Such practices appear to have been fairly localized, but did step up, reportedly especially in Sabah, where newcomer Parti Warisan Sabah (Warisan, or Sabah Heritage Party) took on its progenitor UMNO. Field researchers there documented numerous incidents of cash payments or attempts to buy votes, starting prior to the official campaign period, then accelerating. While the researchers faulted BN operatives most frequently, they also cited numerous such efforts by Warisan workers.[37]

Within a month of the election, referring particularly to Sabah, new PM Mahathir declared that he would void the result and call for new polls where candidates were alleged to have bought votes.[38] Warisan filed challenges to the results in eight seats, partly over procedural issues, but "mostly money politics"; Keadilan challenged a ninth, alleging "rampant vote buying", backed up by thirty police reports from both recipients and distributors, with sums ranging from RM50 to RM1,000.[39] Warisan president Shafie Apdal claims his party, in contrast, "only had money to pay for our transport", presumably referencing the transportation subsidies many parties offer voters to come to the polls.[40] Other states were not immune. Months later, the High Court nullified a Malaysian Indian Congress win in Pahang's Cameron Highlands, on grounds of BN payments to Orang Asli leaders for their electoral support.[41]

Meanwhile, stories of malfeasance peppered the campaign. Particularly well-documented and unrepentant was UMNO division head Jamal Md. Yunos, who distributed RM50 to each participant in a pro-BN campaign rally; he claimed later that all were campaign workers and the funds, wages. Yet the previous day, too, Jamal had joined another BN campaign event, this time with a free meal, entertainment, and lucky draw with prizes of a motorcycle or RM25,000. After a DAP member filed a police report for vote-buying when Jamal promised local fishers RM2,000 each as an "incentive" he would personally redeem if the BN won, Jamal confidently announced a third pre-election event, at which he would present a Mercedes as lucky draw grand prize. He justified these distributions as coming from "sponsors" rather than the party itself.[42]

Then again, a Selangor aid distribution event after the state government had already been dissolved also raised eyebrows: caretaker PH Menteri Besar (Chief Minister) Azmin Ali distributed cheques to students, community groups, and the poor, as well as laptops and tablets. He denied the aid was anything more than a "caring administration's" normal weekly handouts—and his office later clarified that the recipients had applied for this assistance before the legislature had been dissolved, as well as for other grants the caretaker government distributed. Yet Azmin still reminded the crowd, "don't forget to vote".[43]

Immediately after the election came a second phase of (pricier) "vote-buying", centred now around wooing crossovers among legislators, to reconstitute or solidify majorities. Several states sought to resolve hung parliaments. In Sabah, in particular, rumours flew that millions of ringgit were on offer for Warisan state legislators to jump to the BN and perhaps vice-versa. That six BN state representatives jumped ship within days of the election gave the PH–Warisan pact enough seats to control the government. On the one hand, party stalwarts and non-party activists alike worried both about the implications for PH's premise and commitment of an influx of BN members, including elected politicians, into a supposedly reformist coalition. They worried, too, about violating public trust by a post-hoc reversal of the voters' choice of party.[44] On the other hand, such defections could, and did, tip the scales towards PH. Although Mahathir affirmed that the federal government would investigate reports of "people being paid to cross over", the example he gave was of a drop in Warisan's seat total after Election Commission recounts—not alleged party-hopping.[45]

FRAMING CORRUPTION

Beyond introduction of the GST, which changed the economic voters' cost-benefit calculus, a key change in 2018 vis-à-vis previous polls was the unusual salience of questions of rent-seeking and corruption. Concern was sufficiently severe and widespread that observers expected a decline in BN votes (regardless of how those losses translated into seats); unlike in 2013, when the BN still did lose the popular vote, Najib himself no longer held substantial pull. That said, at least some share of voters seem to have been willing until fairly late in the campaign to overlook whatever grouses they had. The much-remarked late swing among voters was surely thanks at least in part to clever PH framing over the course of the campaign.

Surveys in the lead-up to the election fed expectations that scandals, especially the 1Malaysia Development Berhad (1MDB) debacle, would hardly figure in these polls, at least in terms of changing minds on the BN side. (Those voters more firmly in the opposition camp *were* sure to care, but were simply likely to maintain the dissatisfaction with BN they had registered in 2013.) 1MDB is Malaysia's—and among the world's—largest corruption sagas to date. Launched in 2009 to advance national economic development through investments in energy, real estate, and other sectors, 1MDB was in crisis and bogged down by debts by 2015, not least due to apparent political intervention in its business decisions and siphoning-off of funds. Revelations first surfaced that year of around US$700 million had been deposited into Najib's accounts, allegedly from 1MDB. Najib eventually claimed, dubiously, that the funds were from a Saudi donor, to help UMNO win the 2013 elections. Indeed, the *Wall Street Journal* and other investigations noted a "massive patronage machine" for GE-13, entailing hundreds of millions of dollars distributed for schools, hospitals, donations, *umrah* (pilgrimages to Mecca) for village heads, and other grants, with funds channelled through 1MDB's corporate social responsibility arm, Ihsan Perdana Berhad, to UMNO politicians. Although such dispensations may be legal and serve to spread wealth, they ramp up "money politics", being allocated per political rather than economic criteria—and they left 1MDB itself struggling.[46] By the time of GE-14, investigations had largely ceased in Malaysia, but were ongoing elsewhere; US Attorney General Jeff Sessions had, in fact, just reiterated his department's anti-kleptocracy investigation into 1MDB.

PH candidates worked assiduously to make 1MDB meaningful and legible by putting it in terms of household economics, rather than just abstract norms of governance or morality: how much predation cost the average voter. A March 2015 survey found that fully 39 per cent of respondents claimed *no* awareness of 1MDB, with another 30 per cent minimally aware; only 29 per cent knew at least "quite a lot". Awareness increased with income, Internet access, and (less dramatically) youth, and was lowest (by a significant margin) among Malays.[47] In fact, a clean, corruption-free government *was* among the issues voters weighted most heavily, though Malay survey respondents ranked it merely fifth among thirteen priorities identified.[48] Yet few Malaysians saw a personal connection to 1MDB: just under one-third thought they were at least somewhat affected as of March 2015, and just over half were unsure who they should hold responsible. Only 34 per cent faulted the prime minister or federal government.[49]

PH highlighted corruption far more than the BN, not surprisingly. This effort—and the fact of the scandals in question—likely helped the coalition make headway as its message permeated, for example, in FELDA areas (where it promised to investigate malfeasance in the FELDA Global Ventures privatization initiative). But the real challenge was to render 1MDB legible; such "arcane financial skulduggery" of bond issues, government-guarantee letters, and offshore accounts makes for a less clearly compelling narrative than had Najib looted public coffers directly.[50] PH incumbent member of parliament Khalid Samad, for instance, put the 1MDB scandal into real world terms, explaining in a *ceramah* (campaign speech) that expending just RM1 billion, a fraction of the total involved, is equivalent to spending RM5,000 per day for 547 years. Campaign rhetoric from party leaders and ordinary candidates urged voters—using easily grasped terms like *pencuri* (thief) and *penyangak* (rogue)—to assume that without 1MDB losses, the government would not have needed the GST. That connection made Najib's administration culpable for households' *personal* losses, by way of culpability for 1MDB.

The BN essayed to turn the tables. In mid-2017, the government launched a Royal Commission of Inquiry into losses Bank Negara Malaysia sustained in the early 1990s, naming Mahathir, Anwar, former Bank Negara advisor Nor Mohamed Yakcop, and former finance minister Daim Zainuddin as potentially culpable for criminal breach of trust. As critics noted, the inquiry was into actions from decades past, opened only after Mahathir had formed a new political party, and stood in contrast to the BN's obdurate resistance to investigating current scandals.[51] Moreover, the effort served more to imply that no one's hands were clean than to absolve current BN leaders of wrongdoing (and may have reminded voters inclined towards cynicism that UMNO as a whole had a history of under-investigated shady dealings). That implication may perhaps have helped to offset any moral appeal against corruption, but could do little to mitigate PH efforts to quantify household-level effects of present-day rent-seeking.

GE-14 results notwithstanding, the extent to which opposition to corruption sways votes vis-à-vis other issues remains unclear. The individual impact of any one scandal, especially one so convoluted and elusive as 1MDB, may be limited: fault is hard to assign, all the more so since the fact that some who benefited from 1MDB funds while in UMNO had since jumped to PH. Moreover, Najib's claims that he spent these funds, however obtained, for the people's benefit—and the fact that BR1M, other 1Malaysia programmes, and the long litany of projects pursued *is* readily read as distribution of the spoils—might temper Malaysians' negative assessments. Regardless, 1MDB and cognate, also-severe issues of fiscal probity and accountability form part of a policy and ideological package that, coupled with more general concern for economic retooling, surely helped PH make headway not possible previously. Hence, PH's electoral boost from highlighting corruption likely stemmed both from ideological concern with governance and the coalition's having spun these issues as increasing the average voter's economic burden.

CONCLUSIONS

This survey of one election cannot hope to offer any grand conclusions on economic voting generally in Malaysia: the extent to which it matters, and how, will depend in elections to come on the mix of appeals on offer, the specific differences across platforms, and overall economic conditions. But this election does undercut arguments for Malaysian exceptionalism when it comes to voting. If we understand communal alignments, for instance, as being at least substantially driven by economic interests, and voters' flocking to a charismatic leader as not merely a manifestation of neofeudal loyalty, but also as evincing aspirations to return to a developmentalist model from which, at least in retrospect, they feel they benefited more, then Malaysians might be behaving much like anyone else. (That said, the context of pro-bumiputra preferential policies, which both sides pledged to uphold, arguably *is* exceptional as a force shaping *how* voters assess economic self-interest.)

If this pattern continues, it could mean we come to see Malaysian voters more in terms of class alignments—albeit acknowledging the extent to which class and ethnicity overlap and "ethno-class" fractions (Brown 1994, Ch. 6) feature, given intraethnic and intraclass differentiation. Still important, though, in the context of long-term dominant-party rule, is a tipping-point effect. When is it that voters sense that enough of a critical mass is leaning towards change that they are willing to take the risk of losing out on post-election local-area or community goods, via legitimate programmes or more questionable patronage, to be on what they sense will be the winning (other) side—and when do previously unconverted voters tip towards discounting the level of risk involved in the first place, as they grant competing lures credence? A mix of inclinations and calculations surely mattered to the outcome of GE-14, but may also limit the new government's ability to break new ground in economic policy and election platforms. The similarity of platforms and PH's now quasi-communal aspect have left voters expecting *not* to have voted in a new economic—just partisan-political—regime.

Notes

1. My thanks to Lee Hwok Aun and Francis E. Hutchinson for their astute feedback and suggestions. What analytical or empirical flaws remain are my own.
2. Merdeka Center, "Malaysia General Elections XIV Outlook: Prospects and Outcome", 26 April 2018, slide 7.
3. An important exception is Francis Loh's (2003) positing of a developmentalist politics, perhaps coming to supplant a communal orientation.
4. The BN appears to have sought to distract attention from the GST bill by allowing PAS to push forward with a bill to expand penalties under shariah at around the time of its passage. The BN must have known the bill would destabilize Pakatan Rakyat and turn at least some share of Malay attention from economic angst to Islamist aspirations.
5. The GST replaced a narrower sales and services tax, which officials argued would limit the extent of resultant price increases (Narayanan 2014, pp. 2–3).
6. Merdeka Center, "National Public Opinion Survey on Economic Hardship Indicators", 4–14 November 2017, slide 5.

7. Merdeka Center, "Malaysia General Elections XIV Outlook", slide 6.

8. Ibid., slide 8. Perceptions of corruption had been persistently high. As of late 2014, 49 per cent of respondents in Peninsular Malaysia thought corruption had increased in the past year; at that point, 40 per cent deemed corruption "very serious", down a mere 1 per cent from June 2012, and 56 per cent thought the government ineffective in fighting it. Merdeka Center, "Perception Towards Corruption 2014: Peninsular Malaysia Voter Survey", 26 November–5 December 2014, slides 4, 6, 8.

9. The sample covered six states plus Kuala Lumpur; in Johor, scores for corruption and housing were tied. Merdeka Center, "Malaysia General Elections XIV Outlook: Prospects and Outcome II", 2 May 2018, slide 9.

10. Faisal Hazis, "Multicorner Electoral Contest and Voting Factors: Implications and Potential Outcomes", unpublished presentation, 7 October 2017, slide 5; Merdeka Center, "Malaysia General Elections XIV Outlook: Prospects and Outcome II", 2 May 2018, slide 14.

11. Faisal Hazis, "Multicorner Electoral Contest and Voting Factors", slide 6.

12. Ibid., slide 7.

13. Merdeka Center, "Malaysia General Elections XIV Outlook: Prospects and Outcome II", slides 13–16.

14. Faisal Hazis, "Multicorner Electoral Contest and Voting Factors", slide 8.

15. For instance, long-time activist Kua Kia Soong bemoaned the PH manifesto's "cavalier populist policies" such as free water and cheaper cars ("What's Lacking in Pakatan Harapan's Manifesto", *FMT*, 10 March 2018, http://www.malaysia-today.net/2018/03/10/whats-lacking-in-pakatan-harapans-manifesto/), and the activist/intellectual network, The Agora Society, lamented the manifesto's inclusion of "populist, welfarist, reformist and racialist elements" ("The Racialization of Pakatan Harapan", *Malaysiakini*, 18 March 2018, https://www.malaysiakini.com/news/416157). BN proposals drew the same label. Bridget Welsh, for instance, described the "so many promises in the manifestos of all the different parties—all highly populist in nature" ("GE-14: Show Me the Money", *Malaysiakini*, 7 May 2018, https://www.malaysiakini.com/columns/423560).

16. Merdeka Center, "Malaysia General Elections XIV Outlook: Prospects and Outcome III", 8 May 2018, slides 6–7.

17. Ibid., slide 8.

18. Ibid., slides 9–10.

19. "Najib Announces BN Manifesto and More BR1M Goodies", *The Sun*, 8 April 2018, https://www.thesundaily.my/archive/najib-announces-bn-manifesto-and-more-br1m-goodies-FUARCH538518.

20. Kedai Rakyat 1Malaysia, or KR1M shops; Skim Latihan 1Malaysia, or SL1M vocational training programmes, etc., see http://www.1malaysia.com.my for the full array. Offshoots include such programmes as Jelajah Pendidikan Bumiputera, for "exploring education": extending outreach for and access to vocational colleges and other higher education, targeting rural and poor Malays, including through UMNO politician-organized convoys. See https://www.jelajahpendidikan.my.

21. For instance, Rohana, Othman, and Denan (2013), Muhammad Shamshinor et al. (2014); Kajidata Research, "Kajian Tentang Persepsi Rakyat Terhadap Bantuan Rakyat 1 Malaysia (BR1M)", 20–27 February 2017, http://kajidata.com/resources/2017/03/REPORT-BR1M-2017-BM-brief.pdf (accessed 25 July 2018).

22. "Malaysia Presents Populist Budget Targeting Voters Ahead of Polls", *Today*, 27 October 2017, https://www.todayonline.com/world/malaysias-najib-unveils-expansionary-budget-polls-loom.

23. "No Telling What Will Happen at the Polls", *The Edge Malaysia*, 19 June 2017, p. S2.

24. Wangsa Maju, Kuala Lumpur; 1 May 2018.

25. Opalyn Mok, "Want Free Toll Across Penang Bridge? Vote for BN in GE-14, Najib Tells Bikers", *Malay Mail*, 12 April 2018, https://www.malaymail.com/s/1619237/want-free-toll-across-penang-bridge-vote-for-bn-in-GE-14-najib-tells-bikers.

26. Kow Gah Chie, "BN Pledges to Sponsor Mass Weddings in FT Manifesto", *Malaysiakini*, 22 April 2018, https://www.malaysiakini.com/news/421049.

27. "Bentong to Have UTC if Mandate Returned to BN, Pledges Liow", *Malaysiakini*, 15 April 2018, https://www.malaysiakini.com/news/419970.

28. "An Overview of Harapan's Manifesto", *Malaysiakini*, 8 March 2018, https://www.malaysiakini.com/news/414982; Adam Aziz, "Pakatan Harapan Manifesto Aims at Key Voter Groups", *The Edge*, 9 March 2018, http://www.theedgemarkets.com/article/pakatan-harapan-manifesto-aims-key-voter-groups.

29. Leong Meng Yee and Royce Tan, "Gagasan Announces Its Manifesto", *The Star*, 18 March 2018, https://www.thestar.com.my/news/nation/2018/03/18/gagasan-announces-its-manifesto/.

30. Hafiz Noor Shams, "Funding an Opposition's Manifesto Is All About Politics", *New Mandala*, 23 March 2018, http://www.newmandala.org/pakatan-harapan-manifesto/.

31. "Cash Handout for People's Welfare, Not to Buy Votes: Malaysian PM Najib", *Straits Times*, 26 February 2018, https://www.straitstimes.com/asia/se-asia/cash-handout-for-peoples-welfare-not-to-buy-votes-malaysian-pm. The phrase "*makan* (eat) *dedak*", or being bought off by patronage, has recently gained prominence in the Malaysian political lexicon, with Mahathir's take-downs of Najib and his followers. The phrase lends itself well to punnery, as by noting losses to 1MDB as "not chicken feed", PAS' Hadi Awang's warning of UMNO chickens' coming home to roost, and UMNO's Tengku Razaleigh Hamzah stooping to clarify, "I am not a duck". Reme Ahmad, "No Chicken Feed, as Mahathir and Najib Duel over 1MDB's Money", *Straits Times*, 27 July 2016, https://www.straitstimes.com/asia/se-asia/no-chicken-feed-as-mahathir-and-najib-duel-over-1mdbs-money.

32. Trinna Leong, "Cash Handouts Spike as Malaysian Election Nears", *Straits Times*, 28 February 2018, https://www.straitstimes.com/asia/se-asia/cash-handouts-spike-as-malaysian-election-nears.

33. Quoted in ibid.

34. Ibid.

35. "C4 Urges MACC to Act Against Vote Buying", *FMT*, 16 April 2018, http://www.freemalaysiatoday.com/category/nation/2018/04/16/c4-urges-macc-to-act-against-vote-buying/.

36. "Najib Expected to Retain Power Through Massive Vote-Buying: Kroll", *The Independent*, 16 February 2018, http://theindependent.sg/86592-2/.

37. Unpublished Merdeka Center field research data.

38. Viswary Palansamy, "Vote Buying to Be Stopped, Says Dr M", *Malay Mail*, 6 June 2018, https://www.malaymail.com/s/1639025/vote-buying-to-be-stopped-dr-m-says.

39. "Warisan Files Election Petitions to Challenge GE-14 Results", *Perjuangan Rakyat*, 19 June 2018, http://rakyatsproject.org/news/423.

40. Durie Rainer Fong, "Warisan Lawyers Get Leave to Challenge Results", *FMT*, 17 June 2018, http://www.freemalaysiatoday.com/category/nation/2018/06/17/warisan-lawyers-get-mandate-to-challenge-GE-14-results/. Minister in the Prime Minister's Department Paul Low had previously declared transport payments legal, saying these

allowances should not be deemed bribes, since they did not obligate the recipient to vote a certain way; the Malaysian Anti-Corruption Commission disagreed. Sharon Tan, "Travel Allowances for Voters Are Not Bribery", *Malaysian Insight*, 2 September 2017, https://www.themalaysianinsight.com/s/13232.

41. Ho Kit Yen, "Court Nullifies MIC's Election Win in Cameron Highlands", *Free Malaysia Today*, 30 November 2018, https://www.freemalaysiatoday.com/category/nation/2018/11/30/court-nullifies-mics-election-win-in-cameron-highlands/.

42. "Jamal Promises Sekinchan Fisherfolk RM2k Cash for Votes", *Malaysiakini*, 1 May 2018, https://www.malaysiakini.com/news/422429; Wong Kai Hui, "Jamal Rallies Troops, Hands RM50 to 'Workers'", *Malaysiakini*, 2 May 2018, https://www.malaysiakini.com/news/422664; Wong Kai Hui, "Jamal Undeterred by Police Report, to Give out Merc in Next Do", *Malaysiakini*, 2 May 2018, https://www.malaysiakini.com/news/422745. Soon after GE-14, Jamal faced prosecution for actions in connection with his role as leader of the Malay-rights "red shirts" movement.

43. Grace Aisyah Kedayan, "Cash, Laptops, iPads: Azmin Doles out Over RM2mil Worth of Goodies", *Malaysiakini*, 14 April 2018, https://www.malaysiakini.com/news/419876; "S'gor MB's Office: Handouts Not Ad Hoc GE-14 Goodies", *Malaysiakini*, 16 April 2018, https://www.malaysiakini.com/news/420033.

44. "Party-Hopping Betrays Voters, Bersih Warns", *FMT*, 12 May 2018, http://www.freemalaysiatoday.com/category/nation/2018/05/12/party-hopping-betrays-voters-bersih-warns/.

45. "Govt Will Investigate If Party Crossovers After Malaysia GE Involved Corruption: Mahathir", *Straits Times*, 11 May 2018, https://www.straitstimes.com/asia/se-asia/we-will-investigate-if-party-crossovers-involve-corruption-mahathir.

46. Tom Wright and Bradley Hope, "1MDB and the Money Network of Malaysian Politics", *Wall Street Journal*, 28 December 2015.

47. Merdeka Center, "Perception Towards 1Malaysia Development Berhad Controversy", 12–27 March 2015, slides 4–5.

48. Faisal Hazis, "Multicorner Electoral Contest and Voting Factors", 7 October 2017, slide 5.

49. Merdeka Center, "Perception Towards 1Malaysia Development Berhad Controversy", slides 10, 12.

50. Thanks to Lee Hwok Aun for the turn of phrase—and for noting the comparison with Shahrizat Abdul Jalil and the preceding National Feedlot Centre scandal (a.k.a. "Cowgate"): once Shahrizat's family's misappropriation of funds came to light in 2012, the Cabinet minister was obliged to step down (though the saga did not end her political career). See "Malaysian Minister in 'Cowgate' Scandal to Resign", *BBC*, 12 March 2012, https://www.bbc.com/news/world-asia-17335984.

51. Among others, Wan Saiful Wan Jan, "Bank Negara RCI Raises Questions", *FMT*, 25 September 2017, http://www.freemalaysiatoday.com/category/opinion/2017/09/25/bank-negara-rci-raises-questions/.

References

Al Ramiah, Ananthi, Miles Hewstone, and Ralf Wölfer. 2017. "Attitudes and Ethnoreligious Integration: Meeting the Challenge and Maximizing the Promise of Multicultural Malaysia". Report to the Board of Trustees, CIMB Foundation, Kuala Lumpur.

Aspinall, Edward, and Mada Sukmajati, eds. 2016. *Electoral Dynamics in Indonesia: Money Politics, Patronage and Clientelism at the Grassroots*. Singapore: NUS Press.

Barisan Nasional. 2018. *Bersama BN Hebatkan Negaraku*. Kuala Lumpur: Ibu Pejabat Barisan Nasional.

Brown, David. 1994. *The State and Ethnic Politics in Southeast Asia*. London: Routledge.

Gil Sander, Frederico, et al. 2014. *Malaysia Economic Monitor: Towards a Middle-Class Society*. Bangkok: World Bank.

Hicken, Allen, Edward Aspinall, and Meredith Weiss, eds. Forthcoming. *Electoral Dynamics in the Philippines: Money Politics, Patronage and Clientelism at the Grassroots*. Singapore: NUS Press.

Lau Zheng Zhou, Jarren Tam, and Jordan Heng-Contaxis. 2013. "The Introduction of Goods and Services Tax in Malaysia: A Policy Analysis". CPPS Policy Paper Series, 22 October 2013. Bandar Sunway: Asian Strategy & Leadership Institute.

Loh, Francis Kok Wah. 2003. "Towards a New Politics of Fragmentation and Contestation". In *New Politics in Malaysia*, edited by Francis Loh Kok Wah and Johan Saravanamuttu, Singapore: Institute of Southeast Asian Studies.

McAllister, Ian, and Clive Bean. 2000. "The Electoral Politics of Economic Reform in Australia: The 1998 Election". *Australian Journal of Political Science* 35, no. 3: 383–99.

Monroe, Kristen R. 1979. "Econometric Analyses of Electoral Behavior: A Critical Review". *Political Behavior* 1, no. 2: 137–73.

Muhammad Shamshinor, Abdul Azzis, Mohd Azri Ibrahim, Sity Daud, and Farid Wajdi. 2014. "Program Kerajaan dan Pola Pengundian PRU-13 di Selangor". *Geografia* 10, no. 4: 99–114.

Narayanan, Suresh. 2014. "The Impact of the Goods and Services Tax (GST) in Malaysia: Lessons From Experiences Elsewhere (A Note)". *Singapore Economic Review* 59, no. 2: 1450009. https://doi.org/10.1142/S021759081450009X.

Pakatan Harapan. 2018. *Buku Harapan: Membina Negara Memenuhi Harapan*. Petaling Jaya: PKR, DAP, PPBM, Amanah.

Prichard, Wilson. 2009. *The Politics of Taxation and Implications for Accountability in Ghana 1981–2008*. IDS Working Paper 330. Brighton: Institute of Development Studies, University of Sussex.

Rohana Kamaruddin, Akmal Aini Othman, and Zarina Denan. 2013. "Government Sincere Initiatives or Political Motives of 1Malaysia Peoples' Aid: Using Structural Equation Modeling". *Procedia: Social and Behavioral Sciences* 105: 715–22.

Tufte, Edward R. 1978. *Political Control of the Economy*. Princeton, NJ: Princeton University Press.

II
Interest Groups

7

THE RURAL MALAY VOTER IN GE-14
Expectations, Surprise, and Misgivings

Serina Rahman

INTRODUCTION

In the nervous trepidation that was the build-up to Malaysia's 14th General Elections (GE-14), most believed that rural voters held the key to either retaining or taking over the reins of power. There was little understanding of the rural psyche amongst urban reformists (*Star Online*, 4 February 2018) and while some in the then opposition were well aware that it was in the rural heartlands that their narrative fell flat, the results proved that the Pakatan Harapan (PH) coalition was far outdone by the Barisan Nasional (BN) and Parti Islam SeMalaysia (PAS) grassroots networks.

While most analysts expected BN to continue on its downward slide, a pattern that had occurred since the 2008 election cycle, hardly anyone (including the campaigning parties themselves) expected such a spectacular fall from grace.[1] BN and its dominant United Malays National Organization (UMNO) component even lost the jewel in the crown and UMNO's birthplace, Johor, as well as other BN strongholds such as Melaka and Negeri Sembilan to PH. It was a result that many had hoped for but few had dared to imagine.

The widely unexpected outcome was the downfall of a coalition that had been in power for sixty-one years and the first time that Putrajaya changed hands; resulting in claims of a "Malay tsunami" (*Star Online*, 10 May 2018). However, a closer examination of the results revealed that PH won on almost total support by the non-Malay voter, topped up by some Malays who were protesting against the UMNO leadership (Ahmad Fauzi 2018, p. 691). Contrary to most expectations, PAS did not get obliterated in GE-14, but instead retained Kelantan and regained Terengganu, as well as a substantial number of seats in Kedah and Perak. BN continued to retain a good share of the seats in Pahang and Perlis.

Thus, while the overall result was both unanticipated and unprecedented, most of the rural Malay vote remained where it has always been: in the hands of those who maintained the ethnocentric discourse of Malay rights, Islamic superiority and the longevity of the royal houses.

This chapter will provide an insight into the world of rural Malay voters in east and west Johor and Kedah, their sentiments before the general election and how their decision on who to vote for changed (in some parts of Johor) in the days and hours before GE-14. The following sections will demonstrate why the views of rural Malay voters in Johor and Kedah were selected for this analysis. The chapter then traces the reactions the morning after, when the results were clear and rural voters in west Johor realized the extent of BN's fall. A short discussion follows on the continued significance of the rural Malay vote and how the rise to power of a coalition that campaigned on equality has inadvertently led to the deepening of ethno-religious schisms.

The content for this chapter is derived from multiple sources, including long-term ethnographic observation of rural communities on the eastern and western coasts of Johor and Kedah before and after GE-14, as well as informant interviews, informal conversations and focus group discussions (FGDs).[2] This on-the-ground research is further supplemented by media articles and survey reports by a number of other organizations.

The rural vote is not solely Malay; there are also Chinese, Indian and indigenous voters in rural areas, but this chapter focuses solely on the Malays because of the influence of UMNO and the weight that rural Malays have on the outcome of the vote. Analysts have noted that Indian and indigenous votes also had an influence on the GE-14 results, but these aspects are excluded from this chapter. This study only looks at rural issues in Peninsular Malaysia as rural East Malaysian matters are vastly different from those in the west, requiring separate treatment.

THE RURAL VOTE MATTERS

In the build-up to GE-14, the rural Malay voter was one of the most sought-after sectors of the electorate. After declarations of a Chinese tsunami swinging popular support to the Pakatan Rakyat coalition in 2013, it was believed that rural Malay voters had to be won to either take over or hold on to power in 2018. For the first time ever, there was a scent of a possibility that the rural Malay voter in Peninsular Malaysia might move away from UMNO.

According to Politweet.Org, voter categories can be divided into rural, semi-urban and urban seats based on a combination of geographical area, level of urban development and population size. Tindak Malaysia has shown that most rural seats are over-represented, meaning that only a few votes (in the thousands), carry the power to elect a representative. On the other hand, an urban seat can have tens of thousands of votes counting towards the election of a single representative. This means that the weight of a rural vote is far heavier and more influential than that of an urban vote. This was the main reason why the parties were keen to garner the favour of rural voters.

GE-14 was the first time that Parti Pribumi Bersatu Malaysia (PPBM) participated in the elections. Helmed by Mahathir Mohamad, Malaysia's longest-serving former prime minister and now ex-UMNO member, this avowedly Malay nationalist party was seen as one of the main assets of the PH coalition in their attempt to wrest rural Malay votes from BN and UMNO. PPBM members comprise a number of disgruntled ex-UMNO politicians, many of whom left the fold in protest against then Prime Minister Najib Razak's alleged financial transgressions (Wan Saiful 2018a, p. 12).

Parti Amanah Negara (Amanah) was an offshoot of PAS and deemed to be made up of PAS "professionals" who had grown weary of the more strictly orthodox views of the *ulama* (religious scholar) cadre. While Amanah were seen as traitors and outcasts in the north, they were positioned as potential inducements for Malay voters in the south, especially since several of their leadership hailed from Johor (Wan Saiful 2017, p. 12). In the build-up to GE-14, some believed that it was only this new evolution of ex-UMNO members, the leadership of Mahathir Mohamad and the presence of suitably religious Amanah members that could convince the rural voter that their interests will not be forsaken.

Figure 7.1 illustrates the spread of rural, urban and semi-urban votes and the winning party during the 13th General Elections. The map clearly demonstrates how many of the large rural seats were won by the ruling party in the 2013 elections. Of 125 rural constituencies, 78 hold a Malay majority. In GE-13, BN won 108 (88 per cent) of the rural seats. Even though rural voters in all make up only 30 per cent of the population, their significance in terms of the number of both federal and state seats that they represent far outweigh their actual numbers.

Historically, BN has won a disproportionate share of rural seats in Malaysia (including Sabah and Sarawak), with Johor and Kedah being no exception. In the last election, 108 of the 133 seats won by BN were rural seats, while the opposition coalition of Pakatan Rakyat monopolized urban seats; 72 of the 89 seats that it won were urban and semi-urban. Heading into GE-14, BN was said to represent the rural majority and could retain power with just the support of rural and semi-urban seats. It is for this reason that the PH coalition needed to highlight PPBM and Amanah as potential lures for the rural Malay voter.

THE HISTORY OF VOTING IN JOHOR AND KEDAH

The ethnographic study in this chapter focuses specifically on Johor and Kedah. Johor is of particular interest because it is the birthplace of UMNO and has traditionally been the bastion of the party. Kedah on the other hand, is the home state of Mahathir Mohamad and his son, Mukhriz, a popular former Chief Minister when he too was

FIGURE 7.1
Rural, Semi-urban, Urban Seats, and Winning Party (GE-13)

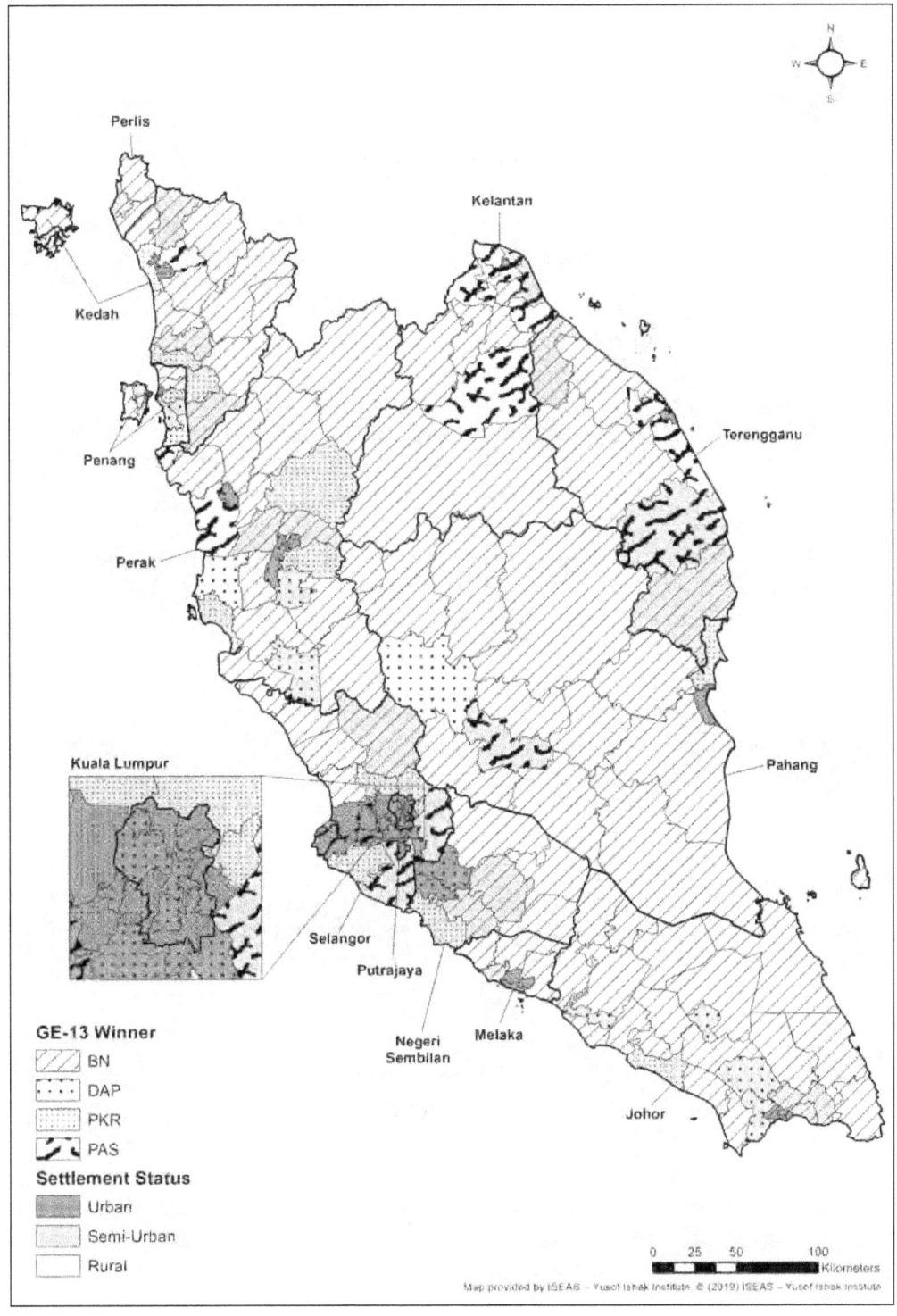

with UMNO. Both states have sizeable rural Malay-majority populations and prior to GE-14 were showing signs of possible transitions to the opposition.

Johor

Johor had always been a bastion of UMNO. Sultan Ibrahim Iskandar once noted that "UMNO was born on palace grounds" (*Straits Times*, 27 December 2015), and that his great-grandfather funded its inception. Since then, UMNO moved from strength to strength in the state. While it was spawned from the anti-colonial movement, UMNO eventually worked with the British colonial powers in negotiations for independence and the creation of the federal constitution. Ironically, in spite of their battle against the British for (among others) their attempt to curtail royal powers and implement equal rights for all races, UMNO followed in the footsteps of the British by continuing to rule and manage the federation by dividing people and power along racial lines (Fahmi 2007).

A number of prominent Johorean civil servants have been influential figures in UMNO, but the party's success in Johor is said to stem from its ability to bring several race-based parties together in a coalition under the BN umbrella. This tactic helped UMNO (through BN) to manage disparate ethnic groups through their community representatives, and on top of that, convince voters to support candidates across ethnic lines. The overarching goal was to keep BN (and thus UMNO) in power for many decades (Hutchinson 2018, p. 6).

With this deft strategy, BN was resoundingly successful in Johor between 1958 and 2008. Only small blips in the record occurred when Kluang was lost in 1978 and Bakri was lost in 2008 to the Democratic Action Party (DAP). In state elections, BN won 85 per cent of total seats, conceding at the most six seats to the opposition. This record is even more significant given that Johor is ethnically diverse, with a population mix similar to Malaysia's overall ethnic breakdown.[3] Given the much smaller number of representatives from the Malaysian Chinese Association (MCA), Gerakan and the Malaysian Indian Congress (MIC) components, Johorean voters have always risen above ethnic boundaries to vote according to the larger BN brand.

Figure 7.2 illustrates the spread of rural, semi-urban and urban parliamentary seats in Johor. Of the seventeen rural seats in Johor, all but two (Segamat and Labis) are Malay-majority seats. In GE-13, all seventeen rural seats were won by BN.

Kedah

Kedah's constituencies are all Malay-majority seats. Between 1955 and 2013, BN or the Alliance dominated Kedah's parliamentary seats, with UMNO taking the most seats within the coalition. The only exception was in 1999 when PAS won eight seats to BN's seven. PAS has been BN's most viable opposition in Kedah and often managed to take one or two seats away from the ruling party, with the exception of 1999. While the preference for BN returned in 2004, the following election saw BN

FIGURE 7.2
Parliamentary Seats in Johor by Urban Status and Ethnicity (GE-14)

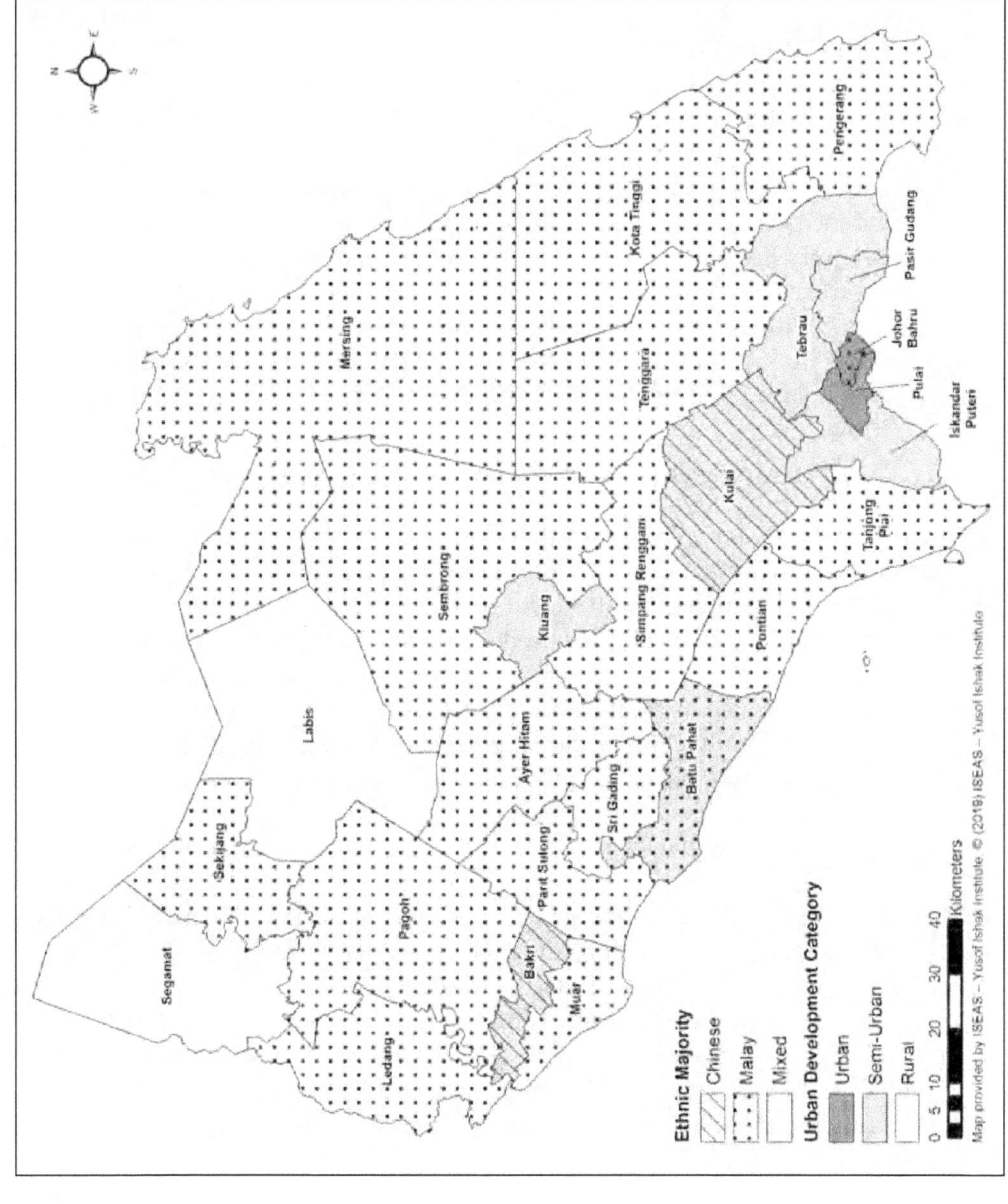

once again losing its majority (winning only four seats) to both PAS (six seats) and PKR (five seats). In 2013, BN once again dominated (ten seats) with PKR hanging on to four seats and PAS taking one seat (one seat went to an Independent).

The significance of Kedah in GE-14 is its status as the birthplace of Mahathir Mohamad. A popular son of the state, his family home in Alor Setar is now preserved and refurbished into a tourism attraction. Mahathir was the member of parliament (MP) for Kubang Pasu from 1974 to 2004, and he is also credited with the development of Langkawi, the state's most popular tourist destination. His son Mukhriz Mahathir became MP for Jerlun in 2008, then stepped down to take up the state seat in Ayer Hitam before becoming Kedah Chief Minister in 2013. While he was undeniably popular as Chief Minister, he was replaced in 2016 through a no-confidence vote by Kedah UMNO leaders. The Mahathir family legacy is strong in Kedah and GE-14 was a test of loyalties between the family and the party that was once their vehicle to power.

Figure 7.3 illustrates the spread of rural, semi-urban and urban parliamentary seats in Kedah. While all seats are Malay majority, nine are rural. In GE-13, six rural seats were held by BN, two by PKR and one by PAS.

ETHNOGRAPHY OF THE RURAL MALAY VOTER

In order to understand the issues that matter to a rural voter, it is necessary to get a clearer picture of conditions and thought processes on the ground. The most important point to note is that the rural voter is not a single homogeneous block. The discussion in this section is based on rural Malay views in Johor and Kedah. Every region has its own idiosyncrasies and unique quirks but some characteristics, especially those related to culture and tradition can be generalized within the wider rural Malay community. This section highlights some features that make a difference to how a Malay rural citizen might vote.[4]

Methodology

The initial study that this chapter is based on is a series of focus group sessions conducted in Johor and Kedah, in three locations. A fishing community on the rural outskirts of the Iskandar Puteri parliamentary seat (southwest Johor), and oil palm farmers, estate workers and Federal Land Development Authority (FELDA) staff and their families in Tenggaroh (FELDA estate in east Johor) were involved in the FGDs and interviews in Johor. In Kedah, the FGDs were held in Yan, a rural community nestled amongst rice fields between Gunung Jerai and the Melaka Strait, on the western shore of Jerai. The participants of these FGDs were all minimum-wage workers from the immediate and surrounding villages—some with relatives or family members who were also fishermen. There was no FELDA community consulted in Kedah.

Aside from the features of the two states mentioned in the earlier section, these three locations were selected for their access in terms of my own long-term observation

FIGURE 7.3

Parliamentary Seats in Kedah by Urban Status and Ethnicity (GE-14)

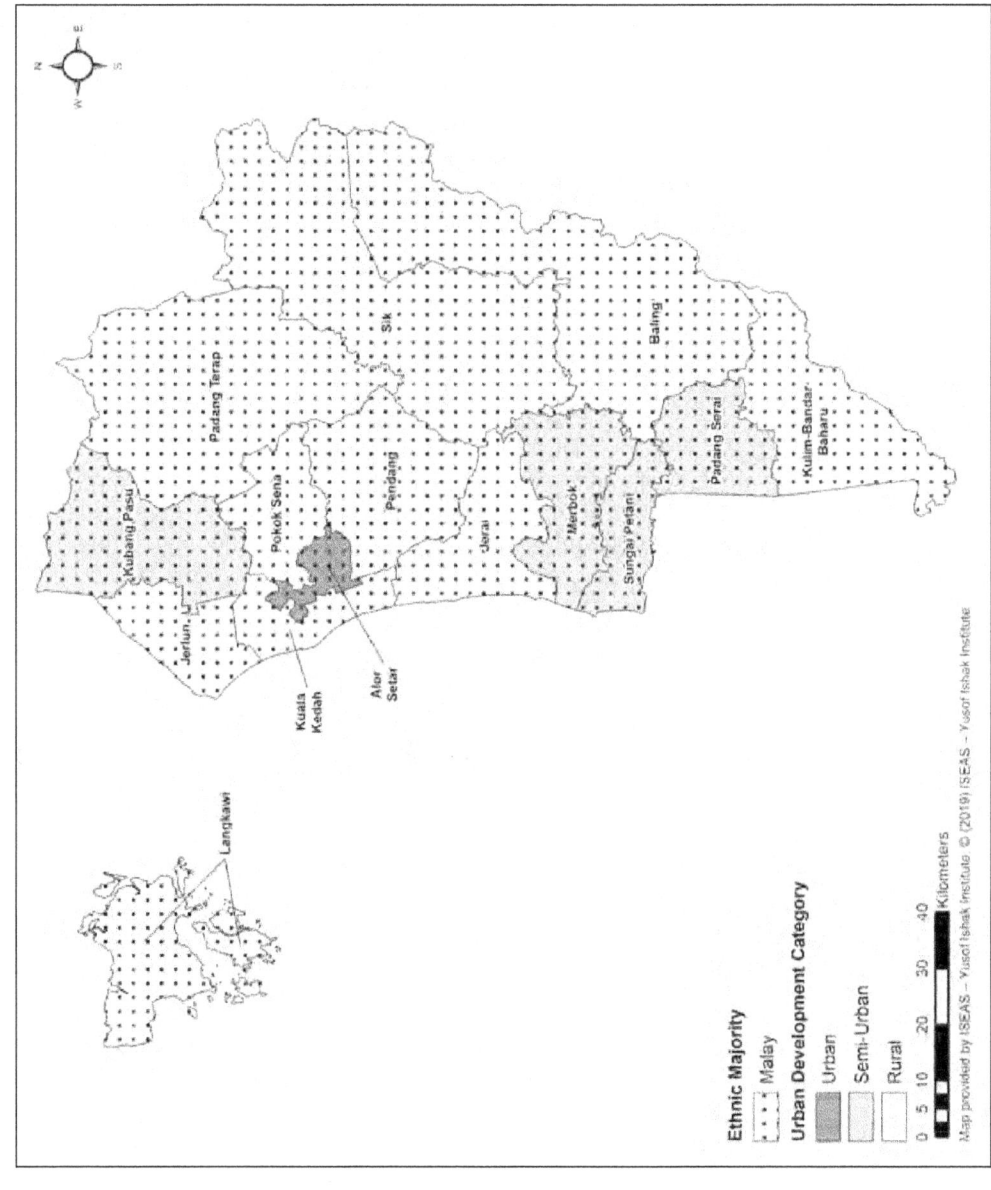

of the communities over the past decade (in Johor), and the plausibility of continued interaction with the community beyond the FGDs, as well as contacts in and around the area (especially in Kedah) who could assist with establishing and maintaining a relationship to monitor long-term changes in local views and opinions.[5]

All FGDs were conducted using the convenience sampling method. In both east and west Johor, selected local community members[6] hosted sessions in their homes over light refreshments. Groups were divided by age and gender to ensure that participants were comfortable discussing the topics at hand. Stratification by age was to enable participants to speak freely without pressure or influence from their elders, while gender separation was necessary to ensure that female respondents were not inhibited by the presence of men when responding. In Kedah, FGD sessions were arranged with the staff of a local company. These participants originated from a number of rural areas near the FGD venues (various locations in Yan, Jerai) and were also separated by age and gender. FGD sessions in Kedah were held at the local branch offices of the host company over light refreshments.

A total of seventy-two people were involved in these extended focus group sessions, split into smaller groups by gender and age (thirty-five years and below, and above thirty-five years). Each focus group had between five and nine people at a time.

The main thrust of the FGDs was to determine how the participants might vote and to better understand the issues that mattered to them. A standard set of questions were asked of each group as follows:[7]

1. What are the needs, wants, problems and issues of the community (that might matter at the ballot box)?
2. Who can provide assistance for the above?
3. What do you think about the current government, ruling party and leaders?
4. What do you think of other leaders and parties (Mahathir Mohamad, Anwar Ibrahim, opposition parties)?
5. Do you know about the 1 Malaysia Development Berhad (1MDB), FELDA, other allegations and what do you think of them?
6. What are the most important criteria when it comes to voting/selecting a representative (race, religion, nominee, party, gender, age)?

FGD sessions usually stretched to about two hours each, with some respondents staying on after the formal discussion to share their personal views out of earshot of other participants.[8]

In addition to the focus group sessions, additional informal interviews were conducted with local informants[9] who are very familiar with rural communities in both states. These conversations provided expert views based on an astute understanding of local conditions. Constant updates of the situation on the ground were received from Kedah after the sessions and an additional visit was made to Langkawi prior to the elections to get a feel of the ground there.

My research over the past decade in Johor examining coastal communities for other studies, as well as my familiarity with rural conditions and people in both east and west Johor have added to the information presented here. Extensive engagement and immersion with local communities and almost daily participant observations of local behaviour, interests, issues and opinions in rural, coastal and island areas over the last ten years have provided additional insight into the possible leanings and evolution of Johor's rural voter.

Beyond this initial study, more recent trends (prior to GE-14) were monitored via online and print media, published reports of surveys by other institutions and organizations, as well as conference and seminar discussions. Some of the material gathered from Johor was further corroborated with the results of a Johor Survey commissioned by the ISEAS – Yusof Ishak Institute and conducted by the Merdeka Center in 2017.[10] The ethnographic discussion generated from this study provides an insight into the psyche of the rural Malay voter, and the basis from which broad expectations of a BN win were generated.

A Peek into the Rural Malay Psyche

In order to better understand rural Malay views and voting decisions, the context of their experiences, thought processes and understanding of the world needs to be clarified. The lived reality of the rural Malay world is far removed from the corridors of power; their priorities, decisions and actions are often misunderstood. The following section hopes to provide more insight into the residents of these parts of Peninsular Malaysia. While they may be geographically close to urban centres of national and state decision-making, they are psychologically very different.

Reverence for Royalty

Malay society is historically feudal; the rural Malay psyche is steeped in tradition (Alatas 1972, p. 111). The Sultan's position at the top of the social hierarchy is a natural state of being. The rest of society accepts their place on the lower rungs (Maaruf 1988, p. 37). To the average rural Malay, respect for the Sultan only comes second to devotion to God.[11] This reverence stems from tales of sacrifice and protection given by royals past. Oral histories handed down through the generations remind the population of their ties to the lords of their lands; rural communities are constantly reminded of their debt to their feudal masters (Milner 2011, p. 18).

This mindset is closely intertwined with the Malay principle of loyalty and indebtedness (Muzaffar 1979, p. 4). It is part of *adat* (tradition) to always remember those who have helped you; to betray the hand that feeds you is a great social sin. Taken in tandem, these beliefs explain why the rural Malay is easily placated with gifts strewn by royalty or others of perceived higher standing. While the little that is given might be but a fraction of the giver's daily expenses, the community receives it with praise and gratitude because of its source and their own perceived position at the bottom of the hierarchy.

This loyalty to royalty is often used to incite voter anger and action at the polls. At BN rallies prior to GE-14 in the rural fringes of a semi-urban seat in Johor, an UMNO party representative used this to their advantage. His plea to the people was as follows:[12]

> Remember the time of Parameswara; from him came our various kings and our Johor royalty. If you vote for the opposition, they will close down the royal institutions. They will remove the power of our Sultan. This is like the pillars that hold up the roofs of our homes, our nation. If they remove this pillar it removes what it means for us to be Malay—our Sultans, our origins. Our roofs and our country will collapse.

In the ISEAS – Yusof Ishak Institute Johor Survey in 2017, 90 per cent of Malay respondents indicated that they were satisfied with the performance of the Johor royalty. Of rural voters, 88 per cent expressed their satisfaction with the royal family. When asked to rank the performance of Johor political leaders, 46 per cent placed the royal family in first place, followed by Khaled Nordin, Johor's Chief Minister, who was selected as top performer by 34 per cent of the respondents.

Respect for Political Leaders

When cultural norms of loyalty and hierarchy are extrapolated to the political context, a favoured politician can step into a position not too far below that of royalty. When they visit a rural community, they are treated like celebrities and the people remember (and are constantly reminded of) the good that the politician has done for them. They can thus do little wrong and any generous gifts given to the community are taken with great appreciation. Stories of excess by those in power have little traction as feudal traditions dictate that pomp and pageantry, as well as exorbitant demonstrations of wealth are necessary markers of high rank (Maaruf 1988, p. 16). This expectation is easily transferred to politicians and other social elites (ibid., p. 155).

The FGDs and conversations with rural people corroborate this. When asked about the allegations of corruption, embezzlement and extravagance, those who are aware of the stories deny the relevance of the accusations to their lives. Their responses ranged from gentle admonishments for believing "fake news" and making judgements about people that they do not know personally, to nonchalance as it is expected of those in the upper echelons of society to behave in this manner. Others noted that those who were complaining were people who had fallen out of favour with the party and thus had other intentions to avenge their dismissal. At BN rallies, the opposition is often referred to as "recycled politicians … who all originated from BN".

At the end of the day, what the politicians did in "their world" made no difference to the respondents' daily struggle for survival. While some said that they had no time for political drama, some of the older respondents pointed out that they did not own smart phones and thus had no access to this news. Typical responses were as follows:

> If they took the money or didn't take the money. I don't know. You cannot believe everything you read or hear. I don't care to know. I do my work and just focus on earning my salary and trying to have enough for my family to eat.[13]

> It doesn't make a difference to us. What they do up there is their problem. We just deal with our problems.[14]

In FELDA communities in particular, the stress on the need to be loyal to those who raised them out of desperate poverty is a common refrain. This view is especially prevalent amongst older FELDA settlers who shared stories of their struggle and difficult conditions in the early days. These first-generation settlers believe they owe their survival and progress to Abdul Razak Hussein, former prime minister of Malaysia and father of former Prime Minister Najib Razak. It was Abdul Razak who started the FELDA scheme in 1953. While they dismissed Mahathir as the prime minister who paid the least attention to them, they firmly believed that the Razak family has their best interests at heart. To them, Najib Razak was the best option to manage Malaysia.

FELDA settlements have always been a BN vote bank (Khor 2017, p. 8). Settlers said they were willing to vote for any component party member— even across racial lines—in order to maintain BN rule. This is because they were aware that UMNO controls the BN coalition and that their Malay rights were safe with the coalition. The DAP was frequently mentioned as a bogeyman. FELDA elders sincerely believed that voting for the opposition would mean the end of Malay benefits at the hands of the DAP. Their greatest nightmare, as they described it, was for Malaysia to go the way of Singapore, where "Malays are marginalized and deprived of opportunities and their rights; suffering at the hands of the Chinese government".[15]

Toeing the Family Line

Hierarchical traditions in rural Malay society also apply to the thoughts and actions of family members. On several occasions after FGD sessions with participants below thirty-five years, eavesdropping elders reminded the younger generation of the debts they owed to the ruling party.[16] They emphasized the need to remain loyal to those who had helped them out of poverty while others maintained that supporting UMNO was a family tradition. It is wholly unbecoming to break with tradition. Some of the more outspoken youths countered with opinions that ranged between the following:

> Yes, it's all good here in FELDA. We are very well taken care of. But if you go into the city it's very difficult for the Malays there. The cost of living—food, rent, transportation, petrol. Okay maybe it's just that the opposition government doesn't know how to manage a state, but it is hard for everyone beyond FELDA.[17]

> We are second-generation FELDA settlers. The benefits go to our parents but we cannot just make them our ATMs. They don't know how expensive it is now to raise children, to send them to school. And we are not always eligible for BR1M. How to survive?[18]

What is the point of voting for the ruling party when they don't find out our problems? Who comes to help us? We tried going to so many people for help. Nothing. In the end that Chinese NGO in Johor Bahru helped us with our medical expenses. A Chinese NGO! If we have to just vote for UMNO because everyone does then maybe there's just no point in voting.[19]

The pressure within the family and community to remain in support of UMNO and BN is strong. Most rural Malay families are generational UMNO supporters, especially in Johor, and to go against family tradition and practice was seen as tantamount to breaching the norms of filial piety. Even in Kedah, some FGD respondents were reluctant to publicly say anything negative against UMNO until the session was over and they were able to share their honest views out of earshot of the others. Many maintained that they often voted in line with family traditions (or publicly supported UMNO) because there was just no point in creating trouble within the family or breaking up friendships.

The Power of Women and Their Networks

Social peer pressure is a tool that Wanita UMNO used with great effect in rural communities. Patriarchy is rife in rural areas and women have little public social standing. But women's networks are the backbone of every community and the avenue through which women are able to establish little spheres of power, control and influence. Rural Malay women have frequent gatherings either for prayer, social support in difficult times or community events such as weddings and ritual feasts. Wanita UMNO members are often prominent participants at these gatherings and are known to frequently provide financial or in-kind support for those in need (Wan Saiful 2018a, p. 21). Many women in rural communities proudly wear their Wanita UMNO affiliation on their sleeves as they gain recognition for their service to the community.

Because a woman's access to a world beyond her home is often through these social events, it is important to the average rural Malay woman to abide by popular movements. When almost everyone else in the community is a Wanita UMNO supporter or member, it is difficult to go against the tide. The need to be part of the in-group means that it is extremely difficult to harbour different political views or profess opinions contrary to the dominant mantra. Rural Malay society is intensely communal. It is highly abnormal to have someone who thinks and acts alone, independently or differently from others. The very real possibility of being excommunicated for being different prevents many women from breaking away or even publicly contemplating a different point of view.

On the other hand, the authority of a woman in her home should also not be underestimated. In discussions with rural women, many professed that they would censure their children if they decided to vote differently from themselves. Many also felt that they were able to wield influence over their husband's views. One woman confidently proclaimed that how she voted determined the voting preference of her entire family:

In the past I was wholly in support of UMNO. My children, husband—we were all the same. But now things are difficult. I am going the other way and my husband and children are all voting with me. I take my whole family. Whoever I support, they support too.[20]

While this FGD participant had made the decision to break away from BN, she did it with the support of her friends. There is strength in numbers when a decision is made to forge a new path. While she was clearly an influence on her family, her gumption in declaring her new allegiance was an anomaly. In all other conversations with rural communities, confessions of empathy for opposition parties were revealed in whispers and only with the assurance that their identities would not be revealed.

Many cited pressure from family, friends and neighbours for their fears. "What would people say if they knew I no longer support UMNO?" was the common refrain. The need to protect the family name and reputation is an intrinsic part of Malay culture, hence the habitual difference between public pronouncements and private action. Public assertions and demonstrations of support for a political party may not necessarily translate into the same action at the ballot box. Perhaps this reluctance to publicly reveal electoral preferences, especially when contemplating a switch to PH or PAS, contributed to PH's unexpectedly high vote haul in some rural and semi-urban areas.

Faith, Fear and Maintaining Favour

Religion is a central pillar of Malay lives (Sulaiman 2018, p. xxi) but fear is a common tool used by rural Malays in matters of faith. The fear of deviating from the right path and forsaking a positive place in the afterlife is deeply embedded in the cultures of rural Malays. Some political parties have successfully tapped on this for votes. Rallies for the ruling party before GE-14 had at least one speaker with religious credentials espousing the values of UMNO and demonising the DAP. It has been very successfully ingrained into rural thought processes that electing the opposition is equivalent to removing Islam as the national religion. By the same token, the nation's prime minister must be a Muslim to ensure the priority status of Islam.

Opposition Malays are deemed "liberal" and *"bebas"* (wild) for a range of reasons, including: the colour of their hair, their desire to eliminate JAKIM,[21] to support and propagate LGBT[22] lifestyles and "Gay Festivals".[23] The fear-mongering is effective. Comments such as *"our jihad is at the ballot box"* is commonly heard and rural Malays often mentioned that they need to have special prayers (*solat al-Istikharah*) for the then ruling party; for guidance and strength to do the right thing in the face of negative influences and emotions. BN rallies attribute the ability of the opposition to spin sweet tales to dalliances with the devil—and evidence that the DAP is *harbi* (a rather derogatory term for a non-Muslim enemy).

As such, in Johor, the general view was that even a Malay-Muslim party such as PPBM that collaborates with the DAP will be "contaminated by this evil" and should not be supported. MCA representatives on the other hand, are said to be non-Muslims that the Prophet has declared acceptable to work with because they bring benefits to Muslims.[24] Homilies like these seemed to be quite effective in garnering the rural faithful to vote for the more outwardly visible "religious" parties and their allies.

In Kedah, on the other hand, the responses given in the FGDs seemed to indicate that PPBM had captured the imagination of the electorate. This was even though theirs was more an ethnocentric approach, rather than a religious one. Some respondents shared that they had seen how the DAP in Penang helped everyone during the 2018 floods, not just the Malays or Muslims, whereas they received nothing because they were not privy to the UMNO or PAS inner circle. While they themselves would not vote for the DAP, they were clearly more open to an alternative to the status quo.

It is interesting to note that Kedah's most viable opposition party throughout history was PAS, and that the 2017 Johor Survey indicated that the second most accepted political party in Johor is PAS, albeit with low percentage support.[25] Yet throughout the FGDs, mention of PAS received only lukewarm responses. In east Johor, the respondents felt that they were a good alternative only because of their Muslim credentials—but it was stressed that this was only if UMNO was not an option. In west Johor, PAS was clearly out of favour as those interviewed saw them as hypocrites who would condemn the government but be first in line to receive benefits. They saw through their claims of religious piety and cited many examples of dishonourable behaviour. In Kedah, mention of PAS was met with a shrug and simple dismissal. With the excitement that PPBM seemed to generate in this northern state, PAS no longer seemed to feature as strongly on the political radar. A number of PAS rallies and election sermons that I observed in Kedah seemed to garner less than fifty people at a time.

Access to Information

While many rural Malays are frequent users of Facebook and WhatsApp, access to news is usually through government print and television media channels.[26] While some information comes to them through Facebook posts and WhatsApp messages, the most effective channel of communication is word of mouth. For rural Malay men, this may transpire at the coffee shop or jetty, while for the women this takes place at social and religious gatherings or the daily morning chat on neighbours' doorsteps. Printed content written in Bahasa Malaysia is always deemed more credible than English sources, but even then the language needs to be accessible to the average rural Malay and not too profound.

Perhaps this is why there is mute condemnation of crass language commonly used by some politicians. Village conversations can be far less refined than those in urban centres and to best get the message across, exchanges need to be in the local dialect. When that is not possible, the regular Bahasa Malaysia spoken amongst friends and family tends to be a little more unseemly than what is expected of usually refined

Malay dialogue.[27] Malay norms intercede, however, if public disrespect is shown to royalty or to elder statesmen. Thus while many now question the intentions and integrity of Mahathir because of his dalliances with the DAP, there is a great distaste at outright personal condemnation of the man. The Malay must above all else be seen to be *bersopan santun* (well-mannered and polite) (Sulaiman 2018, p. xxii). Even in no-holds-barred political exchanges, there are limits.[28]

In urban areas, there are multiple sources of information as well as numerous opportunities to meet representatives of various parties. This is simply not possible in rural areas. In order to enter a rural village and set up a space for a meet-the-public session, the approval of the village head or members of the local committee (AJKKK) must be attained. I have been privy to conversations where villages in support of the ruling party actively mobilize to prevent opposition party members from entering the area or speaking to people.

Even as preparations are made to welcome rallies by BN component parties, there are several caveats to consider. Among these are the guarantee of adequate gifts to the liaison party and those who attend the event. Lucky draw prizes and thank you gifts are obligatory at these rallies; both at the request of local representatives and as customary favours from the campaigning party. In their defence, the local representatives will say that it is the only way to ensure that the rally will be well attended, and to ensure that the villagers get something out of the deal. But it is clear that patronage politics has become part and parcel of life for these communities. A newer, smaller, less well-financed opposition party would therefore have multiple stumbling blocks to overcome in order to gain access to the rural voter.

THE ISSUES THAT MATTERED

Figure 7.4 provides a summary of the issues that were raised by rural voters in Kedah and Johor prior to GE-14. While the importance of some factors (listed in the bottom row) varied in importance between age and gender groups, the top two rows of economic-related problems were the most prevalent issues raised. It needs to be reiterated that these issues were raised almost six months before the election. Between these discussions and voting day, much occurred to influence the final decision at the ballot box.

Common Threads

The FGDs revealed that the common issues of concern to the rural voters in Kedah and Johor are that of daily survival. In all sessions, participants mentioned the effects of the goods and services tax (GST), rising costs of living and the removal of petrol subsidies as matters that added to their daily burden. These were issues that they wanted the government to resolve. Most groups also mentioned that while they had jobs, their salaries remained stagnant even though costs of living increased. This was especially painful for those working in private companies, and they were well

FIGURE 7.4
Matrix of the Main Issues Raised during Focus Group Discussions and Interviews

GST	cost of living	petrol prices	stagnant salaries
lack of job availability	property & land prices	access to assistance	cronyism
Malay rights	protection of Islam	grassroots presence	younger candidates

aware that civil servants were constantly receiving benefits and salary increases from the government.[29]

Several female respondents below thirty-five years mentioned that finding jobs or part-time work (especially in FELDA estates) was hard, and there was little opportunity for them to work near home. While there were two (female) university graduates in the FGDs, they did not mention any problems with their National Higher Education Fund Corporation (PTPN) student loans, a common election topic of the opposition parties. However, they struggled to find their first job and were still unemployed.

The men always raised the problem of not being able to buy land or their own home. They complained about rising land prices (especially in Johor) and their inability to even buy under the "affordable home" scheme.[30] Many were living in rented houses or squatting on other people's land; others shared land with siblings or relatives and had no means of moving out onto their own properties. Rising rental rates were also mentioned as an issue that needed to be resolved.

For the rural voter, these matters and their constant struggle to make ends meet were far more important than politicking, election campaigning and any mention of politicians' scandals or impropriety.

When asked about the usefulness of the 1Malaysia People's Assistance programme (BR1M), almost all responded that BR1M gave them a single pay-out of up to RM1,000, but the government takes back far more through GST and rising prices. In Johor many respondents said that they had trouble getting BR1M payments; either because they had no means to go into the city to process the forms, or they were unable to provide all the documentation that was required, and that their village head or committee were not helpful in the process. Several said that they had been rejected and that many of their friends and family were also declared ineligible for BR1M. In contrast, participants in Kedah seemed to have no problems accessing the payments.

Another common grouse mentioned across the FGD sessions was the problem of the middlemen. These referred to anyone in a position of power above the rural people; community committee members, village heads, UMNO branch heads, and fishing or farming association heads. The standard complaint was that assistance and compensation (for land acquisition due to development, habitat damage or natural disasters) were set aside by the government and its leaders. However, there is a layer of "cronies"[31] who hold the power to disburse these monies, and decide who is eligible to receive it. It was repeatedly mentioned that people in dire need were constantly passed over for a relative or crony.

Corruption at these lower levels of governance acutely affects rural communities. While some were aware that the Malaysian Anti-Corruption Commission (MACC) was arresting government officers for corruption, most felt that nothing came out of the arrests and perpetrators got away with the crimes scot-free. A few noted that corruption charges have been made against lower ranked officers (as scapegoats) while bigger crimes at higher echelons of government are ignored. Some of the respondents felt that the government was doing well in terms of having allocated the funds for the people, but it was the middlemen who made things difficult for the citizenry. Female respondents also mentioned that they deplored the infighting, bickering and favouritism demonstrated by Wanita UMNO.

Other common threads that emerged as a result of the discussion was the importance of Malay rights and Islam as the national religion. For the rural people that I spoke to, the prime minister must be a Malay-Muslim, but there is no gender preference. Indeed throughout the FGD sessions, the participants made it clear that their voting choice depended on the characteristics of the person standing for office, not on his or her party.[32] It mattered more that their representative was present in their lives during special occasions (festive seasons, weddings, deaths, ritual feasts, etc.) than to appear with gifts once every five years. They insisted that they wanted someone who could do the work, fix the problems and produce results. Because many politicians made unfulfilled promises in the past, they would only support someone with a clearly visible track record of providing assistance or that they know personally.

There was also a collective yearning for younger candidates to be put forward. While all participants felt that the presence of more seasoned politicians was necessary as guidance, everyone was keen to see younger politicians taking a stand. This was especially so amongst the younger participants in the FGDs.

As mentioned earlier, the rural vote is not homogeneous. While there are common concerns and issues, there are also many differences between gender and age groups, as well as regions.

East Johor

The respondents in east Johor were overwhelmingly in support of the ruling government and resolutely believed that only Najib Razak and his team could help them with their problems. They did not see a need for a change in the ruling government and felt duty-bound to respond to BN's generosity by remaining loyal to the coalition. FELDA communities in Johor do live well; most report regular salaries which are generous for their needs. Their estates are well kept and have more amenities that the average rural Malay village. While respondents felt the crunch of increased costs of living, the older generation blames it on Chinese businessmen and not the federal government.

Many FELDA children have moved beyond their humble backgrounds to become highly qualified professionals living in urban centres away from the estates. Those who move back to the estates concede that they return only because they have to take care of ageing parents. They lamented that they had no choice but to give up higher paying jobs and that there are few job opportunities in the estates. Their support for the ruling party is not as unwavering as their parents'. During the FGDs, the younger participants often mentioned the difficulties they faced in meeting monthly expenses and how the elders were not aware of the hardship faced by their generation. Displeasure at the government because of this was expressed in hushed voices with furtive glances towards the older generation in the next room. It was clear that there was strong family pressure to remain in support of the ruling party.

When asked if they might vote the other way, these younger participants maintained that the ruling party was the only option because their Malay rights had to be protected. They felt that the opposition did not have a good track record, and they preferred to stick to the proven success of the current leadership. Echoing the sentiments of their elders, they too said that voting for the opposition could result in their suffering the same fate as Malays in Singapore. They also did not want to cause trouble in the family. These respondents felt that any transgressions that the current leadership might be involved in was none of their business. However, when asked their views of the oft publicized allocation of land to second generation settlers, they emphasized that they would only believe it when they see it.

West Johor

This rural edge of Iskandar Puteri has always been in support of BN.[33] However, in 2013, when it was still referred to as the Gelang Patah parliamentary seat, there was a surprise fall to the opposition. Many attributed this to the clout of the opposition candidate but my conversations with people in the area revealed that theirs was a protest vote against the last-minute decision to replace the popular locally born and raised MCA candidate with an UMNO veteran who was a former Johor Chief Minister. Local Malay support for the MCA candidate overcame traditional racial boundaries because they were familiar with him and they had known him as a youth who had grown up fishing with the rest of the community. As a politician he was a constant and regular presence in their villages and they believed that he had their best interests at heart, regardless of his ethnicity.[34] The strength of this loyalty towards him is an indication of the importance of a politician's physical presence in their constituency, and how much the rural voter values grassroots efforts (Dettman and Weiss 2018, p. 744).

The FGDs in west Johor elicited the most differences between age and gender groups. The views of women in this area also differed according to age. The comments of the older women in this community were similar to those of the FELDA elders— only BN can serve them best, even though they were unable to identify local party representatives who could help them in times of need. They too blamed increased costs of living on Chinese businessmen who "abused the GST and raised prices indiscriminately". They did not believe the allegations of corruption against the ruling party. While they conceded that Mahathir Mohamad was once good for the nation, they felt that he had crossed to the dark side by colluding with the DAP, and that he is now a hypocrite that is not to be trusted because he now sits at the same table as his sworn enemies.

The younger women on the other hand were not interested in politics at all. They claimed to be unaware and uninterested in political scandals. To them, their situation and daily struggle were the same no matter who was in power; no political representatives ever came to see them and Wanita UMNO did not include them in their list of beneficiaries. They were unable to get help from village representatives or committees, struggled to find jobs and could hardly make ends meet. Some said they would still vote as it is their duty as citizens, and that they would vote for BN as this is what their family does. But a few were more apathetic and questioned the need to vote when there was nothing in it for them.

The FGDs with the men in this community were rambunctious events where both young and old seemed to vent their frustrations. The men were well versed in all the political narratives and felt that both sides were equally corrupt and problematic. These participants felt that Malaysia should have Singapore's order and systems, and while they felt that Malay rights needed to be preserved, they did not see any problems with the situation in Singapore. Several said that they knew several Chinese Singaporeans who were kind and generous with them, that Malay Singaporeans were doing well, and that they had no issue with the Chinese fishermen from the village who shared the same jetty and struggled as they did at sea. These men maintained that the prime minister had to be a Malay-Muslim so that Islam can be preserved as the primary religion of the nation, but they also noted that they already had Malay-Muslim leaders in power and it was not doing them any good, if not making them worse off.

All the men felt that change was needed but they did not feel that either side could help them. They blamed the increased cost of living on the federal government. While they approved of state government efforts, they attributed this to the Sultan's firm hand. However, they did not see that they could benefit personally from any of the development. In fact, they have suffered as a result of habitats lost and lower fish catch. The men were particularly unhappy with the middlemen who they felt stood in the way of financial assistance or compensation monies that were due to them. They saw corruption at all levels of governance and felt that everyone was able to get away with it, at the expense of rural communities like themselves.

They wanted a younger field of politicians, and those who had the characteristics of the Johor Sultan or the Crown Prince. To them, the Johor royalty embodied the qualities needed in a leader—one who is not afraid to be firm and make unpopular decisions if it is in the best interests of their people, and one who does what they say instead of issuing empty promises. Given the dearth of choices and their lack of faith in both sides, they said that if the weather was bad or if it was good fishing season at sea, they would not waste the day voting. And if they did go to the ballot box, it would be in support of whoever can give them the most immediate benefits.

Kedah

The responses from the FGDs in Kedah were divided along age differences. The older participants spoke along the same lines as the Johor FELDA elders in terms of not being able to trust DAP and the risk of becoming Singapore or Penang. However, they had more positive views of Mahathir Mohamad and his son, and several acknowledged that the Penang government provides assistance to all. They also claimed that UMNO infighting and cronyism meant that they had to repair their homes after the floods without state aid. They also reminisced about happier days of visible progress under Mukhriz Mahathir and commented on a lack of community events or even lighting at state government buildings under the current leadership. The elders in Kedah seemed torn between their nostalgia for the days under Mahathir Mohamad and the need to be supportive of UMNO.

The younger FGD participants were very different in their views. The men were wholly in support of PPBM and claimed that all of their friends and family were with them in moving over to "Parti Bunga".[35] Interestingly, they said that the women they knew remained steadfast UMNO supporters, and they predicted that Wanita UMNO in Kedah will not have anyone to help them put up flags and do heavy work because the men had all crossed over to the opposition. However, the session with women below thirty-five years revealed that they too were in staunch support of PPBM, but they had not discussed it with their husbands or family members. They maintained that they had already decided who to vote for, they did not need to attend any rallies, and they were not going to discuss it with their spouses or families. They revealed that their parents found it hard to leave UMNO.

The common phrase heard in Kedah from all the FGD participants was "*kecewa*" or disappointment. While the older participants conceded that they were disappointed with the trajectory of the nation, they were hesitant to complain or admit that they might want to vote another way. The younger participants, however, were excited and impatient for their turn at the ballot box. While they all received BR1M, they felt that it was not much in view of the rising cost of living and GST. All the younger respondents were struggling to make ends meet with children to feed and put through school. They were also cognizant of the fact that their lives in rural Kedah were not as difficult as friends or family in more urban areas such as Alor Setar and Sungai Petani where costs of living were higher. They said they could not imagine how people in Kuala Lumpur or Johor Bahru can survive.

These younger participants were very well versed in the prevailing political narratives and aware of conditions beyond their state—especially the women. The men said that they were mobilizing for change, and while both genders felt that they were unsure how the opposition might rule, they had faith in the Mahathir family and wanted to give them a chance. They did have misgivings about DAP but they had friends who told them that Penang was actually run far better than how it is portrayed in the media. These respondents wanted Mukhriz Mahathir as prime minister and felt that the only cure for the nation's maladies was a younger generation of politicians who can rejuvenate the economy and put a halt to corruption.

Unlike Johor, there was no mention of the royal family during the focus group sessions and interviews in Kedah. When probed about their royalty and whether their views mattered, I received somewhat blank looks in return. A few whispered in embarrassment because they were unable to remember their new Sultan's name.[36] In Kedah it seems, the rural community are not as attached to their king as they are in Johor.

Additional Developments Prior to GE-14

A visit to Langkawi in early March 2018 revealed that there were more PPBM flags on the roads than BN flags. While BN stations seemed to be rather worn, refurbished containers, PPBM action centres were freshly painted buildings or part of permanent buildings that seemed ready to mobilize for electoral change. Conversations with the Langkawi locals about their views elicited whispered indications of their steadfast loyalty to the Mahathir family. This was despite Najib Razak celebrating Chinese New Year on the island with promises of RM1.3 billion (about S$440 million) in infrastructure improvements (*New Straits Times*, 16 February 2018). Prior to that, BN's popular Minister of Youth and Sports, Khairy Jamaluddin had also stopped in Langkawi to remind the locals that Mahathir's previous contributions to the island was only possible with UMNO support (*The Sun Daily*, 3 February 2018).

Mainland Kedah has also received a lot of attention from the ruling government. 148 residents received Temporary Occupation Licences (TOL) for their homes in Ayer Hitam from Kedah Chief Minister Ahmad Bashah Md Hanipah (*New Straits Times*, 4 March 2018). Najib Razak launched the development of new homes for relocated fishermen in Yan, Jerai and distributed allowances amounting to RM460,000 (about S$155,000) to 1,605 fishermen in the wider region (*Star Online*, 26 March 2018). Following that, the Chief Minister announced the relaxation of local land ownership laws to allow resident Siamese communities to purchase homes originally allocated for Malay-only purchases (*Malaysian Insight*, 26 March 2018). Jerlun and Ayer Hitam were both former seats of Mukhriz Mahathir, and the Siamese community were known to be in support of PH (*Malaysian Insight*, 20 February 2018).

In some Johor FELDA estates, second-generation settlers were given offer letters for newly built affordable homes, part of the 20,000 units promised by Najib Razak (*Malay Mail*, 26 November 2018). A FELDA 2.0 package incorporating new strategies for sustainable environment and economy was launched in February 2018, attracting 10,338 settlers back to the scheme (*New Straits Times*, 27 March 2018). Other recently announced bonuses for FELDA settlers include RM631,821 in allowances for 157 settlers for an intensive planting scheme, RM2.85 million in incentives for 567 settlers, RM1.81 million for 362 FELDA returnees and a promise of RM10 million for necessary infrastructure such as street lighting, road widening and mosques.[37]

In west Johor, 1,814 fishermen were awarded RM2,000 each from the Persatuan Nelayan Kawasan Johor Selatan (South Johor Fishermen's Association), a total of RM3.6 million (about S$1.21 million) (*Utusan Malaysia*, 26 March 2018). Selected fishermen's jetties (*pengkalan*) in west Johor also received RM20,000 each for jetty improvements and repairs, and there were rumours of an additional RM100,000 per jetty to be distributed soon after the elections.[38] New fishing licences were promised, with all the Orang Asli of Sg Temuan receiving theirs before the elections.[39] This was in spite of a long-standing freeze on the issuance of new fishing licences for the west coast of Malaysia since the 1980s because of overexploitation of coastal marine resources (Department of Fisheries, 2013).

Johor's former Chief Minister, Khaled Nordin, launched the Johor Structure Plan 2030 and invited input and suggestions from Johoreans, noting that the state would improve as a team; he was known to take note of citizens' feedback and ideas (*Star Online*, 28 February 2018). BN rallies in the state consistently praised Khaled Nordin's efforts, honoured the support of the Sultan for Johor's development and never mentioned Najib Razak by name. The Chief Minister's successes were repeatedly lauded, especially in ensuring that there were no more squatters in Gelang Patah as every resident now had a legal home. Lucky draw prizes of home appliances and cash were continually distributed at these rallies.[40]

Johor's Sultan (*Star Online*, 28 February 2018) and Crown Prince (*Malay Mail*, 22 August 2018) have always claimed that the royal family is above politics and have no preference for any political party. The Sultan reminded state civil servants to stay out of politics and work for the good of Johor's citizens (*Star Online*, 26 February 2018). While the Sultan insisted that he did not have a preference for either side, he repeatedly stated that there is no place for anyone who incites racial or religious intolerance and hatred in his state.[41] The Crown Prince also clearly expressed his preference for UMNO prior to the elections.[42] While these comments garnered a lot of online retorts, some in rural areas took their opinions as validation of their own discomfort with PH.

SIGNS MISSED

In hindsight, there were countless signs of dissatisfaction that arose in the FGDs and conversations with rural voters. Unfortunately, these were largely overshadowed by the history of BN's unwavering (albeit decreasing) success over sixty-one years, especially in its home state of Johor, as well as traditional Malay fidelity to *adat* and social obligations. It seemed completely unfathomable that Johor would fall (Hutchinson 2018, p. 39).

It was clear that voters were torn between tradition and the ever-increasing difficulties of their daily survival. In west Johor, even as fishermen declared that the country should be led by the Johor Crown Prince because of his willingness to "bluntly speak the truth" and "do what's best for the people", they were also well aware that they suffered the consequences of coastal developments that have links to the royal family.[43] Statements regarding the latter were made only after they checked that the audio recorder had been switched off.

While expectations that displays of wealth are part and parcel of society's top echelon transferred easily from royalty to political leaders and social elites, the desperation of their own financial situation in the face of the flagrant flaunting of wealth[44] stimulated a sense of injustice. Perceived injustice has often been cited as one of the key elements that can trigger revolt against those in power.[45]

The PH coalition's constant attribution of the GST to Najib Razak made headway in rural areas, even though they were less concerned about 1MDB and PH attempts to link GST with those allegations. Several respondents placed the blame for their relentless financial struggle squarely on Najib's shoulders, and also noted that amounts distributed as BR1M did little to offset their woes. When asked about the many promises of financial support and other gifts offered just before the elections, several respondents said that they were always offered the sky at election time. This cycle of voters seemed to be less willing to wholeheartedly believe these promises:

> There is just too much arrogance. Look at them and how they spend money. And we struggle. And they think if they come here and promise us this and that we will vote for them? In the last election they also promised the sky. But after they got into power, they didn't even come to see us—so many promises unfulfilled. Are we to be bought so easily? They give us BR1M but how much do they take in GST? This will never end.[46]

Arrogance was a phrase that constantly came up in informal interviews in Johor and Kedah. Several people felt that Najib had crossed the line in his choice of words when referring to Mahathir. While this anger was more acutely felt in Kedah, where the Mahathir family legacy was more fervently cherished, it also came up in conversations in Johor, where even women who had specifically disapproved of Mahathir's dalliance with the DAP expressed discomfort at the disrespect shown to an elder statesman. Widely spread images of Johor local authorities cutting out Mahathir's photo from campaign banners elicited responses such as this one:

> But what is wrong with Najib? Why is he so petty? Cutting out Mahathir's face from the billboard is just silly. Is he afraid?"[47]

BN Johor's efforts to refrain from featuring Najib Razak in their campaign materials and in their rallies, instead attributing Johor's economic success to then Chief Minister Khaled Nordin was telling. It was clear that Najib Razak was a polarizing figure. Post-election conversations revealed that for some, their vote was a last-minute decision because they simply wanted to get rid of the GST and Najib Razak (and First Lady Rosmah Mansor). Several felt that there was nothing inherently wrong with BN, but it needed new leadership and they believed that voting against them was the only way to make it happen (Serina 2018c, p. 675).

While rural Malays did not necessarily understand issues related to 1MDB, many reflected on their lack of access to benefits in our conversations. While the PH coalition linked corruption to Najib and the UMNO leadership, rural communities were more concerned about corruption and cronyism by village, local committee and fishermen's association heads. Second-generation FELDA settlers (when out of earshot of their elders) also commented that they too were exasperated with promised funds for new recreational facilities on their estates being side-lined by committee heads. On the west coast, a few male respondents below thirty-five acknowledged that even with Malay-Muslims in charge, their lives were getting no better. Johor villagers in particular were cognizant of the fact that this middle level of authority were political appointees with links to the BN government (Serina 2018a, p. 24).

The BN refrain of the trilogy of race, religion and royalty seemed to resonate with East Johor voters, older voters in both north and south of the peninsular and women in west Johor. But younger FGD respondents in Kedah and male respondents in west Johor were more sceptical about doomsday scenarios related to Singapore and Penang. This indicates that the BN mantra that had worked so well for so many decades was beginning to wear thin (ibid., p. 29).

Social and parental pressure to vote for UMNO and BN was strong—this was clear in the way respondents or informants lowered their voices or made sure no one else was around when they wanted to say something negative about the ruling party. Thus, one-off phone interviews or surveys are more likely to result in respondents giving answers that are "safe" or what they think the interviewer would want to hear. FGDs on the other hand provide for more time for the truth to be teased out of respondents.[48] However even within FGDs, some were afraid to reveal the complete extent of their dissatisfaction with the BN government, but the long discussion enabled them to feel comfortable enough to speak frankly with me after the session or at another encounter. My familiarity with some residents in both east and west Johor allowed them to be honest as long as they saw that I was not taking notes or recording them.

While their exact words in these conversations cannot be quoted, the behaviour and their views indicate that there was more dissatisfaction boiling under the surface than is immediately obvious to the casual observer. After the elections, however, some of these respondents seemed to be better able to speak freely, as they explained (with some despair) how they voted:

> ... everyone here supports UMNO. What will they say if they knew that I support the opposition? I did what I had to do. I put up BN flags, I gave out t-shirts. But at the polling booth I voted for PKR. I've had enough of the corruption. But I didn't expect BN to lose completely.[49]

> ... of course I could not say that I do not support BN. What would my parents and in-laws say? I voted for PAS. They are more Islamic. What BN is doing is not Islamic. But I won't vote for PKR.[50]

In the final count, it was the magnitude of voters' socio-economic difficulties (Dettman and Weiss 2018, p. 744) that overcame traditional loyalties and *adat* in the areas I studied in west Johor and Kedah. East Johor voters remained steadfastly in support of BN.

UNDERSTANDING THE RESULTS

While some analysts and polls expected a decrease in support for BN, few foresaw the extent to which it would lose states to the opposition, especially Johor, Sabah and Negri Sembilan (see front endpaper of this book). Even fewer expected PAS to do as well as it did—retaining Kelantan, regaining Terengganu and garnering ninety state seats nationwide (*New Straits Times*, 11 May 2018). Pundits declared the opposition's win a victory for reform and a step towards inclusivity and a maturing of the electorate (*Channel NewsAsia*, 15 May 2018). While urban Malaysia, regardless of race or religion, had indeed been taking steps towards reform over the past few election cycles, the same was not necessarily true in rural and semi-urban areas. Generations of ethnic propaganda and fear-mongering cannot be erased in a decade (*Channel NewsAsia*, 10 May 2018).

Of those interviewed for this study, the FELDA estates of eastern Johor voted to remain with BN, while Iskandar Puteri, a semi-urban seat for which the redelineation added large urban pro-DAP areas such as Skudai, fell to PH. The latter had already been lost to DAP in 2013. As expected, Kedah lost ground to PH, mainly to PPBM.

A closer look at the numbers reveals that many rural Malay voters had in fact stayed within their comfort zones. A Merdeka Center study (*Straits Times*, 14 June 2018) shows that the overall Malay vote was evenly split between PH, BN and PAS. The research showed that 65–73 per cent of Malay votes went to either BN or PAS, which in turn means that about 70 per cent of the Malay voting populace did *not* support PH and voted within racial and religious lines.[51]

While PH won a large number of parliamentary seats, it garnered less than half of the total popular vote. BN won 34 per cent and PAS won 18 per cent of the overall popular vote. Of the Malay voters, BN garnered less than half of the votes, but PH earned far fewer: only about a quarter of the votes. PAS on the other hand earned 28 per cent of Malay popular votes (Ahmad Fauzi 2018, p. 691). PH used China and issues of sovereignty as a concern that was able to sidestep ethnic pitfalls, adeptly spurring urban voters to place national interests first. The association of Najib Razak with 1MDB and Chinese infrastructural and development projects were effective with rural voters, and even enabled civil servants and the army to swing to PH (Malhi 2018, p. 722).

Most northern rural seats remained with PAS (Kelantan, Terengganu and Kedah) and BN (Pahang and Perlis) as PKR was deemed too secular and Amanah were branded as traitors to Islam.[52] While this northern success was attributed largely to PAS' and BN's extensive grassroots network, PAS had less traction in the south where they were not able to use their usual tactic of infiltrating communities through religious schools (Hutchinson 2018, p. 18). The success of PAS' orthodox Islamic approach and campaigning was only successful in majority Malay-Muslim states where their campaign for a corrupt-free government along Islamic mores (*New Straits*

Times, 8 February 2018) removed voters' quandary of choosing between religious priorities and a clean government.

PAS did not make as much headway in central and south peninsular Malaysia (*Straits Times*, 25 May 2018), where rural votes fell largely to BN. Amanah as the more "professional" and moderate Islamic party was more amenable to voters in mixed states such as Johor. Johor's unprecedented fall to the then opposition stemmed from a major swing in urban and semi-urban areas. Much of eastern (rural) Johor remained with BN. It was in west (both urban and rural) Johor and other southern states that Amanah, PPBM and PKR were able to win the favour of semi-urban and urban Malay voters. Having said that, however, analysts have also shown that these wins were sometimes contingent on their being able to demonstrate their Islamic credentials (Hew 2018).

But even as rural Malay voters in Johor opted for the opposition in the hope that it would improve their livelihoods, when the results were revealed, some felt guilty that they had contributed to BN's unexpected fall. Most were also worried that the new government would not help them the way UMNO did in the past; PH is known to have a weak rural support network as this quote reveals:

> I thought I needed to do it [vote for the opposition], but my uncle is right. Who is going to help the fishermen now? What have I done? There is no hope for help from this [PH] government. What are they doing for us?[53]

This view illustrates that the votes that went to PH were done in protest and were not necessarily indicative of a long-term or permanent switch to voting beyond ethnic or religious concerns (Serina 2018c, p. 679). Further examples of the doubt expressed towards the new PH government reinforce this.

Not unlike loud claims by UMNO politicians in the immediate aftermath of the elections, many in Johor's rural areas spoke as if PH taking over government was but a minor aberration and that their time at the helm was limited.[54] Several voters I spoke to commented that if the new government were to fail the Malay people, they would happily bring UMNO back into power.

Even as Johor's generational UMNO supporters either consolidated their positions,[55] wriggled into new roles,[56] or jumped ship,[57] several continued to express concern that there is no longer a party in power than can genuinely champion the Malays and Islam. News of job losses by civil servants[58] and the end of salaries and allowances for more recent recruits for the national volunteer corps (RELA)[59] are taken as evidence that the "Chinese government" is working to disempower the Malays.[60] Additional news of non-Malay-Muslim appointments for the role of Chief Justice, Attorney-General and Minister of Finance added fire to the disbelief (Maidin 2018, p. 809).

These examples demonstrate that rural Malay voters still prioritize issues of race and religion, even as they struggle to cope with still-challenging socio-economic conditions. Discontent and disillusionment expressed by rural voters often only earn dismissive responses in urban areas as a more sceptical electorate question the validity of sweeping comments and denounce incendiary prose. Most blame

UMNO cybertroopers for dissent in the social media space and deem provocative comments by politicians as desperate attempts to cling to power.[61] In rural areas, however, these diatribes actually gain traction and sow seeds of discontent amongst those who continue to struggle to put food on the table.[62]

Since GE-14, several other incidents have demonstrated that ethno-religious schisms have gotten deeper. These include the anti-ICERD rally in Kuala Lumpur in which participants moved away from their party colours of green and blue to protest in white (*Channel NewsAsia*, 8 December 2018); symbolic of how religion has taken precedence over ethno-political issues. The by-election in Cameron Highlands was pitched as a referendum on voters' views of the new regime (*Asian Correspondent*, 7 February 2019). While this cannot be entirely validated, the win by BN's first indigenous Muslim candidate indicates that Malay voters are able to see beyond race to support a candidate of the same faith. Clear evidence of BN and PAS' liaisons on several occasions and Najib Razak's sudden rise in social media popularity in spite of charges levelled against him[63] indicate that voters can be quick to forget if the right ethno-religious diatribes are used to reel them in.

All of these incidences serve to illustrate that while the toppling of the BN regime was wholly unexpected, aside from protest votes in the south and the supremacy of the Mahathir family legacy in Kedah, rural Malay voters did not actually stray far from their comfort zones. As shown above, the majority remained within their ethno-religious boxes, voting for PAS and BN as they always have in the past. In rural areas especially, those who decided that they were willing to take a chance with PH quickly felt regret and remorse; there is little evidence of long-standing change to their views or voting preferences.[64]

CONCLUSION

Initial declarations in the early days after the unexpected results of the 14th General Elections celebrated a Malay tsunami and a new inclusive Malaysia that was able to vote across ethnic lines. More sober analyses beyond the initial jubilation and disbelief revealed a different story.

This chapter has attempted to open a window into the world and psyche of the rural Malay voter. While the build-up to the elections revealed widespread concerns about voters' immediate difficulties and socio-economic struggles, there were always undercurrents of fear of the impending loss of the pillars of Malay identity should a new "DAP-controlled" government come into power. In spite of that, the BN government was toppled.

Deeper investigation into rural Malay voter views post-election indicates that while Kedah's rural voters opted to remain in support of the Mahathir legacy, other rural Malay regions voted along ethno-religious lines, including east Johor where part of this research was conducted. In west Johor, where much of the flip to PH was buoyed by urban and semi-urban voters, rural Malay voters in the semi-urban outskirts voted for PH in protest of Najib and their daily struggles. Not long after the elections, many rural voters regretted their vote for the other side.

While the premise of this publication is to examine how the 2018 elections produced a result that was so widely unexpected, this chapter demonstrates that while the overall outcome was beyond expectations, a closer examination reveals that rural Malay voters in general did not transcend ethno-religious concerns or prove pundits too far wrong. These voters' allegiance to their values was only momentarily sidestepped in the odd desperate attempts to improve their livelihoods and aspire to the golden memories of the Mahathir era. Much of this hope and ambition dissipated soon after the elections. Today, ethno-religious schisms seem to have deepened further as PAS and UMNO continue to gather rural ground and the errors of Najib's old ways seem to have been quickly forgotten as he reinvents himself as a social media hero.

While PPBM is trying to position itself as the new voice of the Malays and begins to tap into available government resources, it now seems to want to continue the patronage practices that worked so well in rural areas. While UMNO and PAS have the grassroots network, they will soon struggle without access to government funds for their outreach. These structural factors could leave the door wide open in the rural fringes of Peninsular Malaysia. However, no matter how the political parties manoeuvre or position themselves, racial divisions and voting priorities in the outskirts of the new Malaysia do not look very different from that of the past.

Notes

1. On the eve of the elections, pollster Merdeka Center predicted that BN would not win the popular vote, but would still be able to retain the government: Tan Hui Yee, "Malaysia Election: Pollster Merdeka Center Expects BN to Win Poll, but Not Popular Vote", *Straits Times*, 8 May 2018, https://www.straitstimes.com/asia/se-asia/malaysia-election-pollster-merdeka-center-expects-bn-to-win-poll-but-not-popular-vote (accessed 20 May 2018). A discussion of BN's progressive decrease in support since the 12th General Elections in 2008 can be found here: Ida Lim, "At 36.42 pc, BN Records Lowest Popular Vote in History", *Malay Mail*, 11 May 2018, https://www.malaymail.com/news/malaysia/2018/05/11/at-36.42-pc-bn-records-lowest-popular-vote-in-history/1629546 (accessed 20 May 2018).
2. These FGDs were conducted in both Kedah and Johor, in three locations, involving a total of seventy-two people. More information on the details of the FGDs can be found in Serina (2018a).
3. Johor's ethnic breakdown is 53.3 per cent Malay, 30.3 per cent Chinese, and 6.5 per cent Indian. Malaysia's overall ethnic breakdown is 50.8 per cent Malay, 21.8 per cent Chinese and 6.6 per cent Indian (2015 figures) Also refer to: "Unjuran Populasi Penduduk 2015" [Residential Population Projections], Portal 1Klik [One Click Portal] https://web.archive.org/web/20160212125740/http://pmr.penerangan.gov.my/index.php/info-terkini/19463-unjuran-populasi-penduduk-2015.html (accessed 12 December 2017).
4. This information is gathered from extensive participant observation, engagement and immersion in rural communities over the past decade, in addition to recent FGD research and other studies carried out specifically for this chapter.
5. I have been immersed in the west Johor fishing community since 2008, where I used participant observation and other anthropological and community empowerment tools to study community responses to urbanization and changes in socio-economic conditions.

This long-term lived experience in the community provided useful background and baseline information to build upon for this assessment of their political views. My extended residence in west Johor but work in the east coast islands also enabled me to make contact with people in Tenggaroh, whom I initially met through their west coast relatives. These were useful starting points to begin the FGDs and continue with follow-up interviews and observation as rural communities need to time to warm up to those who enter their lives to seek information. Increased "familiarity" enables them to speak more freely as they are less concerned about the consequences of what they have to say, should it be "sensitive". In Kedah, initial contact for the FGDs was established by contacts in Universiti Utara Malaysia (UUM), but personal contacts in Yan also facilitated further informal interviews with others beyond the FGDs as well as laid the groundwork to maintain contact with those who were involved beyond the study period to determine changes in views, if any.

6. These selected participants were chosen because of their contacts within the community and ability to gather people for the FGDs. They then became hosts for the FGD sessions. Aside from the age and gender grouping, there were no specific guidelines given with respect to political leaning or affiliation. The hosts were informed that the purpose of the study was to determine voters' election issues and possible political leanings. No cash payments were made in return for the participation.

7. Respondents were allowed to speak freely so that a natural conversation ensued (at times between participants). I only prompted the participants or moved on to the next question when the topic at hand tapered out. At no point did I agree, disagree with or pass judgement on their responses. Occasionally scenarios were presented to the group (such as the suggestion of a female candidate as prime minister) to elicit their opinion on specific concerns.

8. The FGDs were recorded (with permission) but these off-the-cuff conversations were not. Copious notes were taken throughout.

9. These interviewees included but were not limited to: the street cleaners' supervisors, academics (Kedah), government agency staff, business people, academics, NGO staff (Johor) and the average man-on-the-street. Some of these informants requested that their names not be revealed.

10. In this survey, 2011 Johor residents (all Malaysian citizens) were interviewed by phone, of which 55 per cent (1,104 respondents) were ethnic Malay. More details on the results of this survey can be found in several other ISEAS – Yusof Ishak Institute publications.

11. Malaysia's *Rukun Negara* (National Principles) which are recited daily in all schools, ingrains this hierarchy into its citizens from a very young age. The pledge reads as such: *Maka kami, rakyat Malaysia, berikrar akan menumpukan seluruh tenaga dan usaha kami untuk mencapai cita-cita tersebut berdasarkan atas prinsip-prinsip yang berikut: Kepercayaan Kepada Tuhan; Kesetiaan Kepada Raja dan Negara; Keluhuran Perlembagaan; Kedaulatan Undang-Undang; Kesopanan dan Kesusilaan.* (translation: *We, her people, pledge our united effort to attain these ends guided by these principles: Belief in God; Loyalty to King and Country; The Supremacy of the Constitution; the Rule of Law; Courtesy and Morality.*) See also Sulaiman (2018).

12. BN rally held in a village in a semi-urban seat in Johor on 21 March 2018—exact name of location withheld to protect local informants. Speech translated from Bahasa Malaysia verbatim.

13. FGD session in FELDA estate, east Johor: male below thirty-five years (translated verbatim from Bahasa Malaysia).

14. FGD session in rural parts of a semi-urban seat, west Johor: female below thirty-five years (translated verbatim from Bahasa Malaysia).

15. FGD session in FELDA estate, east Johor: male above thirty-five years. Similar sentiments were expressed in almost the same words by female respondents above thirty-five years in both east and west Johor (translated verbatim from Bahasa Malaysia).

16. As the FGD sessions in Johor were held in hosts' homes over light refreshments, they became a bit of an event with children or parents of participants in attendance. While discussions were held in a separate room, other family members would inevitably be listening at the doorway so that they too could contribute their views after the formal sessions were done. Informal sessions with these extended family members and friends then continued for a few hours after the actual FGDs. This did not occur in Kedah as those FGDs were held in branch offices.

17. FGD session in FELDA estate, east Johor: female below thirty-five years (translated verbatim from Bahasa Malaysia).

18. FGD session in FELDA estate, east Johor: female below thirty-five years (translated verbatim from Bahasa Malaysia).

19. FGD session in west Johor: female under thirty-five years (translated verbatim from Bahasa Malaysia).

20. FGD session in Kedah: female over thirty-five years (translated verbatim from Bahasa Malaysia).

21. JAKIM is the Federal Department of Islamic Development Malaysia.

22. LGBT is the common abbreviation for lesbian, gay, bisexual and transsexual people.

23. Part of a speech by an UMNO representative at a BN rally in the rural fringes of a semi-urban seat.

24. Part of a speech by an UMNO representative at a BN rally in the rural fringes of a semi-urban seat.

25. The 2017 Johor Survey by ISEAS – Yusof Ishak Institute revealed that 47 per cent of Malay respondents overall felt that PAS is an acceptable party and 48 per cent of Malay respondents overall were favourable towards PAS (Norshahril 2017, p. 14).

26. These include newspapers such as *Utusan Malaysia*, *Sinar Harian* and *Metro*. RTM is the main broadcaster on rural televisions.

27. An example of a successful local politician in Kedah who knew how to apply the appropriate language in her engagement with the community can be found in this article: Jocelin Tan, "Can Mahathir Swing it in Kedah?", *Star Online*, 5 March 2017, https://www.thestar.com.my/opinion/columnists/analysis/2017/03/05/can-mahathir-swing-it-in-kedah-there-will-be-an-intense-political-battle-for-the-malay-heartland-sta/ (accessed 9 April 2018).

28. This recently came to the fore in this article: Diyana Ibrahim, "Keep Belittling Mahathir and Lose Kedah, Warns UMNO Vets", *Malaysian Insight*, 22 March 2018, https://www.themalaysianinsight.com/s/44327/ (accessed 9 April 2018).

29. In the rural Malay social hierarchy, civil servants are seen to be higher ranked than rural people.

30. While the rural community might be deemed eligible for the affordable homes scheme, they were unable to find the cash to pay for the down payment and other costs required. Rural people, especially fishermen, are usually cash poor and have little savings and irregular incomes.

31. The local meaning to this term is anyone with connections and access to funds,

compensation monies and projects or subcontracted jobs. These could be close family or friends of the person who controls the disbursement of monies or opportunities.

32. This is in contrast to older studies which showed that people voted according to party, not personality. A recent article on a survey conducted to determine how discerning voters are can be found here: Zurairi AR, "Malaysian voters more discerning now, polls suggest", *Malay Mail*, 18 December 2017, http://www.themalaymailonline.com/malaysia/article/malaysian-voters-more-discerning-now-poll-suggests (accessed 10 February 2018).

33. The Iskandar Puteri parliamentary seat was created as part of the redelineation exercise prior to GE-14 and is now the largest constituency in Johor. The fishing community involved in the FGDs were part of the original Gelang Patah seat, which was expanded to include Skudai and Kota Iskandar.

34. A common comment in response to this politician is that they will always remember his efforts for the community *"kami kenangkan jasa dia"*. Again, this is part of the Malay cultural need for loyalty to those who have given them a helping hand.

35. "Parti Bunga" is the local name for PPBM. It is a reference to the hibiscus insignia on the red flags of PPBM.

36. The FGDs in Kedah were held a few months after the death of Sultan Abdul Halim Mu'adzam Shah. While a new king (Sultan Sallehudin Badlishah, the late sultan's younger brother) was proclaimed not long after, the royal installation ceremony has not yet taken place.

37. These bonuses in total come to RM15.29 million (about S$5.15 million). A.R. Raaf and T.N. Alagash, "PM: FELDA settlers, smallholders would suffer if opposition wins GE-14, cancels contracts with China", *New Straits Times*, 25 March 2018, https://www.nst.com.my/news/politics/2018/03/348980/pm-felda-settlers-smallholders-would-suffer-if-opposition-wins-GE-14 (accessed 9 April 2018).

38. Personal communication, fishermen of west Johor: 27 March 2018—name withheld by request.

39. Personal communication, fishermen of west Johor: 8 March 2018—name withheld by request.

40. Personal observation, BN rally in west Johor parliamentary seat, 21 March 2018. The claim of legal homes for everyone in Gelang Patah mentioned by those speaking at the rally were embellishments of the truth as many of the locals in the community were still in the process of applying for land titles at the time of the rally. After the change of government, residents I spoke to said that there was silence from those who had promised them land. The payments made for the application process prior to GE-14 were also not reimbursed.

41. Official Facebook page of Sultan Ibrahim https://www.facebook.com/officialsultanibrahim/posts/497888487044516 (accessed 10 February 2018).

42. In contrast to the claims of objectivity, comments by the Crown Prince were officially released on his personal preference and his expressed appeal to Johor citizens to do what he felt was better for the state. Examples of these comments are discussed in the following online articles: Sadho Ram, "TMJ Shares Why He Doesn't Want Johoreans to Change the Country's 'Skipper'", *SAYS.com*, 8 April 2018 <https://says.com/my/news/tmj-shares-why-he-doesn-t-want-johoreans-to-change-the-skipper-of-malaysia> (accessed 12 June 2018) and Mohd Fahmi Mohd Yusof and Farah Dinah Hassan, "TMJ: Time to Restore the System Damaged by a 93-year old Individual", *New Straits Times*, 8 April 2018, https://www.nst.com.my/news/politics/2018/04/354757/tmj-time-restore-system-damaged-93-year-old-individual (accessed 12 June 2018).

43. Personal communication on condition of anonymity, fisherman (below thirty-five years) after a focus group discussion in West Johor on 6 November 2017.

44. Prior to the elections there were news and social media blitzes on the decadent lifestyles of those in power: from multimillion ringgit weddings to lavish feasts and extravagant shopping trips.

45. Analysts have determined that it is not just a state of poverty or socio-economic difficulties alone that can lead to action against those in power; it is the perception of inequality or experiences of injustice that trigger action. Refer to T. Kharroub, *Understanding Violent Extremism: The Social Psychology of Identity and Group Dynamics*, Arab Centre Washington C.C., 15 September 2015, http://arabcenterdc.org/wp-content/uploads/2015/09/RP-September-25-2015-TK.pdf (accessed 10 February 2018) and T. Abbas, "Muslim Radicalisation's Socio-Economic Roots", *The Guardian*, 29 April 2009, https://www.theguardian.com/commentisfree/belief/2009/apr/29/islam-terrorism-radicalisation-recession (accessed 10 February 2018).

46. Conversation with second-generation FELDA settler, east Johor, 27 May 2018. Translated verbatim from Bahasa Malaysia—name withheld. BR1M refers to an occasional cash pay-out as a form of assistance to those in the lower income bracket.

47. Conversation with storekeeper, east Johor, 27 May 2018. Translated verbatim from Bahasa Malaysia—name withheld. This comment was in reference to a situation in northern Johor where the Election Commission (EC) cut a hole in a billboard that featured a photo of Mahathir Mohamad. In the build-up to the elections, the EC declared that only those standing for elections in the area and party leaders could be featured on campaign material. As this new ruling was arbitrarily enforced, the broad assumption on the ground was that the then ruling government simply did not want Mahathir to be featured in campaign material.

48. This was a view also expressed by Wan Saiful Wan Jan in his presentation on his FGDs in urban Kedah. Also refer to Wan Saiful (2018b).

49. Conversation with entrepreneur, west Johor, 12 May 2018. Translated verbatim from Bahasa Malaysia—name withheld.

50. Conversation with housewife, west Johor, 28 May 2018. Translated verbatim from Bahasa Malaysia—name withheld. The respondent would not elaborate on why PKR did not deserve her vote, she simply maintained that it was better to vote for the more Islamic party.

51. A recent article in the L. Lopez, *Straits Times*, "First 100 days of Malaysia's New Government", 12 August 2018, https://www.straitstimes.com/asia/se-asia/first-100-days-of-malaysias-new-government (accessed 25 September 2018), a Merdeka Center study was cited in a claim that more Malays (roughly 50 per cent) support the new PH government. This is an improvement from the 25–30 per cent support during the elections. This analysis refers to Malays overall; both urban and rural voters. However, a more detailed analysis of the results can be found in S.C. Looi, "In New Malaysia, Malays Still Worry over Race and Religion", *Malaysian Insight*, 14 August 2018, https://www.themalaysianinsight.com/s/87555 (accessed 25 September 2018) corroborate my observations in rural areas. More importantly, 66 per cent of the respondents in this study were in urban areas, with only 21 per cent living or working in rural villages. This indicates that the rates of dissatisfaction with decisions made by the PH government could actually be higher once rural areas are taken into account.

52. Personal observation and communication during pre-election study. Refer to Serina (2018a).

53. Conversation with fisherman, west Johor, 10 June 2018. Translated verbatim from Bahasa Malaysia—name withheld.

54. Also refer to S.J. Zahiid, " 'Shaky' Pakatan Will Fall Before GE15, Zahid predicts", *Malay Mail*, 25 June 2018, https://www.malaymail.com/s/1645493/shaky-pakatan-will-fall-before-ge15-zahid-predicts. These views are parroted by UMNO grassroots members.

55. Personal observation of community behaviour in Johor where new village representatives are not given access to systems and procedures, or regular community members are told to go through older (now replaced) representatives in order to get things done (instead of newly appointed ones) for various reasons. Also refer to *Star Online*, "Wan Azizah to Civil Servants: Serve Govt of the Day or Else…", 22 June 2018, https://www.thestar.com.my/news/nation/2018/06/22/wan-azizah-to-civil-servants-serve-govt-of-the-day-or-else/ (accessed 25 September 2018).

56. Personal observation of community behaviour in Johor where former UMNO supporters discussed how they should move over to PH so that they can continue to receive "project benefits" and other opportunities. These discussions were held immediately after the elections as people tried to work out how to stay on the gravy train with a new government in power.

57. Party-hopping by politicians who are part of a losing party is a common practice in Malaysia. Allegations of bribery and opportunistic alliances are often thrown at those who engage in the practice (usually referred to as "frogs"). More discussion on this can be found in *Free Malaysia Today*, "Party-Hopping Betrays Voters, Bersih Warns", 12 May 2018, http://www.freemalaysiatoday.com/category/nation/2018/05/12/party-hopping-betrays-voters-bersih-warns/ (accessed 30 May 2018).

58. Media reports of civil service job losses such as *Star Online*, "Nur Jazlan Claims Contracts of Civil Servants Nationwide Terminated", 15 May 2018, https://www.thestar.com.my/news/nation/2018/05/15/nur-jazlan-claims-contracts-of-civil-servants-nationwide-terminated/ (accessed 30 May 2018) played on Malay fears as this ethnic group makes up the largest percentage of the civil service. The terminations were actually focused on only politically appointed contracts.

59. An official letter from the office of the Malaysian volunteer corps (Pejabat Jabatan Sukarelawan Malaysia, RELA) announcing the termination of salaries and allowances for its members was circulated (personal observation). Conversations with RELA members, however, revealed that this only applied to recruits who joined the organization in an escalated recruitment programme under the former prime minister and were quickly allowed to earn salaries without having to undergo training. The letter did not apply to older members of more than 10–15 years who have undergone training and are regulars with the organization. RELA is an office under the Home Ministry of Malaysia.

60. Personal observation of Johor rural communities with strong UMNO support: the current PH government is frequently referred to as "that Chinese government"—implying that Mahathir Mohamad is only a puppet being controlled by the DAP. This gels with pre-election chatter on the ground where voters insisted that a vote for PH is a vote for Chinese takeover and control of Malaysia (through the DAP component party).

61. In the build-up to the Sg Kandis by-election, UMNO politician Tajuddin Abdul Rahman accused DAP of a Christian agenda. Excerpts of the speech can be found at A. Lee, "Tajuddin Fires 'Christian DAP' Salvo to Close BN's Sg Kandis Campaign", *Malaysiakini*, 3 August 2018, https://www.malaysiakini.com/news/437314 (accessed 25 September 2018).

62. The abolishment of the GST and the stabilizing of petrol prices are partial fulfilments of two points on the PH 100-day manifesto. With the abolishment of the GST, however, was also a promise to reduce the cost of living, and with the stabilization of petrol prices was a promise to provide targeted petrol subsidies to low-income citizens. The latter halves of these promises have yet to come to fruition. Dissatisfaction with the government has escalated in rural areas with a recent announcement that BR1M (financial assistance scheme for the poor) will be eventually phased out, *Star Online* "PM: Cash Handouts to Stop Eventually", 26 August 2018, https://www.thestar.com.my/news/nation/2018/08/26/pm-cash-handouts-to-stop-eventually-people-should-not-depend-on-govt-to-get-money-without-working-sa/ (accessed 25 September 2018).

63. Also refer to *Malay Mail*, "Now There's a 'Malu Apa Bossku' Song and the Rapper Wants Najib's Forgiveness", 6 February 2019, https://www.malaymail.com/news/malaysia/2019/02/06/now-theres-a-malu-apa-bossku-song-and-the-rapper-wants-najibs-forgiveness/1720317 (accessed 6 February 2019); *Malaysian Insight*, "Sympathetic Malays Embrace 'Rebranded' Najib", 24 February 2019, https://www.themalaysianinsight.com/s/135636 (accessed 27 February 2019); SM Amin, " 'Bossku' Najib Popular in Langkawi Because Pakatan Not Doing Its Job, Say Voters", *Malaysian Insight*, 8 February 2019, https://www.themalaysianinsight.com/s/131287 (accessed 27 February 2019); and Zurairi AR, "From Bijan to Bossku: Najib Taps into 'Rempit' Culture in Working Class Rebranding", *Malay Mail*, 18 January 2019, https://www.malaymail.com/news/malaysia/2019/01/18/from-bijan-to-bossku-najib-taps-into-rempit-culture-in-working-class-rebran/1713790 (accessed 27 February 2019).

64. A number of media articles highlighted why UMNO remains a "safe" party for rural Malays such as: Adrian Chan, "Fight for Rural and Malay Votes Continues", *Star Online*, 12 August 2018, https://www.thestar.com.my/news/nation/2018/08/12/fight-for-rural-and-malay-votes-continues-as-it-ushers-in-the-100thday-anniversary-of-its-historic-g/ (accessed 27 February 2019). Other articles highlighted a study by the Penang Institute and Ilham Centre that showed that Malays are still uncertain about PH and had regrets about their vote, as well as shock at the complete fall of the BN government. These findings corroborated the views that I heard in Johor. Refer to Predeep Nambiar, "Study Finds Malays Still Anxious about Rights under PH Govt", *Free Malaysia Today*, 5 January 2019, https://www.freemalaysiatoday.com/category/nation/2019/01/05/study-finds-malays-still-anxious-about-rights-under-ph-govt/ (accessed 27 February 2019), and Sheridan Mahavera, "Majority of Malays Unhappy with Pakatan but Have Hope, Says Study", *Malaysian Insight*, 31 January 2019, https://www.themalaysianinsight.com/s/129735 (accessed 27 February 2019). Personal communication (22 February 2019) with a reporter (name withheld) canvassing views in a PPBM state seat in Kedah also revealed that voters there were disappointed with the new government as financial assistance provided under the old government had been cut, but no new forms of support had begun under the new government. Many rural Malays that this reporter spoke to also expressed regret at having supported PH in GE-14.

References

Ahmad Fauzi, A.H. 2018. "The Islamist Factor in Malaysia's Fourteenth General Election". *Round Table* 107, no. 6: 783-701. https://doi.org/10.1080/00358533.2018.1545937 (accessed 30 November 2018).

Ahmad, N. 2018. "MB: We Will Develop Johor as a Team". *Star Online*, 28 February 2018. https://www.thestar.com.my/metro/metro-news/2018/02/28/mb-we-will-develop-johor-as-a-team-he-says-ideas-for-state-structure-plan-2030-draft-welcome/ (accessed 9 April 2018).

Alatas, S.H. 1972. *Modernization and Social Change*. Sydney: Angus and Robertson (Publishers).

Asian Correspondent. 2019. "What Lessons Should Malaysia Draw from the Cameron Highlands By-election". 7 February 2019. https://asiancorrespondent.com/2019/02/what-lessons-should-malaysia-draw-from-the-cameron-highlands-by-election/ (accessed 20 February 2019).

Benjamin, N. 2018. "Don't Get Involved in Politics, Johor Sultan Tells Mayors, Council Presidents". *Star Online*, 26 February 2018. https://www.thestar.com.my/news/nation/2018/02/26/dont-get-involved-in-politics-johor-sultan-tells-mayors-council-presidents/ (accessed 9 November 2018).

Cheng, K., E. Ng, and F. Mokhtar. 2018. "The Big Read: Voters Not Swayed by Racial Politics in Malaysia's GE, But How Long Will That Last?". *Channel NewsAsia*, 15 May 2018. https://www.channelnewsasia.com/news/asia/voters-not-swayed-racial-politics-malaysia-general-election-10231158 (accessed 20 June 2018).

Dettman, S., and M.L. Weiss. 2018. "Has Patronage Lost its Punch in Malaysia?". *Round Table* 107, no. 6: 739–54. https://doi.org/10.1080/00358533.2018.1545936 (accessed 30 November 2018).

Department of Fisheries, Government of Malaysia. 2013. "Malaysia's National Plan of Action to Prevent, Deter and Eliminate Illegal, Unreported and Unregulated Fishing (Malaysia's NPOA-IUU)". https://www.dof.gov.my/dof2/resources/user_1/UploadFile/Penerbitan/Senarai%20Penerbitan/Malaysia_NPOA_IUU.pdf (accessed 10 February 2018).

Fahmi Reza. 2007. "First All-Race Political Action and People's Constitution". *Malaysian Bar*, 1 August 2007. http://www.malaysianbar.org.my/echoes_of_the_past/first_all_race_political_action_and_the_peoples_constitution.html (accessed 10 February 2018).

Fairul Asmaini M.P., and M. Muhamading. 2018. "PAS Made the Right Decision Despite Standing Alone". *New Straits Times*, 11 May 2018. https://www.nst.com.my/news/politics/2018/05/368325/pas-made-right-decision-despite-standing-alone (accessed 30 May 2018).

Halid, S. 2018. "Do Not Be Cheated by the Opposition's Empty Promises, Kedah MB Advises Voters". *New Straits Times*, 4 March 2018. https://www.nst.com.my/news/politics/2018/03/341317/do-not-be-cheated-oppositions-empty-promises-kedah-mb-advises-voters (accessed 9 April 2018).

Hassan, H. 2018. "Most Malaysian Chinese Voted PH in Polls, but Malays in 3-Way Split". *Straits Times*, 14 June 2018. https://www.straitstimes.com/asia/se-asia/most-malaysian-chinese-voted-ph-in-polls-but-malays-in-3-way-split (accessed 30 June 2018).

Hew, W.W. 2018. "The Struggle for Political Islam in the 'New' Malaysia". *New Mandala*, 25 June 2018. https://www.newmandala.org/struggle-islamisms-new-malaysia/ (accessed 30 June 2018).

Hutchinson, Francis E. 2018. *GE-14 in Johor: The Fall of the Fortress?* Trends in Southeast Asia, no. 3/2018. Singapore: ISEAS – Yusof Ishak Institute.

Ibrahim, D., and M. Mustafa. 2018. "Dr Mahathir Still Holds Sway over Siamese in Kedah". *Malaysian Insight*, 20 February 2018. https://www.themalaysianinsight.com/s/38806/ (accessed 9 November 2018).

Khor, Y.L. 2018. "The FELDA Quarrel and Its National Ramifications". *ISEAS Perspective*, no. 2017/51, 10 February 2018.

Maaruf, S. 1988. *Malay Ideas on Development: From Feudal Lord to Capitalist*. Singapore: Times Books International.

Maidin, H. 2018. "The Appointment of Malaysia's First Minority Attorney-General and the Communal Discontent against It". *Round Table* 107, no. 6: 809–10. https://doi.org/10.10 80/00358533.2018.1545444 (accessed 30 November 2018).

Malay Mail. 2015. "Johor Prince: I Support Leaders with Integrity Not Political Parties". 22 August 2015. http://www.themalaymailonline.com/malaysia/article/johor-prince-i-support-leaders-with-integrity-not-political-parties (accessed 10 February 2018).

———. 2017. "Second Generation FELDA Settlers Receive Housing Offer Letters". 26 November 2017. http://www.themalaymailonline.com/malaysia/article/second-generation-felda-settlers-receive-housing-offer-letters (accessed 10 February 2018).

Malaysian Insight. 2018. "Kedah Relaxes Conditions to Allow Siamese to Own Homes". 26 March 2018. https://www.themalaysianinsight.com/s/45203/ (accessed 9 April 2018).

Malhi, A. 2018. "Race, Debt and Sovereignty: The 'China Factor' in Malaysia's GE-14". *Round Table* 107, no. 6: 717–28. https://doi.org/10.1080/00358533.2018.1545939 (accessed 30 November 2018).

Milner, A. 2011. *The Evolution of the Malaysian Monarchy, and the Bonding of the Nation*. Bangi: Penerbit Universiti Kebangsaan Malaysia.

Mohamed Radi, N.A. 2018. "Najib Launches FELDA 2.0 Initiative, Settlers' Number Stand at 105,294". *New Straits Times*, 27 March 2018 https://www.nst.com.my/news/nation/2018/02/332003/najib-launches-felda-20-initiative-settlers-number-stand-105294.

Muhammad Zikri. 2018. "RM3.6j Saguhati Nelayan" [RM3.6 million fishermen's gift], *Utusan Malaysia*, 26 March 2018. http://www.utusan.com.my/berita/wilayah/johor/rm3-6j-sagu-hati-nelayan-1.633171 (accessed 9 April 2018).

Muzaffar, C. 1979. *Protector?* Penang: Aliran.

Ngah, N. 2018. "PAS to Prioritise 'Loyal, Professional and Religious Candidate' for GE-14". *New Straits Times*, 8 February 2018. https://www.nst.com.my/news/politics/2018/02/333398/pas-prioritise-loyal-professional-and-religious-candidate-GE-14 (accessed 9 April 2018).

Norshahril Saat. 2017. "Johor Survey 2017: Attitudes Towards Islam, Governance and the Sultan". *ISEAS Perspective*, no. 2017/83, 10 November 2017.

Politweet.Org. 2018. "The Rural-Urban Divide in Malaysia's General Election". http://politweet.wordpress.com/2013/05/21/the-rural-urban-divide-in-malaysias-general-election/ (accessed 10 February 2018).

Serina Rahman. 2018a. *Malaysia's General Elections 2018: Understanding the Rural Vote*. Trends in Southeast Asia, no. 9/2018. Singapore: ISEAS – Yusof Ishak Institute.

———. 2018b. "Commentary: Malaysia Reborn? Does GE-14 Spell an End to Racial Politics?". *Channel News Asia*, 10 May 2018. https://www.channelnewsasia.com/news/commentary/malaysia-general-election-race-card-costs-of-living-concerns-10220262 (accessed 15 May 2018).

———. 2018c. "Was It a Malay Tsunami? Deconstructing the Malay Vote in Malaysia's 2018 Election". *Round Table* 107, no. 6: 669–82. https://doi.org.10.1080/00358533.2018.1545941 (accessed 30 November 2018).

Shagar, L. 2018. "Najib: Barisan Has Proven Its Commitment to Fishermen's Interests". *Star Online*, 26 March 2018. https://www.thestar.com.my/news/nation/2018/03/26/najib-barisan-has-proven-its-commitment-to-fishermens-interests/ (accessed 9 April 2018).

Straits Times. 2015. "Johor Sultan Says Much to Learn from Singapore, Talks about Late Son". 27 December 2015. http://www.straitstimes.com/asia/se-asia/johor-sultan-says-much-to-learn-from-singapore-talks-about-late-son (accessed 10 February 2018).

———. 2018. "What to Make of PAS' Mixed Performance in Election". 25 May 2018. https://www.straitstimes.com/opinion/what-to-make-of-pas-mixed-performance-in-election (accessed 30 May 2018).

Sulaiman, A.B. 2018. *Ketuanan Melayu: A Story of the Thinking Norm of the Malay Political Elite*. Selangor: Vinlin Press.

Sun Daily. 2018. "Unlikely Mahathir Can Develop Langkawi Without UMNO, BN: Khairy". 3 February 2018. http://www.thesundaily.my/news/2018/02/03/unlikely-mahathir-can-develop-langkawi-without-umno-bn-khairy (accessed 10 February 2018).

Tan, Jocelin. 2018. "The Night the Earth Moved". *Star Online*, 10 May 2018. https://www.thestar.com.my/opinion/columnists/analysis/2018/05/10/the-night-the-earth-moved-as-predicted-by-dr-mahathir-the-malay-tsunami-has-taken-place-in-GE-14/ (accessed 25 May 2018).

Tindak Malaysia. www.tindakmalaysia.com/persempadanan (accessed 10 February 2018).

Wan Saiful Wan Jan. 2017. *Parti Amanah Negara in Johor: Birth, Challenges, and Prospects*. Trends in Southeast Asia, no. 9/2017. Singapore: ISEAS – Yusof Ishak Institute.

———. 2018a. *Parti Pribumi Bersatu Malaysia in Johor: New Party, Big Responsibility*. Trends in Southeast Asia, no. 2/2018. Singapore: ISEAS – Yusof Ishak Institute.

———. 2018b. *GE-14: Will Urban Malays Support Pakatan Harapan?* Trends in Southeast Asia, no. 10/2018. Singapore: ISEAS – Yusof Ishak Institute.

Wong, C.W. 2018. "The Truth is Out There". *Star Online*, 4 February 2018. https://www.thestar.com.my/opinion/columnists/on-the-beat/2018/02/04/the-truth-is-out-there-malaysia-is-much-more-complex-than-meets-the-eye-as-we-are-not-just-about-big/ (accessed 10 February 2018).

———, and N. Benjamin. 2015. "Johor Ruler: I'm Above Politics". *Star Online*, 27 December 2015. https://www.thestar.com.my/news/nation/2015/12/27/johor-ruler-im-above-politics-the-interest-of-the-rakyat-always-comes-first/ (accessed 10 February 2018).

Yusof, A. 2018. "Thousands Arrive in Kuala Lumpur from Across Malaysia for Anti-ICERD Rally". *Channel NewsAsia*, 8 December 2018 https://www.channelnewsasia.com/news/asia/malaysia-anti-icerd-rally-in-kuala-lumpur-thousands-arrive-11012828 (accessed 20 December 2018).

Zulkifli, A.S. 2018. "PM Arrives in Langkawi for Two-Day Work Visit". *New Straits Times*, 16 February 2018. https://www.nst.com.my/news/nation/2018/02/336135/pm-arrives-langkawi-two-day-work-visit (accessed 9 April 2018).

8

FROM COUNCIL FLATS TO GOVERNMENT QUARTERS
GE-14 in Urban Malay Constituencies

Adib Zalkapli and Wan Saiful Wan Jan

INTRODUCTION

In recent years, Malaysia seems to have followed a global trend of countries with long-ruling regimes, in that its urban electorate has increasingly voted for opposition parties. At the same time, a majority of rural Malay voters remained loyal to the ruling coalition, Barisan Nasional (BN). Heading into GE-14, searching questions arose: how would the growing number of Malays in urban areas vote, and what would be the consequences of potentially changing preferences?

There have been several attempts in the past to explain the urban-rural divide in Malaysian elections and their wider implications. One example is a study of the 1986 general election, when the opposition won 29 out of 177 federal seats, with the Democratic Action Party (DAP) alone winning 24 urban seats. This result, namely the concentration of opposition footholds in urban areas, and the Alliance-BN's strongholds in rural districts, led many to talk of a political rural-urban divide in place since the 1960s (Ramanathan and Adnan 1988).

In a follow-up study analysing the 1990 and 1995 general elections, Ramanathan (1996) noted that rural Malay voters on one hand, and urban Malay and non-Malay voters on the other, were divided based on their access to the media—implying that rural Malays were more reliant on government-controlled Malay newspapers like *Utusan Malaysia* and *Berita Harian* for information. The same study also noted that in the rural east coast states of Kelantan and Terengganu, the Islamist party, Parti Islam Se-Malaysia (PAS) managed to strengthen its position through the publication and distribution of its party newsletter *Harakah*.

Most recently, Maznah (2015) discussed the outcome of the 2013 General Elections (GE-13) in urban and semi-urban Malay constituencies in a study of parliamentary seats with Malay agricultural settlements managed by the Federal Land Development Authority (FELDA). In that year's General Election, BN, through UMNO, won six of the eight urban constituencies with FELDA settlements. The other two seats were won by PAS, which was then part of the opposition coalition, Pakatan Rakyat (PR). Regarding Malay-majority urban and semi-urban constituencies, BN won only seventeen of forty such seats in GE-13. Consequently, Maznah (2015) argued that urban Malays were more inclined to vote for PR due to their relative economic independence from the state and the belief that the then opposition coalition would not pursue policies detrimental to the interests of their community. The same study also observed that local UMNO branch offices and the FELDA management helped garner support for BN through effective grassroots campaigning.

This chapter seeks to establish and analyse political sentiments in the run-up to and immediate aftermath of the 14th General Elections (GE-14), with a focus on council flats and government quarters—where urban Malays are concentrated, and where crucial contests for this voter bloc took place.

To this end, this chapter will draw on data gathered from focus group discussions (FGDs) held with Malay voters in urban and semi-urban areas in Johor and Kedah to get a sense of their sentiments and voting inclinations. These FGDs, carried out in early 2018, are complemented by fieldwork in urban Malay-majority constituencies in the Kuala Lumpur and Putrajaya Federal Territories carried out during the GE-14 campaign period. This is followed by an analysis of immediate developments following the elections. This chapter will argue that, during GE-14, UMNO attempted to replicate its rural grassroots strategy to drum up support among Malay voters in urban areas. However, this approach had limited success.

This chapter is comprised of seven sections. Following this introduction, the second section will set out the definition of urban and rural constituencies. The following section will set out the context of GE-14, specifically as it pertains to Malay voters. The fourth section will set out the findings of urban Malay voters gleaned from the FGDs. The fifth section will analyse specific electoral contests in urban Malay constituencies. The sixth will then pan out to explore national trends in urban Malay constituencies. The seventh and final section will then examine the results of a number of by-elections held since GE-14.

DEFINING URBAN AND SEMI-URBAN CONSTITUENCIES

There is no conclusive method for classifying parliamentary constituencies in Malaysia. The Election Commission (EC), and the Malaysian government more broadly, have not been able to decisively differentiate between urban, semi-urban and rural constituencies. In a parliamentary reply in 2010, then Prime Minister Najib

Razak stated that urban and semi-urban constituencies have an area of between eight to 250 square kilometres, with each constituency having at least 30,000 voters (*Bernama*, 25 November 2010). These criteria include a vast number of constituencies with varying geographic and demographic characteristics. In addition, their geographic specifications would exclude socially urban constituencies such as: Malaysia's main airport city Sepang (841 square kilometres); the relatively developed Petronas town of Kemaman (2,540 square kilometres); and Gombak (265 square kilometres), a suburb east of the Kuala Lumpur city centre.

Moreover, this explanation was contradicted in the EC's report on the 2018 parliamentary redelineation exercise. According to the Commission, there is no exact formula for determining the number of voters for different categories of constituencies (Election Commission 2018). The 2018 report stated, however, that the EC's work for redelineating parliamentary constituencies is guided by principles set out in the Federal Constitution. These principles include: ease of local administration—where local governments' boundaries are taken into consideration; the availability of government facilities to manage election process; and the maintenance of local ties, to ensure that villages and housing estates are not divided into different constituencies. Similarly, the EC is also not very clear on the physical size of urban and semi-urban constituencies. However, for rural constituencies, the EC seeks to ensure that each electoral district is of reasonable size in order to enable the effective work of its elected representatives.

Due to the lack of clarity on the definition of urban and rural seats, this study adopts the classification used by Politweet, an independent social media research firm based in Malaysia. The firm relies on satelite images provided by Google Maps to classify each seat as urban, semi-urban or rural according to its size and population density (Politweet 2013). Based on the firm's classification, and the EC's 2018 voter registration records, there are forty-three Malay-majority seats in the Malaysian Peninsula that can be classified as urban or semi-urban. Given its greater clarity, this chapter relies on the Politweet classification.

OPPOSITION PARTIES IN THE RUN-UP TO GE-14

In analysing urban Malay votes in GE-14, it is important to revisit the realignment of the opposition alliance, Pakatan Rakyat, that started about three years before the polls. As part of this process, the coalition lost its principal Malay partner, PAS. The void was subsequently filled by two Malay parties: Amanah, which splintered from PAS; and Parti Pribumi Bersatu Malaysia (PPBM), which grew out of UMNO's factional splits and the expulsion of a clique of its top leadership.

PR had been formed after the 2008 General Election, which was characterized by BN losing its majorities in the state legislative assemblies of Selangor, Penang, Perak and Kedah. Unlike in Kelantan, where PAS governed since 1990, no single opposition party had secured a majority of seats in the state assemblies of any of these four states. Thus, the leaders of Parti Keadilan Rakyat (PKR), PAS, and DAP wanted the policies of the state governments under these parties to be coordinated centrally. The outcome led to the formation of coalition governments in the four states, with PKR and DAP representatives appointed as the Chief Ministers of Selangor and Penang respectively, while PAS assemblymen were made Chief Ministers in Perak and Kedah.

One of the biggest challenges of the new coalition in its early days was that the four PR-controlled West Coast states became centres of communal tension, which was partly a result of UMNO's aggressive campaign to delegitimize the state governments—especially among the Malay-Muslim community. In Kedah, the coalition was divided over the demolition of a pig abattoir and the PAS' Chief Minister's decision to set a higher bumiputra quota of 50 per cent for new housing developments (Vinesh 2009). In Perak, the Chief Minister from PAS, Datuk Seri Nizar Jamaluddin was accused of being a puppet of DAP, as the latter controlled most positions in the state executive council (Asliza 2018). Nizar was also criticized by UMNO for the state government's decision to award residents of mainly ethnic Chinese New Villages in Perak freehold land titles. Nizar's government only lasted eleven months, after which it collapsed following the defections of three state assemblymen to BN—which was engineered by the then deputy prime minister and Perak BN chairman Najib.

In Penang, the state faced regular public protests led by UMNO and Malay-Muslim groups affiliated to the party. The situation was perhaps even more heated in Selangor. In September 2009, a group of UMNO grassroots leaders staged a public rally in the state capital of Shah Alam—a Malay-majority city—to protest against the state's decision to relocate a Hindu temple (*The Edge*, 9 September 2009). The protestors marched with a severed cow head, in an apparent attempt to insult the Hindu community.

This was the wave of communal tensions that led to the formation of Perkasa, a Malay rights pressure group led by Ibrahim Ali. Ibrahim was then an independent member of parliament who contested in Kelantan as a PAS-endorsed candidate in the 2008 General Elections. Ibrahim and Perkasa believed that DAP's growing strength was a threat to national security and the strengthening of the Malay special rights was necessary to ensure peace and stability. They stated that any erosion of the special rights would lead to another racial riot similar to what the country experienced in 1969 (Hazlan and Jimadie 2009).

Despite the challenges from UMNO and Malay groups like Perkasa, PR improved its performance in the 2013 General Elections (GE-13). The coalition won the popular vote and increased its number of seats from eighty-two to eighty-nine in the 222-member Parliament. However, the PR coalition failed to hold on to some of the Malay seats it won in 2008, and only DAP made gains in urban areas. Although BN won fewer votes in GE-13 than it did in GE-12, it secured control of the Perak and Kedah state governments, and UMNO won eighty-eight parliamentary seats—up from seventy-nine in 2008.

It was clear from GE-13 that PKR, being a Malay-dominated multiracial party, failed to make inroads into UMNO strongholds. This made PR susceptible to being labelled an urban Chinese-dominant coalition—all the more when DAP held the most opposition parliament seats.

Meanwhile, PAS did slightly worse in 2013—winning twenty-one parliament seats, compared to twenty-three in 2008. Thus, it began to push back against PR's coalitional model and to reassert itself ideologically by reviving its shariah agenda (Mohd Khairuddin 2017). In early 2015, the PAS-controlled legislative assembly of Kelantan passed a law to pave the way for the state government to enforce a stricter version of the Islamic criminal code, otherwise known as *hudud* (Syed Azhar 2015). The move was followed by an attempt by PAS Party President Hadi to table a private member's bill in the Federal Parliament to expand the powers of shariah courts (Zachariah 2015). In the same year, PAS held its party election which saw the defeat of pro-PR party leaders who were against the party reviving its *hudud* agenda. This agenda and the subsequent purge of pro-PR leaders in PAS led to the collapse of Pakatan Rakyat—with DAP leader Lim Kit Siang declaring that the coalition had fallen apart (Lim 2015).

The defeated leaders from PAS led by Mohamad Sabu formed Amanah in September 2015. This new party sought to portray itself as a moderate Islamist party and replaced PAS in the opposition coalition which was then renamed Pakatan Harapan (Wan Saiful 2017).

The new coalition, however, was divided on the role of PAS. PKR president, Dr Wan Azizah Wan Ismail, initially welcomed further negotiation between the new coalition and PAS to work together as a united opposition front. In Selangor, the then Chief Minister and state PKR leader Azmin Ali, dismissed the idea of forming a state-level PH chapter, citing an existing pre-election agreement between DAP, PKR and PAS to govern the state (*Bernama*, 22 October 2015). It appeared that PKR leaders were not convinced that Amanah would be able to play the role of the representative of the Malay-Muslim community. The view that PAS should still be part of the opposition coalition was also shared by prominent electoral reform activist Ambiga Sreenevasan, who feared that three cornered-contests between PAS, PH and BN would lead to opposition votes being split to BN's potential benefit (*Malaysiakini*, 29 August 2017).

While the PH component parties debated how they should work with PAS, Mahathir and Muhyiddin Yassin upon their expulsion from UMNO decided to form an exclusively Malay party PPBM in late 2016. In March 2017, the party subsequently became the fourth member of the PH coalition (Anand 2017). PPBM's decision was later followed by the formation of the Selangor chapter of PH in September 2017, where Azmin convened the first state meeting and announced the leadership line-up. The two developments effectively ended the PH parties' relationship with PAS—making PPBM and also Amanah the representatives of the Malay-Muslim community in the coalition to challenge UMNO dominance.

PRE-ELECTION FOCUS GROUP DISCUSSIONS

In order to shed light on the opinions of Malay voters in urban areas, sixteen FGDs involving a total of 117 Malay-Muslim participants were carried out in the northern state of Kedah and southern state of Johor in January 2018.[1] These two states were selected because they were identified as key battlegrounds by PH, which invested substantial resources in campaigning in these areas. In each state, two urban or semi-urban constituencies were chosen: Kubang Pasu and Sungai Petani in Kedah; and Johor Bahru and Pulai in Johor. Four FGDs were carried out in each constituency, with participants grouped by gender and age (above and below thirty-five).

Three main questions were used to prompt the respondents:

1. What are the issues that concern you most in the run up to GE-14?
2. What do you think of the ruling BN coalition and Prime Minister Najib Razak?
3. What do you think of the opposition PH coalition and their leader Mahathir Mohamad?

Roughly equal amounts of time were allocated to each of the questions, and the respondents were encouraged to comment in a free-flowing fashion, with minimal interruption or guidance. In Kubang Pasu and Johor Bahru, the questions were asked in the sequence above. However, in Sungai Petani and Pulai, the question on PH was asked second, followed by the question on BN.

Overall, the FGDs revealed that respondents in both Kedah and Johor were most concerned about the economic condition of the country in January 2018—a mere four months before the election. Real consternation about the surge in cost of living was expressed. These perceptions were formed by how the economy affected them personally, rather than being based on official statistics. In particular, they felt that prices were rising faster than their incomes, and this affected voters more in urban areas than in rural areas.

For the financial challenges that they faced, the respondents blamed the BN administration. The believed that the policies introduced by Najib changed the focus of support towards the B40 group, while neglecting those in the M40 category.[2] To them, this was an unfair situation, because they believed that as ethnic Malays, they were supposed to enjoy special privileges regardless of their socio-economic status. They also felt that the Najib administration had not helped them transition into the middle class.

Governance and corruption were causes for concern, but not significant enough to be the determining factor in voting. The respondents were generally aware of the various allegations of corruption surrounding the current administration. They agreed that these were weaknesses that must be rectified. Yet, they did not put a great deal of emphasis on these issues.

Regarding issues that were of greatest concern, respondents above the age of thirty-five generally placed a high importance on the position of Islam and the "Malay agenda"—which they assumed could only be defended by Malay politicians from Malay parties. UMNO, the respondents believed, is one such party—despite being in a coalition of more than a dozen parties representing various ethnic and religious minorities. There was no consensus on the definition of the term Malay agenda among the respondents, but some of the examples mentioned included: introducing *hudud* law; increasing budget allocation for government agencies responsible for

Islamic affairs; enforcing Islamic dress code in public places; and increasing Islamic content in the national school syllabus. The respondents also believed that Malaysian politicians have failed in their duties to defend the position of the Malays and Islam.

The same group of respondents were also of the view that UMNO and Najib have been successful in pursuing the Malay and Islamic agenda. UMNO was credited for the construction of local mosques, improvement in Islamic education and the promotion of Islamic culture in government schools such as the wearing of hijab among female students. Some of the respondents cited the establishment of the Islamic Pilgrimage Fund (Lembaga Urusan Tabung Haji), the growth of Islamic finance, and the status of Malaysia's halal certification as among the successes of UMNO-led Islamic initiatives. Upward mobility and access to tertiary education were also attributed to UMNO's affirmative action policies.

The respondents did not trust Pakatan Harapan to pursue the Malay and Islamic agenda. They cited DAP's membership of the coalition, claiming that the party was a chauvinist Chinese party and anti-Islam—citing the party's rejection of shariah law as evidence. It can be argued that the respondents saw the DAP as a dominant party in PH, in the same way that UMNO was the leader of the BN coalition. The perception that DAP was the dominant party in PH was also supported by PAS' departure from the opposition alliance. Some of the respondents believed that the Islamist party played an important balancing role to prevent DAP from overly dominating the opposition coalition. The respondents also believed that PAS was an important link to rural Malay areas for the opposition. Without PAS, the perception was that PH would have to reduce their focus on the Malay agenda in order to secure more mixed seats by winning over the Chinese votes.

Despite the respondents' unfavourable view of PH, they believed that Mahathir's presence as the leader of the coalition would help win Malay support. This view was also shared by respondents who openly declared their support for UMNO. There was also acknowledgement by the respondents that the issue of championing Malay and Islamic agenda could potentially be further exploited by Najib to maintain his popularity ahead of GE-14. Some of them noted that Najib had abandoned his unifying message when he first took over the prime ministership, in favour of Malay-centric messaging.

It can be argued that their replies on Malay and Islamic agenda and complaints on cost of living indicated that the respondents were indecisive. The signs of indecisiveness or even fear were also visible from the body language of some of the respondents. They were uncomfortable with discussing UMNO, Najib and the upcoming election. Some of the respondents also sought assurances of confidentiality out of concerns that their answers might be used against them. The respondents, however, were more open when the discussions moved away from UMNO and Najib to discuss PH.

From the outcome of the focus group discussions, it was clear that although PH addressed the issue of Malay representation in the coalition with the inclusion of Mahathir-led PPBM, it was still largely unable to convince Malay voters that it was a viable alternative to the UMNO-led BN coalition.

THE CAMPAIGN FOR URBAN MALAY VOTES: OBSERVATIONS ON THE GROUND

When the General Elections were called, PH appeared to have resolved two issues, namely the representation of Malays, and the absence of strong leadership. This was achieved by incorporating Amanah and PPBM in the coalition and putting Mahathir forward as PH's candidate for prime minister. However, the coalition's Malay candidates especially from PPBM were no match for UMNO's pool of high-profile candidates. In the Federal Territories of Kuala Lumpur and Putrajaya, UMNO retained two serving Ministers and enlisted two former Cabinet ministers to challenge PH's hold on urban Malaysia. The two territories contain twelve parliamentary seats between them (Figure 8.1). Of these, UMNO contested in five and the remaining PH-controlled non–Malay-majority seats distributed between the BN component members of MCA, Gerakan and PPP.

In the Lembah Pantai constituency, where the mostly Malay, city hall flat dwellers form the bulk of the voters, UMNO fielded former Minister for Federal Territories Raja Nong Chik Raja Zainal Abidin. The seat was won by PKR for the first time in 2008 by Anwar's daughter Nurul Izzah. For the 2018 General Elections, PKR fielded a newcomer Fahmi Fadzil, who has been serving as the party's communications director and political aide to Nurul Izzah. These perceived disadvantages to PKR were compounded by gerrymandering of Lembah Pantai, focused on highly Malay-populated zones.

Meanwhile in the Setiawangsa constituency, where almost 30 per cent of the voters are members of the security forces, former Royal Malaysian Air Force pilot Zulhasnan Rafique was nominated to defend one of UMNO's strongholds. Zulhasnan was first elected MP in 1999 representing the Wangsa Maju constituency. When the Setiawangsa constituency was carved out from Wangsa Maju for the 2004 General Elections, he won convincingly and later successfully defended the seat in the 2008 polls. From 2006 to 2009, he also served as Minister for Federal Territories in the Prime Minister Abdullah Ahmad Badawi's last Cabinet. Zulhasnan was not fielded in the 2013 General Elections and was made Ambassador to the United States in 2016. He resigned as the Ambassador soon after the dissolution of Parliament in April 2018 to contest in GE-14. Zulhasnan's opponent was a former Executive Councillor in the Selangor state government, Nik Nazmi Nik Ahmad. Although an experienced politician, having served in the Selangor legislature since 2008, Nik Nazmi was new to federal politics and his former state constituency of Seri Setia is about 20 kilometres away from Setiawangsa—making him a political outsider in the UMNO stronghold.

Two ministers who served in Najib's last Cabinet were also nominated to defend their respective seats that were allocated by the PH coalition to PPBM candidates— Titiwangsa and Putrajaya. In Titiwangsa, Second Minister of Finance Johari Abdul Ghani contested against the largely unknown PPBM's women wing chief Rina Harun. Johari had wrested the seat back from PAS in 2013. Johari, who is an accountant by training, grew up in the squatter area of Kampung Pandan near the city centre and

FIGURE 8.1
Urban and Semi-urban Malay-Majority Constituencies, 2018

Map provided by ISEAS – Yusof Ishak Institute. © (2019) ISEAS – Yusof Ishak Institute

maintains close ties with the constituency's working class. For years, Johari had made personal donations to enable the poorest of his constituency to perform the *umrah* pilgrimage to Mecca (Ismail 2014). As an MP, Johari also engaged directly with his voters—his weekly "meet the people session" at his service centre was very popular with the city hall flat dwellers of Titiwangsa.

In Putrajaya, UMNO fielded another high-profile candidate, the party's secretary-general and Minister for Federal Territories Tengku Adnan Tengku Mansor. Tengku Adnan had been the MP for the seat since 2004, after the area was carved out from the state of Selangor and turned into a Federal Territory. Putrajaya, the federal administrative capital, is dominated by Malay civil servants and had been considered one of the safest seats for BN. The government quarters that dot the constituency appeared impenetrable to any opposition party. PPBM nominated Dr Samsu Adabi Mamat, a respected academic and political analyst from the National University of Malaysia, who was seen as a political novice.

With four high-profile candidates in the Federal Territories, UMNO appeared to be ahead of PH parties, at least in providing strong leadership for urban Malays. By fielding four former and serving Cabinet members, it can be argued that UMNO was sending a message to the urban Malays that they would be represented at the highest level of the government. In fact, throughout the campaign, Tengku Adnan styled himself as a village head (*ketua kampung*), which is an unelected leadership position used in rural Malay settlements.

Beyond the issue of strong leadership, UMNO's campaign activities in the urban constituencies were also focused on addressing voters' key concerns—race, religion and high cost of living, which had also been listed major areas of concern in the focus group discussions held in Johor and Kedah.

To address the cost of living issue, temporary bazaars were set up in these constituencies to distribute groceries at subsidized prices. These bazaars were, in some cases, set up with the support of Ministry of Domestic Trade, Cooperatives and Consumerism. Officers from the Department of Agriculture could also be seen at some of the bazaars helping with the distribution of subsidized fresh produce. The bazaars were often publicized through leaflets and banners with pictures of UMNO candidates. Throughout the campaign period, the temporary bazaars, officially termed *jualan sentuhan rakyat* (people's sales), were held in all parliamentary constituencies in Kuala Lumpur and Putrajaya. The source of funding for the heavily subsidized goods was never disclosed, but UMNO candidates were happy to take credit for the price reductions as part of the campaign (Zulfadli 2018).

Contributions to Islamic institutions were another theme in UMNO's campaign in these seats. In Putrajaya, a ground-breaking ceremony for a new mosque and an Islamic school was turned into a campaign event for the party's candidate. Similar events planned around Islamic institutions were also observed in other constituencies. Just days before polling, Johari even made a list of his contributions to Islamic institutions in Titiwangsa since he had served as MP in 2013.

In summary, UMNO's campaign can be described as an attempt at replicating the community organization structure commonly found in FELDA schemes. By styling one of its candidates as *ketua kampung*, organizing subsidized bazaars and supporting Islamic institutions to legitimize their positions as community leaders, UMNO attempted to bring the Malays of council flats and government quarters under a leadership structure commonly seen in rural areas.

During the campaign, it was clear Malay candidates from PH were not only seen to be fighting political heavyweights, they were also trailing UMNO in the race to convince Malay-Muslim voters that they would able to protect the interests of the community and their religion. Without access to government resources, PH Malay candidates were also unable to match BN's approach in distributing subsidized goods. PH also had to compete with PAS candidates, who contested with a clear Islamic agenda.

To address the complaints of high cost of living, PH candidates could only pledge to abolish the burdensome GST. PH candidates also relied on national issues such as the 1MDB scandal and allegations of misuse of funds from Malay and Islamic institutions such as FELDA and Tabung Haji in order to win votes. PH, however, managed to partially mitigate the lack of political heavyweights in its ranks with Daim Zainuddin and Rafidah Aziz hitting the campaign trail. The former senior ministers from Mahathir's first administration were leading speakers at several PH's rallies in urban Malay areas and their presence symbolized continuity and stability to the sceptical Malay voters. Daim repeated the line that GST stands for *Government Suka Tipu* (or the government likes to lie), perhaps in an attempt to simplify the campaign message for the Malays.

THE RESULTS IN URBAN MALAY SEATS

In GE-14, BN, PH and PAS contested in forty-three Malay-majority constituencies in urban and semi-urban areas (Figure 8.1). Of these, ten are located in Selangor, six in Kedah, five in the KL federal territories, and four in Terengganu. Kelantan, Pahang, and Perak each contain three seats, and the remainder are scattered across Johor, Melaka, Negri Sembilan, and Penang.

When the results were announced, BN was almost decimated in urban Malay seats (Table 8.1). Out of the sixteen seats that it won in 2013 (fifteen by UMNO, one by MIC), the coalition only managed to retain four seats—all won by UMNO candidates. In contrast, PH parties won thirty-three seats, while PAS won the remaining six urban Malay constituencies (Figure 8.2).

BN also lost the two Kuala Lumpur Malay seats of Titiwangsa and Setiawangsa that were seen as urban UMNO strongholds. While BN managed to hold on to the Putrajaya seat, Tengku Adnan won less than 50 per cent of the valid votes. His victory was made possible by the third PAS candidate who managed to win 14 per cent of the votes.

The situation in Putrajaya was not unique.

In total, twenty-six of the forty-three urban and semi-urban Malay seats were won with a plurality, namely that the winning candidate obtained the largest number of votes, but did not secure more than 50 per cent of the votes (Table 8.2). All four

TABLE 8.1
Winners in Urban Malay Constituencies (GE-14)

State	Parliamentary Seat	Urban/ Semi-urban	Malay Majority or Malay Super Majority	GE-13 Winner	GE-14 Winner	Plurality/ Majority (GE-14)
Johor	Johor Bahru	Urban	MM	BN	PH	M
Johor	Batu Pahat	Semi-urban	MM	PR	PH	M
Kedah	Merbok	Semi-urban	MM	BN	PH	P
Kedah	Kulim-Bandar Baharu	Semi-urban	MM	BN	PH	P
Kedah	Kubang Pasu	Semi-urban	MSM	BN	PH	P
Kedah	Alor Setar	Urban	MM	PR	PH	M
Kedah	Sungai Petani	Semi-urban	MM	PR	PH	P
Kedah	Padang Serai	Semi-urban	MM	PR	PH	P
Kelantan	Pengkalan Chepa	Semi-urban	MSM	PR (PAS)	PAS	M
Kelantan	Kota Bharu	Urban	MSM	PR (PAS)	PAS	P
Kelantan	Bachok	Semi-urban	MSM	PR (PAS)	PAS	P
Melaka	Tangga Batu	Semi-urban	MSM	BN	PH	P
Melaka	Hang Tuah Jaya/Bukit Katil	Urban	MM	PR	PH	M
N Sembilan	Rembau	Semi-urban	MSM	BN	BN	P
N Sembilan	Kuala Pilah	Semi-urban	MSM	BN	PH	P
Pahang	Kuantan	Urban	MM	PR	PH	P
Pahang	Indera Mahkota	Semi-urban	MM	PR	PH	P
Pahang	Temerloh	Semi-urban	MM	PR (PAS)	PH	P
Perak	Kuala Kangsar	Semi-urban	MSM	BN	BN	P
Perak	Tambun	Semi-urban	MM	BN	PH	P
Perak	Lumut	Semi-urban	MSM	PR	PH	P
Perlis	Kangar	Semi-urban	MSM	BN	PH	P
P Pinang	Permatang Pauh	Semi-urban	MSM	PR	PH	M
Selangor	Hulu Selangor	Semi-urban	MM	BN	PH	P
Selangor	Gombak	Semi-urban	MSM	PR	PH	M
Selangor	Ampang	Semi-urban	MM	PR	PH	M
Selangor	Kapar	Urban	MSM	PR	PH	P
Selangor	Kuala Langat	Semi-urban	MM	PR	PH	P
Selangor	Sungai Buloh/Subang	Urban	MM	PR	PH	M
Selangor	Shah Alam	Urban	MSM	PR (PAS)	PH	M
Selangor	Selayang	Semi-urban	MM	PR	PH	M
Selangor	Hulu Langat	Semi-urban	MM	PR (PAS)	PH	M
Selangor	Sepang	Semi-urban	MM	PR (PAS)	PH	M
Terengganu	Besut	Semi-urban	MSM	BN	BN	P
Terengganu	Kemaman	Semi-urban	MSM	BN	PAS	P
Terengganu	Kuala Terengganu	Urban	MSM	PR (PAS)	PAS	P
Terengganu	Dungun	Semi-urban	MSM	PR (PAS)	PAS	M
W.P KL	Setiawangsa	Urban	MM	BN	PH	M
W.P KL	Titiwangsa	Urban	MSM	BN	PH	P
W.P KL	Wangsa Maju	Urban	MM	PR	PH	M
W.P KL	Lembah Pantai	Urban	MM	PR	PH	M
W.P KL	Bandar Tun Razak	Urban	MM	PR	PH	M
W.P PA	Putrajaya	Urban	MSM	BN	BN	P

Notes:
BN = Barisan Nasional
PR = Pakatan Rakyat
PH = Pakatan Harapan
MM = Malay-majority seats (50– 69 per cent Malay voters)
MSM = Malay Supermajority Seats (more than 70 per cent Malay voters)
P = Plurality (more votes than any other candidate)
M = Majority (more votes than all the other candidates combined)

FIGURE 8.2
Urban and Semi-urban Malay-Majority Constituencies and Winning Party, 2018

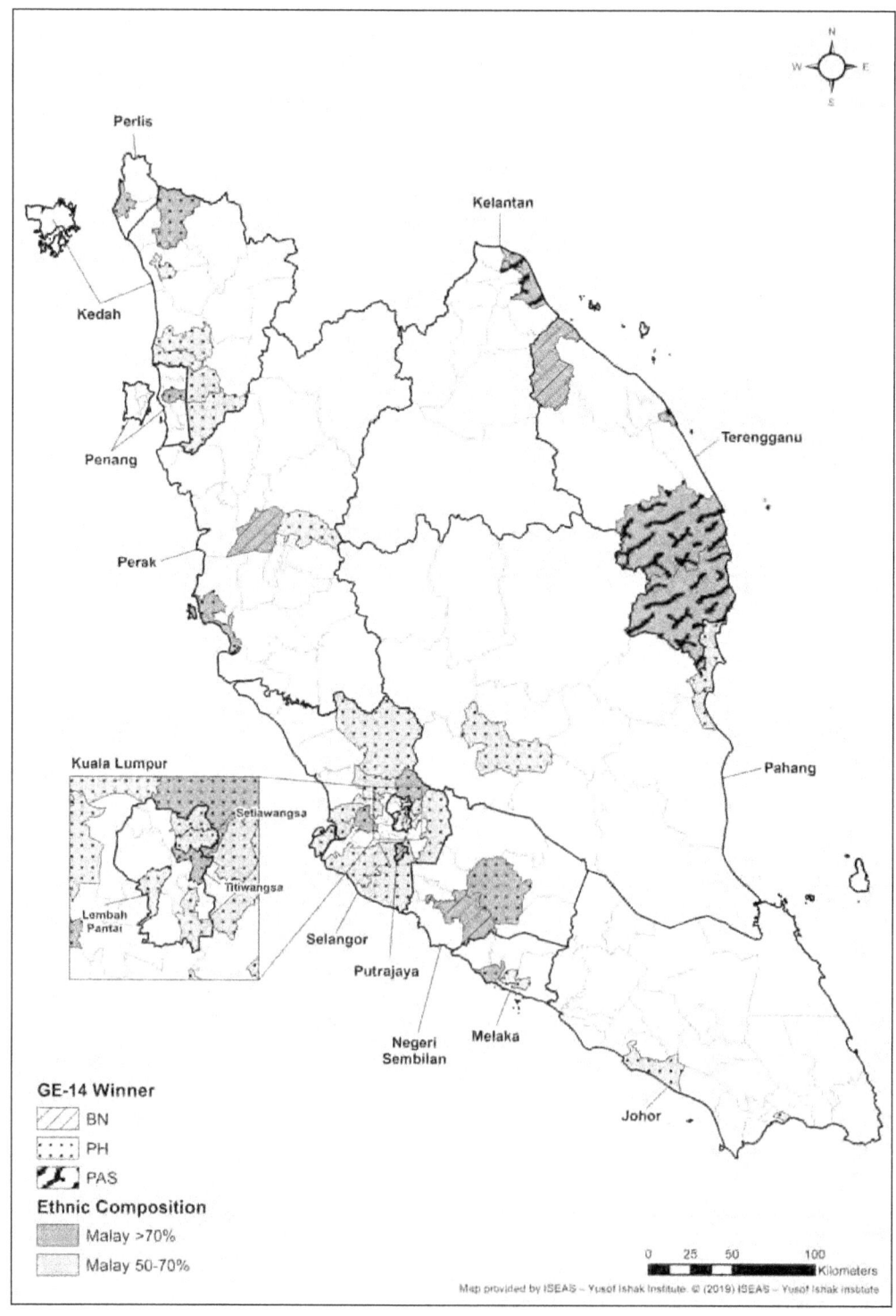

Map provided by ISEAS – Yusof Ishak Institute. © (2019) ISEAS – Yusof Ishak Institute

TABLE 8.2
Winners in Urban Malay Seats by Party (GE-14)

Party	Won by Plurality	Won by Majority	Total
UMNO	4	0	4
PAS	4	2	6
Pakatan-PKR	12	13	25
Pakatan-Bersatu	5	0	5
Pakatan-Amanah	1	2	3

such seats retained by BN were secured in this fashion. Similarly for PAS, four of its six victories were pluralities as opposed to outright majorities. Likewise, fifteen of PH's victories, including Titiwangsa, were secured in the same fashion. The large number of seats won with reduced majorities is consistent with the trend observed during the FGDs that the urban Malay voters did not have a clearly defined political preferences.

PH's thirty-three seats in the urban Malay constituencies certainly contributed to the change of government. Yet of these, eighteen were won with less than 50 per cent of the popular vote. Thus, one conclusion that can be made based on the vote share of each party in these constituencies is that Malay voters were divided almost equally between supporting and not supporting PH.

It can be further argued that an UMNO-PAS partnership could potentially mount a credible challenge against PH in Malay constituencies in the next general election. Although UMNO and PAS failed to challenge PH's popularity in urban Malaysia, both parties emerged as dominant parties in the opposition through the support of rural Malay electorates. With UMNO's fifty-four seats, and PAS' eighteen, following GE-14, Malaysia had a Malay-dominated opposition bench for the first time in Parliament's history.[3]

For PAS, it was the best election performance as an independent opposition party. Indeed, the previous time PAS contested as an independent opposition party in 1986, it won only one parliamentary seat. Amanah, which was formed to take over the role of PAS in the coalition, only managed to win eleven seats. PAS also managed to retain Kelantan despite a very strong challenge from Amanah leaders. Meanwhile in Terengganu, PAS captured the state government from BN. It was clear that traditional PAS supporters were not ready to abandon it for the more progressive Amanah.

The formation of the new government after the election also saw another unprecedented development. For the first time in history, the Malay party that anchored the ruling coalition, PPBM, is a minority party in the government—controlling only 10 per cent of the coalition's seats. As part of the pre-election agreement, PPBM leader Mahathir was made prime minister, despite his party being a minority in the coalition. With the anchor Malay party at the helm of the government being dwarfed by the ethnic Chinese-dominated DAP, and the multiracial

PKR, the new administration had to face allegations from UMNO that it was being controlled by DAP (Ismail 2018).

The results in urban Malay constituencies also negated the conventional wisdom that three-cornered contests with PAS would only benefit BN. PH was able to unseat BN by riding on the 1MDB scandal and rising cost of living. In addition, Mahathir's leadership and the endorsement of former senior ministers Daim and Rafidah compensated for PAS' withdrawal from the opposition coalition. With their experience in government and their simplified campaign message on corruption and cost of living, they helped other opposition leaders navigate the complex maze of council flats and government quarters. Mahathir, Daim and Rafidah not only symbolized Malay leadership of the opposition coalition, but their presence also indicated that a PH government would be guided by experienced hands.

POST-GE DEVELOPMENTS AND CONCLUSION

Without the additional Malay urban seats that PH wrested from BN, the change of government would not have happened. However, some of the unintended consequences of PH's victory are the collapse of the multiracial coalition BN and the emergence of a Malay-Muslim–dominated opposition led by UMNO and PAS. The UMNO-PAS alliance could potentially evolve into a formal political alliance ahead of the 15th General Elections.

In West Malaysia, the People's Movement Party (Gerakan) left BN about a month after the General Elections. BN is now officially left with its original members, UMNO, the Malaysian Chinese Association (MCA) and the Malaysian Indian Congress (MIC). MCA and MIC, however, have no meaningful representation in the coalition as they were almost wiped out in GE-14, winning only one and two seats respectively.[4] In December 2018, MCA even called for the dissolution of BN (Tan 2018).

Even without an official dissolution, Malaysia's first multiracial political coalition has effectively collapsed. This leaves UMNO and PAS the opportunity to shape opposition politics as the dominant parties in the opposition. In the early days of the new government, UMNO and PAS found common causes to fight the fledgling administration. When PH named Tommy Thomas as the new Attorney-General, the first non-Muslim to be appointed to the position, leaders from both UMNO and PAS strongly objected (Zaain 2018; *Suara TV*, 3 June 2018).

Another opportunity for UMNO and PAS to work together came when Mahathir announced at the United Nations General Assembly in September 2018 that Malaysia would ratify the International Convention on the Elimination of All Forms of Racial Discrimination (ICERD). The announcement led to a public protest in December 2018 with PAS and UMNO mobilizing their supporters into the streets of Kuala Lumpur. The two parties shared the view that the ratification of the treaty would undermine the position of Islam. This protest was estimated to have attracted about 50,000 people, forcing the government to backtrack on the announcement.

UMNO-PAS cooperation later went beyond mobilization of supporters for public protests. When the Selangor state constituency of Sungai Kandis was vacated in July

2018 following the death of PH Assemblyman Shuhaimi Shafie, PAS decided not to contest in the by-election to give way to UMNO. The move was reciprocated at another by-election a month later in another Selangor state seat, Seri Setia. In this case, UMNO decided to step aside for PAS. PH successfully retained both seats, but that did not stop UMNO and PAS leaders from maintaining and even strengthening their informal electoral pact.

In November 2018, the Cameron Highlands federal seat in Pahang was vacated by an Election Court that found the BN representative who won the seat at the 2018 General Elections guilty of bribing voters during the campaign. PAS once again decided to stay out of the contest, but mobilized its election machinery to support the UMNO-endorsed candidate Ramli Mohd Nor.[5] PAS President Abdul Hadi Awang also spoke in support of Ramli at an UMNO campaign rally on the eve of polling. PAS' campaign on the ground focused on the need to elect the Muslim Ramli who was contesting against PH's M. Manogaran, a Hindu from the DAP. BN successfully retained the Cameron Highlands seat, and the victory was partly attributed to UMNO-PAS cooperation (Sofian 2019).

In another sign that the UMNO-PAS cooperation could reverse the gains made by PH in GE-14, the ruling coalition lost the Semenyih by-election in March 2019. It was the first by-election since GE-14 that saw the defeat of the incumbent party. Despite the participation of other candidates, the Selangor state seat saw effectively another two-cornered contest between PH's PPBM and BN. Once again, PAS chose to give way to UMNO, but mobilized its campaign machinery to work alongside the latter party.

If there is any silver lining from the increasingly communalist opposition front, it is that the process to delegitimize the government among the Malay-Muslim community has happened largely within the electoral process. As discussed earlier, after the 2008 General Elections, the decline of UMNO and BN was met with racially charged public protests against the PR state governments of Penang and Selangor. Although strengthening a Malay-Muslim political alliance has been the focus of UMNO-PAS cooperation, the two parties were also found to have capitalized on the alleged failure of the PH government to reduce cost of living despite abolishing GST when campaigning at the recent by-elections.

It can be argued that based on UMNO-PAS political messaging after the General Elections, the three issues—race, religion and the cost of living that were high on the list of urban Malay voters before GE-14—will continue to be manipulated by the loose alliance. The battle for the urban Malay votes has not ended with the change of government in May 2018. The same issues are still at play, but with the key players swapping roles.

Council flats and government quarters are symbols of state power. The heavily subsidized council flats have for decades enabled generations of underprivileged Malays to integrate into urban life. They are an important tool for social mobility. For many Malays, government quarters symbolize stability of government employment. At the next General Elections, these symbols of the state will be the key battleground to decide on the future of Malaysia.

Notes

1. This section draws on Wan Saiful (2018).
2. The bulk of those participating in the FGD were M40. There were twelve who were identified as B40, given their estimated household income.
3. UMNO suffered defections after the General Elections leading to reduced number of representatives in the Parliament but remains a formidable opposition in the legislature.
4. MIC was later left with only one seat after it lost the Cameron Highlands seat following a court's decision to hold a fresh election.
5. Ramli was not an UMNO member but contested the Cameron Highlands by-election as a BN direct candidate.

References

Anand, Ram. 2017. "PPBM Officially Part of Pakatan Harapan". *Malay Mail*, 20 March 2017. https://www.malaymail.com/news/malaysia/2017/03/20/ppbm-officially-part-of-pakatan-harapan/1338983 (accessed 20 October 2018).

Asliza Musa. 2018. "Jadikan Sebagai Iktibar". *Utusan Malaysia*, 7 May 2018. http://www.utusan.com.my/berita/politik/jadikan-sebagai-iktibar-1.667179 (accessed 15 October 2018).

Bernama. 2010. "Dewan Rakyat: Persempadanan Pilihan Raya Berdasarkan Jumlah Pemilih Sesuatu Kawasan—Najib". 25 November 2010.

———. 2015. "Azmin Says 'No Need' to Form Pakatan Harapan in Selangor". 22 October 2015.

Edge Markets, The. "Six in 'Cow-Head Protest' Charged with Sedition". 9 September 2009. https://www.theedgemarkets.com/article/update-6-cow-head-protest-charged-sedition (accessed 15 October 2018).

Election Commission. 2018. *Laporan Kajian Semula Persempadanan: Syor-syor Yang Dicadangkan Bagi Bahagian-Bahagian Pilihan Raya Persekutuan dan Negeri Di Dalam Negeri-Negeri Tanah Melayu Kali Keenam Tahun 2018*. Putrajaya: Election Commission of Malaysia.

Hazlan Zakaria, and Jimadie Shah Othman. 2009. "Dr M Launches Perkasa, Group Marches to Police Station". *Malaysiakini*, 27 March 2009. https://www.malaysiakini.com/news/127644 (accessed 30 October 2018).

Ismail, N.H. 2014. "Bermula dari Setinggan Jadi Jutawan, Dermawan dan Kini Ahli Parlimen". *Agenda Daily*, 4 June 2014. https://www.agendadaily.com/Eksklusif-Bersama/bermula-dari-setinggan-jadi-jutawan-dermawan-dan-kini-ahli-parlimen.html (accessed 5 November 2018).

Ismail Sabri. 2018. "ICERD Gugat Kedudukan Orang Melayu dan Anak Negeri Sabah/Sarawak". *dsismailsabri.com*, 23 November 2018. https://dsismailsabri.com/icerd-gugat-kedudukan-melayu-dan-anak-negeri-sabah-sarawak-secara-senyap/ (accessed 6 January 2019).

Kumar, Kamles. 2017. "PPBM Ends Seat Talks with PAS as Pakatan Begins Negotiations". *Malay Mail*, 19 July 2017. https://www.malaymail.com/s/1424491/ppbm-ends-seat-talks-with-pas-as-pakatan-begins-negotiations (accessed 20 October 2018).

Lim, Kit Siang. 2015. "My Forecast That Pakatan Rakyat Might Not Be Around in Two Weeks' Time Seems to Have Come True and What Is Left Are the Funeral Rites". *blog.limkitsiang.com*, 6 June 2015. https://blog.limkitsiang.com/2015/06/06/my-forecast-that-pakatan-rakyat-might-not-be-around-in-two-weeks-time-seems-to-have-come-true-and-what-is-left-are-the-funeral-rites/#more-31364 (accessed 1 November 2018).

Malaysiakini. 2017. "Ambiga Fears Three-Cornered Fights Will Hand BN 2/3 Majority". *Malaysiakini*, 29 August 2017. https://www.malaysiakini.com/news/393584? (accessed 5 November 2018).

Maznah Mohamad. 2015. "Fragmented but Captured: Malay Voters and the FELDA Factor in GE13". In *Coalitions in Collision: Malaysia's 13th General Elections*, edited by Johan Saravanamuttu, Lee Hock Guan and Mohamed Nawab Mohamed Osman. Petaling Jaya and Singapore: SIRD and Institute of Southeast Asian Studies.

Mohd Khairuddin Razali. 2017. "RUU 355 Adalah Dakwah, Bersabarlah". *Harakah Daily*, 9 April 2017. http://www.harakahdaily.net/index.php/berita/77-ruu355/973-ruu-355-adalah-dakwah-bersabarlah (accessed 25 October 2018).

Politweet. 2013. "The Rural-Urban Divide in Malaysia's General Election". 21 May 2013. https://politweet.wordpress.com/2013/05/21/the-rural-urban-divide-in-malaysias-general-election/ (accessed 20 October 2018).

Ramanathan, S. 1996. "Urban-Rural Dichotomy in Malaysian Elections". *Asian Journal of Communication* 6, no. 2: 65–91.

———, and M.H. Adnan. 1988. "Malaysia's 1986 General Election: The Urban-Rural Dichotomy". ISEAS Occasional Paper 83. Singapore: Institute of Southeast Asian Studies.

Sofian Baharom. 2019. "Kemenangan BN Kerana Gabungan UMNO-Pas". *Utusan Malaysia*, 1 February 2019. http://www.utusan.com.my/berita/politik/kemenangan-bn-kerana-gabungan-umno-pas-1.833767.

Suara TV. 2018. "Tommy Thomas Ditolak Kerana Sokong Negara Sekular Kata PAS". 3 June 2018. https://suara.tv/03/06/2018/tommy-thomas-ditolak-kerana-sokong-sekular-pas/ (15 October 2018).

Syed Azhar. 2015. "Kelantan's Hudud Bill Amendments Passed". *The Star*, 19 March 2015. https://www.thestar.com.my/news/nation/2015/03/19/hudud-bill-passed/ (accessed 30 October 2018).

Tan, Vincent. 2018. "MCA to Send Formal Letter to BN to Dissolve the Coalition". *The Star*, 13 December 2018. https://www.thestar.com.my/news/nation/2018/12/13/mca-to-send-formal-letter-to-bn-to-dissolve-the-coalition/2018 (accessed 6 January 2019).

Vinesh, Derrick. 2009. "Azizan Lashes Out". *The Star*, 6 July 2009. https://www.thestar.com.my/news/community/2009/07/06/azizan-lashes-out/ (accessed 20 October 2018).

Wan Saiful Wan Jan. 2017. *Parti Amanah Negara in Johor: Birth, Challenges, and Prospects*. Trends in Southeast Asia, no. 9/2017. Singapore: ISEAS – Yusof Ishak Institute.

———. 2018. *GE 14: Will Urban Malays Support Pakatan Harapan?* Trends in Southeast Asia, no. 10/2018. Singapore: ISEAS – Yusof Ishak Institute.

Zaain Zin. 2018. "Latar Belakang Tommy Thomas 'Tidak Mesra Islam'". *Utusan Malaysia*, 3 June 2018. http://www.utusan.com.my/berita/nasional/latar-belakang-tommy-thomas-tidak-mesra-islam-1.684622 (accessed 30 October 2018).

Zachariah, Elizabeth. 2015. "PAS Lawmakers Rally Behind Hadi on Private Member's Bill". *The Edge Markets*, 8 April 2015. https://www.theedgemarkets.com/article/pas-lawmakers-rally-behind-hadi-private-member's-bill (accessed 30 October 2018).

Zulfadli Sharifudin. 2018. "Jualan Sentuhan Rakyat di Setiawangsa Meriah". *Utusan Malaysia*, 6 May 2018. http://www.utusan.com.my/berita/nasional/jualan-sentuhan-rakyat-di-setiawangsa-meriah-1.666654 (accessed 6 January 2019).

9

THE MAKING AND BREAKING OF MALAYSIA'S FELDA VOTE BANK

Geoffrey K. Pakiam[1]

INTRODUCTION

The study of Federal Land Development Authority (FELDA) settler voting behaviour is nascent but growing. This chapter first outlines the national significance of the FELDA vote, concurrently surveying extant scholarship that has scrutinized the factors influencing FELDA settler voting decisions. It then turns to FELDA parliamentary constituency voting results in 2018, placing them in the context of three previous general elections—a longer term perspective that has been somewhat neglected in previous scholarship. Seen in this manner, the 2018 voting results in FELDA wards—defined here as parliamentary seats hosting at least one FELDA scheme—are both unusual in some ways, and not particularly remarkable in others. Four explanations for the decline in FELDA ward support for Barisan Nasional (BN) since 2004 are discussed: the popularity of Parti Islam Se-Malaysia (PAS) in northern Malaysia; ethnic disparities in voting patterns; schisms within the United Malays National Organization (UMNO), coupled with the rise of alternative Malay-majority parties and their champions; and the uneven distribution of FELDA settlements across Malaysia. To date, support for UMNO remains significant in some FELDA constituencies, but mostly in the southeast region of the Peninsula, where FELDA settlement clusters are especially dense.

SIGNIFICANCE OF THE FELDA VOTE

From the late 1950s to 1990, roughly 120,000 low-income households were recruited by FELDA into over 300 agency-led land development schemes, occupying over half a million hectares of farmland (Figure 9.1). Virtually no Malaysian state has been left untouched by these endeavours, save Penang, Sarawak, and the Federal Territories.[2] The principal beneficiaries of these mostly rubber and oil palm cultivation schemes have been land-starved Malay households, supposedly selected on the basis of age, economic need, agricultural background, physical fitness, functional nuclear family unit, and prior military/security service (FAO 1966, pp. 18–19). Historian Tim Harper has noted that federally subsidized land schemes from the outset were also political creatures, not just in their underlying aims of rejuvenating the Malay rural economy, but as exemplified by the increasingly centrist bureaucratic structures used to perpetuate rural development, themselves the offspring of anti-Communist Emergency campaigns during the late 1940s and 1950s (Harper 1999, pp. 366–67).

How much weight do FELDA voting preferences now have at the national level? One recent estimate—which takes into account the original recruited settlers, as well as their dependants, adult children, and associated workers—pegs the present FELDA voter base at somewhere between 1 to 1.2 million, which would approximate 6 per cent of Malaysia's 2018 eligible voting population of 14.9 million (Khor 2014, pp. 90, 99; 2017, p. 5). But because of what observers have labelled as gerrymandering and malapportionment of electoral seats in favour of BN's predominantly rural ethnic Malay voter base (Lee H.G. 2015, pp. 74–76), FELDA-occupied wards take up a much higher share of parliamentary seats than their voter numbers might indicate; nearly a quarter of all 222 parliament seats, by one estimate (Maznah 2015, pp. 133–35) (Figure 9.2). Indeed, Figure 9.3 suggests that FELDA-occupied seats have a median of roughly 20,000 less registered voters when compared with Peninsular Malaysia's non-FELDA constituencies. Similarly, FELDA-occupied seats usually have higher proportions of ethnic Malay voters than non-FELDA wards in Peninsular Malaysia; over 20 percentage points more on average (Figure 9.3).

Despite this disproportionate seat allocation, FELDA settler voting preferences have generally received only sporadic attention from scholars. FELDA's settler influx only accelerated from the 1970s onwards, rendering their demographic presence relatively insignificant beforehand. At the same time, it is also difficult and time-consuming to amass national-level data on FELDA settlements with sufficient detail and precision. Discussions have accordingly been mostly qualitative and locally bounded, and even these studies are limited by access to what have often been relatively remote rural communities.

Dorothy Guyot is perhaps one of the first scholars to have dwelled on the matter, noting in the early 1970s that Johor BN politicians were co-opting FELDA schemes into their political calculi, doling out FELDA-subsidized land parcels to voters as a reward for political loyalty (Guyot 1971, pp. 385–86). Once chosen, such support for UMNO, as Harold Crouch noted much later, was expected to last across successive

FIGURE 9.1
Peninsular Malaysia: Parliamentary Constituencies and FELDA Schemes, 2004–18

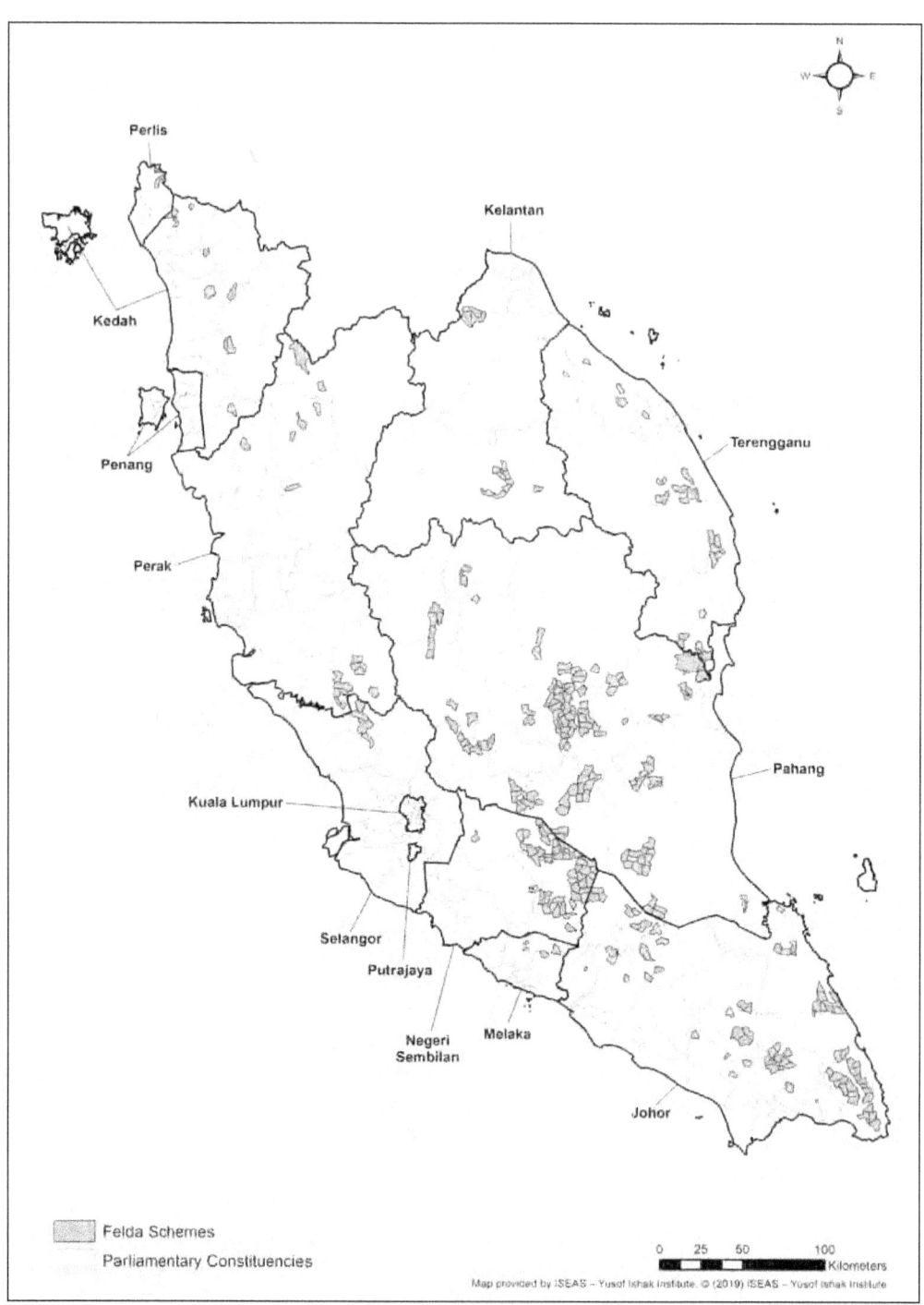

Source: See Appendix 9.1.

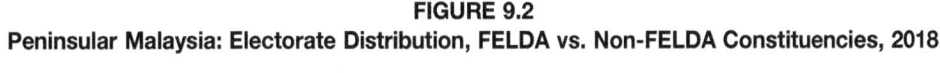

FIGURE 9.2
Peninsular Malaysia: Electorate Distribution, FELDA vs. Non-FELDA Constituencies, 2018

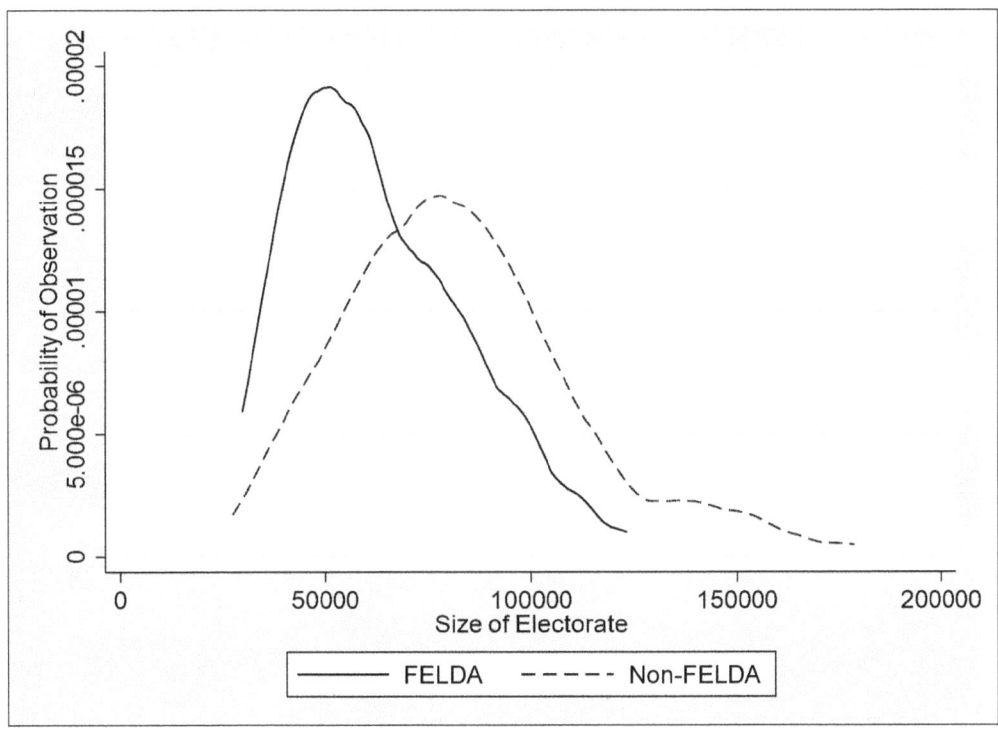

Note: The estimated probability density function graph visualizes the relative likelihood of observing a given electorate size in a Peninsular parliamentary seat.
Source: See Appendix 9.1.

election cycles, failing which settlers could be threatened with expulsion for political disloyalty (Crouch 1996, p. 41).

Halim Salleh has highlighted how persistent settler grievances regarding land rights and low incomes in Pahang have been vulnerable to politicization: UMNO branches have been established in practically every scheme since the 1970s, and UMNO politicians have taken the opportunity to encourage settlers to voice their dissent through party channels, rather than through the FELDA bureaucracy. Nevertheless, settlers in northern and central Peninsular Malaysia have been known to voice unhappiness by voting for non-BN parties since the 1970s, including Parti Sosialis Rakyat Malaysia (PSRM) and PAS. By the early 1980s, small groups of Muslim settlers in Pahang FELDA schemes were already hosting PAS-friendly political meetings within their religious gatherings (Halim 1992, pp. 107–17; Rashila 2003, pp. 129–40). On whole, however, it seems that UMNO politicians at both the state and federal levels were already regarding FELDA settler schemes as "vote banks" by the 1970s, using locally embedded party machinery to repeatedly reinforce the

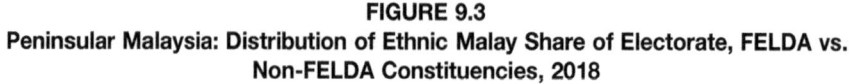

FIGURE 9.3
Peninsular Malaysia: Distribution of Ethnic Malay Share of Electorate, FELDA vs. Non-FELDA Constituencies, 2018

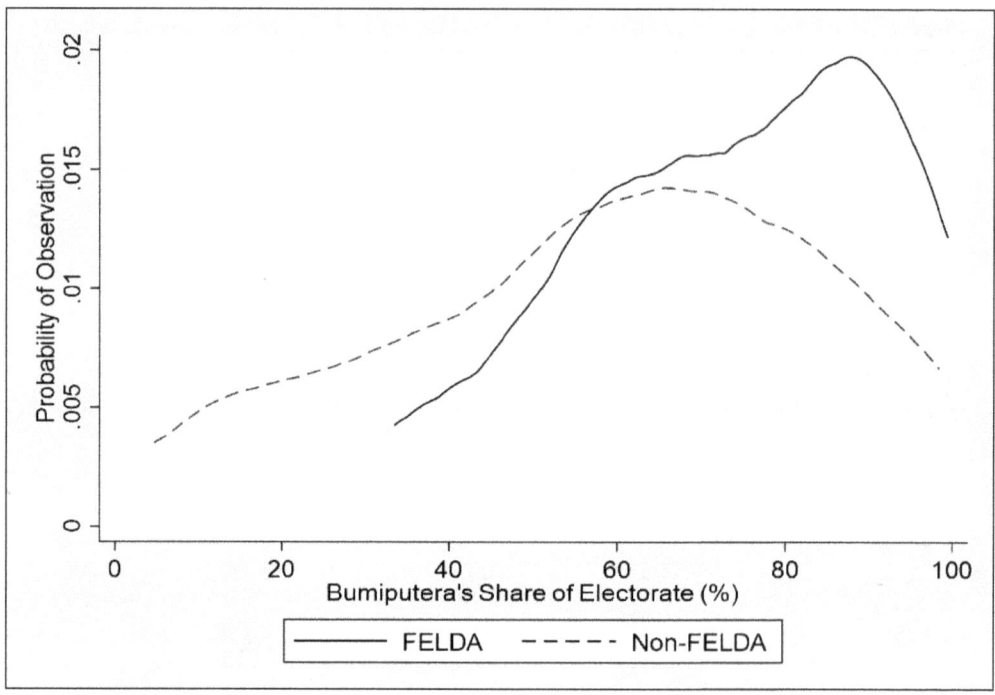

Note: The estimated probability density function graph visualizes the relative likelihood of observing a given Malay share of the voter demographic in a Peninsular parliamentary seat.
Source: See Appendix 9.1.

links between patronage, loyalty, and voting preferences, with largely successful results (Robertson 1984, pp. 286–87).

Recent studies examining 2013's GE-13 results have reignited discussions surrounding FELDA's political significance. Using quantitative databases from research firm Politweet, Merdeka Center, and Malaysia's Election Commission, as well as interviews with politicians and FELDA executives, Khor Yu Leng contended that the opposition coalition Pakatan Rakyat (PR) had failed to win over voters in FELDA areas, effectively increasing FELDA settlements' importance as vote banks for UMNO. At both the parliamentary and state seat levels, many FELDA settlements had voted more strongly for UMNO than in the previous general election. In Johor's closely fought Bukit Permai state seat, a surge of urban and ethnic Chinese swing votes for the opposition was unable to offset FELDA votes for BN. Khor generalized that UMNO's preferential access within FELDA settlements, racially charged campaign rhetoric, a one-off pay-out of RM15,000 to settlers from the June 2012 public listing of FELDA Global Ventures, and promises of housing and land for younger FELDA voters helped maintain support for BN in 2013's elections (Khor 2014, pp. 89–121).

Maznah Mohamad came to even stronger conclusions regarding the significance of FELDA settlements as pro-BN vote banks. Besides contending that money politics, settler indebtedness, and UMNO's penetration of the FELDA bureaucracy had established the "perfect patron-client relationship between FELDA (UMNO's proxy) and the settlers-cum-voters" (Maznah 2015, p. 151), Maznah also postulated that FELDA settlements had an outsized influence on rural Malay votes in general. Using Merdeka Center's national-level geospatial dataset, Maznah identified some 54 out of 222 parliamentary wards containing FELDA settlements. She noted strong correlations between a constituency's hosting of FELDA schemes and the ward's tendency to vote for BN in GE-13, leading her to conclude that these highly corporatized FELDA settlements had helped shore up an even larger pro-UMNO rural Malay vote bank across Peninsular Malaysia in 2013; totalling almost a quarter of all parliamentary wards (2015, pp. 123–57).

In the years following GE-13, however, a number of high-profile corporate scandals affecting FELDA and affiliated enterprises were prompting observers to begin reconsidering earlier assumptions about FELDA constituencies being "fixed deposits" for BN's electoral prospects. FELDA Global Venture's rapid share value loss and possible delisting demoralized many settlers who had purchased shares on credit, only to see them lose more than three-fifths their initial value by mid-2015. Widespread settler indebtedness, worsened by falling commodity prices and late payments for crops and replanting subsidies, gave widespread rumours of cash-flow problems within FELDA added bite. Even before major corporate scandals at FELDA Global Ventures were finally admitted publicly in mid-2017, straw polls by research outfit INVOKE were already indicating considerable settler disillusionment with BN under Najib. Several field studies suggested that many younger settlers lacked a strong sense of political obligation to UMNO, reinforced by stagnating livelihood opportunities (Zaireeni 2014; Serina 2018a, pp. 15–17, 26–27). Observers like Khor highlighted how rapidly expanding telecommunications coverage had enabled social media to penetrate rural areas such as FELDA schemes after GE-13, in all likelihood enabling PH politicians and independent media outlets to amplify information and anti-establishment ideas in the run-up to GE-14 (Khor 2018; Nadirah 2018). It became clear to observers that opposition parties and affiliated non-government organizations such as Persatuan Anak Peneroka FELDA Kebangsaan were generating political mileage from these converging conditions in the run-up to GE-14 (Khor 2017).

Other writers sceptical of the FELDA vote bank argument have taken a different tack, focusing on the extent to which the FELDA vote was being diluted by wider voting trends *within* each constituency. Johan Saravanamuttu (2017) emphasized that FELDA parliamentary wards were "somewhat mixed ethnically … which make them fair game for the Opposition", especially in states like Johor. As mentioned earlier, Khor Yu Leng had already noted growing political polarization along ethnic lines during GE-13, with ethnic Chinese voters swinging towards non-BN parties, and FELDA voters (mostly Malays) settling for BN (2014, p. 108). A fortnight before GE-14's polling day, I published the preliminary results of a geospatial study charting the extent of demographic disparities between FELDA-occupied parliamentary seats, chiefly in terms of voter ethnic composition as well as the numbers of FELDA schemes within each ward (Pakiam 2018). These distinctions were sufficiently striking to suggest a strong correlation between the overall ethnic voter profiles of each FELDA ward and increasing support for non-BN parties since 2004. This observation led to my tentative suggestion that only fourteen FELDA wards represented "reasonably safe" seats for BN in GE-14 (Pakiam 2018, p. 10).

VOTING RESULTS IN FELDA PARLIAMENTARY CONSTITUENCIES

Malaysia's 2018 general elections saw unprecedented numbers of FELDA-occupied constituencies reject politicians from BN, particularly UMNO. In doing so, they helped demolish long-standing presumptions that many Peninsular rural voters—including those from agricultural areas established by FELDA—would invariably vote in BN's favour. Of an estimated fifty-three FELDA-occupied Peninsular wards that marched to the polls on 9 May, twenty-seven seats rejected the ruling establishment. Of these twenty-seven seats, twenty-one were secured by parties under the Pakatan Harapan (PH) alliance, many of them first-time victories. The remainder went to PAS, which retained two FELDA wards in Terengganu, added two new FELDA seats to its Terengganu haul, and recaptured two more in Kedah (Figure 9.4).

Remarkable as 2018's results seem, they need to be tempered by the fact that BN's victory margins in previous elections had already been falling steadily in many FELDA wards since 2008. Figure 9.5 represents the results geographically, noting which political coalition won, and by roughly how much. Measuring and representing this decline requires a bit of simple math, as many more seats saw three-cornered fights in 2018 than in previous elections. Winning vote margins were thus derived from dividing the actual number of additional votes won over the runner-up candidate by the total number of votes accrued by the winner. Done this way, a low score of 0.01 indicates an extremely closely fought seat, whereas a high score of 0.5 meant the seat was an easy win.

In examining these results, several tendencies begin to appear. First, even though only a few seats were captured by non-BN parties between 2004 and 2013 under the first-past-the-post system, BN's vote margins had been generally falling steadily in many FELDA seats since 2004, especially those on the western half of the Peninsula (as indicated by the shift from dark to increasingly lighter shades of grey within BN-held seats). This long-term trend, as we will discuss later, suggests deepening dissatisfaction with everyday economic concerns, identity politics, and unhappiness with what seem to be corrupt and self-serving political elites, even in rural areas.

Second, even in 2018, a further twelve FELDA seats retained by BN candidates scraped by with marginal victories (those in light grey). In Perlis (Padang Besar), Kedah (Padang Terap), Kelantan (Tanah Merah and Gua Musang), Terengganu

FIGURE 9.4
FELDA Parliamentary Constituency Results, 2004–18

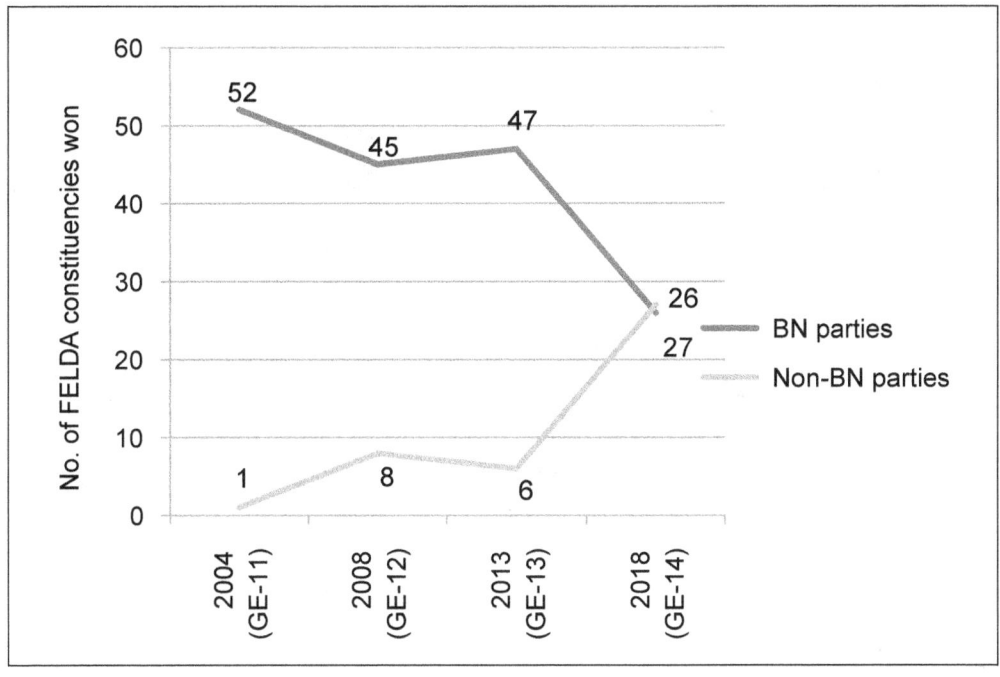

Source: Appendix 9.2.

(Hulu Terengganu and Besut), Pahang (Cameron Highlands, Bera and Kuala Krau), Negeri Sembilan (Jelebu and Jempol) and Melaka (Jasin), seats were subjected to heavy splits in the non-BN vote between PAS and PH. Furthermore, the seats in which PAS candidates came in as runners-up tended to be in the northern half of the Peninsula, in the states of Kedah, Terengganu, and Kelantan. Conversely, PH candidates put on much stronger showings in the Peninsula's southern half.

The PAS Factor

PAS' persistently strong appeal among northern FELDA-occupied seats is somewhat obscured by its previous affiliation with the Democratic Action Party (DAP) and Parti Keadilan Rakyat (PKR) under the Pakatan Rakyat (PR) banner between 2004 and 2013. As Table 9.1 shows, seats that were won by PAS in previous elections under the PR banner tended to stay with PAS in 2018. The only "new" FELDA seat won by PAS in 2018 was Setiu (in Terengganu). Harder to tease out is the extent to which PAS victories in FELDA seats in 2018 owed debts to PAS loyalists, or because PAS' time within the PR coalition allowed cadres to work the ground and deploy the electoral machinery needed to maintain their subsequent vote support levels. There is also the possibility that voters in these seats exercised tactical voting choices in favour of the most likely non-BN party to win, and these approaches produced

FIGURE 9.5
Winning Vote Margins for FELDA Parliamentary Constituencies in Peninsular Malaysia, GE-11 to GE-14[a]

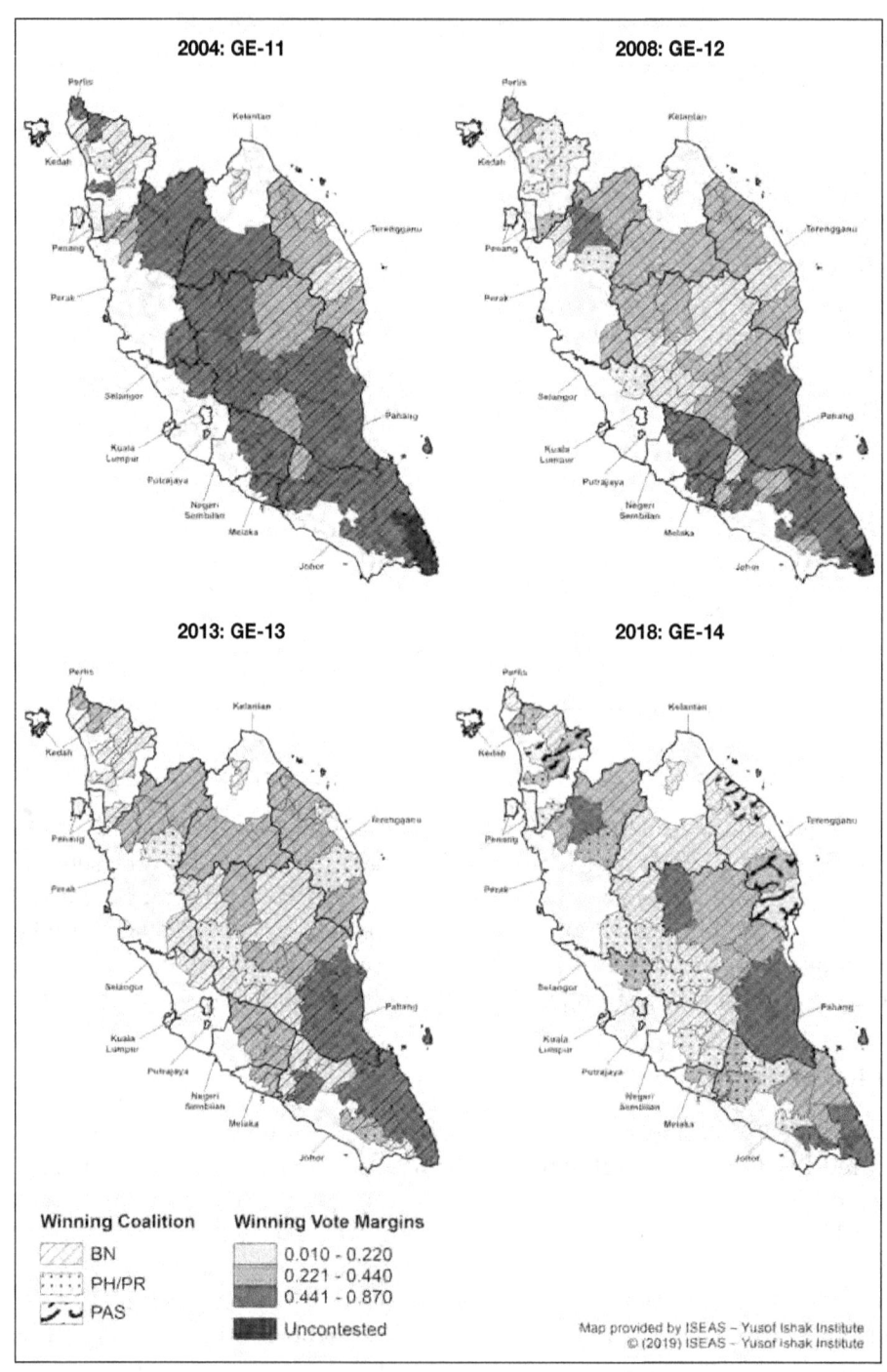

Note: a. PAS, DAP and PKR formed the Pakatan Rakyat coalition between GE-11 and GE-13. Following GE-13, this coalition split into Pakatan Harapan (led by DAP and PKR) and PAS, which cobbled together Gagasan Sejahtera (GS) for GE-14.
Source: Appendix 9.2.

TABLE 9.1
FELDA Parliamentary Constituencies Won by PAS, 2004–18

State	Seat (Seat Code)	Result
Kedah	Pendang (P.011)	Won by PAS in 2004, 2008, and 2018
	Sik (P.013)	Won by PAS in 2008 and 2018
Pahang	Temerloh (P.088)	Won by PAS in 2013 and 2018
Terengganu	Dungun (P.039)	Won by PAS in 2013 and 2018
	Kuala Nerus (P.035)	Won by PAS in 2013 and 2018
	Setiu (P.034)	Won by PAS in 2018

Source: Appendix 9.2.

especially well-defined majorities against BN in these six states (unlike in the twelve seats mentioned above).

Ethnic Preferences

Beyond the PAS factor, ethnic voter preferences within FELDA seats also stood out distinctly. It cannot be overemphasized that in both GE-13 and GE-14, one-third of FELDA wards had less than 60 per cent registered ethnic Malay voters, or more than 25 per cent Chinese voters; what we defined as "mixed" wards (Figure 9.6).

Figure 9.7 and Table 9.2 illustrate this aspect of GE-14's results by juxtaposing FELDA seat election results alongside voter ethnic composition. Wards that ushered in PH-affiliated parties (along the western half of the Peninsula) tended to have ethnically mixed voter demographics (less than 60 per cent Malay voters, or more than 25 per cent Chinese voters). Conversely, seats that voted for PAS or BN tended to be dominated by Malay voter profiles.

These ethnically influenced results are not anomalous. They extend all the way back to at least 2004. Of the forty FELDA seats which had never once fallen under the control of non-BN-affiliated parties between 2004 and 2013, the extent to which BN's vote share slipped over time corresponded strongly with how ethnically mixed each ward's total voter base was (Pakiam 2018, pp. 9–10). In a nutshell, many FELDA seats were highly vulnerable to the growing disillusionment of non-Malay voters with BN's divisive politics and corruption.

Mahathir and the Rise of Alternative Malay Parties

There are, however, distinct limits to how much the ethnic factor and history of voting results since 2004 can explain. A significant number of FELDA seats that saw little decline in BN vote shares since 2004, or came out of the previous GE-13 with a relatively high BN victory margin, ended up capitulating to non-BN-affiliated parties in GE-14 (Table 9.3).

In these wards, as in others, voters of all ethnicities, including Malays, were probably increasingly disillusioned with then Prime Minister Najib Razak's leadership

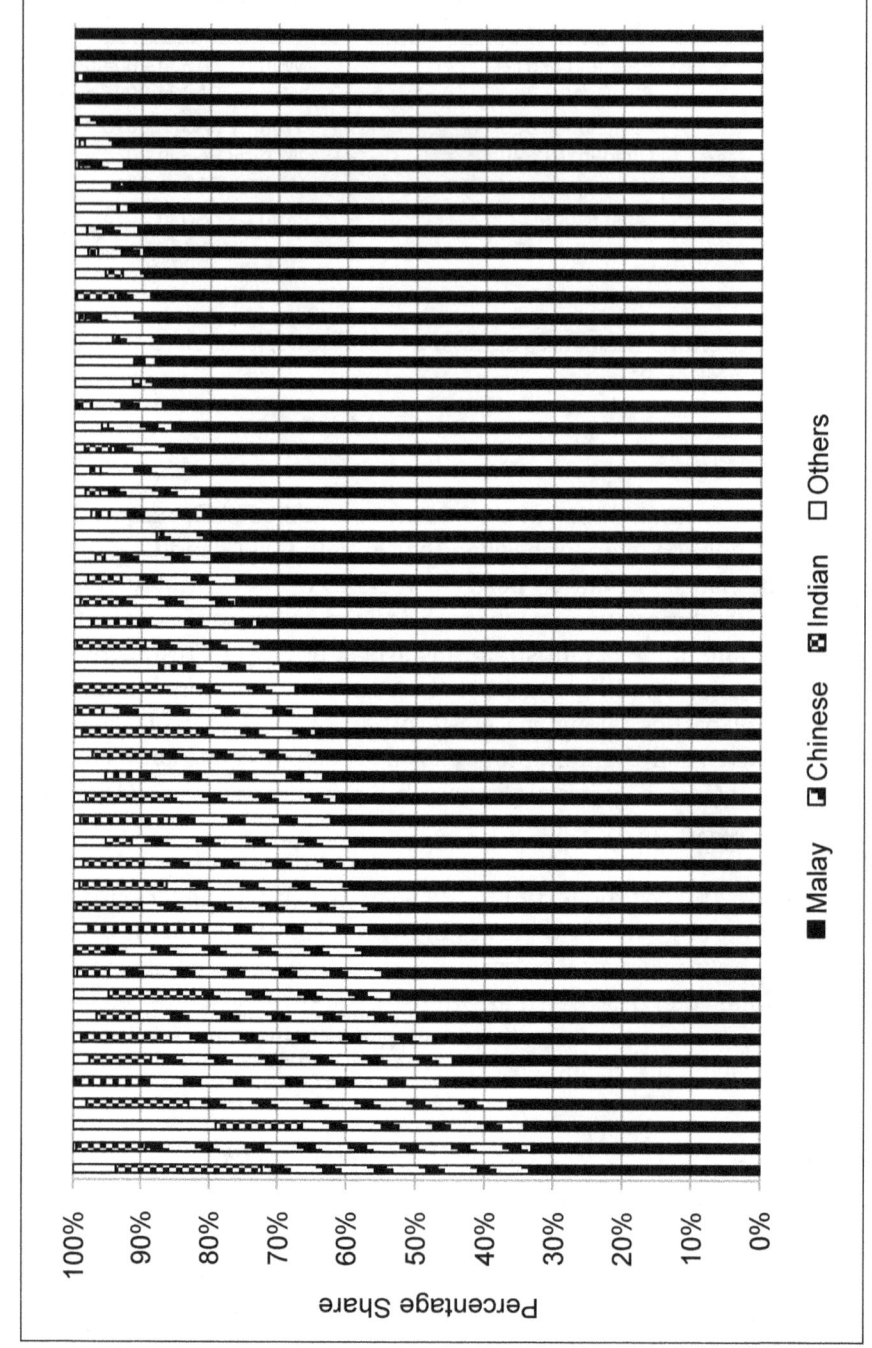

FIGURE 9.6
Ethnic Composition of FELDA Constituencies, 2018

■ Malay □ Chinese ⊠ Indian □ Others

Percentage Share

Source: Appendix 9.1.

FIGURE 9.7

Winning Vote Margins and Voter Ethnic Composition, FELDA Parliamentary Constituencies in Peninsular Malaysia (GE-14)

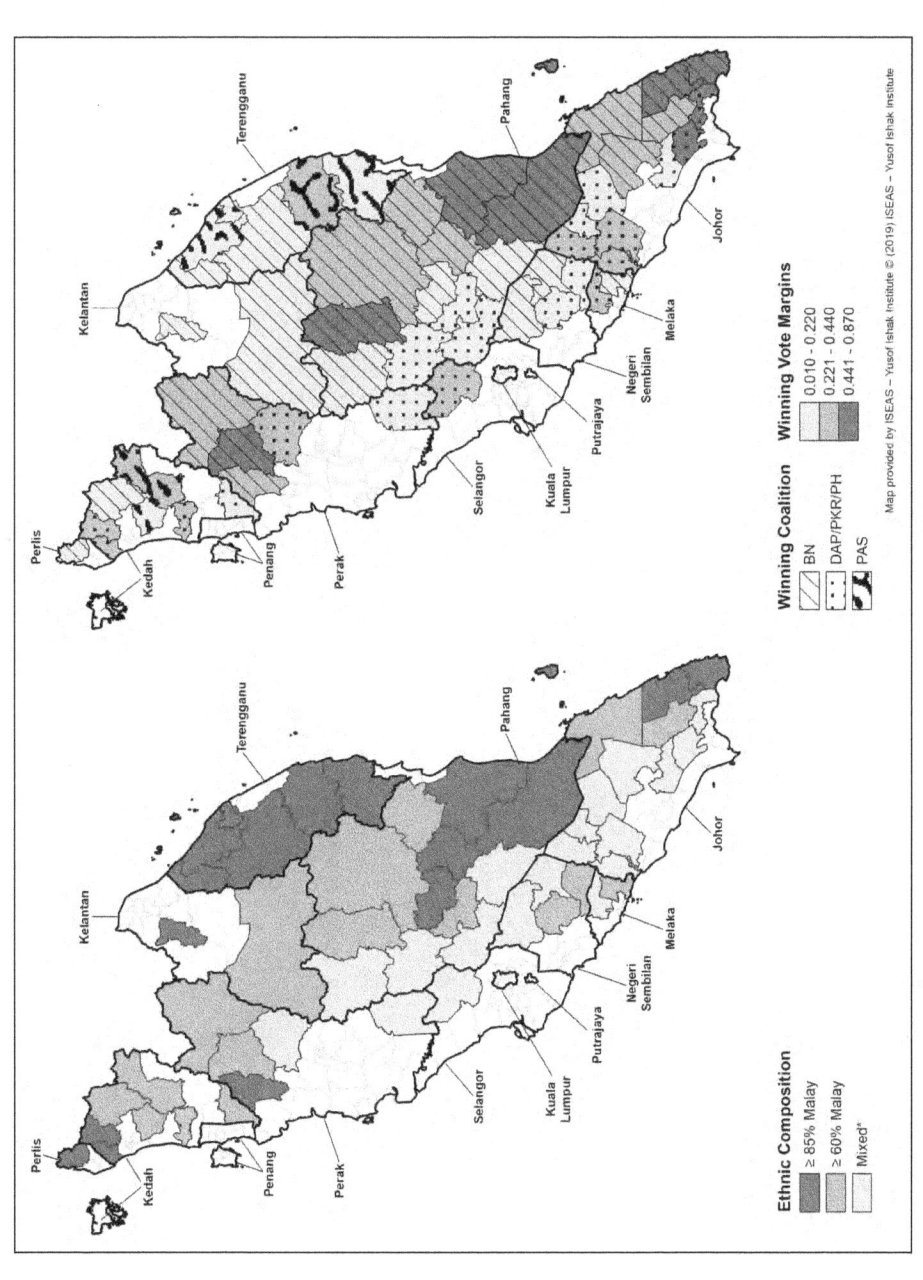

Note: * Mixed seats as defined as those with less than 60 per cent registered ethnic Malay voters, or 25 per cent or over Chinese voters. See Appendixes 9.1 and 9.2 for sources.

TABLE 9.2
Winning Coalitions and Voter Ethnic Composition in
FELDA Parliamentary Constituencies (GE-14)

Winning Coalition	≥ 85% Malay	≥ 60% Malay, < 85% Malay	Mixed	Total Seats Won
GS (mostly PAS)	4	2	0	6
PH	2	5	14	21
BN	11	10	5	26
Total	17	17	19	53

Source: Appendix 9.2.

TABLE 9.3
BN-lost FELDA Wards in GE-14 that Posted High Levels of Support for BN before GE-14

State	Seat (Seat Code)	Pre-GE-14 Voting Preferences	Voter Ethnic Profile	Winning Party in GE-14
Kedah	Jerlun (P.005)	Little change in BN vote in past three elections	≥ 85% Malay	PH-PPBM
	Kubang Pasu (P.006)	GE-13 BN vote 59%	≥ 85% Malay	PH-PPBM
	Merbok (P.014)	Little change in BN vote in past two elections	≥ 60% Malay	PH-PKR
Terengganu	Setiu (P.034)	Little change in BN vote in past three elections	≥ 85% Malay	PAS
	Kemaman (P.040)	GE-13 BN vote 58%	≥ 85% Malay	PAS
Negeri Sembilan	Pilah (P.129)	GE-13 BN vote 62%	≥ 60% Malay	PH-PPBM
	Tampin (P.133)	GE-13 BN vote 62%	≥ 60% Malay	PH-Amanah
Melaka	Alor Gajah (P.135)	GE-13 BN vote 61%	Mixed	PH-PPBM
Johor	Simpang Renggam (P.151)	GE-13 BN vote 59%	Mixed	PH-PPBM

Source: Appendix 9.2.

since 2013, and more importantly, could find suitable alternative political vehicles with whom to lodge their vote. The Malay vote did fracture along multiple lines, with some votes going to PPBM, and some to PH's Parti Amanah Negara. A number of prominent Malay elites who had broken away from UMNO and PAS to join PPBM and Amanah after GE-13 helped consolidate this shift. These included Mahathir Mohamad's son Mukhriz Mahathir (who won in Jerlun) and Maszlee Malik (who won in Simpang Renggam).

This was nevertheless more than simply PH providing an alternative form of consociational politics under which Parti Pribumi Bersatu Malaysia (PPBM) and Parti Amanah Negara could park themselves as perceived champions of Malay rights. After all, PPBM did win seats in mixed wards like Alor Gajah and Simpang Renggam. One political observer found significant numbers of rural voters growing increasingly sympathetic to Mahathir's cause during campaign season because of UMNO and PAS leaders' lack of public respect for the elder statesman (Serina 2018b, pp. 673–74). Mahathir himself tapped into voter emotions during the campaign by painting himself as an underdog who only wanted to "Save Malaysia" (Welsh 2018, pp. 96–97). In all probability, Mahathir's recent leadership of PPBM and PH, charisma, prime ministerial experience, the respect he garnered from voters even in rural areas, coupled with increasing public disdain for Najib Razak—all amplified by social media—played a big role in shifting votes away from BN towards PH.

At the same time, Mahathir's own long-standing unpopularity in Kelantan and Terengganu came back to haunt him in 2018. He had bitterly fallen out with UMNO Kelantan's then leader Razaleigh Hamzah in 1987. Criticisms of him as a materialistic "anti-Muslim" villain resonated especially strongly in northeast Malaysia following his split with Malaysian Islamic Youth Movement's founder Anwar Ibrahim in 1998 (Lee H.G. 2015, p. 71; Wain 2012, pp. 193–213). These lingering associations probably curbed the ability of PH-linked parties to make further inroads into these states. Many in the Peninsula's northeast would have neither forgiven nor forgotten Mahathir's role in presiding over an UMNO-dominant regime that once threatened Kelantan's ex-Chief Minister and PAS spiritual adviser Datuk Nik Abdul Aziz Nik Mat with the Internal Security Act for allegedly promoting religious fanaticism among Muslims, or for cutting off state funding for private Islamic schools in 2002 (Wain 2012, pp. 201, 210). Shortly before GE-14's polling day, Mahathir was barred from visiting the late PAS spiritual leader Datuk Nik Abdul Aziz Nik Mat's grave while campaigning in Kelantan (*The Star*, 7 May 2018).

A REDUCED FELDA VOTE BANK

The limits of Mahathir's personal influence and that of PH in general are perhaps seen most plainly in BN's ability to cling onto twenty-six FELDA seats during GE-14. As noted earlier, twelve of these seats were close scrapes for BN, leaving fourteen seats with significantly higher victory margins. Two other factors—the presence of abnormally high numbers of FELDA schemes in each ward, and the presence of a trusted incumbent BN politician—appear to have worked hand-in-hand to favour BN victories in all of these wards.

While FELDA settler schemes are scattered widely across the Peninsula, they are not evenly distributed. Instead, as Figure 9.1 earlier illustrates, they tend to clump together in a relatively small number of locales, leaving vast areas drained of FELDA voter influence. Out of the 305 FELDA settler schemes known to still be in existence, over half (157, to be precise) are concentrated in just eleven parliamentary constituencies, leaving forty-two constituencies to divide up the rest. At the other end of the spectrum, a whopping twenty-four constituencies have three or less FELDA schemes each. Between these "mega-FELDA" and "mini-FELDA" extremes lie the remaining eighteen "middle-FELDA" constituencies, each hosting between four and nine schemes (Figure 9.8).

Although we have been able to quantify scheme numbers, building estimates of actual eligible FELDA voters per parliamentary constituency—a more accurate measurement of FELDA voter influence, since some schemes contain more households than others—is much more difficult and time-consuming. The exact number of settler households in each scheme is only publicly available up to 2005. We do not yet know of any national-level open data regarding current settler family size and age range, let alone the extent to which household members have moved outstation, working, living, and voting elsewhere. There are scattered independent estimates of discreet localities, including one that pegs Pengerang's 2018 FELDA voter base at around 24,300 individuals, which translates into three-fifths of the ward's total electorate (Razak Ahmad et al. 2018). Blunt estimates of FELDA's vote share per ward suggest considerable similarities between the number of FELDA schemes in each constituency and their constituency vote share (Pakiam 2018, p. 13). Nonetheless, building more accurate estimates is one area ripe for further research, not least because it could help unpack the FELDA vote bank's demographic complexities.

In any case, because of grossly uneven FELDA settlement distribution within the Peninsula, it is entirely possible for political parties to win large numbers of

FIGURE 9.8
Distribution of FELDA Schemes within Parliamentary Constituencies, 2018

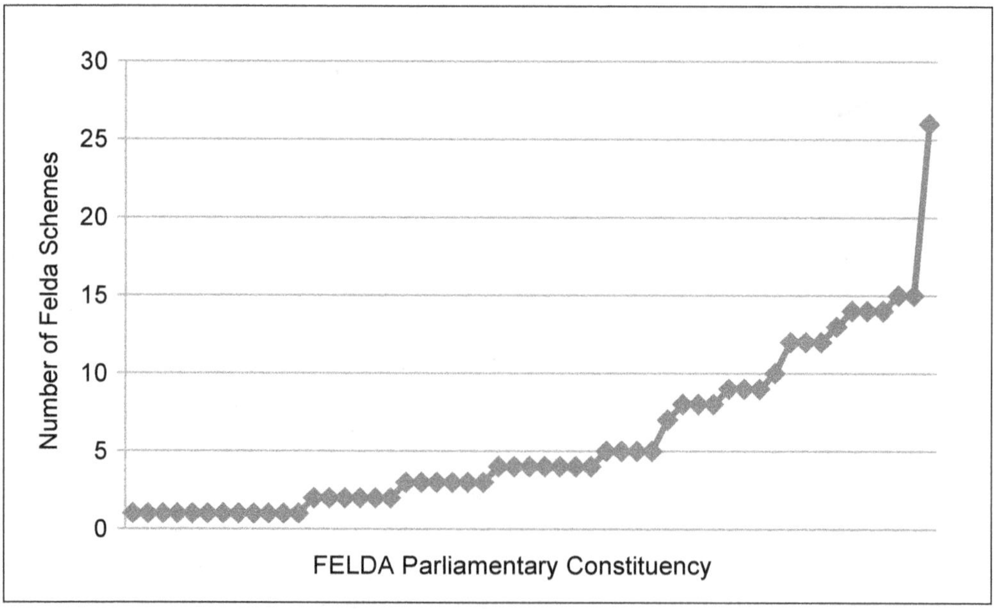

Source: Appendix 9.1.

FELDA seats without a proportionate vote from FELDA settlers. This is exactly what happened in 2018. PAS and PH won more than half the so-called FELDA seats in Peninsular Malaysia, but the number of settlements occupying these seats was actually less than a third of the total number. BN in turn garnered sufficient votes to win twenty-six seats containing a much higher total number of settlements. Such differences can be clearly seen in the average numbers of settlements per seat won by each coalition (Table 9.4).

When BN's twenty-six-seat haul is ranked in descending order of victory margin, three kinds of wards can be identified. The first are seats where UMNO politicians surfaced with relatively clear winning margins (more than 0.2). Fourteen seats fall into this category. They are characterized as having high proportions of Malay voters, and were clinched by UMNO politicians who were typically incumbents from previous elections, if not powerful senior party figures in their own right: Najib Razak, Azalina Othman, and Abdul Latiff Ahmad, to name a few. The only non-incumbent on the list, Halimah Mohamed Sadique, was already popular in Kota Tinggi's neighbouring ward Tenggara in the previous two GEs. In moving to Kota Tinggi, she also benefited from inheriting one of Malaysia's most pro-UMNO wards in history. In Sembrong constituency, where voters were ethnically quite mixed, and there were only five FELDA schemes, UMNO emerged victorious probably because of Hishamuddin Hussein's seniority and command of party resources (Table 9.5).

The other twelve BN-held wards that clinched slimmer victories have more complicated stories to tell. Four of these wards were situated in Kelantan and Terengganu, rendering them more vulnerable to overtures from PAS. Another four—Bera, Jelebu, Jempol and Cameron Highlands—played host to more ethnically mixed voting publics. Despite three of these wards harbouring between thirteen to twenty-six FELDA schemes each, overall support for BN was tepid. Lukewarm

TABLE 9.4
FELDA Settlements in Wards Won by Various Political Coalitions and Parties (GE-14)

		Total Number of FELDA Seats Won in GE-14	Total Number of FELDA Settlements in Seats Won	Average Number of Settlements Per Seat
GS (mostly PAS)		6	19	3.2
PH	PKR	9	29	3.2
	DAP	4	21	5.3
	PPBM	6	15	2.5
	Amanah	2	11	5.5
PH Subtotal		21	75	3.6
BN		26	211	8.1
Total		53	305	5.8

Source: Appendix 9.2.

TABLE 9.5
FELDA Parliamentary Constituencies Won by BN-Affiliated Parties (GE-14)

No.	Parliamentary Constituency (State)	BN Victory Margin, 2018	Ethnic Make-up, 2018	No. of FELDA Schemes	Name of Winning Candidate (Party)	Incumbent?
1	Pekan (Pahang)	0.57	≥ 85% Malay	8	Najib Tun Razak (BN-UMNO)	Yes
2	Kota Tinggi (Johor)	0.55	≥ 85% Malay	9	Halimah Mohamed Sadique (BN-UMNO)	No
3	Pengerang (Johor)	0.52	≥ 85% Malay	12	Azalina Othman Said (BN-UMNO)	Yes
4	Lipis (Pahang)	0.47	≥ 60% Malay	2	Abdul Rahman Mohamad (BN-UMNO)	Yes
5	Lenggong (Perak)	0.46	≥ 60% Malay	3	Shamsul Anuar Nasarah (BN-UMNO)	Yes
6	Rompin (Pahang)	0.45	≥ 85% Malay	15	Hasan Arifin (BN-UMNO)	Yes
7	Mersing (Johor)	0.43	≥ 60% Malay	12	Abdul Latiff Ahmad (BN-UMNO)	Yes
8	Gerik (Perak)	0.42	≥ 60% Malay	2	Hasbullah Osman (BN-UMNO)	Yes
9	Sembrong (Johor)	0.31	Mixed	5	Hishamuddin Hussein (BN-UMNO)	Yes
10	Paya Besar (Pahang)	0.3	≥ 60% Malay	14	Mohd Shahar Abdullah (BN-UMNO)	Yes
11	Tenggara (Johor)	0.29	≥ 60% Malay	7	Adham Baba (BN-UMNO)	Yes
12	Jerantut (Pahang)	0.26	≥ 60% Malay	14	Ahmad Nazlan Idris (BN-UMNO)	Yes
13	Larut (Perak)	0.25	≥ 85% Malay	1	Hamzah Zainudin (BN-UMNO)	Yes
14	Maran (Pahang)	0.23	≥ 85% Malay	12	Ismail Abd Mutalib (BN-UMNO)	Yes
15	Gua Musang (Kelantan)	0.2	≥ 60% Malay	9	Razaleigh Hamzah (BN-UMNO)	Yes
16	Kuala Krau (Pahang)	0.16	≥ 85% Malay	15	Ismail Mohamed Said (BN-UMNO)	Yes
17	Besut (Terengganu)	0.13	≥ 85% Malay	1	Idris Jusoh (BN-UMNO)	Yes
18	Bera (Pahang)	0.11	Mixed	14	Ismail Sabri Yaakob (BN-UMNO)	Yes

continued on next page

TABLE 9.5 — *cont'd*

No.	Parliamentary Constituency (State)	BN Victory Margin, 2018	Ethnic Make-up, 2018	No. of FELDA Schemes	Name of Winning Candidate (Party)	Incumbent?
19	Jelebu (Negeri Sembilan)	0.11	Mixed	13	Jalaluddin Alias (BN-UMNO)	No
20	Tanah Merah (Kelantan)	0.1	≥ 85% Malay	4	Ikmal Hisham (BN-UMNO)	Yes
21	Padang Besar (Perlis)	0.1	≥ 85% Malay	3	Zahidi Zainul Abidin (BN-UMNO)	Yes
22	Hulu Terengganu (Terengganu)	0.09	≥ 85% Malay	3	Rosol Wahid (BN-UMNO)	No
23	Padang Terap (Kedah)	0.07	≥ 60% Malay	2	Mahdzir Khalid (BN-UMNO)	Yes
24	Jempol (Negeri Sembilan)	0.06	Mixed	26	Mohd Salim Shariff (BN-UMNO)	No
25	Cameron Highlands (Pahang)	0.06	Mixed	4	C. Sivaraajh (BN-MIC)	No
26	Jasin (Melaka)	0.01	≥ 60% Malay	1	Ahmad Hamzah (incumbent) (BN-UMNO)	Yes

support may have been due to the fact that most of the BN politicians contesting these wards were doing so for the first time. In the case of Cameron Highlands, which witnessed a five-cornered fight in GE-14, PAS' entry helped transfer votes from both BN and PH (Loh and Chacko 2018). A similar process may have occurred in Kuala Krau, where PAS candidate Kamal Ashaari emerged a strong runner-up in his second outing. These are all signs of long-standing spillover effects stemming from northern Pahang's geographic proximity to states now reaffirmed as PAS strongholds post-GE-14, namely Kelantan and Terengganu (Rashila 2003, p. 140).

All in all, then, only a small cluster of wards with relatively high numbers of FELDA settler schemes—Pekan, Rompin, Maran and Jerantut in Pahang; Kota Tinggi, Pengerang, Mersing, Sembrong and Tenggara in Johor—harboured strong support for BN during GE-14. Confined to Peninsular Malaysia's southeast rump, encompassing just over 30 per cent of FELDA's 300-plus schemes, this eastern Johor-Pahang cluster appears to be all that is left of BN's once-formidable FELDA vote bank.

CONCLUDING REMARKS

Few observers had anticipated the extent to which BN would haemorrhage support from FELDA-occupied seats in GE-14. In hindsight, these losses probably owed much to fragmenting Malay leadership within both UMNO and PAS. Together with former Prime Minister Najib Razak's increasingly egregious political behaviour, several unresolved financial scandals afflicting FELDA and its privatized offshoot FELDA Global Ventures, and the ability of opposition figures to link high-level misdoings with declining settler livelihoods, both PH and PAS managed to break the FELDA vote bank to a certain extent (Saravanamuttu 2018).

At the same time, the decline of BN's FELDA vote fortress was probably at least a decade in the making. Almost four-fifths of all FELDA parliamentary seats had witnessed BN's vote share plummet since 2004, including rural seats harbouring very large numbers of FELDA schemes. BN's 2018 electoral disaster would have been even greater were it not for serious spats in FELDA locales, mostly between PAS and PPBM.

Assuming that all major political parties remain intact before the next general election due by 2023 (neither PPBM nor UMNO may last until then), how FELDA wards vote in future may depend largely on whether Malay votes continue to be split between UMNO and PAS. If these two parties can agree not to contest against each other in the same FELDA wards, PH is likely to face an uphill battle in both eastern Johor and Pahang.

APPENDIX 9.1

FELDA Scheme-Occupied Parliamentary Constituencies, 2004–18

No.	State	Parliamentary Constituency (Code)	Total Electorate, 2018	Malay %	Chinese %	Indian %	Others %	Urban Devt Category (2017)	Total FELDA Schemes	Total Settler Households (2005)
1	Perlis	Padang Besar (P.001)	46,096	86.6	8.5	0.1	4.9	Rural	3	869
2	Kedah	Jerlun (P.005)	54,132	91.2	6.9	0.1	1.8	Rural	2	316
3	Kedah	Kubang Pasu (P.006)	73,881	86.5	8.5	3.5	1.5	Semi-urban	1	376
4	Kedah	Padang Terap (P.007)	46,644	92.1	1.3	0.0	6.4	Rural	2	951
5	Kedah	Pendang (P.011)	74,867	88.8	5.1	0.1	5.6	Rural	1	523
6	Kedah	Sik (P.013)	50,385	93.0	1.5	0.0	5.4	Rural	1	623
7	Kedah	Merbok (P.014)	87,782	68.6	15.1	15.3	1.0	Semi-urban	1	270
8	Kedah	Kulim Bandar Baharu (P.018)	66,587	69.2	17.7	12.9	0.3	Semi-urban	1	180
9	Kelantan	Tanah Merah (P.027)	73,172	96.7	1.9	0.1	1.4	Rural	4	1,278
10	Kelantan	Gua Musang (P.032)	52,524	82.4	5.6	0.5	11.5	Rural	9	2,378
11	Terengganu	Besut (P.033)	86,627	98.1	1.4	0.1	0.4	Semi-urban	1	290
12	Terengganu	Setiu (P.034)	86,247	99.4	0.3	0.0	0.2	Rural	3	912
13	Terengganu	Kuala Nerus (P.035)	86,663	98.7	0.9	0.1	0.2	Rural	1	213
14	Terengganu	Hulu Terengganu (P.038)	73,487	99.1	0.5	0.0	0.4	Rural	3	1,096
15	Terengganu	Dungun (P.039)	90,506	96.0	3.4	0.2	0.4	Semi-urban	5	2,186
16	Terengganu	Kemaman (P.040)	107,593	93.4	5.4	0.6	0.6	Semi-urban	8	3,176
17	Perak	Gerik (P.054)	35,903	69.1	14.1	3.3	13.6	Rural	2	489
18	Perak	Lenggong (P.055)	29,752	83.5	12.7	1.4	2.4	Rural	3	457
19	Perak	Larut (P.056)	49,653	89.7	4.3	5.6	0.3	Rural	1	605
20	Perak	Sungai Siput (P.062)	55,002	34.3	36.3	20.9	8.6	Semi-urban	1	393
21	Perak	Tanjong Malim (P.077)	68,468	55.6	25.6	13.0	5.9	Rural	10	4,164
22	Pahang	Cameron Highlands (P.078)	32,048	34.2	32.3	12.5	21.1	Rural	4	1,194
23	Pahang	Lipis (P.079)	35,294	78.0	15.6	5.2	1.1	Rural	2	256
24	Pahang	Raub (P.080)	57,723	52.1	38.1	6.2	3.7	Rural	4	1,366
25	Pahang	Jerantut (P.081)	63,609	81.8	13.0	2.6	2.6	Rural	14	5,059

26	Pahang	Paya Besar (P.084)	55,135	83.4	12.9	1.9	1.9	Rural	14	5,480
27	Pahang	Pekan (P.085)	88,899	87.8	2.0	0.8	9.4	Rural	8	3,353
28	Pahang	Maran (P.086)	41,036	90.2	6.2	1.5	2.2	Rural	12	4,736
29	Pahang	Kuala Krau (P.087)	47,264	89.9	2.8	2.3	5.1	Rural	15	6,456
30	Pahang	Temerloh (P.088)	75,801	66.5	22.5	8.1	2.9	Semi-urban	2	950
31	Pahang	Bentong (P.089)	67,359	46.5	41.7	9.2	2.7	Rural	8	3,269
32	Pahang	Bera (P.090)	58,711	61.9	29.2	3.7	5.2	Rural	14	5,402
33	Pahang	Rompin (P.091)	61,918	87.7	2.3	1.0	8.9	Rural	15	5,970
34	Selangor	Hulu Selangor (P.094)	100,990	60.4	20.8	16.2	2.6	Semi-urban	4	1,936
35	Negeri Sembilan	Jelebu (P.126)	48,522	65.0	24.1	5.7	5.2	Rural	13	4,191
36	Negeri Sembilan	Jempol (P.127)	72,122	63.4	23.2	12.3	1.1	Rural	26	9,317
37	Negeri Sembilan	Kuala Pilah (P.129)	49,801	77.0	15.8	4.9	2.3	Semi-urban	1	349
38	Negeri Sembilan	Tampin (P.133)	60,765	62.8	23.6	11.8	1.8	Rural	9	4,083
39	Melaka	Alor Gajah (P.135)	70,364	60.8	25.3	12.9	1.0	Rural	4	954
40	Melaka	Jasin (P.139)	73,432	73.5	16.2	9.8	0.5	Rural	1	382
41	Johor	Segamat (P.140)	55,350	46.2	42.8	10.1	1.0	Rural	3	804
42	Johor	Sekijang (P.141)	45,596	59.2	36.2	4.0	0.6	Rural	5	2,382
43	Johor	Labis (P.142)	40,356	38.0	44.9	14.7	2.4	Rural	4	1,382
44	Johor	Pagoh (P.143)	51,512	66.0	29.8	3.7	0.6	Rural	4	1,385
45	Johor	Ledang (P.144)	77,474	55.8	39.0	4.6	0.7	Rural	1	54
46	Johor	Simpang Renggam (P.151)	43,998	59.6	30.8	8.8	0.8	Rural	3	937
47	Johor	Sembrong (P.153)	44,137	60.4	29.2	8.7	1.7	Rural	5	1,823
48	Johor	Mersing (P.154)	48,176	81.5	14.3	1.3	3.0	Rural	12	3,383
49	Johor	Tenggara (P.155)	44,749	74.7	16.1	6.6	2.6	Rural	7	2,917
50	Johor	Kota Tinggi (P.156)	46,677	89.6	8.9	0.8	0.7	Rural	9	4,383
51	Johor	Pengerang (P.157)	40,479	89.6	8.9	0.8	0.7	Rural	12	5,828
52	Johor	Tebrau (P.158)	123,033	47.2	39.4	11.5	1.9	Semi-urban	2	782
53	Johor	Kulai (P.163)	99,147	35.0	54.0	10.2	0.8	Semi-urban	5	1,977
Grand Total									305	114,485

APPENDIX 9.2
General Election Results in FELDA Parliamentary Seats, 2004–18

No.	Parliamentary Seat (Code)	Total FELDA Schemes	Winning Coalition-Party (Vote Margin)				Winner, GE-14
			2004	2008	2013	2018	
1	Pekan (P.085)	8	BN (0.72)	BN (0.73)	BN (0.69)	BN (0.57)	Najib Tun Razak (incumbent)
2	Kota Tinggi (P.156)	9	BN (Walkover)	BN (0.84)	BN (0.81)	BN (0.55)	Halimah Mohamed Sadique
3	Pengerang (P.157)	12	BN (Walkover)	BN (Walkover)	BN (0.83)	BN (0.52)	Azalina Othman Said (incumbent)
4	Lipis (P.079)	2	BN (0.55)	BN (0.33)	BN (0.23)	BN (0.47)	Abdul Rahman Mohamad (incumbent)
5	Lenggong (P.055)	3	BN (0.52)	BN (0.45)	BN (0.31)	BN (0.46)	Shamsul Anuar Nasarah (incumbent)
6	Rompin (P.091)	15	BN (0.48)	BN (0.50)	BN (0.50)	BN (0.45)	Hasan Arifin (Incumbent)
7	Mersing (P.154)	12	BN (0.76)	BN (0.68)	BN (0.60)	BN (0.43)	Abdul Latiff Ahmad (incumbent)
8	Gerik (P.054)	2	BN (0.67)	BN (0.44)	BN (0.38)	BN (0.42)	Hasbullah Osman (incumbent)
9	Sembrong (P.153)	5	BN (0.87)	BN (0.64)	BN (0.47)	BN (0.31)	Hishamuddin Hussein (incumbent)
10	Paya Besar (P.084)	14	BN (0.61)	BN (0.44)	BN (0.32)	BN (0.30)	Mohd Shahar Abdullah (incumbent)
11	Tenggara (P.155)	7	BN (0.73)	BN (0.74)	BN (0.67)	BN (0.29)	Adham Baba
12	Jerantut (P.081)	14	BN (0.40)	BN (0.10)	BN (0.17)	BN (0.26)	Ahmad Nazlan Idris (incumbent)
13	Larut (P.056)	1	BN (0.40)	BN (0.12)	BN (0.24)	BN (0.25)	Hamzah Zainudin (incumbent)
14	Maran (P.086)	12	BN (0.46)	BN (0.42)	BN (0.34)	BN (0.23)	Ismail Abd Mutalib (Incumbent)
15	Gua Musang (P.032)	9	BN (0.49)	BN (0.31)	BN (0.39)	BN (0.20)	Razaleigh Hamzah (incumbent)
16	Kuala Krau (P.087)	15	BN (0.46)	BN (0.33)	BN (0.29)	BN (0.16)	Ismail Mohamed Said (Incumbent)
17	Besut (P.033)	1	BN (0.33)	BN (0.36)	BN (0.24)	BN (0.13)	Idris Jusoh (incumbent)
18	Bera (P.090)	14	BN (0.28)	BN (0.24)	BN (0.10)	BN (0.11)	Ismail Sabri Yaakob (incumbent)
19	Jelebu (P.126)	13	BN (0.72)	BN (0.57)	BN (0.32)	BN (0.11)	Jalaluddin Alias
20	Padang Besar (P.001)	3	BN (0.51)	BN (0.31)	BN (0.35)	BN (0.10)	Zahidi Zainul Abidin (incumbent)
21	Tanah Merah (P.027)	4	BN (0.16)	PR-PKR (0.09)	BN (0.16)	BN (0.10)	Ikmal Hisham (incumbent)
22	Hulu Terengganu (P.038)	3	BN (0.33)	BN (0.38)	BN (0.26)	BN (0.09)	Rosol Wahid
23	Padang Terap (P.007)	2	BN (0.15)	PR-PAS (0.02)	BN (0.22)	BN (0.07)	Mahdzir Khalid (incumbent)
24	Cameron Highlands (P.078)	4	BN (0.61)	BN (0.34)	BN (0.04)	BN (0.06)	C. Sivaraajh
25	Jempol (P.127)	26	BN (0.65)	BN (0.49)	BN (0.28)	BN (0.06)	Mohd Salim Shariff
26	Jasin (P.139)	1	BN (0.68)	BN (0.45)	BN (0.35)	BN (0.01)	Ahmad Hamzah (incumbent)
27	Kulai (P.163)	5	BN (0.56)	BN (0.37)	PR-DAP (0.31)	PH-DAP (0.59)	Teo Nie Cheng (incumbent)
28	Tebrau (P.158)	2	BN (0.81)	BN (0.48)	BN (0.04)	PH-PKR (0.58)	Steven Choong Shiau Yoon
29	Kubang Pasu (P.006)	1	BN (0.51)	BN (0.29)	BN (0.31)	PH-PPBM (0.43)	Amiruddin Hamzah

30	Merbok (P.014)	1	BN (0.52)	PR-PKR (0.12)	BN (0.11)	PH-PKR (0.33)	Nurin Aina Abdullah
31	Hulu Selangor (P.094)	4	BN (0.52)	PKR-PR (0.01)	BN (0.09)	PKR-PH (0.33)	June Leow Hsiad Hui
32	Jerlun (P.005)	2	BN (0.11)	BN (0.11)	BN (0.14)	PH-PPBM (0.31)	Mukhriz Mahathir
33	Pagoh (P.143)	4	BN (0.79)	BN (0.60)	BN (0.49)	PH-PPBM (0.29)	Muhyiddin Yassin
34	Sungai Siput (P.062)	1	BN (0.54)	PR-PSRM (0.11)	PR-PSRM (0.13)	PH-PKR (0.27)	Kesavan Subramaniam
35	Ledang (P.144)	1	BN (0.70)	BN (0.30)	BN (0.06)	PH-PKR (0.25)	Syed Ibrahim Syed Noh
36	Alor Gajah (P.135)	4	BN (0.75)	BN (0.49)	BN (0.36)	PH-PPBM (0.24)	Mohd. Redzuan Yusof
37	Segamat (P.140)	3	BN (0.43)	BN (0.19)	BN (0.06)	PH- PKR (0.23)	Edmund Santhara Kumar Ramanaidu
38	Tanjong Malim (P.077)	10	BN (0.61)	BN (0.26)	BN (0.15)	PH-PKR (0.22)	Chang Lih Kang
39	Kulim Bandar Baharu (P.018)	1	BN (0.35)	PR-PKR (0.25)	BN (0.07)	PH-PKR (0.21)	Saifuddin Nasution Ismail
40	Labis (P.142)	4	BN (0.65)	BN (0.30)	BN (0.02)	PH-DAP (0.20)	Pang Hok Liong
41	Simpang Renggam (P.151)	3	BN (0.75)	BN (0.48)	BN (0.29)	PH-PPBM (0.19)	Maszlee Malik
42	Raub (P.080)	4	BN (0.48)	BN (0.15)	PR-DAP (0.12)	PH-DAP (0.17)	Zulpuri Shah Raja Puji
43	Temerloh (P.088)	2	BN (0.51)	BN (0.11)	PR-PAS (0.04)	PH-AMANAH (0.08)	Anuar Tahir
44	Bentong (P.089)	8	BN (0.62)	BN (0.17)	BN (0.01)	PH-DAP (0.08)	Wong Tack
45	Sekijang (P.141)	5	BN (0.76)	BN (0.55)	BN (0.15)	PH-PKR (0.07)	Natrah Ismail
46	Tampin (P.133)	9	BN (0.76)	BN (0.54)	BN (0.38)	PH-AMANAH (0.04)	Hasan Baharom
47	Kuala Pilah (P.129)	1	BN (0.60)	BN (0.49)	BN (0.39)	PH-PPBM (0.01)	Eddin Syazlee Shith
48	Dungun (P.039)	5	BN (0.19)	BN (0.17)	PAS-PR (0.11)	PAS (0.32)	Wan Hassan Mohd. Ramli (incumbent)
49	Sik (P.013)	1	BN (0.02)	PR-PAS (0.03)	BN (0.13)	PAS (0.26)	Ahmad Tarmizi Sulaiman
50	Pendang (P.011)	1	PR-PAS (0.01)	PR-PAS (0.15)	BN (0.08)	PAS (0.22)	Awang Solahudin
51	Kuala Nerus (P.035)	1	BN (0.16)	BN (0.05)	PR-PAS (0.02)	PAS (0.22)	Mohd. Khairuddin Aman Razali (incumbent)
52	Setiu (P.034)	3	BN (0.30)	BN (0.27)	BN (0.24)	PAS (0.08)	Shaharizukarnain Abdul Kadir
53	Kemaman (P.040)	8	BN (0.43)	BN (0.34)	BN (0.27)	PAS (0.05)	Che Alias Hamid

Data Sources for Appendixes 9.1 and 9.2:
FELDA scheme locations (2004–17) and settler household numbers (2005): Tunku Shamsul Bahrin and Lee (1988), Appendix I; Lee and Tunku Shamsul Bahrin (2006), Appendix A; FELDA (2014); author's own estimates.

Electoral constituency maps (2004–18): Election Commission Malaysia (2007), p. 196; Ahmad Atory Hussain (2009), passim; personal communications with Pearlyn Y. Pang and Benjamin Hu.

Electoral constituency voter figures and election results (2004–18): Election Commission Malaysia (2006); Election Commission Malaysia (2009); Election Commission Malaysia (2015); *The Star*, n.d.

Ethnicity estimates (2013–18): Data collated by Tindak Malaysia; *The Star*, n.d.

Rural-urban classification (2017): Politweet (2018), pp. 22–33.

Notes

1. I would like to thank Cassey Lee, Ooi Kee Beng, Francis E. Hutchinson, Lee Hwok Aun and Norshahril Saat for their feedback on earlier versions of this study. Cassey Lee, Pearlyn Y. Pang and Benjamin Hu made this chapter possible by assisting with statistical analysis, associated charts, and mapping expertise. I am also grateful to Danesh Prakash Chacko and Khor Yu Leng for bringing additional data sources to my attention. The usual caveats apply.
2. This study focuses on FELDA parliamentary seats within Peninsular Malaysia. Sabah hosts another seven to nine FELDA settler schemes in its Tawau and Lahad Datu districts, but the East Malaysian state's peculiar demographic profile and economic trajectory puts it beyond this essay's scope. The analysis also excludes state-level seats (which are nearly triple that of federal parliamentary constituencies) due to time and space restrictions.

References

Ahmad Atory Hussain. 2009. *Politik Melayu Di Persimpangan: Suatu Analisis Pilihan Raya Umum 2008*. Kuala Lumpur: Utusan Publications & Distributors.

Crouch, Harold. 1996. *Government and Society in Malaysia*. Ithaca, NY: Cornell University Press.

Election Commission Malaysia. 2006. *Report of the General Election Malaysia 2004*. Kuala Lumpur: Percetakan Nasional Malaysia Berhad.

———. 2007. *50 Years of Democracy and Elections in Malaysia*. Putrajaya: Election Commission, Malaysia.

———. 2009. *Report of the 12th General Elections 2008*. Kuala Lumpur: Percetakan Nasional Malaysia Berhad.

———. 2015. *Report of the 13th General Election 2013*. Kuala Lumpur: Percetakan Nasional Malaysia Berhad.

FELDA. 2014. "Hubungi Kami: Alamat Rancangan FELDA di Setiap Wilayah". Lembaga Kemajuan Tanah Persekutuan. http://www.felda.net.my/index.php/hubungi/pejabat-wilayah-rancangan (accessed 11 April 2018).

Food and Agriculture Organization of the United Nations (FAO). 1966. "Country Paper: Land Settlement in Malaysia under Federal Land Development Authority". Paper presented at World Land Reform Conference, 20 June – 2 July 1966.

Guyot, Dorothy. 1971. "The Politics of Land: Comparative Development in Two States of Malaysia". *Pacific Affairs* 44, no. 3: 368–89.

Halim Salleh. 1992. "Peasants, Proletarianisation and the State: FELDA Settlers in Pahang". In *Fragmented Vision: Culture and Politics in Contemporary Malaysia*, edited by Joel S. Kahn and Francis Loh Kok Wah. Honolulu: University of Hawaii Press.

Harper, Tim. 1999. *The End of Empire and the Making of Malaya*. Cambridge: Cambridge University Press.

Khor Yu Leng. 2014. "The Political Tussle over FELDA Land Schemes: UMNO Strengthens Its Malay Rural Fortress in 13th General Election". *Kajian Malaysia* 32, no. Supp. 2: 89–121.

———. 2017. "The FELDA Quarrel and Its National Ramifications". *ISEAS Perspective*, no. 2017/51, 12 July 2017.

———. 2018. "Malaysia: The Political Economy of Social Media in GE-14". *Khor-Reports.com*, 21 April 2018.https://www.khor-reports.com/data-analysis/2018/4/21/malaysia-the-political-economy-of-social-media-in-GE-14 (accessed 26 October 2018).

Lee, Boon Thong, and Tunku Shamsul Bahrin. 2006. *Felda's Fifty Years: Land Pioneers to Investors.* Kuala Lumpur: FELDA.

Lee, Hock Guan. 2015. "Mal-Apportionment and the Electoral Authoritarian Regime in Malaysia". In *Coalitions in Collision: Malaysia's 13th General Elections*, edited by Johan Saravanamuttu, Lee Hock Guan and Mohamed Nawab Mohamed Osman. Petaling Jaya and Singapore: SIRD and Institute of Southeast Asian Studies.

Loh, Kai Syuen, and Danesh Prakash Chacko. 2018. "Cameron Highlands: Under the microscope". *Data Tarik*, 20 July 2018. https://datatarik.com/home/2018/7/20/cameron-highlands-under-the-microscope (accessed 26 October 2018).

Maznah Mohamad. 2015. "Fragmented but Captured: Malay Votes and the FELDA Factor in GE-13". In *Coalitions in Collision: Malaysia's 13th General Elections*, edited by Johan Saravanamuttu, Lee Hock Guan and Mohamed Nawab Mohamed Osman. Petaling Jaya and Singapore: SIRD and Institute of Southeast Asian Studies.

Nadirah H. Rodzi. "PH moves in as UMNO Loses in Support in Fortress Felda". *Straits Times*, 16 September 2018.

Pakiam, Geoffrey K. 2018. "Voting Behaviour in FELDA Parliamentary Constituencies since 2004". *ISEAS Perspective*, no. 26/2018, 26 April 2018. https://www.iseas.edu.sg/images/pdf/ISEAS_Perspective_2018_26@50.pdf (accessed 5 September 2018).

Politweet. 2018. "Election Forecast for Pakatan Harapan in Peninsular Malaysia (GE-14)". 11 January 2018, pp. 22–33. https://drive.google.com/file/d/16glv67fwRybQxdKS7X1f FC9R1SN0TSGy/view (accessed 27 October 2018).

Rashila Ramli. 2003. "The Multiple Roles of Rural Malay Women during the 1999 Election: The Case of FELDA J8". In *New Politics in Malaysia*, edited by Francis Loh Kok Wah and Johan Saravanamuttu. Singapore: Institute of Southeast Asian Studies.

Razak Ahmad, Mazwin Nik Amis, Sarban Singh, Ivan Loh, Han Sean Ong, and Mohd Farhaan Shah. 2018. "Felda Voters Could Be Kingmakers". *The Star*, 12 April 2018. https://www.thestar.com.my/news/nation/2018/04/12/felda-voters-could-be-kingmakers-highstakes-battle-set-for-malay-heartland (accessed 15 April 2018).

Robertson, A.F. 1984. *People and the State*. Cambridge: Cambridge University Press.

Saravanamuttu, Johan. 2017. "The FELDA Factor: Why UMNO Cannot Take Its 'Vote Bank' for Granted". *Aliran*, 14 February 2017. https://aliran.com/aliran-csi/aliran-csi-2017/felda-factor-next-election (accessed 5 September 2018).

———. 2018. "The FELDA Factor in GE-14". In *Regime Change in Malaysia: GE-14 and the End of UMNO-BN's 60-Year Rule*, edited by Francis Loh and Anil Netto. Petaling Jaya and Jelutong: SIRD and Aliran.

Serina Rahman. 2018a. *Malaysia's General Elections 2018: Understanding the Rural Vote*. Trends in Southeast Asia, no. 9/2018. Singapore: ISEAS – Yusof Ishak Institute.

———. 2018b. "Was It a Malay Tsunami? Deconstructing the Malay Vote in Malaysia's 2018 Election". *Round Table: Commonwealth Journal of International Affairs* 107, no. 6: 669–82.

Star, The. 2018. "PAS questions why Dr Mahathir wants to visit Nik Aziz's grave". 7 May 2018.

———. n.d. "The Star Online GE 14. Results Overview". https://election.thestar.com.my/. (accessed 11 May 2018).

Tunku Shamsul Bahrin, and Lee Boon Thong. 1988. *FELDA: Three Decades of Evolution*. Kuala Lumpur: FELDA.

Wain, Barry. 2012. *Malaysian Maverick. Mahathir Mohamad in Turbulent Times*. 2nd ed. Houndmills: Palgrave Macmillan.

Welsh, Bridget. 2018. "Saviour Politics and Malaysia's 2018 Electoral Breakthrough: Rethinking Explanatory Narratives and Implications". *Journal of Current Southeast Asian Affairs* 37, no. 3: 85–108.

Zaireeni Azmi. 2014. "The Concept of Gratitude (Budi) in Women's Political Participation: The Case Study of Women in Felda Ulu Tebrau, Johor, Malaysia". *International Journal of Arts and Sciences* 7, no. 5: 525–35.

10

SOCIAL TRANSFORMATION AND THE CONSOLIDATION OF CHINESE VOTES FOR REGIME CHANGE

Ngu Ik Tien and Lee Hwok Aun

INTRODUCTION

Chinese support for Pakatan Harapan (PH) not only remained strong in Malaysia's 14th General Elections (GE-14), consistent with voting trends of the 12th and the 13th General Elections, but was also decisive in rejecting Barisan Nasional's (BN) Chinese-based parties of Peninsular Malaysia and East Malaysia. To understand this momentous swing in Chinese support for the former opposition coalition since 2008, we need to look beyond the election issues and campaign strategies of political parties running up to GE-14. This chapter contends that structural shifts in Malaysia's Chinese society—reflected in the profile and influence of civil society organizations and gravitation away from old, predominantly race-based political vehicles—have moved voters in general towards PH, and that allowed for the realignment of elections that took place in 2008 and 2013.

This chapter is comprised of four sections. After this introduction, the second section reviews the general trends of Chinese votes during general elections from 1959 to 2013 with a focus on the gains and losses of Chinese-based political parties in each election and scholarly interpretations of the results. The third section takes a close look at GE-14 by examining the key issues discussed among civil society groups and the campaign issues and strategies adopted mainly by the candidates belonging to the Malaysian Chinese Association (MCA), the Democratic Action

Party (DAP) and the Sarawak United People's Party (SUPP). The fourth and final section of the discussion looks at social changes within Malaysia's Chinese society.

TRENDS IN CHINESE VOTES (1959–2013)

1959–69: Flux and Contestation

In the years after Malaysia attained independence, political groupings of the Chinese were largely organized along ethnic and ideological lines and divided into MCA, pro-left parties and the underground Communist Party. The pro-left parties[1] were mainly active in the states of Penang, Selangor and Perak where one finds large and concentrated populations of Chinese people (Lee and Heng 2000, pp. 206–7). DAP came onto the scene only after Singapore's People's Action Party (PAP) was compelled to leave Malaysia in 1965.

The 1950s through the 1960s was a period during which Chinese votes were highly fragmented and distributed among national parties such as MCA, DAP, pro-left parties and regional-based parties across the country. The 1969 general election was a watershed event which resulted in the suspension of local elections, banning pro-left parties and enacting several laws that curtailed the freedom of speech.

Chinese politics in East Malaysia took on a different orientation. Unlike the more fluid allegiances in Peninsular Malaysia, the Chinese electorate in Sarawak demonstrated strong partisanship by voting for a single party, the Sarawak United People's Party (SUPP), since its inception in 1959. Moreover, SUPP then espoused a socialist outlook. In Sabah, Chinese-based political parties were divided by locality and dialect,[2] and took a common stance against being incorporated into Malaysia. They subsequently merged to form the Sabah National Party (renamed as the Sabah Chinese Association) and joined the Sabah Alliance.

1974–2004: BN Holds Court, with Ebbs and Flows

The 1950s through the 1960s was a period during which Chinese votes were highly fragmented and distributed among national parties such as MCA, DAP, pro-left parties and regionally based parties across the country. The year 1973 marked the start of a new era, with the formation of the BN unity government, expanded from the Alliance, to include—most significantly for the Chinese community—the co-optation of Gerakan. MCA remained the main vehicle of Chinese political representation from 1974, the first general elections in the BN era. The 1970s saw MCA and DAP oscillate in parliamentary wins, both mutually gaining at the other's expense (Figure 10.1). Political developments in the 1970s also led to the demise of ideologically based parties and the entrenchment of ethnic identification in political discourse and mobilization of MCA, DAP as well as multiracial parties such as Gerakan and SUPP. DAP rose to become the largest opposition party in Malaysia, and its increased popularity came at the expense of the Chinese-based component parties of BN, particularly at the federal level. While DAP performed better in

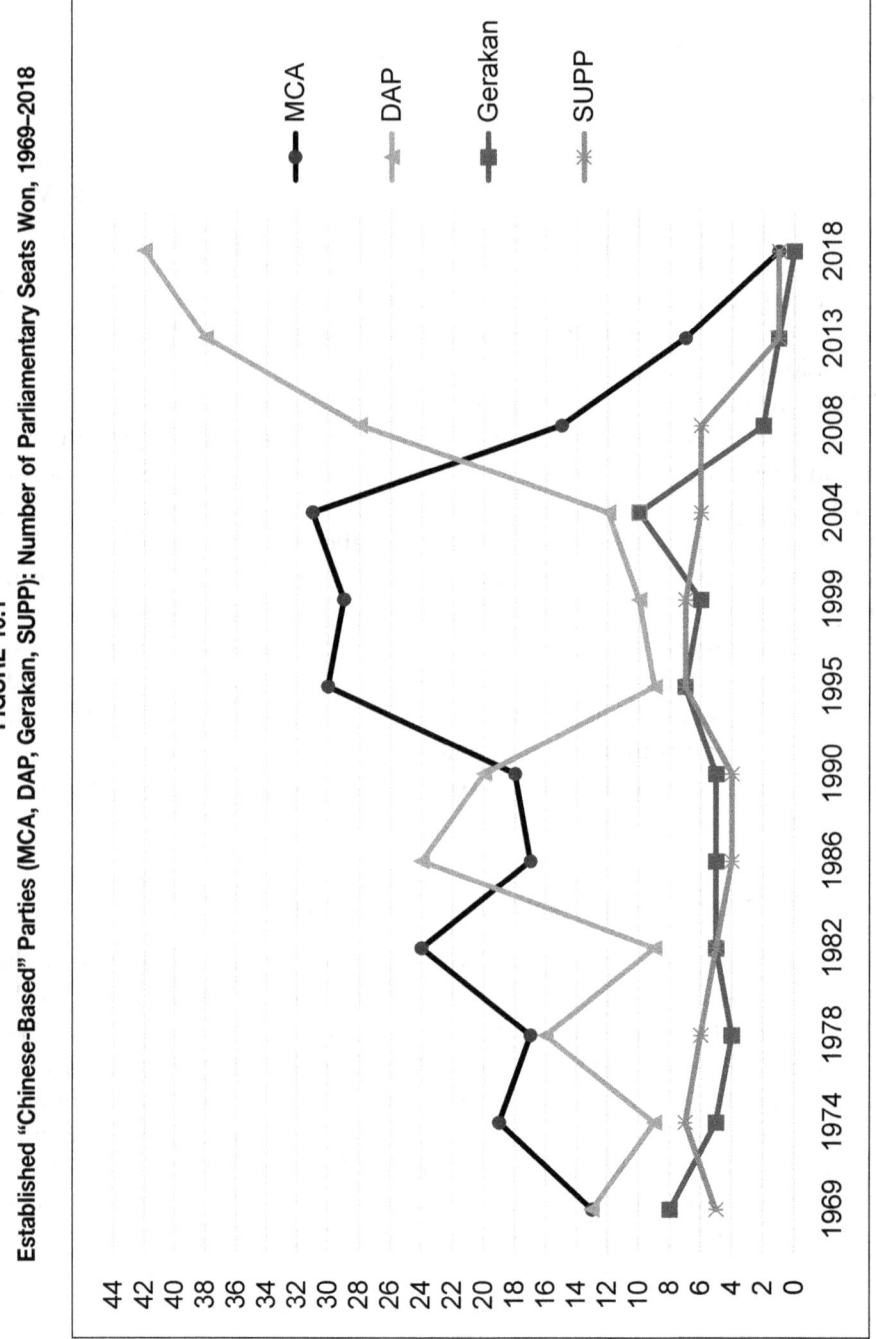

FIGURE 10.1
Established "Chinese-Based" Parties (MCA, DAP, Gerakan, SUPP): Number of Parliamentary Seats Won, 1969–2018

Note: Gerakan, SUPP and DAP are principally urban-based and not exclusively Chinese by constitution. Nonetheless, over much of the five decades these three parties clearly appealed to and depended on Chinese votes.
Sources: Public domain (1969–99); www.undi.info (2004–18).

parliamentary elections, BN candidates fared better in the state elections as voters employed a split voting strategy to ensure that needs for local development were met[3] (Lee and Heng 2000). Political observers noticed that a margin of Chinese votes appeared to swing between BN and the opposition, interpreting the swing voting as a reflection of two main approaches adopted by the community: engagement and intracoalitional negotiation with the UMNO-led BN government, or more open confrontation through DAP (Ng 2003, p. 93).

Such voting patterns persisted throughout the Mahathir Mohamad administration. Along with MCA, Chinese non-governmental organizations (NGOs) and voters in general shared anxieties of being marginalized in policy-making processes. In the 1982, 1986 and 1990 elections, a number of Chinese intellectuals relinquished their posts from Chinese associations to contest in elections under Gerakan or DAP.

However, the 1995 General Elections saw renewed Chinese support for BN. Continuous economic growth, liberalization in cultural, educational and economic policies, and the ideas of *bangsa* Malaysia and Vision 2020 had ignited the hope of some Chinese during Mahathir's leadership. At that point in time, both the ruling party and opposition had equal shares of Chinese electoral support (Ng 2003, p. 104). Chinese support for BN was sustained in the 1999 General Elections even while the country was weathering the Asian Financial Crisis and internal political turmoil after the sacking of Deputy Prime Minister Anwar Ibrahim. While a considerable portion of Chinese voters in Kuala Lumpur swung to the opposition, Chinese voters in other areas stood by BN. Many Chinese were concerned that the BN losses would have led to a repeat of the 1969 race riots and that the victory of DAP—which had formed an alliance with Parti Islam Se-Malaysia (PAS)—might pave the way to an Islamic state (Funston 2000, p. 53). Meanwhile, Loh's (2003) study of Bukit Bendera, a parliamentary seat in Penang Island, provided another dimension by arguing that BN's politics of "developmentalism" had been attractive to the middle and lower classes of Chinese voters, whereas the upper middle class were inclined to vote for the opposition in the hopes of increasing political checks and balances and accountability of the ruling government.

The number of votes and seats held by MCA and Gerakan further increased in the 2004 General Elections after the changing of the UMNO guard from Mahathir Mohamad to Abdullah Badawi before the election. Chinese support for Mahathir had eroded in the latter years, in part due to the quashing of reform appeals made by Suqiu, a consortium of Chinese NGOs. Abdullah was warmly greeted; his gentle and amiable demeanour contrasted with Mahathir's austere and combative disposition. The key promises in the 2004 elections revolved around reforms to education and anti-corruption, issues that especially resonated in the Chinese community. Across BN's decade of buoyant popularity and the Mahathir-Abdullah handover (1995 to 2004), the politics of fear, developmentalism and reform promise helped the Chinese component parties within BN maintain nearly 50 per cent of the community's votes.

In Sarawak, despite its crossover to the Alliance/BN after the 1970 General Elections, SUPP had been fairly successful in carrying its supporter base[4] to Sarawak

BN, much as Gerakan had accomplished in Penang. DAP entered Sarawak's political arena in the late 1970s and made a breakthrough by winning two parliamentary seats in the 1982 general election, although it only won state seats from there until the 1996 state elections. New issues such as money politics, corruption, local development and checks and balances were prioritized by DAP in the 1990s. SUPP sustained a steady presence and popularity in Sarawak in the 1980s, through the 1990s and early 2000s (Figure 10.1). A bigger pro-opposition swing in Chinese-majority constituencies took place in the 2006 state elections, which arguably amounted to a realignment. Arguably, the votes that SUPP lost in 2006 have not yet been recaptured to date.

In the 1970s and 1980s, the Chinese in Sabah were generally alienated by the Islamization and race-based politics of Mustapha Harun, the BN Chief Minister. Instead they turned to and supported Kadazan-led multiracial political parties especially the Parti Bersatu Sabah (PBS) which had been constantly at odds with the federal government over the state of Sabah's interests. The anti-BN sentiment also opened a window for DAP to set its foot in Sabah in the 1978 general elections.

During the Mahathir Mohamad and Abdullah Badawi eras, besides PBS, SAPP and DAP, the Chinese in Sabah also voted for candidates under the Liberal Democratic Party (LDP) and the Peninsular Malaysia-based MCA and Gerakan.[5] This period saw the diminishment of partisan loyalties among Chinese voters and the strengthening of strongman politics that together resulted in the fragmentation of the Chinese vote. In the 2004 elections, each party mentioned above managed to win one or two seats, either at state or parliament levels, by capturing a significant share of Chinese votes.

2008–18: Momentous Change

BN's unprecedented losses in the 2008 General Elections, most significantly the end of the coalition's long-held two-thirds majority in Parliament and relinquishing of five state governments, was coined a political tsunami.[6] States such as Penang, Selangor and Perak on the west coast of Peninsular Malaysia with sizeable Chinese populations all fell into the hands of Pakatan Rakyat (PR), the opposition coalition that formed soon after the elections. BN maintained dominance over the state governments of Negeri Sembilan, Melaka, Johor and Sarawak, where ethnic Chinese account for 20 to 30 per cent of the total state population. Many attributed the political change to new media and the liberalization policies of Prime Minister Abdullah Badawi over public spaces that allowed vibrant civic activism. Another notable trend that emerged was the popularization of street rallies as a means of activism. Between 2007 and 2018, five street rallies demanding free and fair elections were held in Kuala Lumpur and other major cities in Malaysia. BN had lost its two-thirds parliamentary majority and ethnic Chinese participated in these massive public demonstrations against BN, but the events proceeded peacefully, although authorities brutally cracked down on a few occasions.

The spectre of 13 May reprisals, which the government typically conjured when faced with galvanized dissent, had finally faded as an artifice for forestalling public protest. At the same time, ethnic politics persist as a fundamental characteristic and durable strain of Malaysian politics. However, overcoming the psychological barrier of the 1969 riots was arguably a significant factor in sustaining Chinese electoral votes for the opposition beyond the 2008 watershed.

In the 2013 General Elections (GE-13), BN suffered a great loss in popular votes—winning 47 per cent, against PR's 51 per cent—but the coalition managed to retain a simple majority in Parliament and control over ten state governments. The Merdeka Center polls estimated that approximately 85 per cent of Chinese votes went to PR, resulting in a near elimination of all Chinese-based parties in BN. DAP gained the most, its parliamentary seat haul burgeoning from only twelve in 2004 to twenty-eight in 2008 and thirty-eight in 2013 (Figure 10.1). In line with historical patterns, DAP's meteoric rise was mirrored by MCA's precipitous fall, but somewhat in contrast to the 1980s and 1990s, when Gerakan generally held its ground, in 2008 and 2013 this second Chinese-based BN component party continuously declined in popularity. The Chinese electorate's abandonment of BN was most striking on the Peninsula. MCA and Gerakan presence in Parliament were both halved. MCA fell from fifteen to seven parliamentary seats, while Gerakan hung on to just one seat—out of the handful of state seats it contested.

After 2013, the opposition PR coalition became embroiled in internal tussles, most sharply between DAP and PAS, induced by UMNO's overtures to PAS and accommodation of the latter's ambitions to enhance *hudud* law. PAS' subsequent breakaway from PR dented the opposition's numbers in Parliament, but in some ways bolstered DAP's position in the Chinese community. Prime Minister Najib also became embroiled in the 1MDB corruption scandal, which resonated especially among the urban populace. The massive turnout, and conspicuous Chinese presence, at the Bersih 4 rally which called for Najib to step down along with electoral reform demands, signalled the profound, and seemingly entrenched, disaffection with the ruling regime, and with the prime minister in particular. However, whether the electorate was persuaded about PR as a cohesive and credible alternative to BN was another matter, and there remained the possibility that the Chinese, having shown pragmatism over partisanship in the past, might grow lethargic in their opposition leanings and retract support, or even swing back to BN.

Six months before GE-14, media reports indicated that there was growing dissatisfaction among former PR supporters against the then ruling coalition's decisions (Yeoh 2017). Among many issues, PR's cooperation with former Prime Minister Mahathir Mohamad drew pointed criticism, particularly in some activist circles. MCA and Gerakan appeared more energized than in the run-up to GE-13, evidently banking on Chinese opposition-lethargy and UMNO's rallying of Malay votes in the mixed or Chinese-majority seats where these parties would contest. Pakatan Harapan (PH) managed to forge a cohesive alliance, and apprehensions towards Mahathir's return were allayed by polling day. PH secured votes from all ethnic groups, but the overwhelming support of Chinese voters was pivotal to its victory, contributing to its staggering success in multicornered fights on the Peninsula.

Sarawak's politics has seldom mirrored national political developments. A political tsunami did not take place in Sarawak in the 2008 General Elections in which the opposition garnered only two parliamentary seats. However, PR made impressive moves in the 2011 state elections, emerging with twelve DAP seats and three Parti Keadilan Rakyat (PKR) seats in the state assembly hall. The hope to end Sarawak Chief Minister Taib's grip over Sarawak and the wish for stronger checks and balances helped PR to gain considerable votes, causing a huge loss of support for SUPP. The hope of regime change was the main theme in the 2013 general elections. Thus, SUPP Chinese candidates failed to defend any parliamentary seats; Richard Riot Jaem, an indigenous Bidayuh, became the party's sole MP. The following year, the longest-serving Chief Minister of Sarawak Taib Mahmud stepped down and was succeeded by his long-term supporter Adenan Satem. Adenan was very vocal on cultural issues such as the use of English, the recognition of the Unified Examination Certificate, and Islamization trends. He even criticized history textbooks for being too Malay- and Peninsular Malaysia-centric. Under his leadership, BN Chinese candidates wrested back several rural Chinese-majority seats in the 2016 state elections. Adenan died in 2017, and his successor Abang Johari wields less charisma and clout. The loss of the "Adenan factor" clearly contributed to BN's GE-14 losses in parliamentary seats that subsume state legislature constituencies where it is the incumbent.

The fact that DAP only made its first breakthrough in Sabah's elections in 2008 suggests that Sabahan Chinese may possess a stronger sense of regionalism than the Chinese in Sarawak. Furthermore, their continued adoption of the vote-splitting strategy—generally, by supporting the opposition candidate for Parliament and a government candidate for the state assembly—allowed Chinese candidates from BN to survive (Govindasamy and Lai 2014, p. 218). However, this changed in the urban and Chinese-majority constituencies, such as Kota Kinabalu and Sandakan, in GE-13. DAP won four state seats, defeating candidates from local parties such as PBS, SLDP, SAPP and STAR.[7] Sabah DAP secretary Chan Foong Hin (Chen 2013, p. 160) indicated that Sabahan Chinese shared a passion for a government change with the ethnic Chinese across the country. Thus, they selected party over candidates. Urban residents, particularly Chinese voters, perceivably began to regard their predicaments as similar to Peninsular Malaysia Chinese. They were ready to address the urgency of national issues such as good governance and corruption over local interests by selecting national parties over local parties (Govindasamy and Lai 2014). The party system has been relatively weak compared to other states, given the frequent cases of party hopping. The electorate's message in GE-14, however, was loud and clear in Chinese-majority constituencies, all of which voted for opposition candidates of DAP, PKR or Warisan.

CHINESE VOTERS AND GE-14: PUBLIC OPINION, SHIFTING PARTISANSHIP, ELECTORAL SENTIMENTS

While the Chinese electorate voted for Pakatan by an overwhelming majority, the underlying reasons and influences are not homogeneous. The political opinions of a significant portion of the Chinese community are shaped by multiple local groups, mainly civil society groups, political parties and the media. This section examines the issues articulated by prominent Chinese groups and intellectuals who are centred in and around Malaysia's capital of Kuala Lumpur. However, their influence is not limited to the Chinese in Kuala Lumpur, given that their views and activities received considerable coverage by the Chinese language mass media. This posed an interesting dynamic, given that many of these media outlets were also critical of BN and the Najib administration. The latter part of this section analyses the campaign issues and strategies employed by the major Chinese-based political parties such as MCA and SUPP in Sarawak, and DAP of PH during the campaign period.

Transformations in Cultural Values and (Non)Partisanship

Over the past decades, Chinese society in Malaysia has become increasingly liberal in terms of cultural values. Such changes are manifested in their organizational life, ways of political engagement and even the family institution. Traditional Chinese societies such as clan and kinship organizations, many of which were set up during the early migration journeys to Malaysia, have gradually lost their ideological and social appeal to younger Malaysian Chinese. After independence in 1957, national organizations such as Jiaozong, Dongzong and modern political parties were opinion leaders in society, but their influences have diminished since the early twenty-first century. The orientation and focus of Chinese societies also changed over time; their efforts have not just revolved around cultural preservation, including supporting Chinese schools and celebrating traditional festivals, but also individual rights and pro-democracy values.

The rise of non-ethnically motivated social movements and new media in the end of the 1990s have nurtured a new group of activists who are distinct from the traditional leadership in social causes, networking and choice of media. These young activists hold strongly to pro-democracy values such as demanding for accountability by those who hold political power, advocating for individual rights to culture including language and lifestyle and belief in equal citizenship. A sizeable proportion of these activists are in their thirties and forties with affiliations to academic or NGOs. Contrastingly, the *huatuan* (a Chinese acronym for Chinese associations) leadership is dominated by middle-aged Chinese businessmen who are very much concerned about the survival of the Chinese as an ethnic community and the preservation of traditional culture and institutions. Unlike the young activists, *huatuan* leaders would not pick up issues such as Lesbian-Gay-Bisexual-Transgender (LGBT) rights.[8] In terms of their networking strategy, the *huatuan* keep to their ethnic circle and express little intention to establish a cross-ethnic network. When it comes to information dissemination, the *huatuan* rely on Chinese newspapers as a major avenue for the dissemination of information as opposed to the younger activists who are inclined to solely use new media.

Younger activists and *huatuan* leaders represent different generational experiences in some specific areas, significantly in their perceptions of family and the role of women. More and more young people accept that marriage and producing offspring are no longer an obligation but an individual's choice. These choices can explain statistics showing that Chinese have both the lowest fertility rate and the highest mean age at first marriage among all ethnic groups in Malaysia. Changes in perceptions of women's roles are also manifested in the activities held by the women's sections of political parties and societies. For instance, the women's wings of MCA, SUPP and the *huatuan* focus on building sisterhood by organizing social activities and family-based living skills, whereas the women in DAP stress the importance of women's rights and representation in the public sphere. Popular female politicians in DAP include Yeo Bee Yin, Hannah Yeoh and Teo Nie Ching, among others.

In both GE-13 and GE-14, DAP won nearly all the Chinese majority seats across Malaysia, and maintained a staggeringly high win record in all the mixed constituencies it contested, significantly on the back of the Chinese vote. Thus, one question is: what does this outcome say about partisanship and DAP? While these realignments took place in GE-12 and GE-13, the swing to DAP is arguably motivated as much, if not more, by voters' pragmatic calculation than partisanship. Hence, the possibility of swings away from DAP could not be discounted. As early as June 2017, DAP strategist Liew Chin Tong warned that the Chinese support for PH could drop to 65 per cent if Chinese voters were no longer convinced about the possibility of regime change (*Nanyang Siang Pau*, 16 June 2017). The trend was supported by multiple opinion polls that were carried out in 2017 and 2018 indicating that BN might be able to hold on to 20 per cent of Chinese support with a sizeable number of Chinese remaining undecided (Yeoh 2017; Chin 2018).

Party membership numbers indicate that the Chinese electorate has gravitated away from formal affiliation. DAP has a much smaller membership than MCA, PAS and even PKR. BN parties have accumulated their membership base over various decades being in the ruling coalition. However, the disparity remains staggering; UMNO and MCA respectively claim to have 3.5 million and 1.1 million members. PAS has close to 1 million members, despite being in federal opposition—except for a brief spell in the 1970s. DAP's meteoric rise in 2008 boosted its membership, but not as steeply as might be expected. Its register of active members increased from 84,000 in 2008 to 150,000 in 2012 (Democratic Action Party 2012). On the eve of GE-14, DAP counted about 165,000 in its ranks. The party's electoral success and elevation to federal government spurred a slight increase in membership; by March 2019, DAP had registered 173,000.[9] This is partly an outcome of DAP's cadre system that imposes relatively heavier demands on members. A voluminous membership roll does not necessarily translate into mass campaign mobilization and vote-getting; MCA is particularly illustrative.

Nonetheless, DAP's leanness looks exceptional. PKR, its relevant comparator as federal government coalition partner, recorded massive growth soon after GE-14. In June 2018 alone, PKR's membership swelled by 40.5 per cent, from 545,500 to 766,500 (Ong and Hariz Mohd 2018). The spike was clearly induced by upcoming party elections, but nonetheless captures a different internal dynamic—within a non-Chinese-dominant party. Time will shed further light on this perceived shift away from partisanship among the Chinese, but the current signs suggest that fewer and fewer choose direct affiliation.

These trends accord with our observation that many young Chinese who have been working for DAP politicians for several years have not applied for party membership. They actually do not see the need to commit to or be loyal to one political party or organization. Unlike MCA in the 1960s, whose members were recruited mainly from the widespread network of traditional associations and the New Villages (Heng 1983, p. 301), the Chinese voters who voted for DAP candidates are mainly urbanites who do not associate with traditional associations nor live in New Villages. Many of these voters do not regard DAP as a middleman between the Chinese masses and the Malay elites, a role that used to be played by MCA and SUPP during the periods of British colonial and BN rule. Instead, DAP is regarded as an opposition force to the PAS and UMNO conservative fronts and these parties' encroachment on the rights and interests of Chinese and non-Malays.

Expectations that disillusionment and lethargy among Chinese might work against PH did not materialize. Prior to GE-14, some developments raised questions over the ability of PH to maintain its commanding presence in Peninsular urban areas, particularly the Klang Valley, including the movement to abstain from voting or to "spoil" votes (selecting neither BN nor PH). A 4 per cent drop in Chinese turnout at GE-14 also might reflect a segment of registered voters that were not persuaded enough, although the ploy of holding the election on a Wednesday may also have precluded some overseas voters from returning to cast their ballots. DAP's astounding success at the polls—which included Chinese, Indian and Malay candidates—was not just its near 90 per cent win record in parliament contests, but also its gaping margins. The *average* margin of victory in Selangor parliament seats was 75,500, more than double the also massive 36,100 buffer of GE-13. These phenomenal results suggest that the party, along with PH, gained momentum among Chinese voters as 9 May 2018 approached.

Political Debate and Opinion: Chinese Activists and Public Forums

Political debate somewhat flourished prior to GE-14, particularly in activist Chinese circles, springing from a younger community and relatively new organizations. In the run-up to GE-14, seven established Chinese bodies produced a memorandum on Chinese education.[10] Some prominent Chinese businessmen conducted high-profile social events with the prime minister at that time, Najib Razak. However, these events generated few debates and low enthusiasm among the Chinese. Post GE-14, an editorial's note of a local Chinese newspaper criticized the *huatuan* leaders for being conservative and pro-establishment opportunists who have lost their leadership credibility and influence in the Chinese community. The weakening leadership position of the traditional Chinese associations has affected the BN Chinese-based political parties negatively, as these associations were formerly seen as an arm of the parties. Local Chinese associations face the same challenges as the national organizations (Ngu 2014). Only a few have managed to excel, namely the Kuala

Lumpur and Selangor Chinese Assembly Hall (KLSCAH) and the Lim Lian Geok Cultural Development Centre (LLG). These associations are also active members in other coalitions comprised of civil society organizations, such as the Gabungan Bertindak Malaysia (GBM).[11]

Individuals and groups who perhaps demonstrate greater influence over Chinese political opinion are activists who have been inspired by social movements, in particular the 1998 Reformasi and the Bersih 2.0 electoral reform movements along with environmental, student and community movements that took place after the 1990s. Most of them are pro-PH and advocate for regime change. Unlike the leaders of *huatuan* who are not seen as activists but as sponsors, these social movement protagonists have been actively involved in various forms of activism including community organizing, shaping discourse, creating awareness and participating in street protests. Moreover, these activists more readily form cross-ethnic collaborations. Online news portals, social media and seminars are their main channels for networking, thought sharing, and event publicity.

Six months prior to polling day, dozens of forums on issues pertinent to GE-14 were organized in Kuala Lumpur. Among the topics discussed, the leadership of Mahathir Mohamad in the PH appeared to be a highly charged issue among activists who took different stances, with Facebook as the major battleground. As early as the end of 2017, Chinese-language Facebook pages appeared, dedicated to promoting spoilt votes among the Chinese-speaking community (Ronasina 2018; Yeoh 2017). Some activists turned their Facebook pages into semi-public forums and even wrote their postings in three languages—Chinese, English and Malay—addressing opinions from different cultural groups. The main issue contested on Facebook was the deep distrust over Mahathir's sincerity for institutional reform. PH's selection of him as an interim prime minister was seen as a betrayal of the democratic struggle. Some even accused those who agreed to his leadership as unprincipled opportunists. The anti-Mahathir groups also extended their support for the Malay-based hashtag #UndiRosak movement by defending their call for spoiling votes or abstaining from voting.

The broader traction of such appeals to cast a protest vote, particularly beyond the Klang Valley, was arguably intertwined with the perceived prospects of PH actually winning, which in turn hinged on its capacity to garner Malay support. The #UndiRosak movement may have gained some momentum in the initial phase but gradually lost appeal when PH successfully drew large Malay crowds to their political talks. Despite anger at Mahathir, political analysts explained the shift by noting that the desire to change government was much stronger among Chinese voters, who swung further in favour of regime change with a growing belief that the change was possible (Yeoh 2018).

Candidates, Platforms and Outcomes

Various issues were raised at campaign rallies, from general economic concerns to policies with particular resonance among Malaysian Chinese voters, as well as some highly contemporary issues, notably mainland China investments, which ultimately were not as significant as perhaps anticipated. The electoral outcome of GE-14 indicates "uniformity" in Chinese choice of political leadership and ideology in comparison to their political division in the 1950s and 1960s, which was accounted by historian Wang Gungwu (1970).

While in the post-Independence period, the Chinese community was fragmented by language, educational background and political ideology, these dividing factors have waned over time. In fact, over the last twenty years, the top leadership positions in MCA have been dominated by Chinese-language educated local graduates[12] such as Ong Ka Ting, Ong Tee Keat, Chan Kong Choy, Hou Kok Chung, Liow Tiong Lai and Wee Ka Siong. In comparison, the DAP leadership has been able to absorb younger politicians from diverse educational backgrounds, and prominent leaders are not uniformly Western-educated elites. These new generation includes overseas graduates such as Tony Pua and Ong Kian Ming, and local graduates Nga Khor Ming and Anthony Loke, as well as Liew Chin Tong and Teo Nie Ching, who attended independent Malaysian Chinese secondary schools. More importantly, DAP has a considerable number of female representatives in Parliament and state legislative assemblies. In terms of political ideology, the young DAP leaders espouse pro-democracy ideals rather than adopting any political ideology. Tellingly, MCA and DAP candidates did not get into disputes over the existence of Malaysia's capitalist system, the cause of Chinese education or the Chinese proficiency of Chinese candidates, but crossed swords on issues of governance, development policy, and corruption.

As part of the research for this chapter, a dozen political rallies in the Chinese majority and ethnic-mixed parliamentary constituencies of Teluk Intan, Ayer Hitam, Bentong, Damansara, Cheras and Sibu were observed in the run-up to polling day. Ayer Hitam, Bentong and Teluk Intan were, from 2004, characterized by close contests, with MCA holding Ayer Hitam and Bentong by shrinking majorities in successive elections, and Gerakan retaking Teluk Intan by a razor-thin margin in a 2014 by-election. In 2018, the BN incumbents were high-ranking leaders from MCA and Gerakan who held Cabinet ministerial posts. Demographically, these constituencies also contained similar proportions of Chinese among registered voters: Bentong (47 per cent Malay, 42 per cent Chinese), Teluk Intan (41 per cent Malay, 40 per cent Chinese), Ayer Hitam (58 per cent Malay, 38 per cent Chinese).

The main campaign issues of the MCA candidates running for Bentong and Ayer Hitam were local development, Chinese representation in government, cultivation of cordial ties between MCA leaders and China, and apprehension regarding Mahathir's revival. The rhetorical framework of local development was built on the commitment of candidates, their status as part of the ruling government, and their personal connections with officials from China as factors that would help boost local tourism. An interesting point to note is that the BN politicians in Sarawak and MCA speakers in Bentong resorted to local identity by describing DAP campaigners as outsiders who fanned ill feelings among local residents.

Meanwhile, PH, particularly DAP, had been criticized as being unprincipled by having worked with Anwar Ibrahim, Hadi Awang and Mahathir Mohamad despite a number of dishonourable acts by these three politicians, and previous or current racial animosities towards the Chinese. Campaigns generally took harder stances against Mahathir than Hadi; the Islamic state issue was overshadowed by the Mahathir factor and associated cronyism, racism and corruption of his previous twenty-two-year rule. Wee Ka Siong, the BN candidate for Ayer Hitam, who was fluent in Mandarin and Malay gave an informative speech in Yong Peng, a town within the constituency. Wee defended Malaysia's economic performance under Najib Razak, referencing the rise of the Kuala Lumpur Composite Index (KLCI), comprehensive public transportation projects, and the improvement of several international economic indexes during his five-year rule. With respect to the goods and services tax (GST) policy, MCA spokespersons explained that similar policies have been implemented worldwide and that the GST allows government income sources to be diversified. Many MCA rallies as well as DAP's were well equipped with an LED screen and informative slides. The use of these technologies enabled speakers to explain complicated issues with statistics and features and to play back previous utterances that might sow doubt and apprehension towards this alliance of former foes, for example, the criticisms that Lim Kit Siang, Lim Guan Eng and Anwar Ibrahim had lodged against Mahathir.

DAP candidates rode on voters' resentments against GST and the 1MDB scandal that denoted the BN government as a corrupt regime with an unrepentant leadership. DAP candidates were confident in obtaining the majority of Chinese votes but were concerned about maintaining the turnout rates. The DAP candidates believed a Malay swing to the PH would mobilize apathetic and disappointed Chinese voters, as they had long aspired for regime change. The GST issue added fuel to their anti-establishment sentiments.[13]

In addition to the 1MDB scandal and GST concerns, local development issues and the performance of Penang and Selangor governments were frequently mentioned by DAP candidates. Similar to previous general elections, DAP assured their supporters that PH represented a better government that would bring a brighter future to the country. Instead of dwelling on old issues of Chinese education, Islamization and institutionalized racism in the public sector that many voters perceived as structural problems, DAP speakers emphasized corruption issues as immediate threats to the well-being of the nation. The impact of DAP's state leaders' staunch defence of Sarawak autonomy, and its development projects and social outreach in semi-urban and rural communities under the Impian Sarawak banner are difficult to appraise, but cannot be denied as possible factors that burnished the party's brand. While there was diffuse support for the national opposition, variations appeared in different parts of the country. In the isolated districts where non-commercial activities such as traditional farming is the main source of livelihood, local factors carried some weight. Table 10.1 shows the election results for the three parliamentary seats.

TABLE 10.1
Results for the Parliamentary Seats of Teluk Intan, Bentong and Ayer Hitam (GE-14)

	Share of Votes (%)			Majority (No. of Votes)	Registered Voters
	DAP (PH)	MCA (BN)	PAS		
Teluk Intan	54.3%	33.5%	12.1%	11,179	66,487
Bentong	46.6%	43.0%	10.4%	2,032	67,359
Ayer Hitam	43.2%	44.0%	12.8%	303	46,157

Source: http://www.thestar.com.my/GE-14.

DAP candidates won in Bentong and Teluk Intan, but lost in Ayer Hitam despite fielding one of the party's rising young leaders, Liew Chin Tong. DAP prevailed in Bentong and Teluk Intan, with their sizeable shares of Malay voters and about 40 per cent Chinese voters, clearly on the back of overwhelming Chinese support. That the BN candidates were, respectively, president of MCA and Gerakan, underscored Chinese rejection of these parties. In Ayer Hitam, MCA's candidate Wee Ka Siong, defeated DAP candidate Liew Chin Tong, with a slight majority of 303 votes and on the back of Malay support. At the same time, DAP's loss reflects how it has still been largely rejected by the non-urban Malay electorate even though it has been working closely with parties such as the PKR, Amanah and PAS for a number of years. However, DAP made some advances among Indian voters. The DAP candidate won the Teluk Intan seat with a huge majority of 11,179 votes.

In Sarawak, the outlook for PH during the campaign period—based on public opinion surveys and internal strategic assessments—did not see the coalition as having good chances in rural and semi-urban seats.[14] Analysts even predicted that BN had an upper hand in the Sarikei, Sibu and Miri parliamentary seats. However, on the eve of polling day, local informants for this research project shared different stories indicating a DAP victory in those three seats, citing messages circulating among their relatives, colleagues and friends. Other informants, including one in Sarikei, asserted that the BN candidate would lose. There were rumours that party members of SUPP as well as the local people were angered by the thuggish behaviour of the BN candidate's campaigners and that many would vote him out to check his influence in Sarikei. The polling outcome confirmed the informant's projection of the BN candidate's loss. In fact, on the eve of polling day, local gambling wagers on the elections had changed their betting from a slight victory for BN to losses by BN candidates in Sarikei, Sibu and Miri. However, the local context should not be overstated, as national politics played a pivotal role in shaping voters' views. The candidate for Sibu attributed his victory to a swing away from BN among all ethnic groups, despite a lower turnout than the 2013 general elections.[15]

Chinese rejection of BN translates into strikingly painted maps of the community's population distribution and election outcomes (Figures 10.2 and 10.3). The darker shades denote higher Chinese concentration, which is coterminous with urban areas in western Peninsular Malaysia, and throughout Sabah and Sarawak. Uniformly,

FIGURE 10.2
Peninsular Malaysia Parliamentary Constituencies:
Share of Chinese among Registered Voters and GE-14 Winner

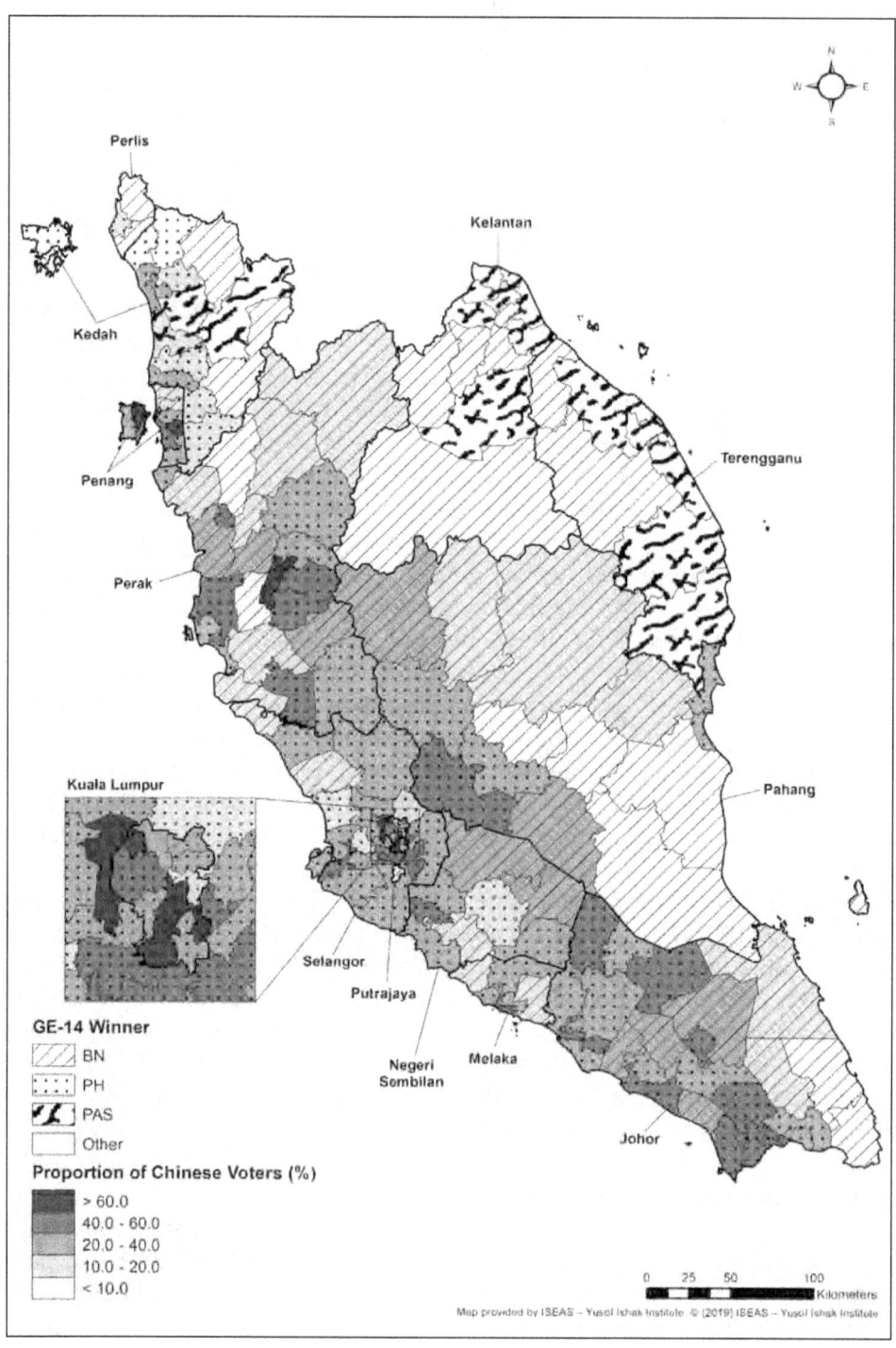

FIGURE 10.3
Sabah and Sarawak Parliamentary Constituencies:
Share of Chinese among Registered Voters and GE-14 Winner

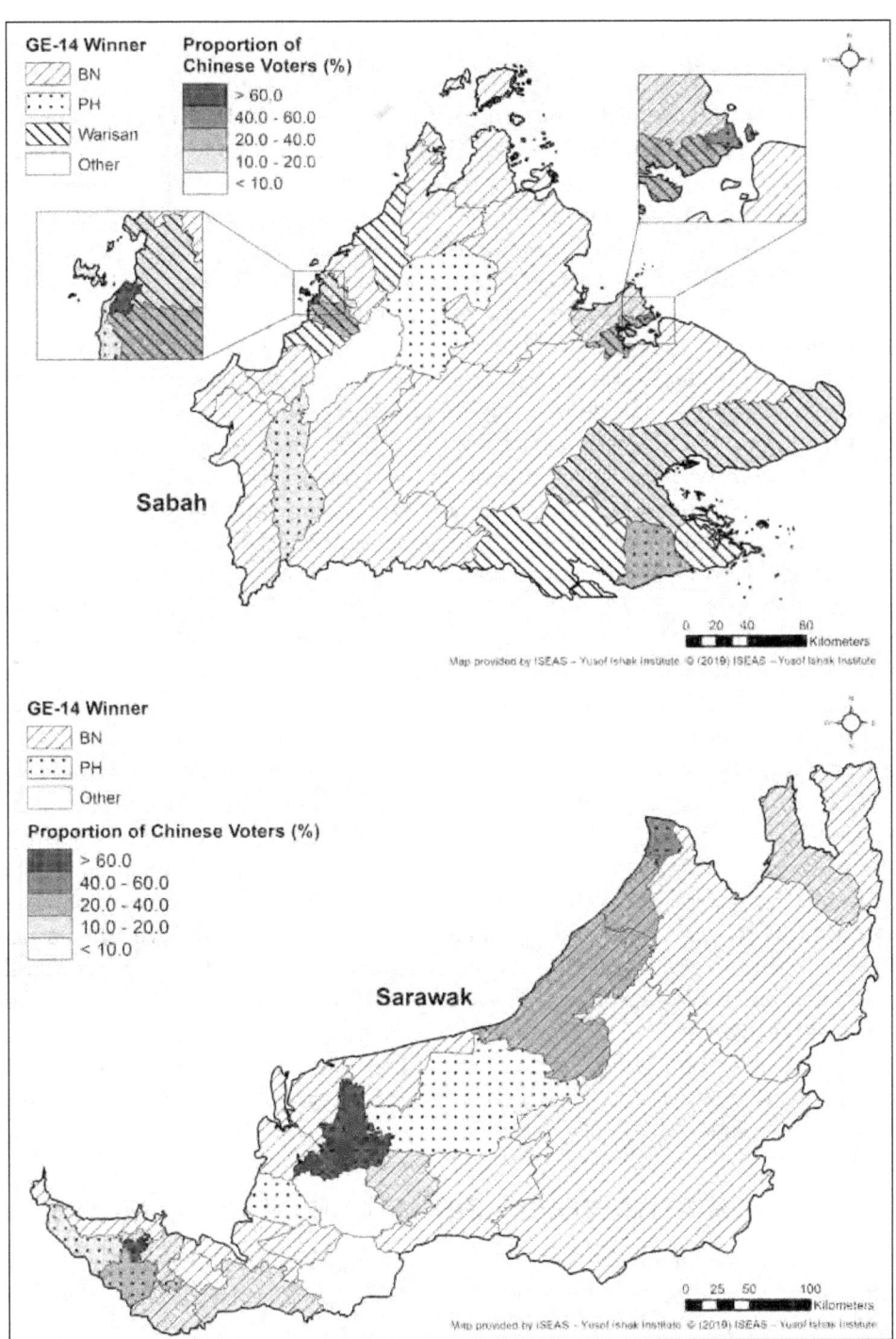

being a Chinese-majority seat corresponded with a win for PH, and mixed seats, with substantial proportions of Chinese voters, also overwhelmingly elected PH representatives.

The China Factor

China was a factor in GE-14 and will perhaps play a role in future elections. As far back as 1974, the visit to China by Abdul Razak, the second prime minister of Malaysia, was viewed as an election strategy to entice Chinese voters shocked by the 1969 race riots. The China card had been left aside in the last few elections but the country's recent massive investments in Malaysia brought it into the limelight again. While UMNO defended China's investment in Malaysia to their Malay supporters, its counterpart MCA cheered the relationship with the hope that China's investments would swing some Chinese votes to BN. By endorsing China's role in Malaysia, MCA was also looking to tap into China's resources that could benefit local Chinese groups neglected by the BN government.

The peripheral Chinese-majority towns such as Yong Peng and Bentong have lagged behind in terms of development. In the Ayer Hitam contest, both Liew and Wee promised to promote local heritage and food to tourists from China in order to revitalize the economies of peripheral towns. In addressing the needs of local, small and medium-sized Chinese enterprises, MCA also promised to use its "connection" with China to open opportunities for business owners. The MCA manifesto openly endorsed the Chinese government's Belt and Road Initiative (BRI), but minimally referred to Malaysia's national economic plans. MCA's dependence on private resources indicated the limitations of its influence in steering government policy to meet the economic needs of Chinese communities in Malaysia.

Contrastingly, DAP politicians appeared to be more cautious about China's investments in Malaysia. Some DAP leaders even reiterated the allegations that had surfaced online, about how investments from China were used as a way to support corruption and the Najib regime. Additionally, local English and online Malaysian Chinese media outlets also showed a certain degree of anxiety about the enormity of Chinese investment in Malaysia. Some feared that investments from China would exacerbate anti-Chinese sentiments among the Malays. Although the general sentiment of Malaysian Chinese towards China's economic power is likely to be positive, the GE-14 election results indicate that the China factor failed to sway votes for MCA or BN. These elections show that Malaysian Chinese voters would vote rationally against China's interests when foreign interests conflict with their own local interests.

CAMPAIGN STRATEGIES AND MEANS OF MOBILIZATION

GE-14 contestants' modes of campaigning and capacity to mobilize support and volunteers capture striking differences between Chinese candidates of the PH and BN coalitions. The main mode for DAP's outreach to Chinese communities, which are predominantly urban, is to hold large outdoor political talks at different venues within the town centre. The DAP candidates interviewed strongly believed in the power and importance of these events. GE-14 underscores the imperative of politicians' face-to-face engagement with the electorate, which social media enhances but does not replace. In addition to luring fence-sitters, the political talks also serve as morale-boosting events for DAP supporters who would then urge their family and friends who live abroad to return to Malaysia to vote.

Since the 2008 elections, political talks in the urban centres organized by DAP have consistently drawn sizeable crowds of people from all walks of life, and droves of Chinese. The highlight of the talk typically features celebrity speakers such as Lim Guan Eng, Lim Kit Siang, Gobind Singh Deo and Nga Khor Ming rather than the candidates themselves. In between speeches, the organizer would play videos and songs professionally composed by the party. As DAP speakers are more sensitive to the cultural preferences of local communities, during the talks in the town of Bentong, Pahang, some speakers gave full speeches in Bahasa Melayu and Cantonese in addition to Mandarin. At another talk in Cheras, a district that hosts a large working-class Chinese population in the downtown section of Kuala Lumpur, virtually all of the speakers delivered their speeches in Cantonese. While in the SS2 neighbourhood of Petaling Jaya, Mandarin and English were the main languages used. This language strategy was also applied in other areas where particular Chinese dialects such as Hokkien, Hakka and Foochow are spoken.

During the campaign period, leaders of MCA and SUPP appeared at many social events that were held by local community organizations or sponsored by their party arms. At those events, political messages were usually subtle, emphasizing local development and political stability. Many of them were open only to invited guests, not to the public. However, these party arms of MCA and SUPP have either been weakened or broken over the past decades. Unlike UMNO, MCA has not been able to use government-linked companies or public agencies as alternatives that UMNO has used to its advantage. This weakening trend has cost BN Chinese-based parties greater voter mobilization. Moreover, the surge of Chinese support for opposition parties over the last ten years has placed traditional Chinese associations under pressure to drop their pro-establishment stance towards political parties. In some organizations, the pro-opposition forces have advanced their influence. For instance, a former DAP campaign manager won the 2018 presidential election of United Chinese Association Sibu, the most prominent Chinese organization in Sibu, Sarawak. The loss of BN as a ruling coalition may further weaken the BN connection with Chinese organizations characterized as a patron-client relationship.

Chinese-based BN parties are fighting against the tide whereas DAP is riding on nationwide change sentiments. The social capital that DAP has received from Malaysian Chinese society has kept the election machinery running vigorously. For instance, campaigns in town areas run by DAP are supported by large teams of diligent and efficient non-party member volunteers. At a talk in Yong Peng, a district town in Johor, we observed dozens of workers moving quickly to dry hundreds of wet chairs set up outdoors after heavy rain. Similarly, the polling and counting agents of DAP largely depended on volunteers.

Other than political talks, a personal touch and the media are the other two major methods used by political parties to reach their supporters and the general public. Door-to-door visits, walkabouts at markets, food courts, and other public areas are common methods employed by political parties. In the GE-14, social media applications especially Facebook and WhatsApp were used extensively. By staying at home or working from any other place with Internet access, people were able to watch the live Facebook feed of Mahathir's speech that played on the eve of polling day.[16] Compared to Facebook, WhatsApp, which requires a relatively smaller volume of data, enabled easier access for rural residents especially people in Johor and Sarawak. However, during the GE-14, the main challenge for BN Chinese-based parties was neither the intensity nor extensiveness of social media usage, but the content of messages that resonated with voters.

CONCLUSION

Malaysian Chinese society has passed through various phases of social transformation and political realignment. The post-World War II era was a highly eventful period for Malaysia. The new nation had: struggled for self-determination and independence from the British; combated the spread of communism; formed a unified and viable new government; and addressed socio-economic challenges, among other issues.

During this period Chinese society was more fragmented than it ever was, reflected in their voting patterns divided among ideologically based, regional and national parties. The next watershed event was the violent racial conflicts that took place in some parts of Peninsular Malaysia in 1969 that led to the sanction of leftist parties and the implementation of major economic and cultural policies that stressed entitlements to the advantage of ethnic Malays.

The Malay-based party, UMNO, leveraged the new ethnic politics to pursue dominance in government and extended its influence into Sabah and Sarawak by grooming the Muslim bumiputra ("sons of the soil") as the heads of both states. Since then, Chinese voters in Peninsular Malaysia have begun to rally behind a few national Chinese-based parties compared to the Chinese in Sabah and Sarawak who continued to favour their local-parties until a much later stage.

For many Chinese, the adversity of being marginalized was cushioned by the comforts of high economic growth in the 1980s and 1990s that gave birth to an urban Chinese middle class. In contrast to modernization theory, the new rich and the middle class remained relatively supportive of the BN government, which over time had become increasingly authoritarian, but also made some concessions that were well received, notably in expanding private higher education. However, the old middle class considered otherwise and was prepared to vote for the opposition as members of the middle class witnessed the rise of government corruption cases in the 1990s that would hurt the country in the long term.

When the ruling elite was split in the 1980s and 1990s, the breakaway force was not convincing enough to persuade a considerable, and multiethnic, mass of people to change the government. However, the large-scale non-religious movement led by former UMNO leader Anwar Ibrahim in the late 1990s, gave a boost to local civil society led by the urban middle class. As a result of the convergence of opposition forces that have evolved for more than a decade, the BN party lost its two-thirds majority in Parliament in the 2008 General Elections. Since 2008, urban Chinese voters have remained loyal to the opposition coalition that has been led by pro-reform and pro-democracy Malay leaders, and these urban voters also constitute a major social force advocating secular state system. Chinese support for the opposition implies that there are real needs in Chinese communities that have long been denied or deliberately neglected by the BN-led government. The ethnicization of state ideology and institutions, a relatively weakening economic position and cultural liberalization that took place over the last decades have maintained urban Chinese votes for the pro-secular opposition.

The politics of Sabah and Sarawak in East Malaysia have seldom progressed in parallel with national political developments. Their regional identities are constructed based on the uniqueness of both states in geography, colonial histories and demographic composition. Despite the differences, ethnic politics remains the underlying political structure that shapes the party system and electoral behaviour. Equally important is the patron-client relationship between local strongmen and their supporters that explains the survival of independent candidates in each election.

Among Malaysia's ethnic groups, the Chinese voted most emphatically for regime change. GE-14 was a culmination of social transformations since the late 1990s, and of electoral shifts manifested in the 2008 General Elections when Pakatan Rakyat breached BN's two-thirds majority and urban Peninsular Malaysia became federal opposition strongholds. That momentum persisted; Chinese support for regime change reached such a height in 2013, estimated at 85 per cent, that the sheer number prompted questions about whether the opposition's popularity could be sustained. Pakatan Harapan was initially not rapturously received, but due to splits in the Malay electorate, depended on exceedingly high Chinese support and voter turnout.

On 9 May 2018, Chinese voters spoke loud and clear; by Merdeka Center's estimate, 95 per cent of Chinese votes went to PH. DAP advanced further, becoming the second largest party in the federal ruling coalition by parliament seats. While it strives to diversify its line-up and leadership and shake the "Chinese party" label, it remains widely perceived as the main party representing interests and issues resonant in the Chinese community. BN's Chinese-based parties MCA and Gerakan on Peninsular Malaysia, and SUPP in Sarawak, already struggling for survival, were sent to the political wilderness. The regime change overwhelmingly desired by the Chinese electorate arrived. The question waiting to be answered, is how these sentiments and affinities will travel in the post-GE-14 era.

Notes

1. The major pro-left parties were the Labour Party, the United Democratic Party and the People's Progressive Party (PPP). These parties won a number of urban and Chinese-dominated seats at the parliamentary, state and local council level elections.

2. The two parties were the Democratic Party from Kota Kinabalu and the United Party from Sandakan. The Democratic Party was supported by Hokkien and Hakka small traders from Kota Kinabalu (formerly called Jesselton) while the United Party was led by English-educated Hakka and Teochew businessmen from Sandakan.

3. Local development, town planning and the maintenance of basic amenities came under the jurisdiction of state and local governments.

4. The Sarawak Chinese Association, a Chinese political party in the Sarawak Alliance, was dissolved after SUPP joined the alliance.

5. The MCA and Gerakan entered Sabah in the late 1990s and started off their first contest in the 2004 General Elections.

6. BN wrested back the Perak state government after three PR state assembly members announced their support for BN in the state assembly.

7. In an internal party fallout, the state assemblyman for Luyang left DAP for MCA, leaving DAP with three state seats.

8. For example, at a talk on "The Way Ahead for New Malaysia" (新马来西亚路在何方) held at KLSCAH on 21 May 2018 one of the speakers identified herself as a lesbian who spoke for the interests of the LGBT community.

9. Personal correspondence with an officer in DAP's national headquarters.

10. The seven organizations are Jiaozong (United Chinese School Teachers Association), Dongzong (United Chinese School Committee Association), ACCCIM (Associated Chinese Chambers of Commerce and Industry of Malaysia), Nantah (Nanyang University alumni), Liutai (Taiwan graduates alumni association) and the Federation of Seven Clan Associations. The Chairman of Dongzong said ACCCIM expressed his organization's agreement to most of the points raised in the memorandum but declined to officially endorse the memorandum.

11. The active members of GBM comprise ethnic and religious-based national organizations like Pertubuhan IKRAM Malaysia, Malaysian Consultative Council of Buddhism, Christianity, Hinduism, Sikhism and Taoism and the Tamil Foundation Malaysia. Together with the other twenty over civil society organizations including Aliran, All Women's Action Society and KOMAS, they aim to foster interethnic understanding and collaboration. Despite being formed less than ten years ago, GBM has been accepted by the civil society groups as an effective platform for the discussion of ethnic and religious issues.

12. "Chinese-language educated" typically refers to people who received their primary education in vernacular schools and have a strong command of Mandarin. However, after completing their primary education, nearly 85 per cent of Chinese students further their secondary education in national schools which use the Malay language as the medium of instruction.

13. Interviews at DAP political rallies: Yeoh Bee Yin in Yong Peng, and Liew Chin Tong in Teluk Intan.

14. Previously in the 2016 state elections, Sarawak BN claimed victories in all the rural Chinese-majority state seats while DAP retained all the urban seats (Ngu 2017).

15. In a telephone conversation with MP for Sibu Oscar Ling (22 May 2018), he expressed surprise at the increased votes of rural Chinese who previously voted for BN in the 2016 state elections.
16. It was reported that the live video of Mahathir's final campaign speech reached 3.3 million views on the eve of polling day.

References

Chen, Hongqian. 2013. "Wanshi jubei, zhiqian dongfeng: di shisan jie daxuan shaba zhengju pingxi" [An Analysis of Sabah Politics in GE13], in *Political Transition: Analysis of the Malaysia's GE13*, edited by Wu Yan Hua and Pang Yong Qiang. Kuala Lumpur: Centre for Malaysian Chinese Studies.

Chin, Emmanuel Santa Maria. 2018. "Invoke: As GE14 Nears, Rise in Undecided Voters". *Malay Mail*, 30 April 2018. https://www.malaymail.com/s/1625753/invoke-as-ge14-nears-rise-in-undecided-voters (accessed 2 July 2018).

Democratic Action Party. 2012. "Laporan Jawatankuasa Tertinggi Pusat Untuk Kongress 2012". https://dapmalaysia.org/arkib/arkib-konvensyen/laporan-jawatankuasa-tertinggi-pusat-untuk-kongress-2012/ (accessed 2 October 2018).

Department of Statistics Malaysia. 2015. "Salaries & Wages Survey Report 2014", 30 June 2015. https://www.dosm.gov.my/v1/index.php?r=column/ctheme&menu_id=U3VPMldoYUxzVzFaYmNkWXZteGduZz09&bul_id=R1pZQ0RqRjY0aFJjcUM4cS9zcUdTZz09# (accessed 2 July 2016).

Funston, John. 2000. "Malaysia's Tenth Elections: Status Quo, 'Reformasi' or Islamization?". *Contemporary Southeast Asia* 22, no. 1: 23–59.

Govindasamy, Anantha Raman, and Yew Meng Lai. 2014. "Kota Kinabalu, Sabah: BN Loses Its 'Fixed Deposit'". In *Electoral Dynamics in Malaysia: Findings from the Grassroots*, edited by Meredith L. Weiss. Petaling Jaya and Singapore: SIRD and Institute of Southeast Asian Studies.

Hazlin Hassan. 2018. "Most Malaysian Chinese Voted PH in polls". *Straits Times*, 14 June 2018. https://www.straitstimes.com/asia/se-asia/most-malaysian-chinese-voted-ph-in-polls-but-malays-in-3-way-split (accessed 30 July 2018).

Heng, Pek Koon. 1983. "The Social and Ideological Origins of the Malayan Chinese Association". *Journal of Southeast Asian Studies* 14, no. 2: 290–311.

Lee, Julian C.H., Chin Huat Wong, Melissa Wong, and Seng Guan Yeoh. 2010. "Elections, Repertoires of Contention and Habitus in Four Civil Society Engagements in Malaysia's 2008 General Elections". *Social Movement Studies* 9, no. 3: 293–309.

Lee, Kam Hing, and Pek Koon Heng. 2000. "The Chinese in the Malaysian Political System". In *The Chinese in Malaysia*, edited by Kam Hing Lee and Chee Beng Tan. Shah Alam: Oxford University Press.

Liow, Sze Xian. 2018. "A Million Members No Guarantee of Votes for MCA". *Malaysian Insight*, 10 February 2018. https://www.themalaysianinsight.com/s/37129/ (accessed 10 June 2018).

Loh, Francis Kok Wah. 2003. "Developmentalism versus Reformism: The Contest for Bukit Bendera, 1999". In *New Politics in Malaysia*, edited by Francis Kok Wah Loh and Johan Saravanamuttu. Singapore: Institute of Southeast Asian Studies.

Mauzy, Diane K. 1979. "A Vote for Continuity: The 1978 General Elections in Malaysia". *Asian Survey* 19, no. 3: 281–96.

————. 1983. *Barisan Nasional: Coalition Government in Malaysia*. Kuala Lumpur: Marican & Sons (Malaysia) Sdn Bhd.

Mohammad Agus Yusoff. 1999. "The Politics of Centre-State Conflict: The Sabah Experience Under the Ruling Sabah Alliance (1963–1976)". *Jebat*, pp. 1–25.

Nanyang Siang Pau. 2017. "Liew Chin Tong: The Chinese Support for PH May Drop to 65%". *e-nanyang*, 16 June 2017. http://www.enanyang.my/news/20170616/刘镇东希盟得票料骤跌至65br-华裔不再对变天抱/ (accessed 31 November 2018).

————. 2018. "Nanyang Editorial's Note". *e-nanyang*, 18 May 2018. http://www.enanyang.my/news/20180518/选边站的华团领袖南洋社论/ (accessed 22 May 2018).

Ng, Tien Eng. 2003. "The Contest for Chinese Votes: Politics of Negotiation or Politics of Pressure". In *New Politics in Malaysia*, edited by Francis Kok Wah Loh and Johan Saravanamuttu. Singapore: Institute of Southeast Asian Studies.

Ngu, Ik Tien. 2014. "Sibu and Lanang: Defeat of the Bosses". In *Electoral Dynamics in Malaysia: Findings from the Grassroots*, edited by Meredith L. Weiss. Petaling Jaya and Singapore: SIRD and Institute of Southeast Asian Studies.

————. 2017. "Repok and Meradong: Challenges in Courting Rural Votes". In *Electoral Dynamics in Sarawak: Contesting Developmentalism and Rights*, edited by Meredith L. Weiss and Arnold Puyok. Petaling Jaya and Singapore: SIRD and ISEAS – Yusof Ishak Institute.

Ong, Andrew, and Hariz Mohd. 2018. "PKR's Membership Spike Sparks Concern Ahead of Polls". *Malaysiakini*, 21 September 2018. https://www.malaysiakini.com/news/444006 (accessed 20 April 2019).

Ronasina. 2018. "#UndiRosak Musuh Baru Harapan". *Malaysiakini*, 22 January 2018. https://www.malaysiakini.com/news/409525 (accessed 18 April 2018).

Saw, Swee-Hock. 2007. *The Population of Malaysia*. Singapore: Institute of Southeast Asian Studies.

Star, The. 2018. "The Star Online GE14 News". https://election.thestar.com.my/johor.html (accessed 1 September 2018).

Strauch, Judith. 1978. "Tactical Success and Failure in Grassroots Politics: The MCA and DAP in Rural Malaysia". *Asian Survey* 18, no. 12: 1280–94.

Wang, Gungwu. 1970. "Chinese Politics in Malaya". *China Quarterly* 43: 1–30.

Welsh, Bridget. 2018. "The GE14 Aftermath: Hope and Healing". *Malaysiakini*, 14 May 2018. https://www.malaysiakini.com/columns/424701 (accessed 18 May 2018).

Yeoh, Cheong Ee. 2017. "Spoilt-Vote Campaign Threatens Core Pakatan Support". *Malaysian Insight*, 5 December 2017. https://www.themalaysianinsight.com/s/25995/ (accessed 20 May 2018).

————. 2018. "Despite Anger at Dr Mahathir, Chinese Vote Will Go to Pakatan". *Malaysian Insight*, 14 March 2018. https://www.themalaysianinsight.com/s/42824/ (accessed 22 April 2018).

11

INDIAN VOTERS IN GE-14
Finding a New Voice?

Anantha Raman Govindasamy

INTRODUCTION

Despite many predictions that Malaysian Indian voters would support Barisan Nasional (BN) in the 14th General Elections (GE-14), the election's outcome revealed that a large majority voted for the Pakatan Harapan (PH) coalition. This was unexpected for two reasons. First, in contrast to Malaysian Chinese voters, who were widely held to have swung towards the opposition in the 2008 General Elections, the Malaysian Indian vote was perceived to have remained solidly behind Barisan Nasional—albeit registering some protest in recent election cycles. Second, despite their long-standing socio-economic marginalization, the Najib Razak administration had spent significant resources on issues perceived as important for Malaysian Indians prior to GE-14.

Beyond BN being swept from power, the coalition's severe defeat in 2018 has called its race-based party structure into question. While BN's prime party, the United Malays National Organization (UMNO) lost a significant number of seats, its other Peninsula-based coalition partners were almost wiped from the electoral map. Like the Malaysian Chinese Association (MCA) and Gerakan, the Malaysian Indian Congress (MIC) performed poorly, losing the majority of its electoral contests with even senior party figures being resoundingly defeated.

The chapter will look at the changing political preferences of Malaysian Indian voters in recent years. In doing so, it will argue that GE-14 indicates a "permanent shift" in this community's voting patterns, from being a loyal supporter of MIC—and through it BN and its race-based formula of governance—to embracing multicultural politics under PH. The beginning of this "shift" in voting preference can be traced back to the 2008 General Elections. However, it deepened in the 2013 General Elections and was consolidated in GE-14.

In order to advance this argument, this chapter will draw on primary statistical and electoral data, secondary sources, as well as field work visits to three constituencies in April–May 2018. Following this introduction, the second section will set out the historical context of the Malaysian Indian community prior to GE-14. The third section will analyse GE-14 as it pertains to Malaysian Indians, through looking at: the number, background and deployment of Malaysian Indian candidates; and the strategies adopted by the two main coalitions to appeal to this voter group. The final section will focus on the outcome of GE-14 and its implications for the future.

THE INDIAN COMMUNITY IN MALAYSIA

The structural shift in the preferences of Malaysian Indian voters is deeply rooted and intertwined with Malaysia's modernization story. Despite their long-standing support for BN, there are three drivers behind a structural migration of Malaysian Indian voters away from the former ruling coalition. They are: the persistence of the socio-economic marginalization of Malaysian Indians; ineffective political representation of the community's interests within BN; and the rise of the Hindu Rights Action Force (HINDRAF). The next paragraphs will look at each of these in turn, before looking at their impact on voting patterns in 2008 and 2013.

Persistent Socio-Economic Marginalization

The socio-economic marginalization of Malaysian Indians is rooted in the colonization of Malaya, when labourers were brought from India to work on commercial rubber and tea plantations. These Indian labourers mainly settled in the isolated rural plantation areas of Perak, Selangor and Negeri Sembilan in the west coast of Peninsular Malaya (Sandhu 1969, pp. 188–89). In fact, in pre-independence Malaya, the British administration systematically controlled the socio-economic and political development of the Indian community. This, in turn, created a largely docile, dependent, and low-waged Indian community (Mahajani 1960, p. 115).

This marginalization was not addressed in Malaysia following independence, due to the overwhelming focus of economic policy on the Malay community. In particular, the New Economic Policy (NEP), implemented from 1971 aimed to eradicate poverty and "restructure society" to achieve parity between the Malay and non-Malay populations (Andaya and Andaya 2001). Later modifications of the policy such as the National Development Policy 1991–2000 (NDP) and National Vision Policy 2001–10 (NVP) retained a focus on addressing the socio-economic status of ethnic Malays (Gomez and Jomo 1999).

Under these frameworks, Malaysian Indians and especially those on rural plantations were largely left out. This marginalization was further exacerbated from the 1960s by the dissolution of plantation estates into commercial land or for the development of new townships for massive state-sponsored industrialization programmes. This pattern continued thereafter and an estimated 300,000 Indians working and living on plantation estates were displaced from 1980 to 2000 (ASLI 2006).

As a result of this process, workers had to leave estates where they had lived for many generations without any alternative housing or meaningful retirement benefits. These displaced Indians migrated to urban areas, with many living in squatter settlements in outlying areas. Some, however, were able to secure employment in nearby industrial zones (Nagarajan 2004, p. 36).

As part of this displacement process, the Malaysian Indian community changed from one that was primarily rural-based to one that was largely urban-based (Table 11.1). Besides creating a large pool of urban poor, this displacement also generated other socio-economic issues: in particular, how and who should be responsible for the resettlement of plantation Indians; what would happen to the temples on the plantations; and who would assume responsibility for building Tamil-language schools in the areas that Malaysian Indians settled.

From 2000, the socio-economic condition of the majority of Indians in urban areas can be summarized as follows: largely based in informal settlements; suffering from a disproportionately high unemployment rate; and experiencing a range of socio-economic challenges, ranging from high school dropout rates to a disproportionately high rate of incarceration. Due to the focus on issues facing the bumiputra community, successive BN administrations have largely failed to address these concerns (Nagarajan 2004, p. 36).

Ineffective Political Representation

In addition to their socio-economic marginalization, Malaysian Indians have not had effective political representation. In part, this stems from their position as the smallest of the three principal ethnic groups in West Malaysia (Table 11.1). Furthermore, the

TABLE 11.1
Malaysian Indians: Key Statistics

Year	Urban Areas (%)	Rural Areas (%)	Total (number)	Proportion of Total Population (%)
1970	34.7	65.3	943,400	9.0
1980	41.0	59.0	1,098,400	8.4
1991	63.8	36.2	1,316,100	7.8
2000	—	—	1,680,100	7.7
2010	79.7	20.3	1,907,800	7.3
2018	—	—	2,100,000	6.2

Source: Department of Statistics, various issues; Saw (2015).

population is dispersed, negating the formation of influential voting blocs in specific parts of the country. Thus, in 2004, Indians did not form a majority in any of Malaysia's 219 parliamentary or 567 state constituencies. Their highest concentration was in the Kota Raja parliamentary constituency where they formed 27.6 per cent of voters. Indians formed between 20 and 24 per cent of voters in a further nine constituencies and 10–20 per cent of voters in fifty-two parliamentary constituencies (Nagarajan 2004). Indeed, in more than half of the country's constituencies, Malaysian Indians constitute less than 5 per cent of voters.

This numerical disadvantage has been compounded by the mechanism through which the Malaysian Indian community has traditionally been represented. MIC, founded in 1946, has been the main political vehicle of the country's Indian community since independence. The backbone of the party's support has traditionally come from poor rural Indians (Muzaffar 1993, p. 220).

In turn, MIC opted to join the Alliance in 1954, otherwise consisting of UMNO and MCA. Under this consociational framework, each member represented its own community's interests and political issues were resolved at the elite level. This model enabled a maximum number of candidates to be pooled and mobilized, and usually enabled the ethnicity of a given candidate to be matched to the predominant demographic in each community. Members of other ethnic groups were persuaded to vote across ethnic lines for members of the Alliance, as they knew that their interests were represented within the coalition as a whole (Lijphart 1977).

However, within this framework MIC has been disadvantaged due to its smaller voter base, as well as tactical decisions made by its leadership. Thus, issues like economic opportunities, language, and civil service employment were contested and settled between UMNO and MCA during the Alliance's early years, but MIC mostly avoided open conflict. The leadership of MIC felt that it would be safer to avoid any direct confrontation with UMNO, and, at the same time, assumed that whatever the MCA won on behalf of the Chinese would also apply to the Indians.

For this reason, V.T. Sambanthan—the MIC president in the 1960s—was accused of not having effectively bargained on behalf of Indians as the MCA had for the Chinese community (Muzaffar 1993, p. 238). In addition, the "May 13 Incident" and the introduction of the New Economic Policy in 1971, changed the dynamics of interethnic bargaining at the cost of the Alliance's smaller members, MCA and MIC (Ampalavanar 1993, p. 338).

MIC also faced considerable internal issues, as it was riven by factionalism, often along caste lines. These splits resulted in periodic leadership crises which, in turn, allowed UMNO undue influence within the party (Ampalavanar 1993, p. 337). For instance, in 1972, the then MIC president V.T. Sambanthan was challenged by his deputy, Manikavasagam. Concerned that any major split in MIC would weaken the newly formed BN, UMNO formulated a peace deal between the two leaders. Prime Minister and UMNO president Tun Razak intervened and proposed that Sambanthan would lead the party until 1973, after which he would step down for Manikavasagam to be the president. Thus, in 1973 Sambanthan resigned as the MIC president and was appointed as the Minister of Labour in Razak's Cabinet (Ampalavanar 1993,

p. 243). The same pattern emerged again in 1997, when MIC president Samy Vellu was challenged by his deputy, Subramaniam. Although Subramaniam lost, with the intervention of then Prime Minister Mahathir, he continued as the deputy president of the party (Milne and Mauzy 1999).

Caste was also frequently used by the MIC leadership to mobilize members during elections and to secure important positions within the party. The formation of the Indian Progressive Front (IPF) in 1987, by former MIC vice-president M.G. Pandithan, was an indication of this trend, as he explicitly mobilized his voters along caste lines (Baradan 2000).

Yet, despite the emergence of new political vehicles to articulate issues for the Indian community, UMNO only engaged with MIC. Thus, persistent requests by the All Indian Progressive Front Party to be part of BN were always turned down by UMNO in order to protect MIC's interests (*Malaysiakini*, 25 April 2007).

This benefited UMNO as it preserved the viability of MIC and maintained the party as the sole legitimate representative of Malaysian Indians. At the same time, MIC leaders demonstrated maximum loyalty and ensured crucial support for the UMNO-dominated BN (Ramasamy 2004, pp. 151–52). In turn, MIC leaders were aware that, without UMNO's support, they would not be recognized as leaders of the Indian community and their Cabinet positions would be in doubt (Nagarajan 2004).

The Rise of the Hindu Rights Action Force (HINDRAF)

HINDRAF was formed in January 2006 as a platform to raise various problems faced by Malaysian Indians, and in particular the urban working class. The creation of the organization is rooted in several trends that affected the Malaysian Indian community from 2000 onwards. This included: the rise in deaths of Malaysian Indians in police custody; Islamization policies; and the demolition of Hindu temples (Case 2010, p. 137). Of these, the last was the most important in galvanizing the Indian community.

From 2000, there was a systematic effort by local governments in states such as Selangor, Negeri Sembilan and Perak, to demolish Hindu temples without proper negotiations or a plan for relocation. The basis for the temple demolition, as cited by the various local authorities, was that these temples were illegal structures and either built without the requisite permits or located on private property (Zurairi AR 2013). In many cases, however, these temples had been built within plantation estates, which were then sold to third parties. Citing the desires of new owners to convert the land for other purposes, the demolition of the temples was often conducted at night with the support from the local police and, in some cases, "thugs" hired by the landlord to clear the premises.

Given its subordinate position within the BN coalition, MIC was unable to find an effective solution to this issue. From 2006, HINDRAF started to organize small-scale seminars and talks in cities like Kuala Lumpur, Seremban and Penang to highlight the socio-economic marginalization of Malaysian Indians. Initially, HINDRAF was perceived as another ineffectual organization. However, persistent action against the temple demolition managed to galvanize the support of working-class Indians. Moreover, HINDRAF's constant attacks on MIC's leadership resonated with middle-class Indians, as well as political parties such as the Democratic Action Party (DAP) and Parti Keadilan Rakyat (PKR) (Reuters, 25 November 2007).

In November 2007, HINDRAF organized a rally against the BN government in Kuala Lumpur, demanding that attention and resources be allocated to the community's key issues. Nearly 30,000 Indians took part in this demonstration. The response taken by the authorities was seen as disproportionate by many, with tear gas being used on demonstrators and many detentions. Of note, HINDRAF's leaders were held under the infamous Internal Security Act (ISA) (*The Star*, 11 May 2009). Later, the Malaysian government declared that HINDRAF had close contact with radical movements such as the Liberation of Tamil Tigers of Eelam (LTTE).

Changing Political Preferences

The perceived inattention to issues facing the Malaysian Indian community as well as the response to the HINDRAF rally affected support levels for BN. In the run-up to the 2008 Malaysian General Elections, HINDRAF leaders and many Malaysian Indian-based organizations were openly calling for Malaysian Indians to vote for opposition parties such as PKR, DAP, and Parti Islam Se-Malaysia (PAS).

When the results were announced, MIC suffered a painful defeat, as it won only three out of the nine parliamentary seats and seven out of the nineteen state seats it contested. Samy Vellu, then minister and MIC president, was defeated in his Sungai Siput parliamentary seat by an unknown personality from PKR (*MySinchew*, 12 March 2008). At a broader level, only 48 per cent of Malaysian Indians voted for BN in 2008 (Case 2010, p. 142). More importantly, HINDRAF scored a moral victory when one of its leaders detained under the ISA won the Kota Alam Shah state assembly seat in Selangor.

Coupled with the shift in Chinese Malaysian political preferences in 2008, the opposition coalition Pakatan Rakyat (PR) managed to deny BN's two-thirds majority in Parliament. The result also forced Abdullah Badawi to step down and paved the way for his deputy Najib Razak to take over as the prime minister of Malaysia (Case 2010, p. 146).

At the beginning of Najib Razak's tenure, there was an attempt to court the Malaysian Indian vote. He immediately released the HINDRAF leaders detained under ISA. Later, Najib Razak managed to convince Makkal Sakthi, a faction within HINDRAF, to join the ruling BN coalition. He also appointed HINDRAF's chairperson, Wathaymoorty, as a Deputy Minister in the Prime Minister's Department. Najib complemented this by establishing a unit in the Prime Minister's Department to study approaches to tackling socio-economic issues affecting the Malaysian Indian community (Ufen 2013, p. 5).

However, accommodating HINDRAF leaders as part of BN was not well-received by right-wing Malay groups like Pertubuhan Pribumi Perkasa Malaysia (Perkasa, or Malaysian Indigenous Empowerment Organization), who argued that the focus should remain on the bumiputras, who had been the coalition's main electoral backers in 2008 (Ufen 2013, p. 6). In the run-up to the 2013 Malaysian General Elections, BN made a last-minute electoral pact with HINDRAF to recognize its influence within the Malaysian Indian community by offering a deputy ministerial post. However, at this point, HINDRAF had disintegrated into more than a dozen factions and its capability to mobilize support was doubtful.

The 13th Malaysian General Elections was conducted on 5 May 2013. When the result was announced, Prime Minister Najib Razak survived a second term in office with a reduced number of parliamentary seats for BN. The incumbent coalition obtained 133 parliamentary seats, while the opposition PR won 89 seats—an increase of seven parliamentary seats from the previous election.

For its part, MIC had been allocated nine parliamentary seats, and only managed to win four, of which all were in Malay-majority constituencies. These four seats were all highly strategic, as they were held by: the MIC party president, Palanivel; his deputy, Subramaniam; the MIC vice-president, Sarawanan; and the MIC youth coordinator, Sivaraj (Table 11.2). The overall support level of Malaysian Indians for BN in 2013 was 45 per cent, a further decline from the 2008 election (Ufen 2013, p. 12).

GE-14: THE CANDIDATES, CAMPAIGN AND ISSUES

This section examines the Malaysian Indian candidates running in GE-14 and the campaigns waged by BN, PH and PAS to attract votes from this group. It then focuses on the election campaign strategies and the issues highlighted by the political parties.

Malaysian Indian Candidates in GE-14

Malaysian Indian voters are largely concentrated in constituencies along the centre and western coasts of Peninsular Malaysia. Beginning in Johor Bahru in the south, they are clustered in seats in Johor, Melaka, Negri Sembilan, Selangor, Perak, western Pahang, Penang, and southern Kedah. In contrast, they are almost entirely absent from the Peninsula's east coast as well as East Malaysia, with no constituency in Kelantan, Terengganu, Sabah and Sarawak having more than 5 per cent of Indian Malaysian voters (Figure 11.1).

TABLE 11.2
Parliamentary Seats Contested and Won by MIC in the
Malaysian General Elections: 2004, 2008 and 2013

Year	2004	2008	2013
Seats Contested	9	9	9
Seats Won	9	3	4

Source: SPR, Warta Pilihan Raya Persekutuan, 2004, 2008 and 2013.

FIGURE 11.1
Proportion of Indian Voters by Constituency in Peninsular Malaysia, 2018

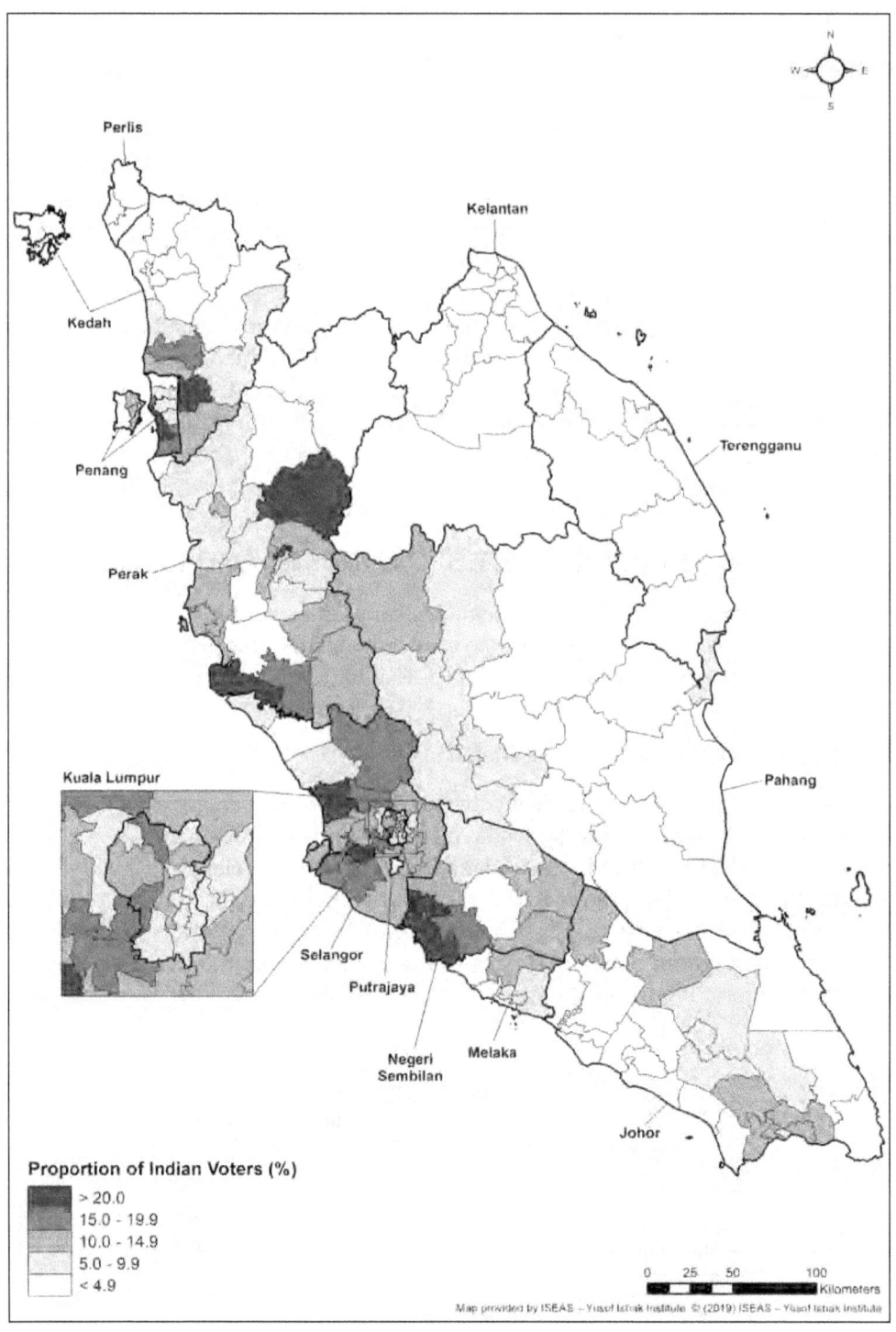

The political impact of their relatively small population is further compounded by their concentration in large, urban and semi-urban constituencies. Of the fifty-eight constituencies where Malaysian Indians constitute at least 10 per cent of the voting population, forty-six are urban or semi-urban constituencies (Table 11.3). These parliamentary seats are affected by the rural bias of the country's electoral process, which rewards rural, Malay-majority, and relatively underpopulated constituencies and penalizes larger, more concentrated and urban seats (Ostwald 2017, p. 10).

However, in an indication of the potentially close electoral outcome, BN and PH invested time and effort in courting the Malaysian Indian vote in GE-14. When the nomination period for candidates ended on 28 April 2018, the number of Indian candidates contesting for the various parties was one of the highest in recent history. At the parliamentary level, thirty-six Indian candidates including three women contested; and a further thirty-six ran for state assembly seats.

For BN, the large number of Malaysian Indian candidates was something of a surprise. In the run-up to the elections, UMNO was rumoured to be eyeing some traditional MIC seats such as Hulu Langat and Cameron Highlands. However, when the final list was announced, MIC was offered the same number of parliamentary and state assembly seats as in GE-13. These seats were located in the following states: Perak (3); Selangor (3); and one each in Johor, Negri Sembilan, and Pahang. At the state assembly level, MIC candidates were apportioned as follows: Johor (4); Selangor (3); Perak (3); Kedah (2); Negri Sembilan (2); Penang (2); Melaka (1); and Pahang (1). Other BN component parties such as Gerakan and People's Progressive Party (MyPPP) nominated three Indian candidates to contest in GE-14 in two seats in Penang and one in the Kuala Lumpur federal territory (Jayasooria 2018).

This final arrangement was not without some internal friction. The MIC retained Cameron Highlands, which had been won by the former MIC president, Palanivel, in 2013. However, MyPPP, one of the smallest component parties in BN, headed by M. Kayveas, wanted the seat to be offered to his party. Indeed, Kayveas threatened to contest against the BN-MIC candidate in the seat and was subsequently sacked by his party leadership for going against the "BN spirit" (*Free Malaysia Today*, 15 January 2019).

TABLE 11.3
Parliamentary Seats by Their Proportion of Malaysian Indian Voters

Proportion of Indian Voters per Constituency	Number of Constituencies and Proportion of Total Number of Constituencies	Number of Urban and Semi-Urban Constituencies	Number of Rural Constituencies
20%<	9 (4%)	7	2
15–19.9%	13 (5.9%)	12	1
10–14.9%	36 (16.2%)	27	9
5–9.9%	38 (17.1%)	22	16
<5%	126 (56.7%)		

Source: Data supplied by Tindak Malaysia, urban/rural classification, Politweet (2013).

Younger people and professionals were less prevalent on MIC's slate of candidates, and most of those mobilized were senior leaders and established party supporters. Indeed, a disproportionate number came from a faction linked to the former MIC president Subramaniam.[1] The most visible of these were Sarawanan and Dewamany, running in in the Tapah and Sungai Siput constituencies in Perak. Sarawanan, who was also the Deputy Minister of Youth and Sports, had been accused by *Tamil Malar*—a leading Tamil newspaper—for his involvement in intimidating a journalist for exposing various corruption scandals against him (*The Sun Daily*, 5 September 2018).

On PH's side, thirteen Indian candidates were nominated to contest at the parliamentary level. Eight of them from DAP, namely: Kasthurrani Patto, Saniswara Nethaji, Ramkarpal Singh, M. Kulasegaran, Sivakumar, Manoharan, Gobind Singh Deo and Charles Santiago. They were fielded in constituencies in Perak, Penang, Pahang, and Selangor. Another five Indian candidates were from PKR, namely: Kesavan, Sivarasah Rasiah, Xavier Jayakumar, Danyal Balagopal Abdullah and Sandhara Kumar. With the exception of one constituency in Perak, the remaining seats were in the southern part of the Peninsula, namely, Selangor, Kuala Lumpur Federal Territory, Negri Sembilan and Johor. Of the thirteen, seven were incumbents and the remainder were running for the first time, entailing a mix of experienced and new candidates. A significant proportion were professionals such as lawyers, academics and retired high-ranking military officers (Jayasooria 2018).

PAS nominated three Indian candidates to contest in GE-14. Kumutha Rahman was nominated for the Johor Jaya state assembly seat in Johor; and Jay Balakrishna and Yougen Mahalingam were nominated for parliamentary constituencies of Batu Kawan and Kampar, respectively (Jayasooria 2018). Although PAS' non-Muslim supporters' club welcomed this move, many argued that this would only split votes in non–Malay-majority areas and not constitute a meaningful challenge to BN or PH (Ho 2018).

The remaining candidates came from smaller political parties such as Parti Sosialis Malaysia which had put forward three candidates, namely, Jayakumar, Kunasekaran and Suresh Kumar to contest in the Sungai Siput, Batu Gajah and Cameron Highlands constituencies respectively. Meanwhile, Puvanandaran and Prabakaran contested as independent candidates in the Klang and Batu parliamentary constituencies (Jayasooria 2018).

The Campaign and Issues

Polling done in the run-up to the election indicated that Malaysian Indians were concerned first and foremost about economic opportunities (43 per cent), followed by corruption (13 per cent) and the country's leadership (7 per cent) (Merdeka Center 2018). Consequently, the manifestos of the various coalitions placed economic and cost of living at the forefront. These were complemented with specific initiatives to tackle long-standing and high-profile issues facing the Malaysian Indian community.

For BN, however, efforts to woo Malaysian Indian voters started before the official campaign period with the announcement of two significant programmes under the Prime Minister's Department: the Malaysian Indian Blueprint (MIB); and the Socioeconomic Development of the Indian Community Unit (SEDIC).

The MIB, announced by Najib Razak in April 2017, was a comprehensive policy document outlining proposed measures for the community. The Blueprint's framework touched on key issues, such as: education; improvement of livelihoods; and provision for better social inclusion. The specific MIB targets included: increasing the proportion of Indians in the civil service to 7 per cent by 2016; lifting the intake of Indian students in public universities by 7 per cent; and a special clearance system to grant citizenship to Indians who were born or had resided in Malaya before 1957. A sum of RM500,000 was allocated under the state-owned investment fund Permodalan Nasional Berhad to distribute shares in publicly listed companies to Indians in the Bottom 40 per cent (B40) income category (*The Star*, 23 April 2017). At the launching of this initiative, Najib stated that the MIB was not "Vetti Pichhu" (political rhetoric) or "Syok Sendiri" (self-gratification) but a genuine policy framework to uplift poor Indians in Malaysia (*The Star*, 23 April 2017).

SEDIC was the enforcement body created to supervise and coordinate the implementation of MIB. The organization received an annual allocation from the government and channelled it to various Indian-based NGOs and training centres to enhance the livelihood of B40 Malaysian Indians. In 2016, RM60 million was allocated to SEDIC and later distributed to various participating entities to target disadvantaged groups such as single mothers, school dropouts, unemployed Indian graduates and youths at risk (*Malaysian Times*, 29 March 2016).

These two programmes were an integral part of the MIC-BN's GE-14 manifesto for the Indian community. MIC launched its four-part election manifesto on 18 April 2018, promising a better future for Indians under BN. This broadly focused on four key areas, namely: to fulfil the basic needs of the Malaysian Indian community; to help realize the potential of children in terms of education; to increase social participation in terms of religious and cultural activities; and finally, to lift the community's average income and wealth (*The Star*, 18 April 2018).

During the campaign period, MIC president S. Subramaniam pointed out that these objectives could only materialize if Malaysian Indians fully supported the efforts of Prime Minister Najib, urging them to retain BN as the ruling party. Subramaniam also promised that MIC candidates would work hard towards achieving the promises set out in the MIC manifesto (*The Star*, 18 April 2018).

In contrast to BN and MIC's channelling of funds to specific organizations, PH's GE-14 manifesto, entitled *Buku Harapan*, proposed that the socio-economic challenges facing Malaysian Indians should be seen as a national issue and handled by the government rather than delegating responsibility to intermediaries (Pakatan Harapan 2018). The manifesto proposed: a sum of RM100 million to be allocated immediately to deal with various problems faced by Malaysian Indians; and additional RM4 billion to be allocated for the next ten years; all partially funded Tamil schools would be upgraded to fully government-funded schools; and additional secondary Tamil schools will be built.

Most importantly, these initiatives outlined by PH would be overseen by the prime minister himself rather than assigning them to specific Indian leaders (Pakatan Harapan 2018, pp. 131–36). Mahathir Mohamad, PH's candidate for prime minister, admitted that during his first tenure, he trusted "middlemen" to tackle problems facing Malaysian Indians, which failed miserably (*Free Malaysia Today*, 5 April 2019). This statement was used to deflect references to initiatives such as Maika Holdings. This corporation, aimed at helping low-income Malaysian Indians and helmed by MIC, was established in the 1980s during Mahathir's previous leadership. It failed due to mismanagement and asset-stripping (Adam Aziz 2018).

The main attraction for Malaysian Indians in the PH manifesto, particularly the working class, was the document's clear approach to dealing with stateless Indians and Hindu temples. The manifesto pledged that stateless Indians resident in Malaysia would have their paperwork resolved within 100 days of PH winning Putrajaya. For Hindu temples, the PH manifesto promised that any temple land dispute would be handled with respect and proper negotiations with all parties involved. In cases of demolition, PH would be committed to providing suitable replaceable land (Pakatan Harapan 2018, pp. 131–36).

On the other hand, PAS' manifesto called "Malaysia Sejahtera" had outlined twenty key points focusing on reducing cost of living and increasing personal income for all Malaysians. The manifesto also promises that if PAS manages to capture Putrajaya, strengthening Islamic values will be the key focus. Like PH, PAS' manifesto also pledged to abolish GST when in power. PAS' manifesto, however, failed to outline any specific programmes geared to Malaysian Indians (*Malaysiakini*, 19 March 2018).

As regards campaign methods, there was a noticeable difference between BN-MIC and PH candidates. MIC candidates waged conservative campaigns, relying on banners and expensive billboards to display pictures of candidates often posing next to Najib Razak.[2] In some working-class areas, it was also reported that MIC supplied free grocery items such as rice packets to woo voters. The mainstream media also gave ample airtime to BN candidates. For example, there were frequent advertisements on the public broadcaster, RTM, as well as Astro's Tamil channels. These featured local celebrities promoting the SEDIC and BN-led initiatives and also urging Indian voters not to be "fooled".[3]

For PH's Indian candidates, fewer posters and banners were used and, instead, campaigning consisted of mobilizing Malaysian Indian voters to attend large events along with the Chinese and Malay communities.[4] This was a common scene in GE-14—large campaign rallies were organized from Penang to Johor with PH heavyweights like Mahathir, Lim Kit Siang and Wan Azizah as the main attraction. In fact, in every PH Indian-contested parliamentary and state constituency, the national leaders of Bersatu, PKR, DAP and Amanah visited during the campaign period. Besides this, to attract young voters, Facebook and WhatsApp were used to circulate campaign information such as PH's election manifesto.

THE RESULTS: OPTING FOR A NEW VOICE?

Despite dips in 2008 and 2013, the widely held assumption at the outset of the 2018 campaign period was that the Malaysian Indian vote could be lured back to BN. Indeed, BN anticipated a boost in support from its economic initiatives and the MIB, targeting 70 per cent of the Indian vote (Gomez and Alagappar 2018). Others held that MIC could win as many as seven parliamentary seats (*New Straits Times*, 1 May 2017).

However, polls carried out during the campaign indicated a broad swing towards PH. And, this swing seems to have accentuated in the final days of the electoral period. Polls seemed to indicate an important change in direction during the campaign. Asked about their voting intentions, 56.5 per cent of those surveyed on 8 May 2018 indicated they would vote for PH, as opposed to 50.8 per cent one week earlier. Conversely, support for BN declined from 49 per cent to 41.3 per cent. As regards PAS, a mere 2.3 per cent stated they would vote for the Islamic party, although this was up from under 1 per cent a week earlier (Merdeka Center 2018).

In the end, an estimated 70–75 per cent of Malaysian Indians voted for PH (*Free Malaysia Today*, 14 June 2018). This was part of broad-based support in urban, west coast constituencies for PH. The result for MIC specifically was a disaster. Out of the nine constituencies where it ran, the party's candidates only managed to win two parliamentary seats. With the exception of Sarawanan and C. Sivaraj, the MIC youth chief, all other candidates lost.[5] Thus, S. Subramaniam, MIC party president and Minister of Health, lost his seat of Segamat, which he had held for fourteen years to Santhara Kumar, a younger and relatively unknown PKR member. Other significant casualties included: Mohana Muniandy, MIC Wanita chief; Prakash Rao, former MIC secretary general; and SK Devamany, MIC deputy president.

In contrast, twelve out of PH's thirteen Malaysian Indian candidates won their electoral contests (Table 11.4). Candidates from both DAP and PKR won their parliamentary seats with impressive majorities. For instance, Kulasegaran, one of DAP's prominent leaders, won the Ipoh Barat seat in Perak—a Chinese-majority constituency—with a massive majority of more than 45,000 votes. Another DAP Indian candidate, Gobind Singh Deo, won the Puchong parliamentary constituency in Selangor—another Chinese-majority seat with a majority of more than 47,000 votes. The same pattern was also visible among PKR candidates. Sivarasa won the Sungai Buloh seat—a Malay-majority constituency by more than 26,000 votes.

CONCLUSION

The GE-14 results confirm that that the structural shift in voter preferences among Malaysian Indians away from MIC and, through it, BN has continued. By and large, Malaysian Indians have decided to move away from race-based political parties, and have sought to choose a different means of political representation than in the past.

TABLE 11.4
Malaysian Indian Candidates Who Won Parliamentary Seats in GE-14

Parliamentary Seat	Winning Candidate and Party	Opposing Candidate and Party
Batu Kawan, Penang	Kasthuri Patto (PH-DAP)	Jayanthi Balaguru (BN-Gerakan)
Jelutong, Penang	Saniswara N. Rayer (PH-DAP)	Baljit Singh (BN- Gerakan)
Bukit Gelugor, Penang	Ramkarpal Singh (PH-DAP)	Low Joo Hiap (BN-MCA)
Sungai Siput, Perak	S. Kesavan (PH-PKR)	SK Devamany (BN-MIC)/
		M Jeyakumar (PSM)
Ipoh Barat, Perak	M. Kulasegaran (PH-DAP)	Cheng Wei Yee (BN-Gerakan)
Batu Gajah, Perak	VN Sivakumar (PH-DAP)	K Kunasekaran (PSM)
Tapah, Perak	M. Sarawanan (BN-MIC)	Mohamed Azni (BN-PKR)
Cameron Highlands, Pahang	C. Sivaraj[a] (BN-MIC)	M. Manogran (PH-DAP)/
		Suresh Kumar (PSM)
Puchong, Selangor	Gobind Singh Deo (PH-DAP)	Ang Chin Tat (BN-Gerakan)
Sungai Buloh, Selangor	Sivarasa Rasiah (PH-PKR)	Prakash Rao (BN-MIC)
Klang, Selangor	Charles Santiago (PH-DAP)	Ching Eu Boon (BN-MCA)
		G. Puvananderan (Ind)
Kuala Langat, Selangor	Xavier Jayakumar (PH-PKR)	Shahril Suffian Hamdan (BN-UMNO)
Batu, Kuala Lumpur Federal Territory	P. Prabakaran[b] (PH-PKR)	Dominic Lau (BN-Gerakan)
Port Dickson, Negri Sembilan	Danyal Balagopal Abdullah[c] (PH-PKR)	V. Mogan (BN-MIC)
Segamat, Johor	Santhara Kumar (PH-PKR)	S. Subramaniam (BN-MIC)

Notes: a. Election subsequently voided.
b. Initially ran as an independent, but subsequently joined PH.
c. Resigned in October 2018 to make way for Anwar Ibrahim.
Source: https://election.thestar.com.my

Despite long-standing grievances regarding the socio-economic marginalization of Malaysian Indians, temple demolitions, and ineffective political representation, BN thought that it could win this community's electoral support with generalized policies dealing with cost of living issues, coupled with targeted initiatives such as the Malaysian Indian Blueprint and SEDIC. Key to this strategy was the mobilization of MIC as part of the incumbent coalition, as well as a substantial number of Malaysian Indian candidates.

This strategy did not work, as nearly three-quarters of Malaysian Indians voted against BN. In urban constituencies where they constitute a substantial voter bank, the swing to PH helped the former opposition coalition win a substantial number of seats. In addition, Malaysian Indian candidates in PKR and DAP did very well in these constituencies.

Conversely, MIC was, by and large, vanquished, retaining only two out of nine constituencies. This result has made them largely insignificant for BN and constitutes a rejection of the traditional consociational model of campaigning used by the former ruling coalition. Should MIC be deprived of the campaign funding and support that it used to enjoy as part of the former ruling coalition, its viability is in doubt.

Furthermore, BN and MIC failed to realize that Indians, since 2008, have not only accepted "the new politics" that had been forwarded by the opposition, but have also moved further to embrace the notion of multicultural politics. This was demonstrated by Indian voters in GE-14 rejecting MIC and instead voting for multicultural parties to represent them.

Looking back at the 2008 Malaysian General Elections, Indian voters, especially working-class Indians, were "practically forced" to vote for parties like DAP and PKR to highlight this community's anger regarding inaction on key issues such as economic well-being and temple demolition. In the 2013 Malaysian General Elections, the voting pattern towards Pakatan candidates was largely sustained, and GE-14 further deepened this trend.

Many of the drivers of the structural shift are social. From its initial position, largely confined to rural plantations, the Malaysian Indian community has now become largely urban. Consequently, its interests are now more effectively articulated and channelled through broader-based and more participatory means. In addition, while it has always been the smallest of the three main ethnic groups, the Malaysian Indian community is shrinking. It is projected that in twenty years, the Malaysian Indian population will drop to 5 per cent. Consequently, Indian voters realize that their future foothold in Malaysian politics will depend on how they can work with other communities in Malaysia. The outcome of GE-14 clearly indicates that Malaysian Indians have shifted their loyalty from race-based parties like MIC and have embraced a multicultural political representation. Political parties in PH such as DAP and PKR have become the new-found political voice to represent the community in Malaysian politics.

Notes

1. These party leaders had supported Subramanian when MIC went through a leadership crisis in 2015. That year, Palanivel lost his membership in the party. Without the approval of the MIC's Central Working Committee, Palanivel had taken the Registrar of Societies (ROS) to court for not ruling against irregularities in MIC. The ROS subsequently appointed S. Subramaniam as the interim president.
2. Fieldwork observation, Cameron Highlands parliamentary constituency, 2 May 2018.
3. Just before GE-14, the Malaysian National Broadcasting channel RTM and paid Tamil channels in Astro Broadcasting Cooperation carried out frequent advertisements to display BN's continuous efforts at uplifting the socio-economic position of Malaysian Indians.
4. Fieldwork observation, Sungai Siput Parliamentary Constituency, 5 May 2018.
5. Sivaraj's victory was nullified in November 2018 and a by-election was held in January 2019. BN directly fielded a candidate, Ramli Mohd Nor, and won the seat.

References

Abdul Rashid Moten. 2009. "2004 and 2008 General Elections in Malaysia: Towards a Multicultural, Bi-party Political System?". *Asian Journal of Political Science* 17, no. 2: 173–94.

Adam Aziz. 2018. "MPs Call for Inquiry into Maika Scandal". *The Edge Markets*, 13 March 2018. https://www.theedgemarkets.com/article/mps-call-inquiry-maika-scandal (accessed 7 January 2019).

Ampalavanar, Rajeswary. 1993. "The Contemporary Indian Political Elite in Malaysia". in *Indian Communities in Southeast Asia*, edited by K.S. Sandhu and A. Mani, pp. 237–65. Singapore: Institute of Southeast Asian Studies, 1993.

Andaya, Barbara W. and Leonard Y. Andaya. 2001. *A History of Malaysia*. Honolulu: University of Hawaii Press.

Baradan, K. 2000. "Still No Entry for Pandithan". *The Sun*, 27 July 2000.

Case, William. 2010. "Malaysia's 2008 General Election-Transition from Single-party Dominance?". *Journal of Current Southeast Asian Affairs* 29, no. 2: 121–56.

Crouch, Harold. 1996. *Government and Society in Malaysia*. Ithaca: Cornell University Press.

Department of Statistics, Malaysia. 2016. "Current Population Estimates, Malaysia, 2014–2016".

Free Malaysia Today. 2018a. "Eliminate MIC, Mahathir tells Indians". 5 April 2018. https://www.freemalaysiatoday.com/category/nation/2018/04/05/eliminate-mic-mahathir-tells-indians/ (accessed 5 September 2018).

———. 2018b. "Report: 95% Chinese but Less Than 30% Voted for PH". 14 June 2018. https://www.freemalaysiatoday.com/category/nation/2018/06/14/report-95-chinese-but-less-than-30-malays-voted-for-ph/ (accessed on 7 January 2019).

———. 2019. "BN Bullied MyPPP, Used It, Says Kayveas". 15 January 2019. https://www.freemalaysiatoday.com/category/nation/2019/01/15/bn-bullied-myppp-used-it-says-kayveas/ (accessed 2 January 2019).

Gomez, E.T., and K.S. Jomo. 1999. *Malaysia's Political Economy: Patronage and Profits,* Cambridge: Cambridge University Press.

———, and P.N. Alagappar. 2018. "Failed Broker State: Malaysia's Indian Poor and the Fall of UMNO". *The Round Table* 107, no. 6: 793–94.

Ho Kit Hen, 2018. "I'm Not Contesting to Split Votes, Says PAS' Indian Candidate". *Free Malaysia*

Today, 4 May 2018. https://www.freemalaysiatoday.com/category/nation/2018/05/04/im-not-contesting-just-to-split-votes-says-pas-indian-candidate/ (accessed 14 April 2019).

Jayasooria, Denison. 2018. "Battling the Hearts and Minds of Indian Voters in GE-14". *Malaysiakini*, 3 May 2018.

Lechumanan. 2013. "GE-13: Wooing Indians with Nambikei". *The Star*, 16 April 2013, p. 14.

Lijphart, Arend. 1977. *Democracy in Plural Societies: A Comparative Exploration*. New Haven: Yale University Press.

Mahajani, U. 1960. *The Role of Indian Minorities in Burma and Malaya*. Bombay: Vora and Co.

Malaysiakini. 2007. "MIC-IPF Merger in Making?". 25 April 2007. http://www.malaysiakini.com/news/66408 (accessed 11 September 2018).

Malaysian Times, The. 2016. "Sedic Making an Impact on B40 Indians". 29 March 2016. http://www.themalaysiantimes.com.my/sedic-making-an-impact-on-b40-indians/ (accessed 5 September 2018).

Merdeka Center. 2018. "Malaysia General Elections XIV Outlook: Prospects and Outcome III". Powerpoint presentation, delivered on 8 May 2018.

Milne, R.S., and D.K. Mauzy. 1999. *Malaysian Politics under Mahathir*. London and New York: Routledge.

Muzaffar, Chandra. 1993. "Political Marginalization in Malaysia". In *Indian Communities in Southeast Asia*, edited by K.S. Sandhu and A. Mani, pp. 211–36. Singapore: Institute of Southeast Asian Studies.

MySinchew. 2008. "Malaysia: Samy Vellu Not to Accept Appointment Offer as Senator". 12 March 2008. http://www.mysinchew.com/node/8504 (accessed 2 January 2019).

Nagarajan, Subramaniam. 2004. "A Community in Transition: Tamil Displacement in Malaysia". PhD thesis, University Malaya.

New Straits Times. 2017. "MIC Targets Winning Seven Parliamentary, 14 State Seats in GE14: Subramaniam". 1 May 2017. https://www.nst.com.my/news/politics/2017/05/235566/mic-targets-winning-seven-parliamentary-14-state-seats-ge14-subramaniam (accessed 15 April 2019).

Ostwald, Kai. 2017. *Malaysia's Electoral Process: The Methods and Costs of Perpetuating UMNO Rule*. Trends in Southeast Asia, no. 19/2017. Singapore: ISEAS – Yusof Ishak Institute.

Pakatan Harapan. 2018. *Buku Harapan: Rebuilding Our Nation Fulfilling Our Hopes*. Pakatan Harapan.

Palanisamy, Ramasamy. 2004. "Nation-Building in Malaysia: Victimization of Indians?". In *Ethnic Relations and Nation-Building in Southeast Asia*, edited by Leo Suryadinata, pp. 145–67. Singapore: Institute of Southeast Asian Studies.

Reuters. 2007. "Indian Protest Rocks Malaysia ahead of Polls". 25 November 2007. https://www.reuters.com/article/us-malaysia-protest/indian-protest-rocks-malaysia-ahead-of-polls-idUSKLR16504820071125 (accessed 2 January 2019).

Sandhu, Kernial Singh. 1969. *Indians in Malaya: Some Aspects of Their Immigration and Settlement (1786–1957)*. New York: Cambridge University Press.

Saw Swee-Hock. 2015. *The Population of Malaysia*, 2nd ed. Singapore: Institute of Southeast Asian Studies.

Star, The. 2009. "Mano I'm Not Linked to LTTE". 11 May 2009. https://www.thestar.com.my/news/nation/2009/05/11/mano-im-not-linked-to-ltte/ (accessed 2 January 2019).

———. 2013. "GE-13: HINDRAF to Partner with Barisan, Waythamoorty". 18 April 2013. https://www.thestar.com.my/news/nation/2013/04/18/GE-13-hindraf-to-partner-with-barisan-says-waythamoorthy/> (accessed 2 January 2019).

————. 2017. "Najib Launches 10-year Blueprint for Indian Community". 23 April 2017. https://www.thestar.com.my/news/nation/2017/04/23/najib-launches-10-year-blueprint-for-indian-community/ (accessed 2 January 2019).

————. 2018. "MIC launches Four Part of manifesto". 18 April 2018. https://www.thestar.com.my/news/nation/2018/04/18/mic-launches-four-part-manifesto/ (accessed 5 September 2018).

Sun Daily, The. 2018. "Sarawanan Denies Sending MIC Members to Rough up Tamil Daily Staff". 5 September 2018. https://www.thesundaily.my/archive/saravanan-denies-sending-mic-members-rough-tamil-daily-staff-video-DTARCH478578 (accessed 2 January 2019).

Ufen, Andreas. 2013. "Introduction: The 2013 Malaysian Elections: Business as Usual or Part of a Protracted Transition?". *Journal of Current Southeast Asian Affairs* 32, no. 2: 3–17.

Warta Kerajaan Persekutuan. 2004. *Keputusan Pilihanraya Umum ke-11*. Kuala Lumpur: Jabatan Percetakan Negara.

————. 2008. *Keputusan Pilihanraya Umum ke-12*. Kuala Lumpur: Jabatan Percetakan Negara.

————. 2013. *Keputusan Pilihanraya Umum ke-13*. Kuala Lumpur: Jabatan Percetakan Negara.

Zurairi AR. 2013. "After Demolition, FT Minister Claims Hindu Temple a Front for Shady Activities". *Malay Mail*, 11 November 2013. https://www.malaymail.com/news/malaysia/2013/11/11/after-demolition-ft-minister-claims-hindu-temple-a-front-for-shady-activiti/560109 (accessed 2 January 2019).

III

States

12

SELANGOR
Pakatan's Home Advantage, Barisan's Hollow Tactics, PAS' Hardy Base

Lee Hwok Aun

INTRODUCTION

In the titanic theatre of Malaysia's GE-14, Selangor did not quite shake the foundations on 9 May 2018, but still served up big surprises. Against widely held expectations of modest results, Pakatan Harapan retained the Selangor state government by a landslide, and wrested a pair of federal parliament seats from its already dominant position (Lee 2018). Moreover, the fledgling coalition secured yawning margins, obliterating the notion that multicornered contests might yield narrow wins. Emphatically, Pakatan Harapan (PH) reaped the advantages of its incumbency and popular administration, while Barisan Nasional's (BN) tactics rang hollow and could not redeem a damaged brand, and Parti Islam SeMalaysia's (PAS) core remained loyal, but its ethnically homogeneous base and parochial platform consigned it to a near wipe-out.

Selangor was a prized trophy heading into GE-14. It is the most populous, prosperous and urbanized state[1] in Malaysia, accounting for 19 per cent of the national population, and together with Kuala Lumpur where millions of Selangorians work, generates 38 per cent of the national GDP. The state's median household income of RM7,225 per month is also 38 per cent above the national median (Department of Statistics 2017). Governing Selangor grants levers to showcase prestige and progress, distribute patronage, determine land use, and oversee state government-linked companies and state-owned entities. Two million registered voters, of which 50.2 per cent identify as Malay, 34.0 per cent as Chinese, 14.5 per cent as Indian, and 1.3 per cent as Others, would decide the winners and losers in the contest for fifty-six state assembly seats and twenty-two federal parliament seats.

It was crucial for PH to retain the state, to shore up its popularity and relevance—and morale, in the event of losses elsewhere. BN declared retaking Selangor as a top priority, and directed the federal government machinery, particularly the Election Commission (EC), towards engineering more favourable conditions. The situation in Selangor was also complicated by PH's continual relationship with PAS, despite the cessation of the Pakatan Rakyat coalition at the federal level. Chief Minister Azmin Ali's calculated truce with PAS until February 2018 seemingly stemmed from fear of a backlash in the Malay electorate should PAS be alienated. Concerns over how Malay votes would be split were coupled with considerations that non-Malay voters might be disillusioned about regime change, and lulled into a lower voter turnout.

With such high stakes and substantial uncertainties, political contestants—both incumbents and challengers—and observers, scholars and citizens, largely remained cautious. Expectations were tempered, perhaps fuelled by past disappointments of change that did not materialize or chastisement for overconfident predictions, and an abiding sense that BN had too much at its disposal. These outlooks were, of course, premised on past experiences and estimations of the regime's resilience, and doubts whether this time would be pivotally different. Previous elections suggested that three-cornered contests benefited BN, and redelineation exercises enhanced BN's performance.[2] Unforeseeable developments in the run-up to GE-14, however, added momentum behind PH's campaign; its prospects of retaining Selangor brightened, but almost no one predicted a comprehensive victory.

This time was far more different than most imagined. GE-14 delivered a massive mandate to PH and a decisive rejection of BN, while also cementing Selangor as PKR's home base. PH won twenty of twenty-two parliament seats and fifty-one of fifty-six State Legislative Assembly (SLA) seats, on the back of 65 per cent of the popular vote, towering above BN's haul of two parliament seats and four state seats, and merely 22 per cent of the popular vote.

Drawing on election data, on-the-ground observations and interviews with key informants, this chapter unpacks GE-14 in Selangor.[3] In anticipation that the Malay vote would be decisive, the research focused on the following parliamentary constituencies and state seats within them, which are Malay majority and contain other features of interest:

- Kuala Selangor, won by the second narrowest margin in GE-13 by UMNO's Irmohizam Ibrahim, challenged by his predecessor (MP for 2008–13), Dzulkefly Ahmad;
- Gombak, Selangor Chief Minister Azmin Ali's seat, and where PAS is headquartered;

- Shah Alam, Selangor's state capital and also a constituency where PAS has a substantial presence;
- Kapar, one of the most aggressively redelineated constituencies, which morphed from a Malay majority into a Malay supermajority.

I survey long-term vote trends, evaluate PH's incumbency strengths and BN's stratagems which caused some consternation over new electoral boundaries and three-cornered fights with PAS. I then report some observations of the campaign period, examine the polling results from a bird's eye view and some zoomed-in angles, which show massive collapse of BN support among Malay voters and further declines in its popularity among Chinese and Indian voters. The anti-UMNO Malay vote was split between PH and PAS, and PH garnered more support among younger voters. On the whole, Selangor is firmly a PH stronghold, but its performance in government and coalition maintenance will weigh heavily on the future of politics in Malaysia's leading state.

A DECLINE FORETOLD?

Selangor has stood out at turning points and tidal shifts in Malaysia's electoral history. In 1969, the hung state assembly—which then included Kuala Lumpur—precipitated a political crisis, culminating in the 13 May riots and subsequent political economic overhaul. BN's formation and government of national unity configuration saw to the coalition's dominance in the 1970s. In the 1980s, BN's slowly but steadily ebbing popularity and UMNO's schisms were also mirrored in Selangor, with BN's share of parliament and state seats declining through the 1986 and 1990 elections. The subsequent rebound and consolidation of BN's rule, on the back of the economic boom of the 1990s, fuelled the regime's most dominant period: 100 per cent of parliament seats, and more than 88 per cent of state seats in the 1995, 1999, and 2004 elections (Figure 12.1). As Ong (2017) notes, Selangor voters have fluctuated more than any other state's, accumulating a track record of showering support on well-run administrations and registering protest from time to time.

The tide turned in the late 1990s. The *Reformasi* ferment of 1999 translated into a marked drop in BN's popular vote, which recovered in 2004, but in retrospect 1995 was actually the high water mark, after which BN's popularity in Selangor has been on a momentous downtrend. In this light, the regime's spectacular 2004 showing rode on the Abdullah Badawi (and redelineation) bonanza, and popular relief and expectancy in the wake of Mahathir's retirement, but was an anomaly in the milieu of an increasingly informed, sophisticated and demanding electorate. BN's administration of Selangor was also marred by the graft associated with Chief Minister Mohamad Khir Toyo, and general lacklustre leadership, evidenced by the dearth of high-calibre federal Cabinet ministers from the state. Selangor voters decidedly swung to Pakatan Rakyat in 2008. Khir Toyo lost his seat, and his downfall was sealed by a conviction in 2011—upheld by the Federal Court in 2015—for acquiring land

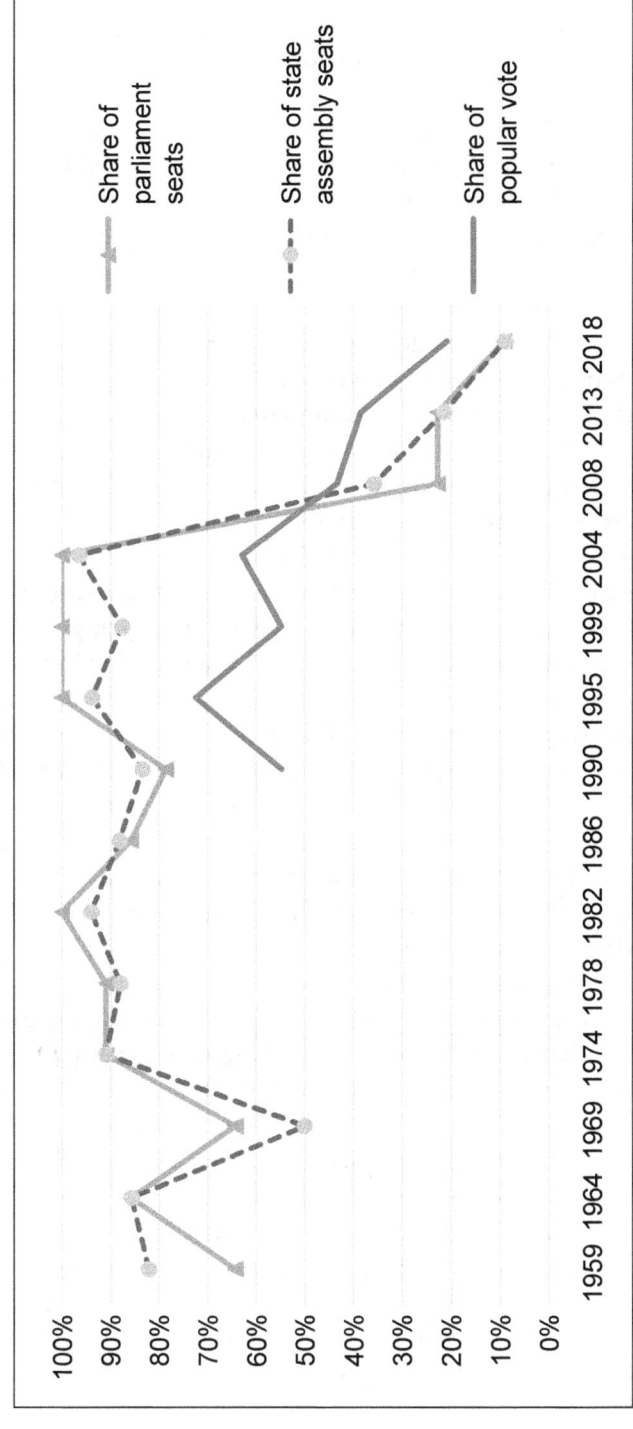

FIGURE 12.1
Barisan Nasional in Selangor: General Election Results, 1959–2018

Note: In 1959 to 1969, Kuala Lumpur was part of Selangor.
Sources: 1959–86: public domain; 1990–2013: Ong (2017), 2018: author's calculations.

and property through corrupt means. BN, continually languid and rudderless, lost further ground in the 2013 elections. The GE-12 and GE-13 election cycles marked a clear break from the past and a reversal of fortune, with Pakatan consolidating its hold on urban, ethnically mixed constituencies, which had previously been the BN's winning formula.

GE-13 results starkly correlated with ethnic composition and geography. Areas with high concentration of Chinese voters resoundingly voted for Pakatan. Mapping the results portrays the pattern of UMNO winning in predominantly Malay, rural northern Selangor (Figure 12.2). The performance of both coalitions' component parties, in terms of win rates and margins, also shows marked contrasts. Pakatan Rakyat's members convincingly won most or all contests, securing 80 per cent of Selangor state assembly and federal parliament seats. PAS made the most gains, at UMNO's expense, and mostly in ethnically mixed constituencies. Pakatan won by large margins and dominated in urban areas, while Barisan Nasional managed victories by slim majorities, and has been reduced to UMNO, with the Malaysian Chinese Association (MCA) and the Malaysian Indian Congress (MIC) suffering comprehensive losses, barring one parliamentary seat for MIC.[4]

From winning the state in 2008 to tightening its grip in 2013, Pakatan Rakyat consolidated its presence in Selangor. The coalition weathered some internal storms. The "Kajang Move" of 2014 was controversial and polarizing, eventually resulting in Azmin Ali's elevation to Chief Minister and the introduction of extensive social policy changes under his administration. However, Pakatan began to fray. In 2015, PAS parted ways with Parti Keadilan Rakyat (PKR) and Democratic Action Party (DAP) in Parliament. Although its splinter party Amanah formed and remained on board, the coalition kept an ambiguous, ambivalent truce with PAS in Selangor. This state level rapprochement, marshalled by Azmin, presumed that alienating PAS would play into BN's hands and mortally hurt Pakatan's defence.

The break-up of Pakatan Rakyat, BN's closing ranks behind Najib Razak and dismissal of 1MDB and other crises, and the federal regime's declared priority of retaking Selangor, set the stage for an eagerly anticipated showdown. With the emergence of Parti Pribumi Bersatu Malaysia (PPBM) and cobbling together of Pakatan Harapan in 2017, the seat balance in the Selangor Assembly was mathematically on edge. PH held twenty-nine seats (thirteen PKR, fourteen DAP, two Amanah), a razor-thin majority out of the fifty-six seats, with PAS holding thirteen and UMNO twelve, and the remaining two occupied by independents—who had left PKR and DAP. Selangor BN has been characterized by weak leadership; its most prominent politician in recent years is Jamal Yunos, an UMNO division chief infamous for provocative stunts and inflammatory statements. Approaching GE-14, the driving question was whether BN's decades-long decline would continue, or be reversed through a vote swing back to the BN fold. Considering the vicissitudes of the past, and the federal resources at BN's disposal and uncertainties over voter fatigue after repeatedly falling short of ultimate, federal regime change, neither PH's hold nor BN's grab was taken for granted.

FIGURE 12.2
GE-13 in Selangor: Malay Share of Voters and Winning Party

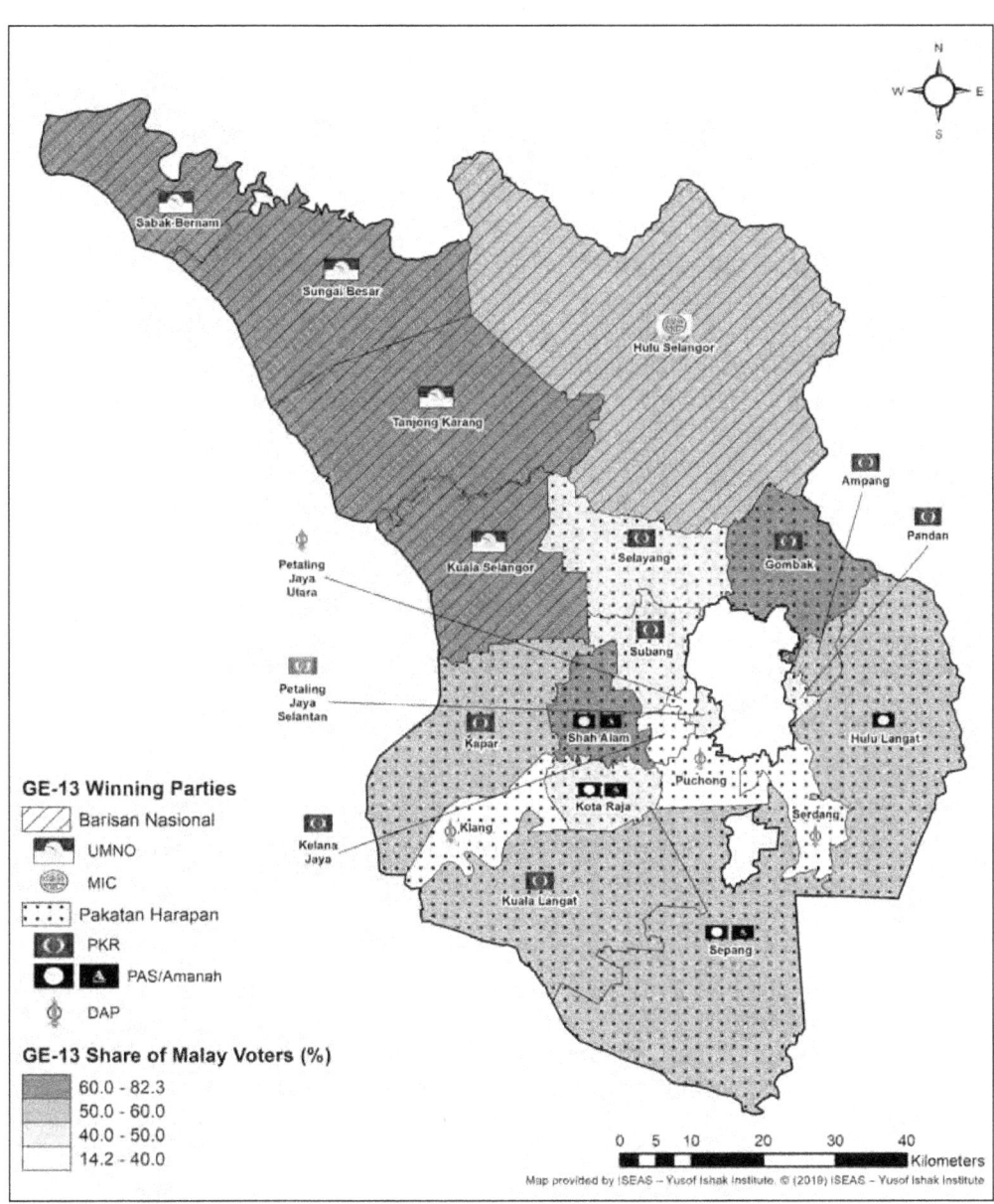

BN'S OFFENCE: HEAVY TACTICS, LIGHT SUBSTANCE

Three-Cornered Fights

The spectre of three-cornered contests across Peninsular Malaysia caused consternation in Pakatan Harapan, not least in Selangor. UMNO's federal machinations and overtures to PAS managed to fracture Pakatan Rakyat, but whether they were tactically orchestrated to set up three-cornered fights is difficult to deduce. UMNO and PAS were unable to establish a pact for the simple reason that they vie for the same Malay-majority constituencies. Indeed, it was widely held that three-cornered contests would benefit UMNO. Multicornered scenarios recur in Sabah and Sarawak, splitting opposition votes and contributing to BN's overwhelming returns at the polls. On the Peninsular, the few breaches in Pakatan Rakyat's seat negotiations of GE-13, which ensured two-cornered fights, played into BN's hands—notably two Selangor state seats, Kota Damansara and Semenyih. These seats were exceptional in that Pakatan's designated candidates were of Parti Sosialis Malaysia and were undermined by PAS' insistence on joining the fray.

Nevertheless, the prevailing outlook towards three-cornered fights was that the anti-BN vote would be split, injecting uncertainties into the equation, despite PH's strong finishes in 2013. Winning margins of GE-13 suggested substantial buffers and "safe" seats. Of Pakatan Harapan's parliament seats held by PKR, DAP and Amanah, eight were won in GE-13 with more than 60 per cent of votes, seven with between 55 per cent and 60 per cent, and three with less than 55 per cent. PAS' only MP (three out of four elected in GE-13 joined Amanah) won with more than 55 per cent. In marked contrast, all four of BN's seats were marginal wins (less than 55 per cent). Similar patterns held in state seats. BN faced wide vote deficits with existing borders.

Redelineation: Malapportionment and Ethnic Gerrymandering

BN seemingly held the trump card of manipulating electoral composition. Electoral redelineation is constitutionally mandated, and has been implemented every two election cycles in the past and was thus overdue. However, a two-thirds parliamentary majority is required to increase the number of constituencies. Thus, BN could not create new seats—but it could still redraw boundaries of existing constituencies. The process was vitiated by some conniving and unconstitutional practices. Here we consider the eventual borders approved in March 2018, two weeks before Najib dissolved Parliament.

The problems of malapportionment and gerrymandering are national in scope (Chacko, this volume) but had particular salience in Selangor, the most redelineated of Malaysia's states in this exercise. Malapportionment, already exceedingly high, was retained or even exacerbated. For parliament seats, the ratio of the largest to smallest grew from 3.94 to 4.05; for the state seats, the ratio dropped from a whopping 4.96 to a still excessive 4.39. The new borders sustained the bias of the rural electorate, BN's inevitably shrinking heartland in highly urbanized Selangor, and continually contravened the one-person-one-vote one-value principle. Figures 12.3 and 12.4 show that average sizes of BN- and PAS-held seats actually shrank, while Pakatan-held seats ballooned. Relocation of voters to voting centres in different state and/or parliament seats also amounts to gerrymandering—altering voter composition without redrawing borders.

FIGURE 12.3
Selangor Parliamentary Seats: Average Size Pre- and Post-Redelineation, by Incumbent

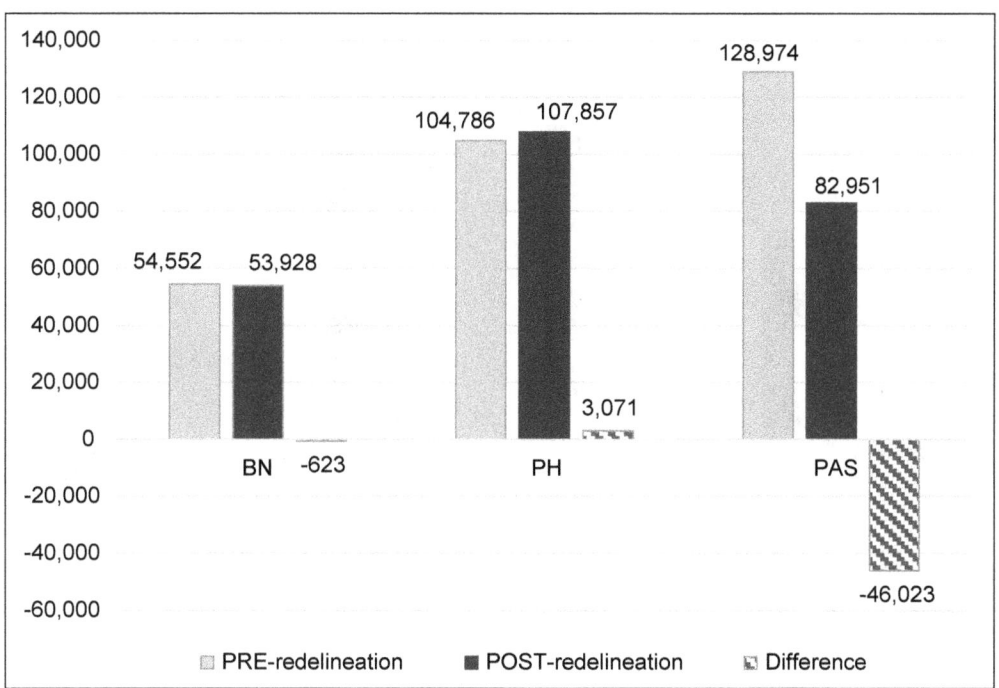

Relative rural to urban bias has benefited BN in the past, but Selangor's highly urbanized demographics—again, the prohibition on increasing the number of seats without a two-thirds parliamentary majority—inclined the EC to engineer supposed advantage for BN through gerrymandering. The process was particularly egregious in Selangor, where the EC presented a first notice of vastly redrawn boundaries with a clear pattern of increased Malay majorities. This triggered organized objections, by citizens' groups and the Selangor government, even from BN members like MCA. In the constitutionally mandated second notice, the EC reverted to a proposal mostly resembling the existing boundaries, which also prompted objections but muddied the process due to the disparity between the first and second proposal. The third and final proposal, in the form of the EC's report to Parliament, morphed back to the first set of borders, without justifying why objections were rejected—and in fact registering assent to some objections. Perhaps most nefariously, the report gave weight to various inputs, largely from federal government sponsored entities, that objected to the second proposal and requested a return to the first. Many of these purported objections were sketchy in content, with incomplete names and dates. The presentation of the report in Parliament on 28 March 2018 was also scandalized by the Speaker's insistence that debate be restricted to one afternoon, with a limit of six participants per side.

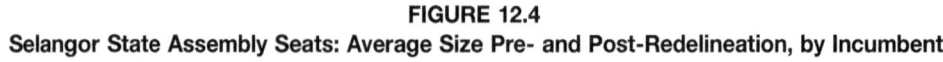

FIGURE 12.4
Selangor State Assembly Seats: Average Size Pre- and Post-Redelineation, by Incumbent

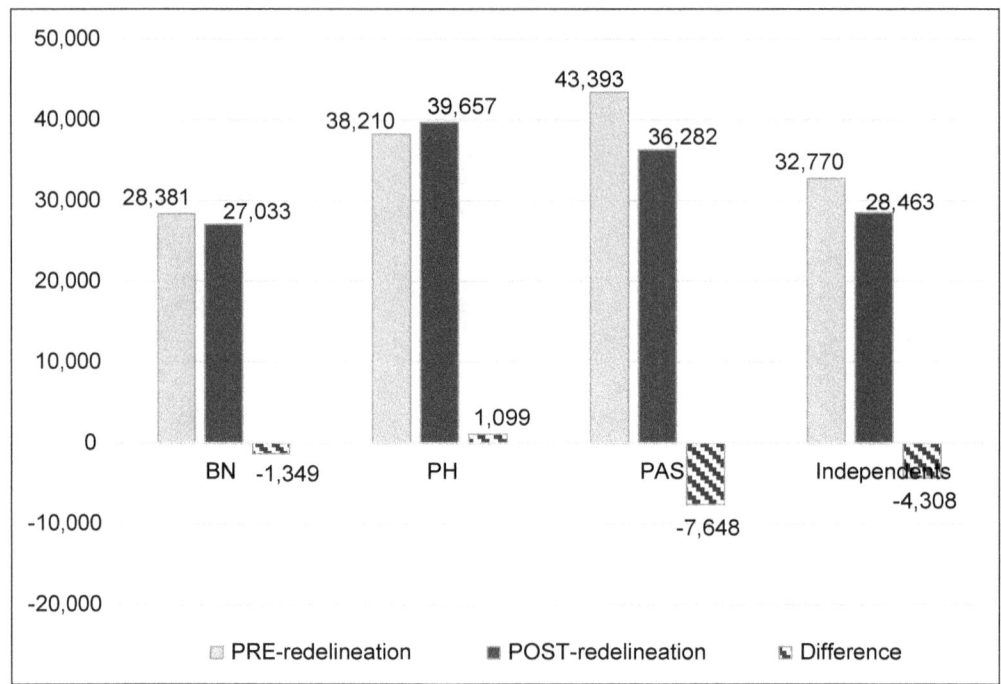

The tactic of inflating Malay majorities translated into increases in Malay-supermajority seats, where Malays comprised more than 60 per cent of registered voters (Table 12.1). In parliamentary seats, Malay-supermajority seats increased from eight to eleven. Among state seats, the number increased from twenty-three to thirty-three. The number of mixed seats were reduced, while Chinese-majority seats were increased—and expanded in size, thus diluting the votes in these constituencies. The exercise was a travesty of Malaysia's electoral democracy, and arguably unconstitutional.[5] Various seats were transformed from ethnically mixed constituencies reflective of the local population, to Malay majorities or supermajorities, apparently to make them more winnable for BN, and non-Malay voters were packed into some seats that BN clearly showed no interest in competing for (Table 12.2). The wanton disregard for orderly administration is reflected in the redelineation of Kapar, Sungai Buloh and Hulu Langat, which had state seats or parts thereof carved in or out of the parliamentary seats (Figure 12.5). Notably, Hulu Langat was held by PAS. The redelineation posed electoral consequences. Based on GE-13 voting patterns, the relocation of voters could cause up to seven PH-held seats to fall to UMNO (*Malaysiakini*, 28 March 2018; *The Edge Malaysia*, 9 April 2018).

TABLE 12.1
Gerrymandering of Selangor Seats: Changes in Electorate Profile,
before and after Redelineation

	Parliament		DUN	
	Before	After	Before	After
Malay supermajority[a]	8	11	23	33
Malay majority[b]	4	3	12	4
Mixed[c]	9	4	8	6
Chinese majority[d]	1	4	13	13
Total	22	22	56	56

Notes: a. Malays ≥ 60 per cent; b. 50 per cent ≤ Malays < 60 per cent majority;
c. no group ≥ 50 per cent; d. Chinese ≥ 50 per cent.

TABLE 12.2
Highest Order Gerrymandering (One Group's Share Changed by ≥10 percentage points)

Change in Profile	Seats Affected	
	Parliament	DUN
Malay majority ➜ Malay supermajority	Kapar Hulu Langat	Paya Jaras Pelabuhan Klang Taman Templer Dusun Tua
mixed ➜ Malay supermajority	Sungai Buloh[a]	Ijok Sementa Seri Serdang Sungai Kandis[b]
Malay supermajority ➜ mixed		Bukit Antarabangsa
Malay majority ➜ mixed		Kajang Kota Kemuning[c]
Mixed ➜ Chinese majority	Subang[d]	
Chinese majority ➜ Chinese supermajority		Bandar Baru Klang

Notes: Previous names: a. Subang; b. Seri Andalas; c. Sri Muda; d. Kelana Jaya.

Soon after Parliament approved the new constituency boundaries, the Dewan Rakyat was dissolved to pave the way for the election nomination, campaign and polling day on 9 May.

BN presented its Selangor manifesto and a fresh cohort of candidates, including young professionals. However, its campaigning veered negative, featuring smears and attacks on Selangor's administration. PAS-Gagasan also projected a populist manifesto and a rather professional (in contrast to clerical) line-up. Both coalitions

FIGURE 12.5
Redelineation of Kapar, Subang/Sungai Buloh, Hulu Langat (Proportion of Malay, Chinese, Indian Voters)

GE-14 Selangor Parliamentary Constituencies

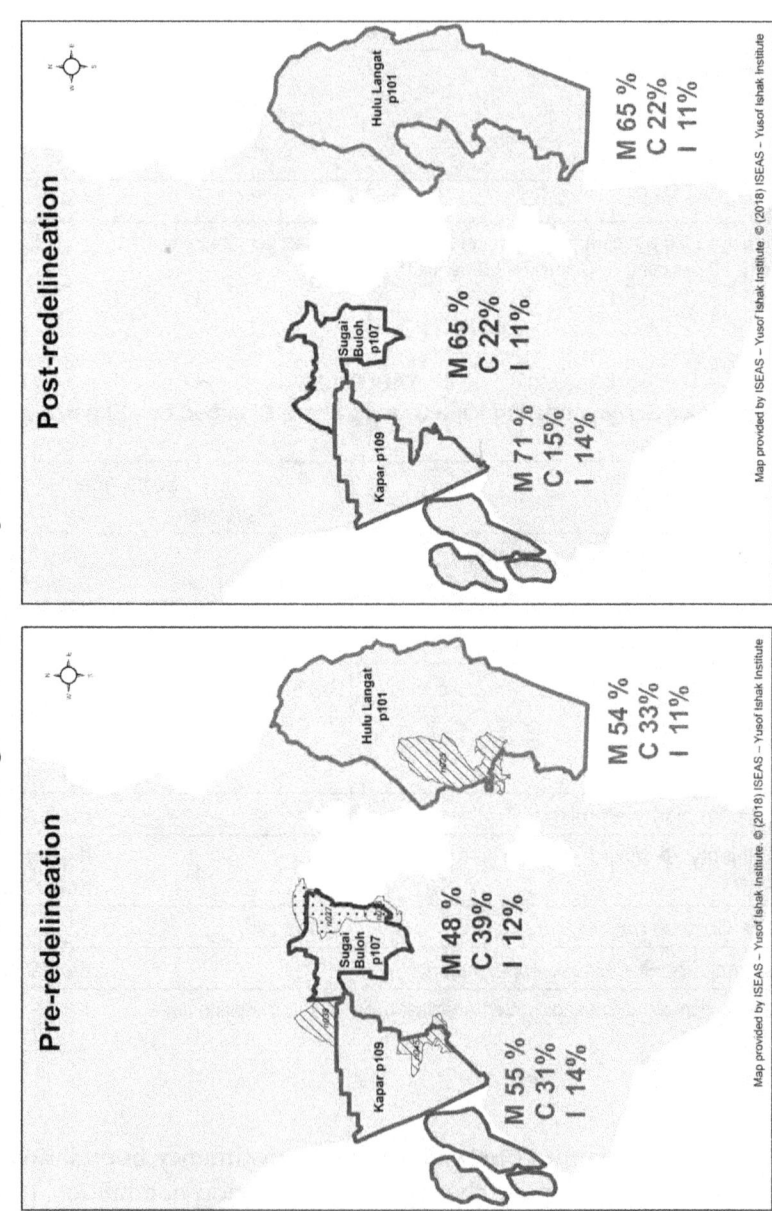

Note: The pre-redelineation map shows state seats that were relocated in part or whole.

dismissed the significance of the 1MDB scandal; indeed, BN's federal manifesto trivialized the problems of corruption.[6] BN set a target of winning thirty seats.

PAKATAN'S DEFENCE: HOME ADVANTAGE, TEMPERED EXPECTATIONS

Incumbency and Popularity

Nearing GE-14, a number of factors worked in Pakatan's favour. The coalition had established a solid presence in the state, after ten years in government and resounding popular mandate in GE-13. Selangor representatives are among the prominent federal opposition parliamentarians. Chief Minister Azmin Ali enjoyed popular support; the array of social programmes rolled out by his administration, from medical card, allowance for mothers (KISS, or Kasih Ibu Smart Selangor), childcare assistance, free Klang Valley bus service, were well received especially by low-income households. Under the Inisiatif Peduli Rakyat, Selangor implemented policies and cultivated an image in line with the objective of administering a compassionate state, not just an industrialized state.[7] These welfare programmes furnished a platform for prospective candidates to foster ties with village chiefs and communities.[8] The maintenance of a functional bureaucracy and clean government, free of major scandal, contrasted with the 1MDB and other scandals engulfing BN. Thus, BN's long-held trump card of being the custodian of development had attenuated over a decade. Both the positives of PH's administration and the negatives of BN's corruption weighed heavily on Selangor's more urbanized electorate.

The state's urbanized and diverse demographics dovetailed with the Pakatan Harapan's coalitional profile. It was also on this basis that PAS' ability to replicate its 2013 successes were seriously doubted, given that it clearly won as part of the coalition and on the back of non-Malay votes, in mixed seats. PAS' narrative remained weak in Selangor, where it had limited appeal beyond the party's base, and any cooperative moves with UMNO-BN would amount to a partnership with another weak party within Selangor.[9] Mindful of the Malay population, especially in northern, rural Selangor, that remained wedded to UMNO, Azmin had assiduously reached out, while also maintaining cordial ties with the Sultan of Selangor.[10]

Nonetheless, Azmin resisted severing ties with PAS, in spite of widening and clearly irreconcilable ideological, partisan and personal fissures in the aftermath of PAS' split from Pakatan Rakyat. He was perhaps cognizant as well of PAS' considerable presence in areas of Selangor, including his Gombak constituency, of which he remained non-committal about defending until very near the dissolution of Parliament. For many months, a strategy of rapprochement with PAS—centred on Azmin and not unanimously shared in Pakatan Selangor—was maintained, further goaded by PAS' declaration of contesting forty-seven out of fifty-six state assembly seats and twenty out of twenty-two parliament seats—and its perceived intention to be kingmaker in the event of a hung parliament, or at least a spoiler to thwart PH. Others held the view that it was strategically more advantageous for Pakatan to clearly break with PAS, to avert portions of the electorate voting for PAS in the hope that the party would remain in Pakatan's state government coalition. Azmin's decision to cut constituency funding for PAS' assemblymen in January 2018, and his mid-February statement that Pakatan-PAS co-operation was no longer tenable, effectively ended the pact, even if his office made no formal declaration dissolving the relationship.

PH was saddled with a few challenges in managing the new and expanded pact. Its newer constituents did not enjoy the recognition and presence of PKR and DAP within Selangor. There were concerns over Amanah's lack of traction and visibility, and possible backlash from PAS; the notion of contesting under the PKR flag was brought up early on.[11] Concerns also arose towards the more outspoken of Amanah's parliamentary incumbents, including Khalid Samad in Shah Alam, and their popular reception, particularly among older, more conservative, and PAS-inclined, voters.[12] PPBM was an even more recent entrant to the political arena, and slated to be competitive in Kedah and Johor, but sought a presence in Selangor.

Cautious Optimism

Despite the incumbency advantages outlined above, the ambient mood within PH could be characterized as cautious optimism. A perceivable majority opinion held that the split Malay vote would yield advantage for UMNO; a minority considered the conditions beneficial to PH. With its popularity decimated among non-Malays, PAS could only contend for Malay votes and thus faced a bleak stand-alone future in Selangor. While it would cobble together the Gagasan Sejahtera alliance with a few minor parties, these partners were too obscure to make a difference. I therefore refrain from applying the Gagasan label; it was all about PAS, to a much greater degree than UMNO-dominated BN.

Electoral prognoses, based on survey trends and simulated results, affirmed the broad circumspection. In December 2017, gerrymandering and three-cornered fights was widely deemed to benefit UMNO, and make various seats more competitive and harder to call.[13] These exercises mostly extrapolated GE-13 vote patterns onto the new constituencies.

Analysis of prospects based on voter composition also yielded cautiously optimistic outlooks.[14] For Selangor's state seats, PH was confident of retaining thirteen Chinese-majority and six mixed seats, making for nineteen safe seats, and thus only needed ten more to reach the majority threshold twenty-nine and avoid a hung assembly.

The direction of pro-PAS votes was difficult to read, but the party was widely expected within PH to play a spoiler role. Parliamentary seat Shah Alam and state seat Hulu Kelang, within Gombak, both with substantial PAS presence, were among the areas in which PH incumbents were concerned about the loss of voters carved out of the constituency.[15] Hulu Kelang's Saari Sungib also contemplated whether frostier reception at mosques that he had experienced would attenuate his popularity.[16] PAS, like PH and BN, projected a technocratic and competent government, tapping into economic anxiety by calling for goods and services tax (GST) abolition. Its Kuala Selangor and Ijok candidates were, respectively, an architect and college administrator.[17] In PH's defence of Kapar, which as a result of redelineation had 71 per cent Malay voters compared to 55 per cent prior to the exercise, Abdullah Sani, the PKR Kuala Langat incumbent, was parachuted in. As a rule of thumb, a Malay candidate was deemed more electable in constituencies with over 60 per cent Malay voters;[18] in Kapar specifically, a Malay would also fare better against PAS' respected Dr Rani Osman.[19] Approaching GE-14, PH set a target of forty state seats.

Electorate Sentiments: Shifting Tide?

PH's incumbency advantages seemed to outweigh BN's gerrymandering and vote splitting in three-cornered contests, but the question of sentiments, specifically pro-PH momentum, pervaded the electoral space in the run-up to GE-14. The prominent issues for Selangor mirrored those at the national level. Widespread economic anxiety and discontent, particularly towards GST introduction, subsidy removals, and high cost of living, was very intense. But would BN's track record of delivering development and public services, and providing burgeoning amounts of Bantuan Rakyat 1 Malaysia (BR1M) cash transfers, placate voters? Voters are clearly mindful of the issues that fall under federal jurisdiction, and thus BN's provision of BR1M cash transfers are negated by GST collected, and most economic woes are attributed to the federal government. BN patronage has also discernibly worn off on Malaysian voters, especially in Selangor, where denizens increasingly view welfare provisions as the state's obligation, and have become more averse to the notion that BN-sponsored largesse must be repaid at the ballot box.

These sentiments were observable in recent years; opinion polls consistently reflected a populace unhappy and anxious about their economic situation. Not much research focused specifically on Selangor, but it is fair to presume that the mood of the state mirrored that of the nation. In Merdeka Center's national surveys of registered voters in early 2018, 51 per cent indicated they were not satisfied with the performance of the federal government, while a minority 43 per cent expressed satisfaction. Public sentiment towards the country's direction can be gauged through polling of the same question over time, including at GE-13. In May 2013, 56 per cent of surveyed voters stated that Malaysia was headed in the right direction; only 32 per cent felt the converse. The share of the electorate responding "right direction" continuously declined in 2014–15, notably with subsidy reductions, GST introduction and the 1MDB scandal, but was on an uptrend from mid-2016. Still, in May 2018 a larger proportion answered wrong direction (49 per cent) than right (44 per cent) (Merdeka Center 2018b).

Loosening affinities were also sensed at the local level. UMNO-stronghold villages previously hostile to other parties were now welcoming PH campaign officers or prospective candidates.[20] Younger voters had indicated in the past that they were less beholden to BN, and this trend appeared to continue. The multiple scandals engulfing Najib and UMNO severely tarnished its image, even if the nitty gritty was too complicated to grasp. The capacity of voters to obtain information, bypassing censored and sanitized reports of the ruling regime's official channels, is not unique to Selangor. Mobile devices and broadband networks have expanded in general, although the extent of connectivity varies across states, with Selangor expectedly among the highest in broadband penetration.[21] Equally, if not more, important to electoral dynamics is the information voters seek and their subsequent response. How Selangorians go about this is difficult to demonstrate empirically, but given the state's high urbanization rate, coupled with high education levels and active civil society, it seems reasonable to presume that voters of the state are above the national average in exercising informed, independent and critical political judgement.

Some local controversies or incidences deriving from abuse by UMNO local elites also played a part. Kampung FELDA Bukit Cherakah is a settlement that previously prohibited any parties besides UMNO and PAS from campaigning, even physically chasing away Pakatan politicians. In January 2018, a condominium development project entailing a land grab allegedly by UMNO branch leaders in collusion with outside players, came to light. The exposé galvanized protest among young adults, who organized themselves and even formally registered an NGO, GGF2, to sustain political pressure behind their cause.[22] Their level of activism may be exceptional, but disaffection towards UMNO were discernible in many other communities.

When and how the tide swung to PH are difficult to ascertain. A number of surveys capturing voter mood and inclination, while analysed and disseminated in the context of Peninsular Malaysia broadly, or Malaysia nationally, again serve as useful references for Selangor, with the caveat that the state is more urbanized and more demanding of government. Sentiments do not equate with political support and voting decisions, and there was a sense of fence-sitting, non-committal voters, or those unwilling to reveal their preferences.[23] While opinion polling performed poorly, judging by the failure to predict the election, surveys did pick up a considerable unsure or non-response rate in consecutive rounds (INVOKE 2018; Merdeka Center 2018b). In INVOKE's national surveys of December 2017 to February 2018, 20–23 per cent did not indicate which party they would support "if the election is held tomorrow", and 12–17 per cent were undecided.

Polls also plotted a longer term downtrend in support for BN. In Merdeka Center's April 2018 survey, Malay support for BN dropped to 41.3 per cent, down from 58.5 per cent in GE-13 in Selangor, the second steepest decline on the Peninsula, after Johor (Merdeka Center 2018a). PH-affiliated INVOKE's national survey of February 2018 reported rising momentum for PH, but found large proportions of undecided voters. Its predictive model, going beyond declared preference of survey respondents, projected momentous wins for PH on Peninsular west coast and a PAS wipe-out, which was widely regarded as overly optimistic. Institute Darul Ehsan (IDE) in March 2018 reported from a Selangor-based survey that support for PH exceeded that for BN in urban and semi-urban areas, among all ethnic groups. IDE's time trend showed increasing momentum for PH, with voter preference rising from 46 per cent in August 2017 to 49 per cent in January 2018 and 56 per cent in April 2018, while BN's remained quite static (31 per cent to 34 per cent to 30 per cent) and PAS' declined (18 per cent to 12 per cent to 12 per cent) (Mohammad Redzuan 2018). The trend held across all groups, but occurred most steeply among the Chinese. Despite these signs of a pro-PH swing, IDE predicted a modest win for PH, with the coalition taking thirty-two Selangor state seats, above twenty-four for BN.

There is the distinct likelihood that PH rode a late wave of popularity, in the wake of the various campaign developments and even after nomination day on 28 April. Internal cooperation made a difference as well. PH's consensus on seat allocations, its manifesto released in March, Mahathir's PM candidacy, and usage of a single logo—PKR's banner—cumulatively demonstrated cohesion and the image of a "government in waiting". Cooperation among PH component members contributed to the energy and outreach of campaigns at the constituency level.[24] Considerably high non-response rates persisted, until and beyond nomination day. In Merdeka Center's tracking surveys, about 15 per cent of respondents stated they were unsure which party to support, even into the campaign period of early May. Modelling voter preference to fill in the gaps, Merdeka Center's prediction for Selangor, released on the eve of GE-14, was more upbeat than IDE's: PH stood to win nineteen parliament seats, with three deemed "too close to call".

GE-14 ON THE GROUND

In following campaigns on the ground, a few observations stand out that are worth a brief note. BN's style and machinery closely resembled preceding elections; it won the paraphernalia war, flooding the streets with banners and posters, and holding events attended by uniformed members and supporters, with free food and gifts on offer. Campaigns utilized social media actively, but unevenly; in many cases, it was difficult to find announcements of activities and to locate *ceramahs*.[25] The federal-level campaign exhibited more cohesion, with a clear appeal to join up with BN, and Najib in particular, to make Malaysia great (*hebatkan Malaysia*) and for development benefits to continue. BN Selangor launched a state-based manifesto, highlighting affordable housing and public transport, resolution to water supply issues, various education provisions, and even very specific promises such as paying consumers 20 sen for bringing their own bag and reducing plastic bag usage. However, BN campaigned negatively, and despite launching a Selangor manifesto and nominating a slate of new and young candidates, its dismal record as state opposition, unremarkable leadership, and absence of a Chief Minister designate, hampered its ability to gain traction. The prominence of Najib in the campaign apparently stoked anti-BN, and especially anti-UMNO, sentiment.

PAS yielded some benefit from UMNO's disrepute. Its people-friendly manifesto, including abolition of GST and expansion of social assistance, tapped into economic anxieties and discontent towards the incumbent administrations. The party also attempted to project a technocratic administration, along with an emphasis on local candidates, and did not openly admit but was clearly mindful privately that its vote base was confined to Malays, which made its winning prospects near impossible in Selangor. On the whole, PAS counted on a loyal base whose vote holds regardless of the prospects, and on UMNO-aggrieved Malays, which ultimately translated into valiant efforts in the face of certain defeat, but in advance of its cause.[26]

The momentum and resonance of PH's campaigns escalated after nomination day through to polling day. The coalition derived support from an evident yearning for government that cares and delivers, and that stewards public resources with integrity. The Selangor government's social assistance programmes were well received especially by low-income populations, and its stable, scandal-free government won favour with a broad swathe. The campaign capitalized on Azmin Ali's popularity, which stood out further in contrast to the dearth of leadership among his adversaries. Concerns over gerrymandering persisted, and prompted efforts to inform relocated voters who may be unaware of their changed voting centre.[27] PH candidates also rode on PH's national cohesion, Mahathir's PM candidacy, and the single logo—PKR's flag—adopted by all constituent parties, and social media dissemination of *ceramahs*, videos and stirring content, particularly through WhatsApp. The volume of flow in these private channels are harder to track. At the same time, BN's chicanery, in deregistering PPBM, holding the elections on a Wednesday, and banning Mahathir's image on posters, evidently backfired, further inflaming protest votes.

The Voters' 9 May Statement: Three Polarized Corners

Selangor voters delivered the state to PH in an astounding landslide. PH won twenty out of twenty-two parliamentary seats, and fifty-one out of fifty-six state seats. PH's popularity far exceeded the national average. In Selangor, the overall popular vote was divided 63.8 per cent for PH, 20.8 per cent for BN and 15.2 per cent for PAS. PH also won by a staggeringly massive margin: averaging 43,361 for parliamentary seats and 16,543 for state seats, while BN only mustered 1,822 and 1,488 respectively. PAS' sole win in the Sijangkang state seat was also by a slim margin of 1,677. The electorate's rejection of BN and PAS and embrace of PH was comprehensive: UMNO lost two parliament seats, MIC one and PAS one; for state seats, PH wrested fourteen from PAS and eight from UMNO, and the two previously held by independents also went PH's way. Within PH, PKR and DAP cleanly swept all of their parliamentary and state contests, and by great distances, while Amanah also won 100 per cent of parliament and almost all state contests. PPBM narrowly lost to UMNO in its only two parliament wins, Tanjong Karang and Sabak Bernam. Tables 12.3 and 12.4 display the win rates and margins, comparing GE-13 and GE-14.

Selangor's electoral map is repainted almost entirely in PH's colours, but to get a fuller appreciation of the new landscape, it is worthwhile tracing out the redelineated borders and marking the second-place finishers (Figure 12.6). The conversion of mixed or Malay-majority to Malay-supermajority constituencies is reflected in the greater coverage of the dark grey areas, compared to Figure 12.2.

TABLE 12.3
Parliament Seats in Selangor: GE-13 and GE-14 Results

Party	GE-13			GE-14		
	No. of Seats Contested	No. of Seats Won	Average Victory Margin	No. of Seats Contested	No. of Seats Won	Average Victory Margin
PKR	11	9	18,512	11	11	39,413
DAP	4	4	36,091	4	4	75,520
PAN				5	5	31,524
PPBM				2	0	
UMNO	10	4	1,786	9	2	1,822
MIC	5	1	3,414	4	0	
MCA	7	0		8	0	
Gerakan				1	0	
PAS	7	4	14,686	20	0	

TABLE 12.4
Selangor State Assembly Seats: GE-13 and GE-14 Results

Party	GE-13			GE-14		
	No. of Seats Contested	No. of Seats Won	Average Victory Margin	No. of Seats Contested	No. of Seats Won	Average Victory Margin
PKR	21	14	7,711	27	27	14,401
DAP	15	15	13,311	14	14	26,461
PAN				7	5	11,224
PPBM				8	5	5,653
UMNO	35	12	2,259	35	4	1,488
MIC/MCA/Gerakan	21	0		21	0	
PAS	20	15	5,210	47	1	1,677

Northern Selangor went from a BN-carpeted territory to a mosaic of BN and PH, with both being the primary adversary as well. PAS continues to struggle in the rural, Malay-majority areas. Its base proved loyal, even in the face of certain defeat in urban seats, to the point that PAS beat BN to second place in Kapar, Sungai Buloh, Kota Raja and Bangi. These results also derive from the further pro-PH swing of non-Malay voters. Indeed, PAS won more votes than the BN component parties in Chinese-supermajority (more than 60 per cent Chinese) areas of Teratai (Gerakan) and Balakong (MCA). Nevertheless, GE-14 decidedly shows that the party, isolated from a broad-based coalition, has negligible chance of securing majority support, nor even of benefiting from vote-splitting in multicornered scenarios. The calculus

FIGURE 12.6
Selangor: Malay Share of Voters; Winner and Second Place (GE-14)

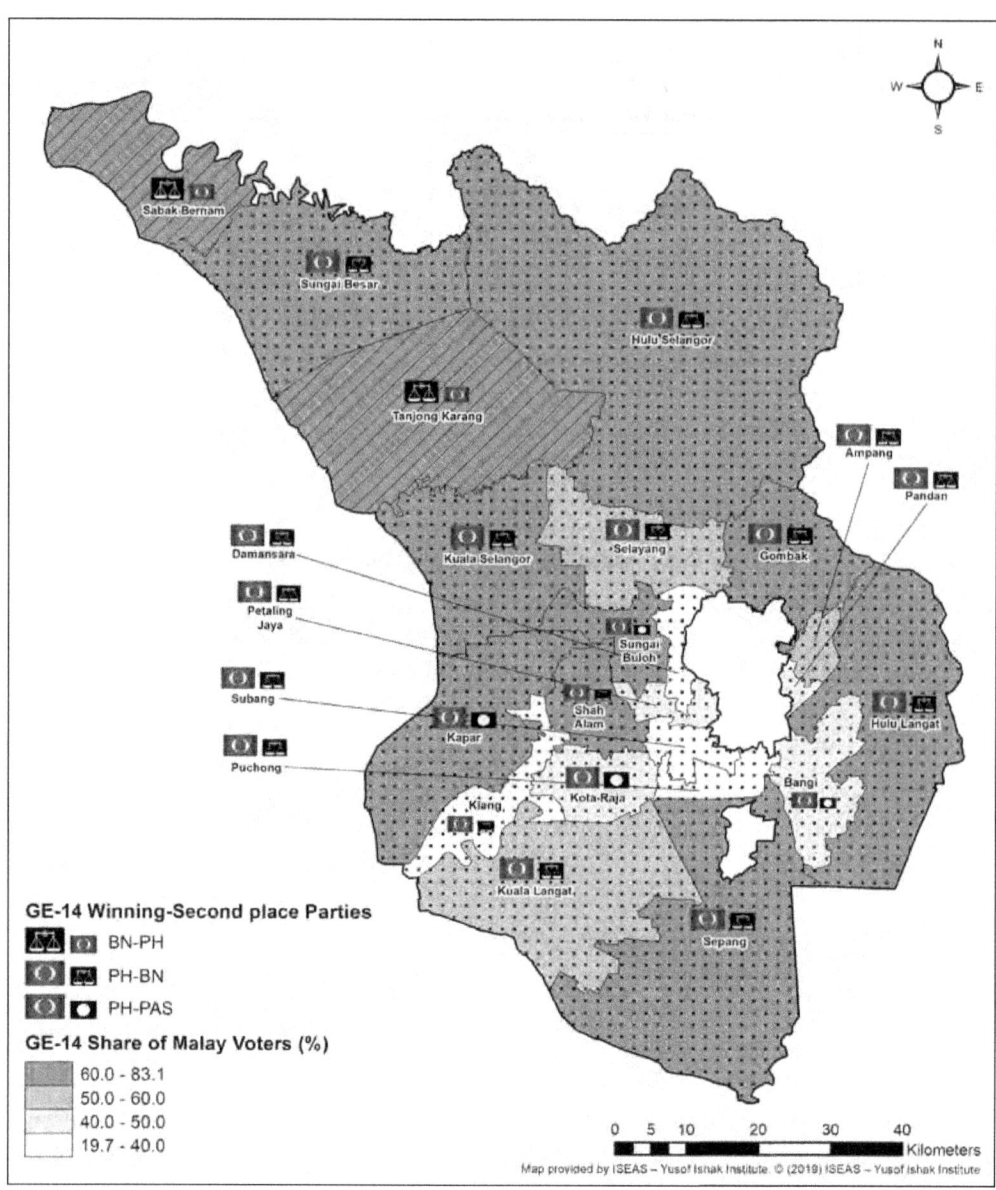

GE-14 Winning-Second place Parties

BN-PH

PH-BN

PH-PAS

GE-14 Share of Malay Voters (%)

60.0 - 83.1
50.0 - 60.0
40.0 - 50.0
19.7 - 40.0

Map provided by ISEAS – Yusof Ishak Institute. © (2019) ISEAS – Yusof Ishak Institute

of Selangor's demographics, and parochialism of PAS' platform, have reduced its presence to the margins.

Ethnic gerrymandering, seemingly designed for BN's advantage, was emphatically negated by Selangorians' rejection of UMNO. In fact, PAS outdid BN in two of the most gerrymandered parliament seats, Kapar and Sungai Buloh. Curiously, BN maintained the allocation of these seats to MIC, even after transmuting them into

Malay supermajorities; which had elicited some expectations that UMNO might contest. Whether this is due to maintaining UMNO-MIC ties or UMNO's lack of confidence is difficult to ascertain, but it is clear that any UMNO candidate would have fallen. Concerns over PH's reduced majorities or even losses, due to the three-cornered fights and redelineation, were utterly confounded.[28]

Ethnic and Youth Patterns

Selangor, like Malaysia, voted in a manner signalling an openness to new political alignments—specifically, to alternatives to the UMNO-BN mode of ethnic parties and its brand of ethnic politics. It is premature to declare an end to ethnic politics; indeed, voting patterns, and the importance of Mahathir's assurance of safeguarding bumiputra special interests, demonstrate the continuing salience of ethnicity in politics, albeit within new partisan and coalitional configurations. Ethnicity and urbanity showed marked correspondence with support for PH. Rejection of UMNO-BN was broad-based, with non-Malay voters overwhelmingly voting against the Najib administration, but Malay voters also significantly registered their disaffection. The Malay vote was, as expected, most decisive.

The preponderant result in the three-way split in Selangor, with PH holding its ground in Malay-majority areas and PAS taking votes from UMNO, was UMNO's collapse and BN's decimation. On the whole, the Malay vote in Selangor was estimated to be split 40 per cent for PH, 40 per cent for BN and 18 per cent for PAS.[29] Early and postal votes constitute just under 2 per cent of all votes cast in both GE-13 and GE-14, but provide insight to the state of Malay establishment support for UMNO, given that they are predominantly police and military personnel. The vote shares mirror UMNO's crisis of confidence. In GE-13, BN secured 77.2 per cent of early and postal votes, while Pakatan Rakyat mustered only 20.6 per cent; in GE-14, BN's share fell to 49.8 per cent, while PH garnered 25.7 per cent and PAS took 24.3 per cent.

A statistical snapshot of parliamentary seat results shows higher shares of Malay voters still corresponding with higher vote shares for BN, but the overall levels were drastically reduced between GE-13 and GE-14 (Figure 12.7).[30] Both UMNO wins, in Tanjong Karang and Sabak Bernam, have among the highest proportions of Malay voters. PH's Malay support was broadly retained across GE-13 and GE-14 (Figure 12.8). Interestingly, PH won overwhelmingly, and substantially above the predicted proportion, in Gombak (Azmin Ali) and Shah Alam (Khalid Samad), two parliamentary constituencies with very large Malay majorities, substantial PAS presence, and prominent Malay incumbents. These results suggest that the Malay electorate held a particular affinity for non-UMNO Malay leaders. Chinese voter presence corresponded with strong support for Pakatan in GE-13 and GE-14, with a higher propensity in the latter (Figure 12.9).

To what extent did young voters drive change? Malaysia's youth have played significant roles in energizing and engendering societal and democratic change, but questions remained over the impacts of BN's overtures to young voters,

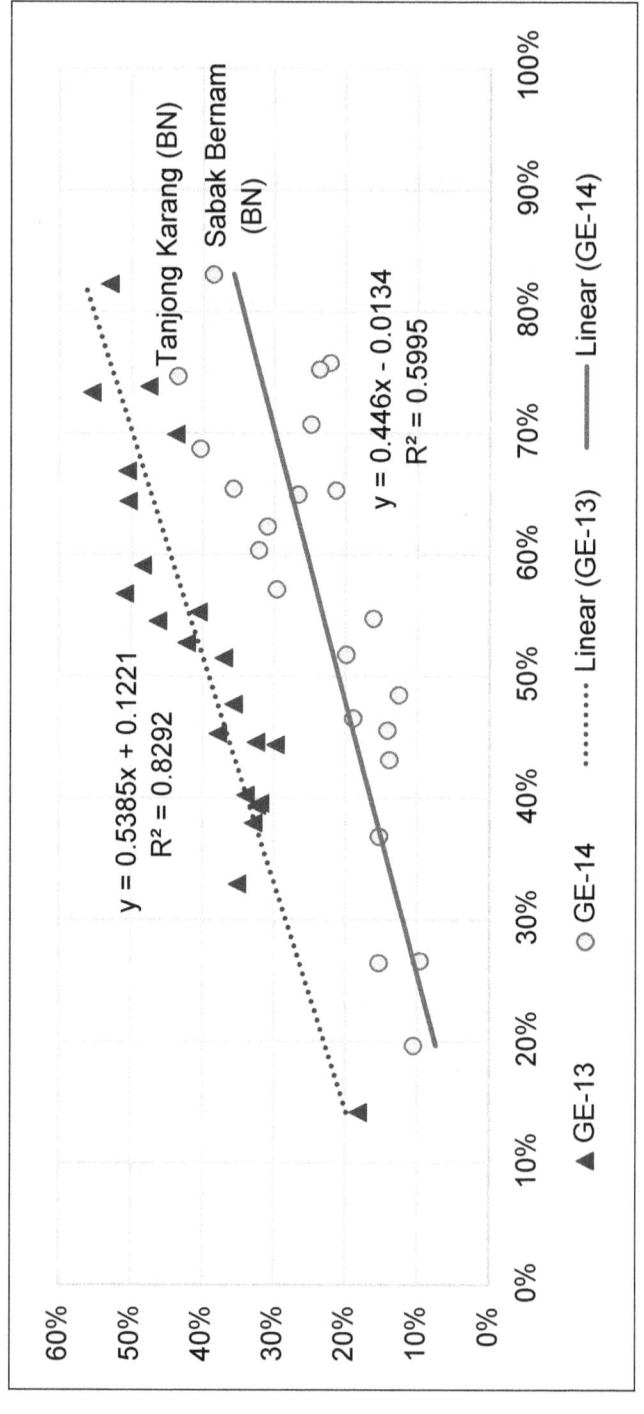

FIGURE 12.7
Selangor Parliamentary Seats (GE-13 and GE-14): Malay per cent of Registered Voters (Horizontal Axis) and BN per cent of Votes (Vertical Axis); Notable Wins

FIGURE 12.8
Selangor Parliamentary Seats (GE-13 and GE-14): Malay per cent of Registered Voters (Horizontal Axis) and Pakatan per cent of Votes (Vertical Axis); Notable Wins

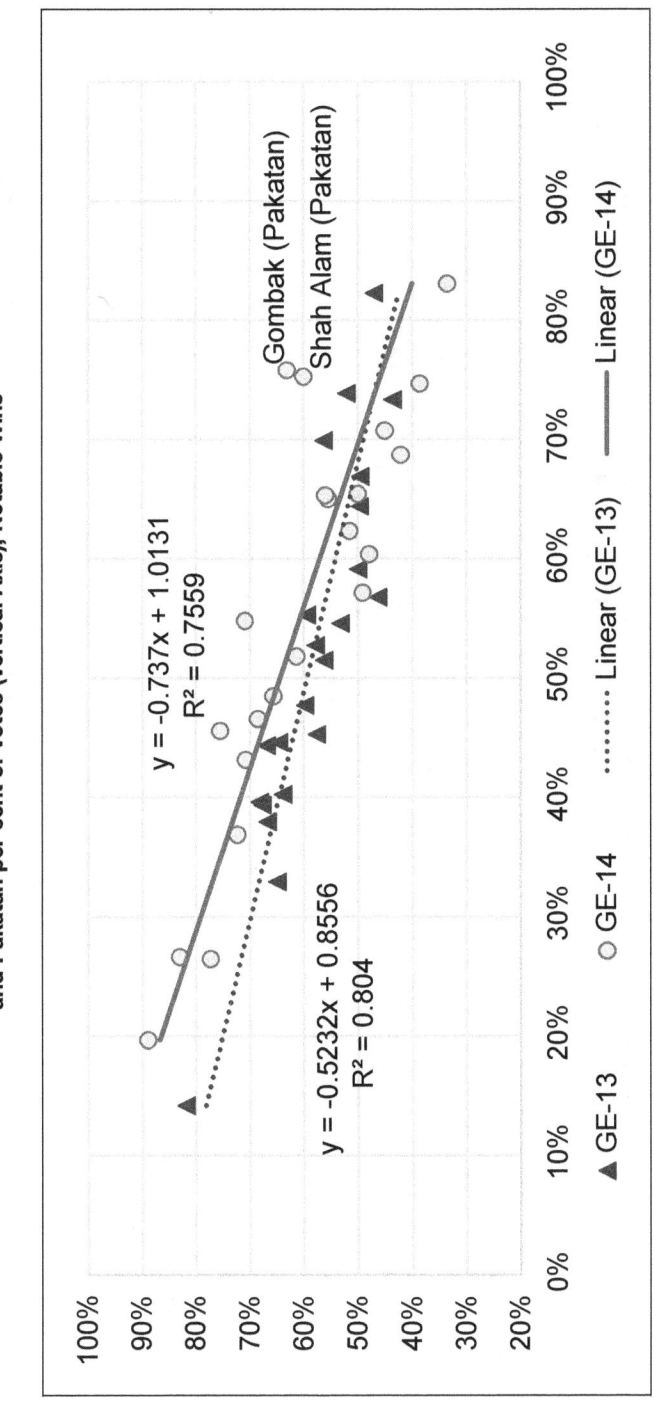

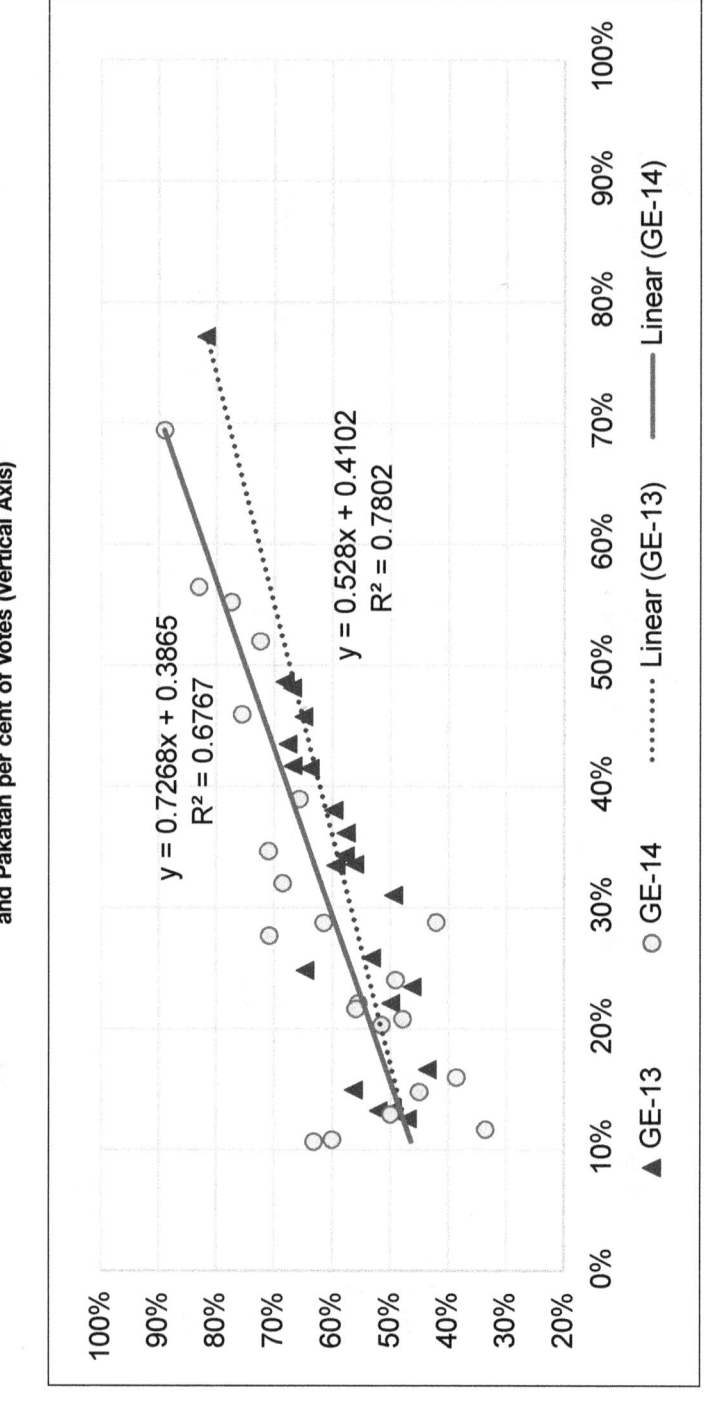

FIGURE 12.9
Selangor Parliamentary Seats (GE-13 and GE-14): Chinese per cent of Registered Voters (Horizontal Axis) and Pakatan per cent of Votes (Vertical Axis)

y = 0.7268x + 0.3865
R² = 0.6767

y = 0.528x + 0.4102
R² = 0.7802

▲ GE-13   ○ GE-14   ⋯⋯ Linear (GE-13)   —— Linear (GE-14)

particularly through the TN50 initiative and its public engagement, as well as various campaign promises targeted at young adult concerns, would let BN reel back some voters. Voting patterns by age are difficult to examine empirically. There are no concentrations of age groups in constituencies that allow for analyses at this level, unlike ethnic composition where there are distinct variations. However, the mechanism for voting provides material to make some broad observations. Voting centres—typically schools—that cater to large numbers of voters sort voters into streams (*saluran*) based on age (specifically the identity card that numerically starts with year of birth). Each *saluran* corresponds with one ballot box for parliament and another for the state seat. *Saluran 1* voters are older than *saluran 2* voters, and so on. Voting data based on *salurans* in Kuala Selangor reflect popularity of UMNO among older voters (*saluran 1*), but falling support for UMNO and rising support for PH among younger voters, in both GE-13 and GE-14 (Figures 12.10 and 12.11).[31] These data exclude voting centres with 1–2 *salurans*. Notably, for GE-14, younger voters are slightly more inclined to choose PAS over UMNO.

The overarching question remains: was PH's caution warranted, or was the writing of BN's demise already on the wall? Did PH enjoy a late surge? The GE-14 run-up and results suggest elements of truth to both. Sentiments were mounting against BN and in favour of PH, partially captured in surveys but also largely missed. Moreover, sentiments do not equal votes. Mounting discontent, anti-UMNO sentiment was observed, but underestimated. The unprecedented circumstances of these elections also posed challenges to attempts to appraise the situation. Swing voters, confronted with the choice of a scandal-tainted regime and a newly cobbled but increasingly credible alternative, were understandably discreet or unwilling to reveal intent—compounded by the existence of a three-way choice.

Evidence points to PH gaining momentum throughout early 2018, in Selangor and Peninsular Malaysia more broadly, and surging during ten-day campaign period, probably more acutely among younger voters. The Mahathir effect is impossible both to deny and to quantify. Among Shah Alam voters, that PH carried all *saluran 1* (senior) voters can be taken as a reflection of Mahathir's impact—given his greater stature among Malaysians with recollection of Malaysia's progress under his previous administration.[32] Mahathir's presence at *ceramahs* also clearly boosted turnout.[33] At the same time, the prospect of UMNO gaining at PH's and PAS' expense may also have been exaggerated. In late 2017, a tide of anti-UMNO rhetoric could be observed in *Harakah*, the party's newspaper.[34] On the whole, the election results also show PAS' base holding steady, neither crossing to PH nor UMNO. We may also surmise that a sizeable portion of Malay protest votes against UMNO went to PAS.

Was PAS a factor in the electoral outcome? Mathematically, the third party/ coalition was inconsequential, although politically, PAS' decision to contest widely influenced election discourses. For parliament seats, PH won with less than 50 per cent of votes only in four seats, and among these the split between UMNO and PAS was rather even. Hence, in simulating shifts of votes from PAS to UMNO, it is difficult to envisage any significantly different outcomes. A 10 per cent shift of PAS votes to UMNO would change the result—i.e. UMNO winning instead of PH—in

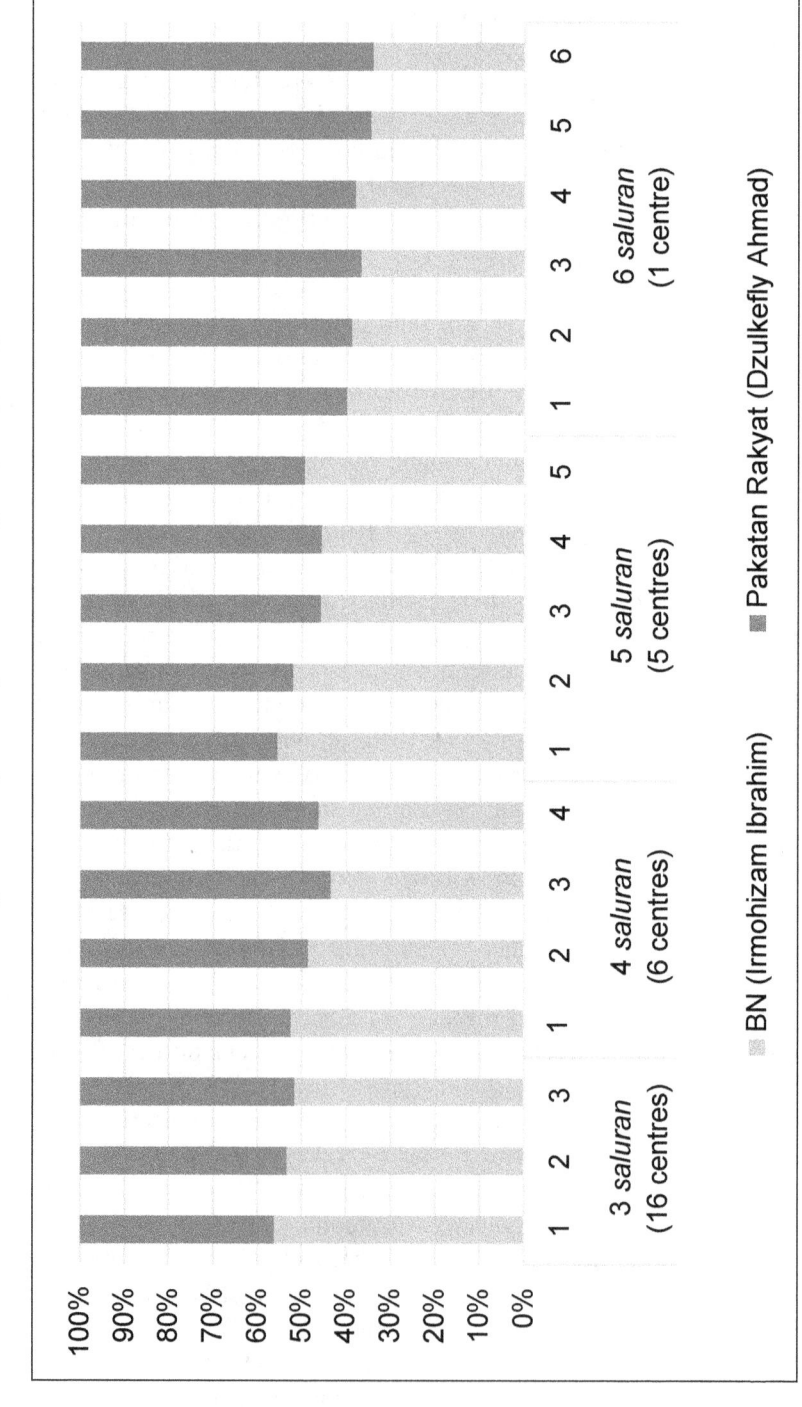

FIGURE 12.10
Kuala Selangor: Votes by *Saluran*, Older to Younger Voters (GE-13)

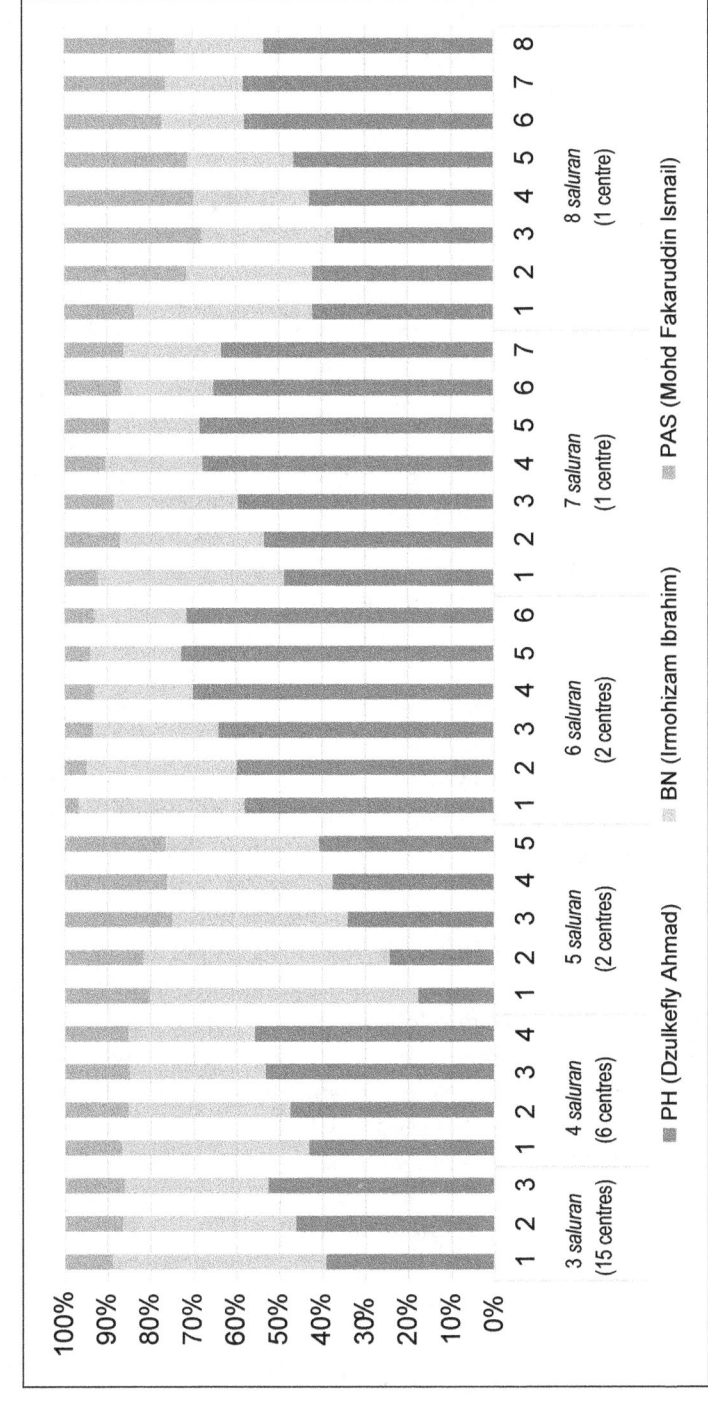

FIGURE 12.11
Kuala Selangor: Votes by *Saluran*, Older to Younger Voters (GE-14)

only one seat, Sungai Besar. In the state assembly, PH won with less than 50 per cent votes in eleven seats. A 10 per cent shift of votes from PAS to UMNO would deliver an UMNO victory in one seat (Sabak), and 30–40 per cent and 40–50 per cent shifts would exert the same effect in, respectively, two seats (Morib, Jeram), and one seat (Permatang). In the other seven seats, UMNO would require more than half of PAS voters to switch.

CONCLUSION

In the run-up to GE-14, three-cornered contests and widespread gerrymandering in Selangor injected some uncertainty to Pakatan's defence, although the incumbent coalition held various advantages that generated expectations that it would comfortably, but not overwhelmingly, retain the majority of seats. The electorate produced a tri-polar outcome. PH enjoyed landslide wins and a new sweep of parliament and state seats; UMNO clung on to a few, while PAS was nearly wiped out. PH bountifully harvested the fruits of its track record and popular policies, coupled with a groundswell of anti-BN, anti-UMNO sentiment. Barisan Nasional's punch proved feeble; gerrymandered borders could not overcome its glaring weaknesses and damaged brand. PAS' base held ground and it drew Malay votes away from UMNO, but its support among all others totally crumbled.

A few implications of GE-14 are worth noting. PH Selangor has enhanced its presence in federal government. Out of twenty-seven Cabinet portfolios, eight Selangor MPs hold ministerial positions (Health; Territories; Economic Affairs; Housing and Local Government; Communications and Multimedia; Defence; Water, Land and Natural Resources; Women, Family and Community Development (who is jointly deputy prime minister)). Additionally, three are deputy ministers (International Trade and Industry; Rural Development; Law). Selangor's over-representation markedly contrasts with the BN's Cabinet profile, but may require rebalancing in future towards more proportionately representing the federation.

PH has a firm grip on Selangor, and PKR in particular, has consolidated the state as its home base, although it will be difficult to replicate the GE-14 landslide of fifty-one out of fifty-six state legislature seats. The Malay ground will continue to be decisive, but it remains to be seen how it will move, between PH, UMNO and PAS. In view of their capacity to shift allegiance in the past and increasing expectations of government, Selangor's Chinese and Indian voters' support for PH also cannot be taken for granted, especially to the heights of GE-14. In a string of SLA by-elections between July and August 2018, triggered by untimely deaths of just-elected representatives, PH held its ground, albeit with concerns over declining popularity among Malay voters. Notably, PKR contested against a de facto UMNO-PAS alliance in Sungai Kandis and Seri Setia, while DAP went head-to-head with MCA in Balakong. A few independents entered the fray, but the opposition did poorly despite the effectively two-cornered fight scenarios. However, UMNO reclaimed the Semenyih seat in a March 2019 by-election, the third in series of momentum-building wins on the Peninsula.

Much will ride on PH's governance of Selangor and the coalition's cohesion in the state. The appointment of Amirudin Shari as Chief Minister mirrors power dynamics—specifically, Azmin's influence—within PKR. This configuration will likely spur factional dynamics in PKR, and may pose challenges for coalition maintenance and inter-party relations, especially with Selangor's proximity to the centre of power in Malaysia. State-federal relations are also in some process of resettlement, particularly in terms of social policy duplication, and PH's administration will need to exercise internal vigilance, in the face of an extremely weak opposition. Selangor's political future thus holds out plenty of continuity, but GE-14 has surely changed the state, and Malaysia as a nation, in ways that will unfold through the decades to come.

Notes

1. Current urbanization statistics are difficult to find. In the 2010 Census, Selangor's urban population constituted 91.4 per cent of the total, slightly more than Penang (90.8 per cent), and well above the national average (71.0 per cent) ("Population Distribution and Basic Demographic Characteristic Report 2010", Department of Statistics, https://www.dosm.gov.my/v1/index.php?r=column/cthemeByCat&cat=117&bul_id= MDMxdHZjWTk1SjFzTzNkRXYzcVZjdz09&menu_id=L0pheU43NWJwRWVSZklWdz Q4TlhUUT09 (accessed 21 January 2019). These statistics have presumably all move upward, and there is little reason to doubt that Selangor remains the most urbanized state.
2. BN's share of seats increased from 70.6 per cent to 84.4 per cent from 1990 to 1995, while correspondingly its popular vote share rose from 53.4 per cent to 65.2 per cent. Comparing 1999 to 2004, BN's popular barely changed, from 63.9 per cent to 63.8 per cent, but the share of seats catapulted from 76.7 per cent to 90.4 per cent (Mohammad Redzuan 2018).
3. The author conducted fieldwork in Selangor over the periods 4–9 December 2017, 11–14 April 2018 and 2–10 May 2018.
4. The author gratefully acknowledges electoral data provided by Tindak Malaysia.
5. In sustaining or exacerbating malapportionment, many redrawn borders contravened constitutional requirements that the number of electors in constituencies "ought to be approximately equal" and that inconveniences and maintenance of local ties should be taken into account (Ooi 2018).
6. 1MDB was deemed not resonant on the ground, where bread-and-butter issues dominated voters' minds, according to UMNO's Irmohizam Ibrahim, MP for Selangor (2013–18) (Author's interview, 8 December 2017). The BN's manifesto, under the slogan "with BN for a greater Malaysia", reduced corruption to a local government problem that could be solved through online procurement.
7. Author's interview with Azmin Ali, 11 April 2018.
8. Author's interview with Juwairiyah Zulkifli, 4 May 2018. Although she was a literal last-minute stand-in for PKR's original candidate for Bukit Melawati, who was disqualified for officially residing in Selangor, Juwairiyah had begun electoral engagement two years prior.
9. Author's interview with Ong Kian Ming, 11 April 2018.
10. Author's interview with Yin Shao Loong, 5 December 2017.
11. Author's interview with Dzulkefly Ahmad, 7 December 2017.

12. Author's interview with Khalid Samad, 5 December 2017.

13. Author's interviews with Tan Seng Keat, Merdeka Center, 8 December 2017; Akmal Nasir, INVOKE, 4 December 2017.

14. Author's interview with Ong Kian Ming, 11 April 2018.

15. Author's interviews with Khalid Samad, 10 May 2018; Saari Sungib, 7 May 2018.

16. Author's interview with Saari Sungib, 7 May 2018. Specifically, there was a 5 percentage point (2,700–2,800 voters) increase in Malay voters (making it the state with the highest share of Malay voters, 86.3 per cent), and an equivalent drop in Chinese voters. Saari had won in GE-13 by a 7 percentage point margin (2,900 votes). The author thanks Elvin Ong for helpful research inputs and joint fieldwork during the GE-14 campaign period.

17. Author's interview with Mohd Fakaruddin Ismail, PAS candidate for Kuala Selangor, 4 May 2018.

18. Author's interview with Xavier Jayakumar, 11 April 2018.

19. Author's interview with Datuk Abdul Halid, Ketua Kampung Rantau Panjang and MP candidate election campaign representative (*wakil calon*), 8 May 2018.

20. UMNO members even shared privately that they were willing to vote against their party (author's interviews with Dzulkefly Ahmad and campaign director M. Sivabalan in Kuala Selangor, 13 April 2018).

21. According to the Malaysian Communications and Multimedia Commission (MCMC), Malaysia's broadband penetration was 103.6 per 100 inhabitants in the first quarter of 2017. Kuala Lumpur registered a rate of 200.2. Among Malaysia's states, Johor led with 138.0, followed by Selangor, at 124.3 https://www.mcmc.gov.my/skmmgovmy/media/General/pdf/1Q17-facts-figures.pdf (accessed 21 January 2019).

22. Author's interview with Faisal Rahman, GGF2 (Gerak Generasi Dua Kampung FELDA Bukit Cherakah, or FELDA Bukit Cherakah second-generation movement), 7 May 2018.

23. Author's interview with Xavier Jeyakumar, PH Selangor's election director, 11 April 2018.

24. Author's interview with Khalid Samad, 3 May 2018.

25. In the four constituencies where the author conducted fieldwork, BN's campaigns operated Facebook pages but with rather scant information. In contrast, PH's campaigns reported more reliably on candidate itineraries, and were generally more energized and substantial.

26. The PAS candidate for Ijok resigned from a stable job to contest in GE-14, in a move described as *pengorbanan* (sacrifice). Party youth and former Chief Minister Khalid Ibrahim were influential in the decision (Author's interview with Jefri Mejan, 4 May 2018).

27. Author's interview with Daroyah Alwi, PH candidate for Sementa, 5 May 2018.

28. Shah Alam's PH campaign expected to hold the seat by a 2,000–4,000 margin, accounting for the outward relocation of 10,000 PH-leaning voters. As in many places, Khalid Samad's eventual victory by almost 34,000 was totally unexpected (Author's interview with Khalid Samad, 10 May 2018).

29. Personal correspondence with Ibrahim Suffian, Merdeka Center's executive director.

30. Saravanamuttu (2015) conducts a similar exercise for GE-13 at the national level, and finds marked ethnic voting patterns, specifically in terms of Malay preference for UMNO and Chinese preference for DAP.

31. We should note that voters are not evenly streamed. The number of voters assigned to

saluran 1 is considerably smaller than the other *salurans* (whose numbers are fairly even), accounting for the slower pace of elderly voters.

32. Author's interview with Khalid Samad, 10 May 2018.
33. Author's interviews with C. David Selvam, Division Chairman, PKR Kuala Selangor and PH Ijok candidate representative, 13 April 2018, 4 May 2018, and with PH Ijok candidate Idris Ahmad, 7 May 2018.
34. Author's interview with Saifuddin Abdullah, PH chief secretary, 5 December 2017.

References

Department of Statistics. 2017. *Household Income and Basic Amenities Survey Report 2016*. Putrajaya: Department of Statistics.

Edge Malaysia, The. 2018. "What New Polls Borders Mean for Selangor". 9 April 2018.

Institut Darul Ehsan (IDE). 2018a. "GE-14: Glimpse of Victory for Pakatan Harapan in Selangor", 5 May 2018. https://www.ideselangor.org/index.php/penyelidikan-footer/item/415-ge14-glimpse-of-victory-for-pakatan-harapan-in-selangor.

———. 2018b. "PRU 14: Pakatan Harapan Dijangka Menang Besar di Selangor" [GE-14: Pakatan Harapan Expected to Win Big in Selangor], 5 May 2018. https://www.ideselangor.org/index.php/penyelidikan-footer/item/414-pru-14-ph-menang-besar-selangor.

INVOKE. 2018. "INVOKE GE-14 Prediction", Presentation at INVOKE GE-14 Prediction forum, Kuala Lumpur, 9 March 2018.

Lee, Hwok-Aun. 2018. "Selangor in GE-14: The Big Prize Fight up in the Air". *ISEAS Perspective, no. 2018/16*, 19 March 2018.

Malaysia. 2010. *Federal Constitution of Malaysia*. Kuala Lumpur: Government of Malaysia.

Malaysiakini. 2018. "Harapan, PAS to Lose Seven Selangor Seats with New EC Borders", 28 March 2018.

Merdeka Center. 2017. "National Public Opinion Survey on Economic Hardship Indicators", press release, November 2017. http://merdeka.org/v4/index.php/downloads/category/2-researches?download=181:nov-2017-economic-hardship-indicators.

———. 2018a. "Malaysia General Elections XIV Outlook: Prospects and Outcome". 26 April 2018. http://merdeka.org/v4/index.php/downloads/category/2-researches?download=183:ge14-26042018-survey-findings-release-27042018.

———. 2018b. "Malaysia General Elections XIV Outlook: Prospects and Outcome II". 2 May 2018. http://merdeka.org/v4/index.php/downloads/category/2-researches?download=184:ge14-02052018-presentation-final-03052018.

———. 2018c. "Malaysia General Elections XIV Outlook: Prospects and Outcome III". 8 May 2018. http://merdeka.org/v4/index.php/downloads/category/2-researches?download=186:ge14-08052018-presentation-final.

Mohammad Redzuan Othman. 2018. "Sidang Media Proses Persempadanan & Pilihan Raya Umum ke 14" [Media Conference on Redelineation and the 14th General Elections], Institute Darul Ehsan, 3 January 2018. https://www.ideselangor.org/index.php/berita-footer/item/384-proses-persempadanan-pilihan-raya-ke-14.

Ong Kian Ming. 2017. "The Battle for Selangor in GE-14 (Part 1)". Media Statement, 26 September 2017. http://ongkianming.com/2017/09/26/media-statement-the-battle-for-selangor-in-ge14-part-1/.

Ooi Kok Hin. 2018. "How Malaysia's Election is Being Rigged". *New Naratif*, 19 March 2018. https://newnaratif.com/research/malaysias-election-rigged/.

Saravanamuttu, Johan. 2015. "Power Sharing Politics and the Electoral Impasse in GE-13". In *Coalitions in Collision: Malaysia's 13th General Election,* edited by Johan Saravanamuttu, Lee Hock Guan and Mohamed Nawab Mohamed Osman. Singapore: Institute of Southeast Asian Studies.

13

GE-14 IN JOHOR
Shock or Just Awe?

Francis E. Hutchinson

INTRODUCTION

Johor, Sabah and Sarawak were traditionally seen as Barisan Nasional's "safe deposits", consistently delivering substantial numbers of parliamentarians and solid state-level majorities to the ruling coalition. Conventional wisdom held that should one or more of these fall, BN's hold on power would be seriously compromised. All three states were lost by BN in the aftermath of GE-14—albeit in different ways.

This chapter, for its part, will focus on Johor. With some 3.7 million citizens and residents, it is Malaysia's third largest state and has the second largest number of parliamentarians. Johor is ethnically mixed as—in addition to its bumiputra majority of 60 per cent—it has substantial numbers of Chinese and Indian voters, comprising 33 and 7 per cent of the state's citizens respectively (DOS 2017).[1]

Johor's level of urbanization of 72 per cent closely mirrors the national average, meaning that many look to it as a bell-wether for national voting trends (DOS 2013). Of the state's twenty-six parliamentary constituencies, nine are urban or semi-urban and ethnically mixed. Many of these are in and around Johor Bahru and—due to long-established manufacturing operations as well as the more recent Iskandar Malaysia special economic zone—are relatively well-off. Conversely, the remaining seventeen constituencies are rural and mostly Malay-majority, grouped in the state's centre or on its coasts.

Johor's unique historical development, due to its lineage of dynamic traditional rulers, early exposure to commodity exports, and multiethnic character make the state important to Barisan Nasional (BN). The United Malays National Organization (UMNO) was founded in Johor in 1946, and the state produced a disproportionate number of the party's leaders and Cabinet members in the immediate post-independence period. For the Malaysian Chinese Association (MCA), the state's large Chinese population and economic importance have meant nearly all of the party's leaders have a connection with Johor, either living there or helming its state branch during their political careers.

Indeed, from the first elections in 1959 until 2013, BN never yielded more than one parliamentary seat or a handful of state seats to the opposition. And, relative to the national average, levels of support for BN in the state remained considerably higher. However, a rather less stellar performance in GE-13—along with unprecedented changes in the country's political context—heralded the beginning of a transformation.

In 2013, five large parliamentary seats in urban areas were lost to the opposition coalition Pakatan Rakyat (PR), as were eighteen state seats. In 2016, one parliamentarian and one state assembly-person crossed the floor to join the newly created Pakatan Harapan (PH). The loss of the second meant that BN was deprived of its two-thirds majority in the state legislature for the first time.

In the run-up to GE-14 in Johor, PH was expected to retain its urban seats and BN looked vulnerable in semi-urban areas as well as some rural seats in the north. Despite this, the prevailing consensus was that BN would retain the state due to the large number of rural Malay-majority seats. This core of electoral support would be shored up by the 2016–18 parliamentary redelineation exercise, which was thought to safeguard certain vulnerable constituencies and tip a number of others. This conservative outlook was bolstered by surveys which indicated that, despite a majority of non-Malay voters supporting the opposition, a majority of Malay voters was still undecided.

In the end, PH won decisively in Johor. This chapter will seek to understand the reasons underlying this unexpected result, and probe whether PH's victory had been widely foreshadowed or was, in contrast, the result of a late surge in support. In order to do this, it will draw on a variety of sources, including: data on parliamentary constituencies and electoral results; newspaper coverage of the elections and polling data; and interviews and personal observations gathered during ten field visits to key constituencies in Johor over the course of 2017 and 2018.

Following this introduction, the second section will analyse the reasons underlying BN's impressive performance in Johor from independence up until 2013. The third section will analyse key dynamics in the run-up to GE-14, including the campaigns, the candidates, and available survey data on voter intentions. The subsequent section will analyse the electoral results and draw out key implications. The fifth and final section will relate these findings back to the question of whether PH's victory was foreseeable or the result of a last-minute surge.

BARISAN NASIONAL IN JOHOR (1959–2013)

Although BN performed well in electoral terms across Malaysia from 1959 until GE-14, its track record in Johor has been outstanding. There are two groups of reasons for this. The first includes three structural factors that favoured the erstwhile ruling coalition across Malaysia, but that worked particularly well in Johor. The second group comprises three dynamics that are unique to the southern state.[2]

Structural Factors

Regarding the generalized structural factors, the first concerns BN's consociational model of politics.[3] Bringing together UMNO, MCA, the Malaysian Indian Congress (MIC), as well as a number of smaller parties, BN was able to capitalize on several advantages. By pooling candidates and then parcelling out constituencies among component parties, the coalition was frequently able to match the ethnicity of candidates with the majority community in each seat. In cases where they did not, BN was still able to persuade a majority to vote across communal lines for their local representative, given that their interests were still represented within the coalition (Horowitz 1993).

Johor's heterogeneous population lent itself well to this model of campaigning, which the various BN component parties put in place in the late 1950s and used consistently since then. Under this arrangement, UMNO was apportioned roughly two-thirds of Johor's parliamentary seats and about 60 per cent of its state seats. These constituencies were largely in rural areas, but also included a number of larger, urban seats in central Johor Bahru. The MCA was awarded the second largest number of seats, usually in urban and Chinese-majority areas, and the smaller MIC and Gerakan were allocated one or two "safe" seats. These arrangements were very stable and tended to change only when parliamentary constituencies were redrawn. Beyond pooling resources, this framework also allowed individual candidates to be fielded in the same constituencies again and again, building up their grassroots networks.

The second structural factor that aided BN's electoral fortunes was mal-apportionment. Due to a pliant Electoral Commission (EC), caps on the degree to which the size of parliamentary and state seats could vary were lifted. Consequently, the number of underpopulated rural, Malay-majority seats in the country increased in number and importance (Saravanamuttu 2016).

Johor was no exception and, its large rural, Malay-majority hinterland was awarded more seats at the expense of urban areas, which tended to be more ethnically mixed. Consequently, eight out of the state's nine urban and semi-urban seats were overpopulated and underrepresented. Conversely, eleven out of its seventeen rural and Malay-majority seats were underpopulated and overrepresented. Within BN, this imbalance worked to UMNO's benefit, as it was allocated the lion's share of overrepresented rural seats (Hutchinson 2018a, p. 11). This overrepresentation of rural seats also increased Johor's electoral importance. Despite having some 2.5 million fewer people than Selangor, it came to have twenty-six parliamentary constituencies versus the latter state's twenty-two.

The third factor favouring BN was Malaysia's first-past-the-post (FPTP) parliamentary system. Common to many Westminsterial systems, this mechanism magnifies electoral victories, conferring parliamentary majorities far in excess of the popular vote. Thus, by way of example, in 2004, BN obtained 79.6 per cent of the popular vote in Johor and 100 per cent of its parliamentary seats. In 2008, its lower level of popular support of 65.3 still translated into 96 per cent of seats. And, in 2013, the corresponding figures were 54.9 and 80.8 per cent, respectively.

Figures 13.1 and 13.2 set out the proportion of BN's share of parliamentary and state assembly seats in Johor from 1959 to 2013. With regard to parliamentary seats, the ruling coalition secured a clean sweep in ten out of the twelve elections up until 2008. In two elections, it lost one seat to the Democratic Action Party (DAP). In 1978, this was the Kluang constituency, and in 2008, it was Bakri. In 2013, in an unprecedentedly strong showing, Pakatan Rakyat extended its holdings to five seats.

This performance is unmatched in other large peninsular states such as Selangor and Perak, which witnessed significant opposition inroads as early as 1969. Other elections which saw large national reversals for BN such as 1990, 1999, and 2008 also had a muted effect in Johor.

Barisan Nasional dominance in Johor was mirrored—albeit to a lesser degree—at the state level. In nine elections, the coalition secured more than 90 per cent of state seats in Johor. In three more elections, namely those of 1959, 1990, and 2008, the ruling coalition secured no less than 85 per cent of the total, conceding only four to six seats to the opposition. In 1969, Johor was a rare exception to the large swing against the ruling coalition, as it yielded a mere two seats to the opposition that year. In contrast, the coalition lost fourteen state seats in Selangor, twenty in Penang, and twenty-one in Perak. In 2008, another bad year for BN nationally, the opposition gained state-level majorities in Kelantan, Kedah, Penang, Perak and Selangor. In contrast, in Johor, this downturn constituted an increase from one to six state seats—out of a total of fifty-six seats in the legislative assembly. In 2013, BN began to show some vulnerability, as the opposition's holdings increased from six to eighteen.

Yet, even within the Malaysian context, this performance is rare. Figure 13.3 sets out the level of popular support for UMNO at the national level as well as for Johor from 1959 to 2013. While broadly following the national trend, with significant dips in 1969, 1990, 1999 and 2008, popular support for BN in Johor was consistently some 10 per cent higher than at the national level—at an average of 70 per cent as opposed to the national level of 60 per cent.

Johor-Specific Dynamics

Consequently, despite BN enjoying the same structural advantages in Johor as it does elsewhere in the Peninsula, there appear to be additional, localized dynamics that account for this extraordinary performance. This chapter contends that there are

FIGURE 13.1
Parliamentary Seats in Johor, 1959–2013

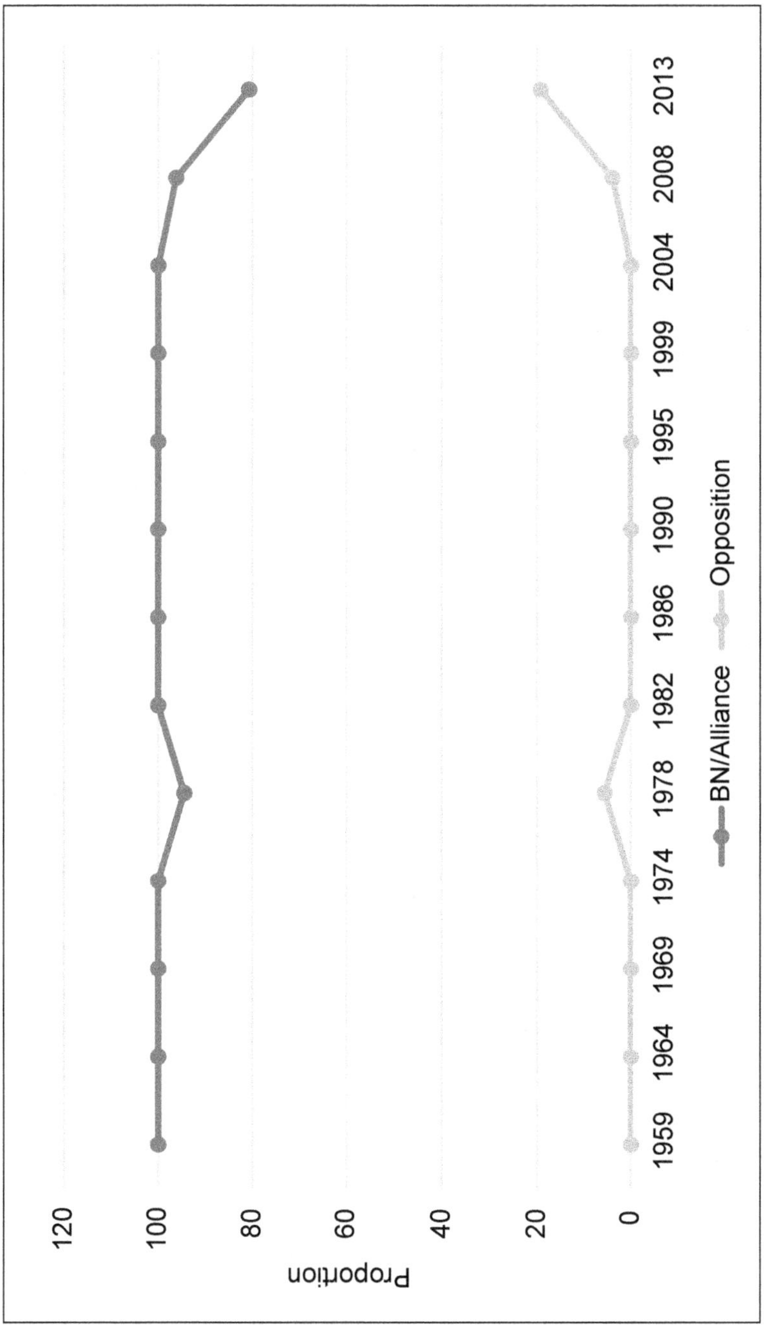

Source: NSTP (1990); Election Commission Malaysia, various years.

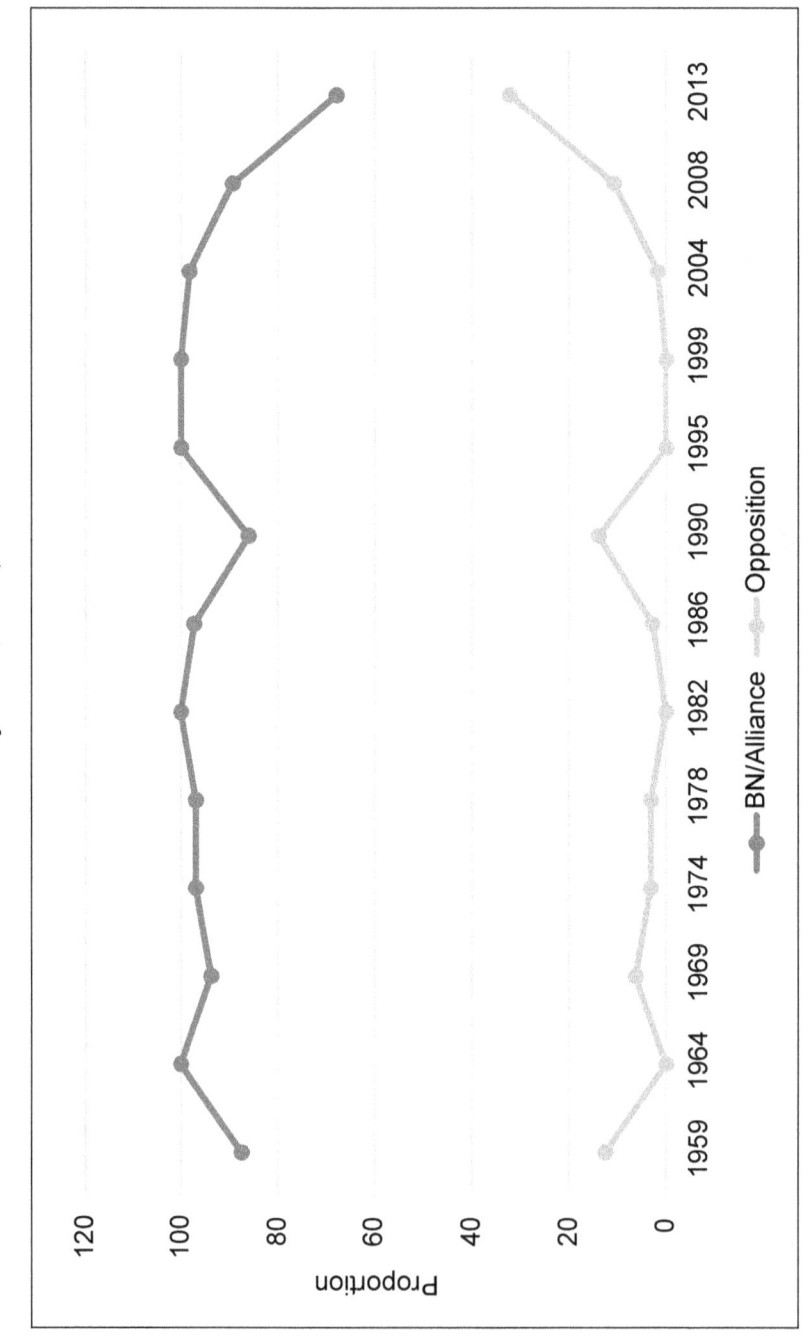

FIGURE 13.2
State Assembly Seats in Johor, 1959–2013

Source: NSTP (1990); Election Commission Malaysia, various years.

FIGURE 13.3
BN Vote Share Nationally and in Johor, 1959–2013

Source: NSTP (1990); Election Commission Malaysia, various years.

three. The first two are directly linked to the state's pattern of development during the pre-independence period, and the third is the localized outcome of a national policy implemented following independence.

The first localized dynamic is UMNO's legacy within Johor. As mentioned, the party was founded in 1946 in Johor Bahru by an eminent local personality, Onn Jaafar. Johor's export-oriented economy had allowed it to develop an expansive state structure that was staffed by a nucleus of local Malays. Its entrepreneurial traditional rulers also sought to maximize autonomy from British influence, striving to retain as much control as possible over senior leadership positions.

Following the return of the British after World War II, the ensuing rejection of the Malayan Union, and the political effervescence in its aftermath, Johor's central location between Singapore and Kuala Lumpur, its highly literate population, and its core of senior Malay bureaucrats meant that its politicians dominated Malaya's burgeoning political scene. Thus, Johorean cadres occupied a disproportionate number of leadership positions within UMNO, its Supreme Council, Youth and Women's wings, as well as the country's first Cabinet (Hutchinson 2015).

This tradition of state-building, protection of Malay rights, and public service still has relevance today.[4] Johor has among the largest, if not the largest, UMNO member bases in the country and an extensive grassroots network—particularly its women's wing (Wan Saiful 2018). This, in turn, results in higher levels of competition for leadership positions. This has been well capitalized upon, with established mechanisms for fielding candidates at the national or state level according to their attributes (Hutchinson 2018a).

The second pertains to the control of Islam. Johor's lineage of traditional rulers invested considerable resources in the religious bureaucracy and education system in the pre-independence period. And, today, the Sultan continues to exercise the prerogative to supervise religious matters and custom in the state, including: making key appointments in the Islamic bureaucracy; overseeing the religious police; licensing of preachers active in the state; and supervising religious education. This tight control on religious matters, as well as the promotion of a traditionalist version of Islam has meant that Johor has not provided a propitious context for the religious outlook promoted by the Islamic party, Parti Islam SeMalaysia (PAS) (Norshahril 2017).

This, in turn, has meant that UMNO's main rival for Malay voters has been unable to establish a foothold in the state. Despite fielding candidates in every election since 1959, PAS only won its first state seat, Senggarang, out of a total thirty-six candidacies in 2004—on a technicality. Only in 2008 and then 2013, as part of a wider coalition, did PAS obtain two and then four seats, respectively.

The third local-level dynamic pertains to the track record of the Federal Land Development Authority (FELDA) in the state. Implemented nationally from 1959 to 1990, this initiative is credited with mobilizing hundreds of thousands of poor Malay families from rural areas onto cleared land for the production of commodities, particularly oil palm. This programme was implemented very effectively in Johor, due to its vast land with agricultural potential, as well as good ties between local leaders and the programme's senior management. In addition, due to its role in selecting beneficiaries and settling land claims, UMNO came to be closely associated with the programme's roll-out (Guyot 1974).

This has translated into exceptional levels of support for UMNO and BN in FELDA settlements. In 2013, 86 per cent of voters in FELDA districts in the state voted for BN, versus 73–78 per cent in Selangor, Kedah, Melaka, Perak and Negri Sembilan; and 61–67 per cent in Kelantan, Pahang, and Terengganu (Khor 2016, p. 106). There are some eighty FELDA settlements in the central and eastern part of the state, many of which are Malay majority and overrepresented.

The GE-13 Turning Point

Yet, despite these advantageous structural factors and local dynamics, GE-13 showed that BN was vulnerable in Johor. Following the downward trend established in 2008, BN's level of popular support fell from 65 per cent that year to 54.9 per cent in 2013. In comparative terms, BN's performance in Johor was substantially better than the national average of 47.4 per cent and, indeed, the outcomes in Kuala Lumpur, Penang and Selangor, where opposition candidates garnered 64, 66.8, and 58.4 per cent of the vote, respectively (Saravanamuttu 2016, p. 227).

Notwithstanding this, GE-13 showed some important—and worrying trends—for BN's dominance in Johor. At the parliamentary level, Pakatan Rakyat retained the seat of Bakri, and won four more seats. Kluang, Gelang Patah, Kulai and Batu Pahat are all semi-urban and—with the exception of the last which has a very small Malay majority—mixed seats. The DAP accounted for four of these victories, and Parti Keadilan Rakyat (PKR) one. These victories came largely at the expense of MCA, which traditionally contested in all of these constituencies with the exception of Batu Pahat.[5]

Relative to 2008, the coalition registered lower levels of support in every single parliamentary seat. Beyond the five seats lost, BN retained a further nine seats with slim margins (defined as less than a 55 per cent majority). Of these seats, three were held by MCA, one by MIC, and five by UMNO. Five are mixed seats, with three in urban/semi-urban areas (Tebrau, Pasir Gudang, Pulai),[6] and two (Labis, Segamat) in rural areas. The other four (Ledang, Muar, Tanjong Piai and Sekijang) are Malay-majority and rural constituencies.

The pattern of a generalized drop in support for BN was also visible at the state level. In 2013, BN carried thirty-eight seats, with UMNO winning thirty-two, MIC three, MCA two, and Gerakan one seat. Of these, a total of eleven seats were won with a slim majority. Eight were Malay-majority seats held by UMNO—indicating some vulnerability in traditional supporter areas. Pakatan Rakyat, for its part, won eighteen seats—up from six in 2008. The DAP took thirteen, PAS four, and PKR one seat. These victories largely came at the cost of MCA, which lost eleven seats.

In other words, based on these trends, BN was in danger of losing the urban vote in Johor in GE-14, as the nine urban or semi-urban constituencies were either in opposition hands or had been retained with narrow majorities. In contrast, BN's key voter base was concentrated in the state's seventeen rural constituencies in the eastern and central parts of the state, most of which have Malay majorities. That said, it was notable that six of them were retained with narrow majorities. See Figure 13.4.

Following GE-13, the political context changed notably, particularly as regards the Malay vote. In 2015, Pakatan Rakyat sundered with the departure of PAS. PAS itself split later that year, with Parti Amanah Negara (Amanah) emerging as an offshoot which, in turn, joined the newly formed Pakatan Harapan. A group of senior leaders from UMNO including Mahathir Mohamad and Muhyiddin Yassin left the party (or were expelled) and formed Parti Pribumi Bersatu Malaysia (PPBM) in 2016. This latter party joined Pakatan Harapan in March 2017.

A survey of Johoreans was carried out in May–June 2017 by the ISEAS – Yusof Ishak Institute. When asked directly which party or coalition they would vote for, 34 per cent indicated that they would vote for BN, and a mere 11 per cent stated that they would vote for an opposition party or the PH coalition. Of key interest is that 27 per cent gave no response and a further 18 per cent professed to not know (Figure 13.5).

At first blush, this indicated substantial possibilities for PH, given the relatively low level of outright support for BN and the opposition's credible showing in 2013. However, when asked specifically about their feelings for the various PH parties, the responses were less favourable. Less than 20 per cent of those surveyed had a positive opinion about the coalition, and they were outnumbered by 44 per cent who had a negative perception. PH did reasonably well among Chinese respondents, with more positive ratings than negative ones. However, negative feelings were particularly marked among Malay respondents and rural-dwellers (Figure 13.6). Other questions pertaining specifically to the awareness of Amanah and PPBM indicated very low levels of support, particularly among Malay voters (Merdeka Center 2017a).

Thus, one year out from GE-14, these findings indicated that while BN was vulnerable, this did not automatically translate into support for PH or the newly founded Amanah or PPBM.

GE-14 CAMPAIGNS IN JOHOR

As with all recent elections in Malaysia, the run-up to GE-14 was long, drawn out, and punctuated by uncertainty. Nonetheless, the various coalitions began to move into pre-campaign mode from early March, when it seemed likely that the elections would be held before Ramadan.

Momentum gathered from the end of that month when the Najib administration began finalizing its preparations. On 29 March, BN's majority in the lower house approved the Election Commission's recommendations for parliamentary redelineation, which was anticipated to shore up support in a number of marginal seats. On 2 April, the BN majority also approved the Anti-Fake News Bill, which opponents feared would be used to clamp down on dissent. And, on 7 April, Parliament and most state assemblies, including Johor's, were dissolved. Nomination day was three weeks later on 28 April, followed by the elections themselves on 9 May.

FIGURE 13.4
Opposition-Held and Competitive Seats in Johor (pre-GE-14)

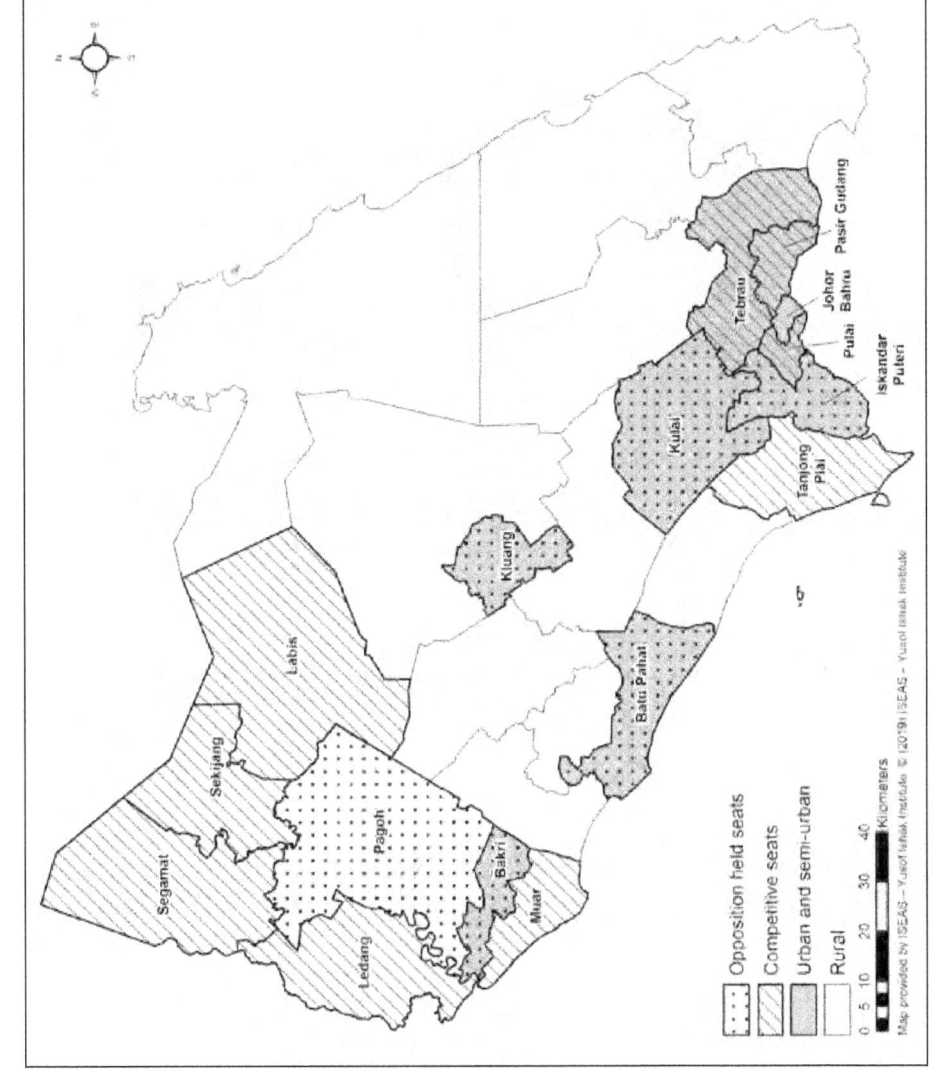

FIGURE 13.5
Parliamentary Voting Preferences in Johor, 2017

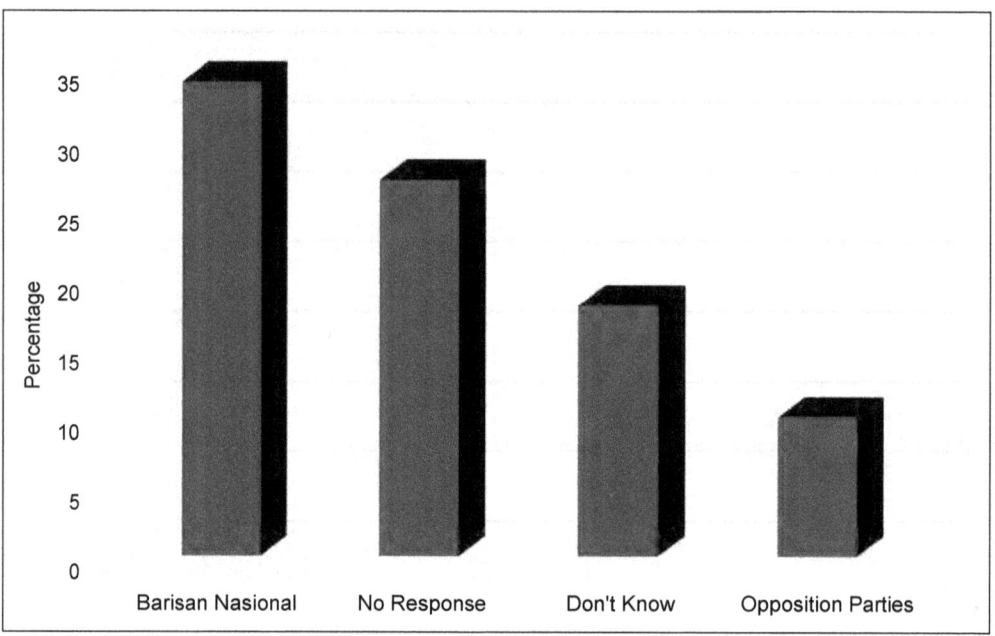

Source: Johor Opinion Survey, May 2017. N=1003.

FIGURE 13.6
Favourability towards Pakatan Harapan, 2017

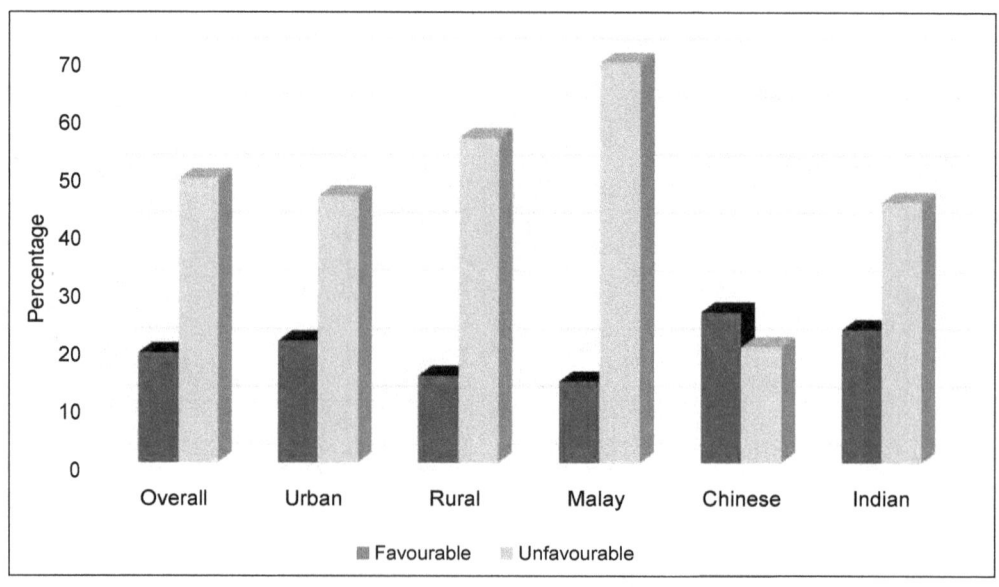

Source: Johor Opinion Survey, May 2017. N=1003.

At both the national and local levels, economic issues were paramount. A nationwide poll in November showed that 72 per cent of Malaysians felt that economic issues were the most important issue, ahead of crime or interethnic relations (Merdeka Center 2017b). A survey carried out in Johor in January 2018 showed broad agreement with this at the state level. Fifty-seven per cent of those surveyed thought the country was going in the wrong direction, with the cost of living and impact of GST, overall unfavourable economic conditions, and poor administration cited as the top issues (Merdeka Center 2018a).

Consequently, all three coalitions campaigning in Johor—BN, PH and PAS—focused on national-level issues and debates, particularly: GST and the elimination of subsidies; 1MDB and related governance issues; and housing. However, where relevant, these national-level issues were tailored to the local context, capitalizing on local-level concerns about the cost of living, affordable housing, as well as crime, as indicated by available surveys (Merdeka Center 2017b).

The next subsections will review the strategies, seat allocations, and salient candidacies of the three coalitions. Following this, it will refer to available survey data on voting intentions in the run-up to the voting.

Barisan Nasional

Barisan Nasional's campaign in Johor was well managed, capitalizing on its established tactics. One additional axis of the campaign was to leverage on the popularity of the incumbent Menteri Besar, Khaled Nordin. Originally from Muar, he was a three-term parliamentarian, and served as Deputy Minister for Higher Education under Abdullah Badawi. In 2013, Khaled relinquished his parliamentary seat of Pasir Gudang and ran in one of its state seats, Permas, subsequently assuming leadership of the state upon his victory.

During his tenure, Khaled was able to earn good marks from the electorate for able management of interreligious issues, municipal services, water supply and housing development, increasing popular support for the Johor state government from 58 per cent in 2013 to 77 per cent in mid-2017 (Merdeka Center 2014, 2017a). In January 2018, 58 per cent of respondents stated that they viewed Khaled Nordin positively, and a full 80 per cent stated that they were happy with the Johor state government (Merdeka Center 2018a).

This personal brand was well capitalized upon, through Khaled's sizeable public relations team, headed by a journalist and former strategic communications professional.[7] Thus, Khaled enjoyed a good presence across traditional and social media, with his office even using the instant messaging service Telegram to highlight significant achievements.[8] Billboards of him were visible across all urban centres in the state early on in the campaign.[9]

Conversely, while BN Johor was able to capitalize on Khaled's personal popularity and good track record, it had to contend with negative perceptions of the Najib administration and the federal government. Fifty-five per cent of Johoreans surveyed were unhappy with the national government, with corruption and poor management listed as key grievances. In addition, Najib Razak only generated a positive reaction from 38 per cent of Johoreans. Thus, while the prime minister did not feature prominently in campaign materials or on billboards, Khaled still had to defend the Najib administration, arguing that Johor's continued development was contingent upon federal support (*Malaysian Insight*, 26 February 2018).[10]

Much of the rest of the BN line-up in Johor consisted of well-established figures, such as: Hishamuddin Hussein (Defence Minister); S. Subramaniam (Health Minister); Nur Jazlan (Deputy Minister for Home Affairs); Wee Ka Siong and Azalina Othman (both Ministers in the Prime Minister's Department); and Shahrir Samad (former Minister for Domestic Trade and Consumer Affairs). That said, five new parliamentary candidates were brought in, and there was considerable renewal of the state line-up, including a substantial number of women.[11]

Continuing its past practice, BN retained its seat-sharing formula—with one change.[12] Thus, UMNO contested in sixteen parliamentary and thirty-five state seats, along the coasts and the interior of the state, as well as the urban seats of Johor Bahru, Pulai and Pasir Gudang. The remaining parties contested in seats along the central spine of the state, running from Tebrau to Labis (Figure 13.7).

Barisan's campaign was largely developmental, focusing on the state's recent high rate of growth and promising more of the same (Kerajaan Negri Johor 2018). Khaled Nordin released a long-term plan for the state entitled "New Decade for Johor", which had six main strategies, of which three focused on economic issues, namely: improving infrastructure; adapting to new international economic trends; and developing human capital. The other three were: improving governance; protecting the environment; and protecting citizens' welfare (Weerasena and Mohd Daud 2018).

Consequently, much mention was made of the state's above-average growth, as well as foreign direct investment (FDI) into and jobs created by Iskandar Malaysia. The New Decade Plan committed to completing large-scale projects such as the KL-Singapore High-Speed Rail, the Pengerang Integrated Petroleum Complex, the Nusajaya High-Tech Park, as well as a range of new initiatives including a redeveloped urban centre in downtown Johor Bahru, tourism facilities, and a drive to improve roads in rural areas (Weerasena and Daud 2018; *The Edge Markets* 14 April 2018).

This was complemented with a plan to address social issues. The most high-profile of these was to expand an affordable housing programme from 16,000 homes completed during Khaled's tenure to 100,000 by 2023 (*New Straits Times*, 15 April 2018). Other initiatives included expanding the network of "fair price" shops across the state, expanding the range of free bus services, and channelling cash transfers to five vulnerable groups, including: women; Orang Asli; the disabled; FELDA settlers; and young people (*The Sun Daily*, 14 April 2018).

Despite Khaled's well-publicized and executed campaign, rumours circulated that he could be substituted as Menteri Besar—particularly in the event of a narrow majority win. Other candidates for the position were mentioned, including Nur Jazlan—particularly following a highly publicized visit by the Sultan of Johor to his house (*Channel NewsAsia*, 17 March 2018). Speculation was further fuelled on

FIGURE 13.7
Seats Contested in by UMNO and Non-UMNO BN Parties (GE-14)

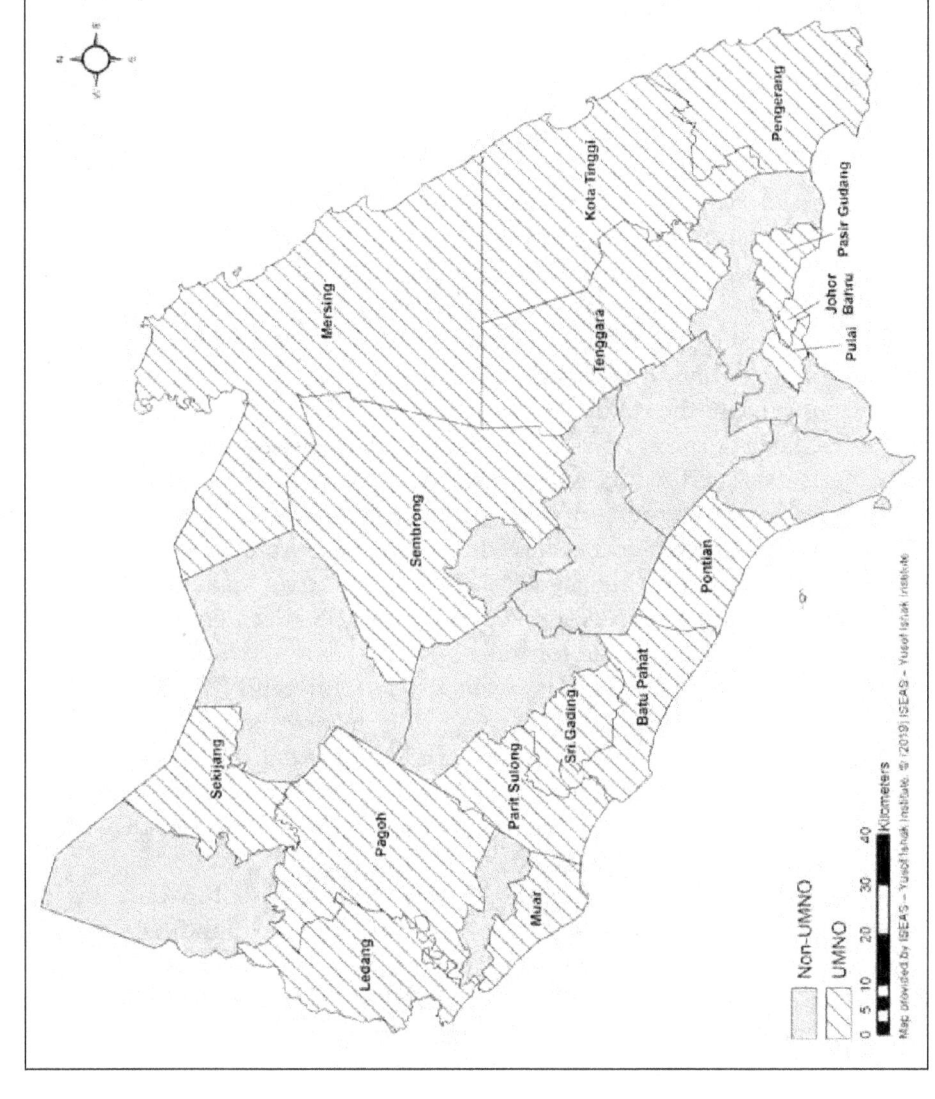

nomination day by Khaled's rather unusual decision to run for both a parliamentary and state seat. In the end, Nur Jazlan only ran for Parliament, eliminating him from the Menteri Besarship; conversely, another candidate emerged. Mohd Othman Yusuf, candidate for the Kukup state seat, was rumoured to enjoy the Sultan of Johor's favour. Yusuf is a member of the Johor Royal Council and Chairman of a large real estate operation Country Garden PV, which has links to the Sultan (*Malay Mail* and *The Star*, 24 April 2018).

Pakatan Harapan

Unlike BN, which was able to rely on an established mechanism for the allocation of territory and seats between its various coalition members, Pakatan Harapan's component members had to undergo protracted negotiations. The first important breakthrough came when Muhyiddin Yassin was named Pakatan Harapan chairman for Johor, as opposed to the previous suggestion of all four party leaders collectively chairing the state-level campaign (Wan Saiful 2018, p. 32).

Pakatan targeted sixteen seats in Johor as well as a simple majority in the state legislative assembly.[13] However, while the numerical target was clear, the seat allocation between the parties was not. One key complication was the departure of PAS, which had borne much of the load of campaigning for state seats. Consequently, the other parties had to step in and compete in new constituencies. Relatedly, many of these were in Malay-majority and rural areas in the state's centre and east, which were widely perceived to be very difficult terrain for PH. While many felt that this was a natural constituency for PPBM, that party's leaders felt that, given the difficulty of winning these seats, it should also be allocated some relatively safer constituencies to compensate for this.[14]

The demands of campaigning were also felt differently by the different parties. DAP and, to a lesser extent, PKR were able to use their existing networks and assets in Johor. However, PPBM and Amanah were entirely new entities, and had to develop a grassroots network quickly. In both cases, this organizational challenge was ameliorated somewhat by their ability to capitalize on assets they brought over from UMNO and PAS, respectively.[15]

For PPBM, the party's organizational and membership base in Johor was centred on Muhyiddin's constituency of Pagoh and surrounding areas, and other senior figures in the campaign such as Shahruddin Salleh and Syed Saddiq were also based in the northern part of the state. Relative to other parts of the country, the party concentrated a considerable amount of resources in Johor, with the aim of making the state its national base—much like PKR's redoubt in Selangor and DAP's in Penang (Wan Saiful 2018, p. 39).

For its part, Amanah was primarily based in and around the state seat of Parit Yaani, the constituency of the party's state chairman, Aminolhuda Hassan. As with PPBM, the fledgling party was helped by the fact that a substantial proportion of its leaders were from Johor, including its vice-president Salahuddin Ayub (Wan Saiful 2017).

DAP was also able to draw on considerable celebrity power, with established national figures such as Lim Kit Siang and Liew Chin Tong running for parliamentary seats in the state. In contrast, PKR had fewer nationally known figures to lead the campaign. Thus, PKR's state head was party veteran Hassan Karim, an established but relatively unknown national figure. Grassroots workers commented that this made campaigning for the party more difficult.[16]

Ultimately, PPBM had to do the heaviest lifting at the parliamentary level. From one seat, Pagoh, the party had to campaign in ten seats along much of the state's eastern seaboard. This proved quite a challenge, with some from the other coalition members observing that their grassroots network was still quite weak. Nonetheless, PPBM's presence, aided by Mahathir and Muhyiddin's legitimacy, was key for PH politicians to enter UMNO heartland seats. In addition, the Javanese background of many of PPBM's candidates was helpful for campaigning in FELDA settlements.[17] PKR was also quite stretched as it had to expand from one seat, Bakri, to campaign in eight parliamentary seats, as well as twelve state seats—many in the east (Figure 13.8). Conversely, DAP was able to capitalize on its existing four parliamentary and thirteen state seats.

Unlike BN, PH did not have a clear candidate for Menteri Besar during the campaign. That said, Muhyiddin Yassin was widely viewed as the most likely candidate for the job, with some people advocating that he serve on an interim basis in the event of a victory.[18]

PH's campaign was very focused on national-level issues, particularly GST and cost of living, along with the broader governance themes of anti-corruption, transparency, and the need to curb the power of the prime minister. Considerable emphasis was placed on the 1MDB corporate scandal, linking the alleged ill-gotten funds with luxury expenditures associated with Najib and, particularly, his wife Rosmah.[19] Other related themes included placing term limits on the prime minister, as well as prohibiting concurrent posts, particularly that of prime minister and finance minister.

Many of these themes were translated into ten state-level pledges which PH promised to implement within 100 days of assuming office. The top three pledges were: limiting Menteris Besar to serving two terms; holding open and transparent bidding for public works; and providing an allocation of free water for low-income households. Like BN, the PH campaign also focused on housing, specifically pledging to make the allocation of affordable housing opportunities more open and transparent, and also working with families in arrears to access financial assistance. Referring to schemes implemented in Penang and Selangor, PH Johor also pledged to provide credit to lower income families to access healthcare. And, as with BN, other pledges contemplated cash transfers to specific vulnerable groups.[20]

Some local-level issues that figured in campaign events and discussions included: a scandal involving the former UMNO state executive councillor, Latif Bandi, who was arrested in 2017 over money laundering associated with real estate deals; demands for compensation from displaced communities arising from large-scale infrastructure projects such as Pengerang Integrated Petroleum Complex; and a perceived influx

FIGURE 13.8
Parliamentary Constituencies Contested in by Different PH Parties (GE-14)

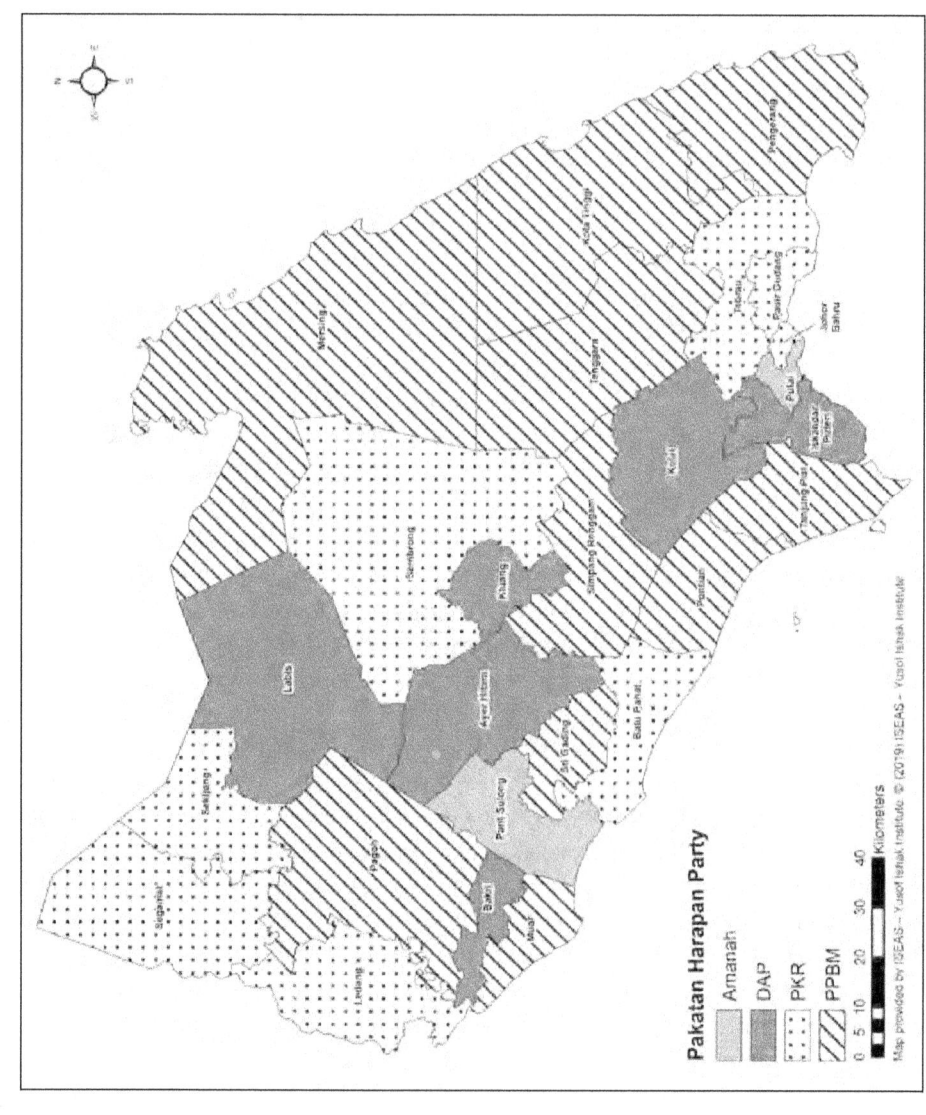

of foreign nationals associated with Forest City, a large-scale luxury housing project promoted by the Johor state government and linked to the Sultan of Johor.[21]

Pakatan Harapan's campaign in Johor began to pick up pace in early March, with the various coalition members opening up local branches in the constituencies that they sought to contest in. *Ceramahs* and large-scale public events were held from mid-March onwards.[22]

PH's campaign was initially hampered by the Registrar of Societies delay in recognizing Pakatan Harapan as a coalition, which meant that members could not use its logo on campaign material. On April 6, in a large rally held in Pasir Gudang, Mahathir Mohamad declared the coalition's decision to campaign under PKR's logo in all parts of the country. This ultimately was seen as fortuitous, as it helped simplify campaigning, projected an image of a solid coalition, and minimized the visibility of the DAP logo in Malay-majority seats.[23]

The event was successful in projecting a united front, with powerful speeches by leaders from all component parties, including: Mahathir and Muhyiddin Yassin for PPBM; Mat Sabu and Salahuddin Ayub for Amanah; Lim Guan Eng for DAP; and Wan Azizah for PKR. The rally was attended by 3,500–5,000 people, including a substantial number of Malays, and marked a turning point in the campaign (*Straits Times*, 7 April 2018).[24] On one hand, the size and composition of the crowd indicated a potential groundswell of support. On the other, it also generated interest from a range of quarters.

The following day, the Johor Crown Prince commented on the rally, urging Johoreans to not be misled by PH, indirectly referring to Mahathir as a "forked tongued" individual and one that had diminished the role of the Sultans in Malaysia. Instead, the Crown Prince encouraged voters to allow the royal family to work with UMNO to address the country's outstanding problems (*Free Malaysia Today*, 8 April 2018).

Over the next few days, there was substantial commentary on social media, with considerable levels of support for Mahathir Mohamad. In turn, many of the postings argued: that younger people should respect their elders; the royal family should not get involved in politics; and the royalty did not understand the difficulty ordinary people had of making ends meet (*Free Malaysia Today*, 8 April 2018; *Straits Times*, 9 April 2018). While many of those commenting were not based in Johor, the criticism was felt by the Crown Prince, who sought to make amends by spending an estimated RM1 million on shoppers at a local supermarket immediately afterwards (*The Nation*, 12 April 2018).

PH's campaign was given another fillip when the Election Commission ruled that only the photos of a given candidate, along with their party president and deputy president, could be used on campaign materials. Due to Mahathir's formal position as chairman (and not president) of PPBM and Anwar's status as de facto leader of PH, their photos had to be removed from PH campaign materials. Pakatan Harapan was able to film and disseminate instances of Election Commission employees cutting out Mahathir's face from PH billboards, yet ignoring BN billboards with photos of Rosmah Mansor and Xi Jinping.[25]

PAS

As with PH, PAS was also affected by the split with Pakatan Rakyat and the 2018 state campaign represented a substantial organizational challenge. The party fielded candidates in twenty parliamentary and forty-one legislative assembly seats, which was a substantial step up from previous campaigns. In addition, the departure of party cadres to Amanah also meant that PAS had to find new candidates. Consequently, 80 per cent of the line-up was comprised of new candidates and, of these, eight ran concurrently for parliamentary and state seats.

This new influx of candidates also meant more diversity, with proportionately fewer being drawn from the *ulama*. According to the PAS state party commissioner, professionals accounted for 60 per cent of candidates, party workers 25 per cent, and *ulama* only the remaining 15 per cent. The candidate for Menteri Besar, Mohd Mazri Yahya, was a cardiovascular surgeon, and other candidates included three university lecturers, a former manager of the FELDA cooperative investment fund, and an army captain (*The Star*, 19 April 2018). There were five female candidates, including one Hindu, Kumutha Rahman, Chief of the PAS Supporters Women's Wing who ran in Johor Jaya, a mixed urban seat.[26]

It is very likely that there was a tacit agreement between UMNO and PAS at the national level on which seats the latter party would run in, in order to facilitate an alliance in the aftermath of the election. Of the six parliamentary seats that PAS did not run in, four were held by senior UMNO figures, including: Shahrir Samad (Johor Bahru); Azalina Othman (Pengerang); Hishamuddin Hussein (Sembrong); and Halimah Mohd Saddique (Kota Tinggi). A fifth was held by Lim Kit Siang (Gelang Patah) and the party may have opted to yield this seat, given the DAP leader's 15,000 vote majority in 2013. The last seat was held by UMNO member Ayub Rahmat (Sekijang), who had very strong Islamist credentials.

Despite the possibility of an elite-level pact between the two parties, at the grassroots level competition was fierce. The PAS manifesto for Johor was well thought-out and, like its PH equivalent, sought to capitalize on cost of living issues and the 1MDB scandal. Consequently, the manifesto stressed the elimination of corruption and a commitment to transparent public administration. Mirroring the PH platform, it also pledged an (increased) allotment of free water for B40 (Bottom 40 per cent) families, as well as widening access to housing through building more affordable lodging, and ending quotas for homes being allocated to political parties. This was to be complemented by a People's Bank to provide loans to first-time buyers as well as M40 (Middle 40 per cent) families. This was supported by a range of welfare payments such as discount card for poor families and a medical support scheme for poor families.[27]

Considerable emphasis was placed on religious issues, particularly empowering Islamic schools and making them more autonomous from state government control. However, there was also an attempt to reach out to Chinese- and Tamil-speakers through increasing the time spent on these languages in the public school system. Other campaign pledges included: reducing smoking areas in the state; combating crime; and increasing parking facilities for people commuting to Singapore to work.

The Polls

In the months and weeks leading up to the elections, polling results consistently indicated that while non-Malays had moved *en masse* to the opposition, the Malay voters were, as yet, undecided.

In January, the social media research firm, Politweet released a projection of election results for Johor, based on the 2017 electoral roll, parliamentary and electoral results from GE-13, and statistically derived patterns for individual voters based on results from 2008 and 2013. The research called the election for BN, but indicated that PH could carry the state if there was a 10 per cent swing across the board—including Malay voters. However, this assumption only held if there was a simple two-way fight between BN and PH. In addition, three-way fights were deduced to favour BN. Furthermore, younger Malay voters in Johor were thought to be more favourable to UMNO than younger voters in other states (Politweet Enterprise 2018).

The Merdeka Center provided a constant stream of analysis in the run-up to the elections, based on periodic surveys across the country, including in Johor. In a report released in late April, the centre indicated that support for BN had slipped substantially among Malays, but from 81.8 per cent in 2013 to 60.9 per cent in 2018. Consequently, while BN had lost the bulk of the Chinese vote, it was still on course to obtain 47 per cent of the popular vote, with PH garnering 42 per cent and PAS the remaining 11 per cent. Thus, in order to win, PH need to get 10 per cent more Malay support and 5 per cent more Chinese support (Merdeka Center 2018b).

While the first two sets of projections were not positive about PH's chances, this was not the case for INVOKE, a PKR-linked data analytics firm. Based on a survey carried out over a two-week period of almost 12,000 voters selected via random stratified sampling and then weighted, in early May, the firm predicted that PH would get twenty-one out of twenty-six parliamentary seats and thirty-nine out of fifty-six state seats in Johor. Barisan Nasional would get the remainder, and PAS would not get any seats. INVOKE specifically singled out Khaled Nordin, Shahrir Samad, and Hishamuddin Hussein as high-profile UMNO politicians that would lose their seats.

In an update published on 8 May, the Merdeka Center maintained that BN was likely to remain in power, with a predicted 100 parliamentary seats relatively secure, versus PH's eighty-three, PAS' two seats, and a further thirty-seven seats too close to call. Interestingly for Johor, BN was likely to retain only seven seats, versus PH's fourteen, with a further five too close to call (Merdeka Center 2018c).

THE ELECTIONS AND THE RESULTS

The elections took place on Wednesday, 9 May. Although the day was later made a public holiday in response to public protests, the timing did raise complications for the estimated 300,000 Johoreans working in Singapore (*Straits Times*, 28 October 2018). The potential impact was thought to favour BN, as outstation workers tend to hail from urban areas in Malaysia, as opposed to the more UMNO-friendly rural areas. Indeed, Deputy Prime Minister Zahid Hamidi raised hackles when he recommended Malaysians in Singapore to not return home if it meant taking time off work (*Malaysiakini*, 13 April 2018).

Many Malaysians, including those Johoreans living in Singapore, travelled back on the night of 8 May, with reports of substantial traffic congestions on main thoroughfares (*The Edge Markets*, 9 May 2018; *Channel NewsAsia*, 11 May 2018). Others were able to vote before going off to work. Overall, the electoral process in Johor took place in an orderly manner.[28]

Polling stations shut at 5:00 p.m. After this, ballots began to be counted, with the first results coming in after 9:00 p.m. The first losses for BN included: Labis (MCA); Muar (UMNO); and Segamat (MIC).[29] At 2:00 a.m., Mahathir called a news conference declaring that PH had obtained a parliamentary majority and control of six state governments, including Johor (*The Star*, 9 May 2018).

The result was a very substantial victory for PH in Johor, which obtained 54.4 per cent of the popular vote, versus BN's 38.6 per cent, and PAS' 7 per cent. Relative to national trends, PH and BN both polled better in the state than they did elsewhere, and PAS' performance was considerably below the average for the country as a whole (Figure 13.9).

While the proximity to Singapore enabled Johoreans working there to navigate around the logistical complications, this did, in the end, affect voter turnout. 1.33 million people out of a total 1.79 million registered voters cast their ballots, which translated into a 74.5 per cent turnout. This was substantially lower than the 87 per cent of eligible Johoreans that voted in 2013 (*New Straits Times*, 9 May 2018; Election Commission Malaysia 2013, p. 150).

As regards parliamentary seats, PH secured a total of eighteen, including all nine urban and semi-urban seats and nine out of the seventeen rural seats (Table 13.1). In terms of the ethnic composition of the seats, PH won in all mixed constituencies, all Malay-majority seats, and five out of the thirteen Malay-supermajority seats (Table 13.2). In geographic terms, this meant that PH took the centre and entire western flank of the state, with three exceptions—the seats of Pontian, Sri Gading, and Ayer Hitam, which were retained by BN (Figures 13.10 and 13.11).

With regard to the state assembly, the performance was similarly sweeping, with PH obtaining thirty-six out of the fifty-six seats. The results broadly map onto the parliamentary ones, with PH taking the more mixed and urbanized state seats within the various parliamentary districts (Table 13.3). The only discrepancy between the different types of seats is the sole state seat won by PAS. The seat, Bukit Pasir, was within PPBM's heartland, but the PH candidate for the seat was disqualified on a technicality. Consequently, the constituency's protest vote went to PAS.

Looking at the performance of the various Pakatan Harapan parties at the parliamentary and state levels, it is clear that while the DAP performed solidly, it essentially only consolidated the inroads made in GE-13. In contrast, PPBM and PKR

FIGURE 13.9
Popular Support in Johor and Nationally (GE-14)

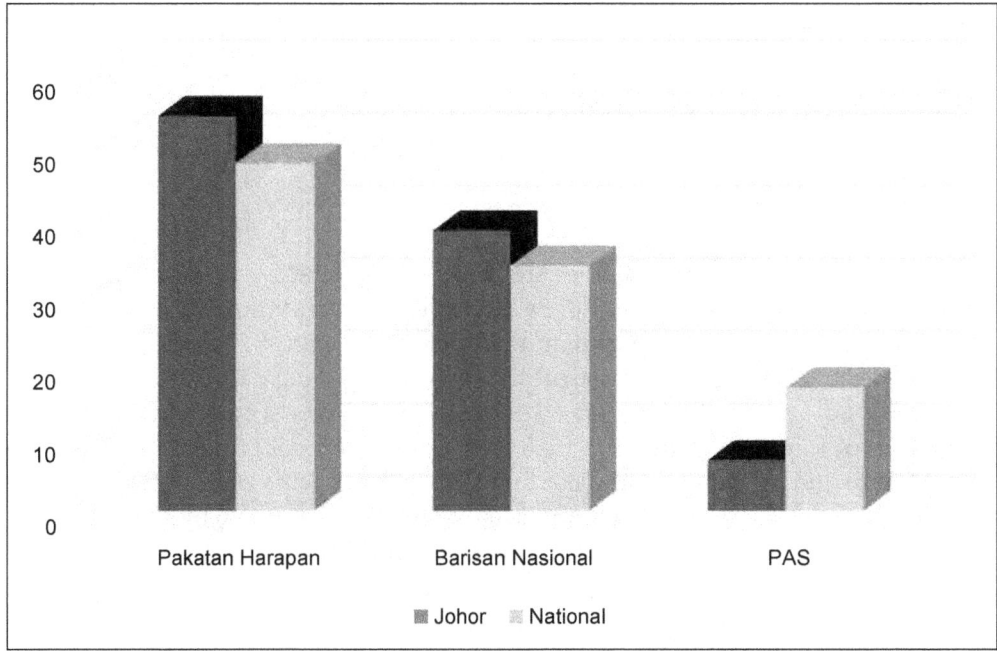

Source: https://graphics.straitstimes.com/STI/STIMEDIA/Interactives/2018/05/malaysia-general-elections-live-results/index.html (accessed 26 December 2018).

TABLE 13.1
Parliamentary Results (Urban/Rural) (GE-14)

Coalition	Urban/Semi-Urban	Rural
Pakatan Harapan	9	8
Barisan Nasional	0	9

Source: Results from http://www.undi.info/ (accessed 26 December 2018); classification of urbanization from https://docs.google.com/spreadsheets/d/1avEv-WaeZwcYsq48GtieTrlh5fdsIVUliBeFGRI8-C0/edit#gid=0 (accessed 26 December 2018).

obtained the bulk of new territories. At the parliamentary level, PKR performed very well, winning seven out of its eight contests. PPBM did less well, winning five out of its ten contests. However, this was also a reflection of the allocation of seats between the parties, as PPBM had to contest in many UMNO heartland seats. Despite its limited presence at the parliamentary level, Amanah did very well in terms of state seats, securing eight—a record for an Islamist party in Johor.

There were, broadly, four messages from the electorate.

TABLE 13.2
Parliamentary Results by Type of Seat (GE-14)

Coalition	Mixed	Malay Majority (51–55)	Malay Majority (56–60)	Malay Majority (61+)
Pakatan Harapan	9	4	2	3
Barisan Nasional	0	0	2	6

Source: Results from http://www.undi.info/ (accessed 26 December 2018).

First, urban and semi-urban areas are no longer hospitable constituencies for BN and, particularly, UMNO. Beyond BN's loss of all non-rural constituencies, UMNO faced particularly dramatic defeats in its three urban seats of Pasir Gudang, Johor Bahru and Pulai. The three highest-profile candidates of the party, Khaled Nordin, Shahrir Samad, and Nur Jazlan were all defeated by margins of approximately 20,000 or more. This stands in contrast to their victories in 2004, all of which were on the back of majorities at or above 30,000. In addition, this swing against BN occurred independently of the popularity of individual candidates, as shown by Khaled's good polling. Furthermore, with the exception of Salahuddin Ayub, who won in Pulai, the other two victorious PH candidates are not well known. Thus, these electoral defeats were referred to as "collateral damage".[30]

Second, non-UMNO BN parties are no longer electorally viable in Johor. Established politicians and party leaders lost their seats such as: MIC president, S. Subramaniam (Segamat); MCA vice-president, Chua Tee Yong (Labis); and the Gerakan secretary-general, Liang Teck Meng (Simpang Renggam). Indeed, the only non-UMNO BN candidate to retain his seat was MCA's Wee Ka Siong (Ayer Hitam), who garnered 303 votes more than his DAP challenger Liew Chin Tong.

Third, PAS is not politically viable in Johor when it competes outside of a broader coalition. Barring Parit Yaani, which it lost to Amanah, PAS won three seats in the state in 2013. In 2018, its sole victory was due to the disqualification of the PH candidate. In contrast, Amanah was able to increase its state seats from one in GE-13 to eight in GE-14. That said, despite PAS' overall low share of votes, its presence did alter the verdict in a number of close contests—most notably Ayer Hitam.

Fourth, UMNO is now really only viable in rural, Malay-majority areas, largely on the eastern flank of the state. However, even here, the party is no longer invulnerable. Of the thirteen Malay-supermajority constituencies, five were won by Pakatan Harapan component parties. And, of these five, four were won by PPBM. All of the seven seats retained by UMNO had smaller majorities than in GE-13, with Parit Sulong looking particularly vulnerable (Table 13.4).

DISCUSSION

Having gone through the context, campaigns, elections, and results, this final section will relate back to the central theme and underlying question of the book—

FIGURE 13.10
Johor Parliamentary Results (GE-13)

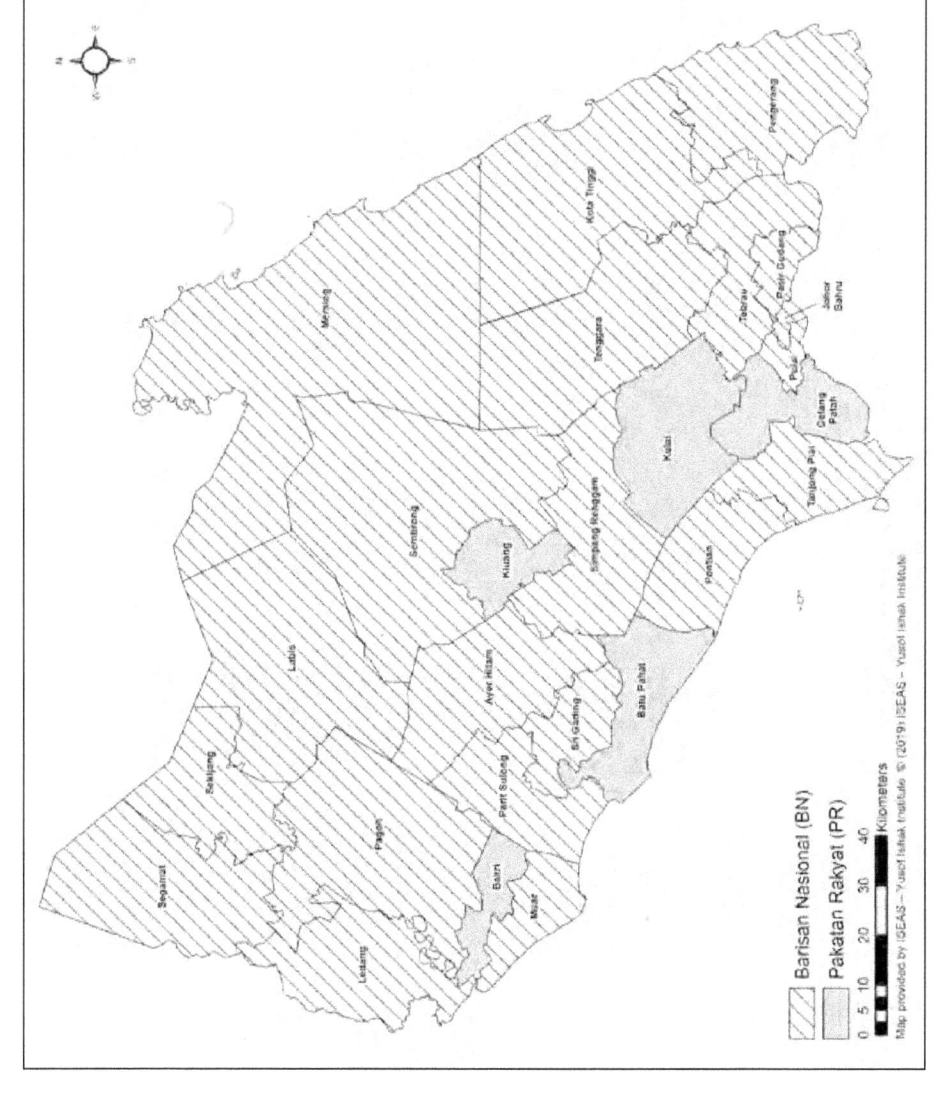

FIGURE 13.11
Johor Parliamentary Results (GE-14)

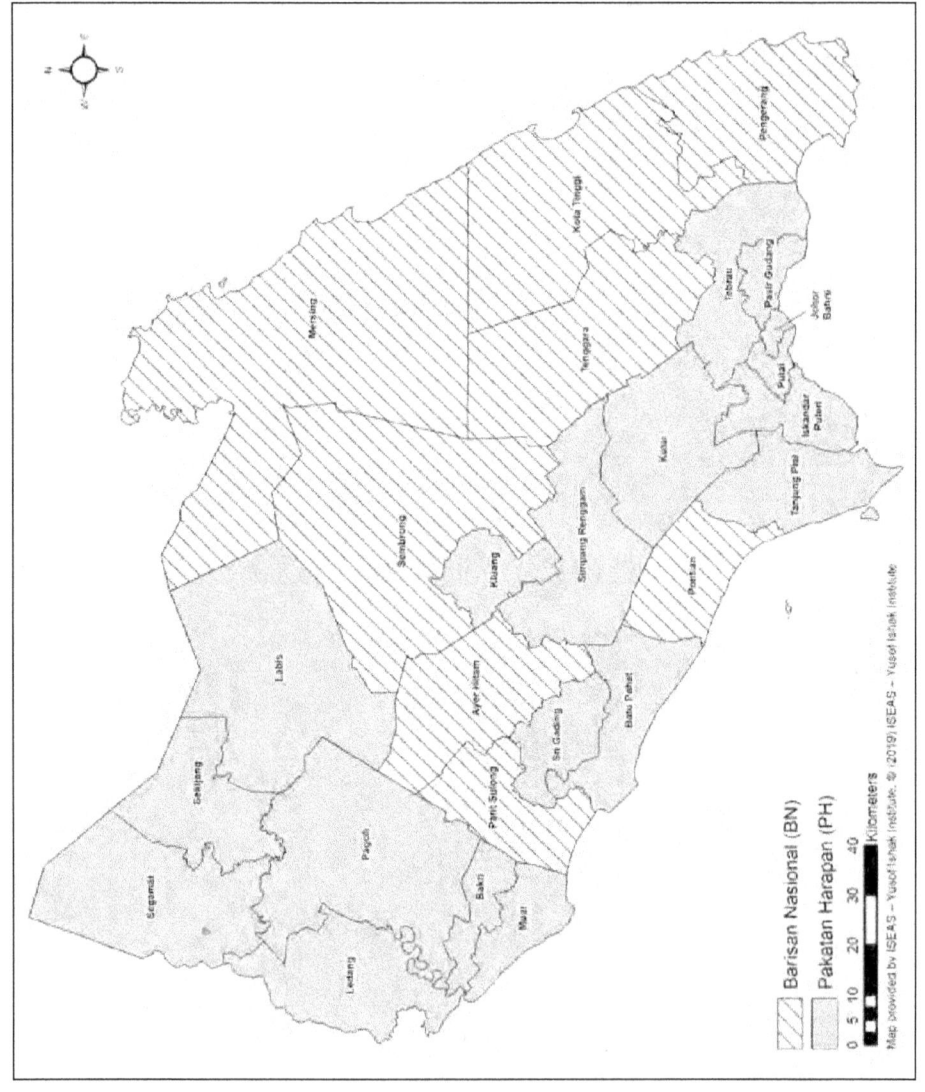

TABLE 13.3
Parliamentary and State Results for Pakatan Harapan (GE-14)

| | Parliamentary Seats | | | |
	PPBM	PKR	Amanah	DAP
Won in GE-13	1	1	0	4
Contested in GE-14	10	8	2	6
Won in GE-14	5	7	1	5
	State Seats			
	PPBM	PKR	Amanah	DAP
Won in GE-13	1	1	1	13
Contested in GE-14	18	12	12	14
Won in GE-14	8	6	8	14

Source: Results from http://www.undi.info/ (accessed 26 December 2018). Italics = seats won by candidates who subsequently changed party affiliation.

TABLE 13.4
Barisan Nasional-Held Seats (GE-14)

Constituency	Person	Party	Malay 56–60	Malay 61+	FELDA	2013 Majority	2018 Majority
Pengerang	Azalina Othman	UMNO		Yes	Yes	22,508	11,417
Kota Tinggi	Halimah binti Mohd Sadiq	UMNO		Yes	Yes	17,196	5,933
Mersing	Latif Ahmad	UMNO		Yes	Yes	24,574	14,621
Sembrong	Hishamuddin Hussein	UMNO	Yes		Yes	15,747	8,459
Parit Sulong	Noraini Ahmad	UMNO		Yes	No	13,727	833
Tenggara	Adam bin Baba	UMNO		Yes	Yes	11,753	6,341
Pontian	Haji Ahmad	UMNO		Yes	No	10,631	6,662
Ayer Hitam	Wee Ka Siong	MCA	Yes		No	7,310	303

Source: Results from http://www.undi.info/ (accessed 26 December 2018).

were there signs indicating PH's victory in the run-up to the election, or was it the result of a last-minute surge? Relatedly, why did the overwhelming majority of analysts, including this writer, get it wrong—anticipating a BN victory, albeit a narrow one?

Having surveyed the trends and evidence, there appear to be four reasons.

First, the sheer benefits of incumbency were thought to render an upset extremely unlikely. This included: BN's well-rehearsed consociational campaign strategy and extensive grassroots network; the first-past-the-post parliamentary system;

malapportionment; control of traditional media; electoral redelineation; and an expanding coercive apparatus (Hutchinson 2018a). Consequently, observers tended to adopt a more conservative approach in analysing possible outcomes.

Second, unlike previous elections which were usually between two candidates, PAS' emergence as a third political force made analysis difficult. Analysts were not used to factoring in three-way contests for their projections, and many continued to use assumptions and patterns from GE-12 and GE-13, which were essentially two-way races (Chan 2018). Furthermore, it was doubly difficult to know how to model three-way races, when there were talks of a possible UMNO-PAS alliance after the elections. This could well have prompted people to vote strategically through opting for their second preference in order to maximize the chances of defeat for their least-favoured party—and this could have played out differently in different parts of the country.

Third, the opinion polls released in the run-up to GE-14 were not very optimistic about PH's chances. More than an accurate reflection of their voting intentions, this was an indication of respondents' unwillingness to share their political affiliations or views to polling firms—either in person or over the telephone. It is likely that this reaction was due to a fear of opprobrium from their respective communities or the authorities. This was compounded by an erroneous assumption that respondents that were undecided would ultimately vote for BN. Thus, while surveys were able to track a decline in support for the incumbents, they were not able to accurately predict how a substantial proportion of the electorate, particularly Malay voters, would vote (Ibrahim 2018).

Fourth, the nature of political discussion has changed in Malaysia. Unlike traditional media or even Facebook, which was pivotal in GE-13, the prevalence of WhatsApp as a preferred means of disseminating information meant that issues and trends informing voter perceptions were off the grid and hard to track. Consequently, it was hard for analysts to detect how and whether PH was making headway or whether people would be motivated to turn out to vote.

With hindsight, the survey results of Johor voters from May to June 2017 were quite illuminating. One year out from GE-14, they indicated a solid core of support for BN, and a very low level of open support for PH. However, most tellingly, more than half of voters either did not know which way to vote or were not willing to reveal their preference. Given the reticence of respondents to openly declare their voting intentions, it is safe to say that, at this point, the majority of voters were dissatisfied with BN and open to other alternatives.

In the subsequent twelve months, PH proceeded to consolidate itself. Most notably, the coalition decided on its leadership structure in 2017, when Mahathir Mohamad was named the chairman, Wan Azizah of PKR the president, and the other party leaders were appointed as deputy presidents of the coalition. Then, in January 2018, Mahathir Mohamad was put forward as the candidate for prime minister.

Furthermore, the cost of living did not improve and the 1MDB scandal continued, providing the opposition with an effective political tool. And, the Najib Razak administration did not improve its popularity through adopting a series of controversial measures, including mid-week voting, restrictive campaign ruling, and additional repressive measures.

Thus, regarding whether the verdict for Johor was a last-minute surge, it seems more likely that it was a steady movement away from BN. One year before the elections, the bulk of voters in the state were disillusioned with the incumbents. In the subsequent twelve months, this was translated into open support for PH. However, due to the reluctance of many voters to publicly declare their intentions as well as the private nature through which much information was circulated, there were few publicly visible signs to augur this shift.

Notes

1. This is calculated on the basis of the 3.3 million Malaysian citizens living in Johor. There are an additional 650,000 foreign residents in the state.
2. This section draws on Hutchinson (2018).
3. For more details on consociationalism, consult Lijphart (1977). For its applicability to the Malaysian context, see Milne and Mauzy (1993) and Horowitz (1993).
4. For an example, consult Zainah (2011).
5. Gelang Patah has traditionally been contested by MCA, but in 2013 the party yielded the seat to UMNO candidate and former Menteri Besar of Johor, Abdul Ghani Othman, who ran against DAP leader Lim Kit Siang and lost.
6. Johor Bahru could conceivably be included in this category. It is a large, urban seat with a slim Malay majority (51 per cent) that was retained with 55.8 per cent of the vote.
7. Ahmad Asri Khalbi, formerly of the *Sun* and Vice-President of Strategic Communications of the Iskandar Regional Development Authority.
8. Interview with Pakatan Harapan coalition candidate A, Johor Bahru, 7 March 2018.
9. Site visits to Muar, Batu Pahat, Kluang, Pasir Gudang and Johor Bahru in March, April 2018.
10. Campaign material in Hishamuddin Hussein's constituency, Sembrong, only focused on the candidate, with scant mention of either UMNO or BN. https://ge14newmandala.wordpress.com/ (accessed 19 December 2018).
11. In a rather ironic twist, UMNO candidates were able to vaunt the relative youth of their senior leaders in comparison to Mahathir Mohamad and Muhyiddin Yassin. Interview with UMNO member and former Central Committee Divisional Secretary, Johor Bahru, 21 April 2018; and PPBM leader from Pagoh, Pagoh, 19 March 2018.
12. In 2013, the previous Menteri Besar of Johor, Abdul Ghani Othman of UMNO, moved to this traditional MCA seat to run—and lose—against Lim Kit Siang. In 2018, this seat was returned to MCA.
13. Interview with Johor PKR leader, Pasir Gudang, 19 March 2018.
14. Interview with PPBM leaders from Pagoh, Kempas, 14 March and Pagoh, 19 March 2018.
15. In an interesting twist, Muhyiddin Yassin allegedly owned the land upon which the Pagoh UMNO headquarters was located. Interview PPBM member, Pagoh, 19 March 2018. Similarly, PAS and Amanah members had to negotiate ownership issues of assets, particularly land titles (Wan Saiful 2017, p. 23).
16. Interview with PH candidate B, Pasir Gudang 19 March 2018.

17. Interview with PH candidate A, Johor Bahru, 7 March 2018; candidate B, Pasir Gudang, 11 September 2018.
18. Muhyiddin Yassin was also considered as a potential interim candidate for Menteri Besar in the early days of the campaign. Interview with PPBM senior state leader, Kempas, 14 March 2018.
19. One campaign poster asked what RM19 billion had been stolen for, and listing a RM1 billion yacht, a pink diamond for Rosmah, a Hollywood movie, as well as a range of real estate deals. Site visit to PPBM branch office in Pagoh, 19 March 2018.
20. PH's Campaign Manifesto—"100 Janji, 100 Hari".
21. Interview with PH candidate B, Pasir Gudang, 13 April 2018.
22. Field trips to Muar, Ayer Hitam, Kluang, Pasir Gudang, Ayer Hitam and Johor Bahru in March and April 2018.
23. Interview with PH candidate B, Pasir Gudang, 13 April 2018.
24. All component parties were represented, with notable speeches by Mahathir Mohamad, Muhyiddin Yassin, Mat Sabu, Wan Azizah, Lim Kit Siang, Mukhriz Mahathir and Salahuddin Ayub. Field trip to Pasir Gudang, 6 April 2018.
25. One notable example is of EC employees excising Mahathir's face from billboards associated with DAP Johor candidate, Liew Chin Tong. https://www.youtube.com/watch?v=NS_TbtG8z1Y.
26. Field trip to Pasir Gudang, which includes the Permas and Johor Jaya state seats, on 28 April 2018.
27. PAS Johor Manifesto, https://www.facebook.com/paskawbakri/videos/1616693205 113262/?epa=SEARCH_BOX (accessed 26 December 2018).
28. There was one short-lived episode of unrest in Ayer Hitam, where voters thought that the ballot boxes were being interfered with.
29. https://ge14newmandala.wordpress.com (accessed 26 December 2018).
30. Interview with PH candidate B, Pasir Gudang, 11 September 2018.

References

Chan Kok Leong. 2018. "Forecasts in Malaysia's Poll Skewed by Islamist Party's Unpredictable Impact". *The Round Table* 107, no. 6: 789–90.
Department of Statistics, Malaysia (DOS). 2013. *Population Distribution and Basic Demographic Characteristics, 2010*. Putrajaya: Department of Statistics.
———. 2017. *Current Population Estimates 2017*. Putrajaya: Department of Statistics.
Election Commission, Malaysia. 2013. *Report of the 13th General Election*. Putrajaya: Election Commission.
Guyot, Dorothy. 1974. "The Politics of Land: Comparative Development in Two States of Malaysia". *Pacific Affairs* 44, no. 3: 366–89.
Horowitz, Donald L. 1993. "Democracy in Divided Societies". *Journal of Democracy* 4, no. 4: 18–38.
Hutchinson, Francis E. 2015. "Malaysia's Independence Leaders and the Legacies of State Formation under British Rule". *Journal of the Royal Asiatic Society* 25 no. 1: 123–51.
———. 2018a. *GE-14 in Johor: The Fall of the Fortress?* Trends in Southeast Asia, no. 3/2018. Singapore: ISEAS – Yusof Ishak Institute.
———. 2018b. "Malaysia's 14th General Elections: Drivers and Agents of Change". *Asian Affairs* 49, no. 4: 582–605.

Ibrahim Suffian. 2018. "Why Opinion Polls Failed to Predict the Fall of BN in Malaysia". *The Round Table* 107, no. 6: 791–92.

Kerajaan Negri Johor. 2018. *Pencapaian Johor 2013–2018: Membangun Dekad Baharu Johor*. Johor Bahru: Pejabat Menteri Besar, Kerajaan Negri Johor.

Khor Yu Leng. 2015. "The Political Economy of FELDA Seats: UMNO's Rural Fortress in GE-13". In *Coalitions in Collision: Malaysia's 13th General Elections*, edited by Johan Saravanamuttu, Lee Hock Guan, and Mohamed Nawab Mohamed Osman. Singapore: Institute of Southeast Asian Studies.

Lijphart, Arend. 1977. *Democracy in Plural Societies: A Comparative Exploration*. New Haven, Yale University Press.

Mauzy, Diane K. 1993. "Malaysia: Malaysia Political Hegemony and 'Coercive Consociationalism'". In *The Politics of Ethnic Conflict Regulation*, edited by J. McGarry and B. O'Leary. London: Routledge.

Merdeka Center. 2014. *Johor Survey*. Singapore: Institute of Southeast Asian Studies.

———. 2017a. *Johore Opinion Survey*. Singapore: ISEAS – Yusof Ishak Institute.

———. 2017b. *National Public Opinion Survey on Economic Hardship Indicators*. Kuala Lumpur: Merdeka Center.

———. 2018a. *Johore Opinion Survey*. 27 January 2018. Kuala Lumpur: Merdeka Center.

———. 2018b. *Malaysia General Elections XIV Outlook. Prospects and Outcome*. 26 April 2018. Kuala Lumpur: Merdeka Center.

———. 2018c. *Malaysia General Elections XIV Outlook. Prospects and Outcome III*. 8 May 2018. Kuala Lumpur: Merdeka Center.

Milne, R.S., and Diane K. Mauzy. 1999. *Malaysian Politics under Mahathir*. London: Routledge.

Norshahril Saat. 2017. *Johor Remains the Bastion of Kaum Tua*. Trends in Southeast Asia, no. 1/2017. Singapore: ISEAS – Yusof Ishak Institute.

NSTP Research and Information Services. 1990. *Elections in Malaysia: Facts and Figures*. Kuala Lumpur: Balai Berita.

Politweet Enterprise. 2018. *Winning Odds for Pakatan Harapan in Johor (GE-14)*. Kuala Lumpur: Politweet Enterprise.

Saravanamuttu, Johan. 2016. *Power Sharing in a Divided Nation: Mediated Communalism and New Politics in Six Decades of Malaysia's Elections*. Singapore: ISEAS – Yusof Ishak Institute and SIRD.

Wan Saiful Wan Jan. 2017. *Parti Amanah Negara in Johor: Birth, Challenges, and Prospects*. Trends in Southeast Asia, no. 9/2017. Singapore: ISEAS – Yusof Ishak Institute.

———. 2018. *Party Pribumi Bersatu Malaysia in Johor: New Party, Big Responsibility*. Trends in Southeast Asia, no. 2/2018. Singapore: ISEAS – Yusof Ishak Institute.

Weerasana, Benedict, and Mohd Daud Mat Din. 2018. *Dekad Baharu Johor: A Summary*. Johor Bahru: Bait Al Amanah.

Zainah Anwar. 2011. *Legacy of Honour*. Kuala Lumpur: Yayasan Mohamed Noah.

Periodicals

Channel NewsAsia
The Coverage
The Edge Financial Daily
The Edge Malaysia Weekly
The Edge Markets
Free Malaysia Today

Malaysiakini
Malaysian Insight
Malay Mail
The Nation
New Straits Times
The Star
Straits Times
The Sun Daily

14

KELANTAN
PAS Settles in on the Balcony of Mecca

Norshahril Saat[1]

INTRODUCTION

In the May 2018 elections, the electoral monopoly of Barisan Nasional (BN) was broken for the first time in Malaysia's history. The erstwhile dominant coalition lost control of its stronghold states of Johor, Melaka and Negri Sembilan to the reconfigured opposition alliance, Pakatan Harapan (PH). However, while these states changed hands from BN to PH, Kelantan resisted the tide, with the Islamic Party of Malaysia (PAS) retaining control of that state for the seventh consecutive time since 1990.

This development was unexpected as, in the run-up to the 14th General Elections (GE-14), many polls predicted that PAS would not retain control of the state. This was due to: a perceived erosion in support for the party; the expected effect that three-cornered fights would have on electoral outcomes; as well as the death of the party's spiritual leader, Nik Aziz Nik Mat. Furthermore, the party's internal schism and the subsequent founding of Parti Amanah Negara (Amanah)—which eventually joined PH—meant that PAS was stretched organizationally and no longer enjoyed a monopoly on religious appeals.

While the implications of three-cornered fights made electoral calculations difficult, opinion polls seemed to indicate that BN would make considerable incursions into the state. However, against prevailing expectations, PAS recorded a convincing victory in GE-14, winning nine out of fourteen parliamentary seats and thirty-seven out of forty-five state seats. BN won the remaining seats in Kelantan and, despite

Amanah's seeming promise, the new coalition did not win a single seat in the state. Beyond Kelantan, PAS performed well in the peninsula's north and east, capturing Terengganu and winning fifteen out of thirty-six state seats in Kedah.

Yet, aside from these considerable achievements, PAS' performance in GE-14 was mixed. While the number of popular votes for the party increased from 1.6 million in GE-13 to more than 2 million in GE-14, PAS' seats in Parliament fell from twenty-one to eighteen. Furthermore, in west coast states such as Selangor, Perak, Negri Sembilan, Johor and Melaka, the party's footprint was substantially reduced. Consequently, the electoral result seen in Kelantan and its neighbouring regions could be the result of localized dynamics.

This chapter focuses on PAS' electoral performance in Kelantan, highlighting the factors that contributed to its success and analysing the reasons for the unexpected results. It seeks to understand why PAS was able to strengthen its grip on Kelantan despite considerable head-winds and how it overcame the challenges of three-cornered fights with BN and PH.

In order to do this, this chapter first analyses PAS' electoral performance in Kelantan since Malaysia's independence, highlighting key events and critical junctures. In the subsequent section, it analyses GE-14, specifically the campaign strategies adopted by the different parties in the state, as well as the contests in a subset of key seats. By way of conclusion, the chapter discusses the reasons why PAS fared much better than expected in Kelantan.

AN OVERVIEW OF KELANTAN'S ELECTORAL HISTORY

As Malays make up 96 per cent of the state's population and Islam is overwhelmingly the predominant religion, Kelantan is essentially ethnically and religiously homogeneous.[2] Due to its religious characteristics as well as its relatively late incorporation into British Malaya, the state has played a pivotal role in the development of Islam in Malaysia, producing prominent religious scholars and anti-colonial leaders such as Tok Kenali, Haji Muhammad bin Said and Abdul Rahman Haji Uthman. The state's demographic composition, overwhelmingly Islamic character, and the prestige of local leaders have led to Kelantan being referred to as *serambi Mekkah*, or the "balcony" of Mecca.

Kelantan has a close association with Parti Islam Se-Malaysia (PAS), which was formed in 1951 by a group of Islamic clerics who split from the United Malays National Organization (UMNO). The party owes its origins to the second Ulama Congress which was organized by UMNO in Kampung Baru, Kuala Lumpur. Congress participants agreed to form a separate body to represent the religious elites, hence the inauguration of Persatuan Alim Ulama se-Malaysia (All Malayan Ulama Organization). In November that same year, the third congress was held, and the organization's name was changed to Persatuan Islam se-Malaysia (Pan Malayan Islamic Organization), which later became a political party (Farish 2014, pp. 38–40). The party was formed in the capital city, but its base has always been in the east coast of the Peninsula, especially Kelantan and Terengganu.

The next sections will analyse PAS' tenure in Kelantan across three time periods, corresponding to the party's: emergence, first tenure in power, and subsequent defeat; return to power, consolidation, and track record in government from 1990 to 2008; and performance in GE-13 in 2013.

PAS' EMERGENCE, FIRST TENURE AND SUBSEQUENT DEFEAT (1959–90)

In the 1959 elections, PAS campaigned at the national level and ran against the UMNO-led Alliance in many constituencies across the country. However, while the Alliance swept most parliamentary and state seats, PAS took the Kelantan state government, winning twenty-eight of the thirty state seats with 63.8 per cent of the popular vote, as well as nine out of ten parliamentary constituencies (NTSP 1994).

In the next two elections, PAS retained control of Kelantan, although its share of parliament and state seats declined. In 1964, PAS secured twenty-one out of thirty state seats and eight of the ten parliamentary seats, yielding seven state and one parliamentary constituencies to the Alliance. In 1969, the party lost a further two state and two parliamentary seats to the ruling coalition.

After the May 1969 racial riots, Abdul Razak enlarged the Alliance coalition—in the form of Barisan Nasional—to include opposition parties on the Peninsula as well as smaller parties in Sabah and Sarawak. In light of the reality of the time, PAS decided to join the expanded BN coalition in 1972. In the 1974 elections, BN, which included PAS as a component member, swept all thirty-six seats in the Kelantan state assembly. The then president of PAS, Asri Muda, was appointed as Chief Minister.

PAS' membership in the BN coalition was short-lived, due to an internal power struggle and BN's divide-and-rule strategy. Subsequently, the PAS president and then Chief Minister of Kelantan Asri Muda was made a federal minister and his rival in the party, Muhammad Nasir, was named the Chief Minister of Kelantan. Once in power, Nasir uncovered corruption scandals involving Asri.

Unhappy with Nasir, Asri engineered a vote-of-no-confidence in the Kelantan state assembly to topple the government. The King of Malaysia, on advice from Prime Minister Hussein Onn, intervened and declared a state of emergency in Kelantan in 1977. No state elections were called, leaving Nasir in power. Upset that the federal government was not on his side, Asri declared PAS would leave BN (Farish 2014, p. 94).

In the 1978 elections, under Asri's leadership PAS contested on its own and won five parliamentary seats in the whole country—two of which were in Kelantan. Nasir, for his part, formed another party, Berjasa (Pan-Malaysian Islamic Front) and contested in the 1978 elections as part of BN, winning seven parliamentary seats in Kelantan. At the state level, out of the thirty-six seats offered, UMNO won twenty-three seats, Berjasa eleven, and PAS only two seats (Farish 2014, p. 95).[3]

Throughout the 1980s, PAS remained as an opposition party in Kelantan, showing little sign of recovering from the 1977 debacle and its internal schism. Thus, in 1982, the party performed poorly, securing ten state seats out of the thirty-six it contested in and, in the 1986 elections, only ten seats out of a total of thirty-nine. At the federal level, PAS secured four out of twelve seats in 1982, and one out of thirteen seats in 1986 (Figures 14.1 and 14.2).

However, despite being in the political wilderness, PAS sought to rebuild itself during this period. The *ulama*—or religiously educated—faction in the party slowly gained a foothold, displacing the former leadership which was more nationalist and socialist in orientation. The *ulama* faction was led by conservative theologians, who supported: the formation of an Islamic state; implementation of *hudud* laws; and creation of a purist Islamic society (Norshahril 2014).

This group, led by Nik Aziz Nik Mat and Yusof Rawa, worked hard at the grassroots level in Kelantan to garner support and promote a strong Islamic character for the party. Influenced by external events, PAS also rode on the wave of the Islamic resurgence taking place in Asia at the time (Muzaffar 1987).

PAS' SECOND TENURE IN POWER
IN KELANTAN (1990–2008)

Reflecting the party's more conservative leadership, in the 1990 elections PAS campaigned on social and religious issues. The Islamic party was also able to capitalize on splits within UMNO. Disagreements between UMNO party president Mahathir Mohamad and senior party figure Tengku Razaleigh Hamzah led to the latter leaving the party to form Semangat 46 (S46) in 1989. PAS thus teamed up with S46 and formed the United Islamic Front (APU) and other smaller parties to contest (Farish 2014, p. 143).

FIGURE 14.1
Kelantan Parliamentary Seats, 1955–86

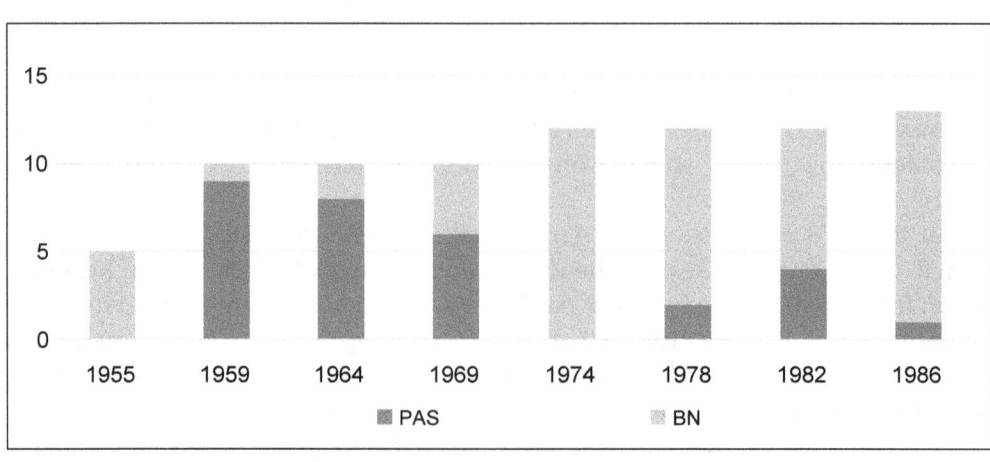

Note: PAS was part of BN in 1974.

FIGURE 14.2
Kelantan State Assembly Seats, 1959–86

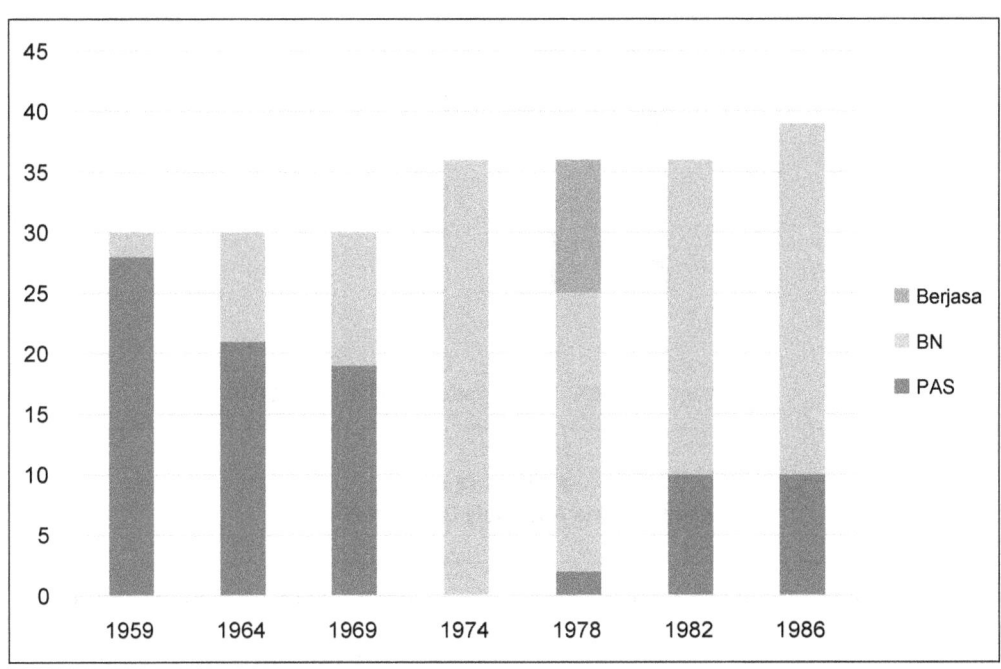

That year, Tengku Razaleigh Hamzah, a member of the Kelantanese royalty and member for the Gua Musang constituency played a leading role in the state campaign. The APU coalition did exceptionally well in Kelantan, with PAS taking twenty-four state seats and S46 a further fourteen seats. At the parliamentary level, PAS won seven seats and S46 the remaining six (Figures 14.3 and 14.4). For its part, BN was unable to secure a single seat in the state. In accordance with the campaign agreement between S46 and PAS, the latter's Nik Aziz became Chief Minister of the state.

With the ascendance of the *ulama* faction within PAS and the party's control of Kelantan, the victory ushered in a new period for PAS. Nik Aziz emerged as a pivotal figure, capitalizing on his popularity to promote Islamization. This involved banning performances deemed not in line with Islamic values, including many traditional practices such as *mak yong* (dance), *menorah* (a dance with Siamese elements) and *wayang kulit* (shadow play). Gender segregation in public places was also introduced, and women were banned from certain activities—including participating in Quran reciting competitions (Norshahril 2012).

However, beyond these practices, what defined PAS' second tenure in power in Kelantan was the call for the implementation of *hudud*. In 1993, the Kelantan state government passed the Shari'ah Criminal Code (II) to introduce *hudud* laws for offences related to theft, robbery, unlawful sexual intercourse (*zina*), intoxication of liquor, and apostasy (Norshahril 2014). While Nik Aziz and other PAS leaders hailed

FIGURE 14.3
Kelantan Parliamentary Seats, 1990–2018

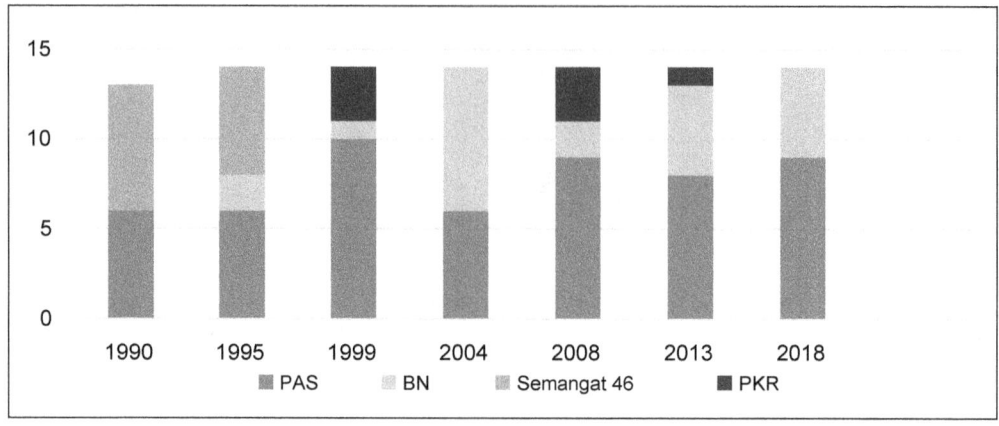

FIGURE 14.4
Kelantan State Assembly Seats, 1990–2018

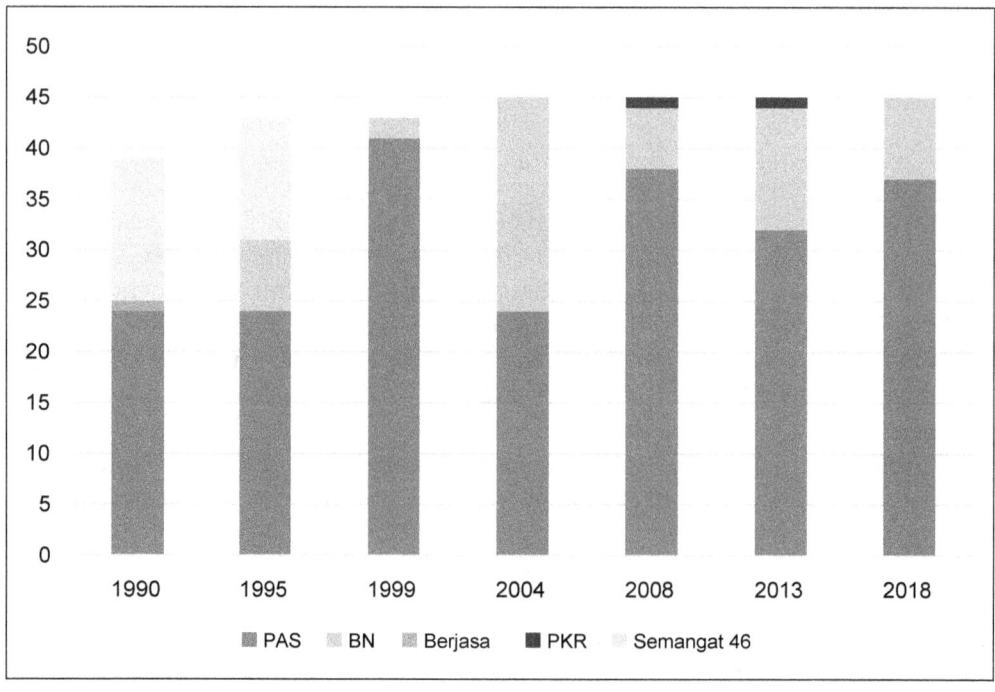

this move as a step towards realizing an Islamic state in Kelantan, the move was blocked by the federal government—which declared it unconstitutional (Mahathir 1995, pp. 63–76).

The national government, led by BN, also resorted to repressive tactics to encourage voters to reject the PAS-led administration in Kelantan. Under Malaysia's heavily centralized federal system, state government budgets are small and also depend on centrally mandated transfers for a significant portion of their revenue. Upon PAS' victory in 1990, federal development funds allocated to the state were reduced, and its proceeds from petroleum revenue withheld (Hutchinson 2014).

The remainder of the 1990s and early 2000s saw a stalemate between the BN-led national government and the PAS administration in Kelantan. Although BN under Mahathir was able to win a two-thirds majority in Parliament in every election, it was unable to recapture Kelantan. Although the ruling coalition made some inroads in the state in 1995, these were reversed in 1999. That year, following the removal of Deputy Prime Minister Anwar Ibrahim, PAS was able to capitalize on disenchantment with UMNO to capture all state seats except for two.

The ruling coalition, riding on the back of Abdullah Badawi's ascension to power, won handsomely at the national level in 2004 and garnered 90 per cent of seats in Parliament. However, in Kelantan, although the ruling coalition secured eight out of the state's fourteen seats, it only took twenty-one seats in the state assembly—leaving PAS with a narrow majority of twenty-four seats.

PAS was able to further entrench its holdings in 2008, obtaining thirty-eight out of forty-five state seats. Beyond support for PAS per se, the party was able to benefit from a national swing to the opposition, which saw the BN government lose its two-thirds majority in the federal government for the first time, along with the control of an additional four state governments (Saravanamuttu 2016). A contributing factor to this performance was the agreement on seat allocations with other opposition parties to avoid three-cornered fights.

PAS' PERFORMANCE IN GE-13 AND SUBSEQUENT DEPARTURE FROM PR

In 2013, although it was able to wrest back control of two states, BN continued its downward trend at the national level. However, as with the previous four elections, the ruling coalition was unable to retake Kelantan. PAS spiritual leader Nik Aziz ran again in 2013, though he did not indicate he would step down from his position of Chief Minister. That said, BN was able to recapture one parliamentary and five state seats compared to the 2008 elections. Figure 14.5 sets out the results of the parliamentary contests in Kelantan in 2013.

In GE-13, PAS won eight parliamentary seats: Pengkalan Chepa; Kota Bharu; Pasir Mas; Rantau Panjang; Kubang Kerian; Bachok; Pasir Puteh; and Kuala Kerai. With regards to the remaining five seats, one, Tumpat, was won by the Pakatan Rakyat component party, Parti Keadilan Rakyat (PKR). The other four were taken by BN, including Jeli and Gua Musang. These are traditional BN strongholds, with senior UMNO leaders helming the seats. Thus, Mustapa Mohamed, formerly Minister of Trade and Industry was the UMNO candidate for Jeli, and former Finance Minister and S46 leader, Tengku Razaleigh Hamzah, the parliamentary candidate for Gua Musang.[4]

FIGURE 14.5
Parliamentary Seats in Kelantan by Party (GE-13)

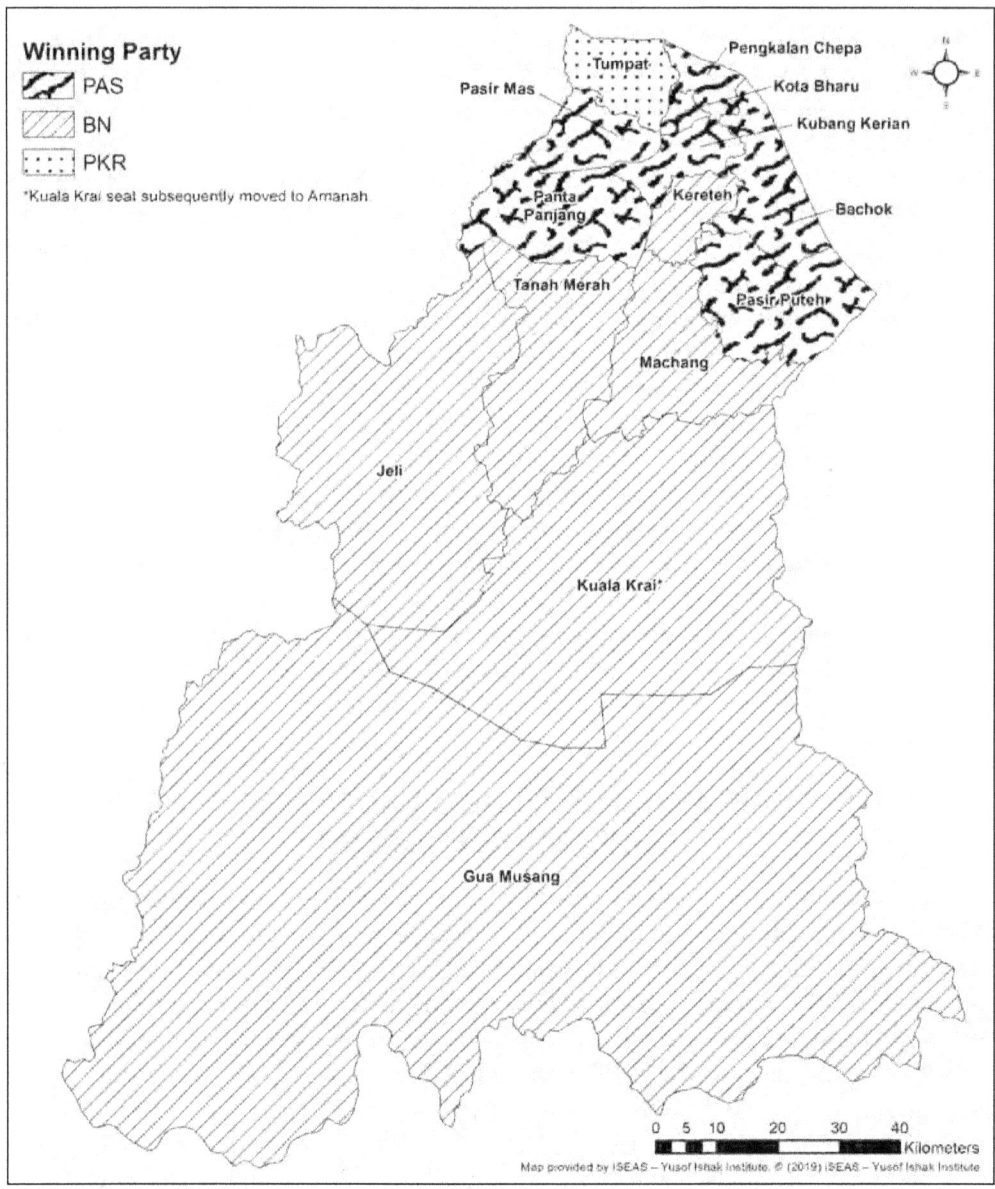

While the seats won at the state level largely corresponded with the parliamentary seats, there are some exceptions. PKR's sole state seat in GE-13, Guchil, was won by Mohd Roslan Puteh. This seat was within the Kuala Krai parliamentary constituency, won by PAS (Figure 14.6). Despite their different party affiliations, this was still acceptable for the Islamic party because it was in a coalition with PKR at that time.

FIGURE 14.6
State Seats in Kelantan by Party (GE-13)

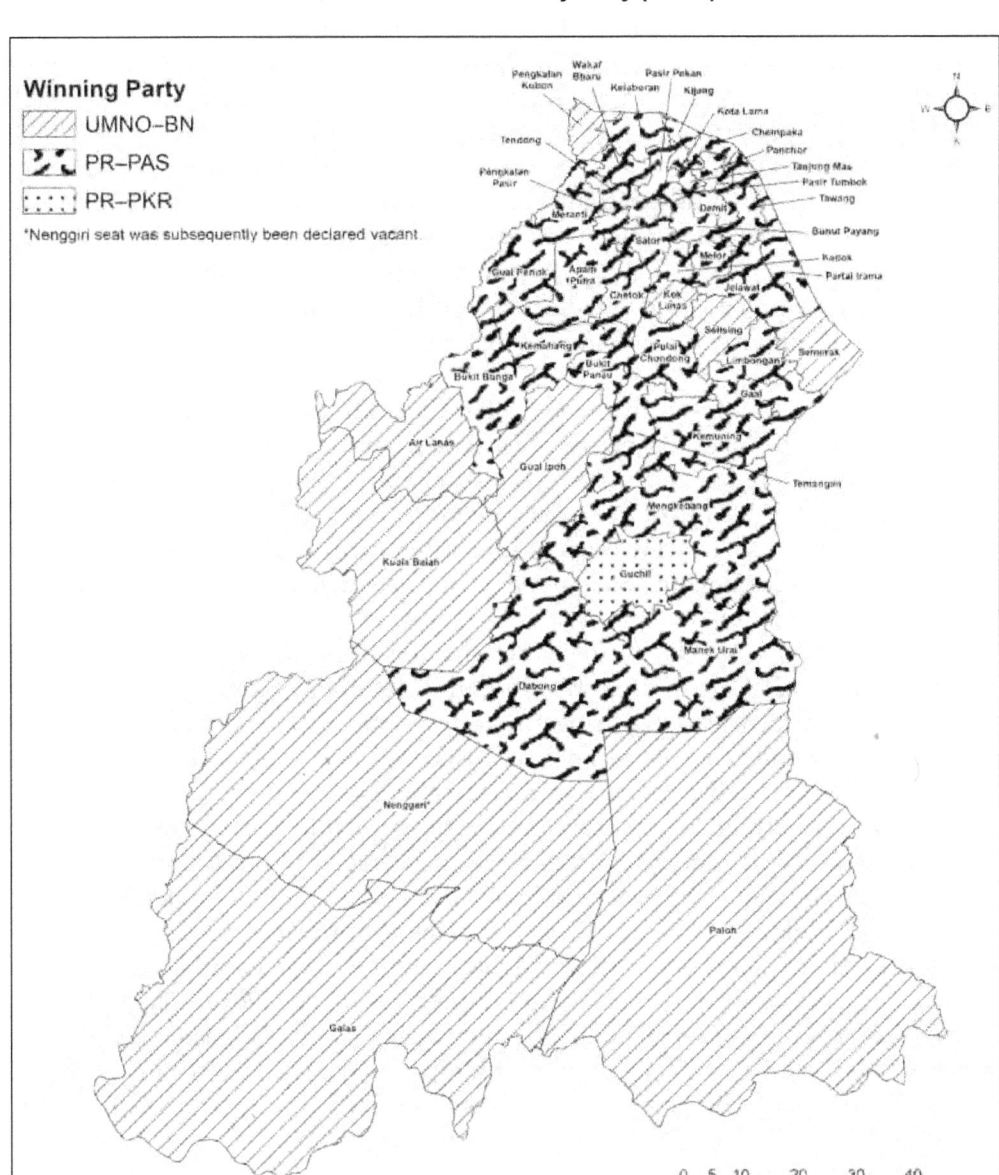

Furthermore, despite belonging to PKR, Mohd Roslan voted in agreement with other PAS members—against his own party's wishes—to support *hudud* laws in 2015 (*Sinar Harian*, 22 March 2015).

However, while PAS was resisting BN's incursions into Kelantan, the picture in 2008 and 2013 was one of stagnation. One possible explanation was that fragmentation within the party—between progressives and conservatives—had already begun, and Kelantanese were not favourable towards PAS' presence in the Pakatan Rakyat (PR) coalition. In particular, the partnership with the largely Chinese Democratic Action Party (DAP)—which was adamant that the country should remain multiracial and would not tolerate the implementation of *hudud* laws—was controversial.

In the subsequent two years, PAS' leadership underwent important changes at the national level as well as in Kelantan. First, Nik Aziz passed away in 2015. While no longer at the forefront of the state's political life, his departure had long-term implications for the party's political direction. Following a short interlude, the most senior leadership of the *ulama* fell to Abdul Hadi, who came from Terengganu, and was associated with the conservative wing in PAS. He later took the party in this direction.

For Kelantan, Nik Aziz's death meant that Chief Minister Ahmad Yakob became the most senior politician for the party. He rose from the party's rank and file, and while he is considered an *ulama* (he is a graduate of Al-Azhar University), he was not as prominent as Nik Aziz, and was seen more as an administrator. In addition, despite Kelantan having the lowest per capita income in Malaysia, the Ahmad Yakob administration was able to demonstrate some improvement in infrastructure, notably road construction and maintenance.[5]

Third, in 2015, PAS made the major decision to leave the PR coalition. Following its departure, the Islamist party formed a third coalition, Gagasan Sejahtera.[6] This fissure affected PAS' electoral prospects in other states, but boosted its standing in Kelantan. Despite the short-term political costs, PAS was seen as being committed to Islam and Malay rights (Hanneeyzah and Zatul 2018).

Fourth, in addition to requiring the party to rebuild parts of its grassroots networks, PAS' organizational coherence was weakened by an internal split within the party between the "progressive-professionals" and "conservative" *ulama*. During the 2014 PAS Muktamar (General Assembly), there were already signs of tensions within the party. The assembly, held in Johor, saw the more dominant camp made up of clerics and *ulama* marginalize the progressives (Khalid 2016). The PAS crisis ended following the subsequent annual general assembly in 2015, when PAS deputy president Mat Sabu, part of the progressive camp, was defeated in the party election. He subsequently left the party and was joined by other PAS progressive leaders, including Husam Musa, to form Amanah (Wan Saiful 2018).

GE-14

It was in this very different context that PAS campaigned in Kelantan in 2018. Beyond the absence of Nik Aziz, the party's "conservative turn" and its split, PAS no longer had the monopoly on the religious vote. In addition, its departure from a broader coalition as well as its campaign pledge to contest across the country constituted a heavy financial and organizational commitment for the party, which had to rebuild networks, raise funds, and field new candidates.

Beyond its own internal dynamics, external factors also shaped PAS' electoral strategies and campaign in GE-14. First, from 2015 onwards, UMNO began to court the Islamic party. During the UMNO General Assemblies in 2016 and 2017, then Prime Minister Najib praised PAS for its commitment in uniting the Malays and Muslims in the country although he stopped short of announcing a formal collaboration with PAS (Norshahril 2018).

While the issue of shariah and *hudud* laws had soured relations between UMNO and PAS in the past, the Najib administration allowed PAS president, Abdul Hadi Awang, to table a private member's bill seeking amendments to the 1965 Syariah Courts (Criminal Jurisdiction) Act. This amendment contemplated raising the maximum sentence of the shariah courts from the existing three years' jail sentence, fine of RM5,000, and six strokes of the cane to thirty years of jail, RM100,000, and 100 lashes of the cane (Chow 2017).

In addition, PAS leaders began to make common cause with UMNO on the plight of the Rohingya in Myanmar. In December 2016, 10,000 UMNO and PAS supporters gathered at the Titiwangsa Stadium in Kuala Lumpur to stage a protest against the Myanmar government over what they call "ethnic cleansing" of the Rohingya people. Both Najib and Abdul Hadi attended the mass protest, demonstrating their solidarity over the plight of Muslims in other parts of the world (Teoh 2016). There were also talks before GE-14 of a possible UMNO-PAS tie up. Even Mahathir in his campaign speeches mentioned that a vote for PAS is a vote for BN, and PAS' motive was to help Najib win (YouTube 2018a).

THE CAMPAIGNS IN KELANTAN

Given the unique context of Kelantan as well as the importance of economic issues in GE-14, the campaigns of the three coalitions were somewhat different in the state than they were elsewhere in the country.

More than in other parts of the country, BN's campaign in the state assumed a religious character. Thus, BN's manifesto for Kelantan contained numerous Islamic references and pledged to change its landscape through the *maqasid syariah* (moderate Islam) approach.[7] UMNO fielded Dr Asyraf Wajdi Dusuki, a deputy minister in the Prime Minister's Office and a religious scholar, to have numerous dialogues with Kelantanese. Beyond his youth and high profile, Asyraf's family line can be traced back to Tok Salehor, a famous Kelantanese cleric. This was complemented by pledges to invest in the state's religious infrastructure including: building a Quran University; expanding the network of *tahfiz* (Quran memorization) schools; and upgrading mosques—including enlarging Masjid Muhammad 1 which was built in 1982 (Mohamad Bakri 2017).

This was complemented with numerous "developmentalist" projects as well as pledges to dramatically improve the state's per capita income—the lowest in the country. Mustapa Mohamed, the Minister of Trade and Industry, was widely rumoured to be BN's candidate for the Chief Minister post, and he became the highest-profile member of parliament (MP) in the state.[8] Referring to the state's low per capita income, Mustapa Mohamed argued that his party devised its manifesto based on what PAS had failed to accomplish over twenty-seven years in power (Rohaiza 2017). Consequently, the coalition pledged to improve the business environment through: reducing land premia and tax rates; improving government administration; and simplifying the procedures for small businesses to obtain licences.

While UMNO clearly sought to play the Islamic card, including fostering closer ties with PAS, it was not clear whether it aimed to forge an alliance with the latter party or simply recapture Kelantan. Judging from statements issued by BN and UMNO leaders, there was some intention to take over the state from a weakened PAS (*Star Online*, 17 March 2018). It is also worth noting that, except for a limited number of established candidates, BN fielded a crop of younger, relatively unknown candidates to contest.

In January 2018, Najib visited Kelantan and promised significant investment in the state, such as: the RM572 million Sungai Kelantan Integrated River Basin Development Project; expanding the Sultan Ismail Petra Airport in Pengkalan Chepa; as well as building the East Coast Railway (ECRL) to connect the Peninsula's East Coast to Kuala Lumpur by train (*Malaysiakini*, 29 January 2018).

Conversely, while UMNO sought to bolster its Islamic credentials in Kelantan, PAS did not make religion an overwhelming part of its campaign platform beyond a general commitment to strengthen Islam as a way of life as enshrined in the federal constitution. PAS also promised to make the Malay language the lingua franca for all subjects taught in schools.

In contrast to UMNO, PAS sought to address cost of living issues directly. Among the party's top promises were: abolishing the GST; resolving the payment of outstanding student loans; offering basic food programmes for the poor; and providing a one-off payment of RM2,000 for women to start work from home. These were indicated in the PAS manifesto entitled *Manifesto Malaysia Sejahtera, 20 Tawaran Utama* (Prosperous Malaysia Manifesto, 20 Key Pledges) distributed during the campaign period.[9]

Rather than holding large-scale rallies, PAS grassroots workers campaigned door-to-door, particularly the party's women's wing (Dewan Muslimat PAS). During the campaign period, PAS' flags and posters were more visible in rural areas than those of other parties.[10] While the photographs of Abdul Hadi and Ahmad Yakob were prominently displayed during the campaign, Nik Aziz's images were prevalent in the form of paintings and murals in the streets.

However, PAS had to counter accusations from PH that it was colluding with BN. Given the acrimonious split between PAS and UMNO in the 1970s over control of the Kelantan state government, this criticism carried substantial weight. News that some PAS members accepted money from UMNO leaders went viral in the social media. Before the elections, there was an audio recording circulated online containing a conversation among PAS leaders. The recording contained the voice of one PAS leader, believed to be Nik Abduh (the son of Nik Aziz), admitting to accepting RM90 million from UMNO. While Nik Abduh initially denied, he later admitted to have Abdul Hadi's blessings for the denial. The matter is currently being investigated by the Malaysian Anti-Corruption Commission (MACC) (*Straits Times*, 14 February 2019).

Within Pakatan Harapan, Amanah was tipped to be PAS' main rival due to its religious credentials and potential attractiveness to the former's support base. As with PAS, it also carried out door-to-door visits. However, despite Amanah absorbing a substantial proportion of PAS' leadership, its grassroots network was weak. PH made ten promises in the Kelantan manifesto: which included to remove car parking fees, to create 20,000 new job opportunities, to build a small harbour, and to complete Kota Bharu–Kuala Krai highway within eighteen months after GE-14. Though it did not mention its candidate for the Chief Minister post, there were rumours that the position would be handed to Husam Musa, Nik Aziz's protégé. Husam was in the Kelantan government when the late leader was Chief Minister. In 2009, when there were rumours of Husam stepping down from the government, Nik Aziz had all but praise for him: "he is a unique leader who is instrumental in not only changing the Kelantan political landscape but also the national politics. Allah did not create Husam for Kelantan, but for all Malaysians." (*Star Online*, 23 November 2009).

Aside from Husam Musa, Nik Aziz's son Nik Omar was the only high-profile campaigner in the state. However, Amanah was unable to convert this backing into popular support. Among Nik Aziz's children, Nik Omar was not in the public eye as much as his brother Nik Abduh, a PAS loyalist. Nik Omar is a teacher, and imam of Pulau Melaka Mosque, where Nik Aziz used to conduct his prayers as well. PAS was able to frame Nik Omar's departure as an act of disobedience to his mother, who had remained with the conservative faction of the party (*Star Online*, 18 May 2018). Many of Amanah's other candidates are not *ulamas*; many are medical doctors.

Another localized dynamics was that Mahathir's prominent role within PH was not an asset in Kelantan. It was due to many public disagreements between the former prime minister and Nik Aziz regarding Islamic law, as well as the sharing of oil revenue and development funds (Hutchinson 2014). Thus, in the run-up to GE-14, PAS supporters and Nik Aziz's family members prevented Mahathir from visiting Nik Aziz's grave (YouTube 2018b). Videos of the failed visit were widely circulated on social media. In contrast to the situation in the rest of the country, PH candidates tended to not refer to Mahathir.

The received wisdom in the days before GE-14 was that PAS would be wiped out in Kelantan. The Merdeka Center's last survey on 8 May, predicted that BN would take eleven out of fourteen parliamentary seats. It predicted that BN will take over Kelantan because of three-cornered fights between BN, PH and PAS. Two weeks before GE-14, Merdeka Center's executive director, Ibrahim Suffian said that, "based on survey results, as of April [2018], BN may win 55 per cent of the vote and Pakatan Harapan [PH] 10 per cent, leaving PAS with 35 per cent" (Sheith Khidir 2018). INVOKE, a think-tank associated with Rafizi Ramli (a member of PKR) predicted that PAS would lose all seats, including in Kelantan. He also predicted that Kelantan would fall to BN (Augustin 2018). However, ordinary Kelantanese whom I spoke to before the election were confident that PAS would retain the state but with a smaller majority.

THE RESULTS

Contrary to the predictions, PAS performed well in Kelantan and improved its performance compared to the 2013 elections. It won nine of fourteen parliament seats, and thirty-seven out of forty-five state seats. It retained the number of parliament seats won in 2013, and gained five state seats.

Figures 14.6 and 14.7 illustrate the seats parties captured during the 2018 election. The grey areas reflect margins of less than 55 per cent of the votes.

The figures show that Kelantan can be divided into a semi-urban north (seats bordering South Thailand) and rural south. Kelantan electoral history shows that the urban and semi-urban seats have always been PAS strongholds, while the rural seats can either be PAS or UMNO strongholds.

During GE-14, fieldwork focused on the following key constituencies: Kota Bharu, Jeli, Kubang Kerian and Pengkalan Chepa (Figure 14.9). These seats were chosen either because they were: BN strongholds; PAS strongholds; or contained state seats where candidates for the position of Chief Minister were running. The following subsections analyse the results from these four parliamentary constituencies and, where relevant, their state seats.

Kota Bharu

Kota Bharu, the capital of Kelantan, is the only urban classified constituency and a PAS stronghold. The seat is one of the smallest in terms of geographical size, but holds the second largest number of registered voters (about 87,000) in the state after Bachok (about 89,900). It is one of the few seats in Kelantan to have a sizeable Chinese community, largely in the Kota Lama state seat, where they comprise 34 per cent of voters.

In 2013, the seat was won by Takiyuddin Hassan, the secretary general for PAS and the party's Chief Whip in Parliament. In 2018, the seat was contested by BN, PAS, and PH (through Amanah). Given the seat's significance, all parties fielded strong candidates to contest. PAS retained Takiyuddin Hassan, and PH mobilized Husam Musa to run in the seat. BN deployed Fikhran Hamshi Mohamad Fatmi, a younger candidate and son of former BN candidate Mohamad Fatmi.

Husam unexpectedly lost the battle. Takiyuddin won 28,291 votes (42.4 per cent), Husam 22,422 (33.5 per cent) and Fikhran Hamshi 16,256 (24.3 per cent). In GE-13, Takiyuddin won the seat with 61.5 per cent while Mohamad Fatmi Che Salleh (BN) obtained 37.3 per cent. The seat is generally a PAS stronghold, and it was unlikely for BN to win the seat in a three-cornered fight. Yet, with BN contesting, it acted as a spoiler party that prevented non-PAS voters from switching to PH's Husam.

PAS also swept all three state seats within the Kota Bharu constituency. Of them, Kota Lama was the most hotly contested, with no less than five candidates running.

FIGURE 14.7
Parliamentary Seats in Kelantan by Party (GE-14)

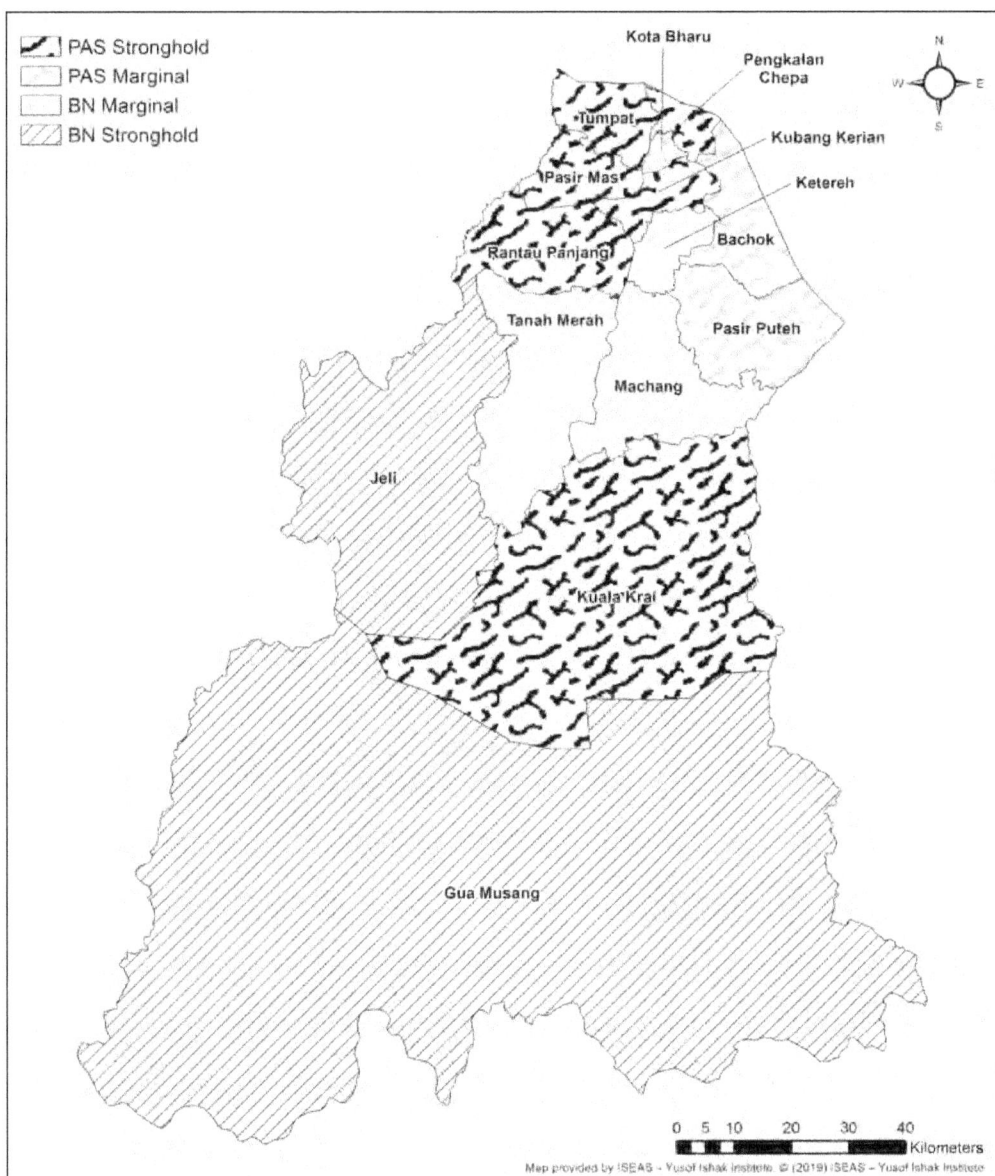

PAS fielded the incumbent, Anuar Tan, a Chinese Muslim. PH sent Tan Sri Abdul Rashid Abdul Rahman, a Parti Pribumi Bersatu Malaysia (PPBM) vice-president and former Election Commission chairman. BN fielded a young Chinese, Chua Hock Kuan, who had been present on the ground for an extensive period. He has been meeting with the villagers and listening to them months before GE-14, and some

FIGURE 14.8
State Seats in Kelantan by Party (GE-14)

Map provided by ISEAS – Yusof Ishak Institute. © (2019) ISEAS – Yusof Ishak Institute

residents I spoke to wanted a young candidate to bring about infrastructural changes to the constituency.[11] The seat was also contested by two independent candidates. In the end, PAS won with 8,410 votes (40.1 per cent), beating PH's 6,965 (26.3 per cent), and BN's 5,502 (26.3 per cent). While PH's Abdul Rashid received a significant number of votes because of his high-profile position, PAS was able to win through appealing to both the seat's Muslim majority and Chinese community.

FIGURE 14.9
Selected Parliamentary Constituencies in Kelantan (GE-14)

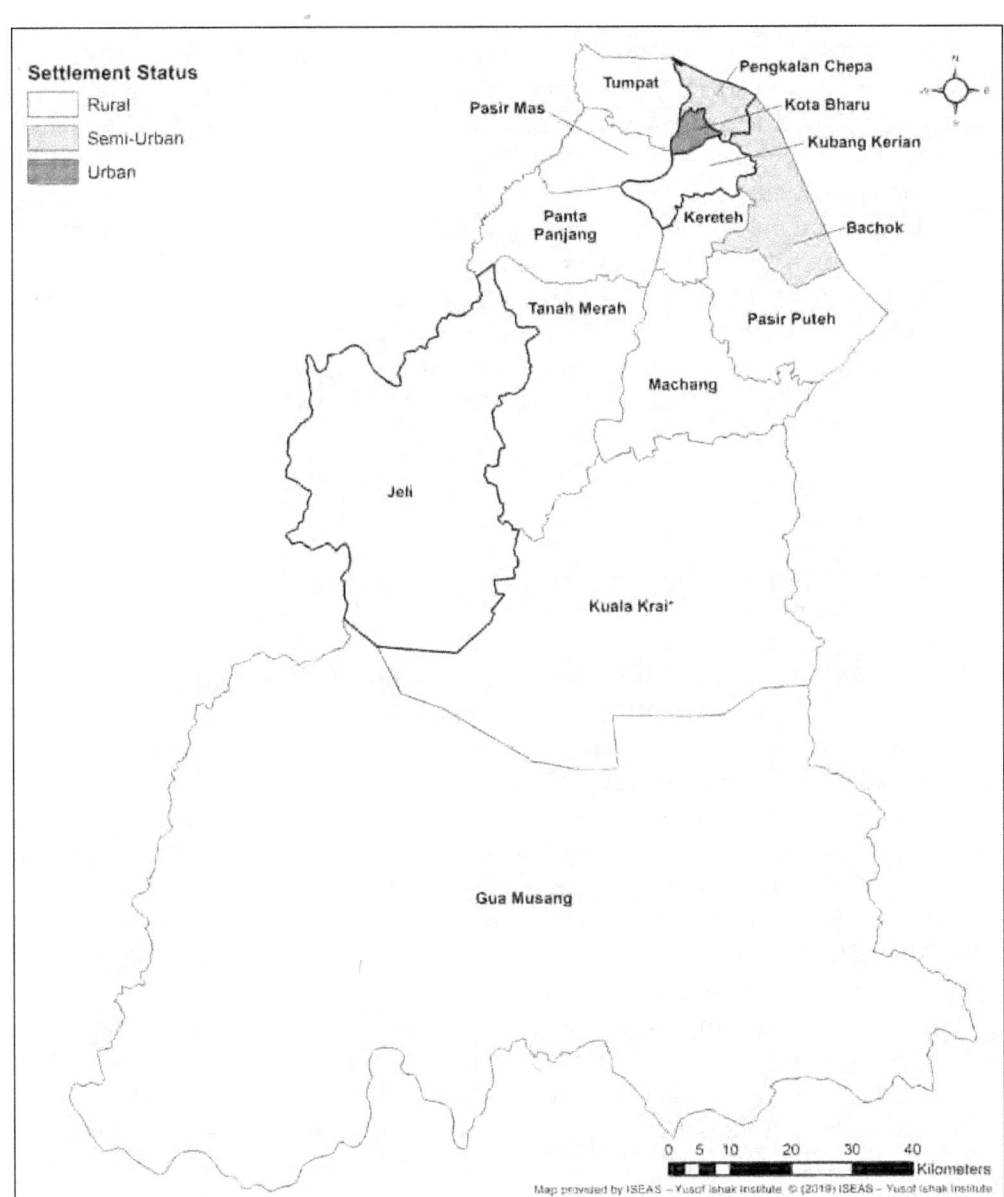

Jeli

As a rural, medium-sized constituency with 47,000 registered voters and a 98 per cent Malay majority, Jeli could be considered a BN stronghold. UMNO veteran and Kelantan Chief Minister, Mustapa Mohamed, had been MP for the seat from 1995 to 2018, except for 1999–2004, when the seat was lost to a PAS candidate. The Jeli parliament seat includes three state seats and, in the 2013 elections all of them were won by BN—albeit narrowly. Of note was Air Lanas, where Mustapa also contested, winning by a mere forty-seven votes.

In the 2018 election, Jeli was contested by BN, PAS and PH (represented by PKR). Although Mustapa had a well-established connection with the constituency, PAS' Mohd Hamid had also been a candidate for the seat for a substantial period. In contrast, PH's candidate, Azran Deraman, was new to the area and not seen to be a serious contender.

Mustapa won the seat through securing 55.9 per cent of the votes. Mohd Hamid received 38.7 per cent, and Azran Deraman a mere 5.2 per cent. BN also managed to retain the Air Lanas seat by a slightly larger margin of 359 votes. The other two seats, Bukit Bunga and Kuala Balah were also won by BN. Mustapa is seen as a clean politician and not involved with the 1MDB issue that tarnished BN. Furthermore, he contested in the same seat despite having almost losing it in 2013. He was also seen as a potential Kelantan Chief Minister if BN won the state.

Kubang Kerian

Despite its proximity to Kota Bharu, Kubang Kerian is a rural constituency with about 72,200 registered voters, of which more than 95 per cent are Malays. Unlike the other two constituencies, Kubang Kerian has an association with the progressive faction in PAS that went on to found Parti Amanah Negara. In 2013, the seat was won by Ahmad Baihaki Atiqullah from PAS. Before 2013, the seat was occupied by Salahuddin Ayub, who subsequently moved to the Pulai parliamentary seat in Johor and was one of the founders of Amanah.

Incumbent Ahmad Baihaki was dropped from the seat in GE-14 because he was rumoured to be pro-Amanah (Zaain and Asma 2018). PAS fielded Tuan Ibrahim, the party's deputy president, to run in the seat against PH's Abdul Halim Yusof (an orthopaedic surgeon). In the end, Tuan Ibrahim won comfortably, securing 56.2 per cent of the vote. The margin of the victory was significant, as PAS was able to secure more votes than the other two candidates combined.

Kubang Kerian is comprised of three state seats, of which one, Salor, was held by Husam Musa of Amanah. In the 2013 election, Husam contested as a PAS member, obtaining 60.3 per cent of the votes against BN's Mohd Nordin Awang's 38.6 per cent. In GE-14, the seat witnessed a three-cornered fight and Husam lost his seat, obtaining a mere 3,617 votes (17 per cent). In contrast, PAS' Saiful Adli obtained 11,206 votes to take the seats, and BN's Mohamad Noordin obtained 6,540. PAS was also able to take the other two state seats in the Kubang Kerian constituency with solid majorities.

Pengkalan Chepa

Pengkalan Chepa was won by Dr Izani Hussin of PAS in 2013, who obtained 57.6 per cent of the popular vote. In 2018, the seat saw a three-cornered fight between BN's

Zaluzi Sulaiman, PAS' Ahmad Marzuk Shaary, and PH's Mohamad Ibrahim. PAS won the seat comfortably with 32,592 votes (54.9 per cent), whereas BN obtained 19,360 (32.6 per cent) and PH 7,435 (12.5 per cent).

The parliamentary constituency is divided into three state seats, and in 2013, all were held by PAS. Of these, the state seat of Chempaka was the most closely watched. In GE-13, the seat was won by Nik Aziz Nik Mat, with a majority of 6,500 votes. Following his death, a by-election was held and contested by five candidates, following which PAS' Ahmad Fathan Mahmood took the seat with an improved majority of 10,000 votes.

In GE-14, Nik Aziz's son, Nik Omar decided to contest in the seat. This was seen by PAS as a betrayal towards the party but also his father's legacy. While Nik Omar was believed to be a favourite during the campaign, he obtained the lowest number of votes (2,418), trailing incumbent Ahmad Fathan Mahmood of PAS, who obtained 10,549, and Mohamed Fareez Noor Amran of BN (7,075 votes). Beyond PAS' smear tactics, Nik Omar's campaign was hampered by his late entry, and his rivals' successful moves to lower his profile—thus, due to PAS' lobbying, he was not allowed to lead prayers at the Kota Bharu mosque.

On the whole, PAS strengthened its grip on Kelantan in GE-14, and clinched important key battles at the parliament and state levels. BN came out second best, with its established candidates such as Mustapa Mohamed and Tengku Razaleigh retaining their seats but many of their younger and less established candidates losing out. Of the three coalitions, PH came off worst, with its component member Amanah losing all of its key contests, not least those waged by two of its high-profile candidates in the state, Husam Musa and Nik Omar.

CONCLUSION: WHY PAS DID WELL

In the run-up to GE-14, the conventional wisdom was that PAS' twenty-eight-year tenure in power in Kelantan would end. Despite the novelty of Parti Amanah and the momentum building up around Pakatan Harapan, surveys consistently indicated that Barisan Nasional would retake the state.

In the end, PAS' electoral victory can be attributed to four main reasons.

First, although it was not covered in the media, PAS was able to utilize its formidable grassroots network to campaign and mobilize voters. This was done through door-to-door visits, often through the party's women's wing, rather than in large *ceramahs*. This grassroots work was not picked up in either the mainstream or social media, leading to its impact being overlooked. This mistaken impression was further compounded by surveys, given that respondents were unwilling to reveal their true preferences (Ibrahim 2018).

Second, while it did not figure extensively in Kelantan, governance issues such as 1MDB did not help Barisan Nasional. Furthermore, given that the cost of living and the introduction of the goods and services tax (GST) were such important issues, it is possible that this negated the criticisms that BN levelled against PAS' economic administration of the state. The relatively positive track record of the Ahmad Yakob government since 2013 also enabled PAS to point to concrete improvements in the state. And, despite a number of high-profile figures, much of BN's slate consisted of lesser known and younger candidates. Consequently, while BN was not decimated, it was unable to significantly expand its footprint in the state.

Third, PAS was able to neutralize the competition for hearts and minds that Pakatan Harapan and, specifically Parti Amanah Negara, posed the party. Apart from Husam Musa and Nik Omar, PH was unable to mobilize charismatic or appealing candidates. In addition, despite Parti Amanah Negara's credible appeals to Nik Aziz's legacy, PAS was able to secure his widow's support to circulate a counternarrative. In seat after seat, Amanah lost its key contests.

Fourth, unlike in other parts of the country, Pakatan Harapan's association with Mahathir Mohamad was a liability rather than an asset. Mahathir's frequent conflict with the PAS leadership during his first tenure as prime minister, as well as Kelantan's financial difficulties following PAS' return to power in 1990 loomed large in the campaign. In addition, the Islamic party was able to neutralize Mahathir's attempts to posthumously make peace with Nik Aziz.

While PAS' performance on the national level was mixed, its consistent performance in GE-14, as well as its deft work and savvy ability to control messaging during the campaign ensured that the party retained control of the balcony of Mecca.

Notes

1. I wish to thank my research assistant Mohd Zaidi Bin Musa for facilitating my fieldwork in Kelantan.
2. For their part, Malaysian Chinese comprise 3.2 per cent of the population and Indians about 0.3 per cent. While a substantial proportion of the Malay population resides in the state's rural areas, the minority groups mainly reside in urban areas, concentrated in the capital Kota Bharu.
3. To understand more about the PAS performance in 1970s, see Farish (2014).
4. Tengku Razaleigh rejoined UMNO in 1996.
5. Based on author's fieldwork observation, 28 April 2018.
6. Gagasan Sejahtera is mainly made up of PAS and two small parties Berjasa and Parti Ikatan Bangsa Malaysia (Ikatan).
7. BN Kelantan adopted the slogan *"Bersama Demi Kelantan"* (Together for Kelantan). Core aims and promises were outlined in manifesto pamphlets disseminated during the campaign period.
8. As will be discussed later, Mustapa won the seat in GE-14, but quit BN to join PPBM.
9. I received a copy of this campaign material during my fieldwork, 29 April 2018.
10. Observations made during fieldwork the last week of April 2018.
11. Interview with Chua Hock Kuan a few days before the elections (Kota Bharu, 29 April 2018).

References

Augustin, Robin. 2018. "INVOKE Predicts 5 States to PH, PAS to Lose Everything". *FreeMalaysiaToday*, 10 March 2018. https://www.freemalaysiatoday.com/category/

nation/2018/03/10/invoke-predicts-5-states-to-ph-pas-to-lose-everything/ (accessed 20 March 2019).

Chow, Melissa Darlyne. 2017. "Hadi Tables Bill to Amend RUU 355 in Parliament". *New Straits Times*, 6 April 2017. https://www.nst.com.my/news/2017/04/227758/hadi-tables-bill-amend-ruu-355-parliament (accessed 20 March 2019).

Farish A. Noor. 2014. *The Malaysian Islamic Party PAS 1951–2013: Islamism in a Mottled Nation*. Amsterdam: Amsterdam University Press.

Hanneeyzah and Zatul. 2018. "PAS Tak Kesal Tinggalkan Pakatan: Hadi". *BH Online*, 11 May 2018. https://www.bharian.com.my/berita/politik/2018/05/424157/pas-tak-kesal-tinggalkan-pakatan-hadi (accessed 20 March 2019).

Hutchinson, Francis E. 2014. "Malaysia's Federal System: Overt and Covert Centralisation". *Journal of Contemporary Asia* 44, no. 3: 422–42.

Ibrahim Suffian. 2018. "Why Opinion Polls Failed to Predict the Fall of BN in Malaysia". *The Round Table* 107, no. 6: 791–92.

Khalid Samad. 2016. *Dari PAS ke Amanah: Berani Berprinsip II*. Selangor: Ilham Books.

Mahathir Mohamad. 1995. "Islam Guarantees Justice for All Citizens". In *Hudud in Malaysia: Issues at Stake*, edited by Rose Ismail. Kuala Lumpur: Sisters in Islam.

Malaysiakini. 2018. "Najib Woos Kelantan with 'Development'". 29 January 2018. https://www.malaysiakini.com/news/410350 (accessed 20 March 2019).

Mohamad Bakri Darus. 2017. "Perubahan di Kelantan perlu bermula dengan impian—Ahmad Zahid". *Bernama*, 5 September 2017. http://pru14.bernama.com/newsbm.php?id=1388802 (accessed 20 March 2019).

Muzaffar, Chandra. 1987. *Islamic Resurgence in Malaysia*. Petaling Jaya: Fajar Bakti.

Norshahril Saat. 2012. "Islamising Malayness: Ulama Discourse and Authority in Contemporary Malaysia". *Contemporary Islam: Dynamics of Muslim Life* 6, no. 2: 135–53.

———. 2014. "The Ulama, Thought-Styles, and the Islamic State Debate in Contemporary Malaysia". *Studia Islamika* 21, no. 1: 47–76.

———. 2018. "UMNO Revival: Reaffirmation of Ideology or Reform?". *ISEAS Perspective*, no. 2018/72, 15 November 2018.

NSTP Research and Information Services. 1994. *Elections in Malaysia: A Handbook of Facts and Figures on the Elections 1955–1990*. Kuala Lumpur: New Straits Times Press.

Rohaiza Ab Rahman. 2017. "Manifesto BN Ambil Kira Prestasi 27 Tahun OAS Tadbir Kelantan—Mustapa". Bernama, 8 October 2017. http://pru14.bernama.com/newsbm.php?id=1398454 (accessed 20 March 2019).

Saravanamuttu, Johan. 2016. *Power Sharing in a Divided Nation: Mediated Communalism and New Politics in Six Decades of Malaysia's Elections*. Singapore: ISEAS – Yusof Ishak Institute.

Sheith Khidir Abu Bakar. 2018. "BN gaining Malay support in Kelantan, says Merdeka Center". *Free Malaysia Today*, 26 April 2018. https://www.freemalaysiatoday.com/category/nation/2018/04/26/bn-gaining-malay-support-in-kelantan-says-merdeka-center/ (accessed 20 March 2019).

Sinar Harian. 2015. "Kagum Adun PKR Sokong Hudud Walau Parti Tolak". 22 March 2015.

Star Online, The. 2009. "Nik Aziz Heaps Praises on Protégé Husam". 23 November 2009. https://www.thestar.com.my/news/nation/2009/11/23/nik-aziz-heaps-praises-on-protege-husam/ (accessed 20 March 2019).

———. 2018a. "Zahid: Now the Best Time to Take over Kelantan". 17 March 2018. https://www.thestar.com.my/news/nation/2018/03/17/zahid-now-the-best-time-to-take-over-kelantan/ (accessed 20 March 2019).

————. 2018b. "Nik Aziz's Son Barred from Leading Prayers at Mosque". 18 May 2018. https://www.thestar.com.my/news/nation/2018/05/18/nik-aziz-son-barred-from-leading-prayers-at-mosque/ (accessed 20 March 2019).

Straits Times (Singapore). 2019. "PAS Leader: I Was Given 'Blessing' to Deny Audio Confession of UMNO Payments". 14 February 2019. https://www.straitstimes.com/asia/se-asia/pas-leader-i-was-told-to-lie-about-30-million-payment-to-party (accessed 20 March 2019).

Teoh, Shannon. 2016. "UMNO, PAS Chiefs in Joint Protest over Rohingyas". *Straits Times*, 5 December 2016. https://www.straitstimes.com/asia/se-asia/umno-pas-chiefs-in-joint-protest-over-rohingyas (accessed 20 March 2019).

Wan Saiful Wan Jan. 2018. "Emergence of Progressive Islamism in Malaysia". In *Islam in Southeast Asia: Negotiating Modernity*, edited by Norshahril Saat, pp. 13–34. Singapore: ISEAS – Yusof Ishak Institute.

YouTube. 2018a. "Jangan Undi PAS Sebab Depa Makan Dedak". 15 April 2018. https://www.youtube.com/watch?v=BMjzmV5G4-A (accessed 20 March 2019).

————. 2018b. "PRU 14: Tun M Dilarang Ziarah Kubur TGNA". 5 May 2018. https://www.youtube.com/watch?v=vI7QJKUWv38 (accessed 20 March 2019).

Zaain Zin and Asma Hanim. 2018. "PAS Kelantan Rombak Kerusi, Gugurkan Pemimpin 'Harumanis'". *Utusan Online*, 25 April 2018. http://www.utusan.com.my/berita/politik/pas-kelantan-rombak-kerusi-gugurkan-pemimpin-harumanis-1.658197 (accessed 20 March 2019).

15

SARAWAK
An Electoral Tremor with
Far-Reaching Consequences?

Lee Poh Onn

INTRODUCTION[1]

The general election of 9 May 2018 was a watershed in Malaysian history. *The Star* newspaper described the outcome as a night when the "earth moved as one Barisan parliamentary seat after another tumbled …" (*Star Online*, 10 May 2018). Driven by rising dissatisfaction with the Barisan Nasional (BN) rule, a deteriorating economy, anger with corruption and the 1MDB scandal, and unhappiness with the goods and services tax (GST), different segments of Malaysians voted across racial lines "sweeping away what many people in the country have for long regarded as an invincible political behemoth" (Lim, Thayaparan, and Netto 2018, p. 3).

The shockwaves were not confined to states in Peninsular Malaysia, but also spilled over to East Malaysia. In Sarawak, the ruling coalition Sarawak Barisan Nasional (Sarawak BN) lost an unprecedented twelve out of thirty-one parliamentary constituencies. This was the first time that opposition parties secured more than one-third of the state's parliamentary seats, leading Pakatan Harapan (PH) to conclude that a Sarawak tsunami had occurred (*Borneo Post Online*, 10 May 2018).

Just as most observers were taken aback by Pakatan Harapan's stellar performance at the national level, the outcomes of the 2018 General Elections in Sarawak were unexpected. The Sarawak state election, held in 2016, had indicated strong backing for Sarawak BN, who won that election resoundingly. In subsequent months, the state government also made progress on a number of hot-button local issues, including negotiations of the Malaysia Agreement to restore Sarawak's rights, recognition of English as a state language, and recognition of the Unified Examination Certificate (UEC) (*Star Online*, 1 February 2018). Consequently, the sitting Chief Minister, Abang Johari Tun Openg, expected Sarawak BN to retain at least twenty-five constituencies, and possibly acquire an additional parliamentary seat or two.

The eventual political realignment after the 14th General Elections (GE-14) was momentous, as the component parties of Sarawak BN departed from the national BN coalition. At present, this grouping—named Gabungan Parti Sarawak (GPS)—is still in power at the state level. Abang Johari has stated that GPS "will cooperate and collaborate with the federal government for national interest, and state rights and interests based on the Federal Constitution and the Federation of Malaysia" (Lee 2018b). Where interests do not coincide, GPS can choose to go their own way and protect Sarawak's interests.

This chapter will explore the reasons underpinning Pakatan Harapan's unexpectedly strong performance in Sarawak in GE-14. It asks first what made Sarawak BN so confident of a repeat performance of the 2016 state election. From there, it seeks to establish why such a large proportion of the state's voters chose the erstwhile opposition. It then draws out the implications for Sarawak GPS in the country's reconfigured political context.

In order to answer these questions, this chapter draws on statistics, secondary sources, as well as field observations and key informant interviews gathered in three key parliamentary constituencies during the GE-14 campaign. Following this introduction, the next section discusses salient structural factors and key events that have shaped Sarawak's current political landscape, providing substantive coverage of the past decades, in view of the lesser general knowledge of the state's history. The third section focuses on the 2016 state elections, in order to understand Sarawak BN's seemingly solid electoral position. The fourth section then analyses general trends running up to, and the outcome of, GE-14 in Sarawak, drawing on fieldwork and interviews. The fifth section analyses the results of the 2018 parliamentary contests in Sarawak. The sixth and final section discusses the ensuing state-level political reconfiguration and then concludes.

SARAWAK'S POLITICAL CONTEXT

Structure and History

Sabah and Sarawak have completely different histories from Peninsular Malaysia (Chin 2014, p. 154). Due to their different colonization processes and later incorporation into the Federation of Malaysia, these two states enjoyed an extensive set of rights distinct from West Malaysian states that are stipulated in agreements signed in 1963. These rights include the use of English and/or Malay as the official language for all purposes, the absence of an official state religion in the state Constitution, and conferring of bumiputra status on all indigenous races (Woon 2012, p. 276).

In addition to this different history, the ethnic composition of Sarawak is distinct from West Malaysia. On the Peninsula, 61.5 per cent of the population is Malay and indigenous, 21 per cent Chinese and 6.3 per cent Indian. In contrast, Sarawak's population is comprised of 75.3 per cent bumiputra, 24 per cent Chinese, and less than 1 per cent Indian (Table 15.1). The bumiputra population is further divided into two large subcategories: 44 per cent is Christian, comprised largely of Ibans and Bidayuhs, and 30 per cent is Muslim, comprised of Malays and Melanaus (*Straits Times*, 5 March 2018). Sixty per cent of the state's population live in urban and 40 per cent in rural areas. Sarawak's urban population is largely concentrated in the cities of Kuching, Miri, Sibu and Bintulu.

Given the circumstances of Sarawak and Sabah's incorporation into the Federation of Malaysia, they have been given a large number of seats relative to their population. Thus, at present, while the state has about 2.6 million people, it has thirty-one parliamentary constituencies—the largest number of any state. Of these, two are considered urban, four semi-urban, and twenty-five rural (Chacko, this volume).

Due to its different ethnic composition, and the fact that there is no one dominant ethnic group, Sarawak's political context is significantly different from Peninsular Malaysia. On one hand, the principal political parties such as the United Malays National Organization (UMNO), the Malaysian Chinese Association (MCA), and Malaysian Indian Congress (MIC) are not present. On the other, like the Peninsula, the state has traditionally been governed by ethnically based parties grouped together into multiethnic coalitions. In West Malaysia there are three broad political groupings. However, in Sarawak's case, they are: Malay/Melanau; the mainly Christian indigenous Ibans; and the Chinese community (Chin 2015, p. 86).

The Early Days

Following the formation of Malaysia in 1963, a multiethnic coalition comprised of six parties won the state's first district elections. From this time until the 1970 state elections, Sarawak's governing coalition was led by Iban Christians. This period was characterized by political turmoil, as the first Chief Minister, Stephen Ningkan, was seen to favour local priorities over national ones. Tunku Abdul Rahman, the first prime minister of Malaysia, eventually sought to oust him through supporting a rival Iban leader. The plan succeeded, but Ningkan contested this in court and

TABLE 15.1
Sarawak Population by Ethnic Group, 2016 ('000) (Projected)

Total Population	Malay	Iban	Bidayuh	Melanau	Other Bumiputra	Chinese	Others
2,580.0	629.0	785.9	215.1	139.8	175.8	618.3	16.2
Percentage	24.3	30.5	8.3	5.4	6.8	24.0	1.0

Source: Statistics Yearbook Sarawak 2016, Department of Statistics, Malaysia, Sarawak, December 2017.

won. The Federal Government declared a state of emergency, and amended the Sarawak Constitution, which reverted control back to Ningkan's successor, Tawi Sli (Chin 2015, p. 87).

Up to 1970, Sarawak's Chief Ministers were also Iban Christians. However, this was to later change with the intervention of the federal government then headed by Tunku Abdul Rahman. The Malay-Melanau faction took over from 1970 onwards. Since then, politics in Sarawak have been relatively stable for over forty years, ruled by a single Melanau-Muslim family (Chin 2015, p. 86). Some have referred to this as "Strongman Politics", especially under Taib Mahmud's rule and also under Abdul Rahman Ya'kub.

In 1970, the first state elections were held and contested by a broad range of ethnically based parties. In its wake, Tun Abdul Razak, Malaysia's second prime minister, cobbled together a coalition comprised of: the predominantly Malay and Melanau Parti Bumiputera Sarawak (BUMIPUTERA);[2] the Malay-majority Parti Negara Malaysia (PANAS); Malay and Melanau Barisan Rakyat Jati Sarawak (BARJASA); and the largely Chinese Sarawak United People's Party (SUPP) (Chin 2015, p. 87). Under this arrangement, Abdul Rahman Ya'kub, a Melanau-Muslim, then became Chief Minister of Sarawak. This signalled the end of a Christian-led government and the beginning of a "dominant Islamic-led native party, with a less subservient Chinese partner" (Woon 2012, p. 279).

Abdul Rahman Ya'kub: Father of Strongman Politics

Abdul Rahman's tenure lasted from 1970 until 1981. In 1973, he merged BUMIPUTERA with another party (Pesaka; Dayak-dominated) to form the predominantly Malay and Melanau Parti Pesaka Bumiputera Bersatu (PBB), which remains to this day, and is arguably Sarawak's most influential political party (Woon 2012, p. 279). Rahman transformed the PBB into a formidable force in Sarawak. By co-opting the politically weak Dayak faction (Pesaka) into PBB, Rahman could field candidates in Muslim bumiputra and Dayak seats. To finance his electoral machinery and to consolidate his power, he established a network of clients through disbursing timber licences and electoral patronage (Faisal Hazis 2012, pp. 101–6, 271). Licences were disbursed to the tune of RM22.5 billion to his allies and family members,[3] representing over half the timber licences issued, during his administration (ibid., p. 101).

Rahman was the first strongman-politician who maintained Muslim bumiputra political dominance in Sarawak, and did not "rock the boat" by overly championing Sarawak's interests. He also passed the Petroleum Development Act in 1974 which allowed Petronas to have ownership over petroleum and gas resources in the state in return for a 5 per cent royalty. All these factors helped to secure the federal government's blessings as it was in line with their interests of staying in power.

Together with Chinese-based SUPP, Rahman was able to ensure the support of Sarawakians from all ethnic groups. This was the most crucial factor. In the 1974 Sarawak parliamentary elections, Sarawak BN (PBB and SUPP) won fifteen out of the twenty-four seats while Sarawak National Action Party (SNAP; then in the opposition) only won nine seats. This was Rahman Ya'kub's first test to show to the central state leaders that he had the capability to win votes (Faisal Hazis 2012, p. 88). Subsequently, he only managed to further consolidate his power; and although there were break-away factions from Sarawak BN from time to time, Rahman managed to quell any opposition and deftly stayed in power.

Sarawak BN roughly follows the consociational model discussed in Hutchinson (2018, p. 5) in his study on GE-14 in Johor. In Sarawak's case, stability was maintained through the representation of Dayak, Malay/Melanau, and Chinese interests in government through its nominally multiethnic parties, each of which was normally dominated by one ethnicity. Consociationalism was also initially manifested in the 1970s by the PBB (dominated by Malay/Melanau and to a lesser extent also had Dayak representation) and the SUPP (predominantly ethnic Chinese party). Later, when the Dayak-based SNAP rejoined Sarawak BN in 1979, there were three parties, with one to represent each of the three ethnic majorities separately.

As new parties were formed from breakaway factions, Sarawak BN was expanded to co-opt such parties into its fold, such as: the Dayak-dominated Parti Bansa Dayak Sarawak (PBDS); the Dayak-dominated Parti Rakyat Sarawak (PRS); as well as the Chinese- and Dayak-dominated Sarawak Progressive Democratic Party (SPDP, now just known as PDP (Progressive Democratic Party) as it is plans to contest in Peninsular Malaysia).

This multiparty coalition model, headed by a Malay/Melanau and PBB, remained the state's governing model to present times. Given its success at securing parliamentary seats and contributing to maintaining BN's parliamentary and also state majority seats, the administration of Sarawak under Abdul Rahman and his successor Taib Mahmud was permitted considerable autonomy by Barisan Nasional.

Taib Mahmud: Master of Strongman Rule

Rahman's failing health prompted him to step down in 1981 and to allow his nephew, Taib Mahmud, to take over (Faisal Hazis 2012, pp. 107–8). Despite their familial linkage, the first few years were not easy for Taib Mahmud, as his uncle tried to topple him, and factional fighting within the Sarawak BN coalition also challenged his mandate. However, this did not stop his eventual rise to become the greatest "strongman" to date.

In short, Taib Mahmud's path to immense power was not smooth all the way. In total, he served as Chief Minister for thirty-three years from 1981 to 2014. Over that period, he led Sarawak BN thorough seven state elections and eight parliamentary elections. He also witnessed the "dissolution and formation of many political parties", and served under three prime ministers of Malaysia (Faizal Hazis 2012, p. 113). Before his ascendancy, Taib worked closely with his uncle, Abdul Rahman Ya'kub, enabling him to learn and then adopt the right strategies for him to eventually remain in power. Of course, his uncle's patronage also helped. While factional fighting by parties within Sarawak BN occurred during his rule, Taib was very deft in handling such schisms and used such opportunities to further split the Dayak into political parties within the Sarawak BN—eventually tilting the power balance to favour the PBB which was dominated by the Malay/Melanaus. His struggles with his uncle, Rahman Ya'kub, who wanted to regain power, were also eventually overcome.

James Chin identified three other reasons—besides political divisions in the Dayak community—that allowed Taib to remain in power. The first was his massive wealth, the second his keeping UMNO out of Sarawak politics, and the last was his ability to consolidate the Muslim vote (Chin 2015, p. 88).

The Sarawak Report exposed massive land grabs by Taib's family and his family's extensive holdings overseas. One source estimated Taib's family to be worth an estimated US$21 billion (ibid.). Such wealth allowed Taib to strengthen his hold on the state through consolidating his network and political support base.

Taib also managed to reach a written agreement with Prime Minister Dr Mahathir, who was then the UMNO president, that the latter's party would not enter Sarawak as long as either person was in power. This allowed Sarawak BN to be highly autonomous, and for Taib to maintain his fiefdom with little or no outside interference. So far, Sarawak has remained the only state in Malaysia without UMNO branches.

Sarawak's autonomy was further strengthened following the *Reformasi* movement, starting in 1998, after which UMNO's grip steadily weakened, despite a popularity spike in 2004. The 2008 General Elections was a game changer and, from 2013, BN became more dependent than ever on Sarawak and Sabah parties. That year, BN's margin of victory was twenty-one seats, and Sarawak alone contributed twenty-five seats. Without Sarawak BN, federal BN would have lost to the opposition. Sabah and Sarawak combined provided forty-seven seats to federal BN, or 35 per cent of all of the ruling coalition's MPs (Chin 2014, p. 181).

The term "safe deposit" has been coined as the number of seats from both Sabah and Sarawak have enabled BN to stay in power. As Sarawak became more vital to BN, it "emboldened Sarawakian leaders to demand for more of the rights stipulated in the 18 Points Agreement that accompanied Sarawak's decision to join in forming Malaysia in 1963" (Lee 2017, p. 3). This, in turn, made the push for state-level nationalism an important aspect of Sarawak-based politics, not just for Sarawak BN, but also opposition parties active in the state.

Besides splitting Dayak loyalties across parties and using his wealth to consolidate his power, Taib also maintained power by utilizing the "politics of developmentalism"—the handing out of "goodies" to constituencies to gain their electoral votes. It was during the 1987 state election that Taib and BN leaders "exploited their political office to dish out 'instant' projects, financial grants and other 'goodies' to Sarawak voters". The number of development projects and grants disbursed out in 1987 were "unprecedented in the history of elections in Sarawak at that time" (Faisal Hazis 2012, p. 140). As this strategy allowed Taib to win, he continued to embrace development as a tool and to use it throughout the 1990s and beyond (ibid., p. 141).

In addition, Sarawak BN also had the resources to use boats and helicopters to reach out to remote areas during the election campaign, which the opposition lacked. The BN campaign machinery—backed by federal and state government agencies—and the rampant practice of vote buying also helped (Faisal Hazis and Kadam-Kiai, 2013, p. 5). In terms of rural outreach, the strategy of co-opting headmen to control villagers was also used to win political support (Faisal Hazis 2012, p. 254). Village headmen were told to be the "eyes and ears of the government" in bringing about rural reforms. The patronage relationship between headmen and elected representatives, and headman and villagers ensured that entire villages would follow the headman in voting for Sarawak BN.

Such was the success that Sarawak BN managed to keep its hold on power from the 1970s onwards at both the parliamentary and state levels as seen in Figures 15.1 and 15.2.

However, the Chinese community grew increasingly unhappy with Taib's money politics, state-level corruption, and the perception that he favoured his family members and political cronies at the expense of the general Chinese community (Faisal Hazis 2011, p. 17). This disaffection was also shared by the non-Muslim bumiputra community, who also felt marginalized by Taib's actions. As a result, Sarawak BN lost nine seats to the opposition during the 2006 state elections, a steep gain from a mere two seats in the prior election. Out of the nine opposition seats, the Democratic Action Party (DAP) held six.

The continuing frustration among the Chinese and non-Muslim bumiputra, resulted in the DAP and Parti Keadilan Rakyat (PKR) making further headway in

FIGURE 15.1
Sarawak's Parliamentary Elections, 1974–2013

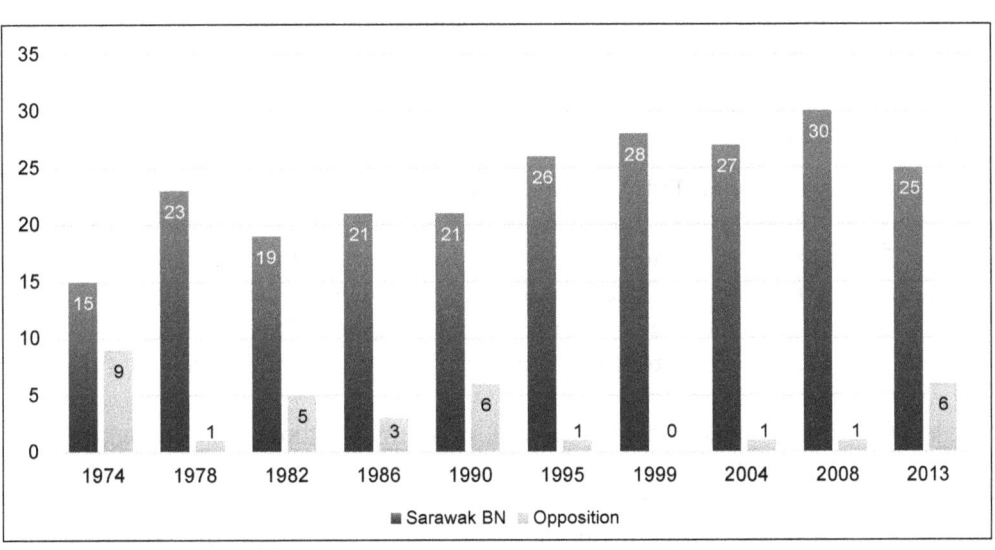

Source: Faisal Hazis (2012) and undi.info.

FIGURE 15.2
Sarawak's State Elections, 1974–2016

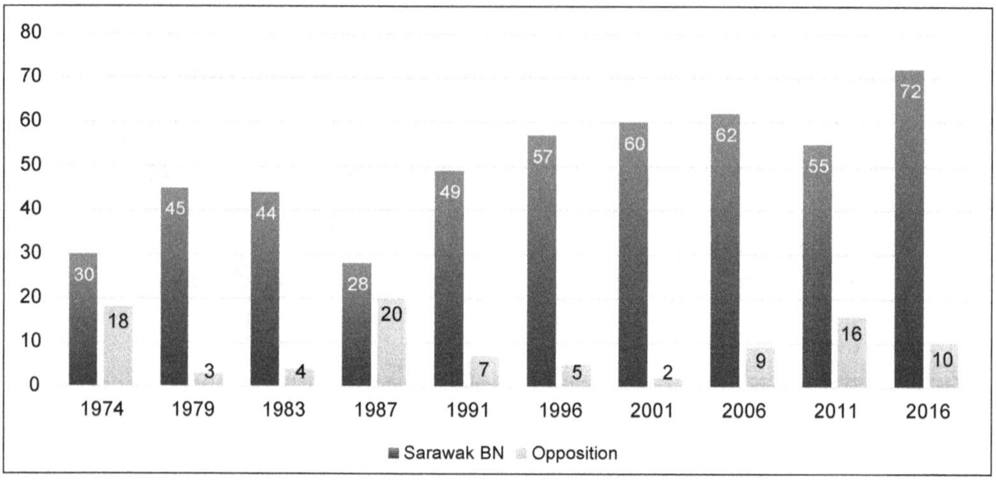

Source: Faisal Hazis (2012) and undi.info.

the 2011 state elections (Lee 2016, p. 3). Also, Taib's refusal to step down became a hot-button issue. The twelve seats won by DAP in Chinese-majority areas, and three that went to PKR, reflected this dissatisfaction.

THE 2016 SARAWAK STATE ELECTIONS

Since 1978, Sarawak has conducted its state legislature elections on its own schedule, without coinciding with the general election.[4] The latest state election in Sarawak, which took place in May 2016, heavily influenced expectations in the run-up to the 2018 General Elections.

The Adenan Factor

Adenan Satem succeeded Taib Mahmud as Sarawak's Chief Minister in 2014. Adenan was well known in the state, and was perceived to be the most trusted lieutenant among Taib's team.[5] Coming from within the ranks, to the surprise of many he turned himself into a reformist leader, which greatly helped secure electoral support during the 2016 state elections. Indeed, Adenan proved to be very much loved and respected by Sarawakians from all walks of life, and was even rarely criticized by PH during their GE-14 rallies.

In 2016, the Adenan factor was said to strongly account for BN impressive showing. He had been quick to establish himself as a no-nonsense and strong leader, advocating a "Sarawak for Sarawakians" stance, criticizing the federal government for its tendency to centralize decisions and strongly supporting demands for autonomy (Weiss and Puyok 2017, p. 5). Adenan also had a cleaner image and was not marred by any major corruption scandals (Mohamed Nawab and Rashaad Ali 2017, p. 41).

The Sarawak government used regional nationalism to its fullest effect, with Adenan Satem promoting the cause of greater autonomy and empowerment for the state during his tenure. Adenan's *53 Principles and Action*, published in 2016, reflected this independent stance strongly and included: reinstating English as the second official language in Sarawak; allowing Christians in Sarawak to use the term "Allah" in their worship; upholding religious freedom;[6] not imposing restrictions on bibles in Bahasa Malaysia in the state; and not recognizing *hudud* law. Adenan also removed bridge tolls, recognized the UEC for entrance into Sarawak tertiary institutions and jobs in the civil service, and froze timber licences.

Adenan also staunchly maintained his predecessors' stance of keeping UMNO out of Sarawak, urging Sarawakians to vote Sarawak BN to "deny UMNO an excuse to take over" (Weiss and Puyok 2017, p. 11; *Borneo Post Online*, 26 March 2014). The fear of what happened to Sabah when UMNO entered into that state was enough of a deterrent, as UMNO was seen to interfere in Sabah's local affairs and also increase racial polarization.

Ineffective Campaigning by PH

On the other hand, the message of *"ubah"* (change) used by the opposition during 2016 state elections was widely seen to be "recycled" from the 2013 General Elections and did not "resonate" with voters. Even the persistent message of economic underdevelopment was adroitly used by Sarawak BN to indicate that only the ruling party could bring about real change. There was really no workable plan to counter Adenan's popularity. Focusing on the 1 Malaysia Development Berhad (1MDB) scandal which involved Najib, allegations of money laundering, mysterious payments of RM2.6 billion into Najib's personal account, and reminding voters that a vote for Adenan was a vote for the corrupt BN government, were not really effective against Adenan's reformist image (Weiss and Puyok 2017, p. 8).

Also, failure by the opposition to form a united front led to multicornered contests, even within the coalition (ibid., pp. 8–9). DAP and PKR contested against one another in six constituencies. In Batu Kitang, for instance, there was a five-cornered fight; in Ngemah, a four-cornered fight. Such multicornered fights diluted the votes among the various opposition candidates in favour of the Sarawak BN candidate (Mohamed Nawab and Rashaad Ali 2017, p. 43). In addition, this was the first time that Parti Islam Se-Malaysia (PAS) contested outside the fold of the defunct Pakatan Rakyat coalition. In this instance, not only was infighting dividing the opposition, but PAS also sought to undermine the position of both DAP and Parti Amanah Negara (Amanah) (ibid., p. 44).

Redelineation

The 2015 redelineation exercise in Sarawak went ahead despite protests and was gazetted on 19 December 2015—just in time for the 2016 Sarawak state elections

(Chacko, this volume). One major issue brought up during the Sarawak state elections was the accusation of gerrymandering by the Election Commission. Redelineation created an additional eleven seats with nine favouring the Sarawak BN. These seats were created in rural and semi-rural areas that were less favourable to the opposition, defying trends in urbanization (Welsh 2016).

After the redelineation, there were twenty-eight Malay/Melanau-majority seats compared to fifteen Chinese-majority seats. This compares to just twenty-five Malay/Melanau seats and fourteen Chinese-majority seats before 2015 (Lee 2016, pp. 2–3). Three new seats were created for Malay/Melanau constituencies (Gedong, Kabong and Tellian), three for Iban majority constituencies (Bukit Goram, Samalaju and Stakan), two for Bidayuh-majority constituencies, two for Orang Ulu constituencies, and one for a Chinese-majority constituency. In total, there were ten new seats created for Muslim and non-Muslim majority seats in the 2016 state elections, and one for the Chinese-majority seat of Batu Kitang.

Bearing in mind that the Chinese make up about 24 per cent of the total population and Malays also about 24 per cent of the total population, the redelineation exercise disproportionately disempowered the Chinese while giving Malays a stronger vote (Mohamed Nawab and Rashaad Ali 2017, p. 44).

The Results of the 2016 Elections

BN Sarawak was comprised of the following component members: the predominantly Malay and Melanau Parti Pesaka Bumiputera Bersatu (PBB); the Chinese Sarawak United People's Party (SUPP); the Iban Parti Rakyat Sarawak (PRS); and the multiracial (Chinese, Iban, Bidayuh) Sarawak Progressive Democratic Party (SPDP) and BN Direct Candidates. These were splinter candidates who contested as BN Direct Candidates under one common Barisan Nasional symbol, who were required to join any BN component party upon winning.

Where the opposition parties are concerned, the DAP, PKR, Amanah, PAS, the State Reform Party (STAR), New Sarawak Native People's Party and Independents contested against BN Sarawak. Table 15.2 provides information on the parties that entered into the Sarawak state elections in 2016. Parti Pribumi Bersatu Malaysia (PPBM) was not in the Sarawak PH coalition at the time of GE-14.

In these elections, Sarawak BN increased its popular vote share from 55.4 per cent to 63 per cent, and secured a massive majority, winning 87.8 per cent of seats (seventy-two out of eighty-two). This was seventeen seats more than the previous state elections, and a higher share of assembly (fifty-five out of seventy-one, or 77.5 per cent). All BN component parties, as well as BN Direct Candidates, won overwhelmingly.[7] Sarawak BN also won all eleven newly created seats (Mohamed Nawab and Rashaad Ali 2017, p. 40).

Out of the ten seats going to the opposition, the DAP held on to seven seats, while PKR retained its three seats. The 2016 state elections regained the ground for Sarawak BN that it had lost in 2011; the opposition lost five seats to Sarawak BN, dropping from the fifteen seats that they held in 2011 to just ten seats. These were

TABLE 15.2
Parties and Candidates—Sarawak State Elections 2016

Coalition/Party		Candidates Fielded	Seats Won
Barisan Nasional	BN	(82)	(72)
United Traditional Bumiputera Party	PBB	39	39
Sarawak United People's Party	SUPP	13	7
Sarawak People's Party	PRS	11	11
Sarawak Progressive Democratic Party	SPDP	6	4
Barisan Nasional Direct Candidate[a]	BN Direct Candidate	13	11
Democratic Action Party	DAP	31	7
People's Justice Party	PKR	40	3
Pan-Malaysian Islamic Party	PAS	11	0
National Trust Party	Amanah	13	0
State Reform Party	STAR	10	0
New Sarawak Native People's Party	PBDS Baru	5	0
Independents	IND	36	0

Note: a. Splinter Candidates who contested as BN Direct Candidates under one common BN symbol were required to join any BN component party upon winning.

all DAP seats. Clearly, the electorate endorsed Adenan's leadership, and apparently some Chinese voters drifted back to the ruling coalition. These factors, in combination with the opposition's inefficacy and the redelineation bias, delivered Sarawak to BN by a landslide.

THE GE-14 CAMPAIGNS IN SARAWAK

Barisan Nasional

Adenan Satem passed away suddenly in January 2017. Abang Johari, who was then the Housing Minister, succeeded as Chief Minister and quickly declared that he would continue with policies initiated by his predecessor (Lee 2017, pp. 2–3). Specifically, Abang Johari reiterated that he would continue to fight for the devolution of power from the federal government to the state, specifically through the fifty-three principles and actions initiated by Adenan Satem which were meant to safeguard the interests of Sarawak.

BN Sarawak reused many elements from the 2016 campaign. Broadly, these elements fall into three broad groups: a continuation of developmentalism; state rights; and multiculturalism. All three frequently referred to achievements from Adenan Satem's tenure. The former Chief Minister's legacy was frequently invoked in campaign activities, and his widow also made campaign appearances, supporting Sarawak BN parties, including the Chinese-majority SUPP[8] (*Star Online*, 5 May 2018).

Developmentalism

A six-point manifesto was launched in April 2018 at the PBB headquarters. The overarching theme of the manifesto was "Transforming Sarawak through Digital Economy". The six thrusts included: regaining and safeguarding Sarawak's rights and preserving its harmony and unity; providing better educational opportunities and facilities; enhancing rural transformation; improving the people's quality of life; initiating new opportunities for progress and prosperity; and practising good governance and integrity (*Star Online*, 9 April 2018). At the same launch, Abang Johari also assured that the government would carry out high-impact infrastructure development projects including roads, bridges, telecommunications, water supply and electricity.

State Rights and Devolution of Power

The drive for greater devolution was frequently referred to and key milestones were cited. In March 2018, Abang Johari announced that Sarawak had complete state rights over mining, which made it the first state in Malaysia to form a state-owned oil and gas company (*Straits Times*, 7 March 2018). Petroleum Sarawak Berhad (PETROS), founded in 2017, would now be able to provide opportunities for the state to earn its own revenues directly through exploration and downstream activities, rather than just relying on cash payments from Petronas. Abang Johari also stated that he would pursue Adenan's objective of raising oil and gas royalties from the present 5 per cent to 20 per cent.

Abang Johari pushed for the establishment of the Development Bank of Sarawak (DBOS) as an alternative financing model for the Sarawak government to promote development projects. DBOS commenced operations on 15 January 2018 (*Borneo Post Online*, 13 January 2019). In April 2018, he announced that the Sarawak Government had acquired the Bakun Dam from the federal government. This would give the state government full control of power generation and supply in the state and attract new mega industries (Lee 2017, p. 3).

Beyond seeking the greater devolution of power, Abang Johari also asked Sarawakians to vote for Sarawak BN to deny UMNO an excuse to enter the state. In constituencies contested by DAP Sarawak, the party was often referred to as one based on the Peninsula, which meant that it would be constrained and unable to independently promote Sarawak's interests.

Multiculturalism

The "Allah ban" was also a non-issue in Sarawak. In Sarawak, Christians can freely use the term Allah in their worship, with no restrictions imposed on using a Bahasa Malaysia bible. In Peninsular Malaysia, this had become a heated issue. The federal government proscribed the use of this word in the 1980s, and the Court of Appeal upheld this decision in 2013—stating that the word Allah is exclusive to Muslims (in Peninsular Malaysia).

UMNO has often used Islam as a tool to secure support from the Malays (Puyok 2017, p. 105). UMNO and PAS have also vied to be the most "Islamic", creating hardline positions despite Malaysia being a multiracial and multireligious society (Chin 2019, p. 9). East Malaysians fear that after half a century of federation, their entire socio-political environment will mirror what is happening in Peninsular Malaysia, destroying their cultural heritage and dividing the state along religious lines (Chin 2015, p. 91).

In March 2018, Abang Johari also announced that the state would amend its laws on conversion, and provide a "standard operating procedure" that would allow individuals to have their conversion reversed. This announcement followed the dismissal of an appeal by three applicants to be heard in a civil court for a reversal in their conversion to Islam (*Straits Times*, 4 March 2018, 5 March 2018).

Abang Johari also persisted with Adenan's policy of using English as the official language of the state with Bahasa Malaysia (*Star Online*, 22 January 2017). Going beyond Adenan's policies, he also wanted Sarawakians to master Mandarin in view of China's rising economic power and assured the Chinese in Sarawak that the government will continue to recognize the UEC (Lee 2017, p. 4).

Fielding of Candidates—Barisan Nasional

The Malay/Melanau and Dayak majority seats were considered safe for Sarawak BN (Chin 2018, p. 183). As such, there was a lower level of campaigning by the incumbent PBB/PDP/PRS MPs of Sarawak BN, who chose to speak at many grassroots, meet-the-people sessions, and launch events, and used flags, posters and banners extensively in the various constituencies, instead of relying on *ceramahs*. The exception was for the opposition Chinese-dominated seats where SUPP candidates campaigned on a larger scale against the PH (DAP) and independent candidates. PBB officials even chipped in during such SUPP rallies to support SUPP candidates in the Chinese populated areas.

Based on the ethnic breakdown in the various constituencies (Figure 15.3), the fourteen PBB candidates campaigned in the Muslim bumiputra and non-Muslim bumiputra constituencies (Santubong, Petra Jaya, Kota Samaharan, Batang Sadong, Batang Lupar, Betong, Tanjong Manis, Igan, Mukah, Kapit, Sibuti, Limbang, Lawas, Puncak Borneo); the four PDP and six PRS candidates contested mainly in the non-Muslim bumiputra seats (PDP: Mas Gading, Bintulu, Saratok, Baram; PRS: Sri Aman, Kanowit, Hulu Rajang, Selangau, Lubok Antu, Julau). It was expected that DAP would only win in their stronghold urban and semi-urban Chinese areas (see Figure 15.3) (Lee 2018c). These were the Chinese-majority constituencies of: Kuching, Stampin, Sarikei, Lanang, and Sibu. SUPP was strategizing to recapture at least some these seats; including the Stampin seat which used to be a safe SUPP seat until 2013 (GE-13). In total, SUPP contested in seven constituencies (Bandar Kuching, Stampin, Sarikei, Lanang, Sibu, Miri and Serian).

SUPP was keen to recapture the Miri seat from PKR. Dr Michael Teo, the incumbent, was seen to be uninterested in being an MP (his attendances at Parliament

FIGURE 15.3
Ethnic Breakdown by Parliamentary Constituency (GE-14)

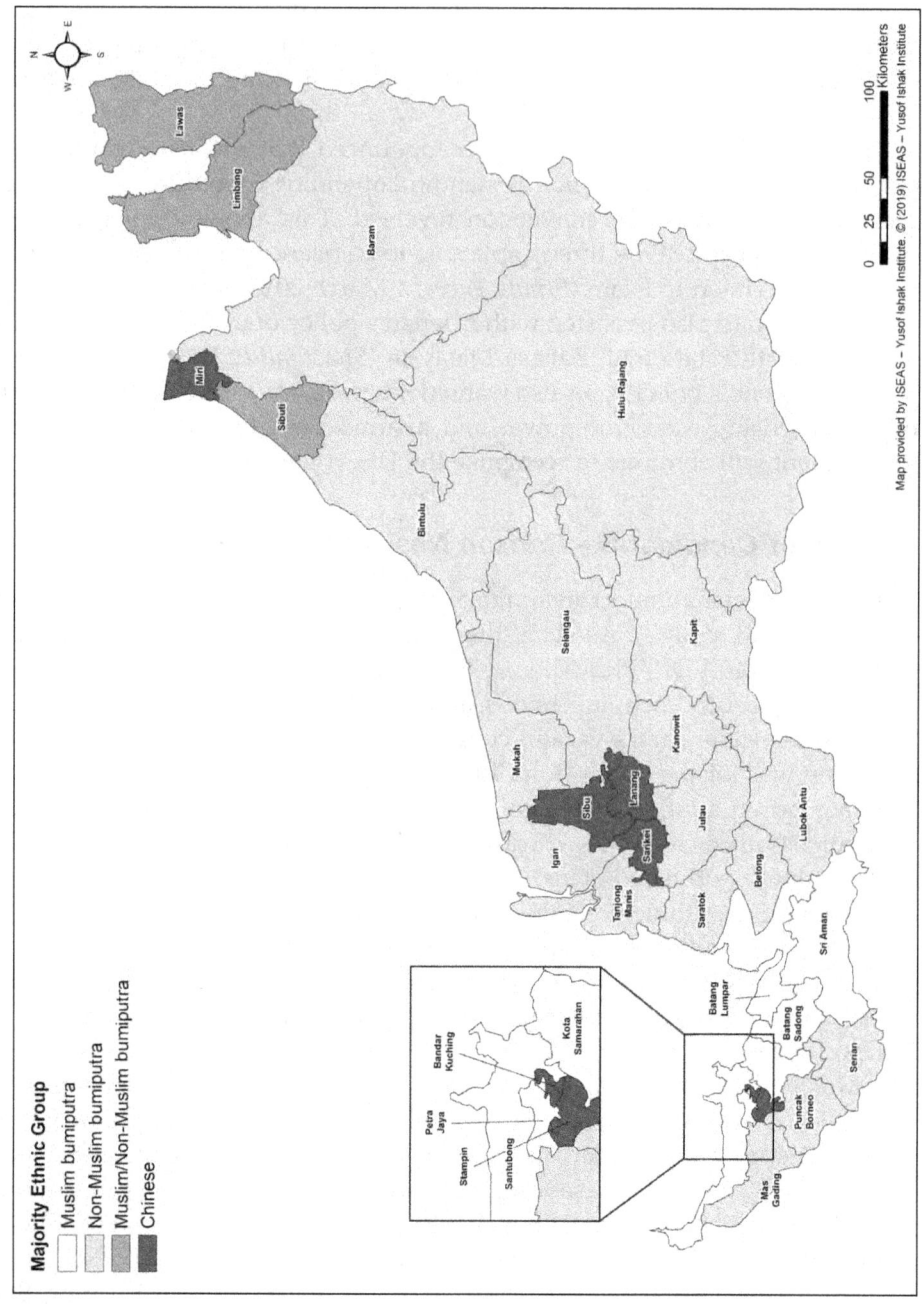

Majority Ethnic Group
- Muslim bumiputra
- Non-Muslim bumiputra
- Muslim/Non-Muslim bumiputra
- Chinese

Map provided by ISEAS – Yusof Ishak Institute. © (2019) ISEAS – Yusof Ishak Institute

were irregular) and he had put forward Bill Kayong to replace him in GE-14. However, Kayong was assassinated on 21 June 2016 and Michael Teo was renominated to contest in that seat. In addition, the bickering between DAP and PKR in the 2016 state elections also made this a shaky seat which the SUPP felt that they could win (Chin 2018, p. 183). Miri was a former BN (SUPP) stronghold which was only lost to PKR in 2013.

Pakatan Harapan

Like BN, Pakatan Harapan did not really develop a new campaign strategy for GE-14, instead basing itself on tactics used in 2016 as well as piggy-backing on the 2018 national strategy. Key elements of the campaign included: questioning BN Sarawak's economic development track record; promising greater devolution to East Malaysia; and governance issues.

Sarawak BN's Economic Development Track Record

PH pointed out that Sarawak BN, in spite of its development rhetoric, had failed to deliver on its promises. For example, the promise to upgrade all dilapidated schools within five years was not fulfilled. In 2018, many of the rural students were still attending classes in such run-down schools (*Borneo Post Online*, 15 April 2018). As of end 2018, the number of such schools stood at 1,020; however, some listed under this category had been repaired but not awarded with the certificate of completion (*Star Online*, 14 November 2018).

Some semi-urban and rural areas have been lacking access to water and electricity even after five decades of development. There is also a wide development gap between rural and urban areas. Rural incomes are about 44 per cent lower than urban incomes. Rural areas still remain very underdeveloped. Only about 60 per cent of households in rural areas have access to piped water, and 51.2 per cent of households are located more than 9 kilometres away from the nearest secondary school.

Youth unemployment stood at around 10 per cent, compared to 5.5 per cent in Penang and 8.8 per cent in Selangor. PH hoped to redress this, not only by reducing youth unemployment by providing 100,000 jobs for Sarawak youths, but also providing a salary of RM2,500 and above.

Devolution and Governance

Unlike Sarawak BN, PH in their manifesto promised that 10 per cent of total oil revenues would be converted into petro cash dividends for Sarawakians (*Borneo Post Online*, 1 May 2018). PH also promised to: give 20 per cent of oil royalties and 50 per cent of all state taxes back to Sarawak (for the state government to take up the financial responsibility of the education and healthcare ministries); and restore Sarawak's status under the Malaysia Agreement 1963 (MA 63), which has only been partially fulfilled.

During campaigning, messages on 1MDB which were used during the 2016 state election were repeated during GE-14. Najib's money laundering activities, the mysterious payments of RM2.6 billion into Najib's personal account, and also the general corruption of the Peninsular BN government were highlighted during these campaigns. PH promised a clean government to replace the corrupt BN government, and it also pledged to ensure prime ministers only serve two terms. *Buku Harapan*, with its ten marquee promises to be delivered in the first 100 days, including GST abolition, targeted subsidies, equalizing minimum wage across East and West Malaysia and raising the level, and setting up a special committee to enforce MA 63, were reiterated on the campaign trail (Pakatan Harapan 2018).

Fielding of Candidates — Pakatan Harapan

DAP fielded nine candidates; five in the Chinese-majority seats of Bandar Kuching, Stampin, Sarikei, Lanang and Sibu, and four in non-Muslim bumiputra constituencies (Serian, Kapit, Bintulu and Mas Gading). PKR focused on the non-Muslim bumiputra and mixed seats, contesting less in Muslim bumiputra constituencies. In the Muslim bumiputra seats, it contested in Petra Jaya and Sri Aman, and in the non-Muslim bumiputra seats, it ran in Betong, Kanowit, Mukah, Puncak Borneo, Saratok, Selangau, Hulu Rajang and Baram. For the mixed constituencies (Muslim and non-Muslim bumiputra), PKR contested in Sibuti, Limbang and Lawas. PKR's incumbent in the Chinese seat of Miri defended that seat. Amanah contested mainly in the Muslim bumiputra seats of Santubong, Kota Samarahan, Batang Sadong and Batang Lupar, and two seats in the non-Muslim constituencies of Tanjung Manis and Igan.

PAS

In Sarawak, PAS was formed by a few Peninsular Malay religious teachers with local Malays as its shadow leaders (Faisal Hazis 2012, p. 163). The party quietly made its entry into Sarawak in the early 1990s through its social engagement programmes aimed at rural Malays (Faisal Hazis 2011, p. 10). The initial intention was also non-political, with a special emphasis on preaching.

The first state liaison office was established in May 1996 but PAS only contested in the 1999 parliamentary and 2001 state elections. Sarawak, due to its multireligious composition, is not receptive towards parties from the Peninsula, especially those with a strong religious leaning. To date, PAS has not won a single state or parliamentary election. PAS has eleven branches in Sarawak located in Batang Sadong, Petra Jaya and Santubong, in the Kuching and Samarahan divisions.

Observations from Three Key Constituencies

Participant observation was carried out in three key constituencies, selected based on their ethnic composition, degree of urbanization, and candidates and parties. Kuching is the state's capital. It is an urban area and a predominantly Chinese seat.

Petra Jaya is also urban and predominantly Muslim bumiputra. Mas Gading is a semi-rural seat, and largely non-Muslim bumiputra.

Bandar Kuching

Bandar Kuching is an urban constituency with 81,856 voters, and an ethnic composition that is predominantly Chinese (89 per cent), followed by non-Muslim bumiputra (6 per cent) and Muslim bumiputra (4 per cent). The seat has been held by DAP since 2004. In GE-13, Chong Chieng Jen (DAP) defeated Tan Khai (SUPP) with a majority of 19,642 votes.

In 2018, Chong Chieng Jen, who was also Sarawak DAP chairman, did not contest in Bandar Kuching, but instead moved to another urban constituency, Stampin, to run against Sarawak BN heavyweight Dr Sim Kui Hian who was State Minister for Local Government and Housing and president of SUPP. Consequently, both candidates in Kuching, Kelvin Yii (DAP) and Kho Teck Wan (SUPP), were new candidates. Kelvin Yii, a medical doctor, is Sarawak PH Youth Information Chief and special assistant to Chong Chieng Jen. Kho Teck Wan is an information technology consultant by training and SUPP's Women's Chief.

This constituency saw fierce campaigning by both candidates supported by their party veterans. As Chong and Sim were the veterans and leaders of their respective parties, Yii and Kho, being less experienced candidates, often had to rely on the drawing power of these two individuals to bring crowds to the *ceramahs*.

DAP based its campaign on the slogan "*Bina Harapan*" (Build Hope) and "*Ubah*" (Change), but also sought to run on the effective and efficient provision of services to their constituents.[9]

The promises that DAP put forward during their *ceramahs* included: abolishing the GST; pledging to increase employment opportunities for the youth of Kuching; returning 50 per cent of state taxes to the Sarawak government; increasing the oil and gas royalties paid to the state from 5 per cent to 20 per cent; and eliminating corruption and nepotism present in the Najib government. The 1MDB scandal featured strongly in the Kuching campaign, with posters of Najib and Rosmah used to illustrate corruption.

DAP *ceramahs* held around town were always very well attended, with around 1,500 to 2,500 attendees. DAP focused on SUPP as a failed party that kowtowed to the national BN party, and never put up a fight when Sarawakian rights were being eroded by the federal government. They argued that if SUPP or BN Sarawak was voted in, it would mean that the corrupt Najib and UMNO would be returned to power. It also had banners that equated SUPP and Sarawak BN to being a puppet of UMNO and Najib. When asked if DAP Kuching was a party from Kuala Lumpur, Kelvin Yii replied that DAP Kuching had autonomy from DAP in Peninsular Malaysia and operated as an independent party.[10]

SUPP's *ceramahs* were also well attended but the crowds were observed to be generally older and about 20 per cent smaller than the DAP's (between 1,200 and 2,000 attendees). The *ceramahs* by both DAP and SUPP were broadcast on Facebook

Live, leveraging off the areas with good Internet connectivity. Kho Teck Wan of SUPP promised to build a stronger economy for Bandar Kuching, through: ensuring that the constituency would be flood-free; promoting urban renewal in the city; boosting Bandar Kuching as a digital hub to create more jobs and attract companies; providing mobile healthcare for seniors and immobile residents; and setting up a taskforce for women.

BN invested significant resources in the election, including flooding the city with banners. The banners asked Sarawakians to think beyond tomorrow in the new age of digitalization and information technology. The campaign message for SUPP was also slick and polished. The catchphrases used by SUPP in their banners included "I'm In", "Sarawakian First" and "Stronger Sarawak". Such catchphrases were also used during the live *ceramahs* that were held in Kuching. The public was asked to think about Sarawak's future, to fight for and regain its rights under MA 63. SUPP also advocated for a stronger Sarawak BN to effectively counter UMNO.

Hence, MA 63 featured strongly in SUPP's *ceramahs*. Pictures of Adenan Satem were flashed to remind the public that Sarawak must continue to fight for its MA 63 rights. SUPP would also highlight the successful establishment of PETROS which brought mining rights back to the state, the purchase of the Bakun Dam which would now allow Sarawakians to purchase cheaper electricity, the development of the RM7 billion Sarawak water grid project that would supply water from the various dams to longhouses and settlements in rural areas, and the rejection of RUU 355 all by the present Abang Johari government.[11] However, on 9 May, Kelvin Yii won by a massive margin (see Table 15.8 below).

Petra Jaya

Petra Jaya has 57,925 voters, predominantly comprised of Muslim bumiputra (74 per cent), followed by Chinese (13 per cent), and non-Muslim bumiputra (12 per cent). In GE-13, Works Minister and Parti Pesaka Bumiputera Bersatu (PBB) senior vice-president Datuk Seri Fadillah Yusof defeated PKR candidate Ahmad Nazib bin Johari by a handsome margin of 21,443 votes.

In GE-14, Datuk Seri Fadillah defended the Petra Jaya seat for the fourth time. He was up against PKR Datuk Ir Dr Nor Irwan Ahmad Nor and PAS candidate Hamdan Sani. Fadillah has been the BN MP for the seat since 2004 and had gained strong support and respect from its constituents. During GE-14, Fadillah carried out a low-key campaign by having walkabouts, and attending community gatherings and events held by the various communities in his constituency.

Often at these events, Fadillah would "remind" his constituents of BN past achievements, what has been done, and what would be done if he were supported by the people. The idea was to "gently" highlight BN's past achievements, and the longer term plans that Sarawak BN (PBB) had for Petra Jaya. His Facebook page during the campaigning period was filled with his visits to the various grassroots areas showing his interaction with his constituents, and included a video reminding locals of Sarawak BN's infrastructure provisions.

The PKR candidate, Dr Nor Irwan, is a first-timer but a local from Petra Jaya. Besides walkabouts and meeting the community, Nor Irwan had to rely more on *ceramahs* to attract potential voters. That Fadillah the incumbent was not from Petra Jaya but Sibu, was played up during the PKR election rallies.

PKR focused its campaign rally on promising to provide more high-income jobs for locals in the constituency. Dr Nor Irwan actively worked the ground as an opposition candidate. Details of his visits to various areas in Petra Jaya, and the problems encountered by residents were highlighted on his Facebook page; which were easily accessible to followers and interested voters. Some of these problems included inaccessibility because of poor quality roads, lack of basic amenities, and also traffic jams in urban areas. In *ceramahs*, Nor Irwan promised to: create opportunities for his constituents to earn a monthly household income of RM3,000 or more; improve infrastructure and public amenities where needed; strengthen safety and peace in the constituency by establishing police stations; lower the cost of living by removing GST; introduce targeted subsidies for petrol; build affordable housing; and remove corruption, among other pledges. However, the effectiveness of the rallies was limited, as there were often only 200–300 attendees.

For PAS, Hamdan Sani wanted to: fight for the removal of GST; scrap the National Higher Education Fund Corporation (PTPTN) debt; form an education endowment facility; grant one-off assistance of RM2,000 for women who began work initiatives from home; and provide basic monthly assistance to the poor through its National It'aam Programmes.[12] PAS generated very little support from voters in the constituency as Sarawakians generally view the party with suspicion, not wanting the "Semenanjung" (Peninsular Malaysia) brand of religion to gain roots in its multicultural and multireligious society.[13]

Flags from BN dominated throughout Petra Jaya, but, in this constituency, PKR also put up a good showing of flags and banners, and established a presence through YouTube videos and *ceramahs*. PAS also displayed its flags and banners but was less prominent than PH or BN. In this constituency, the BN incumbent Fadillah Yusof comfortably retained his seat.

Mas Gading

Mas Gading has 29,617 voters, made up mainly of non-Muslim bumiputra (75 per cent), followed by Chinese (18 per cent), and non-Muslim bumiputra (5 per cent). In a four-cornered fight in GE-13, Anthony Nogeh Gumbek defeated the incumbent, independent candidate Tiki Anak Lafe, by 2,156 votes. Tiki Lafe was the member of parliament in Mas Gading from 1999 to 2013, but was sacked from SPDP (now PDP) after a feud with its president, William Mawan.

The Sarawak BN machinery was careful to craft the message that Nogeh, the incumbent, had been helping the constituency during his five-year term by promoting the planting of commercial crops, like durian and pineapple, to help increase incomes in the area. Since his election to Parliament in 2013, Nogeh has also visited around 80 per cent of the constituency and given grants to various organizations including churches, and helped connect several villages with roads and build decent homes for the poor. The politics of development story featured strongly in all accounts provided by Sarawak BN. The Bau Wet Market had also been upgraded and a new hawker centre was built near Serikin. In April 2018, former PBB Opar Branch chairman, Datuk Peter Minos predicted that Anthony Nogeh, having already established himself over the past five years, would win the seat in 2018 (*New Straits Times*, 16 April 2016).

Some contrasts and similarities could be observed between the campaigns. On nomination day, Anthony Nogeh arrived with a 2,000-strong entourage compared to Mordi Bimol who was accompanied by only 300 supporters at the Bau Civic Centre (*Borneo Post Online*, 29 April 2018). In Mas Gading, Sarawak BN tended to use the more traditional methods of generating publicity and support including press reports of events and community projects attended by Anthony Nogeh, and meet-the-people sessions which in turn provided him with opportunities to reiterate and highlight BN development projects in the pipeline. Mordi Bimol's regular visits, as well as DAP's manifesto of providing jobs, lowering costs of living, and removing the GST featured strongly in his Facebook messages. To reach out to the community, DAP Sarawak opened its first service centre in the constituency in December 2013, taking over the office premises from the former Mas Gading MP, Dr Tiki Lafe.

Mordi Bimol had actively engaged in community work. Over the years, he visited ninety-three villages and familiarized himself with the issues and problems faced by the Bidayuh community in the area. There were some who did not know who to approach when they faced problems with land acquisition, and many also did not have access to proper basic amenities.[14] Villagers also had no access to fixed telephone and mobile lines (*Star Online*, 6 May 2012), and some lacked access to treated water, 24-hour electricity, good roads, clinics, and schools (Mersat 2018, p. 734).[15] Given the lack of basic provisions and protection of land rights, Mordi couched his messages, and a host of campaign promises, in the familiar rhetoric of developmentalism.[16]

Mas Gading was deemed a "hot seat" as Anthony Nogeh won by only a majority of 2,156 seats against Tiki Lafe (incumbent) in a four-cornered fight in 2013. Then Mordi Bimol was involved in a four-cornered fight which he lost. This time it was a straight fight between BN–PDP and PH–DAP. Tiki Lafe, who contested in the 2013 elections, chose not to contest, urging his supporters to vote for DAP (Mersat 2018, p. 733). Patrick Uren, another former candidate, also chose not to contest, saying that he wanted to pave the way for a straight fight between BN and DAP (*FMT News*, 6 May 2018). Anthony Nogeh also suffered from old factionalism within his own party that weakened his voter base.

In terms of banners and posters, BN publicity banners certainly overshadowed DAP's in the township of Mas Gading and also the outlying areas. Campaigning was intense with the whole town of Bau in Mas Gading covered by BN flags and banners and a smattering of DAP flags.[17]

However, the use of Facebook by Mordi Bimol and the uploading of *ceramahs* through Facebook Live, and the use of WhatsApp in announcing venues for daily *ceramahs* may have helped DAP's campaign. Factionalism and the shift of support by former BN politicians (and their supporters) also tipped the scales in favour of

Sarawak DAP. A straight fight between Sarawak BN and Sarawak DAP certainly made battle lines clearer.

On 9 May, this constituency fell to Mordi Bimol from PH (DAP), unseating BN's incumbent and former federal Deputy Minister of Agriculture and Agro-Based Industry, Anthony Nogeh (see Table 15.9 below). Mordi Bimol did not expect to win the seat and did not even campaign in some areas of the constituency as he felt that these were impregnable BN strongholds (*Borneo Post Online*, 10 May 2018).

THE RESULTS

In GE-14, Sarawak BN won nineteen out of thirty-one parliamentary seats, as compared to the twenty-five seats they won in 2013 (GE-13) (Table 15.3). PBB held strong, PDP and PRS split their wins and losses, and SUPP took a beating (Table 15.4). Out of the nineteen seats won by Sarawak BN, six are Muslim bumiputra seats (Table 15.5), ten are non-Muslim bumiputra seats (Table 15.6), and three are mixed Muslim/non-Muslim bumiputra seats (Table 15.7). Figure 15.4 shows the geographic distribution of these demographics, and the electoral results of GE-13 and GE-14.

TABLE 15.3
Parliamentary Election Results in Sarawak (GE-14)

Parties	Contesting	Won
Sarawak Barisan Nasional (BN)	31	19
Democratic Action Party (DAP-PH)	9	6
Parti Keadilan Rakyat (PKR-PH)	14	4
Independents	5	2
Amanah (PH)	6	0
Parti Islam Se-Malaysia (PAS)	5	0
Sarawak Star	3	0
Parti Bansa Dayak Sarawak Baru (PDBSB)	1	0
Parti Bumi Kenyalang (PBK)	1	0
PEACE	2	0
Total		31

TABLE 15.4
Parliamentary Election Results for Sarawak BN Component Parties (GE-14)

Party	Seats Won	Seats Lost
PBB (14 Seats)	13	1
PDP (4 Seats)	2	2
PRS (6 Seats)	3	3
SUPP (7 Seats)	1	6
Total	19	12

TABLE 15.5

GE-14 Results in Muslim Bumiputra (Malay/Melanau) Majority Seats Won by PBB

Constituency	Ethnic Composition	Winner	Votes	Opponent(s)	Votes	Majority
Santubong (Rural)	Non-Muslim bumi: 1% Muslim bumi: 81% Chinese: 8%	BN-PBB Wan Junaidi Tuanku Jaafar (79%), incumbent	26,379	PH-Amanah Mohamad Fidzuan Zaidi	6,894	19,485
Petra Jaya (Urban)	Non-Muslim bumi: 12% Muslim bumi: 74% Chinese: 13%	BN-PBB Fadillah Yusof (68%), incumbent	28,306	PH-PKR Ir Dr Nor Irwan Ahmad Nor GS-PAS Hamdan Sani	13,289 1,350	15,017
Kota Samarahan (Rural)	Non-Muslim bumi: 11% Muslim bumi: 62% Chinese: 11%	BN-PBB Rubiah Wang (70%), incumbent	25,070	PH-Amanah Sopian Julaihi GS-PAS Zulkipli Ramzi	8,078 2,719	16,992
Batang Sadong (Rural)	Non-Muslim bumi: 24% Muslim bumi: 70% Chinese: 5%	BN-PBB Nancy Shukri (83%), incumbent	14,208	PH-Amanah Othman Mustapha GS-PAS Asan Singkro	1,880 978	12,328
Batang Lupar (Rural)	Non-Muslim bumi: 30% Muslim bumi: 67% Chinese: 3%	BN-PBB Rohani Abdul Karim (70%), incumbent	14,204	GS-PAS Wan Abdillah Wan Ahmad PH-Amanah Narudin Mentali	3,927 2,020	10,277
Sri Aman (Rural)	Non-Muslim bumi: 10% Muslim bumi: 72% Chinese: 17%	BN-PRS Masir Kujat (61%), incumbent	14,141	PH-PKR Norina Utot PBDS BARU Cobbold John Lusoi	8,321 538	5,820

Source: undi.info.

GE-14 Results in Non-Muslim Bumiputra (Dayak) Majority Seats Won by BN (Various Component Parties)

Constituency	Ethnic Composition	Winner	Votes	Opponent(s)	Votes	Majority
Serian (Rural)	Non-Muslim bumi: 81% Muslim bumi: 8% Chinese: 10%	BN-SUPP Richard Riot Jaem (70%), incumbent	17,545	PH-DAP Edward Andrew Luwak IND Senior William Rade	7,640 2,234	9,905
Tanjong Manis (Rural)	Non-Muslim bumi: 69% Muslim bumi: 26% Chinese: 5%	BN-PBB Yusuf Abd. Wahab (81%)	11,402	PH-Amanah Mohamad Fadillah Sabali	2,728	8,674
Igan (Rural)	Non-Muslim bumi: 89% Muslim bumi: 7% Chinese: 4%	BN-PBB Ahmad Johnie Zawasi (84%)	10,538	PH-Amanah Andri Zulkarnaen Hamdan	2,043	8,495
Kanowit (Rural)	Non-Muslim bumi: 86% Muslim bumi: 2% Chinese: 12%	BN-PRS Aaron Ago Dagang (65%), incumbent	9,552	PH-PKR Satu Anchom	5,240	4,312
Mukah (Rural)	Non-Muslim bumi: 84% Muslim bumi: 7% Chinese: 9%	BN-PBB Hanifah Hajar Taib (67%)	13,853	PH-PKR Abdul Jalil Bujang	6,853	7,000
Kapit (Rural)	Non-Muslim bumi: 87% Muslim bumi: 3% Chinese: 9%	BN-PBB Alexander Nanta Linggi (79%), incumbent	14,302	PH-DAP Paren Nyawi	3,823	10,479
Betong (Rural)	Non-Muslim bumi: 55% Muslim bumi: 38% Chinese: 7%	BN-PBB Robert Lawson Chuat (60%)	12,517	IND Abang Ahmad Abang Suni PH-PKR Noel Changgai Bucking	4,401 3,802	8,116
Hulu Rajang (Rural)	Non-Muslim bumi: 95% Muslim bumi: 1% Chinese: 2%	BN-PRS Wilson Ugak Anak Kumbong (68%), incumbent	11,834	PH-PKR Abun Sui Anyit	5,519	6,315
Bintulu (Semi-urban)	Non-Muslim bumi: 60% Muslim bumi: 11% Chinese: 29%	BN-PDP Tiong King Sing (57%), incumbent	27,076	PH-DAP Tony Chan Yew Chiew STAR Chieng Lea Phing	20,054 328	7,022
Baram (Rural)	Non-Muslim bumi: 86% Muslim bumi: 5% Chinese: 8%	BN-PDP Anyi Ngau (54%), incumbent	12,171	PH-PKR Roland Egan	10,181	1,990

Source: undi.info.

TABLE 15.7
GE-14 Results in Mixed Muslim Bumiputra/Non-Muslim Bumiputra Seats Won by BN-PBB

Constituency	Ethnic Composition	Winner	Votes	Opponent(s)	Votes	Majority
Sibuti (Rural)	Non-Muslim bumi: 54% Muslim bumi: 24% Chinese: 22%	BN-PBB Lukanisman Awang (55%)	12,214	PH-PKR Jemat Panjang GS-PAS Zulaihi Bakar	8,538 1,617	3,676
Limbang (Rural)	Non-Muslim bumi: 53% Muslim bumi: 28% Chinese: 18%	BN-PBB Hasbi Habibollah (72%), incumbent	12,589	PH-PKR Dr Ricardo Yampil Baba	4,879	7,710
Lawas (Rural)	Non-Muslim bumi: 49% Muslim bumi: 41% Chinese: 10%	BN-PBB Henry Sum Agong (71%), incumbent	10,037	PH-PKR Danny Piri IND Mohammad Brahim	4,037 176	6,000

Source: undi.info.

FIGURE 15.4
Sarawak: GE-13/GE-14 Comparison of Parliamentary Seats

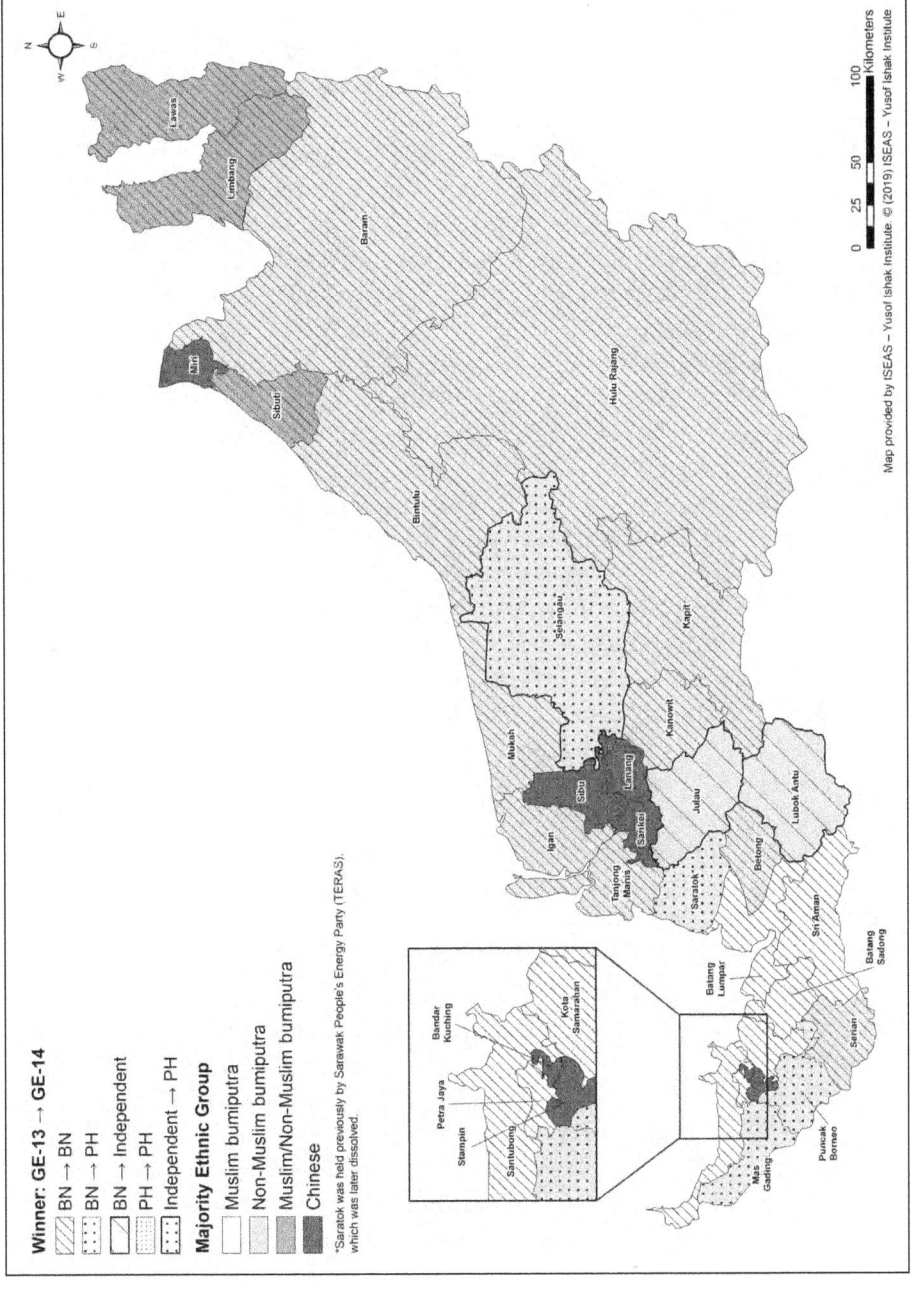

Barisan Nasional Wins

It is instructive to delve deeper into the GE-14 outcome by winning side and ethnic composition. Sarawak parliament seats can be sorted into four generalized categories based on the ethnic and religious profile of registered voters (with the majority group constituting 55 per cent or more in each seat): Malay/Melanau or Muslim bumiputra majority; Dayak or non-Muslim majority, mixed Muslim/non-Muslim bumiputra; and Chinese majority.

BN broadly maintained past patterns of component party allocations, with Malay/Melanau majority seats predominantly contested by PBB, Dayak-majority seats also contested by PBB as well as smaller coalition parties PDP, PRS and SUPP; and PBB fielding candidates in mixed Christian and Muslim bumiputra seats; while SUPP stood in Chinese-majority seats. Tables 15.5 to 15.7 set out each of these ethnic majority seats in turn.

For the Muslim bumiputra seats in Table 15.5, Sarawak BN (specifically PBB) garnered high vote shares, ranging from 61 per cent to 83 per cent. All PBB's candidates were incumbents. The average vote share of the six Muslim bumiputra seats was 71.8 per cent. These predominantly Muslim bumiputra constituencies also included opposition candidates from PKR, Amanah and PAS. However, these candidates performed poorly in these constituencies, and the PBB candidates proved too strong for them. As PAS was no longer in the PH coalition, it engaged in multicornered fights in Petra Jaya with PKR, and in Kota Samaharan, Batang Sadong and Batang Lupar with Amanah. PAS contested mainly in the Muslim bumiputra constituencies, with one candidate in the mixed Muslim/non-Muslim constituency (Tables 15.5 and 15.7).

Ten of the seats that Sarawak BN captured were from the non-Muslim bumiputra (Dayak-majority) constituencies (Table 15.6). SUPP won Serian with a strong majority of 70 per cent, PBB took five seats (averaging 74.2 per cent of total votes cast), PRS took two seats (averaging 66.5 per cent), and PDP won two seats (averaging 55.5 per cent). The average vote share for all ten Dayak constituencies for Sarawak BN was 68.5 per cent. Here PBB shared the victory with its coalition partners, the Dayak-dominated PDP and PRS. However, if vote shares were broken down into the respective coalition parties, it can be seen that PBB and PRS enjoyed sizeable majorities.

The strength of PBB's brand is reflected in its ability to hold seats with new candidates, which was the case in Tanjong Manis, Igan, Mukah and Betong, and also Sibuti. The weaker showing by PDP for both the Baram and Bintulu seats (averaging 55.5 per cent) suggests that it will need to re-examine and strengthen its policies in these constituencies. A mix of opposition non-Muslim bumiputra candidates came from the DAP, PKR, Amanah, and other Sarawakian parties. In Baram and Bintulu, DAP and PKR made major inroads but did not manage to oust PDP.

Three of the mixed constituencies were captured by the PBB (Table 15.7). The average vote share for these three constituencies was 66 per cent, with a considerable difference between Sibuti, where PBB won a relatively low 55 per cent, and the other two. Notably, the candidate for Sibuti was Sarawak BN's youngest.

Pakatan Harapan/Independent Wins

DAP's wins in Bandar Kuching and Mas Gading were discussed above. In addition to these, the party also retained the Stampin, Sarikei, Lanang and Sibu seats (see Table 15.8). The vote shares of the ethnic Chinese majority seats captured by DAP ranged from 54 per cent (Sarikei—three-cornered) to 79 per cent (Kuching), and averaged 64.4 per cent. Two of these seats were urban (Bandar Kuching and Stampin), two semi-urban (Sarikei and Sibu) and one was rural (Lanang). These were previously also DAP seats.

SUPP contested in all five seats but did not manage to wrest any from the DAP. It also did not manage to win the Miri seat from PKR. SUPP fought very fiercely in the seats of Stampin and Miri. At Stampin, it was Sim Kui Hian, the president of SUPP, who contested against Chong Chieng Jen. During the fierce campaign between the two, voters felt that the outcome, though favouring DAP most of the time, could swing to the SUPP because it had put up such a strong combination of campaign of *ceramahs*, posters, banners and popular and nationalistic catchphrases. There was talk that SUPP had employed an outside consulting and advertising agency in order to carry out such an effective campaign during GE-14.[18]

PKR defended Miri (Chinese-majority) and won the Puncak Borneo (Iban-majority), Saratok (Iban-majority) and Selangau (Iban-majority) seats (Tables 15.8 and 15.9). All three Dayak-majority seats (Table 15.9) won were marginal (54 per cent and below, the average vote share was 52.6 per cent), but significant because this was the first time a national-based party had wrested these rural seats from Sarawakian parties.

The Puncak Borneo and Saratok seats (Table 15.9) were lost because Sarawak BN "lacked a succession plan and invited implosion by allowing free-for-all lobbying for candidacy" in these constituencies (Mersat 2018, p. 732). Incumbent James Dawos Mamit did not defend the Puncak Borneo seat. At least twenty candidates lobbied for PBB's leadership for the prized vacancy, and the candidates who lost threw their lot behind PKR's Willie Mongin (*Borneo Post Online*, 27 April 2018).

Puncak Borneo, also a rural seat, was the only seat lost by PBB to the opposition (PKR). Its candidate, Jeannoth Sinel, was tarnished by reported entanglement in a land scandal involving three villages in this constituency.[19] In Saratok, incumbent William Mawan was not selected as candidate due to intra-BN strife, and there were four aspirants who offered to run. When these aspirants were not selected, they refused to support the chosen PDP candidate Subeng Mula, which in turn benefitted Ali Biju from PKR (Mersat 2018, p. 732).

Baru Bian, of the Lun Bawang community, wrested the Iban-dominated Selangau seat (Table 15.9) from Rita Sarimah Insol, a BN Iban candidate. Baru Bian contested in this seat partly because of disputes in native customary rights issues in the constituency. The sacking of Datuk Joseph Entulu Belaun (incumbent in Selangau for three terms) and supreme council member Datuk William Nyallau who were popular among constituents, may also have caused Sarawak BN-PRS to lose support for the seats of Selangau and also Lubok Antu (the seat lost by PRS to independent

TABLE 15.8
GE-14 Results in Chinese-Majority Seats Won by PH (DAP/PKR)

Constituency	Ethnic Composition	Winner	Votes	Opponent(s)	Votes	Majority
Bandar Kuching (Urban)	Non-Muslim bumi: 6% / Muslim bumi: 4% / Chinese: 89%	PH-DAP Kelvin Yii Lee Wuen (79%)	48,548	BN-SUPP Kho Teck Wan	12,575	35,973
Stampin (Urban)	Non-Muslim bumi: 18% / Muslim bumi: 16% / Chinese: 64%	PH-DAP Chong Chieng Jen (64%), incumbent for Bandar Kuching	33,060	BN-SUPP Dr Sim Kui Hian	18,839	14,221
Sarikei (Semi-urban)	Non-Muslim bumi: 32% / Muslim bumi: 5% / Chinese: 63%	PH-DAP Wong Ling Biu (54%), incumbent	16,327	BN-SUPP Huang Tiong Sii / PBK Wong Chin King	13,757 / 392	2,570
Lanang (Rural)	Non-Muslim bumi: 27% / Muslim bumi: 4% / Chinese: 69%	PH-DAP Alice Lau Kiong Yieng (65%), incumbent	29,905	BN-SUPP Kong Sien Chiu / PEACE Priscilla Lau	15,359 / 628	14,546
Sibu (Semi-rural)	Non-Muslim bumi: 25% / Muslim bumi: 12% / Chinese: 63%	PH-DAP Oscar Ling Chai Yew (60%), incumbent	33,811	BN-SUPP Andrew Wong Kee Yew / PEACE Tiew Yen Houng / STAR Tiong Ing Tung	22,389 / 377 / 176	11,442
Miri (Semi-urban)	Non-Muslim bumi: 28% / Muslim bumi: 16% / Chinese: 55%	PH-PKR Micheal Teo Yu Keng (62%), incumbent	35,739	BN-SUPP Sebastian Ting Chiew Yew	22,076	13,663

Source: undi.info.

TABLE 15.9
GE-14 Results in Non-Muslim Bumiputra Majority Seats Won by PH (DAP/PKR)

Constituency	Ethnic Composition	Winner	Votes	Opponent(s)	Votes	Majority
Mas Gading (Rural)	Non-Muslim bumi: 75% Muslim bumi: 5% Chinese: 18%	PH-DAP Mordi Bimol (57%)	12,771	BN-PDP Anthony Nogeh Anak Gumbek, incumbent	9,747	3,024
Puncak Borneo (previously Mambong) (Rural)	Non-Muslim bumi: 68% Muslim bumi: 5% Chinese: 26%	PH-PKR Willie Mongin (55%)	18,865	BN-PBB Genot Sibek @ Jeannoth Sinel STAR Buln Ribos	14,860 795	4,005
Saratok (Rural)	Non-Muslim bumi: 57% Muslim bumi: 36% Chinese: 6%	PH-PKR Ali Biju (52%) Incumbent: William Ikom Mawan (TERAS)	11,848	BN-PDP Subeng Mula	10,859	989
Selangau (Rural)	Non-Muslim bumi: 94% Muslim bumi: 1% Chinese: 3%	PH-PKR Baru Bian (51%)	11,228	BN-PRS Rita Sarimah Patrick Insol	10,742	486

Source: undi.info.

candidate Jugah Muyang—see Table 15.10). Reportedly, the sacked candidates took revenge on Dr James Masing and activated their electoral machinery to support the opposition (Chin 2018, p. 186; Mersat 2018, p. 732).

PH managed to reduce infighting during GE-14, as there were seven three-cornered fights and one four-cornered fight compared to thirteen three-cornered fights and three four-cornered fights during GE-13. The reduction in multicornered fights benefitted opposition candidates by reducing the dilution of votes in the various constituencies.

The Sarawak DAP chairman, Chong Chieng Jen referred to PH's victories in GE-14 as the "Sarawakian tsunami". In total, six Dayak seats fell to the opposition (Selangau, Saratok, Julau, Lubok Antu, Puncak Borneo and Mas Gading—Tables 15.9 and 15.10). However, judging from the seats won, a "Dayak storm" would be more apt term to use instead, as Sarawak BN still retained a majority of nineteen out of thirty-one seats. Also, the seats that were won were in Dayak areas (Mersat 2018).

Sarawak BN still performed strongly, with PBB winning thirteen out of the fourteen seats—nearly all of which enjoyed high voter majorities. The PBB also did very well in the Muslim bumiputra and non-Muslim bumiputra constituencies. Here Amanah and PAS did not succeed in winning any seats, instead losing by wide margins. Sarawak BN's component party, the PRS, also performed well during GE-14. The only worrying coalition member is the PDP, which won by thin margins. Infighting, party-hopping and turmoil over succession and candidacies also undermined various campaigns.

That a number of Dayak seats won by the opposition were only marginal, to some extent, offers hope to Sarawak BN (now GPS) that voter support is still there. However, if ignored, the electoral shift of the Dayak community may be amplified in the next state election or by-election. The PBB brand name remains strong, but the other coalition parties in GPS have lost much support—with SUPP still not able to recover since its defeat to DAP in GE-13. This party performed badly in all the Chinese-dominated seats that it contested in (Table 15.8). The only exception was the non-Muslim bumiputra seat of Serian that its candidate Richard Riot Jaem won (Table 15.6).

Of the twelve seats won by the opposition (PH and independents), four were only marginally won: Sarikei (54 per cent, Chinese), Saratok (52 per cent, non-Muslim bumiputra), Selangau (51 per cent, non-Muslim bumiputra), and Lubok Antu (40 per cent, non-Muslim bumiputra) (see Tables 15.8 and 15.9). Another two non-Muslim bumiputra seats, Puncak Borneo and Julau also hovered at a majority of 55 per cent (Tables 15.9 and 15.10). However, independent candidates surprisingly also won two seats and the opposition (PH and independents) made inroads into a number of rural (Mas Gading, Saratok, Selangau, Lubok Antu, Julau, Lanang) and semi-urban constituencies (Sibu and Sarikei). Figure 15.5 depicts seats won by Sarawak BN and PH, showing that about half of the seats captured by the opposition are in rural and semi-urban areas.

The fall of many Dayak seats points to the need to address the concerns of this community with more care and greater sensitivity. Another observation is that the

TABLE 15.10
GE-14 Results Non-Muslim Bumiputra Majority Seats Won by Independents

Constituency	Ethnic Composition	Winner	Votes	Opponent(s)	Votes	Majority
Lubok Antu (Rural)	Non-Muslim bumi: 90% Muslim bumi: 2% Chinese: 8%	IND Jugah Muyang (40%)	5,834	BN-PRS Robert Pasang Alam PH-PKR Nicolas Bawin	4,775 3,942	1,059
Julau (Rural)	Non-Muslim bumi: 93% Muslim bumi: 1% Chinese: 5%	IND Larry Sng Wei Shien (55%)	10,105	BN-PRS Joseph Salang Gandum, incumbent	8,174	1,937

Source: undi.info

FIGURE 15.5
BN and Opposition Seats in Sarawak (GE-14)

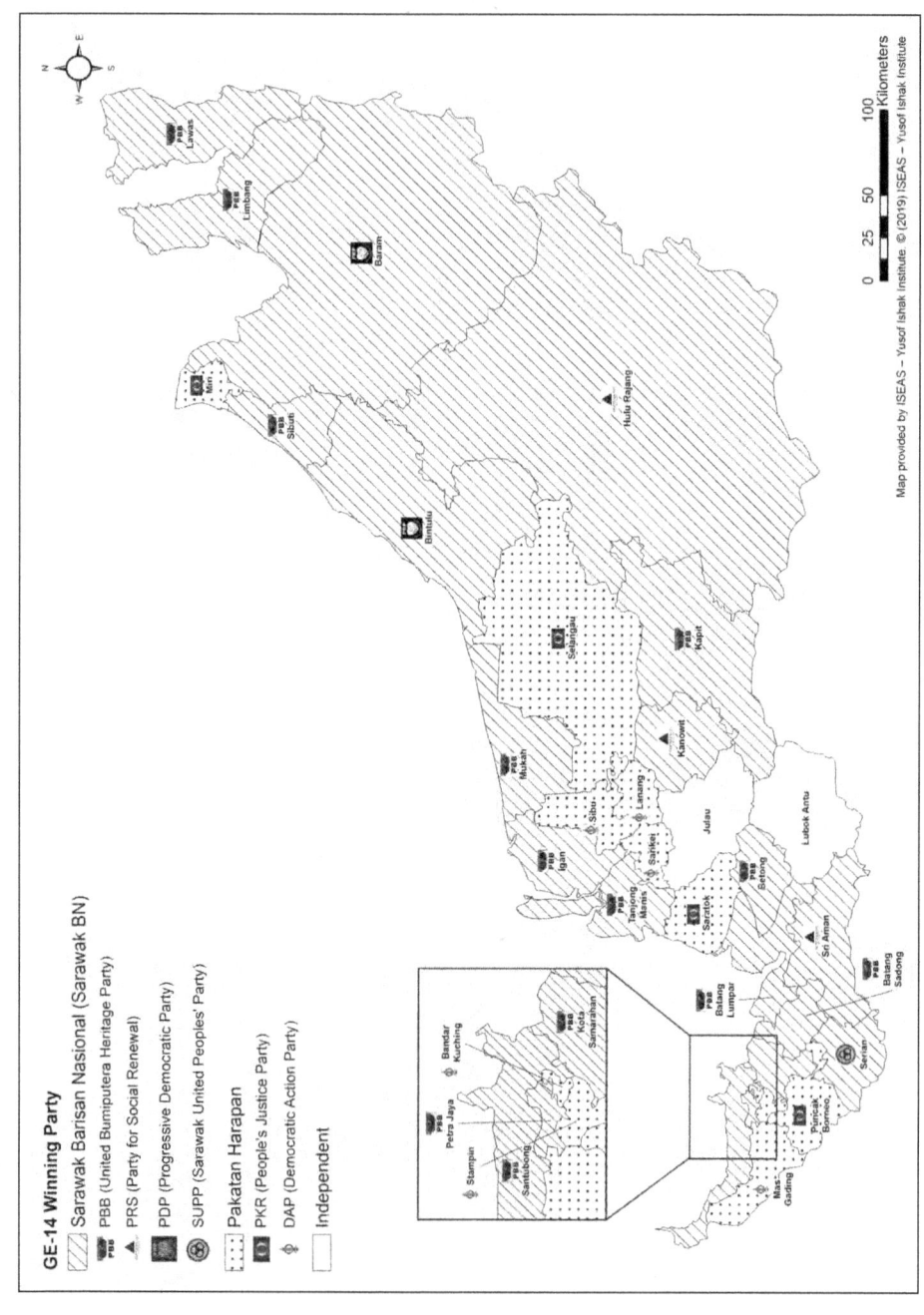

Dayak also supported Chinese candidates, suggesting that voters may increasingly overlook ethnicity. The victory by Baru Bian (Selangau) and Ali Biju (Saratok), both champions of native customary rights, also indicates that the government should pay more attention to concerns of the Dayak community.

CONCLUSION

The outcome of 2016 Sarawak state elections suggested strongly that GE-14 would be a victory call for Sarawak BN. In fact, Sarawak BN was expected to capture more than twenty-five out of thirty-one parliamentary seats. Few fancied the prospects for DAP, PKR and other non-BN candidates beyond the urban, Chinese-majority or ethnically mixed areas. However, as discussed above, this did not happen for a variety of reasons.

On 12 June 2018, Sarawak BN broke away from Barisan Nasional and formed the Gabungan Parti Sarawak (GPS). GPS, which was recognized by the Registrar of Societies (ROS) is made up of the same component parties: the Parti Pesaka Bumiputera Bersatu (PBB); Sarawak United Peoples' Party (SUPP); Parti Rakyat Sarawak (PRS); and Progressive Democratic Party (PDP). As the GPS is made up of the same component parties as Sarawak BN, it should continue to enjoy the support of the same Muslim and non-Muslim bumiputra constituencies. GPS has another advantage in that it is formed by Sarawakians and can contrast its origins with those of Sarawak PH, which has its roots in Peninsular Malaysia.

Sarawak faces challenging times ahead; it is now an opposition-run state with the state government facing a federal Pakatan Harapan government. Severing ties with national BN was a strategic survival move, borne of pragmatism as the BN is no longer the power it once was, and Sarawak, if it remains in a formal alliance with the BN, may also find it difficult to push its concerns at the federal level with the Pakatan government now in power.

GPS can chose to only "cooperate with and support" PH at the parliamentary level in areas where Sarawak interests are safeguarded. Where PH's decisions do not benefit Sarawak, GPS can chose not to support that initiative. Although the PH would not be hostile towards the GPS, it does not mean that it will be fully supportive as GPS is a formal coalition member. We can expect hostilities to increase as the Sarawak state elections draw near in the coming two to three years.

Interesting times lie ahead for Sarawak now with the entry of PPBM, which was launched in the state on 1 December 2018. Dr Mahathir said that PPBM had decided to set up a branch in Sarawak because of "many requests from Sarawakians". In Sarawak, PPBM has invited indigenous natives and other local non-Muslim Sarawak natives—in addition to Sarawak Malays—to join the party. The entry of Dr Mahathir's PPBM into Sarawak politics is something that UMNO failed to do in the past.

Both GPS and PH in Sarawak have the same stance on Malaysia Agreement 1963 and on issues of state nationalism. As Sarawak and Sabah both pursue state nationalism, a new state configuration of federal–state relations may eventually develop. GPS has vowed to focus on Sarawak interests and rights under MA 63; likewise Sarawak PH has also promised that it will look into Sarawakian interests.

Notes

1. I wish to convey my deepest thanks to Francis E. Hutchinson and Lee Hwok Aun for helping me to shape this chapter into its present form, and for their dedicated guidance and their insightful inputs throughout the research and writing stages of this chapter.
2. There are also Iban and Bidayuh membership in the PBB.
3. These clients include his political allies and relatives, Zainuddin Satem, Tajang Laing, Salleh Jafaruddin (Rahman's nephew), Wan Habib Syed Mahmau (Rahman's nephew), former State Secretary Abang Yusuf Puteh, B.R. Adai (editor of *Sarawak Tribune*), Daniel Tajem and Mohd Kamal Hussain (business advisers); and his family members, Norlia Abdul Rahman (daughter), Khadijah Abdul Rahman (daughter), Jamil Abdullah (Rahman's borther-in-law), Polycarp Soon (brother-in-law), Thomas Soon (borther-in-law), among others.
4. Prior to 1978, state and parliamentary elections in Sarawak coincided with one another. However, in 1978, when Parliament was dissolved to make way for Malaysia's 3rd General Elections, Chief Minister Rahman Ya'kub was not ready to face the opposition in a state election. The newly formed Malay Parti Anak Jati Sarawak (PAJAR) posed a credible challenge against Rahman's PBB, which in turn faced factional problems with SUPP. As a result, he postponed the state elections until a year later. This was the first time state elections were held at a different time from parliamentary elections. Since then, state elections in Sarawak have not coincided with the general elections. That Sarawak was not directly under UMNO rule also gave them the leeway to carry out state elections on at their own determination.
5. Adenan had gained prominence in November 1995 when Taib shockingly announced his intention to retire. He was one of three leaders, alongside Abang Johari and Sulaiman Daud, whom Taib had identified as possible successors (Faisal Hazis 2011, p. 12). No clear leader emerged. Adenan was Taib's favourite and a long-time loyalist, but Abang Johari was the most popular and had the strongest grass-roots and federal support (Faisal Hazis 2011, pp. 12–13; 2012, p. 160). Some of the members in PBB believed that Taib wanted to weaken Malay leaders by pitting them against one another in order to consolidate the Muslim Melanau's position in PBB (Faisal Hazis 2012, p. 161).
6. Adenan's support of the Roneey Rebit case, a Sarawakian who wanted to revert back to Christianity from Islam, was also widely viewed by non-Muslims Sarawakians as being progressive (Mohamed Nawab and Rashaad Ali 2017, p. 41). Rebit was converted as a child, and he was made to follow the religion of his guardians; his conversion was however not of his volition.
7. For detailed result, see *FMT News*, 7 May 2016.
8. Author's fieldwork in Sarawak, 3–7 March 2018.
9. Ibid.
10. Ibid.
11. Other forms of assistance include the waiving of excise duties and the provision of interest-free loans to purchase cars below 1,300 cc, reduction on the price of low-cost housing, harmonization of the legal system and the country's management (*tadbir urus*) in line with shariah principles, and returning certain rights to the states.

12. Author's fieldwork in Sarawak, 3–7 March 2018.
13. This involves the strengthening of Malaysia's shariah courts through the proposed amendment of Parliamentary Act (RUU) 355, which pitches a maximum punishment of 30 years in jail and 100 lashes of the cane for shariah-related offences. This could pave the way for the full realization of the PAS' implementation of *hudud* laws in Malaysia.
14. Author's fieldwork in Sarawak, 3–7 March 2018.
15. Ibid.
16. Mordi Bimol promised to help develop policies on native customary rights (NCR) land; propose new plots for existing villages to accommodate the growing population in Mas Gading; ensure that roads to villages in Mas Gading were paved; open agricultural roads throughout Mas Gading, identify existing agricultural firms with the potential of providing high technology access to farmers; promote tourism development in Bau-Lundu-Sematan; and to ensure that education facilities and infrastructure in Mas Gading are in a satisfactory condition especially in boarding schools (*Dayak Daily*, 3 May 2018).
17. Author's fieldwork in Sarawak, 3–7 March 2018.
18. Ibid.
19. This was over his questionable purchase of communal land which belonged to the villagers in Kampung Stabut, Kampung Maang and Kampung Chupak. Such land cannot be purchased and issued with a title (*Star Online*, 11 May 2018; *Borneo Post Online*, 9 May 2018), and this implied that he had "stolen" from his own people.

References

Adenan Bin Haji Satem, Chief Minister of Sarawak. 2016 *53 Principles and Actions*. https://www.sarawak.gov.my/media/attachments/download/2016/JKM%2053%20Prinsip%20&%20Tindakan%20Brochure%20English.pdf (accessed 1 May 2018).

Borneo Post Online. 2013. "'Allah' Ban a Non-Issue in the State". 16 October 2013. http://www.theborneopost.com/2013/10/16/allah-ban-a-non-issue-in-the-state/ (accessed 11 December 2017).

———. 2014. "Adenan 'No' to UMNO's Entry, Warns PKR Leaders". 26 March 2014. http://www.theborneopost.com/2014/03/26/adenan-no-to-umnos-entry-warns-pkr-leaders/ (accessed 3 January 2018).

———. 2015. "Adenan Gives Chong a Poser over Motion". 30 April 2015. http://www.theborneopost.com/2015/04/30/adenan-gives-chong-a-poser-over-motion/ (accessed 30 April 2018).

———. 2018a. "PH Manifesto a Better Deal than BN Recycled Promises—Baru". 15 April 2018. http://www.theborneopost.com/2018/04/15/ph-manifesto-a-better-deal-than-bn-recycled-promises-baru/ (accessed 18 April 2018).

———. 2018b. "4-Cornered Fight Shaping up in Puncak Borneo". 27 April 2018. https://www.theborneopost.com/2018/04/27/4-cornered-fight-shaping-up-in-puncak-borneo/#print (accessed 27 April 2018).

———. 2018c. "Straight Fight in Peaceful Mas Gading". 29 April 2018. https://www.theborneopost.com/2018/04/29/straight-fight-in-peaceful-mas-gading/ (accessed 3 May 2018).

———. 2018d. "State PH Unveils Third Part of Manifesto". 1 May 2018. https://www.theborneopost.com/2018/05/01/state-ph-unveils-third-part-of-manifesto/ (accessed 1 May 2018).

———. 2018e. "Jeannoth Asked to Explain How, from Whom He Bought Communal Land". 4 May 2018. https://www.theborneopost.com/2018/05/04/jeannoth-asked-to-explain-how-from-whom-he-bought-communal-land/ (accessed 7 May 2018).

———. 2018f. "DAP's Mordi Springs Big Surprise in Mas Gading". 10 May 2018, https://www.theborneopost.com/2018/05/10/daps-mordi-springs-big-surprise-in-mas-gading/ (accessed 11 May 2018).

———. 2018g. "PH Secures One-Third of 30 Parliamentary Seats, Triumphs in Predominantly-Bumiputera Areas". 10 May 2018. http://www.theborneopost.com/2018/05/10/ph-secures-one-third-of-30-parliamentary-seats-triumphs-in-predominantly-Bumiputera-areas/ (accessed 12 May 2018).

———. 2019. "DBOS—An Alternative Financing Route for Sarawak". 13 January 2019. http://www.theborneopost.com/2019/01/13/dbos-an-alternative-financing-route-for-sarawak/ (accessed 14 January 2019).

Chin, James. 2014. "Federal-East Malaysia Relations". In *50 Years of Malaysia: Federalism Revisited*, edited by Andrew J. Harding and James Chin. Singapore: Marshall Cavendish International.

———. 2015. "Exporting the BN/UMNO Model: Politics in Sabah and Sarawak". In *Routledge Handbook of Contemporary Malaysia*, edited by Meredith L. Weiss. London and New York: Routledge.

———. 2018. "Sabah and Sarawak in the 14th General Election 2018 (GE-14): Local Factors and State Nationalism". *Journal of Current Southeast Asian Affairs* 37, no. 3: 173–92.

———. 2019. "'New' Malaysia: Four Key Challenges in the Near Term". Lowy Institute, Sydney, March 2019.

Dayak Daily. 2018. "Facing Tough Odds, Mordi Does Not Believe in Surrendering". 3 May 2018. https://dayakdaily.com/facing-tough-odds-mordi-does-not-believe-in-surrendering/ (accessed 5 May 2018).

Faisal S. Hazis. 2011. "Winds of Change in Sarawak Politics?". RSIS Working Paper No. 224, 24 March 2011.

———. 2012. *Domination and Contestation: Muslim Bumiputera Politics in Sarawak*. Singapore: Institute of Southeast Asian Studies.

———, and Stanley Bye Kadam-Kiai. 2013. "Introduction". In *Politics of Local Government in Sarawak*, edited by Faisal S. Hazis and Stanley Bye Kadam-Kiai. Sarawak: Penerbit Universiti Sarawak Malaysia.

FMT News. 2016. "2016 Sarawak Elections—Results". 7 May 2016. https://www.freemalaysiatoday.com/category/nation/2016/05/07/2016-sarawak-election-results/ (accessed 1 May 2018).

———. 2018. "Ex-MP Tells Why He Now Backs DAP Man". 6 May 2018. https://www.freemalaysiatoday.com/category/nation/2018/05/06/ex-mp-tells-why-he-now-backs-dap-man/ (accessed 12 August 2018).

Harding, Andrew J., and James Chin, eds. 2014. *50 Years of Malaysia: Federalism Revisited*. Singapore: Marshall Cavendish International.

Hutchinson, Francis E. 2018. *GE-14 in Johor: The Fall of the Fortress?* Trends in Southeast Asia, no. 3/2018. Singapore: ISEAS – Yusof Ishak Institute.

Kadam-Kiai, Stanley Bye. 2013. "The 1970 Election and its Significance to Sarawak Politics". In *Politics of Local Government in Sarawak*, edited by Faisal S Hazis and Stanley Bye Kadam-Kiai. Sarawak: Penerbit Universiti Sarawak Malaysia.

Lee, Hock Guan. 2016. "Impressive Results Await BN in Sarawak State Elections". *ISEAS*

Perspective, no. 2016/20, 3 May 2016. https://www.iseas.edu.sg/images/pdf/ISEAS_Perspective_2016_20.pdf (accessed 5 January 2018).

———. 2017. "All Signs Point to Sarawak Being 'Fixed Deposit' for BN in GE14". *ISEAS Perspective*, no. 2017/20, 31 March 2017. https://www.iseas.edu.sg/images/pdf/ISEAS_Perspective_2017_20.pdf (accessed 5 January 2018).

Lee Poh Onn. 2018a. "GE-14: A Victory for Barisan Nasional in Sarawak". *ISEAS Perspective*, no. 2018/27, 7 May 2018. https://www.iseas.edu.sg/images/pdf/ISEAS_Perspective_2018_27@50.pdf (accessed 8 May 2018).

———. 2018b. "Free from the Shackles of a Fallen Coalition, Does Sarawak Parties Leaving Spell the End of the Barisan Nasional?". *Channel NewsAsia*, 15 June 2018. https://www.channelnewsasia.com/news/commentary/sarawak-parties-leave-barisan-nasional-end-of-coalition-10430826 (accessed 15 June 2018).

———. 2018c. "Shock in Sarawak: The Dayak Tsunami". *ISEAS Commentaries*, 2018/59, 12 May 2018. https://www.iseas.edu.sg/medias/commentaries/item/7560-shock-in-sarawak-the-dayak-tsunami-by-lee-poh-onn (accessed 12 May 2018).

Lim Teck Ghee, S. Thayaparan, and Terence Netto. 2018. "Anatomy of an Electoral Tsunami". Strategic Information and Research Development Centre, Malaysia.

Mersat, Neilson Ilan. 2018. "The Sarawak Dayaks' Shift in Malaysia's 2018 Election". *Commonwealth Journal of International Affairs* 107, no. 6: 729–37.

Mohamed Nawab Mohamed Osman, and Rashaad Ali. 2017. "Sarawak State Elections 2016: Revisiting Federalism in Malaysia". *Journal of Current Southeast Asian Affairs* 36, no. 1: 29–50.

Mohd Shazani bin Masri. 2017. "Tupong: If It Ain't Broke, Don't Fix It". In *Electoral Dynamics in Sarawak: Contesting Developmentalism and Rights*, edited by Meredith L. Weiss and Arnold Puyok. Petaling Jaya and Singapore: Strategic Information and Research Development Centre and ISEAS – Yusof Ishak Institute.

New Straits Times. 2016. "BN Can Retain Mas Gading with Nogeh: Observer". 16 April 2016. https://www.nst.com.my/news/politics/2018/04/357938/bn-can-retain-mas-gading-nogeh-observer (accessed 15 May 2018).

Pakatan Harapan. 2018. *Buku Harapan: Membina Negara Memenuhi Harapan*. Petaling Jaya: PKR, DAP, PPBM, Amanah.

Puyok, Arnold. 2017. "Ba' Kelalan: Sustaining the Crack in the BN's Rural Dominance". In *Electoral Dynamics in Sarawak: Contesting Developmentalism and Rights*, edited by Meredith L. Weiss and Arnold Puyok. Petaling Jaya and Singapore: Strategic Information and Research Development Centre and ISEAS – Yusof Ishak Institute.

Serina Rahman. 2018. "Malaysia Reborn? Does GE-14 Spell an End to Racial Politics". *Channel NewsAsia*, 10 May 2108. https://www.channelnewsasia.com/news/commentary/malaysia-general-election-race-card-costs-of-living-concerns-10220262 (accessed 11 May 2018).

Star Online, The. 2012. "Mas Gading MP Aspirant Hopeful of Gaining Trust of Constituents". 6 May 2012. https://www.thestar.com.my/news/community/2012/05/06/mas-gading-mp-aspirant-hopeful-of-gaining-trust-of-constituents/#x5er5fAugZeBTmPv.99 (accessed 4 January 2019).

———. 2017. "Abang Johari: We Will Continue Policy of English as Official Language". 22 January 2017. https://www.thestar.com.my/news/nation/2017/01/22/abang-johari-sarawak-to-keep-english-as-official-language/#IydrZTbB403KxZZ2.99 (accessed 3 March 2018).

————. 2018a. "Sarawak BN Confident of Retaining Its 25 Parliamentary Seats". 1 February 2018 https://www.thestar.com.my/news/nation/2018/02/01/sarawak-bn-confident-of-retaining-its-25-parliamentary-seats/ (accessed 5 April 2018).

————. 2018b. Sarawak BN Launches Six-Thrust Manifesto, Including Regaining State's Rights". 9 April 2018. https://www.thestar.com.my/news/nation/2018/04/09/sarawak-bn-launches-six-thrust-manifesto-including-regaining-state-rights/#jGJBuTIjvz0Yfr6E.99 (accessed 26 April 2018).

————. 2018c. "Widow of Former Chief Minister Campaigns for Dr Sim". 5 May 2018. https://www.thestar.com.my/metro/metro-news/2018/05/05/widow-of-former-chief-minister-campaigns-for-dr-sim-former-cms-widow-campaigns-for-dr-sim/ (accessed 28 November 2018).

————. 2018d. "The Night the Earth Moved". 10 May 2018. https://www.thestar.com.my/opinion/columnists/analysis/2018/05/10/the-night-the-earth-moved-as-predicted-by-dr-mahathir-the-malay-tsunami-has-taken-place-in-ge14/ (accessed 25 October 2018).

————. 2018e. "GE14 a Wake-up Call for Sarawak Barisan". 11 May 2018. https://www.thestar.com.my/metro/metro-news/2018/05/11/ge14-a-wakeup-call-for-sarawak-barisan/#LwVj1cDM7tFOoGQo.99 (accessed 12 May 2018).

————. 2018f. "More than 1,000 Schools Still in Dilapidated Category". 14 November 2018. https://www.thestar.com.my/metro/metro-news/2018/11/14/more-than-1000-schools-still-in-dilapidated-category/#7XVZJD8rZmHLHiys.99 (accessed 12 March 2019).

Straits Times. 2108a. "Sarawak Chief Minister Pledges to Amend State Law to Allow Converts to Renounce Islam". 4 March 2018. https://www.straitstimes.com/asia/se-asia/sarawak-chief-minister-pledges-to-amend-state-laws-to-allow-converts-to-renounce-islam (accessed 27 April 2018).

————. 2108b. "Sarawak Could Allow Converts to Renounce Islam". 5 March 2018. https://www.straitstimes.com/asia/se-asia/sarawak-could-allow-converts-to-renounce-islam (accessed 27 April 2018).

————. 2108c. "Sarawak Gains Full Control over State's Oil and Gas Sector as Malaysia Election Nears". 7 March 2018. https://www.straitstimes.com/asia/se-asia/sarawak-gains-full-control-over-states-oil-and-gas-sector (accessed 8 March 2018).

Teoh, Shannon. 2018. "State Oil Rights Not Cure-All for Sarawak". *Straits Times Online*, 8 March 2018. https://www.straitstimes.com/asia/se-asia/commentary-state-oil-rights-not-cure-all-for-sarawak (accessed 26 March 2018).

Weiss, Meredith L., ed. 2015. *Routledge Handbook of Contemporary Malaysia*. London and New York: Routledge.

————, and Arnold Puyok. 2017. "The 2016 Sarawak State Elections". In *Electoral Dynamics in Sarawak: Contesting Developmentalism and Rights*, edited by Meredith L. Weiss and Arnold Puyok. Petaling Jaya and Singapore: Strategic Information and Research Development Centre and ISEAS – Yusof Ishak Institute.

Welsh, Bridget. 2016. "A 'Fixed Result—Sarawak's Electoral Distortions". *MalaysiaKini*, 7 May 2016. https://www.malaysiakini.com/columns/340635 (accessed 13 December 2018).

Woon, Wilson. 2012. "Single Party Dominance in Sarawak and the Prospects for Change". *Contemporary Southeast Asia* 34, no. 2: 274–96.

Zalina Mohd. Desa, and Arenawati Sehat Omar. 2013. "Sarawak State Election 2011: Survey of Malay Voters' Behaviour in BN Critical Areas of N24 Beting Maro and N30 Saribas". *Journal of Techno Social* 5, no. 1: 71–80.

16

SABAH
The End of BN and Start of a New Order?

Tony Paridi Bagang and Arnold Puyok

INTRODUCTION

The 14th General Elections (GE-14) that took place on 9 May 2018 was a significant moment in Malaysia's political history. Against expectations, Pakatan Harapan (PH) defeated Barisan Nasional (BN), thus ending the ruling coalition's dominance after sixty years in power at the federal level.

Sabah, along with Sarawak, had long been seen as Barisan Nasional's "fixed deposit"—states which could be relied upon to deliver large numbers of parliamentary seats. Yet, 2018 was the beginning of a new era in Sabah as, against expectations, a significant proportion of voters supported PH and the newly minted Sabah-based party Warisan. Consequently, BN netted a surprisingly low number of parliamentary seats and the state legislative assembly was evenly split. Following a period of uncertainty, PH, Warisan, and a third party, United Pasokmomogun Kadazandusun Organization (UPKO), secured a majority in the state legislative assembly and formed the state government—constituting a major departure from previous elections.

This chapter traces the GE-14 electoral process in Sabah, analyses key trends and junctures, and then examines the aftermath of this historic election. While the rise of Warisan was largely unexpected, as was the swing against Barisan, various conditions had been building up for such a dramatic shift. The current configuration, including the collapse of BN in Sabah and the emergence of a new state administration, poses important questions for the Kadazandusun, the state's largest ethnic group, and their political preferences.

To this end, this chapter is comprised of six sections. Following this introduction, the second section provides basic contextual information on Sabah, comparing and contrasting it with the situation in Peninsular Malaysia. The subsequent section looks at the lead up to GE-14 in the state, particularly how the various coalitions formed and what issues they sought to highlight. The fourth section looks at the election results at the parliamentary and state levels. The fifth analyses the aftermath of GE-14 in Sabah, and the sixth and final section concludes and looks forward.

CONTEXT

Sabah is one of the thirteen states in Malaysia and one of the country's most ethnically diverse. There are more than forty ethnic and subethnic groups in the state. The Kadazandusun is the largest ethnic group, constituting about 25 per cent of Sabah's population, followed by: Bajau (20 per cent); Chinese (13 per cent); Malay (8 per cent); and Murut (4.5 per cent). Other bumiputras, encompassing more than twenty smaller indigenous groups make up 28.5 per cent, and the remaining 2 per cent are categorized as "Others" (Department of Statistics 2010).

In order to allay fears that they would be overwhelmed by West Malaysia upon their incorporation into Malaysia in 1963, Sabah and Sarawak were allotted a relatively large number of parliamentary seats. At present, Sabah has some 3.6 million people and twenty-five parliamentary constituencies and sixty state seats. In comparison, Selangor, the country's most populated state with 6.4 million people, has only twenty-two members of parliament and fifty-six state seats.

In electoral terms, the indigenous people in Sabah have traditionally been strong supporters of BN, having consistently voted the former ruling coalition to power for its ability to cater to their developmental needs and cultivate strong patronage ties with leaders of bumiputra groups in rural areas. For instance, Loh (2009) argued that the BN victory in the 1999 Sabah state election was due to voters' confidence in the ruling coalition to develop the state and maintain its political stability. Rural people need basic infrastructure such as road connections and agricultural assistance to sustain their economic livelihood, which the BN was able to provide. Such transactional relationships between rural voters and BN leaders were reinforced by the belief that only the ruling party was able to uplift and protect such communities. BN leaders habitually and sternly reminded rural people that if they did not support the ruling coalition, the state's development support would be withdrawn (Puyok 2014; Chin and Puyok 2010).

Consequently, with a brief interlude from 1991 to 1994 when the state was ruled by Parti Bersatu Sabah (PBS), Sabah has been a BN stronghold since 1963.[1] From 1963 until 1991, the state was ruled by coalitions of state-based parties which were, on the whole, ethnically based and friendly to the federal BN government. In contrast, PBS was multiethnic and strongly focused on state-level issues. In 1991, UMNO established grassroots networks and branch offices in the state in order to compete with PBS, and in 1994, an UMNO-led coalition toppled PBS through election wins and post-election defections (Puyok 2011).

From that year onwards, UMNO consolidated its power in Sabah and continued to rule the state until its defeat in 2018. The party's influence in Sabah was largely due to patronage politics and federal support, as well as the lack of viable opposition parties (Puyok 2013a). Although they established bases in the state, the presence of national opposition parties like the Democratic Action Party (DAP), Parti Keadilan Rakyat (PKR) and a handful of local-based opposition parties had very little impact on UMNO. This was due, in part, to these parties' inability to forge a united front. Voters in Sabah were sceptical of DAP and PKR, which they regarded as Peninsula-based parties. Local parties also refused to cooperate with them, calling them "stooges of Malaya" (Puyok 2009).

The role of Sabah United Malays National Organization (UMNO) leader Musa Aman also cannot be discounted. Musa Aman, who was a businessman before entering politics, rose quickly through party ranks and became Sabah UMNO Treasurer in 1992. In 1999, he was appointed as Minister in the Chief Minister's Department and two years later named as Finance Minister. In 2003, Musa Aman took over as Sabah Chief Minister from Chong Kah Kiat. The latter was the president of the Liberal Democratic Party, the Sabah-based BN component party. This change in leadership ended a rotation system which had been established in 1994, which allowed the various BN member parties taking turns to helm the state.

Due to his tenure from 2003 to 2018, Musa Aman became the only Sabah Chief Minister to last more than ten years. Puyok (2013a) argues that:

> Musa (sic) realized that in order to remain strong in local politics, he had to tackle three things: one, a continued support from the people, second, undivided loyalty from other state BN component parties and third, good relations with the federal government. Musa Aman did well in all three except that once in a while he had to deal with one or two disgruntled state BN leaders who were unhappy with Sabah UMNO's dominance. If the 2004 and 2008 elections results are anything to go by, they clearly show that the Sabah BN Government is strongly supported by the people. Inter- and intra-party rivalries (sic) were also successfully defused by Musa Aman. Any attempts at undermining his leadership were dealt with accordingly, thanks to Musa Aman's politics-business acumen. Musa Aman made good federal-state relations one of his top priorities. He knew that the exclusive (or combative) approach to federal-state relations would not work, given the experiences of his predecessors. (2013a, p. 236)

The total dominance of BN in Sabah can be seen in their performance at the parliamentary and state levels in 2004 and 2008. In both elections, the ruling coalition secured twenty-four out of twenty-five parliamentary seats and fifty-nine out of sixty state seats (Figures 16.1 and 16.2). Elsewhere in the country, this solid performance was only matched in Johor, the birthplace of UMNO, and Sarawak, BN's two other "fixed deposits".

FIGURE 16.1
Sabah Parliamentary Seats, 2004–13

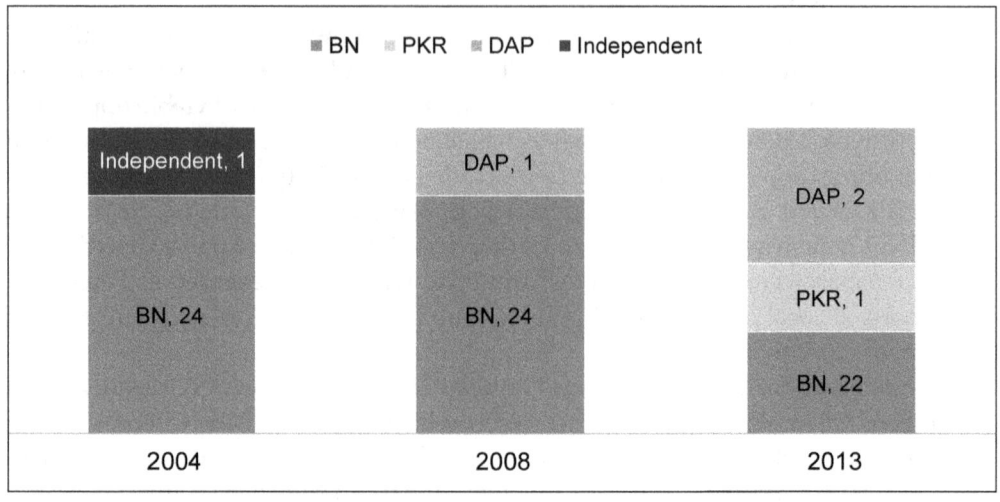

FIGURE 16.2
Sabah State Assembly Seats, 2004–13

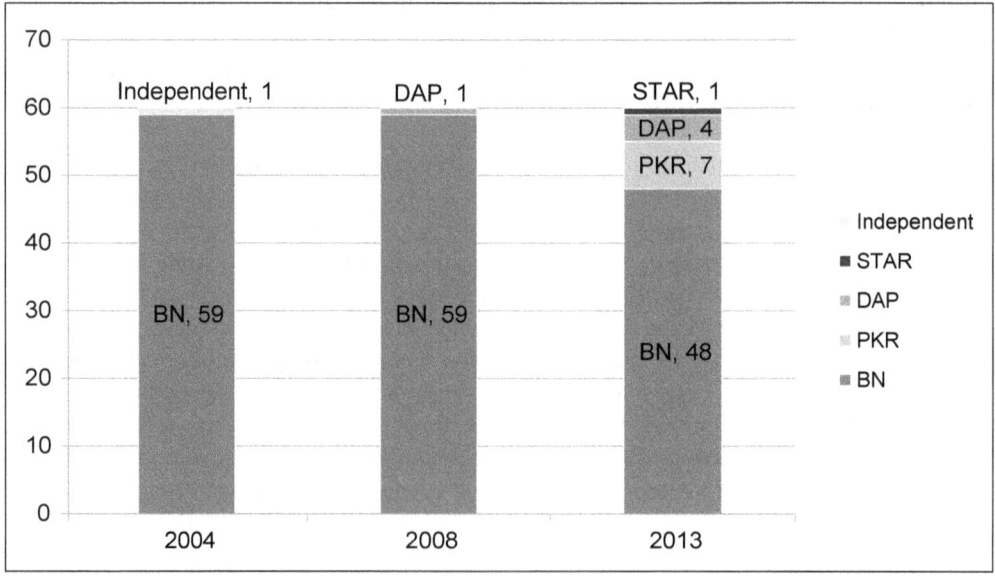

Nonetheless, despite BN's endurance and Musa Aman's dominance, the ruling coalition's grip was weakened in GE-13. In that year, the DAP and PKR managed to win three parliamentary seats and eleven state seats, largely in Kadazandusun and Chinese areas (Puyok 2013b). Their campaign strategies focused on issues such as illegal immigrants, Islamization, UMNO domination, ethnic marginalization and religious freedom. The Kadazandusun felt that they were affected by the illegal immigrant issue because foreigners with fake Malaysian Identification Cards (ICs) were allegedly registered as citizens and allowed to vote, thus changing the state's demographic structure. The Kadazandusun also accused their leaders within BN of being subservient to UMNO. The Kadazandusun were also told that if BN returned to power, there would be no religious freedom as Christians would be prevented from using the word Allah.

Consequently, many Kadazandusun who used to support BN member parties such as PBS, UPKO, and to some extent, Parti Bersatu Rakyat Sabah (PBRS), began to support opposition parties such as PKR and DAP. However, in the 2008 and 2013 elections, even though support for members of Pakatan Rakyat grew, the shift in voter preferences was not strong enough to weaken BN.

THE LEAD UP TO GE-14

While GE-14 had a seismic effect on Malaysia in general and Sabah in particular, what transpired before the election is important for understanding the dynamics and eventual result.

The run-up to the 2018 general election in Sabah was marked by important national and state-level political dynamics. At the national level, the 1MDB scandal as well as the goods and services tax (GST) were salient issues in Sabah. At the local level, feelings regarding autonomy for Sabah and devolution of revenue and responsibilities to the state level were quite strong. These feelings were a hold-over from GE-13, when they had featured quite prominently during the campaign. Other local-level issues that featured prominently included: the Malaysia Agreement 1963 (MA 63); the percentage of oil royalties that should accrue to the Sabah state government; and number of illegal immigrants in the state and their treatment by the authorities. Many Sabahans felt that the federal government failed to honour the MA 63 and deliberately attempted to change Sabah's distinct culture and character.

In addition, Sabah's political context was dramatically reconfigured by the emergence of Parti Warisan in October 2016. The party was founded by Shafie Apdal, a Bajau from Semporna in eastern Sabah. Formerly a senior BN leader, he had been Minister for Rural and Regional Development and UMNO vice-president. However, he was suspended from UMNO in mid-2016 for raising questions over the 1MDB scandal. He swiftly proceeded to form the new party with several key Kadazandusun leaders.

As Warisan's founding president, Shafie sought to portray himself as a leader for the people, someone willing to deal with the general needs of Sabahans, and a champion for the state's rights. Warisan was able to garner support along Sabah's east coast in the predominantly Muslim bumiputra areas comprising of Bajau, Bugis and Suluk communities as well as among UMNO members in other parts of the state.

However, despite the presence of several Kadazandusun leaders, voters from this ethnic group were initially sceptical of the party due to Shafie's ethnicity and track record at the federal level. This is where the roles of deputy Warisan president Darell Leiking, the Penampang MP who left PKR to join Warisan, and vice-president Peter Anthony, were crucial for establishing support. Darell was a popular leader among young Kadazandusun in Penampang, while Peter was known to many in the interior through a Kadazandusun-based non-governmental organization (NGO) of which he is president.

In the run-up to GE-14, the state's political parties began to team up, resulting in five groupings.

BN in Sabah was comprised of UMNO, PBS, UPKO, PBRS, the Malaysian Chinese Association (MCA), Liberal Democratic Party (LDP) and the Malaysian Indian Congress (MIC).

The second coalition was PH, comprised of PKR and DAP. Shafie Apdal's Warisan aligned itself with PH, hoping to ride on the opposition coalition's rising popularity especially in the Kadazandusun and Chinese areas. Compared to other local-based opposition parties, Warisan was relatively successful in projecting itself as the party that Sabahans had longed for. In a short period, Warisan's founding president Shafie Apdal was able to promote himself as the new Sabah champion.

The third coalition was Gabungan Sabah, comprised of Party Solidarity Tanah Airku (STAR), Sabah Progressive Party (SAPP), Parti Harapan Rakyat Sabah (PHRS), and Parti Perpaduan Rakyat Sabah (PPRS). The GS' constituent members were led by prominent political figures in Sabah such as: Jeffrey Kitingan of STAR; Lajim Ukin of PHRS; former Chief Minister Yong Teck Lee of SAPP; and Mohd Arshad Abdul Maulap of PPRS.[2]

Two small local parties Parti Cinta Sabah (PCS) and Parti Kerjasama Anak Negeri (AN) constituted a fourth coalition. The PCS (headed by Wilfred Bumburing) and Anak Negeri (led by Henrynus Amin) decided to ink a political pact in an attempt to capture the Kadazandusun state seats (Inus 2018a). PCS was relatively more established and was known to champion state rights and development which focused on the Kadazandusun Murut areas (Lee 2018a). AN was a relatively new party, and its main aim was to protect the interest of "Anak Negeri" or the native peoples of Sabah. Given their relatively small size, the PCS-Anak Negeri political pact agreed to use a common party symbol and common manifesto. This arrangement would enable resources to be shared, and allow each party to ride on the other's popularity among different voting blocs.[3]

The fifth contestant was Parti Islam Se-Malaysia (PAS), which attempted its luck by contesting in eight parliamentary seats and eighteen seats in the state legislative assembly. These seats were predominantly Muslim bumiputra majority constituencies where PAS sought to attract Muslim voters. In contrast to other Peninsula-based parties, PAS did not make a pact with any Sabah-based parties. The Islamic party campaigned on a platform of: strengthening Islamic institutions; upgrading the management of native land; respecting state rights as contained in MA 63; and giving Sabah autonomy in managing large-scale infrastructure projects (*Borneo Post*, 19 March 2018).

On 7 April 2018, the waiting game for the dissolution of Parliament and state assemblies ended. Before the dissolution of the Sabah state assembly, Chief Minister Musa Aman met the Yang di-Pertua Negeri for his consent for the elections to proceed with the existing number of sixty state seats. This meant that the new additional thirteen seats that had been gazetted in the state constitution in 2016 were not created, raising doubts about the legality of the exclusion of the new seats.[4]

The Gabungan Sabah coalition and PCS took legal action to compel the state government not to dissolve the state assembly, demanding that the government either repeal the thirteen additional seats or get Parliament to approve it (Lee, Joibi, and Fatimah 2018). Musa Aman then argued that the existing sixty seats were still legal as the national Parliament had not yet approved the additional seats nor had the Yang di-Pertuan Agong consented to them. The High Court of Sabah subsequently dismissed both GS and PCS applications (Anjumin 2018).

Official campaigning started right after nomination day on 28 April 2018.[5] Given that polling day was set on 9 May 2018, there were only eleven days for campaigning. The decision to hold the elections on a Wednesday made voting difficult for Sabahans, particularly those working in Peninsular Malaysia but who were still registered in their home state. Existing legislation required them to return to vote in the constituencies where they were registered.

In terms of the various campaign strategies, Sabah BN complemented the national BN manifesto named *Bersama BN, Hebatkan Negaraku* (With BN for a Greater Malaysia) with a state-level equivalent. The Sabah manifesto was called *Tanah Airku Maju* (My Homeland Has Progressed) and was launched by the chairman of Sabah BN, Musa Aman on 25 April 2018. In recognition of sentiments regarding state's rights, Sabah BN pledged twenty commitments in its manifesto, including to:

> safeguard the rights of Sabah in the Malaysia Agreement 1963; further strengthen the relationship amongst religions and races; further spur the poverty eradication agenda and create more affordable housing; continuously address the issue of illegal immigrants; empower Eastern Sabah Security Command (ESSCOM) by increasing its assets and membership; create more employment opportunities; be more efficient in land management; reduce the gap of development between rural and urban areas; and increase human capital development (Lajiun 2018).

On the other hand, Gabungan Sabah focused on its drive on restoring Sabah's rights and status. In its manifesto unveiled in March 2018, GS promised "to restore Sabah as an equal partner in the federation, to resolve the Sabah identity cards issue by granting them to genuine Sabahans, to resolve Sabah claims, to reclaim oil and gas rights and to elevate the status of native courts" (*Star Online*, 4 March 2018). The slogan of *Ini Kalilah...Tukar!* (It's the Time...Change) was chanted by its supporters, although less prominently than during GE-13.

Warisan and PH agreed to work together to contest against BN. Knowing the fact that Sabah was a "fixed deposit" for BN, and taking into account his trajectory as a senior UMNO leader, Shafie had to work with PH in order to convince the people in the state. Thus, the campaign focused on Najib Razak's alleged wrongdoings.

PH's manifesto for the state included pledges to: reduce people's burden; strengthen government institutions; spur sustainable and equitable economic growth; return Sabah and Sarawak to the status accorded in MA 63; and create a Malaysia that is inclusive, moderate and respected globally (Pakatan Harapan 2018).

Although it was a new state-based party, Warisan was expected to pose a formidable challenge to BN. To quell fears that Warisan was dominated by a single race, Shafie worked to assure people that Warisan was a multiracial party representing all Sabahans (*Borneo Post*, 18 Feruary 2017). Warisan campaigned on its manifesto themed *Aku Janji Warisan*, which featured thirteen points that covered people's rights, improving the deficiencies of the BN administration, as well as a development plan to improve quality of life and increase the efficiency of public services (Fiqah Roslan 2018).

During the campaign, both manifestos were mentioned interchangeably by Warisan and PH. However, Warisan candidates tended to focus more on state rights and reforms, with the tagline "In God We Trust, Change We Must". Meanwhile, PH focused on the national agendas relating to governance, along with assuring Sabahans that the state would be treated as an equal with West Malaysia.

THE RESULTS

Relative to previous electoral battles, GE-14 was rather different in that it was being contested by five groupings: BN; Warisan-PH; Gabungan Sabah; PCS-AN; and PAS. Consequently, there were multicornered fights in almost all seats. At the federal level, there was one straight fight, eight three-cornered, eleven four-cornered, three five-cornered and two six-cornered fights. At the state level, out of the sixty constituencies, only two were straight fights, with the rest between at least three candidates, if not more. Traditionally, multicornered fights were taken to favour BN, as they split the protest vote. However, in GE-14, the multicornered contests gave rise to a range of permutations, in some cases benefiting BN, in other cases Warisan-PH or Gabungan Sabah.

At the parliamentary level, BN fielded candidates in all constituencies, and its component members were apportioned the following seats: UMNO (14); PBS (5); UPKO (4); PBRS (1) and LDP (1) (Table 16.1). Collectively, Warisan-PH covered all constituencies, with Warisan fielding sixteen candidates and PH nine, of which PKR ran in six and DAP the remaining three. Gabungan Sabah ran in twenty-three constituencies, with PHRS contesting in fourteen and STAR five seats. PCS and PAS ran in eight seats each.

Warisan-PH did spectacularly well in GE-14, securing a total of fourteen seats. Broadly, there were several important shifts in voter preferences in 2018 (Figure 16.3). In Muslim bumiputra areas, Warisan did very well on the east coast seats of Silam, Semporna, and Kalabakan. Along with its coalition partners, it was also able to take other Muslim bumiputra seats such as Kota Belud, Sepanggar, Putatan and Papar in the northwest, as well as Batu Sapi near Sandakan. In Chinese and mixed seats, Warisan-PH won in Kota Kinabalu, Tuaran and Sandakan, and in non-Muslim

TABLE 16.1
Parliamentary Results in Sabah (GE-14)

Political Parties	Total Seats Contested	Total Seats Won
Barisan Nasional (BN)	(25)	(10)
UMNO	14	7
PBS	5	1
UPKO	4	1
PBRS	1	1
MCA	—	
LDP	1	
Gerakan	—	
Warisan	16	8
Pakatan Harapan (PH)	(9)	(6)
DAP	3	3
PKR	6	3
Gabungan Sabah	(23)	(1)
STAR Sabah	5	1
Harapan (PHRS)	14	0
PPRS	2	0
SAPP	2	0
Parti Cinta Sabah (PCS)	8	0
PAS	8	0
Total		25

Source: Authors' compilation from https://election.thestar.com.my/sabah.html

bumiputra, predominantly Kadazandusun seats such as Ranau and Tenom. Broadly, within the opposition coalition, Warisan performed well in Muslim bumiputra seats, while PH cleanly swept Chinese-majority or ethnically mixed seats.

For its part, BN retained ten seats out of the twenty-two it held before the election. There were mostly Muslim bumiputra seats in the centre of Sabah, such as Kinabatangan, Beluran, Libaran and Kudat, as well as the west coast such as Kimanis, Beaufort and Sipitang. It also retained a small number of non-Muslim bumiputra seats, such as Pensiangan and Kota Marudu.

Despite running in twenty-three seats, Gabungan Sabah did not perform well. PHRS lost all of its fourteen contests and STAR was only able to secure one non-Muslim bumiputra seat, Keningau, from BN.

At the state level, BN fielded candidates in all constituencies, and its component members were apportioned the following seats: UMNO (32); PBS (13); UPKO (6); LDP (six); MCA (2); Gerakan (2) and PBRS (1). UMNO contested mostly in the predominantly Muslim bumiputra areas comprised of Bajau, Malay, Suluk, Bruneian, Kadayan and Bisaya voters. PBS, UPKO and PBRS candidates were fielded in the mixed and non-Muslim bumiputra constituencies comprised of Kadazandusun and Chinese. BN only managed to retain twenty-nine seats, prohibiting it from forming a government with a simple majority.

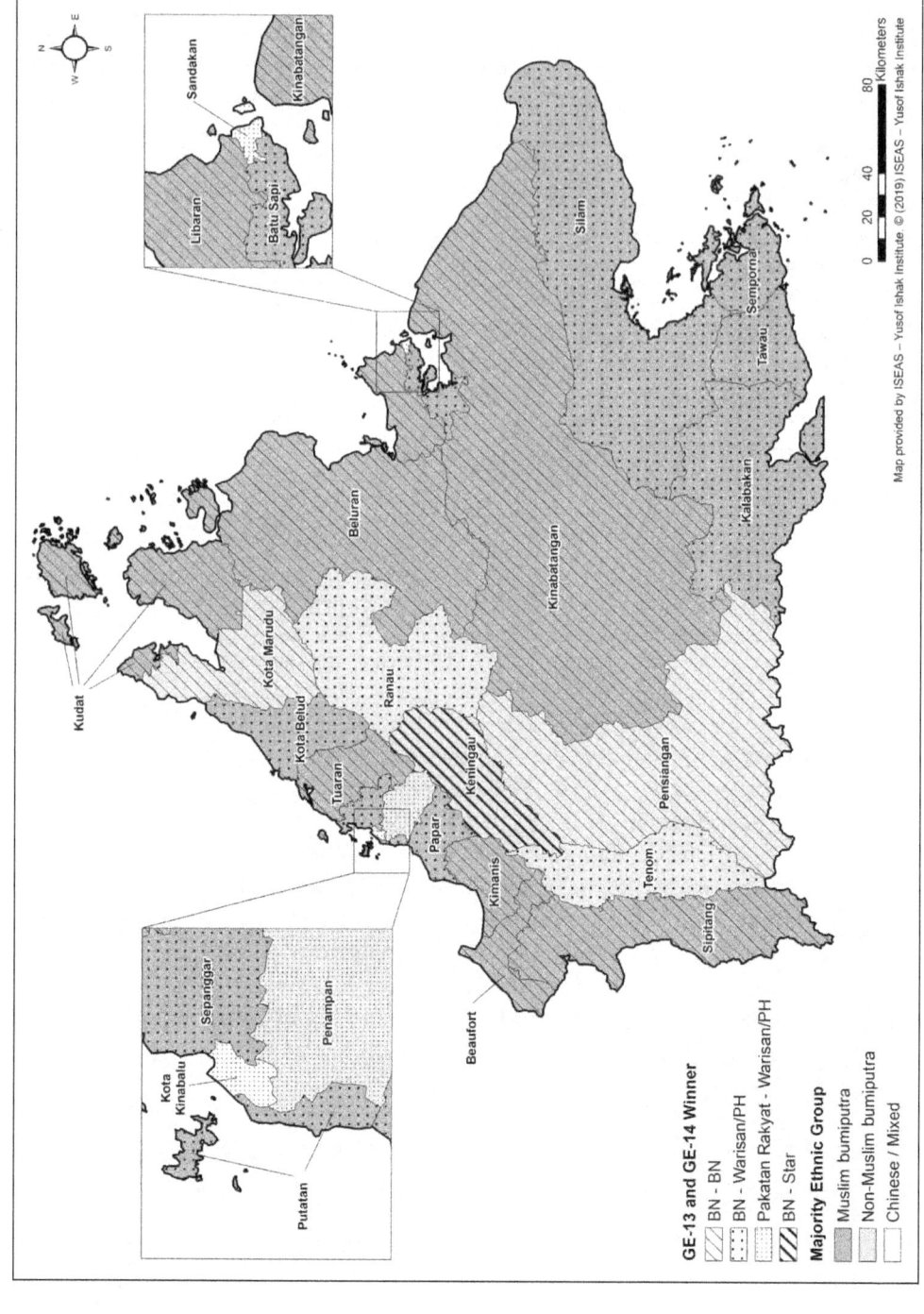

FIGURE 16.3

Sabah Parliamentary Seats: Winning Parties and Ethnic Composition (GE-13 and GE-14)

On the other hand, Warisan contested forty-five seats and managed to secure twenty-one seats, while DAP and PKR won six and two seats, respectively. DAP fared very well, losing only one out of the seven seats where it contested. In contrast, PKR won only two out of its eight seats.

With regard to the other groupings, despite their vocal defence of Sabahan rights and autonomy, GS did not perform well, with only one member party, STAR, netting two seats. PHRS, PPRS, and PKS failed to win any seats. PAS and PCS also did not secure any seats.

In terms of broad changes in voter sentiments, unlike the parliamentary contests which showed a clear shift in preferences from BN to Warisan-PH, the picture at the state level is more diverse. Warisan-PH dominated in urban area state legislative assembly (SLA) seats, mirroring the parliamentary results, specifically, winning 75 per cent of votes in Chinese-majority areas and 63 per cent in ethnically mixed areas. However, in the Muslim-majority areas in Sabah's eastern half and portions of the west coast, the seats were split between BN and the Warisan-PH alliance, indicating the ability of Warisan to gather votes from Malays and Bajaus (Figure 16.4; refer to Figure 16.3 for ethnic composition). Along the north-to-south belt of non-Muslim bumiputra constituencies west of Sabah's centre, the popular vote was also quite evenly split, with BN performing better than Warisan-PH specifically in the Kadazandusun areas. Despite the strong anti-BN sentiment among the Kadazandusun electorates, many still regarded BN as the better option. This differentiation in preferences between the parliamentary and state levels suggest that a majority of people voted for a change at the federal level as most of controversial issues were national-based and directly associated with BN and Najib.

THE AFTERMATH

Initially, the GE-14 results for the Sabah state assembly failed to determine the winner and the rightful party to form a new government. It appeared to be a deadlock situation for the state as Sabah BN and the Warisan-PH were tied at twenty-nine state seats each. In the Sabah state constitution, there are no clear provisions for a hung assembly situation. In this context, STAR emerged as the kingmaker.

People started to speculate that there might be a high possibility that Warisan-PH, under Shafie's leadership, would form a government in alliance with STAR. Jeffrey Kitingan, the leader of STAR, had been very vocal criticizing the BN state administration as well as promoting local rights (*Star Online*, 8 May 2018). Consequently, this was thought to preclude him from supporting the BN faction in the state legislative assembly. Nonetheless, both BN and Warisan-PH attempted to woo his party's allegiance. Early reports indicated Jeffrey was more willing to work with Warisan and PH, but no official deal was sealed between Jeffrey and Shafie. At the same time, BN also tried to secure his support (*Straits Times*, 10 May 2018).

The contest to form the new state government reached its peak on the afternoon of 10 May 2018, when Musa Aman, the incumbent Chief Minister, claimed that BN

FIGURE 16.4
Sabah State Assembly Seats: GE-14 Winners

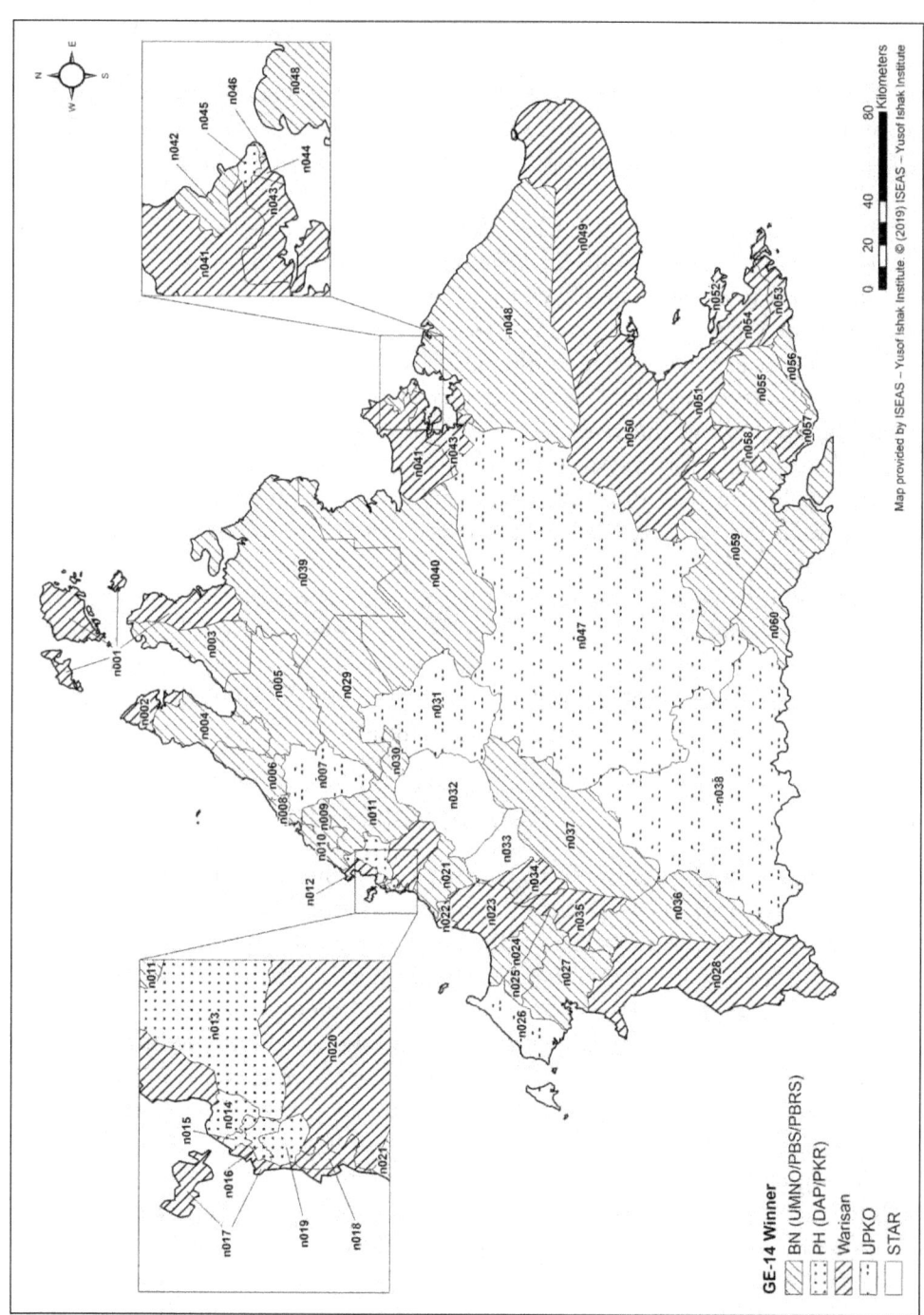

GE-14 Winner
- BN (UMNO/PBS/PBRS)
- PH (DAP/PKR)
- Warisan
- UPKO
- STAR

Map provided by ISEAS – Yusof Ishak Institute © (2019) ISEAS – Yusof Ishak Institute

had won the race for STAR—thus securing a majority of thirty-one seats. He rushed to the Istana Negeri to seek an audience with the Yang di-Pertua Negeri.[6] At 11:00 p.m. Musa was sworn in as the Chief Minister of Sabah (*Star Online*, 11 May 2018).

This dashed the hope of many opposition supporters who wanted to see a change of government in Sabah. Jeffrey Kitingan's role in enabling Sabah BN to remain in power received a great deal of attention, with hundreds of Sabahans taking to the streets in Kota Kinabalu on the night of 10 May (Katrina Khairul Azman 2018). The protesters chanted "*Sabah Ubah*" and recorded their action live on social media. Rumours about the involvement of money politics also circulated, including an allegation that Kitingan was paid RM20 million and also offered a Deputy Chief Minister's post in the BN state government. The allegation led the Malaysian Anti-Corruption Commission (MACC) to subsequently raid his house and confiscate about RM80,000 cash (Gomez 2018).

However, this did not end the struggle for control of the state government. On the same day, prior to Musa seeking an audience at the palace, Madius Tangau, the acting president of the BN component member UPKO, unexpectedly announced that his party would leave BN and join Warisan to form the state government (Lee 2018b).[7] This was despite the fact that five UPKO assemblymen had pledged their support to Musa Aman during a press conference earlier that same day (Zam Yusa 2018). According to Madius, the party supreme council unanimously agreed to leave BN in line with the wishes of the Kadazandusun or Momogun[8] communities (Fatimah Zainal 2018b).

On 11 May, less than twenty-four hours after Musa Aman was sworn in as the chief minister, two UPKO assemblymen made a U-turn, instead pledging support to Warisan-PH and Shafie Apdal (*Borneo Post*, 12 June 2018). Of the party's other three assemblymen, two subsequently left UPKO, with one joining Warisan and another becoming a government-friendly Independent. On the same day, another four UMNO assemblymen quit their party and joined forces with Warisan.

The defection of six BN assemblymen to Warisan-PH meant Musa no longer had a majority in the assembly, and calls began demanding his resignation. Under the Sabah state constitution Article 7(1) states:

> if the Chief Minister ceases to command the confidence of a majority of the members of the Legislative Assembly, then, unless at his request the Yang di-Pertua Negeri dissolves the Assembly, the Chief Minister shall tender the resignation of the members of the Cabinet.

The Istana Negeri reportedly handed an official letter to Musa Aman notifying him that he was no longer the Chief Minister of Sabah, effective 12 May 2018 (*New Straits Times*, 14 May 2018). Despite this, Musa did not resign or dissolve his Cabinet.

On the other hand, as six BN assemblymen vowed their support to Shafie, Warisan obtained a total of thirty-five seats and was able to form a new government. At a press conference on the evening of 11 May 2018, Shafie revealed that he had sent a letter to the Yang di-Pertua Negeri regarding his majority support in the state assembly (Joseph 2018). The following day, Shafie was sworn in as Sabah's 14th Chief

Minister, ending UMNO's twenty-four years at the helm. Despite their limited number of seats, UPKO was well accommodated in the new state government. In order to recognize the importance of the Kadazandusun, UPKO members Madius Tangau and Ewon Benedick were appointed as the Deputy Chief Minister and Minister of Rural Development, respectively.

On 17 May 2018, Musa Aman filed a writ of summons against the Yang di-Pertua Negeri and Shafie Apdal, seeking a declaration that he, Musa, remained the lawful Chief Minister and that the swearing in of Shafie was unconstitutional (*Daily Express*, 18 May 2018). Musa's decision to bring the case to the court received reactions from various parties. According to the former deputy Speaker of Sabah Legislative Assembly and the secretary-general of PBS, Johny Mositun, Musa was lawfully right to insist that he was the legitimate Chief Minister as he can only be removed from office through a vote of no confidence in the State Assembly. Likewise, Masidi Manjun, BN assemblyman and the former State Minister of Tourism and Culture observed that the legal action by Musa should be viewed as upholding respect for and compliance to the rule of law and the state constitution (*Borneo Post*, 5 June 2018).

The political crisis persisted, even though Shafie had started his duties as Chief Minister. On 19 May, the Yang di-Pertua Negeri lodged a police report which was believed to have a connection with Musa's swearing-in on 10 May 2018 (*Daily Express*, 25 May 2018).[9] Shafie also applied to the court to strike Musa's legal suit on the ground that he had no reasonable grounds to challenge his appointment and that Musa's actions amounted to a "scandalous, frivolous and vexatious" abuse of the court process. In Shafie's affidavit, he also questioned Musa's swearing-in on 10 May 2018 as it was alleged that it was done under duress in line with the police report lodged by the Yang di-Pertua Negeri (*Borneo Post*, 5 June 2018).

On 6 June 2018, Musa withdrew his first lawsuit against the Yang di-Pertua Negeri and Shafie, but filed a new writ of summons that would not require him to appear in court. This was seen as part of his intention not to return to Malaysia, as he had been out of the country since 14 May 2018 (Chan 2018). However, on 5 September 2018, Musa returned to Sabah and was sworn in as Sungai Sibuga assemblyman (Vanar and Stephenie 2018a).

CONCLUSION

Sabah's voters showed they were capable of exercising their democratic rights by choosing the government of their choice, amidst some of the most crowded and intense multicornered contests of GE-14.

Despite BN's well-oiled campaign machinery and development promises, the coalition lost immense ground to Warisan. The results also show that developmentalist politics hold less clout over indigenous voters than before. In some areas, delivering development projects and promising new ones remain effective campaign strategies. Nonetheless, the voting pattern also shows a shift from parochial sentiments to concerns over a broader set of issues such as governance, economy, and leadership.

More voters, including in the rural areas, supported national-based parties such as PKR and DAP that campaigned heavily on national issues such as the 1MDB, Najib's financial scandal, and Malaysia's economic performance. Thus, while state-based issues such as autonomy and MA 63 are still popular, local-based parties cannot continue to depend on these issues to remain relevant in future elections.

Shafie's down-to-earth approach worked well among many voters who voiced their dissatisfaction with BN more openly than before. In addition, Warisan played a key role in garnering support for Warisan-PH in Malay and Bajau areas. Thus, BN's dominance especially in Muslim bumiputra majority constituencies was eroded. The Chinese and mixed seats in urban areas firmly supported PH members PKR and DAP. However, the results in other areas such as the Kadazandusun-based constituencies were mixed—with the opposition failing to capitalize on this group's disenchantment with BN. This constitutes a challenge to Warisan, which claims to represent all ethnic groups in Sabah.

With BN's disbandment and the formation of the new Warisan-PH-UPKO coalition government, Sabah is set to enter into a different phase of its political history. However, the newly minted governing coalition has a number of important challenges to face.

First, it remains to be seen how long the new coalition of Warisan-PH and UPKO will last. There are signs that Warisan and UPKO supporters do not trust each other, with well-publicized disputes between key leaders in the early days of the coalition government.[10] One fault line concerns the Kadazandusun community. Do UPKO and its leaders advocate for the community, or is it represented by Kadazandusun members in Warisan, such as Darrell Leiking and Peter Anthony? Furthermore, there are also members of this ethnic group in PKR and DAP.

Second, this fault line crosses coalitions, as BN member PBS garnered more than 40 per cent of the popular vote in Kadazandusun areas—which is more than what UPKO and Warisan obtained. This raises the question of whether Warisan-PH can confidently claim to represent all communities in Sabah. Should various parties with a better claim to political representation emerge, the new state government may be under threat.

A new opposition coalition called Gabungan Bersatu Sabah (GBS) was announced on the 24 October 2018.[11] Coalition members include UMNO, STAR, and PBS, with other smaller parties such as PPRS and SAPP expected to join. Despite having UMNO as a member, GBS is not associated with BN at the federal level. The aim is to compete with Warisan-PH in representing as many ethnic communities as possible.

Despite the reconfiguration of Sabah's political context and the importance of local-level issues, the state will still continue to be affected by developments in West Malaysia's political context. On one hand, UMNO is a key member of GBS, despite the coalition's disassociation with BN. On the other, despite promises to the contrary, PH component member Parti Pribumi Bersatu Malaysia has begun opening local branches in Sabah.

Sabah welcomes a new political order, but awaits to see what changes and what takes root.

Notes

1. Upon the establishment of Malaysia in 1963, the Sabah Alliance formed the first government in the state. The coalition comprised the: United National Pasokmomogun Kadazan Organization (UPKO); United Sabah National Organization (USNO); Sabah Chinese Association (SCA); and Sabah Indian Congress (SIC). All these political parties were established in the wake of the formation of Malaysia and were ethnically based (Ongkili 1989). The Sabah Alliance governed the state from 1963 until 1967, following that the USNO-SCA Alliance ruled the state from 1967 until 1976. This coalition secured the mandate to rule Sabah until the emergence of a multiracial party known as Parti Bersatu Rakyat Jelata Sabah (BERJAYA). The formation of BERJAYA was a result of strained relationships between the USNO-SCA government and BN government in Kuala Lumpur. BERJAYA ruled the state from 1976 until 1985. Tun Fuad Stephens led the BERJAYA government for few months before he and three other ministers perished in a helicopter crash in June 1976. Harris Salleh took over the state leadership until 1985. The BERJAYA government was subsequently defeated by Parti Bersatu Sabah (PBS) in 1985. PBS which was founded in 1985, was led by Joseph Pairin Kitingan, a former BERJAYA leader who rose through the party ranks to challenge Harris. PBS was the second multiracial party to govern Sabah after BERJAYA.
2. STAR Sabah was headed by a well-known political figure, Jeffrey Kitingan. His party had been very vocal in fighting for Sabah's rights and autonomy. Its base support came largely from the Kadazandusun in the interior of Keningau. Meanwhile, SAPP party was a state-based opposition party led by the former Chief Minister, Yong Teck Lee. SAPP was one of the component parties in BN before but it withdrew from the ruling coalition in 2008. Parti Harapan Rakyat Sabah (PHRS), or known as Harapan, was headed by the former UMNO leader, Lajim Ukin. Lajim was the MP for Beaufort constituency from 2008 to 2013 under UMNO. In GE-13, Lajim failed to retain Beaufort under PKR's ticket but he won the state seat of Klias. As the Janang Gayuh or Paramount Leader of the Bisaya community in Beaufort, Lajim enjoyed strong support from the Bisaya people (Bagang 2014). Another local-based opposition party was PPRS led by Mohd Arshad Abdul Mualap, a former civil servant turned businessman. He was an independent candidate in the 2013 General Elections who contested against Musa Aman in the Sungai Sibuga state seat. The Parti Cinta Sabah (PCS) was headed by Wilfred Bumburing, the former UPKO deputy president while Parti Kerjasama Anak Negeri (AN) was led by Henrynus Amin who was the former secretary-general of PBS. Both parties promoted the rights of the indigenous people of Sabah.
3. Senior AN party member, personal communication, 19 May 2018.
4. When the 2016 redelineation exercise commenced, the Election Commission (EC) complied with the state legislature's two-thirds' majority decision to increase the number of state seats from sixty to seventy-three. Out of the thirteen new seats proposed by the EC, six were Muslim-majority, four mixed, two non-Muslim-majority and one Chinese-majority. However, the thirteen new seats were not included in GE-14 as Sabah redelineation proposals were excluded from the EC report tabled in Parliament and approved on 28 March 2018.

5. However, campaign activities had been ongoing for a considerable period of time. For instance, in the Kuala Penyu state constituency, the BN's machinery organized Program Negaraku @ Komuniti 2017 which was held in Menumbok, Kuala Penyu. The programme was officiated by the Kuala Penyu assemblyman Limus Jury. Program Pemimpin Bersama Petugas Jalinan Rakyat @ JR was also organized by Wanita UMNO Beaufort which was held at Pa' Musa Hall, Beaufort on 19 October 2017 and Malampai Hall on 23 October 2017. Isnin Aliasnih, Beaufort UMNO Chief Division was the guest of honour for both programmes. Likewise in Papar, another constituency, a programme known as Kupi-Kupi Gabungan Sabah (GS) Zon Mengundi Ovan Kosopon was held on 1 February 2018 at Kg Bolotikon Papar which aimed to give an explanation on GS' political struggles (SAPP 2018).

6. It was reported that Musa attempted to seek an audience earlier that day—at about 1:30 a.m.—but was resisted by the palace (*Star Online*, 11 May 2018).

7. As in Peninsular Malaysia, there are no laws banning MPs or SLA members from crossing the floor to join other parties.

8. Momogun communities refer to the Dusunic, Paitanic and Murutic ethnic groups in Sabah. Despite being usually labelled as Kadazandusun, some disagree with the term and prefer to be known as "Momogun".

9. There were rumours saying that Musa intimidated the Yang di-Pertua Negeri over his swearing-in as Chief Minister. However, Musa denied all the allegations of criminal intimidation and also regretted dragging the Yang di-Pertua Negeri into the legal suit over his appointment (*Daily Express*, 25 May 2018).

10. For instance, the UPKO deputy secretary-general, Georgina George criticized Christina Liew for her failure to acknowledge UPKO's support to form the present government during her state assembly motion of vote of confidence in Shafie as Chief Minister (*Borneo Post*, 12 June 2018).

11. Musa announced that he would leave Sabah UMNO and might join PBS. This was confirmed by Pairin when he announced his party's exit from BN, to form Gabungan Bersatu Sabah with Sabah STAR as this move would lift the spirits and aspirations of Sabahans (*Star Online*, 12 May 2018). However, to date, there is no official news on the status of GBS' formation even though Jeffrey claimed that the idea of forming an opposition bloc in Sabah is in the pipeline (Patrick 2018b).

References

Anjumin, E.C. 2018. "Applications Rejected, Contest is for 60 Seats". *New Sabah Times*, 24 April 2018. http://www.newsabahtimes.com.my/nstweb/fullstory/23268 (accessed 29 August 2018).

Bagang, Eric. 2015. "Limus Jury Education Foundation Provides Recourse to Financially Less Fortunate". *New Sabah Times*. 30 November 2015. http://www.newsabahtimes.com.my/nstweb/fullstory/1503 (accessed 1 September 2018).

Bagang, Tony Paridi. 2014. "Beaufort, Sabah: Whither Lajim Popularity?". In *Electoral Dynamics in Malaysia: Findings from the Grassroots*, edited by Meredith L. Weiss. Petaling Jaya and Singapore: SIRD and Institute of Southeast Asian Studies, 2014.

Borneo Post, The. 2017. "Shafie Insists Warisan is Multiracial". 18 February 2017. https://www.pressreader.com/malaysia/the-borneo-post-sabah/20170218/281621010095867 (accessed on 25 November 2018).

———. 2018a. "Kuala Penyu to be Top Attraction". 14 January 2018. http://www.theborneopost.com/2018/01/14/kuala-penyu-to-be-top-attraction/ (accessed 1 September 2018).

———. 2018b. "PAS Sabah Launches Manifesto for GE14". 19 March 2018. https://www.theborneopost.com/2018/03/19/pas-sabah-launches-manifesto-for-ge14/ (accessed 5 May 2019).

———. 2018c. "PBS Calls for Calm Till Court Judgement". 21 May 2018. http://www.theborneopost.com/2018/05/21/pbs-calls-for-calm-till-court-judgement/ (accessed 6 August 2018).

———. 2018d. "UPKO Sacrifices Principles for Stability". 12 June 2018, p. 2.

———. 2018e. "Shafie Applies to Strike out Musa's Lawsuit". 5 June 2018. https://www.theborneopost.com/2018/06/05/shafie-applies-to-strike-out-musas-lawsuit/ (accessed 12 July 2018).

———. 2018f. "UPKO Leader Regrets Christina's Failure to Acknowledge Significance of Party's Support". 12 June 2018. https://www.pressreader.com/malaysia/the-borneo-post-sabah/20180612/281578061365572 (accessed 9 August 2018).

Chan, Julia. 2018. "Musa Files Fresh Suit in Seeming Bid to Avoid Returning to Malaysia". *The Malay Mail*, 6 June 2018. https://www.malaymail.com/s/1638990/musa-files-fresh-suit-in-seeming-bid-to-avoid-returning-to-malaysia (accessed 6 August 2018).

Chin, James and Arnold Puyok. 2010. "Going Against the Tide: Sabah and the 2008 Malaysian General Elections". *Asian Politics and Policy* 2, no. 2: 219–325.

Chok Sim Yee. 2018. "Musa No Longer CM—Istana Negeri". *Borneo Post Online*, 14 May 2018. http://www.theborneopost.com/2018/05/14/musa-no-longer-cm-istana-negeri/ (accessed on 6 August 2018).

Constitution of the State of Sabah. (n.d). www.lawnet.sabah.gov.my (accessed 12 May 2018).

Daily Express. 2018a. "Musa Takes TYT, Shafie to Court". 18 May 2018.

———. 2018b. "Musa Denies the TYT's Claims". 25 May 2018. http://www.dailyexpress.com.my/news.cfm?NewsID=124811 (accessed 6 August 2018).

Department of Statistics. *Population and Housing Census 2010*. Kuala Lumpur: Government Printer, 2010.

Doksil, Mariah. 2018. "PCS, Anak Negeri Sign Political Pack". *Borneo Post*, 17 March 2018. http://www.theborneopost.com/2018/03/17/pcs-anak-negeri-sign-political-pact/ (assessed 31 August 2018).

Fatimah Zainal. 2018a. "Gabungan Sabah Files Appeal against Court Decision to Strike out Case against PM, EC". *The Star Online*, 3 May 2018. https://www.thestar.com.my/news/nation/2018/05/03/gabungan-sabah-files-appeal-against-court-decision-to-strike-out-case-against-pm/ (accessed 5 July 2018).

———. 2018b. "Madius: UPKO Made 'the Boldest of Decisions' in Leaving Barisan". *The Star Online*, 10 May 2018. https://www.thestar.com.my/news/nation/2018/05/10/madius-upko-made-the-boldest-of-decisions-in-leaving-barisan/#EuVdDV7YHBf0ql5j.99 (accessed 2 August 2018).

Fiqah Roslan. 2018. "Warisan Manifestos Promises Prosperity". *Borneo Post*, 28 April 2018. https://www.pressreader.com/malaysia/the-borneo-postsabah/20180428/281616715981349 (accessed 3 May 2018).

Gomez, Elton. 2018. "MACC Raids Jeffrey's home". *Borneo Post Online*, 22 May 2018. https://www.theborneopost.com/2018/05/22/macc-raids-jeffreys-home/ (accessed on 25 May 2018).

Hana, N.Z., and Z. Zafira. 2016. "Muhyiddin, Mukhriz Sacked from UMNO, Shafie Suspended".

News Straits Times, 24 June 2016. https://www.nst.com.my/news/2016/06/154389/muhyiddin-mukhriz-sacked-umno-shafie-suspended (accessed on 5 May 2019)

Inus, Kristy. 2018a. "PCS, Anak Negeri Join Forces, Target 25 Kadazandusun Murut State Seats". *News Straits Times*, 16 March 2018. https://www.nst.com.my/news/politics/2018/03/345846/pcs-anak-negeri-join-forces-target-25-kadazandusun-murut-state-seats (accessed 20 July 2018).

————. 2018b. "Sabah UMNO's Election Machinery Not Affected by Leaders Departure". *New Straits Times*, 29 April 2018. https://www.nst.com.my/news/politics/2018/04/363292/sabah-umnos-election-machinery-not-affected-leaders-departure (accessed 5 September 2018).

Joibi, Natasha. 2018. "Musa Aman to Return to Malaysia against Doctor's Advice". *Star Online*, 21 August 2018. https://www.thestar.com.my/news/nation/2018/08/21/musa-aman-to-return-to-malaysia-against-doctors-advice/#UPrjKivs946jE6Dq.99 (accessed 29 August 2018).

Joseph, Neil Brian. 2018. "Shafie Commands a Majority". *Borneo Post*, 12 May 2018, p. 1.

Katrina Khairul Azman. 2018. "Disappointed Sabahans Stage Protest after Jeffrey Joins BN to Form State Govt". *Says*, 11 May 2018. http://says.com/my/news/sabahans-protest-against-bn-led-state-government (accessed 1 August 2018).

Lajiun, J. "Sabah BN Launches Manifesto". *Borneo Post Online*, 25 April 2018. http://www.theborneopost.com/2018/04/25/sabah-bn-launches-manifesto/ (accessed 5 August 2018).

Lee, Stephenie. 2018a. "State Rights and Development among Key Points in PCS' Manifesto". *Star Online*, 21 January 2018. https://www.thestar.com.my/news/nation/2018/01/21/state-rights-and-development-among-key-points-in-pcs-manifesto/ (accessed 31 August 2018).

————. 2018b. "UPKO Leaves Barisan; Joins Warisan to Form Coalition Government". *Star Online*, 10 May 2018. https://www.thestar.com.my/news/nation/2018/05/10/upko-leaves-barisan-joins-warisan-to-form-coalition-government/ (accessed 2 August 2018).

————, Natasha Joibi, and Fatimah Zainal. 2018. "Sabah Assembly Dissolves, but Legal Questions Linger". *Star Online*. https://www.thestar.com.my/news/nation/2018/04/07/sabah-assembly-dissolves-but-legal-questions-linger/> (accessed 25 November 2018).

Loh Kok Wah, Francis. 2009. *Old vs New Politics in Malaysia: State and Society in Transition*. Petaling Jaya: SIRD and Aliran.

Means, Gordon P. 1963. "Eastern Malaysia: The Politics of Federalism". *Asian Survey* 8, no. 4 (April): 289–308.

Mohd. Agus Yusoff. 2006. *Malaysian Federalism: Conflict of Consensus*. Bangi: UKM, 2006.

New Straits Times. 2018. "Istana Negeri Hands over Letter Stating Musa Aman No Longer CM". 14 May 2018. https://www.nst.com.my/news/nation/2018/05/369275/istana-negeri-hands-over-letter-stating-musa-aman-no-longer-cm (accessed 15 May 2018).

Ongkili, James. 1989. "Political Development in Sabah, 1963–1988". In *Sabah: 25 Years Later 1963–1988*, edited by J.G. Kitingan and M.J. Ongkili, pp. 61–79. Sabah: Institute for Development Studies (Sabah).

Pakatan Harapan. 2018. *Buku Harapan: Membina Negara Memenuhi Harapan*. Petaling Jaya: PKR, DAP, PPBM, Amanah.

Patrick, Tracy. 2018a. "Pairin to Put Retirement on Hold to Defend Tambunan?". *Free Malaysia Today*, 12 April 2018. https://www.freemalaysiatoday.com/category/nation/2018/04/12/pairin-to-put-retirement-on-hold-to-defend-tambunan/?fmt=1 (accessed 1 September 2018).

————. 2018b. "New Opposition Bloc Gabungan Bersatu Still on, Says Jeffrey". *Free Malaysia Today*, 6 June 2018. https://www.freemalaysiatoday.com/category/nation/2018/06/06/new-opposition-bloc-gabungan-bersatu-still-on-says-jeffrey/ (accessed 15 June 2018).

Puyok, Arnold. 2011. "Political Development in Sabah, 1985–2010: Challenges in Malaysian Federalism and Ethnic Politics". IRASEC Discussion Paper 9. Bangkok: Institute of Contemporary Southeast Asia, French Embassy, 2011.

————. 2013a. "Sabah's Rise to National Prominence and Deepening UMNO Dominance". In *Awakening: The Abdullah Badawi Years in Malaysia*, edited by Bridget Welsh and James Chin, pp. 226–37. Petaling Jaya: SIRD.

————. 2013b. "GE13: Political Awakening in Sabah?". *ALIRAN*, 5 August 2013. https://aliran.com/aliran-monthly/2013/2013-4/ge13-political-awakening-in-sabah/ (accessed 9 May 2019).

————. 2014. "Kota Marudu and Keningau, Sabah: Personality, Patronage and Parochial Politics". In *Electoral Dynamics in Malaysia: Findings from the Grassroots*, edited by Meredith L. Weiss. Petaling Jaya and Singapore: SIRD and Institute of Southeast Asian Studies, 2014.

Ram, Sadho. 2018. "Sabah Musical Chairs to End with Shafie Swearing in as Chief Minister Tonight". *Says*, 12 May 2018. http://says.com/my/news/sabah-musical-chairs-to-end-with-shafie-swearing-in-as-15th-chief-minister-tonight (accessed 14 May 2018).

SAPP. 2018. "Kupi-Kupi Gabungan Sabah". http://www.sapp.org.my/ms/Activitiy/2018/01/Kupi-Kupi-Gabungan-Sabah-GS-Zon (accessed 15 June 2018).

Star Online, The. n.d. "The Star Online GE-14". https://election.thestar.com.my/sabah.html (accessed 10 May 2018).

————. 2018a. "Gabungan Sabah Launches New Manifesto". 4 March 2018. https://www.thestar.com.my/news/nation/2018/03/04/gabungan-sabah-launches-new-manifesto (accessed 20 August 2018).

————. 2018b. "Highway Will Boost Kiulu". 23 March 2018. https://www.thestar.com.my/news/nation/2018/03/23/highway-will-boost-kiulu-najib-new-link-will-ease-access-to-valleys-famed-ecotourism-attractions/ (accessed 1 September 2018).

————. 2018c. "With Jeffrey's Backing, Musa Sworn in as Sabah CM". 11 May 2018. https://www.thestar.com.my/news/nation/2018/05/11/with-jeffreys-backing-musa-sworn-in-as-sabah-cm/ (accessed 11 May 2018).

————. 2018d. "Musa Aman: I Am Still Sabah Chief Minister". 12 May 2018. https://www.thestar.com.my/news/nation/2018/05/12/musa-aman-i-am-still-sabah-chief-minister/ (accessed 12 July 2018).

Straits Times. 2018. "Malaysia GE: Hung Assembly in Sabah Sees Intense Political Horse-Trading". 10 May 2018. https://www.straitstimes.com/asia/se-asia/malaysia-ge-hung-assembly-in-sabah-sees-intense-political-horse-trading (accessed 11 May 2018).

Tan Chee Khoon. 1986. *Sabah: A Triumph for Democracy*. Petaling Jaya: Pelanduk Publication.

Vanar, Muguntan. 2018a. "Gabungan Sabah launches manifesto". *Star Online*, 4 April 2018. https://www.thestar.com.my/news/nation/2018/03/04/gabungan-sabah-launches-new-manifesto/#1c15dkhqSuqr4S55.99 (accessed 30 August 2018).

————. 2018b. "Musa Aman Claims Simple Majority in Sabah Amidst Shifting News on Horse Trading". *Star Online*, 10 May 2018. https://www.thestar.com.my/news/nation/2018/05/10/musa-aman-claiming-simple-majority-in-sabah/ (accessed 2 August 2018).

————, and Stephenie Lee. 2018a. "Musa Aman Sworn in as Sungai Sibuga Assemblyman".

Star Online, 5 September 2018. https://www.thestar.com.my/news/nation/2018/09/05/musa-aman-sworn-in-as-sungai-sibuga-assemblyman/ (accessed 13 September 2018).

———, and Stephenie Lee. 2018b. "Court Rules Shafie is the Legitimate Sabah Chief Minister". *Star Online*, 7 November 2018. https://www.thestar.com.my/news/nation/2018/11/07/court-rules-shafie-is-the-legitimate-sabah-chief-minister/ (accessed 8 November 2018).

———, et al. 2018. "Shafie Sworn in as Sabah CM as Well". *Star Online*, 13 May 2018. https://www.thestar.com.my/news/nation/2018/05/13/shafie-sworn-in-as-sabah-cm-as-well-musa-was-made-the-states-leader-on-thursday/ (accessed on 5 August 2018).

Zam Yusa. 2018. "Sabah BN Assemblymen May Go Local, Ditch UMNO". *Free Malaysia Today*, 10 May 2018. https://www.freemalaysiatoday.com/category/nation/2018/05/10/sabah-bn-assemblymen-may-go-local-ditch-umno/ (accessed 11 May 2018).

IV

Personal Perspectives

17

LEMBAH PANTAI, KUALA LUMPUR
And Together, We Will Fell Goliath!

Fahmi Fadzil

HOPELESS CAUSE TO HOPEFUL WIN

9 May 2018 will live forever in the minds of Malaysians as the day we thought would never come—and yet it did. It was the black swan of black swans; the perfect storm of perfect storms.

Going into the campaign, no one thought that I would win in Lembah Pantai. From the outset, the odds looked stacked heavily against me:

- The incumbent, Nurul Izzah Anwar, had vacated the seat, and Barisan Nasional (BN) was playing it as though she was "running away" in fear;
- The government had just completed a redelineation exercise, blatantly gerrymandering Lembah Pantai such that: two key areas that previously supported Parti Keadilan Rakyat (PKR), namely, Brickfields and Jalan Puchong, were carved away to other constituencies; and about 8,000 police votes in Bukit Aman, which is seen to be traditionally a BN vote bank, were carved in;
- I was up against Raja Nong Chik, an experienced UMNO "warlord" who was once a federal minister;
- I was a political "novice", having never run in an election before;
- PKR's traditional ally, Parti Islam Se-Malaysia (PAS), was running against both Pakatan Harapan (PH) and BN, which meant the Malay vote was split.

In this light, it is not difficult to see how I was the "dark horse" in this fight.

Yet all of these factors combined to become the perfect smokescreen, giving the impression that Lembah Pantai was a walkover for BN— thereby enabling my team and me to operate as political underdogs.

Knowing that we had nothing to lose, we ran a "guerilla-style" campaign, offering myself as an upstart and "clean-slate" candidate in direct contrast to BN's Raja Nong Chik. We created huge posters (some as large as the sides of buildings) unlike any seen before; we challenged BN to a debate (which they obviously refused to attend); we even made a video that featured me in *Gol dan Gincu*, a popular TV series that I had acted in many years ago. I suppose all of these got people talking, on top of the general sentiment favouring PH.

On Election Day, at almost every polling station I visited, people would ask me for a selfie. I still did not fully believe we would win, but in retrospect, this was a further sign of the winds of change that had been blowing, subtly and surely, across the country.

TURNING POINTS: BUKIT AMAN; DAVID AND GOLIATH (AND THE STONE); RIDERS OF BN'S APOCALYPSE

I began to contemplate that this election was going to be different from early voting day, 5 May 2018. It was the first time I was given the opportunity to step into Bukit Aman, the national headquarters of the Royal Malaysian Police. I was intimidated from the start. Yet on that day, I spent almost the entire day shaking hands and posing for selfies with police officers. I found the reception to be quite good, although I felt that it would be very difficult to win them over.

After polls closed, I was sitting outside the gates of Bukit Aman with my team— waiting for the ballot boxes to be escorted to the holding centre at the District Police Headquarters (Ibu Pejabat Polis Daerah (IPD)) Brickfields—when I met a plainclothes policeman whom I believed was part of the Special Branch. We started talking, and he told me almost nonchalantly, "Sir, if you win, please look after all of us." I didn't expect him to say that, and so I took that to be a signal of sorts.

I would end up losing the Bukit Aman polling district, where I received about 800 votes—fifty less than PAS, whereas the majority went to BN. Yet, what was peculiar was that the turnout rate was nearly 10 per cent less than at other police stations. All in, I estimated some 1,000 potential police voters did not cast their votes or were not able to, for whatever reason. And in a close race like Lembah Pantai, this mattered.

Another key turning point for me was a series of rallies I gave, especially one in the leafy neighbourhood of Bangsar. This area has always been well known as an opposition bastion, so we organized a number of rallies and house meet-ups. At one such rally in Lucky Garden, on a rainy evening in the presence of several hundred (if not nearly a thousand at one point) attendees, I spoke about having misrepresented myself in the early part of the campaign:

> At the start of this campaign, I called myself the underdog, the "David" in this fight against the BN "Goliath". But as the campaign wore on, I realized that I was very wrong. No, I was not David. You, the *rakyat*—YOU are David. I am but a stone. And together, we will fell Goliath!

The usage and then turning of this Biblical narrative on its head, in a rally for an educated and politically aware audience, again got the people talking. To this day, I would encounter people who tell me, "I was there that night in Lucky Garden, when you spoke about David and Goliath."

However, since Lembah Pantai had some 63 per cent Malays (up from 55 per cent in GE-13, pre-gerrymandering), it was not enough to focus on areas like Bangsar. And for this, I had some unexpected help.

One day during the campaign period, a friend and ardent supporter suddenly messaged. "Fahmi, someone wants to support you. Can you come by my office now?" Feeling that this was something urgent, I said yes. And then I realized who it was—Tun Daim Zainuddin. "He wants to come and help in Lembah Pantai", my friend added. Without thinking twice, I immediately arranged for an event that evening in the heart of Kampung Kerinchi—a predominantly Malay area regarded as UMNO's fortress.

That evening, Tun Daim came, although I was told he would not speak. His mere appearance should have sent a clear signal, especially since he campaigned for Raja Nong Chik against Nurul Izzah in GE-13! But that night, the audience and I coaxed him to say a few words, and he went to town hammering Dato' Sri Najib and BN. To me, this was beyond belief.

And it got better; Tun Daim's cameo foreshadowed the grandmaster's. I had been trying to invite PH's Prime Minister designate, Tun Dr Mahathir Mohamad, to campaign in Lembah Pantai. But I was not successful. Suddenly, a few days later, I was pleasantly surprised to be told that Tun Mahathir would make a brief, 15-minute appearance in Lembah Pantai before adjourning for a massive rally in Putrajaya.

Mindful of the momentum we could build on, I pushed to have his presence felt in Kampung Kerinchi.

The rally that night had several thousand attendees—there seemed to be as many local voters as curious outsiders. Tun Mahathir spoke next to me on stage for a good 15 minutes. This was the heart of UMNO that he struck at, and along with other "guerilla" strategies which included working with influential locals to reach out to local voters, we made some massive inroads to the point that we flipped a polling district that we had not won since 1999.

MAJOR CHALLENGES: BRANDING, FUNDING, SECURITY

Among the challenges my campaign faced was the need to get my name/identity/branding out there. Lembah Pantai had been held by Nurul Izzah for two terms (2008–18), and she had built an effective brand and image. The BN challenger, Raja Nong Chik, was also generally understood to be visible because of his being the

UMNO Division Chief as well as his position as the Minister of Federal Territories (2009–13), which enabled him to have access to many government agencies and resources.

We addressed this challenge largely by greater use of social media platforms including Instagram and Facebook, as well as applications such as WhatsApp, which enabled us to have direct communications with voters on a one-to-one basis.

I also leveraged both local and international media interest in Lembah Pantai, on how the uphill challenge in this constituency was reflective of the trials and tribulations PH faced in overcoming BN.

Another high hurdle to clear in elections was the reality that logistics, volunteers, even posters need to be paid for. Even though candidates for Parliament can spend up to RM200,000, the challenge is both in raising that amount as well as keeping expenses to spend within that figure. Financing is an uphill battle for any first-timer, but it was especially steep for my campaign, having to face a "warlord" like Raja Nong Chik who not only comes from UMNO but also is from a wealthy background.

The only way to overcome this was to do many small fund-raising events and house meet-ups, and to get influencers to persuade their colleagues or connections to support my effort.

All of this can only happen if the overall narrative was laid out: That I was a political neophyte, which also meant I was not influenced by the "corruption" of UMNO; that I stood for change; that I stood a chance to defeat UMNO and PAS in Lembah Pantai; and that PH stood a chance to defeat BN and become the Federal Government.

Thankfully, I had many friends and supporters, people from the arts, and even some acquaintances who believed in the cause and helped in many ways. Some came to volunteer their time or services during the campaign. Some supported by printing banners or posters. Some dropped by the main operation centre to drop off cakes or drinks.

We became an "insurgent" political movement in Lembah Pantai.

This wasn't the first time that PKR was facing Raja Nong Chik, and past experience suggested we might also encounter security challenges. During his contest against my predecessor, Nurul Izzah Anwar, in the 13th General Elections in 2013, thugs were employed to disrupt some of our programmes.

During one rally in Kampung Kerinchi where Anwar Ibrahim was speaking in 2013, thugs started throwing eggs and rocks at the stage which resulted in a number of people getting injured. In one area, Perumahan Awam Sri Pahang, a volunteer was threatened by a parang-wielding UMNO local chief (in 2018, this person was convicted of criminal intimidation).

Going into GE-14, it was not difficult to imagine that similar thuggish tactics were going to be used again.

Various precautionary measures were used including hiring a security team, releasing the details of programmes only on that day itself to make sure our movement could not be hijacked or sabotaged, as well as having contingencies should thugs attempt to disrupt the campaign events.

Although the stakes for Lembah Pantai as well as the Federal Government itself were even higher this time, thankfully, we did not face as tough a time in terms of security as we did in GE-13. I cannot be certain why this was the case; perhaps it was because Nurul Izzah was not contesting, or that because most thought that I was a walkover. Even so, there were incidences where I was personally confronted by some local thugs, although these were localized and the security team managed to control the situation.

LESSONS FROM A POLITICAL JOURNEY: TELL A STORY, GET LOCAL INFLUENCERS

When I started the campaign, having had no experience of running as a parliamentary candidate, I did not really know what to expect. I just knew that I had to spend as much time on the streets, in the markets, knocking on doors, meeting voters and shaking hands.

But that alone was not enough. You had to have a convincing story: about yourself (the candidate), why you were involved in this campaign, why this fight means a lot to you, and why a vote for you should mean a lot to the voter you are shaking hands with. And you need to tell that story consistently throughout the entire campaign.

Being an arts practitioner perhaps gave me a slight advantage in terms of this storytelling.

I felt this was important because the narrative BN spun for Lembah Pantai was that "Nurul Izzah is afraid, and she is running away because she knows she will lose". As such, I had to create a narrative that "it's not Nurul Izzah who's running away, but Fahmi Fadzil who's come to stay".

There are generally three areas in Lembah Pantai: Bangsar (demographically mixed, economically wealthy), Kampung Kerinchi (predominantly Malay, mainly poor and working class), and Taman Seri Sentosa (demographically like Bangsar, but poor).

Since we only had about eleven days of campaigning, what was critical was to build a network of local influencers.

In one area, partly due to the shifting political tectonic plates that resulted in Dr Mahathir and Parti Pribumi Bersatu Malaysia (PPBM) joining Pakatan Harapan, former UMNO chieftains ended up openly campaigning with me, going door to door and house to house.

In another, local influencers organized house meetings (*ceramah kelompok*) that were attended by nearly a hundred voters each time, which is quite unprecedented. To me, building this local coalition of believers was essential to winning Lembah Pantai.

Through local interactions, I became aware of issues close to the communities, including the strong sentiments that Kampung Kerinchi residents felt towards the disappearance of their land—and heritage—on official maps, replaced by the moniker of posh commercial blocks. Restoring the name of Kampung Kerinchi became one of my manifesto promises.

DAWN OF THE REFORM ERA, RISE OF THE RIGHT

The PH government has stated its intent clearly from the outset that this would be a reform-oriented administration. Certain targets will be harder to achieve, particularly those that require a two-thirds parliamentary majority such as amending the Constitution to limit the prime minister to two terms.

Parliament has also seen, for the first time, a cohort of eighty-nine MPs (40 per cent) that are first-time parliamentarians. This means that MPs can change the way that Parliament is done—in fact, the Speaker has already initiated numerous reforms, including creating six new select committees, with more to come. This will help ensure that more bills will be scrutinized, and hopefully enable a more thorough and intelligent discourse at the highest level.

Putrajaya itself has embarked on a number of major reforms, including: its commitment to make the Malaysian Anti-Corruption Commission (MACC) independent; fixing the systemic rot in the Federal Land Development Authority (FELDA), Tabung Haji and other key institutions; enabling more academic freedom in universities and reforming the education system itself in stages; as well as other commitments.

But only time will tell.

Much remains in flux within the federal opposition. Post–GE-14, BN, and UMNO above all, must undertake massive reforms, especially in terms of their position on the political spectrum. Within the space of a year, the party has gone through three presidents (Najib Razak, Zahid Hamidi, and currently Mohamad Hassan). Its traditional partners—the Malaysian Chinese Association (MCA) and Malaysian Indian Congress (MIC)—also appeared to be prepared to leave the coalition; it remains to be seen if UMNO's dalliance with PAS will ultimately benefit or betray the spirit of BN. Najib's public relations "Malu Apa Bossku" tactic will not do much to endear BN to the masses, as Najib is more focused on his own political future due to the whirlwind of court cases he is in.

But ultimately, I think the reformation of BN would be good for democracy in the long run, *if* it reforms.

A great fear enveloping much of the Western world is the rise of populism and the Right, especially the Far Right. In Malaysia, while the Far Right may not be as politically visible, I do believe that race- and religion-based parties like UMNO and PAS stand a chance of becoming more right-wing and extremist. This is manifested in some early political actions such as the anti-ICERD (International Convention on the Elimination of All Forms of Racial Discrimination) rally, anti-Rome Statute, as well as the increased use of exclusivist and divisive political rhetoric.

While it is unlikely that either party will abandon democratic norms, I can foresee that as PH itself balances between its urban core group of supporters and the need to reach out to a wider, more rural base (traditionally PAS and UMNO supporters), there may be a "race to the bottom" in terms of outdoing each other in order to present one's party as being "more Malay/Islamist" than the other.

This would not bode well for Malaysia, and I believe is a peril that must be defused early.

"ONE-TERM" GOVERNMENT?

Lastly, and most ominously, there may be a tendency to judge PH and the effectiveness of its reform programme before its time, which may lead people to echo the BN propaganda that this administration will end up being a "one-term" government.

We should recall that a swallow does not make a summer. This first year (2018–19) of PH in Federal Government, I would like to argue, is akin to Pakatan Rakyat's first year (2008–9) of administering Selangor and Penang. It took Pakatan Rakyat some time before it grew comfortable with administering both states.

Even so, this is no excuse to rest easy. On the contrary, PH will need to redouble its efforts, in staying attuned to constituents' personal, local and national concerns, and in communicating how the reforms PH is fighting for will not only be good for the future of democracy in Malaysia but also be good for the Malaysian economy (and especially the pockets of the *rakyat*).

As I am writing this, Merdeka Center has just released its March 2019 survey that reports PH support levels at 39 per cent versus 66 per cent in August 2018. But I believe that Putrajaya has stated its position clearly, that it will not be swayed in fixing the problems in institutions like FELDA and Tabung Haji, solving the mystery of 1MDB, as well as correcting the deals of major projects like ECRL. The result of these fundamental corrections will only be felt, most likely, within the first half of 2020.

Until then, we must continue to work harder to make sure the faith of the *rakyat* is not betrayed.

18

KAPAYAN, SABAH
Silent Winds of Change

Jannie Lasimbang

ENTERING PARTY POLITICS

On 6 January 2017, I decided to join the Democratic Action Party (DAP) because of its commitment to the struggle of women in Malaysia. DAP had demonstrated sincerity and resolve in empowering women in politics.

In 2015, the party's leadership made a constitutional change to set a minimum quota of 30 per cent of women at the Central Executive Committee (CEC) level. It was a positive step to encourage more women to participate in politics, especially at decision-making levels—an initiative many women saw as a turning point for DAP's campaign. At the ground level, party leaders consciously started to appoint women leaders in all Sabah parliamentary seats where DAP is active, and to hold talks with women leaders to engage their participation. These women leaders, in turn, mobilized other women, especially in Sandakan, Penampang and the state's interior, to be actively involved in gearing up for GE-14.

In March 2017, DAP Sabah appointed me Ketua Wanita (Women's Chief) and a member of the DAP State Committee, because there were vacancies following the crossover of seven DAP committee members to Parti Warisan Sabah. Although I had worked in the non-governmental organization (NGO) sphere for more than thirty years, as someone who was new to politics, I still had to lot to learn about internal party dynamics. The crossovers, coupled with recently concluded and divisive party elections, posed major challenges to DAP Sabah's preparation for GE-14. However, thanks to the firm advice by Lim Kit Siang to immediately appoint replacements, DAP Sabah was able to move forward.

I had no idea about party structure when I joined, but there was speculation that state elections might be held as early as May 2017, so I immediately began to mobilize support from women voters. My forte is in building networks, so organizing existing Sabah women leaders into campaign teams was easy enough, especially with very supportive DAP state and national leaders. A personal challenge then was the internal friction between the DAP Sabah chairman and the then Kapayan Assemblyman and DAP Sabah deputy chairman, Edwin Bosi, which already existed when I joined DAP. When the schism became irreconcilable and the party resolved to move on with new leadership, I was appointed as the coordinator for the Kapayan state assembly constituency, which lies within the Penampang parliamentary seat. Campaigning and building support in an environment surrounded with internal party conflicts meant I needed all the patience and goodwill I could muster.

The interparty dynamics within Pakatan Harapan (PH), which comprised Parti Keadilan Rakyat (PKR) and DAP in Sabah, also affected the campaign in the Kapayan constituency towards the end of 2017. Warisan's entry to form a three-party alliance prompted negotiations for the parliamentary seat of Penampang just before GE-14. PKR, which had won Penampang in GE-13, as well as Moyog, the other state seat within Penampang, wanted to swap seats with DAP, but DAP stood firm in keeping Kapayan, which it had won for the first time in GE-13. Penampang's incumbent Darrell Leiking defended the parliamentary seat while Jenifer Lasimbang stood in the Moyog state seat—both under Warisan.

With the other new and established opposition political parties in Sabah eyeing Kapayan, including Parti Kerjasama Anak Negeri (PKAN), Parti Cinta Sabah (PCS), Sabah Progressive Party (SAPP) and Party Solidariti Tanahair Ku (STAR), DAP had to build an understanding to avoid splitting votes that would give the advantage to Barisan Nasional (BN). It is worth mentioning here that there was a tacit understanding with PKAN to refrain from fielding a candidate in Kapayan. The STAR/SAPP coalition again fielded Chong Pit Fah, who had stood as the SAPP candidate in GE-13. Prior to 2013, BN had held it over many election cycles, partly due to multi-cornered fights.

GEARING UP, GETTING VOTES

For me and for DAP Sabah, the speculation that Sabah would call early state elections was a blessing as it provided the impetus to gear up for the election. By March 2017, the Sabah team in DAP's national office organized numerous training and support activities, focused on registering voters, producing publicity materials, and upscaling social media and campaign strategies. For me and other DAP candidates making a debut in party politics, this prolonged period of "campaigning" from February 2017 to May 2018 helped us to build a solid team and get very well acquainted with our constituency—thus equipping us to conduct the election campaign with minimal financial resources.

In Kapayan, my key opponent, Goh Fah Sun, was from the Malaysian Chinese Association (MCA). Having been designated Barisan National's (BN) candidate months earlier, he had the advantage of an early start in establishing his campaign team. As a businessman, he also had his own finances to fund many programmes and activities, apart from the financial backing of BN's government machinery.

During the campaign, it was obvious that the key concerns of the Kapayan constituents were mainly on economic issues and the uncaring attitude of the BN administration. Business was deteriorating, small infrastructure development was absent, while prices of goods were going up. Single mothers, elderly, the poor and the sick felt their needs were not met, and yet they kept hearing of corruption scandals involving billions of ringgit.

I focused my campaign on reaching the Kadazan voters through house-to-house visits as I feared they may be susceptible to vote-buying. I understood from my house visits that they kept their strong desire for change inside their hearts since many were from the civil service and feared negative repercussions if they were seen as supporting the opposition. I met the urban, Chinese voters mostly through walkabouts and *ceramahs* in the numerous commercial centres in Kapayan. These activities, and the connections that I established since January 2017, gave clearer and clearer indications that the DAP would experience an even bigger vote swing than GE-13.

Nonetheless, I was not overconfident or complacent because about 7,000 new voters were registered in Kapayan, many of whom were young voters as well as a number that were allegedly brought in from other constituencies. There was also a fear that with the redelineation exercise that was passed by the Sabah State Assembly, the Lido voting district would be moved to the neighbouring Luyang seat. My outreach to youths in Kapayan was not very fruitful, as many young voters are not very bothered with politics or elections. I was pleased, however, that there were many voters supportive of a woman candidate.

Against expectations of a closer contest, I am proud to say I garnered the biggest majority for all the state seats in Sabah. Kapayan has 33,675 registered voters, out of which I received 19,558 votes, compared to 6,308 for MCA's Goh Fah Sun and 1,318 for Solidariti's Chong Pit Fah. The result was humbling for me in view of the very apparent show of BN flags, billboards and partying everywhere in Kapayan. The wind of change obviously swept voters' hearts silently.

CHANGING GOVERNMENT

Various developments in Sabah politics were signalling the possibility of an explosive showdown. Parti Warisan Sabah was formed in October 2016 but was visibly and actively on the ground only in mid-2017, so there is no doubt that Warisan made a dramatic impact in Sabah during GE-14. The tough negotiation process by top

Warisan and Pakatan Harapan (PH) national leaders, and their efforts to convince PH Sabah component parties to pick up momentum for a change in Sabah, entailed much sacrifice from PH Sabah, which had to revisit the seat allocations it had settled in November 2017.

Negotiations between Warisan and PH meant that some seats, where PH had already spent money and energy to build campaigns, were relinquished to Warisan. Within PH, DAP and PKR fared much better compared to Amanah, which ended with no seats at all to contest. While DAP accepted the strategic advantages of allying with Warisan, supporters and leaders were strongly affected by the sacrificing of the Sook, Tanjung Aru and Karamunting seats to Warisan. DAP had maintained a consistent presence in these constituencies and worked intensively on the ground since 2016. The party had cultivated a strong urban base and successfully managed defections.

In GE-14, DAP fielded candidates in seven seats in the state legislature and two in Parliament for Sabah. All were successful except the Bingkor state seat, which was won by STAR. The loss in Bingkor was the result of split votes and an overfocus on BN. For PKR, its large number of losses was already expected in view of the serious internal conflict that the party leadership was unable to contain, plus the vote-split in almost all the areas contested by the party.

Vote-splitting has repeatedly been used by the BN to split the opposition vote, and GE-14 was no exception. This tactic was successful in constituencies that were not very leader-centred; where constituents could be swung by sentiments; and where there was an abundance of individuals who could profit from such a divisive tactic. Because this has an almost guaranteed outcome, it was especially difficult for Warisan and PKR to win in such seats. Both parties either lacked strong candidates, or they lacked a firm political strategy to overcome sentiment-based politics used by STAR, Parti Harapan Rakyat Sabah (PHRS) and even by emerging parties like Parti Kerjasama Anak Negeri (PKAN) and Parti Kerjasama Sabah (PKS). Split votes significantly account for Warisan's and PH's losses to BN as well as United National Pasokmomogun Kadazan Organization (UPKO) in twelve state seats (Pitas, Matunggong, Kadamaian, Tamparuli, Kiulu, Klias, Kundasang, Paginatan, Tambunan, Bingkor, Balung and Sebatik), and seven parliamentary seats (Kota Marudu, Kimanis, Beaufort, Sipitang, Keningau, Pensiangan and Libaran).

GE-14 has therefore shown yet again that efforts to split votes can seriously affect results of any election, and strategies to empower voters and shame political opportunists should be put in place.

STAYING TOGETHER

Despite the fragile Warisan-PH alliance in GE-14, it was enough to create the wave needed for the dramatic swing—albeit one that resulted in a hung assembly. Some believe the turn of events following 9 May created by STAR were not altogether unexpected as it was apparent from the start that the party's allegiance was with

BN. However, few expected the decision by UPKO to take its turn as kingmaker and usher in a new Warisan-led government in Sabah.

GE-14 demonstrates that to effect an epic change, coalition party leadership must have a shared vision, and the message must be transmitted to voters who want change. GE-14 presents a powerful lesson that money and machinery cannot stop people when they work together to put an end to a corrupt, arrogant and uncaring government. This serves as a good reminder for any government that comes into power.

At the same time, although the GE-14 result in Sabah was desirable, the opaque party-to-party seat negotiation process prior to the election left a bitter taste for the coalition partners, especially PH parties. Analyses of party strength and candidates for certain constituencies were haphazard and without strong basis. The current Warisan-PH-UPKO alliance continues to be a fragile marriage, and lacks a formal interparty mechanism to discuss how to make inroads into BN-held areas. Without such a mechanism in place, arrogance, denial, and competition for control may imperil the coalition. A transparent and cohesive seat negotiation process should involve all coalition partners sitting at the same table.

19

PASIR GUDANG, JOHOR
Fortitude Amid Defeat

Khaled Nordin

RUNNING IN PASIR GUDANG

I strongly believe that contesting a parliamentary constituency is so much more than merely winning the seat in an election. It is about serving others, and standing up for your principles. You must believe in your vision, and the narratives the people should subscribe to in the next coming decades. As a leader, contesting, or winning a seat in an election is not an end by itself.

It has always been my stance and principle that this is the area where an elected representative should actively serve; where he or she is present for the constituents. There needs to be a strong connection with the people and the entire local community. Only then, will you be able to understand their concerns, their needs and their wants.

In my case, Pasir Gudang has always been the place where my family and I live. I know the people there, and they know me well too. This has been the case since the last few elections. I understand their concerns and I have been working to address them one by one. I want to see them grow, and treated justly by those who are above them. Most of my constituents are from low- and middle-income families. They are hardworking and honest individuals, earning a decent living in their respective fields, trying to chase the "Malaysian Dream".

But as wages are stagnant and prices of basic goods increased, someone must take care of them, speak and console their postmodern uncertainties. Therefore,

I naturally decided to contest in Pasir Gudang. Certainly, I was aware that there were other safer seats which were easier to win. But winning is not the main point. Serving the people is what matters. If I cannot connect on a personal level with the people and I am a stranger to them, it defeats the whole idea of becoming a *wakil rakyat*.

BARISAN NASIONAL'S CAMPAIGN IN JOHOR

There were three key focuses in our party's campaign. Firstly, an offer to ensure and improve the well-being of Johoreans. Secondly, to position the state as the southern economic powerhouse with substantial and meaningful contributions to Malaysia. And thirdly, to push and prepare Johor to become a strong competitor especially to its neighbour, Singapore. The strategy was called "Mengejar Singa" or generally translated as "Chasing the Lion" (Bait al Amanah 2018).

These three goals were to be achieved by executing what was called the "Johor Hi-5"—an umbrella concept that encompasses five main focuses, approaches and initiatives for the state over the next ten years, such as: crafting a sustainable and prosperous economy; developing comprehensive infrastructure; advancing skills, knowledge and talents; expanding high-performance leadership; and, lastly, nurturing an Islamic as well as a culturally rich society (Barisan Nasional Negri Johor 2018). The party aimed to elevate Johor to become the best state in Malaysia in terms of its politics, economy, society and environment.

With regards to the economy, we had planned to further develop each district according to its specific strengths, needs and niche potential. We did not assume that all parts of the state need a similar narrative and economic programme. For instance, Muar, as the world's eighth largest producer of furniture and high-tech wood products, was approached with the aim of developing its fullest potential in this specific economic sector. Another example is the district of Mersing, whose attributes include the sea, white sands, beautiful islands and natural beauty. Creating a concrete jungle here would not be viable. Therefore, we planned for Mersing to be the "Fisheries and Maritime Economic Hub" of the state. This included the development of a fish processing centre in the district to further drive the fisheries and maritime industry for domestic and regional consumption.

We also believe in empowering future leaders and the workforce of the state through education. To this end, we offered to reduce the cost of education by extending the interest-free education loan scheme (*Qard Hassan*) to more Johor-born individuals. Realizing that technical and vocational skills are critical and in high demand in the state, we proposed increasing disbursements from the Johor Skills Training Fund to students from RM2,500 to RM5,000 within five years.

Special and different approaches were required when dealing with young voters. In this light, our manifesto contained a specific section catering only to the youth of Johor. The party promised to address the needs of Johor youth by offering to create 5,000 job opportunities in skilled occupations including the furniture industry, as well as 5,000 job opportunities in the oil and gas industry in Pengerang.

The second key focus in Johor Barisan Nasional's campaign was to highlight our proven track record and the need for a continuation of excellent performance. This idea was motivated and supported by the outstanding performance of Johor's economy, particularly in its GDP growth and levels of foreign direct investment, which surpassed other developed states in Malaysia such as Penang and Selangor (Bait Al Amanah 2017). This performance was the result of practical and fresh policies, good governance and political stability. In fact, a large fraction of Johor's development was supported and facilitated by the federal government. Therefore, retaining and maintaining such excellence is critical for the state's future development.

The third key focus was on the candidates themselves. Selecting and naming candidates requires the party to be more than strategic, and many considerations must be weighed. The party leadership at the central level must be briefed and convinced of an entire spectrum of political sentiments in the state which, in themselves, are unique. For example, Johor is one of the states with the highest concentration of Federal Land Development Authority (FELDA) settlements in the country. The attitude of the majority Malay-Muslim voters in these constituencies is different from the rest of urban Johor. Therefore, the right candidates who are familiar with the local context and sentiments are needed so that they are able to better represent the interests of the FELDA settlers.

The party had emphasized to the voters that there would be no parachute or "imported" candidates—those who are not local and not from Johor—fronted by us. This was in contrast to our opponent who named many outsiders as representatives for the local people. For us, that was an irresponsible approach since the concerns of locals will be best understood and addressed by those living in their respective constituencies and not any politician who was sent by their party to simply fill in the quota.

"Kita Pilih Biru": A New Paradigm for Johor's Election Campaign

Apart from the "Johor Hi-5" and "New Decade of Johor", we also introduced a new paradigm for the election campaign. We designed the narrative of "We Choose Blue" (*Kita Pilih Biru*), referring the official colour of Barisan Nasional (BN). This was supposed to be seen as a mass support movement from the people for BN and its candidates, instead of the normal and straightforward plea of "Vote for Barisan Nasional" (*Undilah Barisan Nasional*). This is a fresh and unprecedented approach to the election, and was well received by everyone.

At the same time, in Johor, there is a state-level nationalist narrative known as the *Bangsa Johor* identity (Mohamed Nawab and Rashaad 2018), which played an active role in shaping the minds of the electorate. According to a study, nine out of ten Johoreans identify strongly with the narrative (*Malay Mail*, 19 November 2017), because of the royal family's successful portrayal as a custodian of moderation and interethnic harmony in the state (Chong et al. 2017). The Sultan of Johor was participating actively in the affairs of the state's politics and other arising issues, after seeing the 2013 elections which were characterized by a further weakening of BN's performance. He saw an opportunity to get more involved in the public sphere by being reactive to various issues of the state.

Therefore, the "We Choose Blue" campaign paradigm encapsulates the mass imagination of all Johoreans for an economically developed and socially progressive state. This is done for the party to subtly move away from political rhetoric of race and religion towards a needs-based approach. Furthermore, this paradigm coexists side by side with the nationalist *Bangsa Johor* narrative.

We also realized the importance of exploring and utilizing social media outlets like Facebook, Twitter and Instagram as well as creating simpler and clearer political messages. Our opponents were ahead of us in this aspect pre-GE-14. Cybertroopers were used to deliver messages through online platforms, especially to provide and make viral, alternative views on many issues.

Addressing National and State Issues

As a party, and a coalition of various parties with various focus and strengths, it is natural that we were not without certain major challenges. First, when it came to national issues, we were arguably "troubled" and hugely affected by various allegations as well as specific policies. This includes: the transfer of RM2.6 billion into the United Malays National Organization (UMNO) party president's personal account; the corporate governance issues pertaining to 1 Malaysia Development Berhad (1MDB); as well as the goods and services tax and the rising cost of living.

Apart from that, addressing state-level issues was equally important, especially when it came to the attack by Tun Mahathir and discontented local Johoreans on the development of the Forest City mega property project owned by the Chinese developer (Beech 2018) as well as corruption allegations against one of BN's state legislative assemblymen (Kili 2017).

I cannot emphasize enough that the party has tried its utmost best to address all the issues and any misperception, misconception and misrepresentation of them. It was a tough task. We were forced to take all measures and steps that could help us clear the air. For that, approaches taken by the party included publication of the benefits of, as well as clarifications of and the reasoning behind, certain economic programmes in question. This was due to the fact that, as much as those issues and concerns were legitimate, there were too many misrepresentations, and too much manipulation of facts and misunderstandings. It is pertinent that we deliver our side of the argument. We also trained and coached candidates and speakers for campaign rallies to ensure they were prepared and fit to present our alternate narratives and arguments to the people.

I can verify that explanation and clarification of national issues was critical and crucially important. Those must be done through discourse that can be easily understood by the people, both in urban and rural Johor. The failure to communicate and conceptualize our views to cater to varied demographic needs may be safely said as one of the many reasons why, according to our Johor GE-14 analysis, the vote share and winning margins for BN in large constituencies of more than 70,000 voters were low (Bait Al Amanah 2019).

Furthermore, despite being the so-called bastion of Malay support and votes, the FELDA constituencies in mostly northern Johor showed a considerable drop in voter turnout among the Malay electorates, even when they were in Malay-majority constituencies (Bait Al Amanah 2019). This could signify several things. Perhaps we did not address their concerns effectively, or some were perhaps put off by internal FELDA factors, such as controversies related to the corporate governance of FELDA Global Ventures (FGV) (Hutchinson 2018).

CAMPAIGN CHALLENGES

Candidate Selection

First, rumours that Johor would receive a new Menteri Besar from BN—that I was no longer the Menteri Besar candidate from BN—were widely circulated across the state. This was completely untrue and it pushed me to clarify in a media statement that, as far as BN was concerned, given the mandate, I was the candidate for Menteri Besar. My media statement managed to generate confidence among the party election team and supporters. Yet, the rumour could not be quashed and in fact instilled enough doubts among people over who the next Menteri Besar would be.

Second, I had to manage the frustration and retaliation of the previous Batu Pahat MP who was not named as a candidate during GE-14. In his dissatisfaction, he accused and attacked me and the party as a whole, which was totally against the spirit of putting the party first over self-interest. This was certainly very unhealthy and caused another setback to the party. Moreover, it happened when the election was just around the corner. The recurring conversation between this MP and the party president, who was also the Prime Minister, created uncertainty and widespread speculations. Finally, the party president announced his new candidate. This overall debacle was uncalled for and would not have happened if candidates put the party's interest first over their political ambitions.

The "Mahathir and Najib Factor"

The popularity of Tun Dr Mahathir Mohamad was seen to be more mixed in Johor. Most of the Malays, especially those who had lived through the premier's previous administration, believed that he had betrayed the "ideals" of UMNO and the country by leaving the party. He also had previously clashed with the Johor royal family and questioned the need for a state-level nationalist narrative of *Bangsa Johor* (Jalil 2016). But what was crucial then was the fact that the former prime minister, Datuk Seri Najib was not a popular figure in Johor. Being accused of multiple corruption scandals and breach of trust, his presence and influence failed to resonate with the Johor electorate. Therefore, the state campaign machinery focused on the past achievements and future socio-economic plans for Johor. We also developed our own manifesto, with the intention of solving local problems and propelling the state's economy using local talents and wisdom.

9 MAY 2018

When the counting of the votes commenced, it was noticeable that many of the candidates from my party would not be re-elected. Subsequently it became clear and official that we not only lost our seats, we also lost the state. Some of the state's senior executive councillors did not make it either. I specifically recall the current UMNO Johor State Liaison Chief, Datuk Ir. Hasni Mohammad calling me over the telephone, asking about the current situation. I told him that we might lose the state and the federal government to the then opposition and I myself would not get re-elected.

The party's defeat in the 14th General Elections (GE-14) was a humbling experience. The most excruciating part of it, perhaps, was to know that we had failed to convince the people that we deserved to continue governing the state. Despite our continuous efforts to share the state's prevailing performance in the economy and its development marching towards GE-14, as well as our plans for the future, we have to admit that the people decided to send a strong signal to us, to the state, in fact to the whole nation, that Malaysia is now a mature democracy. Like in many democracies, we are prepared to accept the consequences when the concerns of the people are not effectively addressed, or when good governance is not a part of the mainstream political discourse.

Personally, the thing I remember the most is that my whole family helped out with the campaign and the entire journey. They were there throughout the thick and thin of campaigning. Also, I was so blessed to have a very hardworking team of young and aspiring people, working day and night in one way or another to ensure success. Unfortunately, it was not meant to be; but I still credit every single one of them, friends and family for working together in this campaign. Without them, it would have been an impossible task.

MALAYSIA MOVING FORWARD

The last general elections have shaped Malaysia in ways we had never imagined. Like any other instances of change of government, there are promising aspects and perils that accompany it.

The country has experienced a smooth and peaceful change of government. This is a strong and impressive sign of a healthy and stronger democracy. A healthy and stronger democracy is good for Malaysia. GE-14 has also witnessed the emergence of many young leaders from both sides. In the case of UMNO, our young candidates have successfully secured the seats in Layang-Layang and Panti constituencies. Many political parties are now committed to prepare and highlight young capable leaders.

At the same time, Pakatan Harapan's (PH) victory will allow and encourage Malaysia to compare and evaluate the performance of not only the current government, but also the previous one. This is definitely a healthy and good development.

Nevertheless, it is undeniable that the Malaysia Baru PH government is a fragile political coalition. Splinters and internal divisions within the coalition will create continuous political instability and uncertainty for Malaysia. There are too many U-turns and flip-flops in their policies. For instance, pre–GE-14, China was viewed as a bad trading partner and a country with the intention to control the Malaysian economy. But now, the government is encouraging trade and collaboration with China in various aspects of the economy and repeatedly emphasizing that country's importance for Malaysia's economy and trade. Similar contradictions can be seen in the appointment of politicians or politically affiliated people to be in universities and higher learning institutions.

It is easy to conclude that the appointment of many incompetent and inexperienced members of parliament (MP) has led to "Kakistocracy". We even witnessed a situation where those incompetent MPs lied about their tertiary qualifications and, worse, were defended by their fellow party members. It will not only diminish the confidence among the people, but also outsiders including international investors.

Failure in implementing the election manifesto has also resulted in continued dissatisfaction and anger among the people vis-à-vis the abolishment of highway tolls and the student debts under the National Higher Education Fund Corporation (PTPTN), minimum wages of RM1,500 and low fuel prices (*Free Malaysia Today*, 17 August 2018).

Clearly, this will hinder the government from focusing on developing the country and its economy. Focusing on unnecessary aspects such as the third national car, the ratification of International Convention on the Elimination of All Forms of Racial Discrimination (ICERD) and the resurfacing of old narratives when in foreign policy, such as against Singapore with regard to the 1962 Water Agreement and the disputed territorial waters is not helpful.

With no new approach and grand plans for the country's economy and social cohesion, the future of "Malaysia Baru" remains uncertain and precarious.

References

Bait Al Amanah. 2017. *Johor Development Report 2016*. Kuala Lumpur: Bait Al Amanah.
———. 2018. *Dekad Baharu Johor: A Summary*. Kuala Lumpur: Bait Al Amanah.
———. 2019. *Johor GE-14 Analysis*. Kuala Lumpur: Bait Al Amanah.
Barisan Nasional Negeri Johor. 2018. "Barisan Nasional Johor Manifesto".
Beech, H. 2018. "We Cannot Afford This: Malaysia Pushes Back against China's Vision". *New York Times*, 20 August 2018.
Chong, Terence, Lee Hock Guan, Norshahril Saat, and Serina Rahman. 2017. *The 2017 Johor Survey: Selected Findings*. Trends in Southeast Asia, no. 20/2017. Singapore: ISEAS – Yusof Ishak Institute.
Free Malaysia Today. 2018. "We Over-Promised, Dr M Tells Ruling MPs", 17 August 2018.

Hutchinson, Francis E. 2018. *GE-14 in Johor: the Fall of the Fortress?* Trends in Southeast Asia, no. 3/2018. Singapore: ISEAS – Yusof Ishak Institute.

Jalil Hamid. 2018. "Bangsa Johor Concept Now More Relevant Than Ever, Says Johor Ruler". *New Straits Times*, 30 August 2018.

Kili, Kathleen Ann. 2017. "Ex-Johor EXCO Latiff Bandi, Two Others Charged with Money Laundering RM35.7 million". *The Star*, 14 June 2017.

Mohamed Nawab Mohamed Osman, and Rashaad Ali. 2018. "Localising Victory: GE 14 and the Electoral Contests in Johor and Kelantan". *JEBAT: Malaysian Journal of History, Politics, and Strategic Studies* 45, no. 2: 367–85.

20

KETARI, PAHANG
Protest and Loyalty,
Confidence and Desperation

Young Syefura Othman
Translated by Mohammad Syafiq Suhaini

NOVICE IN A HOT SEAT

As a political newbie, it was no easy feat to stand for elections in the 14th General Elections (GE-14) as a Democratic Action Party (DAP) candidate in Ketari, Pahang, a state assembly seat expected to be hotly contested. I was initially surprised when the party leadership asked me to contest there. I knew that as a DAP candidate and an outsider to the neighbourhood, I would have to surmount multiple hurdles. The profile of Ketari's electorate—48 per cent Malay, 44 per cent Chinese, 5 per cent Indian and 3 per cent Orang Asli—made it potentially very competitive in the event of a multicornered fight. Nonetheless, I saw this opportunity as a sign of my party's confidence in my abilities to deliver a state seat within the Bentong parliamentary constituency, and accepted the challenge wholeheartedly.

In GE-13, DAP together with Pakatan Keadilan Rakyat (PKR) successfully captured the Ketari constituency. This victory was partly due to the vote from the Parti Agama Se-Islam Malaysia (PAS) camp which was then part of Pakatan Rakyat (PR) coalition, who voted against the ruling Barisan Nasional (BN) government. This time around, however, the opposition coalition Pakatan Harapan (PH) was without PAS as a partner and would be campaigning under the PKR banner. Despite initially mixed reactions from coalition members, including DAP itself, PH leaders managed to convince the coalition that this was the best way to display interparty unity and strength. Further, DAP candidates would have a fair chance at victory in an ethnically mixed but substantially Malay constituency like Ketari if they stood under the PKR banner.

In any case, PH's participation in Ketari in GE-14 would be a crucial trial by fire. The three-cornered fight with PAS and BN would mean that PH had to face a potential loss of support from the PAS members and Malay supporters that they enjoyed in GE-13.

ENTRENCHED LOYALTY, ACTIVATED PROTEST

I first met the Ketari PH supporters towards the end of 2017, right after the leadership informed me that they wanted to field me as candidate there. Some thought that my chances for victory were considerably low, given that I was not local to the area. Others were surprised that I was the first Malay candidate fielded by the DAP in that constituency.

Other Malay voters, especially the supporters of the United Malays National Organization (UMNO), were particularly hostile. One house visit incident when I was doing my rounds in Ketari's UMNO quarter particularly stood out. I knocked on the door of a man in his forties, who refused to let me in. Instead, he hurled vulgarities, calling me a blood traitor for being a DAP candidate, and brandished the 13 May incident before me and my team of volunteers. It was only later that I noticed the huge BN flag proudly displayed outside his house.

The unstinting Malay support for BN, despite clear allegations of their financial scandals, was something to truly worry about. Even Dr Mahathir's political manoeuvring to outbid UMNO and its chairman, then Prime Minister Najib Razak, had failed to win over Malay BN supporters to his new party, Parti Pribumi Bersatu Malaysia (PPBM) or the PH coalition.

However, there was one house visit that perhaps signalled positive things to come. Just like the previous house, there was an UMNO flag displayed outside. I was initially hesitant to knock, out of fear that history would repeat itself. To my relief, the elderly house owner was kind enough to invite us in. In the discussion that ensued, I noticed that he indicated a slight preference for a political change that he thought was long due.

As Nomination Day approached on 28 April, it was clear that BN would do all that they could to secure a victory in GE-14. Reports were emerging from all over the country that the Election Commission (EC) was actively trying to disqualify PH candidates over the slightest fault. Furthermore, the EC announced that polling day would fall on a Wednesday, a working day. This bizarre announcement could work in BN's favour by preventing the vast majority of young working voters from casting their vote. However, this move had the opposite effect, incensing the electorate and stirring them to action.

The situation in the Ketari state seat was no different. Government agencies like the EC and the National Registration Department were effectively used by BN to their advantage. The BN candidate for Ketari, for example, was registered at an address outside of Pahang, which would effectively render him unfit to contest in any constituency in the state. The EC approved his application anyway and gave all sorts of reasons to justify their decision.

Why did BN pull off such unscrupulous moves so early in the election? Was it out of an extreme desperation to win, or was there something else that they knew that PH was unaware of?

VOTER GROUPS

Throughout GE-14, there was one group of voters who was the constant talk of the election pundits; these were called the "silent voters", made up of the undecided and those who did not outwardly display any signs of political affiliation, either because of their occupation, their social status or out of fear of a backlash from their family members.

What was certain about these silent voters was that many of them were civil servants. Before any of them would throw in their support for PH, they wanted assurance that they were on the right side of history. Further, they wanted to be sure that PH was strong enough to form a government following their victory. This latter point was important, because many were afraid of facing repercussions should BN return to power instead.

Realizing the importance of this electoral bloc, I made it a point to reach out to them through my house visits. Done this way, it not only gave them the privacy they needed to show their support, but it was the only way I could engage with them, as they could not attend any of the usual campaign events, like rallies or speeches.

I was pleasantly surprised to learn that most of these silent voters turned out to be Malay PH supporters. Many felt that the time was right for them to vote BN out of the government. I had to admit that I was disappointed with Malay voters after a dismal turnout during one of PH's rallies in Ketari. However, after learning this, it gave me the motivation to work even harder to convince, persuade and eventually win the majority vote.

The situation over at the Federal Land Development Authority (FELDA) plantations, however, was an entirely different matter altogether. The FELDA settlers constitute roughly a quarter of the Ketari electorate, making them one of the largest electoral blocs in the seat. Here, support for PH remains stubbornly low, despite multiple efforts to woo them over. Moreover, opposition supporters tended to be from the PAS camp. Support for BN still remained strong, despite the many scandals that have plagued FELDA, like heavy debts and financial mismanagement. Many landowners were indebted to the BN government for their efforts in incorporating FELDA, thereby securing their lands and livelihood. The fact that Najib was the son of one of FELDA's pioneers, Tun Razak Hussein, also helped to boost BN's standing among the landowners.

Non-Malay support, however, rested firmly with PH. The Malaysian Chinese Association (MCA) and the Parti Gerakan Rakyat Malaysia (Gerakan) tried multiple tactics to court the non-Malay vote, including politicizing racial issues. These efforts invariably failed, as voters perceived the two parties' subservience to UMNO.

The Chinese vote in Ketari was of particular importance. Just like in GE-13, the Chinese voters were clear and resolute in their support for PH. I had to make sure that this support was sustained for GE-14 as well, as it seemed clear that the Chinese vote could not climb any higher than it already did in GE-13. Furthermore, many of the Chinese voters whom I met assured their support for me, and encouraged me to refocus my efforts on the majority Malay population instead.

CONFIDENCE AND DESPERATION

The tension became palpable as polling day drew closer. The once-confident BN turned desperate and despondent in their campaigning. There were rumours that the BN had engaged in vote-buying over at Bentong and also in Ketari. Further, two BN bigwigs, Pahang Menteri Besar and one of Bentong's state seat candidates, Adnan Yaakob, and Bentong Parliament candidate, Liow Tong Lai, appeared on television, making a last-minute appeal for support.

The campaign period climaxed on the night of 8 May, with PH chairman Tun Dr Mahathir's address to the entire nation. This event, widely publicized for a few days, spurred BN chairman Najib Razak to do likewise. PH live-streamed Tun Dr Mahathir's speech on the Internet, whereas Najib used TV networks. Everyone was guessing what both sides would say. Some expected Tun Dr Mahathir to announce new pledges that might help reel in some support in the last hours.

Anyone could observe the stark difference between the two men's speeches. Tun Dr Mahathir was calm, collected, and repeated his campaign points. He appealed to his fellow Malaysians to stand up and be courageous in the face of a momentous change. Tun Dr Mahathir also announced that the Thursday and Friday after polling day would be declared as public holidays, should PH be elected into power.

Najib Razak, on the other hand, seemed tense. Should BN be given a renewed mandate for the next five years, Malaysians would enjoy a five-day toll-free travel for this year's Aidil Fitri. Najib also promised tax exemption for all working youths under the age of twenty-six for the 2017 tax year. To many, these were clear signs of BN's grasping at the straws; for others, they were convinced that BN was sure to lose this time around.

WINNING KETARI: HOW AND WHY

9 May 2018, 0800 hours. The voting had officially begun. PH was worried that many working voters would not come down to give their voice at the ballot. A low voter turnout rate would certainly mean PH's defeat. However, we witnessed

a mass movement of voters across Malaysia. For us in Ketari and Bentong, located at the start of the East Coast Expressway, we saw an upsurge in traffic overnight. The Karak Expressway was also thick with cars since the night of the cooling-off period until polling day.

Despite such encouraging signs, however, by 12:00 noon voter turnout was disappointingly low at 53 per cent. I began making the rounds to the various polling stations in Ketari to check on voter turnout levels, and instructed my team to call everyone out to vote. At 3:00 p.m., with only two hours left to vote, the proportion of voters who had cast their ballots was still only 69 per cent. At one of the FELDA polling stations in Ketari, I was told by a PH volunteer that they saw very few people coming out to vote. We suspected that voters in the FELDA plantations, most of whom were UMNO and BN supporters, had either boycotted the elections, or did not return home to vote. I felt that my chances of winning were good, even if the turnout rate might be lower than we had hoped for. Thankfully, the worst case scenarios did not transpire; the official count shows that at the close of polling, 84 per cent of Ketari voters had cast their ballots.

That night, PH Bentong HQ tallied the election results according to *Borang 14* compiled from all voting streams.[1] I found out that we had won both the Bentong parliamentary and Ketari state seats. The results reflected a highly polarized community. For the Ketari state seat, the Chinese vote not only remained strong for PH, but also increased. In urban areas and housing estates, we also managed to win over a significant majority of Malay voters. In the FELDA areas around Ketari, however, PH only managed to scrape 10 per cent of the vote, while BN and PAS received the same amount of votes. On the whole, I won the elections with 51 per cent of the vote, with a lead of 3,710 votes over my opponents.

It is difficult to determine whether PH's victory in the Ketari state seat, Bentong parliamentary seat and in many other places across the country was due to a late surge in popularity, or other indicative signs that we might have missed during the course of campaigning. There were, of course, some clues here and there, which gave us an inkling of the amount of support that we would receive in GE-14, like the mounting people's dissatisfaction against BN. Similarly, there were times when BN failed to see the signs of impending defeat; nonetheless, they persisted and pressed ahead.

BN's unscrupulous tactics and later, knowledge of their defeat, would be the final nail in their coffin: their desperate antics to win at all costs had managed to tilt many undecided voters over to PH's side. Further, their gamble to push for a three-cornered fight in all constituencies in an attempt to weaken PH support had failed spectacularly, and instead worked in PH's favour. All that PH needed was a small swing vote from the majority Malay voters to ensure a comfortable lead over its opponents.

Taken together, BN's blindness to voters' signals, the support swing from the undecided voters and the failed three-cornered fight strategy contributed to PH's victory in GE-14.

Note

1. Borang 14 (Statement of the poll after counting the ballot) is a form that records the parties' official ballot count. Only election officials are allowed to write on the form, in the presence of counting agents.

21

CEMPAKA, SELANGOR
Keeping the Faith

Iskandar Abdul Samad

The Parti Islam Se-Malaysia (PAS) contested in Malaysia's GE-14 as a "gentleman". Despite our main rival resorting to "ungentlemanly" strategies, PAS adhered to the rules of the game. We did not follow the same path, although we knew that the campaign trail would be tough and one-sided. PAS campaigned the traditional way, presenting to the people what we have to offer and highlighting our success in Kelantan.

PAS had the most complete manifesto compared with the other parties, where we not only presented our short-term but also long-term policies. It was entitled "A Master Vision of Well-Being for the Country" (*Wawasan Induk Negara Sejahtera*) and it charts out the direction of the nation up to 2051.

I was part of the committee that evaluated the manifestos of the various PAS State Liaison Committees. We were very meticulous in ensuring that what they wanted to offer was practical. We wanted to know where the money to fund their programmes would come from. We wanted to know the exact calculations, the exact dollars and cents—not some figures plucked out of the sky.

This was obviously different from the Pakatan Harapan (PH) coalition. They promised the sky and surely the voters fell for it. However, in the end, the coalition had to admit that some of their promises were made without detailed statistics and are impossible to fulfil.

PAS also had to endure the malicious lies spread about the party. PH not only attacked Barisan Nasional (BN) with the 1 Malaysia Development Berhad (1MDB), but PAS was also at the receiving end. There were allegations that PAS received funds from 1MDB. In addition, PAS was also accused of receiving funding from UMNO. This was an illogical accusation as we were contesting against UMNO-BN, so why would they give us money to challenge them?

These allegations and accusations were made without any proof whatsoever. Social media was effectively used to influence voters. Sometimes I wonder how can you call yourself a Muslim when you can spread untrue stories? Maybe it was the case of the Machiavellian principle of the end justifying the means, but Nicolo Machiavelli was not a Muslim. Islam would never condone any slanderous act.

PAS campaigners on the ground were often rudely accused of receiving money from UMNO and 1MDB. When challenged to show the proof, the accusers would have no answer but would only refer to the stories circulated on social media or through rumours. They were so emotionally charged that they would believe any story heard from anyone.

I must admit that we failed to control the narrative on social media. Even if we had, we would have had no chance as we were supposed to show proof that we were innocent. This was akin to the skewed form of justice in the Deep South of the United States back in the 1920s and 1930s where Blacks were deemed guilty until proven innocent. Just imagine being accused of stealing a car but the prosecution could not produce the car nor any witness to the crime. PAS had to go through this experience in GE-14.

A year after the election and after the victors had received their sought-after titles, the world has yet to see the proof that could link PAS to 1MDB and UMNO. The Malaysian Anti-Corruption Commission (MACC) even confirmed that PAS did not benefit from 1MDB. Even ex-Prime Minister Najib Razak who had been "pronounced guilty" before any trial, is still a free man and moves around unhindered.

Although under pressure and provoked to the maximum, PAS did not follow the same path of its political rivals. Our campaign was more focused on explaining what the party had to offer. The achievements of the Kelantan state government were also highlighted. There were very few personal attacks or baseless allegations. We could if we wanted to be like PH, but being an Islamic party, we are the standard bearer of Islamic politics in Malaysia and we would not stoop to the same level as our rivals. The PAS president constantly reminded us to be like a fruit tree. It is natural for a fruit tree to have stones thrown at it. When someone throws a stone at a fruit tree, it will only throw back its fruits.

The voters in GE-14 were overwhelmed by emotion. The hate and anger towards Najib and his wife Rosmah was very cleverly stoked for more than two years before the election. This, together with promises such as eliminating GST, abolishing highway toll charges and forgiving debts to the National Higher Education Fund Corporation (PTPN) led to voters giving the mandate to PH.

Local politics were swept aside in the tsunami. The track record of candidates was not a factor in GE-14. I do not think that my ten-year record as a state assemblyman was considered when my constituents voted. My party workers were told by voters that they were sorry that they did not vote for me, but they wanted to kick Najib out. Whatever I did for the past ten years was no match for their hatred towards Najib and Rosmah. The voters were very emotional and there was no way that we could win the argument.

The last general election showed us that national sentiment can totally eclipse local sentiment. Before GE-14, I believed that local sentiment could carry a candidate towards victory, but I was wrong. All those leaflets, posters, banners and short video clips of my achievements in my constituency seemed pointless when the voters had already made up their mind no matter what the consequences could be. This propaganda was very effective in preventing voters from choosing PAS, even when the party was represented by high-calibre candidates. The narrative was that voting for PAS was like voting for BN.

However, I fail to see the correlation between kicking out Najib and rejecting PAS. Voters could also kick Najib out by voting for PAS, and voting for my party should not be equated with voting for BN. PAS had no relationship with UMNO or BN at the time. This was where the propaganda that PAS had received money from UMNO played its part. Until today we have yet to see the proof. We can only hope that those that spread this false news are punished in the hereafter, because there was no action from the Election Commission.

In GE-14 we saw many unknown personalities winning their seats because they were on the right side of the national sentiment and riding on the wave. However, this is dangerous because incompetent candidates were voted in. Today we hear many complaints about members of parliament and state assemblymen failing in their duties. In my opinion, the voters should not be complaining. They chose their representatives and they will have to live with this for the next four to five years.

In Selangor, our position was quite awkward. Up until the dissolution of Parliament we were part of the government. After that, we were the opposition and not part of the caretaker government. However, only the members of the caretaker administration were seen by the voters as the government of the day. This gave PH the edge over us.

According to a survey before the election, less than 20 per cent of the people in Selangor were unhappy with the policies of the state government. Therefore, we knew that it was going to be an uphill struggle to displace the PKR-led coalition.

We were part of the Selangor state government for ten years and we campaigned on the basis of our track record in government. However, PH also ran on the same record. For example, we spoke about the Rumah Selangorku affordable housing initiative. This also featured in PH campaigns. But, since we were no longer part of the government, it was the words of PH that attracted the most attention. In essence, we were battling against two governments, the state government and the federal government.

At the state level, I could not see how the Selangor PAS manifesto could match the state manifesto of PH. This was simply because the voters considered their manifesto to be a continuation of the success achieved by the previous state government. The people were happy with the state government for the past ten years, so why change?

It was true that we were part of the previous government, but we were swept aside when we were linked to 1MDB and UMNO. Furthermore, we failed to successfully project ourselves as the next state government simply because we did not have a candidate for the Menteri Besar position. Pakatan Harapan was led by Mohamed Azmin Ali, who was seen as the future Menteri Besar. PAS, on the other hand, did not name their candidate. We only announced that our candidate would be known after we had won the election. How can you get people to vote for you when they do not know who will lead them? Barisan Nasional did the same in the 2013 General Elections. They did not announce their candidate for the Menteri Besar post and, consequently, their state seats were reduced from twenty to twelve.

In GE-14, PAS contested the general elections alone for the first time since 1995. PAS initially had a link with PKR, although the Pakatan Rakyat coalition was dissolved long before GE-14. However, in 2017, the PAS Muktamar had approved a motion to sever all ties with PKR. The motion was adopted unanimously.

This decision put us in a quandary in Selangor. PAS was still part of the state government, but we had severed all links with both PKR and DAP. In order to make our presence legitimate, we argued that we were appointed by the Sultan and only the Sultan could remove us. Furthermore, the links severed were political while governmental links still remained. Politicians can be creative!

Our three State Executive Councillors were able to work with the Menteri Besar and the State Executive Councillors from PKR and DAP without any problem. I believe this was also true for our Councillors at the local government level. The disagreements were not in Selangor nor among those in government, but elsewhere in Malaysia or with those outside government. Even if we had disagreements, we would try our very best to resolve them. This happened because we had people with the right temperament in government to manage this awkward position.

Although the fate of any electoral cooperation was sealed at the 2017 Muktamar, this did not stop PH from trying to entice PAS. Some of their leaders openly invited my party to join them. I remember Tan Sri Muhyiddin Yassin announcing in the media the deadline for PAS to respond. To me, this was baffling because we had never indicated any intention of joining PH.

The most contact between PAS and PH occurred in Selangor as we were in government together. Azmin invited some of us to his office after Exco meetings to discuss cooperation between PAS and PH. He once suggested that seats held by the respective parties would not be contested by other parties in an effort to reduce the number of three-cornered fights. But, the decision was not in our hands.

I have always advocated electoral cooperation. I believe that PAS should form an electoral pact with other parties. If not at the national level, then maybe in Selangor. However, it would be almost impossible to have two separate arrangements, namely, one for Selangor and another for the whole country. The difference between PAS and DAP was also as how the Malays would describe "like the earth and the sky".

In the end, as decided at the Muktamar, PAS entered GE-14 without any electoral pact with any major party except with a few other minor parties. However, I am more comfortable to describe that we are on our own as the contribution from these minor parties, although warmly welcomed, was minimal.

That said, even today, I still believe that PAS should not be alone. We need to establish strategic partnerships with other parties or even non-governmental organizations. Therefore, I was elated when PAS decided to work with UMNO— although prior to this I would not have touched the latter party with a ten-foot pole. The situation had changed. When in government before GE-14, I strongly believed that we should work with PKR and DAP, but now after GE-14 we should work with other opposition parties.

So, what happens now? After GE-14, the situation is totally different. Whether it is for the better or for worse, it depends on who you are talking to. Immediately after the formation of the new government, many were hopeful, but after more than a year has passed, they are disappointed.

The new government failed to fulfil many of its promises. Although lowering the cost of living or increasing household incomes may take time, promises to lower the price of petrol to RM1.50, remove toll charges for highways, or abolish PTPTN loan repayments should have been fulfilled within 100 days. The life of the lower and middle-income earners have not improved, and the change of government means nothing to them.

To many Malay-Muslims, although the Prime Minister is a Malay-Muslim, the current federal government is Chinese-dominated. Whether this is true or otherwise depends on what you consider as Chinese-dominated. They say that the Malay-Muslims have lost key ministries such as finance and communications and multimedia, as well as many more key government posts. This is the opinion of many Malay-Muslims whom we meet at the grassroots. Maybe the typical Damansara or Bangsar crowd would have a different opinion but, despite being the loudest or most vocal, they are not the majority.

With this new government, Islam is also perceived to be under threat. Malay-Muslims are feeling insecure. The attack on Prophet Muhammad (Peace Be Upon Him) and Islam in the social media, ratification of the International Convention on the Elimination of All Forms of Racial Discrimination (ICERD), ratification of the Rome Statute and the demand to abolish the matriculation quota are issues that are like petrol being thrown onto a house on fire.

Malay-Muslims do not see the new government protecting them and their religion. They do not see the Malay-Muslim leaders of PH having the courage to defend them. Nobody has yet to be prosecuted for the death of fireman Muhammad Adib Mohd Kassim. Their feeling towards the government is that of animosity.

I do not see that Malaysia Baru has resulted in a united Malaysia. Everyone seems to be moving to the right of the political spectrum. Everybody seems to be fighting for the interest of their race. Malaysia Baru is actually bad news for Malaysians. We do not trust each other anymore.

I have no doubt that the next election, GE-15, will be fought along racial lines if the current political climate prevails. GE-13 was different, as Pakatan Rakyat still existed and PAS was part of it. Racial harmony was still there. Whether in the Pakatan Rakyat or BN coalitions, we could see interracial cooperation.

Although they have Malay-based parties in PH, in GE-14 less than 30 per cent of Malays voted for PH. A year after the election, these Malay parties have failed to prove their worth. Their role is seen to be very minimal. We have deputy ministers from non-Malay parties performing better than ministers from the Malay parties. Some have even called these Malay ministers *pelakon tambahan* (supporting actors) instead of being the leading stars.

So, where do we go from here? We surely cannot continue to mistrust each other. Everybody will lose. Someone will have to give in. There is a need for a compromise. The Malays would naturally say they have given more than they should have during independence.

Do not blame the current situation on UMNO or PAS. It will be an insult to Malay-Muslims to blame political parties for provoking them. They are reasonable and intelligent enough to realize the situation they are in today without requiring political parties to remind them. This is the age of social media. You make up your own mind. No one can control how you think unless you feed them with lies and play the hate card. Many who are vocal today are not politicians but are individuals that are unhappy with the current situation.

The cooperation between UMNO and PAS should not be seen as a threat to racial harmony. The two parties have been at loggerheads since the 1950s. This recent development should be welcomed rather than despised. It will reduce conflicts in Malaysian society. Previously we had PAS members and UMNO members not talking to each other for years, but today they can sit side by side at weddings. Previously, we had PAS members refusing to eat chicken slaughtered by UMNO members. But today they can work together in the community. Is this a bad thing? Why do some people want to see Malay-Muslims continue to fight with each other? Why do some people label this cooperation as an "unholy alliance"?

This is unless you profit from the split among the Malays and their unity will threaten your hold on power. People who are divided are easily controlled. Other races are able to unite or work together without attracting criticism—whether it is under a non-governmental organization or another form of umbrella body, or whether for common interests like the economy, human rights or education. However, for these people, Malay-Muslims cannot or must not unite to pursue common goals.

PAS is not a racist party. Racism is not tolerated in Islam. Although the non-Muslims, especially the Chinese, rejected PAS in GE-14, my party continues to work with all races. In GE-14 only 5 per cent of the Chinese voters in my constituency voted for me, but I still attend functions at the Chinese temple when invited and still entertain lion dance groups during Chinese New Year. PAS has a Supporters' Wing comprised of non-Muslims, which is very active all year round. During GE-14, members of the Supporters' Wing actively campaigned for our candidates throughout the country. We also had Chinese and Indian candidates representing PAS in the election. So, why are we called racist?

Although they deserted us in GE-14, PAS will not desert non-Muslim voters. I am glad that, apart from cooperating with UMNO, we are also talking to the Malaysian Indian Congress (MIC) and the Malaysian Chinese Association (MCA). A new form of electoral pact involving not only Muslims but also non-Muslims is required to save Malaysia as the Quran tells us (49:13), "We created you from a single (pair) of a male and female, and made you into nations and tribes, that ye may know each other (not that ye may despise (each other)."

22

BIG DATA AND BOLD CALLS
How INVOKE Saw What Everyone Missed

Rafizi Ramli and James Chai

INTRODUCTION

INVOKE Malaysia remains the only organization in the world to have correctly predicted Malaysia's 14th General Elections (GE-14). All other research houses and political scientists pointed to a comfortable or narrow victory for the incumbent, Barisan Nasional (BN) coalition (Zurairi 2018). Only INVOKE maintained its prediction—since January 2017—of a historic Pakatan Harapan (PH) victory.

Malaysian research houses like Merdeka Center for Opinion Research, Kajidata Research (*Malay Mail Online*, 4 May 2018), and Ilham Centre (Kaur 2018), as well as political analysts from Universiti Kebangsaan Malaysia and Universiti Sains Malaysia, had all predicted a comfortable BN victory (*The Sun Daily*, 14 February 2018). Merdeka Center and political analysts even floated the possibility of BN regaining a two-thirds majority in Parliament (*The Sun Daily*, 7 May 2018). Prominent international research houses and news sites like FT Research (*Malaysiakini*, 19 April 2018), Oxford Economics (*NST Business*, 11 April 2018), the Economist Intelligence Unit (Economist Intelligence Unit 2018), *Reuters* (Sipalan and Menon 2018), CIMB Investment Bank Research (Ridzwan 2018), HSBC Global Research (Incalcaterra et al. 2018), Hong Leong Investment Bank Research (*NST Business*, 9 April 2018), Maybank Investment Bank Research (Zarina Zakariah 2018) similarly predicted a BN victory.

The reason for these discrepancies could be attributed to the methods used for prediction. Quantitatively, only INVOKE managed to use Big Data analytics for its prediction to construct a more accurate representation of voters' inclinations across the country. The process of installing a Big Data warehouse with the necessary tools, talents and expertise is expensive and prohibitive for many research institutions.

Qualitatively, an observer's perspective of the Malaysian political climate is limited by Najib Razak's government that masked the true political and economic sentiment of the masses. His government ensured that the local and international media were constantly showered with positive economic numbers to indicate that the country was doing well. Due to the intrinsic connection between economic and political stability in Malaysia, many political observers had taken the marvellous economic numbers as an indicator that the government was still strong.

Malaysia's GDP growth numbers witnessed a dramatic increase from 4.2 per cent in 2016 to 5.9 per cent in 2017. This GDP number was also higher than the 5.0 per cent figure that was recorded in 2015. Not only was the year-on-year increase impressive, but it was also one of the highest figures in the region because the global economy at that time was at a slowdown. World Bank estimated that Malaysia's GDP would stay at 5.4 per cent in 2018 (the year of GE-14), and the International Monetary Fund put it at the same level, as did Bloomberg and the World Economic Forum. Almost every research house that focused on Malaysia had predicted a BN victory being aided primarily by a supposedly good economy.

However, during the same period, INVOKE through its Big Data analytics found that the economic sentiment on the ground plummeted to an all-time low. When most research houses predicted the economic sentiment to increase between the third quarter of 2017 to the first quarter of 2018 due to the impressive GDP numbers, INVOKE's data showed that the overall economic sentiment index had fallen from 41.9 per cent in the third quarter of 2017 to only 38.1 per cent in the first quarter of 2018. The latter number being the lowest ever recorded in the country's recent history. Further statistical methods also revealed that GE-14 was largely decided on the economy.

What this means is that without Big Data analytics as a method to predict political outcomes, many signs would have been missed. Although this does not fully explain why most research houses did not obtain the right prediction, it does prove that INVOKE's Big Data analytics is a competitive edge in the sphere of political predictions.

INVOKE played a dual role in GE-14. It was primarily a Big Data institution that collected insight into voting behaviour of each constituency in the country and, subsequently, predicted how these voters would vote in GE-14. Besides this, INVOKE also played a crucial role in shaping the political opinion of fence-sitters to vote for pro-reform candidates in the PH coalition. INVOKE's efforts were primarily concentrated on marginal seats that could tilt the balance in favour of the opposition coalition. This chapter explains both our predicting and shaping roles.

Predicting the Vote

In simple terms, Big Data analytics refers to the deployment of specialized technologies to make sense of large, varied and complex datasets. The term "Big Data" received its first spotlight around 2001 where Doug Laney, a former analyst at Meta Group Inc., introduced the mechanism of a system that could deal with the volume, velocity and variety. It was only a decade after that that the public started to pay close attention to Big Data analytics. Barack Obama's 2008 presidential campaign opened a new frontier of Big Data analytics where it was successfully deployed to secure his victory through the digital platform.

Although there is no set number of rows and columns required for Big Data analytics, any dataset that has 100,000 rows and above would benefit significantly from this technique. The purpose of using Big Data analytics is to determine if there are hidden patterns and correlations that are previously unknown or unverified through the naked eye. Once this information is analysed and visualized, users are able to make informed decisions to maximize the intended outcome and optimize the cost.

The good thing about Big Data analytics is that it leads to the formulation of predictive models and statistical algorithms which may help predict an election.

To do this effectively and efficiently, however, INVOKE had to use specialized analytics systems and software, and also high-powered computing systems. This was the only way to process and analyse extremely large volumes of data points (amounting to millions) in a short amount of time. The agility of predictions in Big Data analytics enabled INVOKE to uncover many behavioural patterns outside of politics to determine voting behaviour with higher accuracy each time.

For example, INVOKE conducted the largest political survey in the history of Malaysia. In January 2017, INVOKE published its findings based on the 104,340 matched and completed respondents. The survey was conducted from 25 December 2016 to 15 January 2017. The survey successfully telephoned 8.36 million Malaysians using INVOKE's proprietary interactive voice response (IVR) recorded voice tool. In the same month the survey was completed, INVOKE was able to publish findings on the inclination of votes in a three-cornered contest between BN, PH and the Islamic Party of Malaysia (Parti Islam Se-Malaysia, PAS).

At that time, the survey had already found a dramatic loss in Malay support for the incumbent BN government, at only 40 per cent (Figure 22.1). INVOKE also found that the Chinese votes for remained high, but not to the high support level of the previous general election (Figure 22.2). However, it was also observed that the core challenge of the Chinese votes lies not in the support level, but the ability to get them out to vote.

Following on these observations, INVOKE made several simulations based on the different levels of support and with reference to the June 2016 by-elections in Kuala Kangsar and Sungai Besar, including:

- Non-voting remains the same, and Chinese voter support is at the by-election levels, i.e., approximately 51 per cent;
- Non-voting remains the same, and Chinese voter support is at the 13th General Elections (GE-13) level, i.e., approximately 85 per cent;
- Half of the non-voters vote for PH, and Chinese voter support is at the by-election levels;

FIGURE 22.1
Percentage of Malay Support for Each Coalition in January 2017

% of votes by coalition/party
Malay voters only

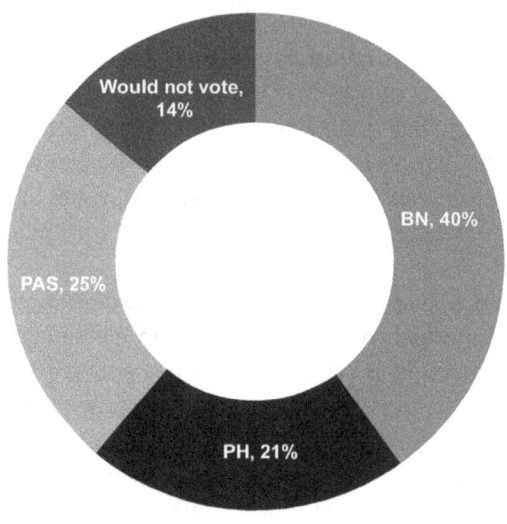

Only 4 out of 10
Malay voters
surveyed are likely to
vote for BN in a
3-corner contest

Note:
• *PH support level includes PPBM*
• *All surveys were conducted in Malay*

Source: INVOKE (2017).

FIGURE 22.2
Percentage of Chinese Support for Each Coalition in January 2017

% of votes by coalition/party
Chinese voters only

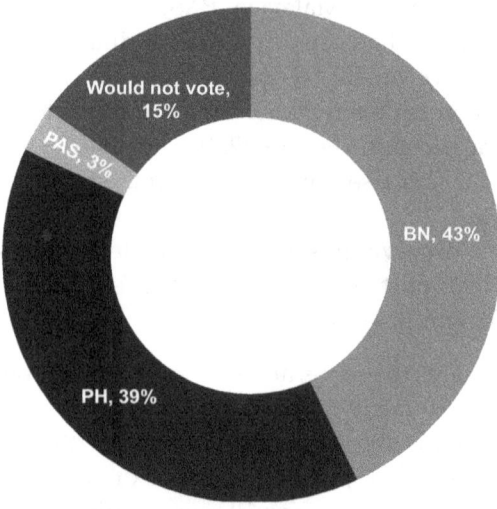

Source: INVOKE (2017).

- Half of the non-voters vote for PH, 38 per cent of PAS voters vote for PH, and Chinese voter support is at the by-election levels;
- Half of the non-voters vote for PH, 38 per cent of PAS voters vote for PH, and Chinese voter support is at the GE-13 level.

The numerous simulations were generated based on our reading of the political scenario at that time. The last simulation (half of the non-voters vote for PH, 38 per cent of PAS voters vote for PH, and Chinese voter support is at the GE-13 level) indicated that a victory for PH was likely if the simulation were to materialize the next day. INVOKE found that PH would win 126 seats (fourteen seats more than required to obtain a simple majority in the Malaysian Parliament), whereas BN would win only ninety-six seats. In other words, PH would secure its first-ever victory over the BN coalition. The final simulation was the closest simulation to the final GE-14 results.

The survey findings were refined with other survey results that exposed more intricately the demographic differences and patterns, apart from broader surveys to determine the economic sentiment and voting transferability from one party to the other. Logically, the more one learns about the voting behaviour and attitudes of one particular profile of voters, the more accurately one can predict the actual vote that would be cast on GE-14.

The INVOKE public event that generated the hugest wave in the public psyche was the "INVOKE GE-14 Prediction" that was held on 9 March 2018, at the Grand Hibiscus Hall, Swiss Garden Hotel, Kuala Lumpur. The closed-door forum was attended by approximately 400 people which comprised ambassadors, foreign mission officials, academics, politicians, journalists, corporate giants, and the general public. The video was published on all social media platforms including Facebook and Instagram and has collectively amassed over 150,000 views.

The important observation that could be derived from Figure 22.3 at that time was that the support for the incumbent BN government had dropped drastically on a monthly basis to February 2018, at a rate of at least 6 per cent per month. On the other hand, the Malay support for PH had correspondingly increased in those few months. The voters who refused to answer or were undecided in the survey questions—collectively regarded as fence-sitter voters—were predicted to be PH voters since their profiles matched those of a PH supporter. Other pollsters predicted that the surveyed respondents who refused to answer or were undecided would vote for BN, but this turned out to be the exact opposite.

The difference in the predictions lies in the questioning method and matching accuracy. INVOKE's survey questions follow a tested decision tree to prompt more honest answers by the respondents even though they refused or stated their indecision on the straightforward question of who they would vote for. INVOKE has extracted the key profile and characteristic of a PH voter and had used this to determine if the similar profile and characteristics are present in the fence-sitter voters. In other words, if the fence-sitter voter shared similar frustration for the cost of living, price

FIGURE 22.3
Percentage of Malay Support for Each Coalition in March 2018

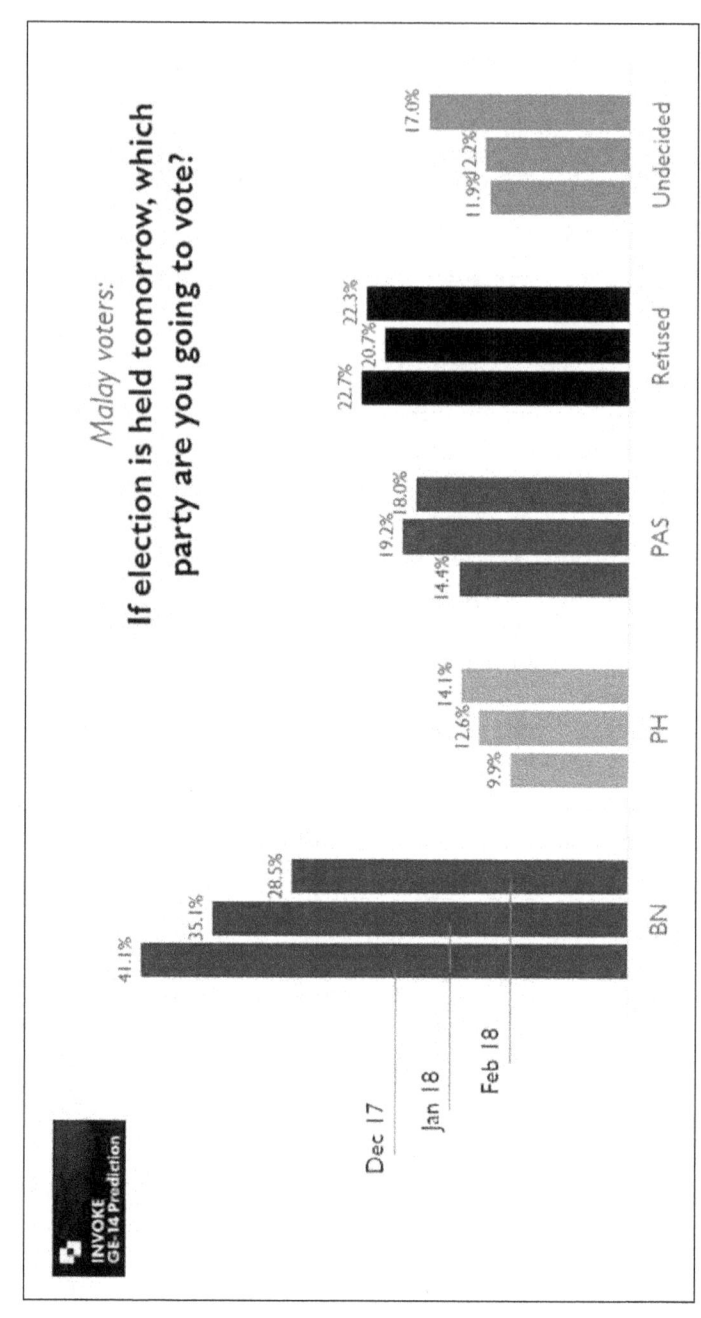

Malay voters:
If election is held tomorrow, which party are you going to vote?

Source: INVOKE (2018).

of goods, corruption, and Najib Razak's administration, then it is likely that the fence-sitter voter would be prompted to vote for PH in GE-14.

Additionally, the matching accuracy was increased by repetition to ensure that there is a reliable method of getting closer to what these fence-sitters would vote for. Repetition and frequency of surveys helped mitigate the risk of error.

On the other hand, the Chinese voter support levels also showed that the Chinese support had returned to the level of the previous general election, that is a split of 80 per cent for PH and 20 per cent for BN (Figure 22.4). Chinese voters who started to announce their support for PH increased in roughly the same magnitude as the decline in the "undecided" category of Chinese voters. Once again, this showed that the Chinese support could carry the PH coalition through in GE-14.

In the end, INVOKE's overall prediction of a PH victory, based on PH winning a pivotal majority on the Peninsula, was largely reflected in the actual results of GE-14.

Shaping the Vote

Once INVOKE was able to gain an insight into the voting behaviour of each voter profile in each constituency, INVOKE was also equipped with the ability to target these voters with the right campaign message to maximize voter knowledge.

The mainstream media was monopolized by the BN coalition, and that means that there is zero airtime given to any other party or coalition. The opposition had started to make substantial gains by campaigning through the digital platform in GE-12 (2008) and GE-13 (2013). In GE-12, the opposition deprived the BN of its precious two-thirds majority that had conferred an iron grip on the Parliament and government; in GE-13, the opposition made its largest gain by securing 89 out of 222 seats in Parliament.

For GE-14, INVOKE adopted a more sophisticated digital strategy centred on data analytics. Data analytics here refers to more continuous, repetitive, and frequent collection and analysis of the data on a large scale. The purpose is to get to a more predictive and intelligent understanding of the past, present and future. Data was focused at every step of the process. We conducted preliminary data analytics to segment voter groups based on their inclination and behaviour, then sent microtargeted messages to them, rather than generic campaign rhetoric. These messages, designed for particular visual and psychological impact, were also matched to voter profiles to enhance positive response. We subsequently ran post-campaign analytics to assess the performance of each posted message so that we could make improvements.

To elaborate, preliminary data analytics enabled INVOKE to divide and categorize voters based on demographics and predicted behaviour. For instance, if the intention was to target fence-sitter voters, then voters with a roughly equal likelihood of voting for each party or coalition—for instance, 25 per cent each for BN, PH, and PAS—could be drawn out of the database. Further, that group of fence-sitter voters could be divided with more precision into gender, race, religion, constituency and others.

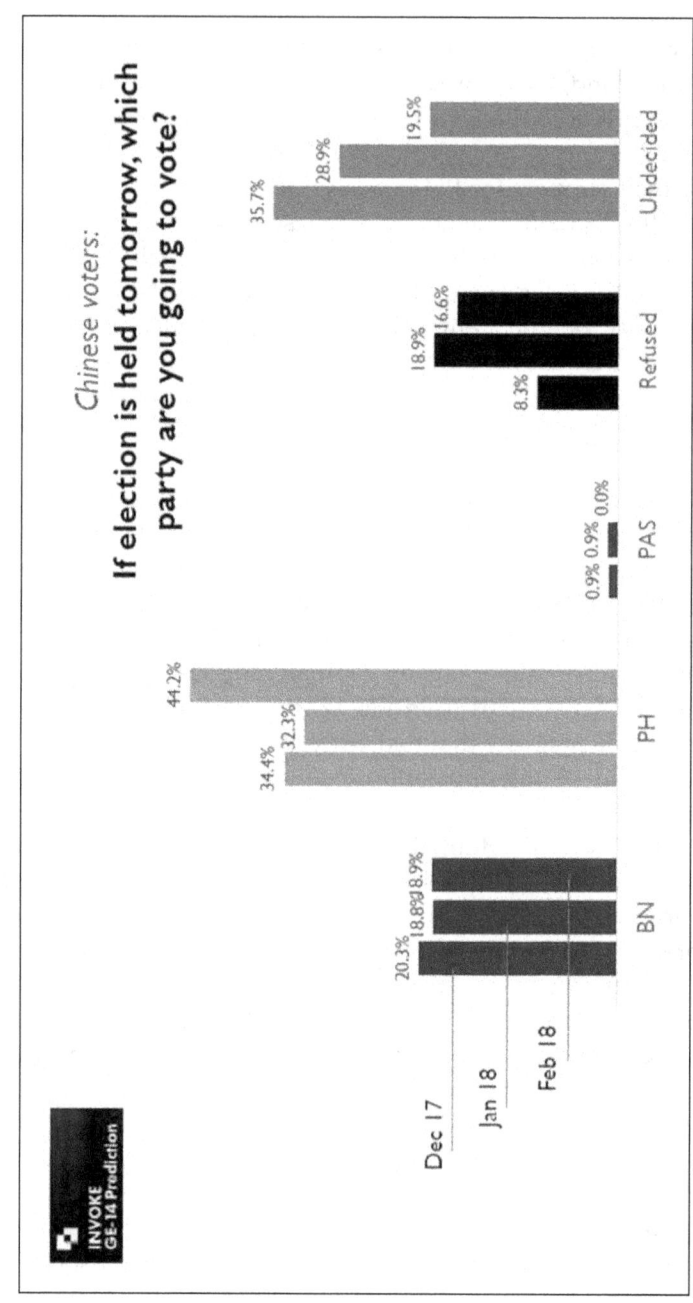

FIGURE 22.4
Percentage of Chinese Support for Each Coalition in March 2018

Chinese voters:

If election is held tomorrow, which party are you going to vote?

Source: INVOKE (2018).

Each voter category serves a different purpose. The voters who are regarded as hard-core and loyal supporters of selected coalitions would be targets for call-to-action in the form of volunteering, donating, and digital advocacy. For instance, a voter group with a percentage of supporting PH at an 85 percentage rate would be targeted for donations. Moreover, a voter group with a percentage of supporting BN at an 85 percentage rate would be ignored since it would otherwise be a waste of resources to focus on someone who would not change their mind to vote for any other coalition than BN.

The fence-sitter voters with a roughly equal distribution of across all three coalitions would be the primary target for persuasion since this was the battleground. In terms of the constituency, the marginal seats are considered the primary target of political campaigns. Marginal seats are seats that are won with less than 55 per cent of the popular vote, which means that a small swing in voters' inclination could unseat the incumbent.

The reason for segmenting voters into smaller groups was to ensure that the campaign messages sent to each of these voters was particularized to their preferences. A microtargeting technique entails understanding voter groups as much as possible before creating and sending effective campaign messages to them. In other words, the microtargeting technique circumvents the traditional targeting techniques that are one-size-fits-all and rely on messages that are as generalized as possible. In the past, politicians have always relied on using a single and unified message that would hopefully work in the urban Selangor areas, as well as the rural Pahang areas. Most of the time, this does not work since no two voters are alike. Instead, what must be done is to create campaigns that would emphasize what the audience in that particular area cares for.

A common example is that the campaign messages on corruption and abuse of power would work better in urban parliamentary seats like Subang (P104) and Petaling Jaya (P105), but would be less effective in Jempol (P127) where the issues of cost of living mattered more. INVOKE's microtargeting reached the level of producing different messages to different clusters of voters in the same constituency. The type of messages received by these voters depend highly on their profiles. For example, a Malay housewife between 50 and 60 years old, who is unreceptive of politics, would receive an advertisement on cooking recipes that will be subtly linked to the rising cost of living in the country.

Segmenting voters would also ensure the resources allocated for microtargeting are optimized. As stated above, the most aggressive political campaigning would take place at marginal seats and with fence-sitter voters across the country. On the other hand, the political campaigning in safe seats or for hard-core and loyal supporters would be reduced, and resources would be redirected elsewhere. The strategic allocation of resources that is informed by voter segmentation would ensure that resources are allocated at optimal levels. Big Data analytics helps this process by updating the effectiveness and efficiency of the allocation process in a short amount of time. This means that decisions would be made and changed quickly based on the most updated information.

Besides setting the parameters of microtargeting, INVOKE also employs "psychographic" posters and videos—with content that will likely resonate with the voters and induce them to take action. For fence-sitting voters, the main objective is for them to view enough targeted campaign messages so that they are better informed as to whom to vote for in the general election. For voters with a low percentage of turning up to vote, campaign messages will be primarily on encouraging voters to turn up on election day to vote. This includes content that promotes election day car-pooling around the voter's constituency, peer support for voting, and other messaging geared towards getting out the vote.

After sending out the campaign messages to the selected voter groups, INVOKE would collect the data on the performance of each post and analyse them accordingly. The primary intention of collecting these data and conducting post-campaign analytics is to improve on the segmenting and microtargeting process to determine what worked and what did not. For instance, INVOKE could determine if the psychographic message published met its objective of having high levels of relevance to the voter that is targeted, or if the post's content needs revision or if the target audience needs refinement.

METHODOLOGY

Big Data utilizes surveys, which are simpler in form and widely understood, but also generates further information and seeks to fill gaps. The information garnered from public opinion polls can be very useful, but is limited to the questions asked and the responses given—which in turn depends on respondents' willingness to answer. It might be helpful for us to explain the methodology of our data generation and analysis.

INVOKE's Big Data operations comprised four elements:

1. Building a large database and constructing representative voter samples
INVOKE accumulated a massive raw database that is constantly enriched and refined, drawing on new survey (online and offline) data points. The database is constantly cleaned (extract, transform, load) to ensure accuracy and validity, and ensure that the data warehouse is scalable and adaptable to be used for different research needs.

Conventional surveys would randomly select a sample to reflect the ethnic profile of the population of a target research area. INVOKE's Big Data is able to take this a few steps further by having richer random stratification of the population so that each strata is more representative and detailed. The intention is not only to get a sample size that is large enough but one that also has the power to represent each voting behaviour distinctly and accurately.

Each stratification is informed by a set of variables that data analytics has shown to be important for obtaining a representative sample, including age, gender, ethnicity, state, urban-rural classification and others. There is a total of twenty-four strata constructed by INVOKE.

For instance, a stratum would have a person's demographic profile including the age, gender, race and others (age between 21 and 30, male, Chinese, etc.) and the survey result collected of that person in that strata should represent the survey result of a different person in the same stratum. INVOKE generates random voters only after identifying the specific strata. Upon obtaining the survey result for each stratum, further randomized sampling is done for the strata to ensure consistency, validity and reliability.

In other words, INVOKE's technique is not only reliant on randomized and large sample sizes, but they are preceded with a stratified technique to ensure that they are truly representative of the entire Malaysian voting population. The high accuracy rate of 90–93 per cent of the parliamentary and state seats predicted in GE-14 is a testament to the success of this method.

Surveys are done frequently to ensure that the data is timely. Demographic data are tested constantly for verification purposes, and data on political behaviour and inclination changes more frequently, approximately on a quarterly basis.

2. Survey question design

The process of designing survey questions for political prediction is intricate since respondents are less likely to answer political questions truthfully, or may not respond at all if the matter is deemed too sensitive. For instance, INVOKE encountered multiple and continuous problems of respondents refusing to answer whom they would vote for if the general elections were to be held the next day. This problem was particularly profound in the months leading to the general election. This is commonly experienced in surveys of a political nature; around the world, voters still regard these questions as private and confidential. The disinclination to respond is compounded in Malaysia by threats signalled by the BN government against individuals, especially civil servants, who openly support the opposition. Voters who start to prefer the opposition coalition would prefer to refuse to answer or state that they are undecided. The share of respondents who refused to answer or said they were undecided increased as the country inched closer to GE-14.

Recognizing this problem, INVOKE had to carefully formulate a responsive decision tree analysis for the survey questions to provide additional features to the data. This way of formulating the survey questions would ensure that other subsidiary questions would assist INVOKE in getting closer to a right prediction of who they would vote for, even when they refused to answer the main question of whom they would vote for. The decision tree analysis is constantly improved upon so that it prompts honest and complete responses by the respondents. These additional features would prove to be vital in the predictive models that are developed of this Big Data analytics work.

3. Call centre systems, high bandwidth connectivity, specially trained call centre executives

INVOKE deployed a state-of-the-art interactive voice response (IVR) system that could make up to 300 calls at any one time, and up to 100,000 numbers in two hours.

After filtering, probing, and assessing, the call centres at INVOKE could garner more than 100,000 completed responses within two days, which is equivalent to the global standard. The high bandwidth connectivity also ensured that there was high speed to operate the data structure of a large capacity.

These call centres were also aided by data scientists who actively evaluated the best day and time to call individual respondents to maintain high response rate and high response quality. More optimal day and time were selected to call these respondents, the respondents are more likely to accept calls and are more likely to give complete and honest answers.

Besides that, call centre executives were trained rigorously to operate consistently and adaptively so that the results obtained are not misleading or unreflective of respondents' true intentions. To cover the diversity of the voters in Malaysia, the IVR and live callers were well versed in Malay, English, Mandarin and Tamil, in proportions representative of the country's population.

The survey results were extracted and cleaned before we conducted further analysis. First, our data scientists ensured that the responses were matched and verified. We tested responses by matching and verifying with reference to other demographic data. Responses that were found to provide information inconsistent with demographic data, which might subsequently impair the credibility of our findings, were subsequently discarded.

It is important to note that, like any other statistical processes, INVOKE's call centre services were also susceptible to bias. The most notable biases include those of BN supporters who refused to pick up or complete the survey questions due to the perception that INVOKE was opposition-led and Chinese voters who have traditionally been more conservative in revealing their political leanings for fear of government repercussions. However, these biases are minimized in the overall scheme of prediction since they probably contributed to a more conservative prediction by INVOKE in the end.

4. Suitable mathematical modelling to profile a national audience
INVOKE has in-house data experts to fit the data into several mathematical models and assess the accuracy of those models. Then, they propose the best models to use to maximize accuracy and scalability while minimizing computation time. Formulations are then devised so that the machines self-learn and self-improve to ensure that future results are finer and more comprehensive.

The usage of cloud computing solutions widely contrasts with legacy technologies like SAP or SAS systems which are limited by the capacity of the in-house computers. Cloud computing solutions enable massive scalability to make quicker and more voluminous predictions.

By applying suitable mathematical modelling in profiling the national audience, INVOKE has achieved the highest messaging efficiency in the world. INVOKE's platform served 1 billion social media campaign impressions to a voting population of 15 million—this translates to sixty-seven social media campaign messages delivered directly and individually to each voter. The closest international competitor only managed to reach six social media campaign messages per voter; and this means that INVOKE was at least ten times more efficient than the closest competitor in terms of volume. Effective targeting techniques at a low cost were only made possible with highly accurate mathematical models. It is safe to say that INVOKE's profiling methods are the widest and most profound in the field of Malaysian politics, and this explains the accurate prediction of the election outcomes of GE-14.

Besides learning from existing datasets and survey results, INVOKE also triangulated social media data collected from Facebook, Instagram, Twitter, and LinkedIn. This triangulation was done with care and consideration since the social media data were found to have lower accuracy rate and lower representational value compared to the data that is collected and stored in-house. However, social media data still had its utility as it covered behavioural data that is otherwise absent from INVOKE's survey results. The triangulation of social media data with INVOKE's data is also important in optimizing the overall cost of reaching the voting audience. The cumulative deployment of INVOKE's data, social media data, and lookalike functionalities on social media platforms provide INVOKE more tools than others to obtain the lowest cost possible for each post.

Further, INVOKE also fully deployed its volunteers to conduct canvassing since 2016 to collect and verify more data in order to get a more accurate picture of Malaysians' voting inclination. This included going door-to-door to houses of voters who were identified by prior analysis to be swing voters. These volunteers conducted face-to-face surveys to garner voter sentiment.

Dissemination

Microtargeted dissemination of campaign messages meant that the PH's manifesto promises were particularized to the voters in that constituency. To track the effectiveness of these campaign messages, post-campaign analytics were conducted on every social media post to ensure that the dissemination process is also refined and improved. Facebook remained the most effective channel of dissemination whereby the reaching and tracking of messaging effectiveness was most conducive for Big Data analytics.

Other social media platforms like Instagram, LinkedIn, and Twitter similarly were effective tools of messaging dissemination albeit slightly weaker compared to Facebook. WhatsApp was crucial in winning the general election as many ordinary voters were intent on spreading information about the choices available in GE-14 to sway the public opinion on their favour. INVOKE participated in WhatsApp chain messages to ensure information that was spread had a consistent basis. The problem, however, was that the trackability of WhatsApp was the least effective and the messages could not reach the numbers of thousands or millions within the same space of time compared to other social media platforms. WhatsApp campaigning was most effective when activists, volunteers and ordinary voters took their own initiative to spread campaign messages on other social media platform like Facebook and spread it to their WhatsApp groups. WhatsApp remains a private and sacred space for many where trust is a crucial element. That is why the dissemination of information was most effective when it is spread by someone they know.

LESSONS LEARNED

In the realm of GE-14 political predictions, INVOKE stood out for being the only organization to have correctly foreseen the triumph of the PH coalition as the government of Malaysia.

Besides predicting the overall victor, INVOKE has also successfully predicted most of the winners and losers of each parliamentary and state seats. We accurately called 87.2 per cent of parliamentary seats, and 81.8 per cent of state legislature seats, which corresponded with PH winning seven out of eleven state governments in Peninsular Malaysia. Our overall prediction that PH would win approximately 120 seats in Parliament (including PH's electoral ally Warisan's seats) was almost identical to the final tally. The state governments that were correctly predicted were Kedah, Penang, Perak, Selangor, Negeri Sembilan, Melaka and Johor. These predictions were consistent since January 2017, approximately seventeen months before GE-14.

INVOKE also correctly pointed out the correlation between the drop in BN's Malay support and the increase in the number of fence-sitter voters, which may have significantly contributed to the victory of PH. We were able to detect this trend through our decision tree analysis, which indicated that most of the fence-sitter voters would likely vote for PH, although they did not directly state their preference to vote. The high number of mixed seats, with substantial presence of Chinese voters or urban Malay voters, also tilted the balance in favour of PH. Our stance that three-cornered fights would benefit PH, which went against the conventional wisdom that such scenarios give advantage to BN, held true.

Discrepancies

INVOKE predicted that PAS would not win a single seat on the parliamentary level. In the end, PAS secured a total of eighteen parliamentary seats, primarily concentrated in Kelantan and Terengganu. PAS' wins came at the expense of BN, and hence barely affected PH's results, but nonetheless holds out some lessons.

A few factors account for our incorrect prediction of PAS' downfall. Through a post–GE-14 survey, INVOKE found that most PAS voters resorted to tactical voting in their constituencies. PAS voters in Kelantan and Terengganu regarded PAS as the strongest contender in the opposition. Thus, they would not risk voting for PH because, in their minds, that would mean Najib's BN government would retain power. The post–GE-14 survey also found that the machinery of PH in Kelantan and Terengganu was weak; in most constituencies, the flags of PH (under PKR's banner) were not obvious, or they were mostly overwhelmed by PAS.

Statistically, INVOKE found it difficult to differentiate a PAS voter from a PH voter in Kelantan and Terengganu since they shared most of the similar characteristics. For example, both PAS and PH voters wanted to get rid of Najib Razak as prime minister, both voters intend to abolish the goods and services tax (GST), and both voters were voting on economic reasons like the cost of living issue. INVOKE also did not conduct further surveys, particularly in Kelantan and Terengganu to find out how much premium was attached to a religious party or leader to delineate in detail a PAS and a PH voter. In the end, the voters in Kelantan and Terengganu did not act similarly to the rest of the PH voters, and they chose to vote tactically in favour of PAS.

The other area that PAS has a strong presence in was in Kedah, where a sizeable portion of the state is historically dominated by the Islamic party. The similar pattern to Kelantan and Terengganu emerged in this state from the post-election survey to show that the PH machinery was comparatively weaker in the parts where PAS dominated and induced similar voting attitudes by the voting population in the state. In other words, voters who chose PAS in these areas were tactical voters who thought that only the Islamist had a fighting chance in GE-14. This unusual pattern that is only unique to Kelantan, Terengganu and parts of Kedah could be explained by the fact that PAS' presence is all-encompassing in these places where religion, politics, and community permeates every part of these voters' lives.

These explain the discrepancies in the predictive outcomes of INVOKE about Kelantan and Terengganu. However, it is also important to note that the shortcomings in predictive inaccuracy by no means invalidate and discredit the findings of INVOKE's predictions. No prediction is fool-proof nor is it designed to be. Every prediction has a possibility of turning out otherwise due to a host of other uncontrollable variables. The difference between cases of accurate and inaccurate predictions is whether the methodology used was consistent and sophisticated and whether the inaccurate predictions would have been accurate had the set of uncontrollable variables been minimized. This was the case for INVOKE.

THE FUTURE OF BIG DATA CAMPAIGNING

Traditionally, politicians decide on how to campaign through their daily interactions with voters on the ground or by instinct. This method is extremely flawed since individual politicians have a limited view of voter sentiment. Most of the time, the voter sentiment of one constituency differs significantly from another, and they are not representative of the overall voter sentiment in the country. In Malaysia, political parties campaigning based on a single and unified message is problematic as each constituency responds differently. This results in low and sporadic effectiveness.

The introduction of a data-driven approach in political campaigns meant that not only would the political parties gain an insightful understanding of their strengths and weaknesses in each constituency early on, but they were also to respond accordingly by tailor-making their campaign strategies.

Dashboards of each constituency and the overall voting inclination of the Malaysian population are extremely valuable to politicians, and we have seen a surge in interest by politicians locally and globally. For instance, since Barack Obama's successful 2008 presidential campaign, no mainstream political party in the United States of America and other developed countries would risk another political campaign without Big Data analytics to research and strategize. An interesting example is Taiwan, where Big Data analytics is deployed in every political sphere imaginable, like the popularity rating of each member of the legislature, and the probability of the nominations for selected political posts in the country. The trackability and reliability of data-driven solutions in political campaigning also mean that responses against changes of voter sentiment could be undertaken well.

Although Big Data campaigning is applied in more and more political campaigns around the world, INVOKE remains the only organization to have successfully done this in Malaysia. During GE-14, there were rumours about the then BN government engaging a London-based Big Data outfit Cambridge Analytica and its parent company SCL Group. This was subsequently denied by the former government when the outfit was involved in an alleged criminal act of data theft. At the time, Cambridge Analytica's website proclaimed that it was responsible for political advisory work for BN and the Kedah state government since 2008.

Regardless of the veracity of these claims, more and more political parties and coalitions are recognizing the value of Big Data in running election campaigns. However, the key to success, as we have learned, depends very closely in the presence of a dedicated team of data scientists, campaign managers and coordinators, political consultants, field workers, supporting staff and others. At its height, INVOKE's total staff numbered 125. Effective deployment of a Big Data political campaign hinges on a dynamic and capable team, since the effort of setting up Big Data machinery is tedious, laborious, and expensive.

Grassroots Campaigning

INVOKE's success in using Big Data to win GE-14 altered the way campaigns are run in Malaysia. It is an open secret that political campaigns are expensive. A parliamentary seat requires at least RM250,000 to cover the basics: cost of t-shirts, party flags, place rentals for volunteers, and stipends for field workers. That means to have an edge in the campaign, you require more funds, and Malaysian politicians have traditionally relied on big donors who can contribute hundreds and thousands or millions of ringgit to ease the financial burden. The trouble with this form of campaign fund-raising is that the politicians are directly or indirectly beholden to the whims of the select few elites who expect something in return for their contribution. This is unhealthy for Malaysia's democracy because it creates a politics that serves the interest of the few who are rich and powerful.

That is why INVOKE's success in raising funds through the grassroots channel has altered how campaigns could be run in the country. Effective targeting and persuasive campaign messaging had helped INVOKE raise US$2.5 million (RM10.4 million) through crowdfunding over one year (INVOKE 2019). Most of the donations were smaller than US$10 each (RM41.59).

Besides using the crowdfunded money to drive the Big Data analytics and online campaigning, the money was also used to fund the campaign of 106 pro-reform candidates for GE-14. These candidates had to sign a statutory declaration that promised, among other things, to:

- stay loyal to the service of the Malaysian people;
- pay a penalty of RM20 million each to a people's trust fund if they decided to party-hop after winning their seats; and
- declare their assets to the public.

Each candidate who signed the statutory declaration received direct funding and also the full backing of INVOKE in terms of data analytics and surveys, and its digital campaign targeting tools to maximize the candidates' chances of winning. In the end, 95 per cent of the candidates ended up triumphant in their campaign against their political opponents.

Microtargeting and Democracy

The usage of microtargeting techniques achieves the aim of tailor-making the content that is most suitable and interesting to the particular voter. This means, with effective microtargeting, voters will no longer be exposed to political content that they have little to no interest in, and this will make the democratic process more meaningful by having a more informed electorate.

The problem with the usual course of politics is that what is typically covered on the mainstream media is uninteresting to the masses. This includes the daily political jostling for power and gossipy posturing among politicians. None of these seem close enough to the lives of the people who are more consumed with day-to-day concerns that are particular and specific to them. By understanding the most pressing concerns of each voter, the content that reaches this voter would be more relevant and meaningful in their participation in politics. The assumption is that the more an electorate knows about the political issues of the day, the more meaningful the democracy is. Informed decisions beat blind participation.

However, there is a concern relating to ethics in microtargeting. Some salient criticisms against microtargeting in political campaigns are that voters may be emotionally manipulated in making decisions, or the messaging may deviate from true and accountable election promises, or that voters may be misled to act in a way that will produce net detriment to society.

To counter that, the people who use the technology of microtargeting must be ethical in deciding how far they are willing to go in serving the needs of a certain political campaign. Big Data organizations must collectively abide by rules and not trespass on boundaries. The needs of the political campaigns do not allow the campaign to exceed the ethical and legal boundaries which are otherwise present outside the digital sphere.

Secondly, the electorate themselves ought to be wary of online information. As the use of online tools and content matures, the voters should also develop self-regulation in filtering information for its validity and credibility before consuming them.

Thirdly, the social media tools available are increasingly guarding against malicious and deceptive content that is spread through its space. The approval process has become increasingly extensive, and the types of allowable content are increasingly strict. That means the hurdles that currently exist would force content creators to be more careful in their microtargeting efforts so that the end users (voters) are ultimately protected.

CONCLUSION

INVOKE's efforts in the GE-14 should not be discounted. It has brought a sea change to how political campaigns are run in Malaysia. Not only was INVOKE a central house that stood out for rightly predicting the election results—with more audacity and veracity than anyone else—we were also responsible in using Big Data analytics and microtargeting techniques to help win the historic election for the PH coalition in the end.

These collective efforts in the years preceding the GE-14 has changed the elitist financing method of political campaigns into a grassroots crowdfunding method. It has also changed the nature of politics and democracy from one that is centred among the select few personalities at the top, into one that is driven by ordinary people on the ground. Most of all, it has added an empirical and scientific way of deploying data into a field traditionally driven by subjective impulses and instincts. The days of politicians knows best have given way to a data-based political assessment.

Winning the election was icing on the cake.

References

Economist Intelligence Unit. 2018. "Barisan Nasional Coalition Set to Win Another Term". *The Economist*, 9 April 2018. https://country.eiu.com/article.aspx?articleid=386598022 &Country=Malaysia&topic=Politics.

Incalcaterra, Joseph et al. 2018. "The Mother of All Elections: Malaysia Announces General Election". HSBC Global Research, 11 April 2018. http://www.fullertreacymoney.com/ system/data/files/PDFs/2018/April/24th/Malaysian%20Elections_HSBC.pdf.

INVOKE Centre for Policy Initiatives. 2017. "Preliminary Results and Observations from a Survey of 104,340 Voters to Gauge Voter Preferences in a 3 Corner Contest". 19 January 2017.

———. 2018. "INVOKE GE-14 Prediction". 9 March 2018.

Kaur, Minderjeet. 2018. "GE-14: Swing in Malay Voters Not Enough for PH to Take Over". *Free Malaysia Today*, 27 March 2018. https://www.freemalaysiatoday.com/category/ nation/2018/03/27/GE-14-swing-in-malay-voters-not-enough-for-ph-to-take-over/.

Malay Mail Online. 2018. "BN Likely to Prevail in Battle for Malaysia, Kajidata Survey Finds".

4 May 2018. https://www.malaymail.com/news/malaysia/2018/05/04/bn-likely-to-prevail-in-battle-for-malaysia-kajidata-survey-finds/1627156.

Malaysiakini. 2018. "Financial Times Expects BN to Win Amid Signs of Growing Malay Disquiet". 19 April 2018. https://www.malaysiakini.com/news/420596.

NST Business. 2018a. "Stock Market Investors Expect Comfortable BN Win in GE-14". *New Straits Times*, 9 April 2018. https://www.nst.com.my/business/2018/04/355278/stock-market-investors-expect-comfortable-bn-win-GE-14.

———. 2018b. "Oxford Economics Research Firm Predicts Comfortable BN Election Win". *New Straits Times*, 11 April 2018. https://www.nst.com.my/business/2018/04/355887/oxford-economics-research-firm-predicts-comfortable-bn-election-win.

Ridzwan, Amir. 2018. "BN Expecting to Win Viewed as Positive for Market, Says Analyst". *The Edge Markets*, 9 April 2018. https://www.theedgemarkets.com/article/bn-expecting-win-viewed-positive-market-says-analyst.

Sipalan, Joseph, and Praveen Menon. 2018. "Explainer: Why Scandal-Hit Najib Is Expected to Win Malaysia's Election". Reuters, 10 April 2018. https://www.reuters.com/article/us-malaysia-election-explainer/why-scandal-hit-najib-is-expected-to-win-malaysias-election-idUSKBN1HH1BF.

Sun Daily, The. 2018a. "BN and Najib Have Upper Hand in GE-14, Say Analysts". 14 February 2018. https://www.thesundaily.my/archive/bn-and-najib-have-upper-hand-GE-14-say-analysts-YUARCH526173.

———. 2018b. "BN to Romp Home to GE-14 Victory, Analysts Predict". 7 May 2018. https://www.thesundaily.my/archive/bn-romp-home-GE-14-victory-analysts-predict-KUARCH545937.

Zarina Zakariah. 2018. "Bursa to React Positively if BN Wins the GE-14: Maybank IB". *New Straits Times*, 10 April 2018. https://www.nst.com.my/business/2018/04/355533/bursa-react-positively-if-bn-wins-GE-14-maybank-ib.

Zurairi AR. 2018. "GE-14 Results: How It Went So Wrong for Pundits". *Malay Mail Online*, 29 June 2018. https://www.malaymail.com/news/malaysia/2018/06/29/GE-14-results-how-it-went-so-wrong-for-pundits/1646711.

Conclusion

23

MISSED SIGNS OR LATE SURGE?

Lee Hwok Aun and Francis E. Hutchinson

INTRODUCTION

Regardless of events in years to come, 9 May 2018 will be regarded as a crucial juncture in Malaysia's history, as the 14th General Elections (GE-14) reconfigured the country's political context in many and far-reaching ways. What from afar looks like a binary preference between Barisan Nasional (BN) and Pakatan Harapan (PH) is actually a mosaic of changes in the country's increasingly diverse electorate. From their base in urban areas in Peninsular Malaysia, PH expanded into semi-urban areas at the expense of the United Malays National Organization (UMNO) and, particularly, smaller BN component parties. Support for Parti Islam Se-Malaysia (PAS) spread outwards from Kelantan into Terengganu, as well as parts of Pahang and Kedah. In East Malaysia, the newcomer Warisan made substantial inroads into BN heartlands in Sabah. And, Sarawak, while not experiencing the same local-level swing against the incumbent, was nonetheless carried along by the momentum.

Through a multipronged approach to GE-14, this book has sought to shed light on the various factors behind these shifts in voter sentiment. It has done this by, first, looking at the context within which voters act, in terms of: the institutional rules of the game; the wider economic environment; and the availability of financial inducements. From there, it explored the perspectives of different interest groups, seeking to identify key issues facing them and the means used by the competing coalitions to attract their support. This was then complemented by an analysis of political issues and trends in key states, including three on the Peninsula (Selangor, Johor and Kelantan), and the two East Malaysian states of Sabah and Sarawak. Lastly, essays from a selection of "players" in the election provided personal perspectives on the lead-up to the election and its immediate aftermath.

In addition to seeking to deepen our understanding of GE-14 through these four approaches, this book has also sought to explore the question of whether the generalized surprise at the results was due to: signs being overlooked or misread; or the result of a late surge in support for PH and PAS at the expense of BN. While important for guiding the research carried out for this book, the question is not actually binary. Indeed, the answers that have emerged from the preceding chapters indicate a complicated and changing reality with elements of both.

So, the question is not simply whether we missed signs, or whether there was a late surge away from BN. The more important and interesting task is to unpack the elements of truth on both sides. The twenty-two chapters of this book have shed light on the prelude, culmination and denouement of GE-14. In concluding, we draw on our contributing authors' astute observations and scholarly analyses, and discuss the missed signs heralding BN's downfall and the factors that gave PH a late surge in its march to victory.

We address both sides in turn, organizing our discussion in each case into five aspects. These points are not mutually exclusive, but rather intertwined and complementary. In line with this project's focus on the run-up to and results of GE-14, our direction remains primarily retrospective. However, in recognition of this watershed moment in Malaysia's history, we finish with brief reflections on the country in the post–GE-14 era. We consider the ways the PH government and the new opposition have reshaped Malaysia, and contemplate the open questions surrounding new political dynamics, promised reforms and power transitions.

MISSED SIGNS?

With regard to missed signs, the generalized contention of observers, analysts and pundits that BN would retain power in GE-14 clearly overlooked a number of important indicators of the prevailing—if latent—mood. What, then, were these signs and why were they missed?

BN's Structural Advantages

Shaped by experience as well as the manifold expressions of BN's power, many held that the momentum of reform would dissipate against the perceived solidity of the incumbent coalition's pervasive influence. This overestimation stemmed more from looking too much to the past, rather than observing trends in the present.

Building on the strong, cohesive state inherited at independence (Esman 1972), BN was able to accumulate a formidable arsenal of structural advantages in the following years. Malapportionment and the resulting rural bias benefited UMNO with its rural strongholds, and the redelineation exercise preceding GE-14 concentrated Malay votes in targeted constituencies to engineer perceived advantage. This was further exacerbated by the docility of oversight agencies such as the Election Commission (EC), which had been unable or unwilling to address long-standing issues such as irregularities in electoral rolls, including: involuntary voter deregistration; inaccurate entries; and unsolicited address changes (Chapter 2, Ostwald; Chapter 3, Chacko).

These BN-favouring conditions were further augmented by historical precedents. Despite considerable momentum in the run-up to the 2013 General Elections, Pakatan Rakyat's rally cry of "This time" (*Ini kalilah*) was unfulfilled. The momentum for reform was stymied by those very same advantages of incumbency, such as malapportionment, compliant electoral oversight bodies, and control of traditional media. Thus, despite winning the popular vote, Pakatan Rakyat was unable to secure a parliamentary majority. And, although BN registered a significant number of electoral defeats, UMNO actually increased its number of parliamentarians. Consequently, both Najib Razak and UMNO exuded an air of expectation in the last days of campaigning.

In addition, three-cornered fights in Malaysia's first-past-the-post (FPTP) system had previously split opposition votes to BN's advantage and this was widely anticipated to happen again in GE-14. States and constituent groups that had come to the ruling coalition's rescue were expected to deliver again. Most salient among these were the "safe deposit" states with the largest number of parliamentary seats, namely: Sarawak (thirty-one seats); Johor (twenty-six); and Sabah (twenty-five). The outlook for Sabah's GE-14 contests was for an exceedingly high incidence of multicornered fights, and in Sarawak's recent 2016 elections, BN won by a thunderous landslide (Chapter 15, Lee P.O.; Chapter 16, Bagang and Puyok). Analysts also highlighted the impact of Federal Land Development Authority (FELDA) voters, whose presence correlated with strong showings for BN and who are heavily concentrated in the centre and south of the Peninsula, including Johor (Chapter 9, Pakiam; Chapter 13, Hutchinson).

To be clear, incumbency advantages did not exclusively benefit BN. Indeed, PH leveraged on the popularity of its ten-year administration of Selangor state to bountiful effect, overpowering the prejudiced gerrymandering of the BN-subservient EC (Chapter 12, Lee H.A.). Likewise, PH resoundingly prevailed in three-cornered fights in Penang. PAS' resolute defence of Kelantan reaped the returns of a well-regarded state government (Chapter 14, Norshahril).

However, BN's attempts to engineer structural advantages were premised on past voting patterns——chiefly, solid Malay support, and the benefit of three-cornered fights. Such extrapolations also weighed heavily in political observers' outlook for GE-14. The possibility that three-cornered contests could favour PH was, of course, considered and not dismissed. Yet, barring INVOKE, very few confidently forecasted that as a likely outcome.

Economic Discontent

Economic issues predominated in the election, and accordingly are among the indicators that researchers and analysts did not fully appreciate. While the realm of "correct" estimation is subjective and abstract, it is fair to say the vast majority of analysis focused on the economy at large and its continued growth.

GE-14 acutely tested the theory of economic voting and the practice of patronage. Governments seeking re-election at a time of buoyant economic conditions tend to be rewarded for delivering the goods. BN was riding comfortably on robust macro data—steady economic growth, relatively low inflation and little unemployment—bolstered by its targeted development programmes for the bumiputra and Indian communities.

However, various analyses suggest that the disparity between the macro picture and lived realities have widened. Statistical estimations, albeit derived from the small sample of Malaysia's past elections, yield instructive findings. In past elections, better economic results on the eve of elections corresponded with improved returns at the ballot box, and vice versa.

Yet, this time was different. The statistical relationship between economic variables and electoral outcomes was weaker in GE-14 compared to past elections (Chapters 4 and 5, Yeah and C. Lee). The macro data failed to capture deficiencies on the ground, including sluggish wage growth among low-wage workers. Inflation rates, while relatively low, evidently did not adequately reflect persistently high cost of living, which had been a source of hardship and grievance for years. In addition, house prices and related debt burdens are excluded from the consumer price index—limiting the validity of this indicator (Chapter 4, Yeah).

While survey data signalled potential voter retribution, the strongest expressions of this possibility arose from anecdotal data and personal observation (Liew 2018). BN's introduction of the goods and services tax (GST) and removal of various subsidies on basic items placed a target on their chests—one that PH and PAS could blame for household financial burdens. Indeed, the centrality of the GST issue in both of their campaigns bears testament to its deep unpopularity and electoral impact.

In response, BN dug in its heels and made the case for new and improved sources of government revenue. This was complemented by assurances of the continuation and even expansion of social assistance—especially BR1M cash transfers. This second aspect was an important change in the form of political patronage that had unfolded over the past decade (Chapter 6, Weiss). Nearing GE-14, BN reminded voters of the material gains to be enjoyed with re-election. However, PH and PAS assured voters that these would not be taken away and promised to immediately repeal GST—substantially neutralizing BN's traditional appeal to developmentalism.

Najib Razak and UMNO: Tainted Reputations

The former prime minister was ultimately a greater liability for BN's cause than anticipated. Najib Razak was undoubtedly in a fight for his political survival but, in the run-up to GE-14, seemed to shift up a few gears. However, he could not wash off the taint of corruption hanging over him, nor dissociate himself from his wife

Rosmah's pageantry and profligacy. The BN regime, and UMNO in particular, also lost popularity by association with Najib, and more generally for being perceived as self-serving, venal, and arrogant (Chapter 7, Serina).

In some ways, the Najib factor made a late appearance, and hence his effect specifically on the election, post-April 28 nomination day, was difficult to foresee. BN's Najib-fronted campaign, canvassing the Peninsula with his portrait and broadcasting his achievements and promises, came as somewhat of a surprise, given his unpopularity in many circles. As noted by the former Menteri Besar of Johor, Najib's prominence hurt their standing (Chapter 19, Khaled). BN's attempted outreach to Indian voters, centred on Najib, utterly flopped (Chapter 11, Govindasamy).

Conventional wisdom holds that anti-Najib, anti-UMNO sentiment percolated through urban areas but did not penetrate significantly to the rural populace. The map of GE-14 results suggests that this dichotomous simplification generally held true—although rural voters had mixed feelings and should not be regarded as homogeneously favouring the status quo (Chapter 7, Serina). In addition, there are many voters who live in urban areas but are registered in rural constituencies, thus making this distinction less dichotomous.

However, voters in semi-urban constituencies considerably turned against UMNO and BN; in retrospect, the electoral dynamics in these social demographics were highly significant, but not readily apparent. Some of BN's reliable Malay vote banks—notably, civil servants—expressed displeasure with the federal government, sometimes openly but often discreetly. The fear of revealing their inclinations was palpable in research work (Chapter 8, Adib and Wan Saiful) and on the campaign trail (Chapter 20, Young Syefura).

Revelations of Najib's kleptocratic behaviour seemed a bridge too far for many Malays in Selangor, who viewed these acts as sullying Malay dignity (*maruah*) and shaming the nation (Chapter 12, Lee H.A.). The widespread presence of PAS, regarded as a safe haven for registering protest, pulled votes from UMNO. This was the case in Kelantan, where 1MDB-related matters was used to counter claims from BN that the state had not benefited from PAS rule (Chapter 14, Norshahril).

National Issues Matter

A popular notion in the run-up to GE-14 held that it would boil down to personal issues and material, "rice bowl" concerns, which overshadowed all else. In particular, national issues surrounding corruption, abstract notions of governance, and the 1MDB and other financial scandals with their arcane intricacies and distance from everyday lives, were taken to be of scarce import. This perspective was bolstered by surveys, which continuously indicated that economic issues were paramount (Ibrahim 2019).

Despite this, the election results indicated that issues of national scope and importance made a difference for PH. These issues weighed in from different angles. The raft of financial scandals plaguing the Najib administration and incredulous attempts to forestall investigation and perpetrate cover-ups elicited strong reactions in the urban areas. Corruption was perceivably a main factor in the further swing among Chinese and Indian voters away from BN (Ibrahim 2019). Among rural Malays—who could be more forgiving of misdemeanours and deferential in the face of incomprehensible fraud—a palpable ill-feeling still lingered, towards UMNO's perceived excesses, arrogance and breach of public trust (Chapter 7, Serina). This was compounded by scandals related to a FELDA-owned subsidiary, FELDA Global Ventures, which directly affected many settlers who had purchased stocks in the company (Khor 2017).

Veiled Preferences, Firm Undercurrents?

Reading voters' preferences, inclinations and choices involves a blend of observable response and underlying uncertainty, but preceding GE-14 the mood and momentum were difficult to discern. Public polling throughout 2017 captured more decided votes for BN than for PH, but many were undecided or declined to answer. Were the "fence-sitters" neutral or already leaning one way? The substantial share of the electorate that apparently took a "watch and wait" stance could plausibly reflect voters' decision to observe how PH would emerge, given that BN was a known quantity. Presumably, voters leaning away from BN would also be more apprehensive about revealing this intention in a survey (Ibrahim 2018). However, a majority view assumed that these "fence-sitters" would either ultimately support BN or, at a maximum, not vote.

Exceptions to the mainstream were few, hence the predictions of BN's defeat by INVOKE stood out. Their utilization of Big Data methods to construct voter profiles and predict voting outcomes beyond survey revelations yielded an overall prediction of PH winning GE-14, with strikingly accurate calls for Peninsular west coast states (Chapter 22, Rafizi and Chai). However, as with most other assessments, INVOKE's model also projected the decimation of PAS. The Merdeka Center's eve of polling day predictions likewise only called two parliament seats going to PAS, both in Kelantan (Merdeka Center 2018c).

This could be due to three factors. First, the Islamic party's traditional campaign methods of grassroots outreach and door-to-door campaigning escaped the attention of analysts, who focused more on visible campaign paraphernalia such as banners and billboards (Chapter 14, Norshahril). Second, it is possible that a substantial number of voters understood—tacitly or explicitly—that in order to achieve change, they needed to vote tactically, one way in west coast states and another in east coast states. Third, the dynamics of three-way fights in Malay-majority constituencies were not well understood, giving rise to a number of unexpected outcomes. One of the biggest conclusions is that PH won a substantial number of seats by obtaining a majority of non-Malay votes as well as a portion of the Malay votes, with the remainder of the Malay votes split between PAS and BN. This then turned the conventional wisdom of BN benefiting from three-cornered fights on its head.

OR LATE SURGE?

With regard to the surge, was there also a groundswell of anti-UMNO or anti-BN feeling and, consequently, momentum for either PH or PAS? On one hand, since its thumping victory in 2004, BN had steadily lost ground in 2008 and 2013, yielding increasing numbers of seats and retaining others with ever-smaller margins. On the other, the formation of a cohesive opposition coalition as a credible alternative emerged relatively late in the run-up to GE-14.

Coalitional Cohesion and Credibility

Indeed, the opposition was sorely weakened by the 2015 split between PKR and the Democratic Action Party (DAP) on one side, and PAS on the other. Beyond sundering the parties' potential voter base, it also forced DAP-PKR on one hand and PAS on the other to expand into new constituencies handled by their former partners—straining them organizationally and financially in the process.

Pakatan Harapan was formed in September 2015 with DAP, PKR, and PAS' splinter party Amanah. However, in this form, it was still not clear that the grouping would be electorally competitive outside urban areas. It was only when UMNO's internal strife in 2016 gave rise to the splinter parties of Parti Pribumi Bersatu Malaysia (PPBM) and Warisan, who then joined PH, that BN faced a politically viable opponent.

Nonetheless, circumstances required that PH gain cohesion, credibility and traction in a short space of time and, by most accounts and survey data, the initial reception from the public was tentative. In mid-2017, PH made important organizational strides by settling on the leadership structure of the coalition. And, PH also enjoyed a late surge in the months before GE-14, especially with developments that unfolded from late 2017 and early 2018. These included seat allocations, the *Buku Harapan* manifesto, and Mahathir's nomination as prime minister.

Informal campaigning prior to Parliament's dissolution set the precedent of all PH parties being represented and delivering *ceramahs*, which were live-streamed to global audiences and posted on social media after the event. This practice continued, and gathered momentum during the official campaign period running up to 9 May.

This show of cohesion and comportment as a government-in-waiting, with a clear national platform and local flavour, benefited PH in Kuala Lumpur and Sabah, as recalled in the participant accounts of Fahmi (Chapter 17) and Lasimbang (Chapter 18), as well as across the country. In contrast, BN's campaign reached out to its base, but struggled to extend beyond its core demographic. In addition, certain tactics, including holding the election on a Wednesday and banning PPBM at the dissolution of Parliament, may well have backfired and increased the number of protest votes (Chapter 20, Young Syefura).

The Mahathir Factor

Mahathir was appointed Pakatan Harapan chairman in July 2017 and prime ministerial candidate in January 2018—with an agreement to later hand over the reins to Anwar Ibrahim, who would first need to secure a royal pardon. Mahathir's position at the helm was, therefore, not a late development. Furthermore, the explicit statement of PH's choice for prime minister *prior* to the election was an advance, and a significant difference from prior years.

The effect of Mahathir's leadership, and the swelling number of UMNO stalwarts and Mahathir's formidable former Cabinet members who joined PPBM and PH's cause, lends credence to the claim that the "Mahathir factor" was a significant momentum-builder. Apprehensions among Chinese voters towards Mahathir, voiced by a vocal, albeit minority segment, eventually almost completely dissolved (Chapter 10, Ngu and Lee H.A.). Even statistically, a Mahathir campaign visit was found to have a positive and significant relationship with PH's vote share (Chapter 5, C. Lee). Within the Malay electorate, Mahathir was an assuring presence in a particular context. Defending Malay interests featured prominently and fervidly in GE-14, with battle lines drawn between an unprecedentedly UMNO-centric BN, PAS and PH. "Malay rights" was reported as the top driver of voter choice among Malays, ahead of governance and service delivery, which Chinese and Indian survey respondents held most important (Merdeka Center 2018b).

The longest-serving prime minister steadied PH's occasionally unwieldy and ill-disciplined ship, and his kinetic nonagenarian presence galvanized troops. His seniority and track record, while making some question his intentions in returning to politics—especially with caustic attacks on Najib—also added to his charisma and authority, and provided a sympathetic shield when the latter fired back. The Merdeka Center's surveys instructively found that leadership increasingly mattered as the campaign progressed. Comparing the findings of sampling before and after nomination day, the share of respondents that regarded "having credible leadership" as one of two main factors influencing their vote doubled, from 10 per cent to 20 per cent (Merdeka Center 2018c).

Economic Rescue

Economic discontent pervaded Malaysia, but did any features of PH's campaign give it more traction to tap into those sentiments, and increase momentum in terms of popularity? The *Buku Harapan* manifesto, launched in early March 2018, with GST abolition as the paramount pledge, was very positively received and surely boosted the coalition's popularity. Indeed, it would appear that, at that time, many voters were unclear on the mechanics of the elimination of the GST—namely that it would replace the previous sales and services tax (SST) regime—instead only focusing on the suppression of the former (Ibrahim 2019).

The overarching narrative of economic rescue also resonated with swathes of the electorate. The distillation of a tome of promises down to ten to be delivered in the first 100 days enhanced the focus, clarity and appeal of PH's campaign. These pledges included: reintroducing a fuel subsidy; encouraging Employees' Provident Fund (EPF) savings for stay-at-home mothers; abolishing road tolls; providing relief for PTPTN borrowers; resolving FELDA settlers' woes; and investigating financial scandals among others (Pakatan Harapan 2018).

Surveys carried out in the months since have shown several of these pledges to be particularly appealing, not least relief for PTPTN borrowers and the EPF provisions (Merdeka Center 2019). Of course, not all of these pledges were financially viable, a fact that was later admitted by Mahathir Mohamad (*Straits Times*, 16 August 2018). However, they were effective in neutralizing the substantial economic incentives targeted at key interest groups such as civil servants, retirees, village heads, and farmers released by the Najib Razak administration in Budget 2018 and again in early April 2018 (Yeah 2017; *New Straits Times*, 5 April 2018).

Notwithstanding talks at the elite level between the Islamist party and UMNO, grassroots members took campaigning very seriously. Cognizant of the polling numbers, PAS also made economic issues the centrepiece of their platform. Thus, the repeal of GST, eliminating PTPTN debts, housing affordability, and increased transfers to B40 (Bottom Forty or low-income) families figured prominently in their campaigning (*Malay Mail*, 18 March 2018; Chapter 14, Norshahril).

Simple, Resonant Messaging

While PH's manifesto clarified the main planks of their campaign, the cause was also bolstered by simplifying the message and speaking in terms that resonated on the ground. The effects kicked in as the campaign wore on. Mahathir, and other popular speakers like Mat Sabu, helped translate complex economic troubles and scandals into common terms, plainly and simply accusing Najib and BN of theft rather than kleptocracy. PH also increasingly connected GST with scandal bailouts, Najib's corruption and Rosmah's ostentation, which while logically and empirically questionable, was deployed to popular effect on the campaign trail (Tapsell 2018).

Consistent campaigning, with the attendance and participation of all component party leaders was important. As more people attended these events, this drew attention to the messaging and organizational coherence. Thus, events like the 6 April rally in Pasir Gudang caught national attention for their: high-level attendance by party leaders; clear, consistent, messaging across all member parties; and large crowd size, with cross-ethnic representation (Chapter 13, Hutchinson).

Last-Minute Decisions

The underlying frustration at the cost of living, an out-of-touch national leadership, and a compromised governance context had created a nucleus of potential opposition supporters. In the face of persuasive economic arguments and presented with a viable political alternative, voters began to gravitate towards first, PH, and secondly PAS.

The proportion of the electorate that made the decision at the last minute is difficult to ascertain. INVOKE's surveying from December 2017 to February 2018 reported persistently substantial levels of respondents—between 20 to 22 per cent—refusing to provide an answer on which party they would vote for, and the proportion who declared themselves "undecided" actually rose from 12 per cent to 17 per cent (INVOKE 2018).

It is reasonable to assume that some portion of fence-sitters turned against BN, or PH-leaning voters decisively swung towards their choice, in the course of the election campaign. That this period lasted a mere eleven days provided a very narrow window for observing such electoral dynamics. This was made more difficult by the role of social media and particularly WhatsApp. Other types of media such as Facebook are more public, but WhatsApp is a much more private method of circulating data and, consequently, harder to monitor or study. Furthermore, microtargeted messaging, such as that carried out by INVOKE, possibly influenced decisions or induced supporters to vote and to persuade family members and friends to do likewise.

Merdeka Center's tracking surveys remain the primary, consistent data source on voter preferences. An early April 2018 opinion poll reflected a longer term momentum: Malay support for BN was down from 60.4 per cent in GE-13 to 52.5 per cent. Trends varied by state and, among Malay voters, BN lost ground most sharply in Johor and Selangor, but retained similar levels of support in Kedah, and registered slight increases in Terengganu and Kelantan.

Asked which party respondents most preferred as their representative, in the week before 9 May: 28 per cent selected BN; 13 per cent PAS; 29 per cent PH; 15 per cent were not sure; and 9 per cent declined to answer (Merdeka Center 2018c). Another survey conducted by a team at the International Islamic University (IIUM) found that support swung away from BN after nomination day.

LOOKING FORWARD

What changes and continuities lie ahead in Malaysia's political landscape, coalitional dynamics and possibilities for reform? What can we expect down the road? By way of conclusion, the paragraphs ahead will concentrate on five key issues in post-GE-14 Malaysia and related challenges that the new administration will have to handle.

First, will the new, reconfigured political order remain intact? At the time of writing, the PH-Warisan grouping has lasted more than a year, but may face challenges in the long term. These include stresses internal to the new ruling coalition, the emergence of an UMNO-PAS alliance, and an opportunistic Gabungan Parti Sarawak (GPS) in Sarawak.

With regard to internal stresses, a large section of the electorate has signalled a desire for new modes and priorities—most saliently, shifting away from BN-style ethnic politics and extending more autonomy to Sabah and Sarawak. From a normative perspective, such changes are also widely regarded as positive for Malaysia's democratic progress.

However, PH negotiates a polity in flux and a society polarized anew. The new ruling coalition finds itself in an uncomfortable situation. Its support base consists of a preponderant share of non-Malays and a segment of urban-based Malays (largely in Selangor). Regarding the non-Malay electorate, Chinese and Indians, having shifted to new political vehicles of DAP and PKR, have shown themselves less partisan and less wedded to ethnic politics—but hold high expectations of change and increased opportunity (Chapter 10, Ngu and Lee H.A.; Chapter 11, Govindasamy).

The gradually solidifying alliance of the UMNO-PAS pact and their successes in three by-elections have posed a formidable challenge to PH. Beyond the specific by-election victories, this pact exposes the new ruling coalition's tenuous appeal to many Malay voters as well as the vestiges of loyalty to BN in many rural constituencies (Chapter 7, Serina). That said, the UMNO-PAS pact may contain the seeds of its own electoral demise due to the overlap of desirable seats for the two parties, as well as their limited appeal in mixed seats as well as East Malaysia. Nonetheless, in the short to medium term, this arrangement could put PH on the back foot.

Last, the prevalence in local-level sentiment in Sabah and Sarawak, as well as the different denouements in each in GE-14 shows that the refraction of Peninsular-based politics and dynamics onto East Malaysia yields different outcomes. The upcoming state elections in Sarawak in 2021 will be decisive, with both PH and GPS competing for seats—signalling a potential dissolution of the latter's independent stand.

PH's second set of challenges revolves around the numerous economic promises made during the GE-14 campaign, which the new administration is now expected to deliver on in the near term. Relative to the heady days of the 1990s and early 2000s, Malaysia's growth trend is lower. Furthermore, the outlook is less positive—given headwinds such as the US-China trade war, slowdowns in major economies, and weak business sentiment (World Bank 2019).

Reports on the ground suggest that large groups of people are still struggling to cope with cost of living issues. And, while the elimination of GST was a very good tactical move by PH, the reinstatement of the SST regime did not go unnoticed by voters. Furthermore, the latter tax's narrower base has left a shortfall in revenue that needs to be covered by other means (Lee 2019). The frustration regarding cost of living issues has not been helped by the lack of progress on campaign promises such as alleviating student debt or abolishing highway tolls (*The Star*, 24 February 2019; 25 May 2019). The breadth and nuances of the manifesto also provide fodder for the opposition. With so many promises made, it is easy to point out failures, and in the process to sometimes omit key details—as exemplified even in some chapters of this volume. And, in the event of an economic downturn, the country's relatively high levels of debt may constrain countercyclical expenditure (World Bank 2019).

Third, institutional and democratic reforms are crucial, both in terms of keeping election promises and consolidating the fundamentals for Malaysia's further maturation. BN's long tenure at the federal level and in most state governments, meant relatively few opportunities for politicians in the opposition to gain administrative experience. Consequently, PH's first Cabinet was predominantly comprised of newcomers to federal administration, complemented by several senior state-level leaders.

The first year thus constituted a steep learning curve for the incoming administration, particularly given the country's difficult and complex issues. However, the honeymoon is clearly over, with the onus now on delivering results. Yet, there are issues with the civil service, whose capacity has been affected by rigidity, overcentralization, and other suboptimal practices, resulting in falling levels of government effectiveness (World Bank 2019).

Furthermore, legacies of the BN period remain, further inhibiting the possibilities for reform. This was seen with the veto of the anti-fake news bill by the BN-appointed majority in the Upper House (Dewan Negara) (*Bernama*, 12 September 2018). Discursive legacies also frame issues, as seen by the push-back against Malaysia ratifying the Rome Statute of the International Criminal Court, which was framed by UMNO politicians and the Johor royal house as an assault on the autonomy and prestige of the country's sultans (*Straits Times*, 5 April 2019).

Pakatan Harapan has been clearer and more consistent in tackling corruption and acts of illegality than its BN predecessor. The passing of a motion in early July 2019 to make the declaration of assets by members of parliament and their spouses mandatory was an important victory (*Malay Mail*, 1 July 2019). Yet, in other areas, the new administration has been less consistent. The direct appointment of the new head of the Malaysian Anti-Corruption Commission (MACC), Latheefa Koya, by Mahathir in June 2019 raised questions, as this contradicted earlier pledges to consult Parliament on high-level appointments (*Malay Mail*, 7 June 2019).

Looking ahead, the possibilities for reform will be constrained by internal fault lines within PH on key issues ranging from Malay privileges to education, and from religion to affirmative action. The Mahathir administration is charting a new overarching narrative of "shared prosperity", addressing inequality in its manifold dimensions, including class, ethnicity and region, and encompassing various forms, such as income, opportunity, and wealth. This new vision will assuredly redesign and rebrand the staple themes of inclusivity, sustainability and unity. However, the credibility and traction of the shared prosperity agenda will ride on how it negotiates the contending demands for preferential treatment and equal opportunity, and how effectively it delivers benefits, especially to the B40 as well as M40 (Middle Forty or middle-income households). Another potential area of discord will be the next redelineation exercise, which will take place after the next election, but before the subsequent one. The degree to which malapportionment between oversized, mixed and urban constituencies and undersized, Malay-majority, and rural seats is significantly addressed is very likely to raise tensions within the PH coalition and require lengthy behind-the-scenes negotiations.

Fourth, the Malaysian political context is continually evolving, as are the means through which politicians and citizens engage with each other. The move away from traditional media towards social media has been underway for some time. However, if GE-13 was the "Facebook election", GE-14 was definitely its WhatsApp equivalent.

While both BN and PH used this to their respective benefit during the campaign period, it remains to be seen how and in what ways the new administration will be able to engage successfully and meaningfully with citizens. One challenge will be for the new parties, PPBM and Amanah, to develop their party machinery. And, all PH member parties will need to target the middle part of the Peninsula that resisted their outreach campaigns. UMNO in particular has formidable grassroots networks that have provided an anchor for many communities and settlements. It also remains to be seen how and whether the new administration can establish itself in a meaningful way in the PAS-controlled states of Kelantan and Terengganu. Despite PAS' electoral pact with UMNO, the Kelantan state government has dropped its long-standing legal suit against the federal government, following PH's pledge to pay outstanding oil royalties (*The Edge*, 21 May 2019). This bodes well for some form of cohabitation in the months to come.

Last, the leadership transition from Mahathir to a successor remains fraught. Despite initial pledges that the mantle of leadership would be transferred from Mahathir to Anwar Ibrahim within two years, there has been some opacity on the timing and the manner in which this would occur. Indeed, at the time of writing, Mahathir had gone on record to state that—his age notwithstanding—the new timeline was three years, although this was later amended to refer to the time needed to complete the most outstanding reforms (*The Edge Financial Daily*, 25 June 2019). Furthermore, seventeen MPs have left UMNO to join the ranks of PH, the bulk of which have gone to PPBM, increasing the relative size and influence of the party within the opposition coalition. These two developments have the potential to derail or split the sitting administration, requiring deft handling in the months ahead.

Malaysia is in an acute phase of flux. The peaceful transition of power shows the nation's ability to cope with change. More change is in store, but the direction and magnitude remain to be seen, as political mandates and manoeuvres, policy achievements and shortfalls, and electoral undercurrents and mood swings, play out. GE-14 has underscored: the complexity of Malaysia's polity and society; its present unpredictability; *and* the abiding potential for surprise.

References

Bernama. "Dewan Negara Rejects Bill to Repeal Anti-Fake News Act". *The Star Online*, 12 September 2018. https://www.thestar.com.my/news/nation/2018/09/12/dewan-negara-rejects-bill-to-repeal-anti-fake-news-act#wFgTWGO8bDRYqBwP.99.

Chan, Kok Leong. 2018. "Forecasts in Malaysia's Poll Skewed by Islamist Party's Unpredictable Impact". *The Round Table* 107, no. 6: 789–90.

Esman, Milton. 1972. *Administration and Development in Malaysia: Institution Building and Reform in a Plural Society*. Ithaca: Cornell University Press.

Hutchinson, Francis E. 2018. "Malaysia's 14th General Elections: Agents and Drivers of Change". *Asian Affairs* 49, no. 4: 582–605.

Ibrahim Suffian. 2018. "Why Opinion Polls Failed to Predict the Fall of BN in Malaysia". *The Round Table* 107, no. 6: 791–92.

————. 2019. "Malaysia One Year After GE-14". Paper presented at seminar on "Malaysia's Pakatan Harapan One Year On: Challenges and Outlook", ISEAS – Yusof Ishak Institute Singapore, 19 June 2019.

INVOKE. 2018. "INVOKE GE-14 Prediction". Presentation at INVOKE GE-14 Prediction forum, Kuala Lumpur, 9 March 2018.

Khor Yu Leng. 2017. "The FELDA Quarrel and Its National Ramifications". *ISEAS Perspective*, no. 2017/51, 12 July 2017.

Lee, Cassey. 2019. "The Malaysian Economy Post-GE-14". Paper presented at seminar on "Malaysia's Pakatan Harapan: One Year On", ISEAS – Yusof Ishak Institute, Singapore, 6 May 2019.

Liew, Chin Tong. 2018. "How I Could See the Malay Tsunami Coming". *The Round Table* 107, no. 6: 787–88.

Merdeka Center. 2018a. "Malaysia General Elections XIV Outlook: Prospects and Outcome". 26 April 2018. http://merdeka.org/v4/index.php/downloads/category/2-researches?download=183:ge14-26042018-survey-findings-release-27042018.

————. 2018b. "Malaysia General Elections XIV Outlook: Prospects and Outcome II". 2 May 2018. http://merdeka.org/v4/index.php/downloads/category/2-researches?download=184:ge14-02052018-presentation-final-03052018.

————. 2018c. "Malaysia General Elections XIV Outlook: Prospects and Outcome III". 8 May 2018. http://merdeka.org/v4/index.php/downloads/category/2-researches?download=186:ge14-08052018-presentation-final.

Pakatan Harapan. 2018. *Buku Harapan: Membina Negara Memenuhi Harapan*. Petaling Jaya: PKR, DAP, PPBM, Amanah.

Tapsell, Ross. 2018. "The Smartphone as the 'Weapon of the Weak': Assessing the Role of Communication Technologies in Malaysia's Regime Change". *Journal of Current Southeast Asian Affairs* 37, no. 3: 9–29.

World Bank. 2019. "Malaysia Economic Monitor, June 2019: Re-energizing the Public Service". International Bank of Reconstruction and Development, Kuala Lumpur.

Yeah Kim Leng. 2017. "Malaysia's 2018 Budget: Balancing Short Term Needs and Long-Term Imperatives". *ISEAS Perspective*, no. 2017/88, 24 November 2017.

Periodicals
The Edge
The Edge Financial Daily
Malay Mail
New Straits Times
The Star
The Straits Times

INDEX

Note: Page numbers followed by "n" refer to endnotes.

Perlis

Kelantan

Kedah

Terengganu

Penang

Perak

Kuala Lumpur

Pahang

Selangor

Putrajaya

Melaka

Negeri
Sembilan

Johor

April 6th, 2018

Barisan Nasional (BN)

Pakatan Harapan (PH)

Malaysian Islamic Party (PAS)

Independent

Perlis

Kelantan

Kedah

Penang

Terengganu

Perak

Kuala Lumpur

Pahang

Selangor

Putrajaya

Negeri
Sembilan

Melaka

Johor

May 9th, 2018

Barisan Nasional (BN)

Pakatan Harapan (PH)

Malaysian Islamic Party (PAS)

Independent

0   25   50   100
                              Kilometers

Map provided by ISEAS – Yusof Ishak Institute © (2019) ISEAS – Yusof Ishak Institute

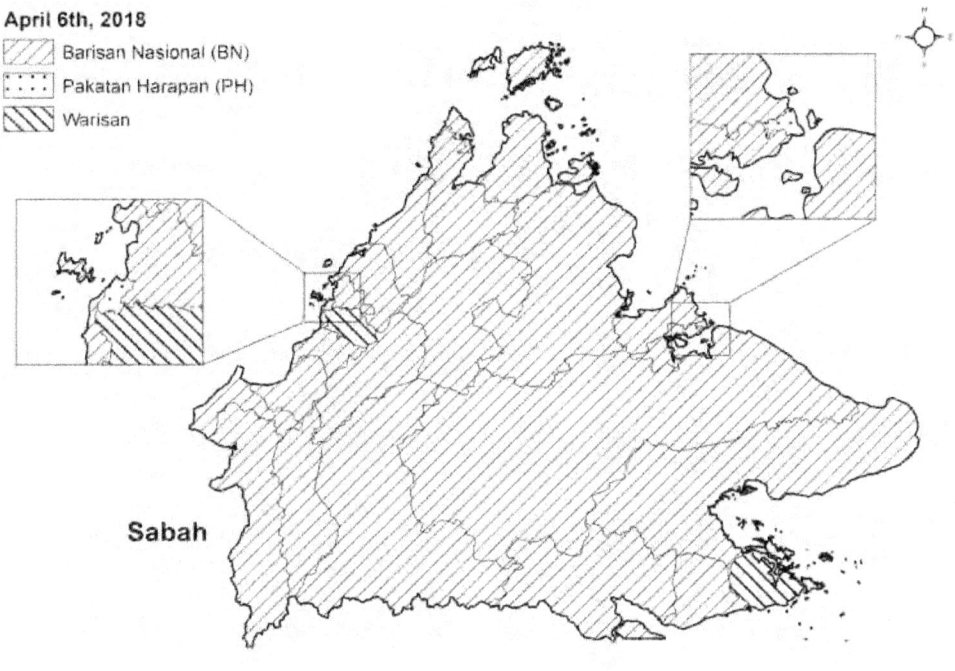

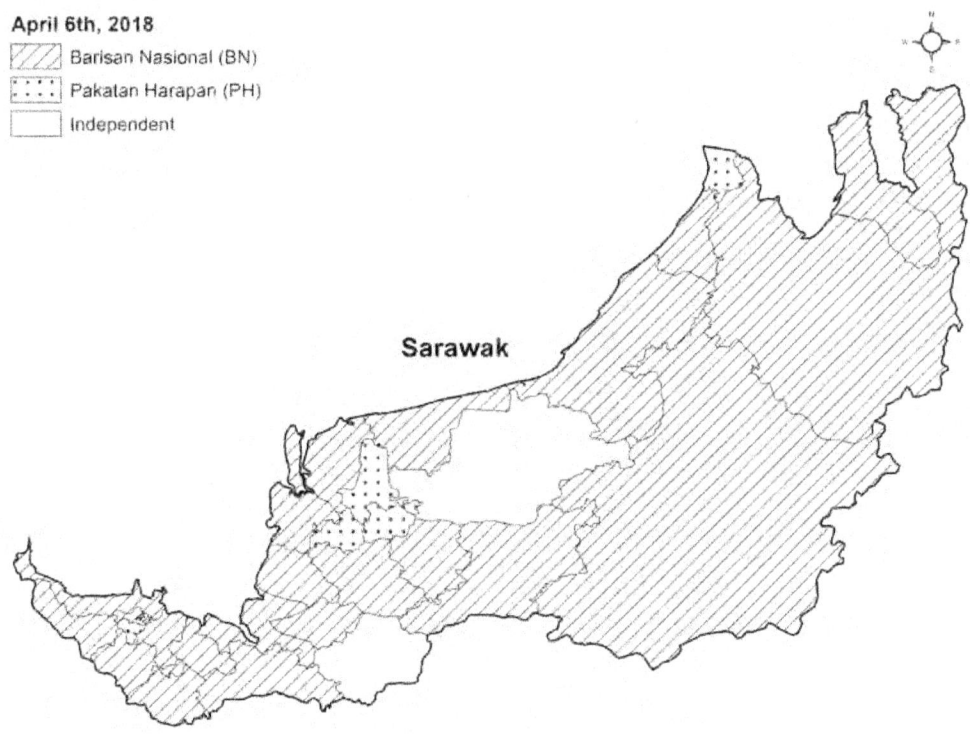

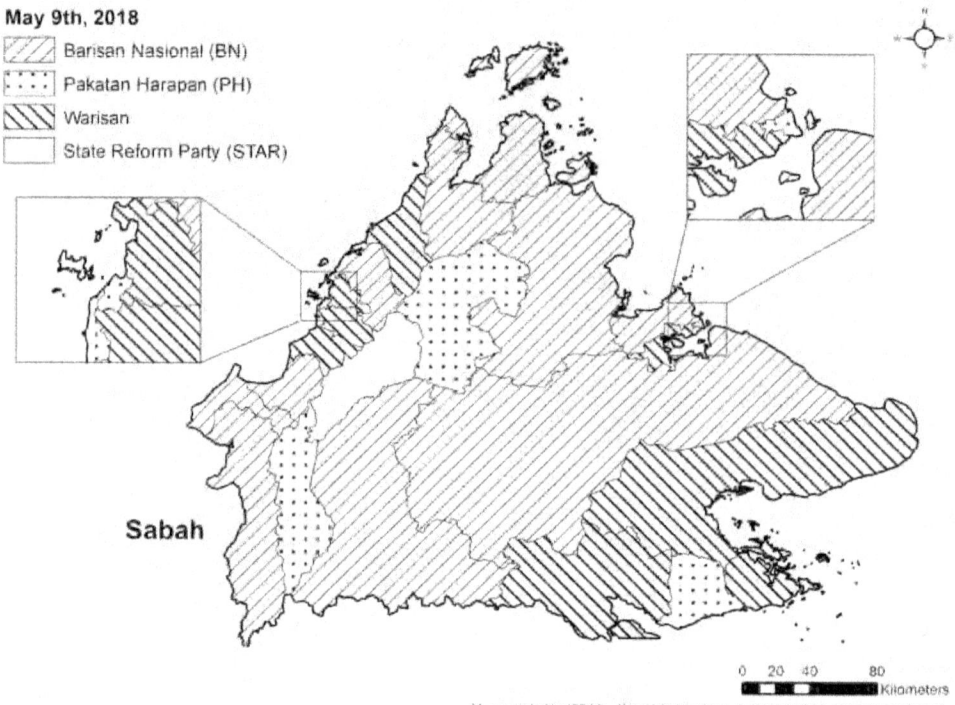

May 9th, 2018
- Barisan Nasional (BN)
- Pakatan Harapan (PH)
- Warisan
- State Reform Party (STAR)

Sabah

0 20 40   80
Kilometers

Map provided by ISEAS – Yusof Ishak Institute. © (2019) ISEAS – Yusof Ishak Institute

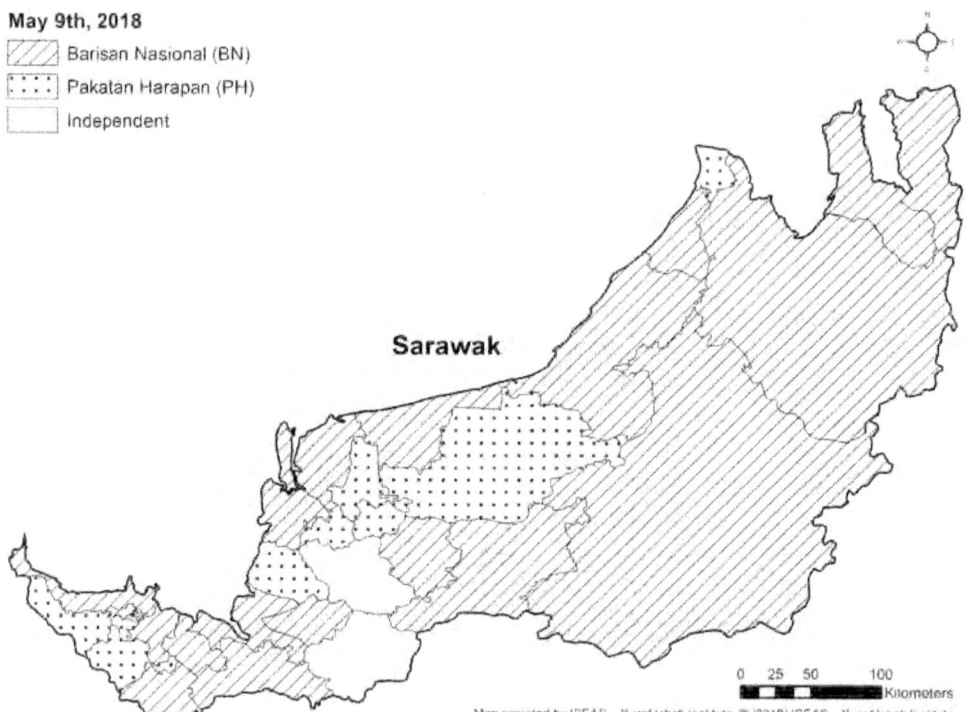

May 9th, 2018
- Barisan Nasional (BN)
- Pakatan Harapan (PH)
- Independent

Sarawak

0 25 50   100
Kilometers

Map provided by ISEAS – Yusof Ishak Institute. © (2019) ISEAS – Yusof Ishak Institute

www.ingramcontent.com/pod-product-compliance
Lightning Source LLC
Chambersburg PA
CBHW081425270326
41932CB00019B/3101